Troubleshooting & Maintaining Your PC All-in-One For Dummies®

W9-BEV-428

My PC

PC purchase date: _____

PC make and model: _____

PC serial number: _____

PC manufacturer:_____

PC dealer: _____

Manufacturer's Web support page: _____

Manufacturer's phone support number: _____

Customer number: _____

ISP's phone support number: _____

Startup key to press to enter Setup program:
F1, F2, Del, Enter, other: _____

Startup key to press to display Boot menu:
F10, Enter, other: _____

Mantras of the Troubleshooter

- Change causes trouble. Recall the items you changed recently and you can better pinpoint the problem and devise a solution.
- Rarely do you need to reinstall Windows. Use the System File Checker to repair damage to Windows. Reinstall only after an unrecoverable disaster.
- Restart Windows to cure common ills.
- When your computer is more than five years old, the problem is most likely the computer itself. Buy a new one.
- Resist the temptation to upgrade Windows. Rather than upgrade, buy a new PC with the latest version of Windows preinstalled.
- Back up. Back up. Back up.
- Use Safe Mode for troubleshooting only; do not run applications or finish your work in Safe Mode.
- If the optical disc doesn't format, throw it away.
- The best way to troubleshoot disk storage is to understand what a file is.

For Dummies: Bestselling Book Series for Beginners

Troubleshooting & Maintaining Your PC All-in-One For Dummies®

General Software Troubleshooting

- Run Windows Update for the latest software versions.
- Use the Update Driver button in a device's Properties dialog box to ensure that you have the latest software drivers.
- System Restore can save your butt. Set restore points often. Restore your system whenever it goes hinkey.
- If the computer runs fine in Safe Mode, the problem isn't with Windows itself.
- Regularly scan your PC for viruses and spyware.
- Use the Task Manager to determine which programs have stopped running.

Network Troubleshooting

- Run a firewall.
- There's no need to run multiple firewalls. A single hardware firewall on the router works best. If you don't have one, run a software firewall.
- Share folders on the network in Windows Vista by using the Advanced Sharing button to access the Sharing tab in the folder's Properties dialog box.
- When restarting the network, turn everything off. Then turn on the modem, the router, any switches, and, finally, the PCs attached to the network.
- Ensure that the wireless NIC has been enabled on your laptop; check for a small switch somewhere.

General Hardware Troubleshooting

- Is it plugged in?
- Is it connected?
- Is it turned on?
- Press and hold down the power button for five seconds to turn off any computer.
- Hot things cause trouble. Ensure that the console's air vents are unobstructed and that the fan is on. Touch a power supply brick to ensure that it's not too hot. If it is hot, disconnect the power supply.
- Check the Device Manager for conflicts detected by Windows.
- Swap out questionable hardware with hardware that works to help pinpoint the problem.
- The printer must be on and online or selected before you can print.

For Dummies: Bestselling Book Series for Beginners

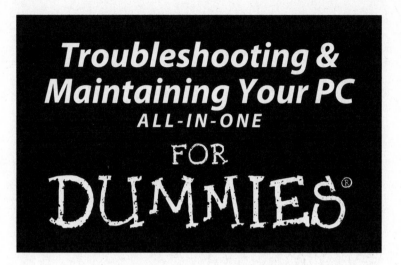

Troubleshooting & Maintaining Your PC
ALL-IN-ONE
FOR DUMMIES®

by Dan Gookin

WILEY

Wiley Publishing, Inc.

Troubleshooting & Maintaining Your PC All-in-One For Dummies®

Published by
Wiley Publishing, Inc.
111 River Street
Hoboken, NJ 07030-5774

www.wiley.com

WILEY

About the Author

Dan Gookin has been writing about technology for way, way too long. He has contributed articles to numerous high-tech magazines and written over 110 books on personal computers, many of them accurate.

Dan combines his love of writing with his gizmo fascination to create books that are informative, entertaining, and not boring. Having sold more than 14 million titles translated into over 30 languages, Dan can attest that his method of crafting computer tomes seems to work.

Perhaps his most famous title is the original *DOS For Dummies*, published in 1991. It became the world's fastest-selling computer book, at one time moving more copies per week than the *New York Times* #1 bestseller (though, as a reference, it could not be listed on the NYT bestseller list). That book spawned the entire line of *For Dummies* books, which remains a publishing phenomenon to this day.

Dan's most popular titles include *Word 2007 For Dummies*, *Laptops For Dummies*, and *PCs For Dummies* (all published by Wiley). He also maintains the vast and helpful Web page www.wambooli.com.

Dan holds a degree in communications/visual arts from the University of California, San Diego. Presently, he lives in the Pacific Northwest, where he enjoys spending time with his sons playing video games inside while they watch the gentle woods of Idaho.

Dedication

To Cosette. Thanks for the love and attention. You will be missed.

Publisher's Acknowledgments

We're proud of this book; please send us your comments through our online registration form located at http://dummies.custhelp.com. For other comments, please contact our Customer Care Department within the U.S. at 877-762-2974, outside the U.S. at 317-572-3993, or fax 317-572-4002.

Some of the people who helped bring this book to market include the following:

Acquisitions, Editorial, and Media Development

Senior Project Editor: Mark Enochs

Acquisitions Editor: Katie Mohr

Executive Editor: Greg Croy

Copy Editor: Rebecca Whitney

Technical Editor: James F. Kelly

Editorial Manager: Leah Cameron

Media Development Project Manager: Laura Moss-Hollister

Media Development Assistant Project Manager: Jenny Swisher

Media Development Assistant Producer: Josh Frank

Editorial Assistant: Amanda Foxworth

Sr. Editorial Assistant: Cherie Case

Cartoons: Rich Tennant (www.the5thwave.com)

Composition Services

Project Coordinator: Patrick Redmond

Layout and Graphics: Samantha K. Allen, Ana Carrillo, Reuben W. Davis, Nikki Gately, Christin Swinford, Christine Williams

Proofreaders: Evelyn W. Gibson, Jessica Kramer

Indexer: Broccoli Information Management

Special Help: Susan Christophersen, Elizabeth Kuball

Publishing and Editorial for Technology Dummies

Richard Swadley, Vice President and Executive Group Publisher

Andy Cummings, Vice President and Publisher

Mary Bednarek, Executive Acquisitions Director

Mary C. Corder, Editorial Director

Publishing for Consumer Dummies

Diane Graves Steele, Vice President and Publisher

Composition Services

Gerry Fahey, Vice President of Production Services

Debbie Stailey, Director of Composition Services

Contents at a Glance

Table of Contents

Introduction

If trouble were predictable, it wouldn't be a problem. The problem with trouble, however, is that it's unpredictable.

You hold in your hands a big ol' book that could potentially be the largest volume ever written on the topic of personal computers. The subject is troubleshooting. It's vast. That's mostly because there hasn't been a computer yet invented that didn't have trouble following it like a shadow on a sunny day.

The computing experience should be a pleasant one. And it can be — if you're informed and able to deal with the troubles you encounter. This book helps you along that journey in an informative and entertaining way. Welcome to *Troubleshooting & Maintaining Your PC All-In-One For Dummies*.

Woe Is Computer

A byte of prevention is worth a megabyte of cure.

My philosophy on troubleshooting is that it's easier to do when you understand how the computer works. This philosophy is opposite of what most people expect, which is to look up a specific condition and find a specific cure for it. Although many people like that approach, it has two problems.

The first downfall with the look-it-up approach is that you don't learn anything. Because there's a method behind PC madness, often, the same solution exists for multiple problems. After you understand why things go wrong, it's not only easier to fix them — it's also possible to prevent them in the first place.

The second difficulty with the specific-solution approach is that it would make this book even larger. With millions upon millions of potential hardware and software configurations available in all the PCs in the world, it would take one huge book to document every problem and its solution. This book is big enough already!

This book takes a simple approach: Look up the problem, learn a bit about what might have caused it, and then arrive at a solution. The notion is that when trouble arises again later, you will have the experience to deal with it in a practical manner. Because most PC troubles have a common origin, this solution works.

Married to troubleshooting is the topic of maintenance. The two topics go hand in hand; with proper maintenance and care, your computer runs better and more reliably, often negating the need for much troubleshooting in the first place!

Before moving on, please be aware that there's a difference between trouble and an event that's merely annoying. For example, if the text you print from an e-mail message is tiny, it's annoying, but it isn't a bug. Though specific annoying problems such as that one might not be covered in this book, you'll still find a solution here. That's the beauty behind my philosophical approach to troubleshooting. After all, using Windows shouldn't be a frustrating experience.

About the For Dummies Approach

As a *For Dummies* title, this book doesn't delve into the technical. It doesn't start out easy and then become immediately technical and cryptic. And this book never disrespects you as a reader.

It's entirely possible to be a smart and clever (and, I might add, attractive) computer owner and not know a darn thing about what a computer is or how it works. That's fine with me. This book doesn't assume that you're a computer expert or that you want to become one. The subject is troubleshooting and maintaining your computer. Anyone who owns a PC can read and understand this book well enough to fix their computer woes.

This book may appear to be overburdened with humor. I admit that writing about things in an entertaining manner is a weakness of mine. Troubleshooting can be a serious topic, and this book treats serious issues with respect. But there are times when I feel that the amusement value is necessary to keep the mood light. Computer repair and maintenance need not be a grim topic.

Who Are You?

Allow me to make some assumptions about who you are and why you're reading this introduction.

First, I assume that you're human, or at least posing in human form while visiting Earth from whatever planet or dimension you hail. If so, welcome. Please wait until I've completed my death ray plans before you proceed with your mission to annihilate humanity. Thank you.

Second, you have a PC. That's the generic term for any computer running Microsoft Windows. So, if it runs Windows — whether the computer is a Dell, a computer made by Joe the Nerd, or an iMac — it's a PC as far as this book is concerned.

Even though you're holding a *For Dummies* book, I must make some assumptions about how well you know your computer. The text assumes, for example, that you know how to start the computer, use the mouse, type, and perform other basic computer activities. If you can read and send e-mail or play a game of Spider Solitaire, you have enough computer literacy to understand this book and handle the chores I set forth.

Finally, you're using Windows on your PC. It can be either Windows Vista or Windows XP. Both versions are covered here. You should be aware, however, that Windows Vista has far better tools for PC troubleshooting. Unlike many of my colleagues, I happen to enjoy Windows Vista. (Well, most of the time.)

How This Book Works

This book is composed of six *minibooks*, each of which addresses a computer troubleshooting or maintaining topic. The minibooks are split into traditional chapters, all geared to a specific subject within the minibook topic. Then the chapters are split into sections consisting of paragraphs, words, and then letters. So, as long as you understand the alphabet, you'll understand this book.

Here are some other important things to note about how this book works:

Cross references: Because this book contains six Chapter 1s and six Chapter 2s and so on, those chapters in other minibooks are referenced by the book they belong to. So, when you read "See Book II, Chapter 2," you know in which minibook to find that Chapter 2. Chapters within the same minibook are referred to as just plain chapters, such as "See Chapter 2."

Windows Vista versus Windows XP: When this book refers to *Windows*, it means both Windows Vista and Windows XP. Otherwise, specific mention is made of Windows Vista or Windows XP.

Procedural steps: This book presents numbered steps to accomplish specific tasks. Sometimes, two sets of steps are available — one for Windows Vista and the other for Windows XP. When there are only subtle differences between the versions of Windows, this book breaks up steps and procedures by offering an A or B step for Windows Vista and Windows XP, respectively.

Typing stuff: When you're supposed to type something, that text appears in **bold type**. In the context of a step, where the text is normally bold anyway, the stuff you type appears in regular roman text.

The Enter key: Do not press the Enter key until you're directed to do so. And even then review what you type before you type it just to ensure that you got everything typed properly.

Period: Do not press a period at the end of any text you type, unless I explain that the period is needed. Unlike sentences in English, computer commands don't end with a period.

Filenames and text commands: Windows lets you type filenames or text commands in either upper- or lowercase letters. This book uses lowercase, often using `monospaced text` to present the command name or filename.

How the DVD Works

This book features a companion DVD. The DVD contains some sample software coupled with a small PDF file I've written to describe the software. None of the software is required for using this book; it's just bonus software I've thrown in. All the software is available either free or as a demo on the Internet. So, right away, you can rest assured that you're not missing any software when you pick up a copy of this book in the 80-percent-off remainder section at your local Book Nook.

The DVD primarily contains lovely videos that I created to assist you in working through some of the more technical topics in this book. The videos comprise the majority of the DVD's contents.

There are two types of videos:

A walk-through of any complex steps listed in this book: Sometimes, despite all my flowery prose, it's difficult to explain on paper how something works. So the video shows you, step-by-step, how to troubleshoot or maintain your PC.

A demonstration of how to do more physical tasks, such as clean a computer or yank out a hard drive: That video uses an actor (myself because I'm cheap) to demonstrate the concept.

All the videos on the DVD are referenced in this book. You'll see the On the DVD icon and a video number. Then pop in the DVD and use that number to find the video you're looking for. For more on how to use the DVD, see Appendix A.

If the DVD is missing, my guess is that someone probably took it. That happens at libraries and when you buy used books. I cannot supply you with a replacement DVD. You can, however, visit my YouTube page to view some videos or teasers from this book:

`www.youtube.com/dgookin`

Terms and Stuff to Know

Here are some vital tips you should keep in mind regarding how this book presents information and deals with certain topics regarding PC troubleshooting and maintenance. The rest of the book assumes that you know this basic introductory information:

The PC: This book refers to your computer as a PC, which is short for *personal computer*. The nomenclature is traditional. If you have a computer that runs Windows — even when it's a Macintosh — it's a PC.

Laptops and notebooks: All the information in this book refers to both desktop and laptop computers, except where noted. Book III is specific to laptops, however.

I use the term *laptop* to refer to a portable PC. Some folks prefer the term *notebook*.

The specialized Tablet PC is basically a laptop with a writeable screen. Any information specific to a Tablet PC is noted in the text.

Windows versions: You can assume that when I refer to *Windows* in this book, the information applies equally to both Windows Vista and Windows XP. Otherwise, I specify when the information is specific.

As far as naming things goes, in Windows XP the prefix *My* is applied to various key windows: My Computer and My Documents, for example. Windows Vista dropped the My prefix. Also, in Vista, the network window is named Network; in XP, it's My Network Places.

The Windows Control Panel: Often, this book requires you to use the Windows Control Panel. For the sake of brevity, I reference the Control Panel in its Classic view, where icons represent categories.

To use the Control Panel Classic view in either Windows Vista or Windows XP, choose the link on the left side of the window to switch to Classic view. That saves you time (and saves me precious typing molecules).

Icons Used in This Book

I'd like to think that everything in this book is a tip, but for those special, worthy items, you'll find this icon lurking nearby.

A reminder of something not to do, something to avoid, or something that can cause serious trouble is flagged by the bomb icon.

This icon flags text that's important enough to remember or reminds you of something you may have forgotten that bears repeating.

Extra information on the topic is available on the DVD in video form. The paragraph next to this icon indicates which video to view.

When the urge to blurt out something nerdy overwhelms me, I feel the urge to use this icon to supply a warning sign. You're free not to read any technical text near this icon.

Other images are found in the book's margins, including icon images from Windows itself. When those icons appear, such as the icons used to represent items in the Control Panel, they appear in Windows Vista.

Where to Go Now?

Feel free to start reading this book in any minibook, chapter, or section. Everything is self-contained, so there isn't really a reason to read one section before another. For those rare times when it helps to know information located elsewhere in the book, I provide a cross-reference. But it's not necessary to read the book from front to back.

Final Thots

I can't believe I wrote the whole thing.

This book has been the most massive undertaking of my writing career. Not only is it a big, fat book on PC troubleshooting and maintenance, it's a big, fat book that covers two versions of Windows. In addition to the writing, this book includes videos on many topics presented in the text. All that stuff took time to do, and I appreciate that my publisher didn't lean on me too heavily during the process; I hope to regain full use of my left knee soon.

Here's my e-mail address:

dgookin@wambooli.com

That's my real e-mail address. All the mail you send to me there pops up on my screen, and I read it. I also promise to answer all my e-mail. If you want a quick response, type a *short* e-mail message. The longer the message, the longer it takes me to get around to reading and responding.

Although I promise to respond to all e-mail, I can only answer questions regarding this book. I cannot troubleshoot your PC for you. Consider e-mailing your ISP, software developer, or PC manufacturer or dealer for technical support.

This book also has a companion Web page:

```
www.wambooli.com/help/troubleshooting
```

The Web page contains any needed updates or errata, plus answers to common questions, if there are any.

Thank you for choosing my book,

Dan Gookin

Book I
Hardware

Contents at a Glance

Chapter 1: Let There Be PC

In This Chapter

- ✔ Powering on the PC
- ✔ Diagnosing hardware
- ✔ Finding the operating system
- ✔ Loading the operating system
- ✔ Logging in
- ✔ Making personal settings
- ✔ Using the computer
- ✔ Ending your PC day

The computer that isn't on doesn't require much troubleshooting. In the Off state, your typical PC is a very realizable beast, merely taking up space yet packed with digital possibilities. Yet once you flip that switch (well, metaphorically speaking), trouble looms with the full potential of a three-year-old wandering an antique store with an open-face peanut butter and jelly sandwich. Disaster can happen right away when the power is turned on. An immense help in understanding PC start-up problems is to know exactly how a computer rousts itself out of electronic slumber.

This entire chapter borders on what I believe to be typically nerdy information, but when your goal is to fix a sick PC, knowing the sequence of start-up events helps you pinpoint exactly what to fix when things go awry.

In the Beginning, There Was Power

During the initial power-on phase, your computer transforms itself from a chunk of quite useless expensive electronics into a chunk of quite useful expensive electronics.

What happens

You press the power button. When the PC is off, pressing the power button turns it on again. It works that way whether the computer was properly shut down, put into hibernation, or has met an untimely or inopportune demise.

The computer's *power supply* does its job: It starts converting alternating current into direct current. *Alternating current* comes from the wall socket. *Direct current* is used inside the computer to power its circuitry and motors.

What could go wrong

A lack of power from the wall means that your computer remains quiet. To ensure that a wall socket is properly supplying juice, try this test: Plug a lamp into the socket. If the lamp works, the problem is with the computer's power supply. If the lamp doesn't work, buy a copy of *Troubleshooting Lamps For Dummies*, available at fine bookstores everywhere.

When the wall socket is operating properly, the problem lies with the PC's power supply. Such issues are easy to detect. The power supply on every PC also contains a fan: If you can hear the fan spinning, the power supply is getting power. You may need to open the case to ensure that the power supply is properly connected to the computer's main circuitry, the motherboard.

✦ Power supply problems can be random and unpredictable. Mostly their impact is on the heat inside the computer case. That causes a number of weird events, but those things don't happen when the computer is in Safe mode. See Book II, Chapter 3 for information on Safe mode.

✦ Refer to Chapter 8 for information on opening a computer's case. You also find information there on replacing a bum power supply.

The First Test: Hardware Self-Diagnostics

Once abuzz with electricity, the computer's internal components spring to life. It could be a chaotic ballet of confusion, but one thing is in charge: the processor.

The processor, also known as the *central processing unit* (CPU), is the computer's main chip. It's the boss. The main dude. *El Comandante Supremo*. In a PC, the processor goes by the name Pentium or Athlon, or pick your own science fiction theme.

What happens

Being the chip *in charge* means that the processor knows what to do. As it receives power, the processor "jumps" to a location in memory where it begins executing instructions. Those instructions place the computer in a diagnostic or self-checking mode. The computer inventories its various components.

A *POST*, or *Power-On Self Test,* is performed, in which the computer basically checks its own hardware. Memory is tested and its size determined. Control is passed to various subsystems (network, video, audio, and power management, for example), which also perform their own inventories and tests.

Information may be provided on the screen as feedback during this stage. Most PCs, however, display a start-up, or *splash,* screen. The screen may or may not divulge what's happening inside the computer. When it does, you may see a memory count or seemingly random numbers or letters on the display. That diagnostic information is intended for troubleshooting (*very* nerdy troubleshooting, as in oscilloscope troubleshooting).

✦ One important message revealed at this point is which key or key combination to press to enter the computer's Setup program. See the section "Your PC's Setup Program," a little later in this chapter.

✦ Note that just because hardware passes the POST doesn't mean that everything is well. Computer hardware also needs software to control it. If the software isn't working, you may still have a problem.

What could go wrong

Problems that come up immediately are signaled using the console's speaker. The pattern of beeps dictates the type of problem, though the pattern isn't consistent across all PC hardware. Generally speaking, the problem indicated by a beeping speaker is either in the power supply or the display adapter (video system).

When the power supply and video system are working, problems with other devices are indicated by messages appearing on the screen.

At this point, the only real way to fix the problem is to identify and replace the defective hardware. The message on the screen indicates what the problem child is, such as the video system, network, or other subsystem. Make a note of whatever error message appears. Then deal with the issue by replacing the hardware.

✦ Replacing internal hardware is covered in Chapter 8.

✦ Refer to Chapter 7 for tips on troubleshooting hardware by swapping it out.

✦ Sometimes, replacing hardware doesn't work, such as when the hardware is part of the motherboard. The motherboard replacement operation is more of a brain transplant than a simple hardware swap. I recommend that you contact the computer manufacturer or your dealer for help. Or, honestly, buy a new computer when the motherboard goes bad.

✦ The computer may operate with defective hardware, but that's no excuse to avoid fixing or replacing it.

Your PC's Setup program

At some point during this stage, you can enter the PC's Setup program. I call it the Setup program, though sometimes it's called the Hardware Configuration Menu. Whatever. A prompt appears on the splash screen indicating which key or key combination to press to enter the Setup program.

The key to press is often F1, though also common are Del (or Delete) or F2 or some key combination, such as Alt+F1. The only way to know for certain is to check the screen when the computer starts or refer to the manufacturer's documentation (scant though it may be).

You use the Setup program to configure your PC's hardware. You can do things such as set the computer's clock (date and time), set the order in which storage devices (such as a hard drive or CD-ROM drive) are searched for an operating system, enable or disable hardware components, set security options, and other often technical tasks.

Using the Setup program is simple: Although each program is different, most of them are easily manipulated using the keyboard. A simple menu system is used to select things, and helpful information is displayed to show you which keys you should use to select, choose, or set options.

When you're done changing things, you're given the option to either save the new settings and restart the PC or quit without saving.

✦ Make a note on this book's Cheat Sheet of which keys are required in order to enter your PC's Setup program.

✦ Various other chapters in this book reference using the Setup program.

✦ Another key you can press at start-up is F10 to enter the Boot menu. See Chapter 2 for a discussion of that menu.

✦ Some PCs don't display a message telling you which key to press to enter the Setup program. In that case, try F1.

✦ If the PC has a special Support type of button on the keyboard, such as the blue ThinkVantage button on some Lenovo PCs, press that button. Though pressing that button may not open the Setup program directly, it may display a menu from which you can enter the Setup program.

The Search for an Operating System

The computer hardware can check itself out, but that's about it. To run a computer, you need software. The final task that the PC's hardware takes, after all that checking and testing, is to find and load an *operating system*, the main piece of software in the computer. The process is called *bootstrapping*, or just *boot*.

What happens

A program encoded in the computer's hardware works to find an operating system on one of the PC's mass storage devices. Running this program is the last step in the computer's start-up process.

Originally (back at the dawn of the 1980s), the PC loaded its operating system from a floppy drive and then the hard drive was searched. Today, however, that order can be changed; the computer can load the operating system from a hard drive, an optical drive, a USB drive (flash drive or external drive), a network, or a media card.

After the operating system is found, it's loaded into memory. It takes over the computer system, continues to load itself, and sets up the rest of Mr. PC for you to use and enjoy.

✦ Technically, the PC hardware loads and executes the first portion of the hard drive into memory. That portion is the *Master Boot Record,* or *MBR.* You find the term MBR used quite a bit when diagnosing PC start-up problems.

✦ The Master Boot Record may also contain information about disk partitions. See Chapter 4 for a scintillating discussion.

✦ When you have multiple operating systems installed on the PC, you see a *Boot menu,* where you can select which operating system to load. The boot menu is displayed by a Boot Manager program. In that type of PC configuration, the Boot Manager is given control by the hardware. The *Boot Manager* isn't an operating system; it's merely a program that helps you select and load an operating system. Chapter 2 coughs up more information about the Boot menu and Boot Manager.

What could go wrong

The hardware may be unable to find the *Master Boot Record* on the hard drive (it could be missing or damaged). That doesn't mean that the operating system is gone — merely that it's lost. Missing operating system error messages are described in Chapter 2. Fixing the problem depends on the error message, so directions for where to go next are also found in Chapter 2.

When the boot order is changed, your computer may attempt to load an operating system from a device that lacks an operating system. An error message may or may not be displayed when that happens. Refer to Chapter 2 for how to deal with such a situation by changing the boot order.

A damaged operating system or storage media can muck up the works. A fouled operating system is a software problem. Fixing it involves using a recovery disk or the recovery partition of your PC's hard drive. See Book II, Chapter 8 for more information.

When the hard drive is damaged, you can still attempt to recover the operating system. The recovery process confirms whether the storage system can be used or needs to be replaced.

The boot loader

A *boot loader* is a special program that appears just as your PC's hardware is passing the baton of control to an operating system. The boot loader primarily dwells on the start-up hard drive in the master boot record, though it's found on any bootable media. Like an operating system, the boot loader is transferred from the storage device, loaded into memory, and executed. But keep in mind that the boot loader isn't a full operating system.

The job of the boot loader is to help you choose an operating system for your computer. Some boot loaders do nothing more than continue the process of loading the computer's only operating system. But many boot loaders are more complex.

For example, a simple type of boot loader may merely display a menu from which you choose an operating system to use. Other more complex boot loaders might offer partitioning and disk management and disk resizing tools.

✦ Windows features the boot loader NTLDR. The *NT* came from Windows NT, where the NT stood for New Technology. I assume that LDR somehow translates into *loader*.

✦ A common boot loader is the LILO, or *Linux Loader*. LILO displays a list of operating systems, you choose one, and then the operating system loads.

✦ The most popular boot loader today is GNU GRUB. GRUB stands for Grand Unified Bootloader. It's often used after installing Linux on a PC.

✦ The GRUB settings file is edited only from the Linux partition for which it was installed. You cannot modify GRUB's menu from within GRUB itself. The configuration file, named either `grub.conf` or `menu.lst`, is found in (or linked to from) the `/boot/grub` directory.

✦ Running Windows on a Macintosh involves the Boot Camp boot loader.

✦ Operating system management programs, like Partition Commander and Partition Magic, also dwell in the Master Boot Record and serve the same purpose as a boot loader. (As this book goes to press, Partition Magic isn't compatible with Windows Vista.)

Operating System Initialization

The operating system loads itself into memory in a multistep process that's way too boring to detail here. Various mystery steps take place until you log in.

What happens

Lots of stuff happens:

Windows begins to load itself into memory and check out the computer's hardware. This investigation isn't completely thorough (Windows is quite forgiving), which is why errors can crop up later as you use the computer.

If you press the F8 key just before Windows loads (the timing is quick), a special start-up menu is displayed. See the section "Start-Up Menus" in Chapter 2.

If the system is recovering from hibernation, information is loaded from disk into memory as the computer resumes its operation.

What could go wrong

When something amiss is detected in your PC's hardware or in the *driver* software that controls the hardware, Windows places the system in *Safe mode*. Refer to Book II, Chapter 3 for how to deal with Safe mode.

If anything is wrong with Windows itself, you see an error message specific to the problem. At that point, however, it's fairly certain that Windows is the problem. The solution is to repair Windows. Refer to Book II, Chapter 8.

Log On to Windows

After Windows has successfully forced itself upon your PC, its final act is to run the program WINLOGON.EXE, the *Windows Logon Manager*. The visual effect is that you see a logon window, prompt, or thingy where you can log in to the computer.

It's possible, but not recommended, to configure Windows XP to forego the login. Refer to Book II, Chapter 5.

What happens

You select or type your account name and then type a password. If multiple accounts are set up on the same computer, you choose your account from a list.

If you wait at the logon screen and the computer doesn't crash, you can be certain that the start-up problem takes place with one of the personalized start-up programs that run after you log in. See the section "Personalized Start-Up," just ahead in this chapter.

What could go wrong

Your account might be missing. In that case, you have a number of choices. The option I recommend is pressing the F8 key as Windows starts and choosing Last Known Good Configuration from the start-up menu. Refer to Chapter 2.

You can also repair a missing account by using the recovery console, which is covered in Book II, Chapter 8.

The most common mishap is to forget your password. Passwords are covered in Book II, Chapter 5.

Windows XP offers two types of login: a graphical one and one using the more stolid Windows NT–style logon dialog box. Refer to Book II, Chapter 5 for information on changing the Windows XP login style.

Personalized Start-Up

After the prisoner identifies himself to the warden, or, rather, after you log in to Windows, a series of steps takes place to make your computing experience personal. Problems occurring at this point are due to those programs being loaded as the computer starts.

What happens

Logging in confirms who you are. Windows proceeds to load personal information about you and configures itself according to your preferences. Windows then loads the rest of itself into memory; specifically, the parts that deal with user interaction and program management. Any start-up programs are run as well.

When you get to this point, Windows updates the last known good control set. Those settings are used when you choose to restart the computer using the Last Known Good Configuration. Refer to Chapter 2.

Eventually the dust settles and you start using the computer. Any chaos that ensues at that point is most definitely *not* due to a start-up problem.

What could go wrong

Start-up programs can run things aground quickly, but another issue with a start-up program is how to disable it if you decide that it's no longer needed. Those issues are dealt with in Book II, Chapter 2.

Use Your PC

At some point, the Windows start-up ordeal ends and you're free to use your computer. Ta-da!

What happens

Oddly enough, even when you choose not to do anything with your computer, it doesn't sit still. A PC running Windows is a beehive of activity. Various programs, called *services,* scamper hither and thither. Windows own programs continue to run, such as the Task Scheduler, which help the computer perform tasks like networking, disk maintenance, and other routine stuff.

What could go wrong

Services can often run amok or die. Worse, some services are entirely unnecessary. Shutting them down, as well as monitoring them, is covered in Book II, Chapter 2.

The most common PC problem is when it runs slowly. That could be due to a number of reasons; therefore, Chapter 4 in Part II dwells on the topic at length.

The Last Thing You Do

After toiling (or playing or wasting time) with your computer, you eventually turn it off. As far as troubleshooting goes, turning off the computer again presents a slate of issues that may crop up. Those are covered in Chapter 3.

The most important thing about any computer isn't the hardware or the software. No, it's the stuff you create, the *data.* No matter what happens to your PC, preserving that data must be your top priority. The best way to ensure that your data stays with you is by creating a secondary, *backup,* copy of all your important creations, settings, savings, and stuff. Refer to Book VI, Chapter 1 for details.

Chapter 2: Birth Pangs

In This Chapter

✔ Solving start-up hardware problems

✔ Dealing with the BIOS password

✔ Losing an operating system

✔ Changing the boot order

✔ Using the Boot, F8, and F5 menus

✔ Facing the ugly recovery menu

*N*ot everyone gets out of bed the same way. Sure, some folks are superstitious about which foot hits the ground first. But I'm specifically addressing the issue of whether you energetically bound out of bed with a sunburst of energy or slog it through like a slow winch dragging a moss-covered log from a mud swamp. Although people exist on both sides of the bed (so to speak), computers seem to consistently and with enthusiasm jump to life at the start of their day. When they don't, that's when you turn to this chapter for troubleshooting assistance.

✦ When troubleshooting start-up problems, it helps to understand the process a computer goes through to get out of bed in the morning. Consider reading Chapter 1 for details on the PC's start-up process if you haven't already.

✦ Book II, Chapter 2 covers information on programs that may run when the computer starts, also leading to high-tech anguish.

The Onset of PC Heartbreak

Nothing beats that feeling when you arrive at your PC, set down a hot cup of coffee, take your seat and get ready to start a fresh, productive day. Well, nothing except seeing something unwanted on the screen. This section addresses those issues of initial woe.

✦ Initial woe is almost always a sign of hardware trouble. Replacing a bum part fixes the problem.

✦ Unlike other, typical PC trouble, problems occurring during start-up might not be due to some recent change in the computer. Even so, consider what you've changed in your computer: added new hardware, modified a software setting, or updated Windows. Those issues may have caused the problem.

✦ As long as the problem isn't with the PC's hard drive (storage system), your data stored in the computer is probably safe. Replacing the bad hardware fixes the problem without damaging your data. Even so, you risk damaging your data when taking your PC into the shop for repair; sometimes, the technicians replace or erase the hard drive. Or, of course, when the hard drive is the problem, it needs replacing anyway. That's why I recommend backup; see Book VI, Chapter 1.

Nothing — I see nothing

The loud silence of nothing when you turn on a PC means that it has a power supply issue. Check the following items in this order:

1. **Is there power?**

You cannot compute when the power is off. Likewise, you cannot compute during a *dip,* commonly called a *brownout.* That's a situation when the power is on, but running at a low voltage. Lights work, but motors don't. If the lights are on (dimly) but your computer doesn't work, you may be experiencing a dip. Wait it out, or check with the power company.

You might be tempted to run your PC from a UPS, or uninterruptible power supply. Don't. Use the UPS only to save your stuff and then properly shut down the computer. (If you have a generator, you can run the computer from its power, but not from a UPS.)

2. **Is the power supply on the computer operational?**

Do you hear the fan? Are any lights on? If not, the power supply may need replacing. See Chapter 8.

3. **Is the monitor on?**

Obvious question, and even I have fallen prey to this maddening problem.

4. **Is everything connected?**

Both internally and externally, cables must be plugged in and wires firmly seated. Especially if you just moved the computer, a cable can become unplugged easily.

Inside the PC is a different story: It doesn't happen often, but cables can wiggle loose — especially due to wide variations in the internal case temperature. See Chapter 8 for more information on venturing inside a PC's case to check the cable connections.

If you complete these steps and still cannot pinpoint the origin of the nothingness, the issue is most likely too large for you to resolve on your own. Before toting the computer into the shop, however, consider its age. Old computers die. That means that they don't start. If your PC is more than eight years old, it might just have expired. To fix that problem, buy a new computer.

✦ One way to confirm a dip is to check to see whether the refrigerator or furnace fan is running.

✦ Some uninterruptable power supplies (UPSs) beep during a brownout. A few models feature a digital display that may graphically show that the voltage is subnormal.

✦ It's possible to use a laptop when the power is off. Well, if the laptop has a charge in its battery and nothing else is awry. Refer to Book III for information on troubleshooting laptop start-up issues.

POST errors

The *POST* is the Power-On Self Test that all computers go through when they first start. (See Chapter 1 for the details). A computer that fails the POST has hardware trouble.

Your PC may or may not beep when it first starts. If you hear two or more beeps where there was one before, the PC may have either a power supply problem or a video system problem. Otherwise, the PC's splash screen is displayed. Any POST errors after that point are displayed on the computer's monitor.

What you can do with a POST error depends on the error message. Some error messages are cryptic. One POST error message that appeared on my PC was 58. *Hmmm.*

Text messages can be just as bad. For example:

```
Resource allocation conflict on motherboard
```

Whatever.

You can choose from two solutions for such puzzling start-up messages:

The first solution to try is to enter the PC's Setup program and determine whether the issue can be resolved there. Often, any errors encountered during the POST are flagged in the Setup program, or at least information is provided to help you resolve the issue; for example, to resolve a hardware sharing conflict. See Chapter 1 for more information on the PC's Setup program.

The second solution is to contact the manufacturer or your computer dealer to see what's up. If the computer is under warranty and the problem is severe, the manufacturer or dealer has an obligation to fix it.

✦ Some PCs sport error feedback on an LCD or through colored lights on the console. For example, a red light blinking three times on an HP computer might mean that the processor isn't installed or has popped out of its socket.

✦ Don't think that every code you see on the splash screen is a POST error. Many PCs display information during start-up that is completely normal and expected.

✦ POST error beeps vary in their number and variety. Generally, they refer to a problem with the power supply, memory, or video system.

✦ A common POST error is a missing keyboard or mouse. In fact, one of the most comic errors from the early days of the PC went something like this: "Keyboard missing, press any key to continue."

✦ If you have access to another computer and the Internet, you can search for specific POST errors. Many PC manufacturers list the lot on their support Web sites.

✦ Obviously, audio error messages work only when the PC's internal speaker works.

CMOS errors

PCs that are getting on in years may experience persistent start-up errors relating to a dead motherboard battery.

Yes, your computer has an internal battery. That battery keeps track of the time while the computer is turned off. On ancient computers, it also maintained something called the *CMOS* (say "see moss"). So a telltale sign of a CMOS error, and therefore a dead PC battery, was that the word *CMOS* appeared in the error message. For example:

```
98304K
162-System Options Not Set
163-Time & Date Not Set
The following configuration options were automatically
    updated:
Disk 1: 2428 Mbytes
If you are running Unix, you need to configure your system
    using the COMPAQ User Diagnostics diskette.
Total memory installed: 98304 Kbytes
Diskette Drives
CMOS checksum invalid, default values loaded
F1: Save Changes Compaq Deskpro 4000
```

To the trained eye, the information in this start-up text error message says a lot. Don't concern yourself with those details, just note the line that says, "CMOS checksum invalid." That's the clue: The PC needs a new battery.

Refer to Chapter 8 for more information on opening the computer's case.

There's a BIOS password!

I do not recommend setting the so-called BIOS password. That's an option in many PC Setup programs where you can lock out access to your PC at the hardware level. The password you set is recorded in the computer's non-volatile memory along with other system settings. Upon starting the PC, you're prompted to type the password to continue.

The problem with BIOS passwords is that people forget them. To make life easier, PC motherboard manufacturers have made it simple to reset or work around the password, which effectively renders the thing useless.

If you have forgotten the BIOS password, check with the motherboard manufacturer (or your computer dealer) to see whether a *backdoor* password is available. For example, the Phoenix-brand motherboard has the backdoor password PHOENIX, which you can type at the BIOS password prompt to gain access to the computer.

The time-honored solution to resetting the BIOS password is to open the computer's case and then remove and replace the motherboard's battery. Doing so erases the non-volatile memory and resets the password. Some motherboards also feature a *jumper,* which can be removed or reset to erase or disable the password.

✦ To find out which motherboard you use, pay close attention to your PC's splash screen. The motherboard (or chipset) manufacturer, as well as the version number, is often displayed. If that doesn't work, contact your dealer for support and write down the specifics for your computer's motherboard model number or type and the chipset version on this book's Cheat Sheet.

✦ Backdoor passwords are widely known and published extensively on the Web. That makes them seriously insecure.

✦ Refer to Chapter 8 for information on opening the PC's case.

✦ I say this in my other computer books, and I repeat it here: Do not use the BIOS password. The mere fact that it's so easy to recover from a missing BIOS password means that the thing is utterly useless in the first place. Trust me: Even if you don't know how to recover a BIOS password, the bad guys most certainly do!

"Did my PC secretly restart?"

If you leave your computer on all the time, you may show up one morning and discover that Windows has automatically restarted itself; rather than see the desktop, you see the logon screen.

The main reason the computer has restarted itself is that you have Windows Updates install automatically. That's okay. For some updates, an automatic restart is done. You can confirm that by looking at the pop-up bubble that appears in the notification area, describing that updates were recently installed. No problem there.

✦ If the computer restarted and there were no updates, it might indicate a restarting problem. See Chapter 3, the section "Problems with Restarting."

✦ The power company might be to blame: A power outage or "dip" in the middle of the night can stop or restart your computer.

✦ Refer to Book II, Chapter 1 for information on Windows Updates and how to configure Windows to not automatically restart itself for updating purposes.

Operating System Trouble

You can't do squat on a computer until an operating system is loaded into memory. The process of loading the operating system is handled by the computer's *boot loader,* which is part of the PC's hardware. The boot loader's job is to transfer information from the computer's mass storage (typically a hard drive) into memory. It sounds simple, but a plethora of things can go awry.

The horrifying, blinking cursor

The screen is dark. In the upper-left corner is a flashing bar. Off and on. That's the blinking *cursor.* It's a bad sign: It means that the computer is waiting to load an operating system from somewhere, anywhere. It's not the end of the world, though, because it means that the problem might be easy to fix.

First thing to check: Is a memory card sticking out of the console like a tiny diving board or an impudent tongue? If so, remove the card and restart the computer. The same thing might happen with an MP3 player or iPod: Remove the device and restart the computer. What happened was that the PC, because it's stupid, tried to start itself using the memory card (or iPod) rather than the hard drive. Removing the memory card fixes the problem.

Mostly, when an operating system is missing, it means that that the computer's *boot order* must be changed. Refer to the next section.

Changing the boot order

The *boot order* is the sequence of storage devices that the computer's hardware checks to find an operating system. As luck would have it, an operating system could lurk in several places:

Hard drive: This is the main boot device for most PCs, selected first for reasons of tradition. More than one hard drive may be in your computer, and those hard drives may be *partitioned* into separate, *logical* drives. All that's okay. The *Master Boot Record* (MBR) on the primary hard drive holds a map that indicates where the operating system can be found or provides a boot menu to select an operating system.

Optical drive (CD-ROM/DVD): Even when you don't choose the optical drive as the primary boot device, many PCs automatically detect a bootable disc in the optical (CD or DVD) drive. When that happens, an option is displayed on the screen, something like "Press Enter to boot from the CD or DVD." By pressing the Enter key, you direct the computer to start from that disc on the fly.

Network (Ethernet): Rather than load an operating system from the PC's own (local) storage devices, the network option directs the computer to load its operating system from the network. On start-up, the network adapter makes a request to a server for an operating system to load, which it then downloads from the server.

USB device: The USB device can be a memory card or an external disk drive. This option is useful for laptops that lack an optical drive, allowing you to install or upgrade your PC's operating system. It also allows you to boot from a memory card.

You set the boot order in the PC's Setup program. Generally, the steps go like this:

1. **Restart or turn on the computer.**

2. **Press the key or keys to enter the Setup program.**

Refer to Chapter 1 for information on the PC's Setup program. As a reminder, the most common key used to enter the Setup program is the F1 key.

Ensure that you press the key to enter the Setup program or menu. Do not press the key to enter the boot menu, which is a different item (and is covered later in this chapter).

3. **Choose the menu option or options to display the boot sequence.**

The option may not be obvious from the Setup program's main menu, not to mention that the Setup program is in text mode. Various computers I've researched display the menu that changes the boot order in these ways:

Startup⇨Boot

Boot⇨Boot Device Priority

Advanced BIOS Features⇨(various priority submenus)

System⇨Boot Sequence

Figure 2-1 illustrates a typical Boot Sequence screen found in a PC Setup program screen that I made up.

```
                        System Setup
  Main   Advanced   Security   Power   Boot   Exit
  Boot Menu    Boot Sequence

       1. Hard Drive
       2. Floppy Drive          (not present)
       3. Optical Drive
       4. Network Controller
       5. USB Device

  Do not boot from:

       6. USB floppy drive
       7. USB Flash Drive


       Press F6 to move an item up; F7 to move
       an item down. Press F10 to save,
       ESC to cancel.
```

Figure 2-1:
A typical
Boot
Sequence
screen.

4. **Set the boot order.**

Use whichever keys or techniques are required in order to set the sequence in which the hardware searches the storage devices for an operating system.

5. **Save the changes and exit the Setup program.**

The computer restarts with the new settings.

You might see other options in addition to those that set the boot sequence search order. For example, there might be a way to exclude certain devices from being searched. This might be a good idea for USB media cards that may stop up your PC's start-up sequence or for legacy floppy drives.

You may see supplemental or submenus as well: for example, menus for each of the devices — hard drive, optical drive, and external drive. That way, for instance, when multiple optical drives are present, you can choose which to use as boot devices and which to ignore.

Additionally, you might find boot options to turn off or on for each boot device. For example, your PC's Setup program may allow you to disable or enable booting from the optical drive. If it's disabled, you can't boot from a CD or DVD no matter where the optical drive is in the boot sequence order.

✦ Booting from the network happens only when the network card is configured as a boot device. Not all network cards have such a feature. It can also happen only when the network is active and the cable is connected.

✦ For the longest time, PCs looked first to the floppy drive to start the computer. That's why the floppy drive was drive A, the first drive. When the floppy drive didn't contain a diskette, the computer then looked to the first physical hard drive for an operating system. (See Chapter 4 for more information on what the first physical hard drive is.)

The No Operating System sisters

Several start-up error messages have similar causes and solutions, yet each of them has a tendency to induce heart palpitations. These messages appear before an operating system is loaded, and they indicate that the computer is having difficulty in finding the operating system:

```
Invalid Partition Table
Missing Operating System
Operating System Not Found
Non-System Disk or Disk Error
```

Each of these error messages is caused by a similar issue: a faulty Master Boot Record or partition table. You can easily address this situation; Chapter 4 provides a good explanation of the jargon. Fixing the problem is the domain of the Windows Recovery Console, which is covered in Book II, Chapter 8.

"Press any key to boot from the optical disc"

When you insert a bootable disc into your PC's optical drive, you may see a message prompting you to boot the computer from that disc. The message varies, but reads something along the line of

```
Press any key to boot from the CD or DVD
```

This message is *not* a sign of trouble. It merely means that you stuck a bootable disc into the optical drive — and you configured your PC's Setup program to look for an alert to the presence of such a disc. No problem: Wait out the message, and the computer starts up normally. Or, if you press Enter (the "any" key), the computer starts using the optical disc.

Never start your computer from an unknown disc, such as one burned by a "friend" who is "giving away" a "free" copy of Windows or some other software program illegally. That's how computers become irrevocably infected with malware. (See Book IV, Chapter 4 for more information on *malware,* or evil software.)

Removing a boot loader

To remove a boot loader, you must rewrite the storage system's *Master Boot Record* (MBR). That's where the boot loader dwells, so all you need is a tool to raze the existing boot loader like a bulldozer would raze a perfectly good old government building to make room for a new, more expensive government building.

Rather than use a bulldozer on your PC's hard drive (and it would work, but not well), you need to use the recovery console to rewrite the MBR. Directions for doing so can be found in Book II, Chapter 8.

+ Refer to Chapter 1 for more information on what a boot loader is and how it plays a role in the way your PC starts.

+ If problems persist after fixing the MBR, the boot manager wasn't the source.

+ A corrupt or missing boot loader prevents the computer from starting — well, specifically, starting from the hard drive. You can still boot the computer from an optical disc, a USB drive, or a media card.

+ I don't recommend removing the Boot Camp boot loader when you're running Windows on a Macintosh. Even when you plan on using only Windows on your Macintosh, it would just be a bad idea to remove the option for starting OS X.

Start-Up Menus

Before your PC can get up and dance, you may encounter, or desire to encounter, one of a multitude of start-up menus and options. Some are for troubleshooting purposes, and others may present options for starting the computer, selecting an operating system, or placing Windows into Safe mode. This section covers many of those menus and choices.

✦ If you're using a boot loader, you see its menu when you first start your computer. Refer to Chapter 1 for more information on the boot loader.

✦ Though you don't see a menu per se, you do have the option of pressing one or more keys when the computer starts. One key allows you to enter the PC's Setup program (see Chapter 1), and the second presents a boot menu, described in the next section.

The boot menu

The first possible menu you can see for starting your PC is what I call the *boot menu*. I don't believe it has an official name, but it's an option available on many computers.

To view the boot menu, you press a special key when the computer first starts. The key to press is described on the PC's start-up or splash screen. Often it's the F10 key, though it may be some other key, such as the blue ThinkVantage button found on many Lenovo keyboards. Pressing that key displays a boot menu, similar to the one shown in Figure 2-2.

```
                    Boot Menu


Choose a Startup Device:


        Hard Disk
        Removeable Drive
        CD/DVD
        Network
```

Figure 2-2:
A typical
boot menu.

Use the menu to select a storage device containing the operating system you want to start. The PC then attempts to load an operating system from the chosen device.

Unlike setting the boot order in a PC, the boot menu is used to select a *temporary* start-up device; the option you choose from the boot menu doesn't become the primary way the computer starts from now on. This is why the boot menu is often called the Alternative Startup Device option on some PCs.

The F8 menu

Perhaps the most well-known of the PC's boot-up menus is the Advanced Boot Options menu, commonly called the F8 menu. That's because the menu appears when you press the F8 key just after Windows starts. In fact, you have to be quick: The F8 key must be pressed *before* the Windows start-up screen (the logo) appears.

Figure 2-3 illustrates what the F8 menu looks like in Windows XP. The Windows Vista version has similar options available, as described next.

```
Windows Advanced Options Menu
Please select an option

    Safe Mode
    Safe Mode with Networking
    Safe Mode with Command Prompt

    Enable Boot Logging
    Enable VGA Mode
    Last Known Good Configuration (your most recent settings that worked)
    Directory Services Restore Mode (Windows domain controllers only)
    Debugging Mode
    Disable automatic restart on system failure

    Start Windows Normally
    Reboot

Use the up and down arrow keys to move the highlight to your choice
```

Figure 2-3: The F8 boot menu.

Repair Your Computer: This option starts up repair and recovery options on certain PCs, essentially booting the computer into the RECOVERY partition of the main hard drive (in Windows Vista only). See Boot II, Chapter 8 to find out how to use this tool.

Safe Mode: In Safe mode, the computer starts and only Windows is loaded — no add-on drivers or software. Safe mode is a good tool for tracking down problem programs, as covered in Book II, Chapter 3.

Safe Mode with Networking: Safe mode is started and networking abilities are loaded. This option is required when you need to access the network to assist with troubleshooting.

Safe Mode with Command Prompt: Windows runs in Safe mode but displays a text-only interface, which is useful for troubleshooting graphics problems or when you're not completely befuddled by the command prompt and actually enjoy using the computer that way.

Enable Boot Logging: Selecting this option directs Windows to write detailed information about the start-up process to a file named `ntbtlog.txt`. See Book II, Chapter 7 for information on reviewing this log file.

Enable low-resolution video (640 x 480): Choosing this option starts the PC in a very low-resolution video mode, but not in Safe Mode. This setting is useful for tracking down video problems (see Chapter 6). Note that in Windows XP, this selection reads Enable VGA Mode.

Last Known Good Configuration: This item starts Windows using the most recently saved system configuration information. This option is good for when you experience start-up problems after a Windows update or software upgrade.

Directory Services Restore Mode: Selecting this option is necessary only when using a Windows Domain Controller. If such a concept befuddles you, rest assured that you'll most likely never need to choose this option.

Debugging Mode: This item is used for programming purposes. It starts something called the Windows kernel debugger. Whatever.

Disable automatic restart on system failure: A gem, this item prevents the vexing and endless "There is a problem, so I will restart" type of problem. Refer to Chapter 3 for more information.

Disable Driver Signature Enforcement: This Windows Vista option allows the computer to run drives that don't have proper identification (signatures). Doing so is risky when you're uncertain of the driver software or the developer's reputation, but it's often necessary in order to run a computer when troubleshooting.

Start Windows Normally: Choosing this option continues the Windows start-up process on its merry way, as though nothing ever happened. La-di-da.

Reboot: This item is available only in Windows XP. Choosing Reboot restarts the computer.

When the F8 menu is visible, you can press Ctrl+Alt+Delete to restart the computer. This works because Ctrl+Alt+Delete is hard-wired on PCs as the software restart switch.

✦ You have to press the F8 key almost *immediately* after the PC's hardware splash screen appears. I often just press and hold F8 to ensure that the menu shows up, though the computer beeps at you when the keyboard's buffer is full (but that's not a bad thing).

✦ Why the F8 key? I don't know.

The F5 menu

Another start-up menu, though not as popular as the F8 key menu, is the F5 key menu. It works the same way: You press the F5 key just as the computer starts, and hopefully before the Windows logo appears. What happens after pressing F5 depends on your version of Windows.

In Windows Vista, the F5 key summons the Windows Boot Manager, which displays a list of operating systems known to Windows. You can choose one from the list. Often, when no other version of Windows is installed, as shown in Figure 2-4, you just choose to start Windows Vista.

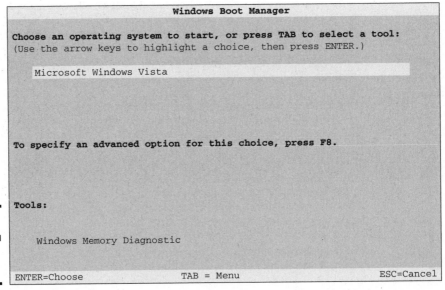

Figure 2-4:
The F5 menu in Windows Vista.

In Windows XP, the F5 menu looks similar, though it's missing the Tools portion of the Windows Vista menu (refer to Figure 2-4). When only one operating system is installed on the computer, what you see when you press the F5 key looks just like the F8 menu (refer to Figure 2-3), but with the addition of one menu item at the end: Return to OS Choices Menu.

You use the F5 menu to choose an operating system, though the menu itself isn't a boot loader per se. It's more of a way to manage multiple versions of Windows installed on the same PC, which in and of itself I think is a nutty concept.

Controlling the F5 menu is done by using the Startup and Recover dialog box, covered in the next section.

✦ There's no point in using the F5 menu unless Windows is installed multiple times on your computer. Often, it's easier to use a boot manager to configure your PC with multiple operating systems.

✦ In MS-DOS, pressing the F5 key at start-up disabled the AUTOEXEC.BAT and CONFIG.SYS files, preventing them from being executed. Adding the line

```
SWITCHES=/N
```

to the CONFIG.SYS file disabled the F5 key from working when the computer started. Since Windows 98, however, the F5 key has worked as described in this section.

Start-up and recovery options

The options for the various start-up menus are kept in the Startup and Recovery dialog box. Here's how to venture to that dialog box:

1. Open the System icon in the Control Panel.

This book assumes that you're using the Control Panel Classic View (see the Introduction).

2. In Windows Vista, choose the link Advanced System Settings from the left side of the window; if prompted with a User Account Control warning, click Continue or type the administrator's password to continue.

The System Properties dialog box presents itself.

3. Click the Advanced tab.

4. In the Startup and Recovery area, click the Settings button.

The Startup and Recovery dialog box appears. Figure 2-5 illustrates the dialog box for both Windows Vista and Windows XP; they have only subtle differences between them.

Figure 2-5: The Startup and Recovery dialog boxes.

Windows Vista   Windows XP

The list of operating systems at the top of the dialog box includes only those that Windows itself knows about — the same items that would appear on the F5 boot menu. (See the section "The F5 menu," earlier in this chapter.) Other options relate to that boot menu as well.

The bottom section of the Startup and Recovery dialog box deals with how Windows handles a crash, including the infamous Automatically Restart option that you might consider unchecking at this point.

5. **Close the dialog box by clicking the OK button, and close any other open dialog boxes or windows.**

If you installed Linux or some other operating system on your PC, the computer uses a special boot loader as the computer's start-up menu, not the Startup and Recovery options in Windows.

Don't get excited about the memory dump options; that information is useful only when you're a programmer — specifically, someone working for Microsoft who has a way to fix the Windows code using the "dump" information.

Windows Error Recovery menu

One ugly start-up menu that you don't want to see is the Windows Error Recovery menu. It has two flavors, with one menu showing up for start-up problems and the other for shutdown problems. The shutdown version is covered in Chapter 3, and the start-up version is shown in Figure 2-6.

```
                      Windows Error Recovery

Windows failed to start. A recent hardware or software change might be the
cause. To fix the problem:

   1. Insert your Windows installation disc and restart your computer.
   2. Choose your language settings, and then click "Next."
   3. Click "Repair your computer."

Other options:
If power was interrupted during startup, choose Start Windows Normally.
(Use the arrow keys to highlight your choice.)

      Safe Mode
      Safe mode with Networking
      Safe Mode wth Command Prompt
      Last Known Good Configuration (advanced)
      Start Windows Normally


Description: Start Windows with its regular settings
```

Figure 2-6:
The
Windows
Error
Recovery
menu,
start-up
version.

The first thing suggested by the Windows Error Recovery menu is to use the Windows Recovery Console, as described by the three steps shown in Figure 2-6 (and covered in Book II, Chapter 8).

The bottom part of the window contains commands similar to those on the F8 menu, including Safe mode options.

I recommend first choosing the option Start Windows Normally. If you see the error message again, choose Last Known Good Configuration.

When the problem persists, try Safe mode to determine whether the problem exists in Windows itself or in some other program or driver on the computer. See Book II, Chapter 3.

Chapter 3: Death Throes

In This Chapter

↳ **Understanding PC shutdown**

↳ **Controlling the power button**

↳ **Dealing with shutdown woes**

↳ **Using power management**

↳ **Discovering hibernation**

↳ **Fixing restart issues**

You don't actually turn a computer off. That's old-school thinking. Computers today go through a *shutdown* process: They methodically plod through a set of steps to ensure that all the knots are unwound and the loose ends tightened. Then, after the software has determined that all its tasks are in the Happily Ever After stage, the operating system directs the hardware to turn itself off. The hardware complies. That's how it's supposed to work. When things go awry, when the computer acts like a stubborn four-year-old and refuses to be put to bed, that's when you turn to this chapter for assistance.

To Quit or Not to Quit?

As with starting a computer, it helps to understand the PC shutdown process to appreciate where and how things can run amok. Unlike starting a computer, however, the case of shutting down a computer involves choices: You don't always need to turn a computer off. In fact, I leave my computers on pretty much all the time. I do, however, employ some of the alternative, "almost shutdown" options. This section describes the details.

Shutting down a PC

Turning off a computer was once as simple as flipping the On–Off switch to the Off position. As with most electronic gizmos, a computer no longer sports a true On–Off switch. No, it has a *power button*. Unlike when you turn the PC on, seldom do you use the power button to turn the thing off.

When you shut down a PC, the following things happen:

User Check: When other users are logged in to the computer (using another account on the same PC), you're alerted. Do you really want to shut down? Those users may be running programs or have unsaved documents. Clicking No cancels the operation, which is the proper thing to do. (Also see the section "Someone else is logged in!" later in this chapter.)

Program Close: Windows shuts down any programs or processes that you've begun, or that "belong" to you. It sifts through that list and sends each program the shutdown signal. If a program contains unsaved data, you're prompted to save the data to continue. (Or, you can click the Cancel button, which stops the entire shutdown operation.) When a program cannot be stopped, you're prompted to end it, which is discussed later in this chapter, in the section aptly titled "End now?"

User Logout: After programs (and processes) belonging to you, the human, are stopped, Windows logs you out, ending your Windows session.

Windows halted: After you're gone, Windows begins shutting down bits and pieces of itself. These programs, services, and processes are all ended, and Windows ensures that they end properly and have no social issues or gripes.

Shutdown signal: When Windows is done with itself, it sends a signal to the computer's power-management hardware to turn off the power. If that feature isn't present, a message appears on the screen, something like "It is now safe to turn off this computer and get back to real life."

The shutdown process may seem overly formal. After all, a program will stop when it's told to stop or when the electricity stops. Indeed, years ago, computers were routinely shut down by flipping off the power switch. But there's something unnerving about *grinding* to a halt.

By properly shutting itself down, the computer avoids the issue of *digital detritus*. For example, an improper shutdown causes some programs to leave pieces of themselves around like clutter from an explosion. Clutter builds. Rather than deal with the clutter, you should make sure that the tasks the computer does are sanely and systematically shut down.

Another advantage to a proper shutdown is that any looming errors not detected when the computer is running might show up during the shutdown process. Often, that's the only way to identify and troubleshoot an issue.

Ending your Windows day

You have several choices for quitting your computer duties:

Switch User: You remain logged in to the computer and your programs continue to be open, but choosing this option allows another user to access the computer.

Log Off: You can end your Windows session, save your stuff, and quit programs, but Windows remains on and ready for others to use the computer.

Lock: Not a complete log-out, this option allows you to protect your stuff by displaying the Windows logon screen. You must type your password or log in as another user to get into the computer. (Obviously, this option works best when all accounts are password protected; see Book II, Chapter 5.)

Sleep: The computer is put into a low-power consumption mode, saving energy. Also known as Stand By, this mode may put the entire computer into low-power mode or only the monitor or hard drives. In this power-saving mode, the computer comes back to life quickly, usually with the press of a key or jiggle of the mouse.

Restart: The computer is shut down and then started again when this option is chosen. Also called a *reset* or, if you want to get nerdy, a *warm boot.*

Hibernate: The best power-saving mode, with this option the computer is shut down and turned off. But information in memory is saved so that when the computer turns on again, you simply resume your former activities (after logging in, of course). Hibernation saves the most power, but it takes longer to restart the computer than either Sleep or Standby mode because you're literally turning it on again.

Shut Down/Turn Off: When this option is selected, the computer is shut down: You're logged out of your account, which closes your programs and allows you to save your data. Windows then shuts itself down, and eventually the computer turns itself off.

The Switch User, Log Off, Lock, and Sleep options don't turn off the computer. The Restart, Hibernate, and Shut Down options do turn off the system.

See the next section for information on where to access these commands and options.

Finding the shutdown options

Choosing a shutdown option first involves finding where that option dwells in Windows. For a software shutdown, the location varies, but generally speaking, you need to look to the bottom of the Start button menu.

Windows XP sports two options at the bottom of the Start button menu: Log Off and Turn Off Computer. Neither button does what it claims; instead, another menu appears, as shown in Figures 3-1 and 3-2.

Figure 3-1: Windows XP Log Off options.

Figure 3-2: Windows XP shut-down options.

Choosing the Log Off options from the Windows XP Start menu displays the Log Off Windows options, shown in Figure 3-1. Both options allow someone else to use the computer; Switch User suspends your session, and Log Off ends it.

In Figure 3-2, you see the Turn Off Computer window, which contains *four* options. The visible options are Stand By (to enter Sleep mode), Turn Off, and Restart. The fourth option is Hibernate. It becomes visible when you press the Shift key; the Stand By text is replaced by the word *Hibernate*. (Hibernation is available only when it has been turned on, as described later in this chapter.

The only option not available in either window is Lock. To lock a Windows XP computer, you press the Win+L key combo. That trick also works for Windows Vista.

In Windows Vista, the shutdown options are found at the bottom of the Start menu, as shown in Figure 3-3. Unlike in Windows XP, all these options are clustered near the same spot and pretty much all of them are listed.

Figure 3-3:
Windows
Vista
shutdown
options.

Lock button   Shutdown menu

Sofware power button

Unlike in Windows XP, all the shutdown options are available on the Windows Vista shutdown menu (refer to Figure 3-3). You also notice that a Lock button exists, which locks the computer. It does the same thing as the Lock command on the Shutdown menu and the Win+L key combination. (I enjoy how Microsoft occasionally hits you over the head with a command.)

Windows Vista also sports a software power button (refer to Figure 3-3). That button can be assigned the functions Shutdown, Hibernate, or Sleep, as described later in this chapter.

You may notice that the Hibernate command is missing on the shutdown menu in your version of Windows Vista. That means that you activated hybrid sleep. When hybrid sleep is on, the Hibernation option isn't available on the shutdown menu. See the section "What is hybrid sleep?" later in this chapter, for more information on hybrid sleep.

Setting the power button function

The poor power button sits in the real world, often used only to turn on the computer. How sad. But you can use the power button to turn the computer off as well. That's because the power button is *programmable*. It can do anything you want it to do, including nothing.

To set the power button's function, follow these steps for Windows Vista:

1. **Open the Control Panel's Power Options icon.**

2. **Click the link Change Plan Settings found beneath the selected plan.**

   More than one link is titled Change Plan Settings. Choose the one under the plan with the highlighted radio button.

3. **Choose the link Advanced Power Settings.**

   The Power Options dialog box appears.

4. **Click the plus sign (+) by the item titled Power Buttons and Lid.**

5. **Click the + next to the option Power Button Action.**

6. **Click the button next to the word Setting to choose a power button function.**

   The word next to Setting is really a button you can click. There can be four options: Do Nothing, Sleep, Hibernate, and Shut Down.

   Because this is Windows Vista, you can also set the function for the software power button:

7. **Click the + next to the option Start Menu Power Button.**

8. **Choose an option for the Start menu power button.**

   The options are Sleep, Hibernate, and Shut Down.

9. **Click OK to dismiss the Power Options dialog box and confirm your choices.**

10. **Close the Control Panel window.**

Watch Video 131 on the companion DVD to see me work through these steps on your screen.

Follow these steps to set the power button's function in Windows XP:

1. **Open the Control Panel's Power Options icon.**

   The Power Options Properties dialog box appears.

2. **Click the Advanced tab.**

3. **In the Power Buttons area, choose the power button's function from the drop-down list beneath When I Press the Power Button On My Computer.**

   The five options are Do Nothing, Ask Me What to Do, Stand By, Hibernate, and Shut Down.

   The Ask Me What to Do option displays the standard Shutdown window (refer to Figure 3-2).

4. **Click OK and close the Control Panel window.**

You must have hibernation activated before you can use hibernation as an option for the power button. See the section "Activating hibernation," later in this chapter, for the details.

You can assign the power button to hibernate the computer in Windows Vista, even when hybrid sleep is active. See the later section "What is hybrid sleep?"

Shutdown Malaise

Shutdown problems don't carry the weighty burden of start-up issues, or, really, other typical PC problems. That's probably because shutting down is what you do at the *end* of the day. Also, shutdown issues don't often have an effect on starting the computer. (Well, just hope that's the case.) Regardless, this section contains some good information on dealing with PC troubles and tribulations that happen during the shutdown process.

General shutdown advice

A big reason for shutdown issues in any PC is that the computer's software isn't up-to-date. Old hardware without proper software to support it may work fine when the computer is on. But when you shut down the PC, you have trouble as the older hardware and its equally old software fail to follow proper procedure. So a blanket rule for fixing just about any shutdown issue is to ensure that your computer is using the latest software drivers. Refer to Chapter 7 for information on how to check and update drivers.

Another useful hint: Check the logs. A shutdown problem that causes an error message generates a log entry in Windows. Refer to Book II, Chapter 7 for more information.

Turning off a stubborn PC

The computer's power button may seem feeble, but there's a sneaky way to turn it into a true Off switch: Press and hold the power button for five to eight seconds. After that length of time, the computer turns itself off.

Using the power button to forcibly turn off a computer is a desperate measure. Yes, it's necessary, but it shouldn't be the way you always turn off the computer. Try to troubleshoot shutdown issues. Do not ignore them.

Slow shutdown

The most common reason that a PC takes a long time to shut down is that it's installing updates. Windows Vista displays information right on the screen when updates are being installed. Just wait. But, often, third-party device drivers may not display information. My advice is to be patient.

How long should you wait? That depends on how much time you have. If you interrupt an update process, at best you have to go through it again and at worst you corrupt Windows. (Corrupting Windows is the only time you really need to reinstall the operating system.)

A good way to determine whether the computer is stuck or just thinking is to examine the hard drive light on the console. When the light is flashing, the computer is simply busy. It's best that the light flash at irregular intervals, however, because a regularly flashing light may indicate that Mr. Computer is stuck in a loop. In that case, force a shutdown as discussed in the preceding section, "Turning off a stubborn PC."

The shutdown process may be slow simply because the PC is slow to begin with. Refer to Book II, Chapter 4 for information on pepping up a slow computer.

Someone else is logged in!

If you're one of the smart folks who bothered to set up multiple accounts on a single PC (one for everyone!), you may have seen a shutdown error message similar to the one shown in Figure 3-4. It's a good message; nothing to panic over.

Figure 3-4:
Someone's
in the PC
with you.

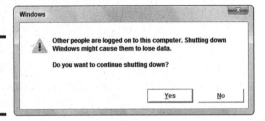

Unless it's an emergency, click the No button when you're greeted by a message such as the one shown in Figure 3-4. That's because (as it says) the other person may have open, unsaved files. Only when you really need to shut down or restart (such as during a power outage) should you click the Yes button.

When you click the No button, log out of your account. Then use the login screen (which automatically shows up) to determine who else is logged in. Get that person to log in, save their stuff, and then shut down or restart the computer.

A variation on the warning message shown in Figure 3-4 happens when others on the network are using your computer. The message might say something like "Others on the network are using this PC." In that case, it's generally okay to proceed.

End now?

The dialog box is titled End Program, but just about everyone I know refers to it by its key button, End Now. It's shown in Figure 3-5, and it occasionally shows up on the computer screen when you shut down or restart the PC. The issue is a program that's stuck or one that's running but that Windows cannot shut down.

Figure 3-5:
Killing off a program.

To continue the shutdown process, click the End Now button. Or, in some cases, you can wait it out, and Windows eventually shuts down the program automatically.

A Windows Vista variation on the End Now situation is a full screen message stating, "The following programs are still running" and then listing the programs. Click the Cancel button to stop the operation, or click the red button to continue. (The red button's text varies, depending on whether you're shutting down or just logging off.)

+ Don't fall into the trap of just clicking the End Now button! Occasionally, the message is flagging a program that you must manually shut down, such as the Command Prompt program mentioned in Figure 3-5. In that case, click the Cancel button in the dialog box and then return to the stuck program, save, and quit. You can then shut down or restart the PC.

+ A common culprit of the End Now syndrome is the Rundll32.exe process. Don't freak out! In Windows, Rundll32.exe is responsible for running (get it?) a number of processes. The problem is most likely not with the Rundll32.exe program itself, but rather with whichever process Rundll32.exe is running. Refer to Book II, Chapter 2 for information on processes in Windows.

"The computer was improperly shut down!"

Whether it was intended to or not, sometimes the computer does crash. This book would be a lot thinner if computers didn't crash often enough.

In the early days, a computer that was improperly shut down warned you the next time it started. A message appeared on the screen, alerting you to the improper shutdown. These days, the computer doesn't display the message; instead, it just automatically does a disk check to fix any problems caused by the improper shutdown.

Face it: Sometimes you have to "improperly" shut down a computer that has gone haywire. And, sometimes the power just turns off, and shuts down the PC immediately. It's okay! Don't freak out! Today's operating systems recognize and recover from such shutdown mishaps.

If you see the message often, you need to troubleshoot it. Often, the culprit is a program that hangs or hogs memory and makes the shutdown process impossible. Refer to Book II, Chapter 2 for information on hunting down such naughty programs.

Windows Error Recovery menu

Sometimes the boo-boos caused by Windows at shutdown aren't known until you restart the computer. In some of those cases, you see the Windows Error Recovery menu, shown in Figure 3-6. Yes, it's a Text mode screen that appears as soon as Windows starts to load.

The Window Error Recovery menu is basically an abbreviated form of the F8 menu; in addition to the standard F8 menu options, it has Safe mode options and the Start Windows Normally option.

+ If the error appears to be random, select the Start Windows Normally option and, after Windows starts, check the logs to see which program may have improperly shut things down. See Book II, Chapter 7 for information on reviewing the logs.

✦ You can use the Safe mode options to attempt a System Restore operation, but that works only when you've recently updated hardware or software in your PC. Refer to Book II, Chapter 8 for information on System Restore and to Book II, Chapter 3 for Safe mode.

✦ When this error is chronic, you really need to pay attention to your computer. Something is wrong that needs fixing. Because Windows recognizes the error, it's most likely not a hardware problem. See Book II, Chapter 8 for various Windows recovery options.

✦ The other Window Error Recovery menu, the start-up version, is covered in Chapter 2 of this minibook; refer to the section uncreatively named "Windows Error Recovery menu."

Figure 3-6:
Windows
Error
Recovery
menu,
shutdown
version.

Windows Error Recovery

Windows did not shut down successfully. If this was due to the system not responding, or if the system was shut down to protect data, you might be able to recover by choosing one of the Safe Mode configurations from the menu below:
(Use the arrow keys to highlight your choice.)

   Safe Mode
   Safe Mode with Networking
   Safe Mode with Command Prompt

   Start Windows Normally

Seconds until the highlighted choice will be selected automatically: 30
Description: Start Windows with its regular settings

ENTER=Choose

Power Management Issues

Way back when, hardware engineers set out to enhance the way computers manage power. Various solutions culminated in a set of software protocols and hardware goodness called the *Advanced Configuration and Power Interface (ACPI)*.

Although ACPI serves many computers well, by managing power, sleeping hardware, and saving lots of energy year after year, it can also be a source of woe. For example, Windows XP often fails to detect ACPI hardware in a computer, so the feature is never installed. Or, worse, ACPI is improperly detected and you end up with a computer that falls into a coma instead of falling asleep.

This section discusses some common power-management messes.

Activating power management in Windows XP

To ensure that Windows XP is taking advantage of your computer's power management prowess, follow these steps:

1. **Open the Control Panel's Power Options icon.**

2. **In the Power Options Properties dialog box, click the APM tab.**

If you don't see the APM tab, your computer is fine and ready to go: skip to Step 4.

3. **Click the option Enable Advanced Power Management Support.**

4. **Click OK to dismiss the Power Options Properties dialog box, and then close the Control Panel window.**

The computer should now properly manage power options, like Sleep mode.

If you continue to have problems with Windows XP and power management, visit the computer manufacturer's Web site to check for new power-management driver software. You can also use the Windows Update service to confirm that your computer is using the most current drivers. Refer to Book II, Chapter 1.

Enabling power management for specific devices

Occasionally, you find a Power Management tab in various Properties dialog boxes for devices capable of power management. You can use that tab to enable or disable the power management features of specific devices, such as the networking adapter shown in Figure 3-7.

To find those devices, you use the Device Manager. Heed these steps:

1. **Open the Control Panel.**

2a. **In Windows Vista, open the Device Manager icon; click the Continue button or type the administrator's password to continue.**

2b. **In Windows XP, open the System icon, click the Hardware tab, and then click the Device Manager button.**

3. **Open a category to view the devices available in that category.**

4. **Open a device to view its Properties dialog box.**

5. **Click the Power Management tab in the Properties dialog box to control power management for that device.**

Typically, you see an option to enable the power management features, plus maybe another option specific to the device.

6. **Close the various dialog boxes and windows when you're done.**

Figure 3-7:
Power
manage-
ment for
specific
gizmos.

The devices I've found with a Power Management tab in their Properties dialog box include keyboards, mouse or pointing devices, network adapters, and some of the system devices. There may be others as well.

Note that it's possible to configure your PC's mouse or keyboard to *not* wake up the computer from Sleep mode. That's done on the Power Management tab of the device's Properties dialog box; simply remove the check mark next to Allow This Device to Wake the Computer. In Windows XP, the command is titled Allow This Device to Bring the Computer Out of Standby.

Activating hibernation

Hibernation must be activated, in both Windows Vista and Windows XP.

In Windows Vista, hibernation can be activated, but remember that when hybrid sleep is also activated, Hibernation doesn't appear as an option on the Shutdown menu. (Hibernation can, however, be assigned to the software power button, as described in the section "Setting the power button function," earlier in this chapter.)

To quickly activate hibernation in Windows Vista, follow these technical but efficient steps:

1. **Pop up the Start menu.**

2. **Choose All Programs⇨Accessories.**

3. **Right-click on the Command Prompt item.**

4. **Choose Run As Administrator.**

5. **Type the administrator's password or click Continue.**

   The Administrator Command Prompt window appears — in all its ugly text-mode glory.

6. **At the command prompt, type** powercfg -h on **and press Enter.**

   That's **powercfg**, a space, a hyphen, the letter **h**, a space, and then **on**.

   There's no feedback for the command.

7. **Type** exit **(and press Enter) to close the Administrator Command Prompt window.**

To deactivate hibernation, repeat these steps but substitute the word **off** for **on** in Step 6.

To activate hibernation in Windows XP, follow these steps:

1. **Open the Control Panel's Power Options icon.**

2. **Click the Hibernate tab.**

3. **Place a check mark by the option Enable Hibernation.**

4. **Click OK, and close the Control Panel window.**

After hibernation is active, the next step toward using it is to find the option, as described in the following section.

Finding hibernation

Hibernation is easier to find in Windows XP than it is in Windows Vista. Of course, it's not obvious in Windows XP; to see the Hibernation setting, you must press the Shift key while viewing the Turn Off Computer window (refer to Figure 3-2). When the Shift key is held down, the Stand By option changes to Hibernate. Click the Hibernate button to hibernate the PC.

On Windows Vista, the Hibernation option appears on the Shutdown menu (refer to Figure 3-3). That is, unless you have hybrid sleep active (see the next section). But in that case, you can easily assign hibernation to the software power button's function, as described earlier in this chapter; see the section "Setting the Power Button function."

It's possible that the Disk Cleanup tool renders hibernation inoperable. When using Disk Cleanup, be sure that you do not remove any hibernation files, such as the Hibernation File Cleaner. Refer to Book VI, Chapter 2 for more information on Disk Cleanup.

What is hybrid sleep?

Somewhere between Sleep mode and hibernation is the Windows Vista feature *hybrid sleep*. It's like hibernation in that information stored in memory (RAM) is saved to disk, but the computer doesn't fully turn itself off. Instead, as in Sleep mode, you can quickly resume computer operation by touching a key or moving the mouse.

The advantage of hybrid sleep is that you can quickly resume computer operations *and* avoid the risk of losing data if the power goes out. But to use hybrid sleep, it must be activated. Here's how:

1. **Open the Power Options icon in the Control Panel.**

2. **Choose the link Change Plan Settings beneath the selected plan.**

3. **Choose the link Change Advanced Power Settings.**

   The Power Options dialog box appears, similar to the one shown in Figure 3-8.

Figure 3-8:
Activating hybrid sleep.

4. **Open the item Sleep by clicking the + sign.**

5. **Open the item Allow Hybrid Sleep.**

6. **Click on the blue text next to Setting, and choose On from the button menu.**

7. **Click OK to confirm your choice and activate hybrid sleep.**

8. **Close the remaining dialog boxes and windows.**

When hybrid sleep is active, choosing the Sleep command places the computer into Hybrid Sleep mode.

  ✦ Hybrid sleep is a Windows Vista feature.

  ✦ If you have disabled hibernation, the hybrid sleep feature in Windows Vista may not function properly. Specifically, hybrid sleep may not recover any unsaved data if it's on and the power goes out. See the previous section for information on enabling hibernation in Windows Vista.

Recovering from a PC coma

Occasionally, a PC may go to sleep and not wake up. It gets stuck. The problem isn't as common as it once was, but the solution is the same: Turn off the computer. Refer to the earlier section "Turning off a stubborn PC."

Yes, it's okay to forcibly turn off a computer when it's in a coma.

When you turn on the computer again, your next task is to update the PC's power-management driver software. To complete that task, you can phone your dealer for more information, but they'll probably direct you to the manufacturer's Web site. After you're there, look for the Support or Download Drivers link. Find the latest power-management driver software for your PC and update it.

You can also use the Windows Update service to ensure that your computer has the latest power management software. See Book II, Chapter 1.

If the problem persists, don't use Sleep mode for your PC. For example, on one of my older, more stubborn computers, I don't use Sleep mode. Instead, I simply turn off the monitor when I'm not using my computer.

Problems with Restarting

Restarting a computer is a common and often necessary task. Even if you're a fan of leaving a computer on all the time, you'll find yourself restarting it every so often for a number of reasons, from installing or updating software to fixing bugs.

Two ugly restart issues may plague you. The first is the random restart, which is unexpected. The second is the automatic restart, or re-restart, which is unwanted. This section covers both.

Restarting Windows often cures many minor ills.

Random restarts

An unexpected restart is a sign of trouble. I'm not talking about the computer requesting a restart — one of those "Restart now?" type of dialog boxes. Nope. I'm talking about the computer just going off into la-la land in a rude and discourteous manner.

Poof!

A random restart is most likely, though not exclusively, a hardware error. The primary culprit is the power supply:

✦ If the power supply lacks the proper wattage to power the PC's hardware, it randomly restarts or dies. The solution is to replace the power supply with a beefier model. See Chapter 8.

✦ If the power supply is just flaky, it needs replacing anyway.

✦ When the power supply's fan fails to keep the computer cool enough, the PC restarts because of the heat. You can buy a power supply with more fans or buy a supplemental fan for your PC.

Other hardware glitches may also cause random restarts, so if the problem isn't in the power supply, it can be difficult to pinpoint.

Don't rule out software glitches: Poorly installed and corrupt software can randomly crash a computer. You can use the Windows logs to help determine which programs may be causing the random restarts. See Book II, Chapter 7 for more information.

Automatic restarts

For the sake of troubleshooting, an automatic restart is really more of a re-restart. What happens is that the computer restarts and then restarts again. Restart, restart, restart. The problem is that you can configure Windows to automatically restart on an error, in which case the computer ceaselessly restarts and coincidentally drives you mad.

You can choose from a couple of solutions for automatic restarts. The first solution is to disable the feature. Obey these steps:

1. **Open the System icon in the Control Panel.**

2a. **In Windows Vista, choose the link Advanced System Settings on the left side of the window; click the Continue button or type the administrator's password to continue.**

2b. **In Windows XP, click the Advanced tab in the System Properties dialog box.**

3. Click the Settings button in the Startup and Recovery area.

4. Remove the check mark by the item Automatically Restart.

5. Click OK and close the other dialog box and then the Control Panel window.

The second solution is to take advantage of the start-up menu that disables automatic restarts. This solution comes in handy when the restart takes place. See Chapter 2, the section "The F8 menu," for more information.

Chapter 4: Mass Storage Issues

*A*ll parts of your computer system are necessary. Everything you buy or attach to the main computer console is something you need in order to put the *personal* into personal computer. Yet, of all the hardware components that make up your computer system, the most important is the mass storage system. It has nothing to do with being Catholic.

Mass Storage Overview

It's easy to ignore the basics of computer science, so I will. Suffice it to say that storage is one of the key components of any computer system. This section provides an overview of the PC's storage system. By reading through this information, you'll have good insight into not only names and functions but also the general storage troubleshooting process.

A computer's storage system really has *two* components: long term and short term. Both are required. Short-term storage is the computer's memory, or RAM. Long-term storage, or *mass storage*, is the domain of the disk drives and media cards. That's what's covered here.

Understanding mass storage

Three different types of storage are found on a PC, though there are similarities and overlaps between the different types. I like to classify them this way:

✦ Hard drive

✦ Optical drive

✦ Removable media

The typical PC comes with hard drive and optical drive storage. Removable media includes digital media cards, but also other types of storage, including external hard drives, oddball drives (magneto-optical and tape drives, for example), and antique floppy drives, which I hear are still used in parts of North Idaho. Even the optical drive is considered removable media because you can yank out the disc.

Detailed information about these types of storage is offered in the remainder of this chapter.

✦ The *disk* is the media on which information is recorded. I prefer using the term *storage media* instead of *disk* because computers are now bridging the gap between spinning disk storage and solid-state storage. Solid-state storage doesn't spin, unless you accidentally leave a thumb drive in your pants and put it through the wash.

✦ The drive is the part of the mass storage unit that reads the disk. A hard drive contains a hard disk; you insert an optical disc into a CD or DVD drive; media cards are placed into a media drive or media card reader or are connected directly to a USB port.

✦ The PC's hard drive cannot be removed. It's fixed in place, which is why you may see a hard drive referred to as a *fixed drive* in some obscure manuals.

Finding mass storage in Windows

Windows Vista provides ready access to storage media in your computer via the Computer window, shown in Figure 4-1. In Windows XP, the window is titled My Computer, and it looks similar to the one shown in Figure 4-1.

Figure 4-1: The Computer window shows a PC's storage devices.

Windows assigns storage media in your computer by using a letter of the alphabet, a *drive letter*. The main hard drive is usually (though not always) drive C. The drive letters are then assigned to any additional storage media from letters D on up. In Figure 4-1, you see the following:

Hard drives: Drives C and D are two logical drives on a single physical drive, though it's difficult to determine that from Figure 4-1. Like most PCs sold today, drive D is used for recovery purposes. Drive F is a second, internal physical drive that I installed myself. Hard drive J is an external backup drive, which I also installed myself.

Optical drive: Drive E is the optical drive.

Media drives: Drives G, H, I, and K represent media drives accessed through the PC's media card reader.

You might also see a network drive, as shown by drive N at the bottom of Figure 4-1. That drive isn't part of your computer system; network drives accessed by your computer can be *mapped* to unused drive letters. They appear primarily in the Network or My Network Places windows, and they have "plumbing" beneath their drive icon, as shown in Figure 4-1.

The number of disk drives available on your computer is different. You may have more, you may have less.

✦ Drive letters are followed by a colon, as in C: or D:.

✦ A single physical hard drive can be divided into multiple *logical* hard drives. In Figure 4-1, drives C and D are two logical drives on a single physical hard drive. See the section "Partitions," later in this chapter, for more information.

✦ You can reassign and change the drive letters, which is covered in Book VI, Chapter 2.

✦ The icons shown in Figure 4-1 for the removable media drives are specific to that computer. Most versions of Windows use the generic removable media drive icon, shown in the margin, to represent media drives.

✦ Optical disc icons change depending on the disc's contents. For example, a musical CD uses a custom music icon (refer to Figure 4-1).

Using the Disk Management console

The Computer/My Computer window is used for file management. To control the disk drives in your PC, you use the Windows Disk Management console. Here's how to summon that window:

1. **Open the Control Panel.**

2. **Open the Administrative Tools icon.**

3. **Open Computer Management.**

4. **In Windows Vista, click Continue or type the administrator's password when prompted by the User Account Control warning.**

5. **Beneath the Storage heading (on the left side of the console window), choose Disk Management.**

   The Disk Management console appears, as shown in Figure 4-2. It looks similar in both Windows Vista and Windows XP.

Figure 4-2:
The Disk Management console.

6. **Close the Disk Management console when you're done, and close the Control Panel window if it's still open.**

You can use the Disk Management console to get your disk drive knuckles dirty. Later sections in this chapter describe a few of the things you can do.

Understanding Medea

Jason of Argonauts' fame took home Medea, princess of Colchis, as his wife. Then he betrayed her. She grew jealous and sought revenge, killing just about everyone, depending on which version of the tragedy you read. But you're probably more interested in *media* than in Medea.

Adding drives and media

There are a few issues with adding new items to your PC's storage system. It can be done in two ways.

First, you can insert storage media into those drives that accept removable media: the optical drive and all the various media card readers. Simply stick the media into the drive. After a few moments, the operating system recognizes the media and *mounts* it into the disk system.

In Windows, where drives are preassigned letters, the media you insert is accessed through the drive letter. In other words, to use the media card inserted into drive H:, you use the drive H icon in windows or the designation H: when referring to the drive in the pathname manner.

Note that the drive letter isn't changed; only the media referenced by the letter.

Second, you can add storage to a computer system externally, often by plugging the drive into the PC's USB port. After a few moments, Windows recognizes the drive's addition, updates itself to use the drive, and finally assigns the drive a letter.

You can confirm that an external drive has properly been added by opening the Computer or My Computer window.

In addition to adding an external hard drive, you can add external removable media drives, such as an optical disk or media card reader. In that case, you still need to add media to the drive. What that means is that although an external, removable media drive is given a drive letter, you cannot access the drive until you stick some sort of media into the drive.

✦ Also refer to the later section "AutoPlay issues" for information on how to handle newly mounted media in Windows.

✦ Some older PCs running Windows XP may not have USB 2.0 adapters. If so, you cannot successfully use most external USB drives, including flash or "thumb" drives. Windows alerts you to the problem. The solution is to buy a USB 2.0 adapter and install it.

✦ It's okay to attach a drive with media already in it. For example, you can connect a media card reader with a media card already in it and the computer deals with it just fine. Attaching such a reader works just like adding an external hard drive or attaching a digital camera to the PC; the media reader is added and then the media is read.

Removing media

Windows has no problem recognizing new drives or media, but there can be issues with removing media — especially when the media is still being used.

To properly remove media from a drive, follow these steps:

1. **Open the Computer or My Computer window.**

2. **Click to select the icon for the drive containing the media you want to remove.**

3a. **In Windows Vista, click the Eject button on the toolbar.**

3b. **In Windows XP, choose the link Eject This Disk from the list of System Tasks on the right side of the window.**

For an optical disc, the drive should eject the disc. For a media card, however, you need to manually remove the card from the reader.

4. **Close the Computer/My Computer window.**

When the computer is still using the removable media, you're warned; you cannot remove media that's being used, that has unsaved files on it, or that is somehow being accessed by the computer. This warning is a good thing in that it prevents the data stored on the media from being corrupted.

When you have trouble removing media, close any open applications. Then try ejecting the media again. If that fails, shut down the computer. You can safely remove any media when the computer is shut down.

Removing drives

The media is the thing that stores computer information; the drive is the thing that reads the media. Just as media can be removed (see the preceding section), you can also remove any drives or media card readers attached to your computer.

In Windows, you can remove the drive whether it contains media or not. But you must let Windows know that the drive is going bye-bye or else Windows gets angry at you. To prevent that, follow these steps for Windows Vista:

1. **Open the Computer window.**

2. **Right-click on the drive you want to remove.**

The drive can be empty, or it can have media attached.

3. **From the pop-up menu, choose Safely Remove.**

4. **After the confirmation message appears, disconnect the drive from the computer.**

For both Windows Vista and Windows XP, you can use the Safely Remove icon in the notification area to disconnect external disk drives or media card readers. Here's how:

1. **Review the Computer window to confirm the letter associated with the drive you want to remove.**

I urge you to follow this step because today's PCs can sport several drive letters and not always assign the same letter to a removable device.

2. **Point the mouse at the Safely Remove Hardware icon in the notification area.**

   You know that you found the right icon when the pop-up bubble says Safely Remove Hardware. (Also see the margin art at the end of this section.)

3. **Click the Safely Remove Hardware icon.**

   A pop-up list appears, detailing any removable hardware that's attached to your PC.

4. **Choose the hardware you want to remove from the list.**

5. **When prompted that it's "Safe to Remove Hardware," disconnect the device.**

For an external hard drive, you can either unplug the USB cable or merely turn off the drive's power; it doesn't matter which at this point.

 ✦ The Safely Remove Hardware icon for Windows Vista is shown in the margin.

 ✦ The Windows XP version of the Safely Remove Hardware icon is shown in the margin.

 ✦ There's a difference between removing (ejecting) media and unmounting the drive that reads that media. Ejecting media doesn't disconnect the drive or media card reader.

Hard Drive Stuff

Your PC's main storage device is the hard drive, also called a *hard disk drive, fixed disk,* or, if you're over 50, a *Winchester drive.* Boy, does that bring back memories. For regular PC use, you need to know that the hard drive is the drive C thing people talk about and that you cannot remove it from your computer without using a screwdriver or modicum of explosives. Beyond that, and for troubleshooting purposes, you need to know a bit more about the hard drive. That's why I wrote this section.

Eventually, the hard drive is going to be replaced by a solid-state drive (SSD). The SSD is basically a large, fast flash memory drive — a big media card. SSDs are available today, though their cost per gigabyte is prohibitive when compared to traditional, spinning hard drives. The SSD proves more reliable than the hard drive because it lacks moving parts, but some of the terminology in this section remains the same, as do the troubleshooting issues.

Hard drive technical trivia

A hard drive is basically a tiny box. It contains the hard disk, which is a stack of disks, or platters. The box also contains read/write heads, which read and record information on both sides of the several disks inside the drive. Oh, there are a lot more details than that, but for troubleshooting, you don't need to know the trivial stuff.

The hard drive dwells in a *drive bay* inside your PC's bosom. The bay has room for more than one drive; a typical PC can sport up to two physical hard drive units. Larger PCs have room for more; smaller PCs may have room for only one drive.

The drive is connected to the computer via two cables: One is a data cable, and the second is the power cable. Figure 4-3 illustrates the connections and other trivial stuff.

Figure 4-3:
Typical,
naked hard
drive.

Mounting screws (both sides)

Impressive gibberish

Power supply interface

SATA interface

No matter what the hard drive internals are, the computer treats the hard drive as a single unit — a data storage device. But within that single physical drive can be multiple logical drives. It's important to understand how that works.

To prepare a hard drive for use in Windows, you go through these steps:

1. **The hard drive is low-level formatted, which is done at the factory.**

2. **The hard drive is partitioned into one or more logical drives.**

3. **The partitions are formatted.**

4. **One partition is selected as the active partition, the one that will contain the operating system. (This step is required on only the first physical hard drive.)**

5. **The operating system is installed on the active partition.**

Full detail on using these steps is provided in Book VI, Chapter 2. For now, it's important to note what is a physical hard drive and what is a logical hard drive. The next section covers the details.

✦ The process of formatting a hard drive organizes the disks into individual chunks where data is stored. There's a lot of jargon surrounding this process: cylinder, track, and sector, for example.

✦ The hard drive formatting process explains why the hard drive's rated size is never equal to its formatted capacity. For example, a standard 500GB hard drive formats out to about 465GB. The missing storage space is used by the formatting process and, according to law, some of the bytes must be given over to the federal government in lieu of taxes.

✦ Two types of interface are used to communicate between the hard drive (and optical drive) and the PC's motherboard. Older PCs use the Advanced Technology Attachment (ATA) interface, and newer PCs use the Serial ATA, or SATA interface. Both types basically control how fast data can be moved to and from the hard drive to the processor.

Partitions

A single physical hard drive can become one or more logical hard drives. In fact, it's those logical drives you see in the Computer or My Computer window (refer to Figure 4-2). That's because Windows can use a hard drive only after it's been prepared for use, and part of that preparation includes partitioning and formatting.

To determine how your PC's hard drives are partitioned, refer to the Disk Management Console window, which was covered earlier in this chapter. Open the Disk Management Console window, and check out the list of drives on your PC.

Each physical hard drive is named starting with Disk 0. (Computer nerds use zero, not one, as the first number.) On your computer, you should see Disk 0 listed along with its partition(s). One of those partitions is most likely drive C, the main hard drive. Another partition commonly found on today's PCs is drive D, a "recovery" drive. Figure 4-4 shows the relationship between the partitions, or logical drives, and the drive icons you see in the Computer or My Computer window.

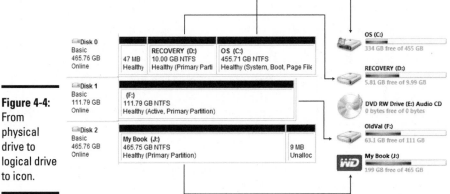

Figure 4-4: From physical drive to logical drive to icon.

If your computer has a second hard drive, you see it listed as Disk 1. That drive may have one or more partitions as well, which is illustrated in the Disk Management console window. Those logical drives also map out to icons in the Computer or My Computer window.

You can close the Disk Management console window when you're done looking.

+ All hard drives must have at least one partition.

+ Disk 0 is the first physical hard drive inside your computer. Any additional hard drives, internal or external, are numbered Disk 1, Disk 2, and so on.

+ Each drive is partitioned into one or more logical drives. Those logical drives map out to the drive letters and icons you see and use in Windows.

+ Each partition has a format, such as NTFS or FAT32, for example. The format explains the method by which the drive was formatted and how data is written (or stored) to the drive.

+ Another name for a partition, or logical drive, is *volume*. This isn't a loudness thing; instead, think of a volume in a book.

The Master Boot Record

The most important part of the hard drive is the Master Boot Record, or MBR. It's the first part of the first physical hard drive (Disk 0) in your PC. The MBR contains two vital items:

✦ A map, or *partition table,* describing how the hard drive is divided into smaller, logical drives.

✦ The *boot loader,* or the program used to find and load an operating system from one of the drive's partitions.

A host of errors are associated with a bad, corrupt, or missing MBR. These error messages appear when the computer starts, obviously before the operating system is loaded. Here's a sampling of the error messages and how to deal with them:

Invalid Partition Table: A nasty error message indicating that the partition table is damaged or missing or contains questionable information.

Operating System Not Found: Not a deadly error message, this one might indicate that the partition table doesn't have an active partition set. That means that the computer doesn't know which partition to look at for an operating system.

Missing Operating System: This message most likely implies that the partition table is damaged. The MBR is saying that a bootable partition is available but there isn't any information about where to find the partition.

Non-System Disk or Disk Error: An old error message often surfacing when non-bootable floppy disks were left in their drive, and the computer tried (by default) to boot from those disks.

When you see one of the first three error messages, the solution is to run the Windows Recovery Console. You can use the FIXBOOT or FIXMBR utilities to address the issues, by repairing the MBR and restoring things to normal. See Book II, Chapter 8 for the details.

When a hard drive is damaged beyond repair, it must be replaced. Book VI, Chapter 2 offers details. After installing a new disk, be sure to restore your old files from a backup. See Book VI, Chapter 1 for information on backing up your stuff.

+ Refer to Chapter 2 for additional information on problems plaguing PCs when they start.

+ The MBR also contains information identifying the disk, called a *disk signature*. The disk signature information, however, isn't used by the operating system.

Optical Drive Death and Misery

Don't worry: Your PC's optical drive is a robust beast. It's far more reliable than the old floppy drives. Hopefully, mankind has kept all the world's floppy drives ready so that we can hurl them at an invading fleet of space aliens. Such a brutal move would devastate any potential galactic foe.

This section contains some hardware troubleshooting tips for your PC's CD or DVD drive, which I refer to collectively as the *optical drive*.

Also refer to Chapter 7 for information on troubleshooting sound problems that might be related to the optical drive.

Is the drive dead?

It's easy to determine whether an optical drive is dead: Does the tray eject? If not, the drive could be dead. When the drive has a light and the light isn't lit, that's another sure sign. But the only way to know for certain is to open the PC's case, as described in Chapter 8.

When the drive is getting power and the tray slides in and out, you need to check the media. Is the disc okay? The easiest way to determine that is to try the disc in an optical drive that works. If the disc is okay and the drive doesn't recognize it, the drive is probably dead.

+ In Windows XP, recordable optical drives may seem to vanish from the My Computer window after you uninstall CD/DVD recording software. That's due to a sloppy uninstallation. See this Web page for information on how to address the issue:

    http://support.microsoft.com/kb/314060

+ The good news is that optical drives are cheap and easy to replace. Again, see Chapter 8.

+ The drive cannot read a disc that has been inserted upside down. Likewise, a nonrecordable drive cannot read blank discs.

"A disk is stuck in the drive!"

Whether the computer is on or off, you can easily eject a stuck disk. Look for the drive's "dimple" hole. Figure 4-5 helps you find the hole; it's a tiny, pin-size hole found on the face of every optical drive.

Insert a bent paper clip into the hole. Push! The drive tray pops out a bit. Then you can remove the disc.

Figure 4-5:
Where
to find an
optical
drive's
dimple hole.

Here

The program won't install

When you install a new program, the theory goes that when you insert its optical disc into the computer, the program automatically installs. When it doesn't, follow these steps:

1. **Open the Computer or My Computer window.**

2. **Right-click the optical drive icon.**

3. **From the Shortcut menu, choose the command Install or Run Program.**

If the Install or Run Program command isn't available, choose AutoPlay instead.

The install or setup program on the disk should now run and install the software. If it still doesn't, choose the Open command in Step 3, or just double-click the optical drive icon. From the window that opens, locate an icon named `setup` or `install` and open that icon to begin installation.

✦ The optical drive isn't always drive D.

✦ Refer to Book II, Chapter 6 for more information on program installation problems.

AutoPlay issues

When you stick a disc into the optical drive, any number of things might happen. When the computer doesn't know what to do, it presents you with a list of options in the AutoPlay dialog box.

Software installation discs have built-in AutoPlay. A file named `autorun.inf` exists in the disc's root folder. It's a text file that Windows reads when the disc is inserted. The file contains instructions that describe which icon to use for the disc, as well as which program to automatically open when the disk is inserted.

When a disc without an `autorun.inf` file is inserted, the Windows AutoPlay function takes over. You've probably seen the dialog box displayed, as shown in Figure 4-6. Basically, you choose a disc type so that Windows can more properly display the information stored on the disc or so that Windows can deal with the disc's contents (music and video, for example).

Figure 4-6:
The typical AutoPlay dialog box.

You can customize the AutoPlay settings, creating preset options for various types of discs or controlling whether AutoPlay is used.

 In Windows Vista, configuring AutoPlay is done by using the AutoPlay icon in the Control Panel. The AutoPlay window displays a list of different disc types, along with menu buttons from which you can choose which actions to take.

In Windows XP, you control the AutoPlay feature by following these steps:

1. **Open the My Computer window.**

2. **Right-click the optical drive icon.**

3. **Choose Properties from the pop-up menu.**

4. **In the drive's Properties dialog box, click the AutoPlay tab.**

5. **Use the dialog box's drop-down list to choose a disc type.**

6. **Choose the action to take from the Actions area.**

7. **Click the OK button when you're done.**

The idea here is convenience: If you always rip your CDs into Media Player, choosing that AutoPlay option for all music CDs you insert into your PC saves you time.

+ One of the AutoPlay options is Take No Action. That means that when you insert a disc, you aren't visually assaulted by an AutoPlay dialog box.

+ One of the disc types in Windows Vista is Software and Games. If you choose the Take No Action item for that type of disc, your software doesn't automatically install.

+ Another option is Ask Me Every Time or Prompt Me Each Time to Choose an Action. That's the opposite of the Take No Action option in that each time you insert a disc, you always see the AutoPlay dialog box.

+ The AutoRun command on the optical drive's shortcut menu automatically runs whichever program is specified in the `autorun.inf` file.

The drive doesn't record

To make your own optical disc, you need a PC that sports an optical drive that lets you record discs. When you don't have such a gizmo, don't expect to be making many of your discs.

The key to knowing whether your optical drive can record discs is to read the drive's faceplate. Recordable drives often have the word *recordable* or *recorder* on them. If not, you see the common R, +R, -R, or RW, or any of those variations, on the drive.

In Windows XP, you need to confirm that recording abilities have been activated for a recordable optical drive. Mind these steps:

1. **Open the My Computer window.**

2. **Right-click the optical drive icon.**

3. **Choose Properties from the shortcut menu.**

   The drive's Properties dialog box appears.

4. **Click the Recording tab.**

   You should see the dialog box shown in Figure 4-7. If you don't, it means that the drive isn't recordable. Go to Step 6.

5. **Place a check mark in the box next to Enable CD Recording on This Drive.**

6. **Click OK.**

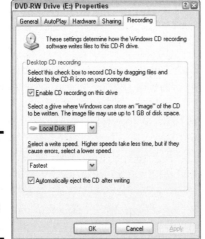

Figure 4-7:
Enabling
recording
goodness
in Windows
XP.

If the drive still doesn't record any discs, the drive itself may have a problem. See Chapter 8 for information on replacing a bum optical drive.

+ When it's difficult to tell whether the drive is recordable, you can rely on the Device Manager to confirm things for you. By opening the DVD/CD-ROM Drives category, you can confirm that you have a CD-R/RW or DVD-R/RW by checking the device's name. Refer to Chapter 7 for more instructions on using the Device Manager.

+ For information on recording optical discs, refer to my book *PCs For Dummies* (Wiley Publishing), available only in the fourth dimension.

Optical disc disposal

You can throw out an optical disc, but check with your local refuse company to see whether optical discs have a special classification. If so, dispose of the discs according to the proper methods.

Never burn a disc. The discs give off toxic fumes. The toxic fumes are also present when you microwave a disc, in case that thought has ever crossed your mind.

The most secure way to dispose of an optical disc is to shred it. Many common paper shredders feature an optical disc slot (that can also be used to shred old credit cards). Use a shredder when you're concerned about the disc contents landing in the wrong hands.

The disc doesn't record

Optical discs come in many recordable flavors. Always ensure that you get the right disc for your drive. For example, a DL, or Dual Layer, disc cannot be recorded as a DL disc in a non-DL drive. If your recordable drive is older and doesn't recognize the RW format, don't buy RW discs.

In some cases, software might be specific about the type of disc you record to. For example, DVD-making software might prefer that you use the more compatible DVD-R format for a video rather than the more efficient DVD+R format.

Some discs are duds. When a disc doesn't record, toss it out. Try another. If you end up tossing out all the discs, the problem is most likely with the drive and not the discs (which means that you need to untoss the discs.)

✦ Ensure that any optical disc recording software you're using is up-to-date. That way, you can eliminate any recording problems with older software.

✦ Most television DVD players read the DVD-R format and have trouble reading the DVD+R format. Also note that a DVD must be formatted for playing in a television DVD; you cannot "play" a DVD with data on it.

On cleaning an optical drive

I don't recommend using optical drive cleaners. Back in the old days, floppy disk cleaners really worked, removing build-up on the floppy read/write heads and often improving performance and readability. But the floppy read/write heads actually touched the disk. An optical drive uses a laser.

Optical drives are sealed. There's no way inside of them, other than through the drive tray (well, or an industrial can opener). I don't recommend either blowing air into an open optical drive or using a vacuum to suck the air out. If the drive is shot, it's shot: replace it. New optical drives aren't prohibitively expensive.

Although I don't recommend cleaning an optical drive, I can heartily recommend cleaning a disc. First, simply wipe the disc with a damp cloth. Wipe from the center outward; don't wipe around the disc in a circle. If you have a special disc cleaning solution, use it as well as any special disc cloth. The idea behind cleaning is to remove things that may interfere with the laser reading the disc but not scratch the disc by cleaning it.

Professional Data Recovery

One of the reasons that few people back up their computer data is that they know professional data-recovery services exist. Similarly, the reason that many people back up is that they know how much the professional recovery-services cost.

Yes, your data is important to you. Yet whereas a business considers a $10,000 charge to recover a hard drive an "expense," a mere mortal, such as myself, considers such a charge merely "expensive." It's much cheaper to back up, and I hammer away on that topic ad nauseam in Book VI, Chapter 1.

You have to consider two issues for using a professional data-recovery service: cost and time. Both issues are related, given the old adage that "Time is money." In this case, the quicker the time, the more the money.

For an individual, I don't recommend using professional data-recovery services. The cost is just too prohibitive. And I would never trust any bargain basement data-recovery service. Nope, just back up. Trust me.

The backup philosophy also holds true for businesses. For mission-critical data that cannot be backed up right away, I recommend using a RAID system. (RAID stands for Redundant Array of Independent Disks.). Then you back up the RAID when you can. And in those desperate situations when you need professional data recovery, brace yourself for the cost. Don't get all cheap on me, either.

Chapter 5: Pain in the Printer

In This Chapter

- ✔ Understanding the printer
- ✔ Locating printer stuff in Windows
- ✔ Confirming the printer driver
- ✔ Cancelling printing
- ✔ Dealing with output ugliness
- ✔ Unjamming
- ✔ Printing the page properly
- ✔ Doing envelopes

A printer is part of your computer system and at the same time its own, separate device. Today's computers are little computers in themselves, complete with the whole input-out-storage paradigm, but suited to only one task: getting information from the digital world onto paper in the real world. When that task falls short, turn to this chapter for some printer troubleshooting.

Marginal Printer Stuff

If Heracles were to have 13 labors rather than 12, I'm certain that one of them would be to try to connect a Lexmark printer to a computer running Windows Vista. Folks, there's a reason that computers aren't sold with a printer in the same box. My guess is that the printer and computer secretly despise each other — like they were once married or lived in the White House together.

The result of your digital labors is the printed copy of your stuff. This section covers some of the places in Windows where printing takes place, or where it *should* take place when everything goes well.

Amazing printers

If you're using an old printer with your computer, you're missing out on some of the latest tricks. Although older printers share today's printers fancy displays and full-text messages, the newer models often sport one of those handy Cancel buttons. Nothing beats that.

The printer connects to your PC using a USB cable. Older printers use a specific printer cable called, remarkably, a *printer cable*. If you have an older printer, ensure that you get a *bidirectional* printer cable, which is more compatible with the printer's features, allowing communications between the printer and computer.

Printers also plug into the wall.

Most printers feature power management abilities, just like your computer. That means the printer can be left on all the time and doesn't consume an abundance of electricity. Still, I recommend turning off the printer when you don't plan on using it for great lengths of time.

+ Yes, there are wireless printers. They mostly use the Bluetooth standard, which means that troubleshooting involves knowing about not only printers in Windows but also Bluetooth wireless communications. My advice is to avoid wireless printers, but if you just can't help yourself, use the Bluetooth icon in the Control Panel when doing troubleshooting.

+ I don't recommend those all-in-one printers — the gizmos that combine printing with scanning, copying, and faxing. Some of those models are pretty good, but most provide marginal performance at best. And, when the fax component stops working and you have to have it repaired, you then lose the printing and scanning abilities too — unless you go buy a new printer.

+ Get to know your printer. Discover how the paper goes in: face down or face up, and top edge first or top edge last or whatever. Often, a set of icons on the paper tray describe the paper's orientation. Make a note of it.

+ If you have an older or cheaper printer without a text display, know what the lights mean. Perhaps even label the lights with a Sharpie so that you can remember. English beats international icon hieroglyphics every day!

+ Always have plenty of paper and ink available for the printer.

+ Some printers feature a button called *on-line* or *select*. That button controls communications between the printer and the computer. When it's on, the printer is ready to print. Taking the printer off-line or deselecting it means that the printer is on and can be configured (or fixed), but nothing can be printed.

Printing in Windows

Before Windows (and I recognize that I'm addressing a very old crowd here), various applications were responsible for their own printing duties. That means you had to configure your printer for each and every program you owned. If you're really old, you probably remember writing your own *printer driver*. That was a solitary duty as in those days there was no Internet. Oh, these bones. . . .

Windows handles all printing duties for you. The process works basically the same in every program: Press Ctrl+P to summon the Print dialog box, as shown in Figure 5-1. If need be, adjust settings in the dialog box; otherwise, just click the Print button to print. Or, you can click a Print toolbar button to quickly print a document.

Figure 5-1:
A typical
Print dialog
box.

The printer must be on and ready to print and have plenty of paper and ink for the printing process to be successful.

Here are some general printer notes:

✦ Save paper! Use the Print Preview command before printing. Proof your document. Print only when everything is ready to print.

✦ A Range option allows you to set the starting and ending pages. Some Print dialog boxes (refer to the one shown in Figure 5-1) offer a more flexible plan: You can specify individual pages or a range or a combination of both. Separate individual pages with commas; a range of pages with a hyphen. For example:

        2,4,9-16

This range prints pages 2 and 4 and then all pages 9 through 16.

✦ When a Selection option is available, only the text or items selected in the document are printed.

✦ Some printers can print on both sides of a sheet of paper. It's called *duplex printing*. When that's not available, print all the odd pages first. Reinsert the pages in the printers face down, and then print all the even pages.

✦ If the stack of paper comes out of the printer in the wrong order (the first page is on the bottom), consider printing in *reverse* order. An option to do so can generally be found in the Printer's Properties dialog box; click the Properties button in the Print dialog box.

✦ The Print to File option is dubious. Rather than send information to the printer, you save the same raw data in a file. There isn't much you can do with the file, sadly. Rather than use Print to File, I recommend using the Adobe Acrobat Writer program to create a PDF file. You can also use the Microsoft XPS format, though it's not as popular.

✦ Color options are often available, but not in the Print dialog box itself: Click the Properties button in the Print dialog box, and then use the printer's Properties dialog box to set color options.

✦ Printing a color document in grayscale (no color information) saves color ink. It's a good trick to use for drafts.

✦ When the Collate option is used, multiple documents print one after the other. When documents aren't collated, all the first pages print first, and then the second pages, and so on.

✦ The infamous printer error message PC Load Letter means that the printer is out of paper. PC in this case stands for Paper Cartridge, Load Letter means to load letter-size paper.

Using the Page Setup dialog box

The Print dialog box (refer to Figure 5-1) is where settings are made that affect how things are printed, but it's not the only place to look for some printer problems. Another location is the Page Setup dialog box, shown in Figure 5-2. To access the Page Setup dialog box, choose the File⇨Page Setup command.

Figure 5-2: The Page Setup dialog box.

Printing Windows

You can print documents and graphics using applications in Windows, but what about printing Windows itself? That's a sticky point: Windows own folder windows lack a Print command. If you want to print a list of files in a folder, you have to use a third-party utility or the command prompt to do so.

To print the desktop, press the Print Screen key. That sends a snapshot of the desktop to the Clipboard. Similarly, Alt+Print Screen captures the front (or top) window to the Clipboard. You can then paste that image into any application that accepts graphics, such as Windows Paint. From there, you can print the image.

The Page Setup box may appear to have nothing to do with printing, but it has a lot to do with how the page you print is formatted. That includes some items you might think would fall into the Print dialog box, which do not:

Margins: To set your document's margins, you use the Page Setup dialog box. In the Page Setup dialog box example shown in Figure 5-2, you click the Margins tab to specify how far out the text is displayed on the page.

Paper size: When printing on a sheet of paper of a special size, you must use the Page Setup dialog box to set that paper size.

Paper orientation: Whether printing longways (landscape) or normal (portrait), you choose the page orientation in the Page Setup dialog box.

Paper source: When your printer has more than one paper tray, that source is chosen in the Page Setup dialog box, not in the Print dialog box.

Printing is the mechanical job of putting a document on paper with ink. The duties of the Page Setup dialog box are really document formatting, not printing.

   ✦ In some applications, the Page Setup command on the File menu might be titled Document Setup.

   ✦ Sometimes you access the Page Setup dialog box by pressing a button — for example, in the Print dialog box.

   ✦ Office 2007 applications take a different path to the Page Setup dialog box. To view the Page Setup dialog box, click the Page Layout tab on the Ribbon. The Page Setup area contains commands found in the Page Setup dialog box; to see that dialog box in person, click the Dialog Box Launcher in the lower-right corner of the Page Setup area. (See my book *Word 2007 For Dummies,* from Wiley Publishing, for details.)

REMEMBER

✦ When you choose another paper size in the Page Setup dialog box, don't forget to stock your printer with that new paper size. The printer's display may remind you of the paper swap, or it may not.

✦ Not every printer is capable of printing to the full edge of a piece of paper. Many printers cannot print within one half-inch of the paper's edge. Some printers can go further, but usually one edge of the page is required to help pull the sheet through the printer. On that one edge you must have a margin.

Dealing with printers

In Windows, printer activity has its locus in the Printers window. In Windows Vista, the window is called Printers, and it contains a handy toolbar with buttons, as shown in Figure 5-3. In Windows XP, the window is called Printers and Faxes, and the relevant printer commands appear on the task-bar on the left side of the window.

Toolbar   "Show more" button

Figure 5-3:
The Printer
window.

Default printer   Available printers   Additional tools

The buttons and menu, or the various printer tasks, appear in the Printers window only when a specific printer is selected.

The easiest way to summon the Printers window is by choosing the Printers or Printers and Faxes command on the Start menu. That command is available, however, only when the Start menu is configured to show it. Follow these steps:

1. **Right-click the Start button and choose Properties.**

2. **In the Taskbar and Start Menu Properties, click the Customize button.**

3. **In Windows XP, click the Advanced tab.**

4. **Scroll through the list and put a check mark by Printers (in Windows Vista) or Printers and Faxes (in Windows XP).**

5. **Click OK and then click OK again to close the open dialog boxes.**

The Printers window lists all the printers available to your computer and the software you use.

✦ If you desire a shortcut icon for the Printers window, open the Control Panel and right-click either the Printers or Printers and Faxes icon. From the pop-up menu that appears, choose Create Shortcut. In Windows XP, click Yes to confirm that you want a shortcut icon placed on the desktop.

✦ You use the Printers window to install a new printer on your PC. Use the Add a Printer button or link and then work through the steps in the wizard to configure the printer.

✦ You also use the Printer window to remove printers from your computer. Although you physically unplug the printer, you remove the printer's icon by deleting it from the Printers window.

✦ If your printer doesn't appear in the window, it may not have been installed or it could have been accidentally removed. Check the printer's USB cable and power cord.

✦ A network printer must be connected to the network, turned on, online, stocked with paper and ink, and ready to print before it works as a printer.

✦ I recommend *not* removing the printer drivers (software) when you disconnect a printer. That way, the job of reinstalling the printer later is easier.

✦ For more information on adding and setting up a printer, refer to my book *PCs For Dummies* (Wiley Publishing), first published on the planet Earth 21 years before the Zaglaxian invasion.

Checking the printer driver

Like most things in a computer, your printer requires both hardware and software to function in a sane manner. The printer itself is the hardware. The software is a *printer driver* that controls the printer, helping Windows talk to the printer and cajole it into printing things in a pleasing manner.

The printer driver is installed when you first set up or add the printer. To check on the printer driver, follow these steps:

1. **Open the Printers or Printers and Faxes window.**

2. **Right-click a printer icon and choose Properties from the shortcut menu.**

3. **In the printer's Properties dialog box, click the Advanced tab.**

   The Advanced tab in the printer's Properties dialog box lists the current driver associated with the printer, as shown in Figure 5-4.

Figure 5-4:
Checking on the printer driver.

The name for the printer driver should match your printer. If not, you can reset the driver by choosing another one from the drop-down list.

4. **Close the printer's Properties dialog box when you're done.**

If the driver is all screwed up, the best solution is to delete the printer: choose its icon in the window and choose Delete This Printer from the toolbar or task list. Then use the Add as Printer button or link to add the printer again.

Working with print jobs

When you print something in Windows, you're creating a *print job*. That's a good, general name for anything you print: printing is handled by the operating system and not by individual programs. Therefore, what you print becomes a duty, or "job," for the operating system, and not for the application you used to create that document.

Print jobs are associated with whichever printer you're using. In Windows, to view the print jobs, you use the Printers window and open the icon for the printer you're using. Print jobs are listed in the window, as shown in Figure 5-5.

Figure 5-5:
Print jobs
waiting in
the queue.

Print jobs don't wait in a line. No, they wait in a *queue*. In fact, the term
printer queue is an ancient computer term, dating back to before the French
and Indian war. I believe Benjamin Franklin coined it.

You can adjust items in the queue or cancel or pause printing.

To adjust an item, simply drag its icon up or down. That changes the order
in which it prints.

To pause or cancel an item, click to select it. Then from the Document menu,
choose Pause or Cancel, respectively. Other items on the Document menu
include Resume, which continues printing a paused job, and Restart, which
can be used to reprint a document from the beginning.

Cancelling a print job

About the only real reason to use a printer's window is to cancel something
sent to the printer. Sadly, the Print window, covered in the preceding section, isn't really effective for doing that: You probably won't see a full printer
queue window. Today's printers pack lots of memory, so the jobs slip off
into the printer's memory rather than wait in the computer's memory.

If you see a print job looming and you want to cancel it, choose Document⇨
Cancel. Even so, doing that doesn't unsend any information inside the printer's
memory. Some printers can hold dozens of pages, so cancelling a print job may
not immediately abort printing. That can be frustrating.

To best cancel a print job, go to the printer itself. If your printer sports a
Cancel button, use it. That stops the printing almost immediately.

For printers that lack a Cancel button, try taking the printer off-line: Press
the On-line or Select button. A few lines or pages may continue to print, but
eventually the printer stops. Remove the last sheet of paper, if necessary.
Then reset the printer or, if the printer lacks a reset button, turn it off.

By resetting or turning off the printer, you erase any remnants of a document in memory. That way, the unwanted print job doesn't continue to print when you put the printer back on-line.

Using the Printing Troubleshooter

The Windows Help system contains a number of useful troubleshooting tools, which can often guide you to a quick solution through step-by-step questions. To visit the Printing Troubleshooter in Windows Vista, follow these steps:

1. **Pop-up the Start menu and choose Help and Support.**

2. **In the Windows Help and Support window, type** troubleshoot printer problems **and press Enter.**

3. **Choose the first item in the list.**

   The item is titled Troubleshoot Printer Problems.

4. **Work through the troubleshooter by choosing the questions that apply to you and then following the answers.**

In Windows XP, obey these steps:

1. **Open the Printers and Faxes window.**

2. **From the links on the left side of the window, choose Troubleshoot Printing.**

3. **Follow the steps in the wizard to help solve your printing conundrum.**

The wizards are generally good, but also refer to the later section in this chapter, "General Printer Problems."

An option to troubleshoot a printer is presented when the printer is first installed. After printing a test page, you can choose to troubleshoot at that time; in Windows Vista, click the Troubleshooting link; in Windows XP, click the Troubleshoot button.

Visiting the Print Management window

Windows Vista features a Print Management console, shown in Figure 5-6. It's a central location for printing and has more features than the Printers window, but it's not really a secret or powerful place that only the gurus know about.

Figure 5-6:
The Print
Manage-
ment
console in
Windows
Vista.

 To visit the Print Management console in Windows Vista, open the Control Panel's Administrative Tools icon and then open the Print Management item. Click Continue or type the administrator's password to continue.

The Print Management console can quickly help you reference jobs that your PC is printing on multiple printers; choose the Printers with Jobs item on the left side of the console window. You can control multiple jobs across all printers by cancelling or pausing those jobs in bulk in the Print Management console window.

Close the Print Management console window when you're done, and realize that there's little you can do there unless you're printing a lot of stuff.

General Printer Problems

The first step in diagnosing printer problems is to determine whether the problem lies with the printer itself or with the application you're using. Generally speaking, the Print Preview command helps you determine whether your software is up to snuff or the printer has gone hinkey. The information in this section also helps determine the source of the problem and potential solutions.

Print Preview lies

Yes, I've written that Print Preview can help determine whether the problem is with the printer or specific to your software. Although that statement is true for the most part, in some situations the Print Preview command *lies*.

First, remember that there's most likely one edge of the paper that your printer cannot print on. For the other three edges, the margin may be all the way up to the edge of the page, or it might be a half an inch or so away from the edge. The fourth edge, however, is required by the printer to feed the paper. Regardless of what Print Preview says, you can't print on that edge of the page. The solution: Draw in the document's margins.

Second, some features have problems being implemented properly. I'm thinking specifically of Microsoft Word's annoying page border feature. The problem is with Word, not with the printer, but it's difficult to determine because the Print Preview window shows the border present.

To fix the page border on a page in Word, set the border from the *text*, not from the edge of the paper.

Finally, ensure that you haven't set your application or the printer itself to print in *Draft mode*. That mode is used for quickly printing a document without fancy things like text formatting or graphics. If that's the case, disable Draft mode in your application or in the printer's Properties dialog box.

Wrong colors, streaks, madness

For the content of your document or even its formatting, when the printed page looks ugly, chances are that the printer itself is to blame. The chief motivator of the ugly printing demon is your printer's ink supply.

Weird or faded colors indicate that one of the color ink cartridges is low. Some printers inform you of that fact, and others don't. Sadly, if you use an ink cartridge that contains multiple ink colors, you must replace the entire thing. Yep, that's how they make their money!

Dark streaks down the page might indicate that ink or something gunky got on the printer's paper-feeding mechanism. But for a laser printer, the streaks often mean that the toner is old. Replace the toner cartridge.

+ Replace the ink cartridges in an inkjet printer when they're empty. Obey your printer! Using ink cartridges that are too low on ink can damage some printers.

+ It's possible to extend toner life in a laser printer. The first time you see a Toner Low warning, remove the cartridge and gently rock it from side to side. Replace the cartridge and the warning message should no longer appear. When it does, replace the cartridge at once!

Weird characters on the page

Unless you're writing fiction and the weird characters are part of your narrative, what I'm referring to is what appears to be random letters, numbers, or symbols that appear on the printout. Typically, the characters appear at the top of each page. They may be the same on each page, or they may be different.

First, confirm that you didn't screw up the document's header by using the Print Preview command. Some documents print with an automatic header.

For example, your Web browser or the Windows Notepad program may automatically insert a header on your document. But that text doesn't look exactly "weird."

Second, update the printer software driver. Refer to the section "Checking the printer driver," earlier in this chapter, to confirm that the proper printer driver is chosen. If not, directions in that section explain how to delete and then add your printer again — hopefully, with the proper driver.

You can also visit the printer manufacturer's Web site to check for new or updated driver software.

Page after page of gobbledygook

I've seen a printer spew out endless pages of nonsense — and I'm not just speaking about the time I did consulting for a particular political cause, either. I'm talking pages of junk. That often happens for one of two reasons.

The first reason is that printing was somehow interrupted. The stream of data flowing from the computer to the printer had a hiccup, so the printer is misinterpreting the information. The solution is to stop the printer, cancel the print job, and then restart the printer and resend the print job. (Print again.)

The second reason for the junk may be an improper printer driver. See the section "Checking the printer driver," earlier in this chapter, for instructions on how to check the printer driver and change it to something better.

Printer jams

The number-one cause of printer jams is, of course, paper. Paperless printers seldom jam, but, sadly, they just don't sell that well. You probably have a printer that uses real paper, so it may jam someday.

The first solution to a printer jam is to find the jam and remove the paper. If the printer is smart enough to tell you where the jam occurred, heed its advice. Otherwise, follow the paper's path from tray to output, by opening various printer hatches and covers to find the errant sheet. Remove the jammed sheet and then resume printing.

✦ If the one page that jammed needs to be printed again, use the Print dialog box to print only the single sheet that jammed. See the earlier section "Printing in Windows" for details.

✦ Some printers may not recover from a paper jam until you open and close the cover.

✦ I don't recommend turning off a printer to recover from a jam; when you do, you often have to reprint the entire document.

✦ Some printers are smart and recover well from a jam, reprinting the page that was jammed.

✦ Sometimes the printer says it's jammed, but there's merely a misfeed from the paper tray. Remove the paper and fan it out, to get some air between the pages. Then try printing again.

✦ Avoid using overly thick paper in your printer, because it tends to jam.

✦ If you must use thick paper, check to ensure that your printer doesn't have a straight path type of option, where the paper simply moves from the front of the printer to the back without going through too many turns.

Page orientation

Consider yourself fortunate when the printer has on the paper tray a little icon or hint that explains how the page feeds through the printer. This icon comes in especially handy when printing on letterhead or the back side of a sheet of paper. Figure 5-7 explains how the icons work, though the icons you see on your printer may be subtly different.

If your printer lacks such an icon, feel free to create your own. Or, write a hint and tape it to the printer. For example, on my laser printer where I print checks, it says, on the paper tray, "Checks go in face down, top toward you." (That's the lower-right example from Figure 5-7.)

Envelopes must eat, too

Years ago, it was common for computer users to keep a typewriter handy. The only reason to relish the office relic was that the typewriter could still be used to type an address on an envelope. Happily, those days are long gone.

Most printers have an envelope slot, feeder, or tray. The better printers even let you stack up envelopes for mass mailings. Finding the tray is the first step in printing an envelope. The second step is to ensure that the envelope is properly oriented.

One sample printing can determine the envelope's orientation. If the printer has icons for envelope orientation, heed them. If not, refer to the preceding section and create your own envelope icons. (Curiously, the envelope icon on my printer is backward, so I made my own icon with a Sharpie.)

After working through the mechanical part, your next most difficult task is getting your software to print an envelope. That's not as difficult as it sounds: An envelope is merely a sheet of paper, one of a specific size. Use the Page Setup dialog box to choose the envelope size from the list of paper sizes. *Ta-da!* Just format the envelope "document" accordingly, and then print.

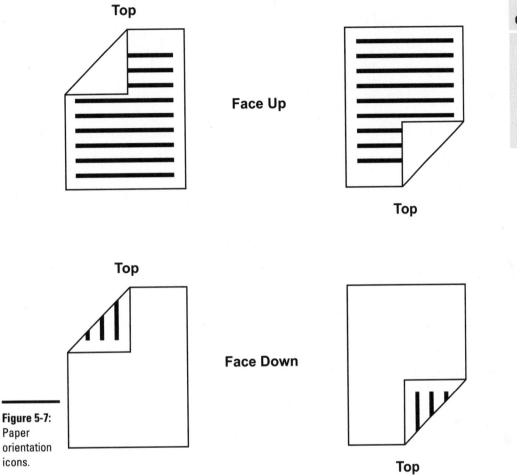

Top

Face Up

Top

Top

Face Down

Figure 5-7:
Paper
orientation
icons.

Top

✦ High-end printers often feature an envelope-feeder option, which allows a massive number of envelopes to be shot through the printer at a time.

✦ Some applications feature an Envelope command, which can be used to print a single envelope or more. In Microsoft Word 2007, use the Envelopes button in the Create area on the Mailings tab; in older versions of Word, you use the Tools⇨Envelopes and Labels command and click the Envelopes tab in the dialog box.

✦ Those peel-and-close envelopes work best in a laser printer. Because laser printers use heat to fuse the toner to the paper, the heat can also seal an empty envelope.

Chapter 6: Seeing Trouble

In This Chapter

✔ Understanding the video system

✔ Getting info on the display adapter

✔ Using a second monitor

✔ Swapping out parts

✔ Adjusting the display

✔ Installing new driver software

✔ Using the video troubleshooter

Some people think that the computer *is* the monitor. On an iMac, that may be true, but most PCs still have a separate monitor and console. The actual computer part is inside the console; the monitor merely represents the computer's face. So what's on a face anyway? Can you see the monitor? Is the image all funky, or is there even an image? When it comes time to troubleshoot what you see on the computer screen, this chapter is the one to turn to.

The PC Graphics System

The monitor isn't your PC's graphics system. No, it's only the part you see. To best help troubleshoot PC graphics problems, you need to know more than what you see. This section helps you understand all the background info that makes troubleshooting easier.

Know the terms

When speaking about that TV-like thing connected to your computer, you use three words: *monitor, screen*, and *display*. Here's how and when to use them:

Monitor: A monitor is a chunk of computer hardware. It's the gizmo that displays images created by the computer's graphics adapter, which is located inside the console.

Screen: The screen is the part of the monitor that displays an image: text, graphics, the Windows desktop, games. All that information shows up on the screen part of the monitor.

Display: The display is the image you see on the screen. For example, the display may show you the Windows desktop, some icons, and a window with a picture of Jessica Alba frolicking in the surf.

Here are some more points that may help you clarify the differences:

+ When you clean the monitor, you're cleaning the entire thing: base, back, top, and screen — unless you're a teenage boy, in which case you clean only the top part.

+ Cleaning the screen doesn't clean the display; by cleaning the screen, you're removing dust, fingerprints, and sneeze globs. See Book III, Chapter 4 for information on cleaning an LCD monitor; refer to Book VI, Chapter 4 for information on cleaning a CTR (glass screen) monitor.

+ When you clean the display, basically you're clearing off windows, icons, and other graphical information. It's a software thing.

+ Yes, the nerds like to say "Clear the screen." They really mean "Clear the display."

Graphical system overview

The key to understanding, and therefore troubleshooting, computer graphics is to know that the brains of the operation lie in the *display adapter,* which is inside the computer console. Figure 6-1 illustrates a typical PC graphics system.

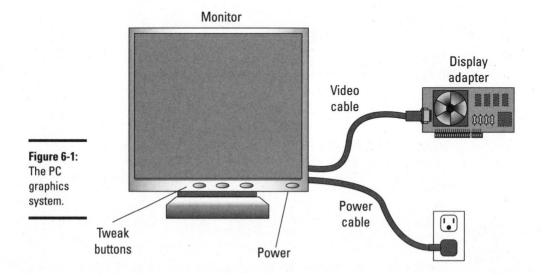

Figure 6-1:
The PC graphics system.

Monitor

Display adapter

Video cable

Power cable

Tweak buttons

Power

The image is generated inside the PC using the display adapter hardware. That image is then sent to the monitor, which displays the image. Technically, all the action takes place inside the console, with the display adapter. That gizmo determines the graphics abilities of your computer.

The monitor plays a smaller role in your PC's graphics system. Its main contribution is its screen size. It also has some technical aspects, which are covered later in this chapter.

✦ Figure 6-1 shows the PC's display adapter as an expansion card, which is common for high-end graphics. Most PCs, however, use a display adapter that's built into the computer's motherboard.

✦ The display adapter might also be called the *graphics adapter.* That term hearkens back to an era when PC monitors displayed mostly text. To display graphics, you had to buy special graphics hardware (a graphics adapter).

The display adapter

The only visual part of the display adapter you see on your PC is the spot where the monitor's video cable plugs in. Well, if you have a translucent computer console, you might be able to see the display adapter inside. Regardless, there are two common types of video connector, as illustrated in Figure 6-2: VGA and DVI.

Figure 6-2:
Two
common
display
adapter
connectors.

VGA   DVI

Analog   Digital

Other information about the display adapter must be gathered from within Windows. You can look in two places: the Adapter's Properties dialog box, which is covered in the next section, and the Device Manager, covered elsewhere in this minibook.

✦ The best way to ensure that you're properly using your PC's display adapter is to keep its software (the device driver) up to date. See the section "Updating drivers," later in this chapter.

✦ DVI stands for Digital Visual Interface. It's also called the *digital* connector.

+ The DVI connector shown in Figure 6-2 is a *female* connector. The male connector (found on the video cable) may not have a pin for every hole in the female connector. No, the pins aren't missing: there are five types of DVI connector by design. The female connector accepts each type of DVI male connector and uses the differences to help the hardware identify and properly use the monitor.

+ A mini-DVI connector is also often found on laptop computers. See Book III for more information.

+ VGA stands for Video Gate Array, and commonly (though incorrectly), Video Graphics Adapter.

+ The VGA connector might also be known as the *analog* video connector.

+ The VGA connector is of a similar size to the old PC serial port. Note that the VGA connector, however, sports 15 holes rather than 9.

+ Adapters are available for connecting VGA and DVI monitors to DVI and VGA adapters, respectively. A bonus with the DVI-to-VGA adapter is that it might also let you easily attach a second monitor to your PC. See the section "That second-monitor thing," later in this chapter.

Display adapter info

Video performance is based on two factors. The first is the graphics processor. A nice, beefy graphics processing unit (GPU) makes your PC's graphics shine. A nice 3D physics engine makes all the difference when playing games.

The second thing that affects the PC's video system is the amount of dedicated video memory available. A display adapter with 256MB of video memory is a good baseline for computer games. More memory makes things better, but the cost also comes into play; more memory is expensive, and unless your PC has a beefy GPU and a 3D physics engine to help things out, more memory isn't worth it.

Sadly, both the GPU and video memory are things you cannot change after buying the graphics card. You can replace a graphics card, but you cannot upgrade an existing card the way you can, say, add more memory to your PC.

To discover which type of display adapter is in your PC, as well as how much memory it sports, you need to view the display adapter's Properties dialog box. You have various ways to get to that dialog box, depending on which version of Windows you have.

To view some basic information about your PC's display adapter hardware in Windows Vista, abide by these steps:

1. **Right-click the desktop and choose Personalize from the shortcut menu.**

2. **Choose Display Settings in the Personalization window.**

   The Display Settings dialog box appears.

3. **Click the Advanced Settings button.**

   The display adapter's Properties dialog box is shown.

4. **If necessary, click the Adapter tab.**

The display adapter's information appears, similar to what's shown in Figure 6-3.

Figure 6-3:
Display adapter information.

For Windows XP, follow these steps to see information about your PC's display adapter:

1. **Right-click the desktop and choose Properties from the pop-up menu.**

2. **In the Display Properties dialog box, click the Settings tab.**

3. **Click the Advanced button.**

4. **In the display adapter's Properties dialog box, click the Adapter tab.**

The information displayed looks similar to the Windows Vista version of the dialog box (refer to Figure 6-3), but some of the more detailed information is missing.

Although the dialog box doesn't say whether the display adapter sports a GPU or 3D physics engine, it does tell you an important piece of information: the name of the adapter. In Figure 6-3, it's NVIDIA GeForce 8800 GT. That information comes into play when updating graphics drivers, as covered later in this chapter. More revealing, however, is the video memory information displayed in the dialog box.

In Figure 6-3, the adapter has 1790MB of video memory available. That's a total figure; 512MB of video memory dwells directly on the adapter card. That's a good thing. The rest, 1278MB of video memory, is shared with main computer memory.

Close the dialog box and any other open windows when you're done absorbing the information.

✦ You get the least measure of performance from a video adapter that shares all its memory with the computer's main memory. For basic computer use, however, that's okay; beyond e-mail, word processing, and the Internet, you don't need truly beefy graphics to run a PC.

✦ In Windows XP, a display adapter that shows 0MB or some other low value is doubtless sharing main memory. If you want better video, you need to upgrade with a new display adapter.

✦ A great improvement in video games can be had by replacing the PC's display adapter with a newer model that sports at least 256MB of video memory. Refer to Chapter 8 for information on replacing a video adapter.

The monitor

The PC's monitor merely does what the display adapter tells it to do, but that doesn't imply that the monitor is lacking in smarts. Fortunately, most of the stuff the monitor does is automatic, such as self-adjust to whichever resolution the display adapter demands.

The monitor sports two tails: one for power and the other to connect to the computer — specifically, to the display adapter.

There are two flavors of monitor: LCD and CRT. The LCD is now more popular because of its size and because it's flat and lightweight. It also consumes less power. CRT monitors — the older, bulkier glass monitors — might still be around, but they aren't that popular any more.

On the monitor, you find a power switch plus a series of adjustment buttons. Most current monitors sport four buttons, which are used in combination to help manipulate an onscreen menu. Using the menu is covered in the section "Adjusting the monitor," later in this chapter.

Monitors are gauged by their size. As on a television set, the monitor's size is measured diagonally on the screen. In addition to the diagonal size, the monitor's aspect ratio is used to determine the relationship between the screen's horizontal and vertical sides. Figure 6-4 helps you understand the ideas behind monitor size and aspect ratio.

Figure 6-4:
Measuring a monitor.

4:3 aspect ratio

16:9 "widescreen" aspect ratio

Here are some additional trivial details about a computer monitor, without getting too technical:

Contrast ratio: The difference between the monitor's brightest white and darkest black. Some monitors get high points for showing truly rich blacks.

Dot pitch: The distance between a monitor's pixels as measured in millimeters (mm). The closer the distance, and the smaller the dot pitch value, the sharper the image on the monitor. There's a relationship between the dot pitch and screen size as far as resolution is concerned.

Luminance: The monitor's brightness.

Refresh rate: The number of times per second that the monitor's image is displayed. The refresh rate is measured in hertz, which is why you may see the term displayed on the screen when the monitor changes resolution. Refresh rate might also be referred to as *frequency*.

Resolution: Images displayed on a monitor using tiny, colored dots, or *pixels*. The monitor displays images using a given number of pixels horizontally and vertically, which is referred to as the screen resolution. The resolution is set by the display adapter and controlled via software (Windows).

Viewing angle: Important for LCD monitors; determines how well the monitor can be seen when you're not staring straight at it, which is an angle of 0 degrees. The closer the viewing angle is to 180 degrees, the easier it is to see the monitor.

One key issue with monitors is *glare*, or the reflection of light off the monitor and into your eyeballs. The best way to reduce glare is to position the monitor so that bright lights aren't reflected on the screen. Don't compute with your back to a bright window. When you can't move the monitor or remove the glare, buy an antiglare screen for the monitor.

✦ Another monitor type is the *plasma*, though it's less trendy for computers than it is for large, wide-screen televisions.

✦ Pixel is a combination of the words *picture element*. It's the smallest dot of color that can be displayed on a monitor. Images on the screen are composed of thousands of individual pixels.

✦ LCD monitors may have a limited set of resolutions that they can adapt to. For example, the monitor may accept resolutions of only 800-by-600 or 1024-by-768 pixels. Other resolutions may not render properly and can damage the monitor. The only way to know for certain is to check the documentation that came with the monitor.

✦ LCD stands for liquid crystal display.

✦ CRT stands for cathode ray tube.

✦ CRT monitors are still preferred by graphic artists and gamers. For graphic artists, the analog nature of the CRT monitor better reproduces colors that match the real world (because the CRT monitor is analog, not digital). For games, the CRT monitor's update rate is faster and more responsive than an LCD monitor.

✦ Aspect ratios other than 4:3 and 16:9 are used, though they're not as common.

✦ A wide-screen monitor doesn't share the same amount of screen real estate as a traditional 4:3 computer monitor. Despite identical diagonal measurements, a monitor with a 4:3 aspect ratio has more square inches of screen than the wide-screen monitor. That's one reason why 4:3 monitors are a bit more expensive than the wide-screen versions (and why monitor manufacturers push the wide-screen format).

✦ Some monitors feature dual inputs. For example, they can be used with two computers or perhaps take two different types of signals. A problem with such monitors is that they may appear broken when they're simply not receiving a signal through the proper input. The solution is to change inputs using the monitor's controls.

✦ The nerdy term for a computer monitor is a VDU, or visual display unit.

✦ See Book III, Chapter 4 for information about cleaning an LCD monitor and screen; Book VI, Chapter 4 describes how to clean a standard or CRT monitor.

That second-monitor thing

Certain editions of Windows have the ability to power two monitors. All you need to complete the picture are two monitors plus two display adapters or one display adapter that can handle two monitors.

The easiest way to tell whether your PC has this ability is to check the Display Properties dialog box to see whether a second, phantom monitor shows up. In Figure 6-5, you see that the display adapter has the ability to use two monitors, though the second monitor (number 2) isn't activated.

Primary monitor

Display monitor numbers on the screen

Secondary monitor

Drag monitor around

Figure 6-5:
Second-monitor things to note.

Selected monitor

Settings for selected monitor

Activate secondary monitor

Identify main monitor

To use the second monitor, select it and then choose the option Extend The Desktop Onto This Monitor in Windows Vista; in Windows XP choose Extend My Windows Desktop onto This Monitor.

The taskbar shows up only on the main monitor, or monitor 1. (To see which monitor is which, click the Identify Monitors button in Windows Vista; the Identify button in Windows XP.) To switch main monitors, click to select the new main monitor and then put a check mark by the option titled This Is My Main Monitor in Windows Vista; in Windows XP choose Use This Device As The Primary Monitor.

Each monitor has its own resolution and color settings. To change the settings, choose the monitor from the menu in the center of the dialog box and then set the Resolution and Colors. Changing the resolution changes the monitors' relative sizes in the window. You can then drag the second monitor around to adjust how they relate to each other.

Drag a window between the two monitors to see how their positions relate. In fact, you can use the Display Settings or Display Properties dialog box for that test.

Click the OK button when you're done arranging the dual monitors.

+ The easiest way to set up dual monitor hardware is to buy a dual monitor adapter. They come in both VGA and DVI models.

+ Display adapters with a digital connector can drive two VGA monitors. You need to purchase a DVI to dual VGA adapter to make this happen.

+ Most laptops have the second-monitor ability built in. It allows them to easily use external monitors and video projectors for making presentations. See Book III for more information on troubleshooting laptop computers.

+ To swap the Windows Vista Sidebar to the other monitor open the Windows Sidebar icon in the Control Panel. In the Windows Sidebar dialog box, choose the monitor number from the menu by the item titled Display Sidebar On Monitor.

+ Changing the main monitor doesn't change its number. To change the numbers, you have to swap the monitors display adapter connectors on the PC.

+ Do not remove a monitor while the computer is in hibernation. Doing so can prevent the logon screen from showing when the computer restarts.

+ Monitor *mirroring* is when you display the same image on both monitors. This is a feature used in laptops for presentations. See Book III.

Captain Video the Troubleshooter

Sometime in the future, heroes of freedom will swoop down from distant mountaintops, ably assisting computer users with their PC's video system troubles. Until then, you have the information in this section to help you.

Seeing nothing

When you see nothing, the first thing you should try is opening your eyes. That often solves the problem right away.

When you see nothing on the computer monitor, check the basic hardware first: Is the monitor turned on? Is it plugged in? Is the monitor properly connected to the display adapter on the console? If the monitor has dual inputs, is the proper one selected?

A computer or monitor in sleep (low-power) mode shows its power-on LED in an amber color instead of the normal green. If so, the problem is with the video signal not reaching the monitor.

Press the monitor's menu button, as described in the later section "Adjusting the monitor." If the monitor's menu appears, the monitor is fine and the problem is with the display adapter.

✦ When a monitor has dual inputs, be sure that the proper input is selected. This type of checking is the same as my general "check to see whether it's plugged in" advice, but usually you need to press a button or switch on the monitor to ensure that the input is coming from the proper connection.

✦ Monitors are never something you should try to fix on your own. Never open a monitor's case.

✦ When a monitor is dead, throw it out. Do so properly, according to whatever rules govern the disposal of computer equipment for your locale.

Swapping solutions

Because the PC's video system contains two parts, you have to check two hardware things for the source of the trouble: the monitor and the display adapter. To do forensic troubleshooting, it helps to swap out the parts to determine specifically where the trouble lies.

Obviously you cannot swap out a monitor and display adapter unless you have spares lounging about. But when you do have a spare monitor or display adapter, you can use them to help troubleshoot.

Start with the monitor:

1. **Turn off the computer and monitor.**

2. **Unplug the monitor and disconnect it from the console.**

3. **Attach the replacement monitor.**

4. **Turn on the computer.**

Assuming that you know the replacement monitor works, the computer should display an image on the screen. If not, the problem lies with the display adapter.

You can use similar steps to troubleshoot a display adapter. Heed the directions in Chapter 8 for installing a display adapter, but instead replace the current adapter with one you know works. If that fixes the problem, you know that you need to buy a new display adapter.

✦ The replacements you use for swapping must be working for the swap to be an affective troubleshooting tool.

✦ This trick still works when the display adapter is part of the motherboard: simply plug a video adapter into one of the PC's expansion slots. If it works, the problem is in the video circuitry on the motherboard. Buy a new display adapter.

Adjusting the monitor

No monitor is perfect, and the manufacturer recognizes that. So each monitor features its own adjustment menu, along with a set of confusing buttons you can use to access and manipulate the menu, thereby honing your monitor's screen to graphical perfection.

The typical monitor has five buttons: one power button and then four buttons to manipulate the onscreen menu. Usually, two buttons have arrows or triangles on them, and then two other buttons manipulate the menu commands. The types and designs of the buttons differ from monitor to monitor.

Generally speaking, pressing one of the buttons (or the button labeled with a menu icon) displays the on-screen menu. A menu example is shown in Figure 6-6. You then use the arrow or triangle buttons to select a menu item. The other two buttons are used (somehow) to manipulate the item and adjust the monitor.

The on-screen menu eventually disappears after a period of inactivity. Or sometimes it disappears when you press the main menu button while viewing the main menu.

✦ One key feature found in many on-screen monitor menus is Auto Tune or Auto Adjust. Use that feature to quickly have the monitor adjust to the image the display adapter is sending.

✦ If the LCD monitor has regions on the screen that appear fuzzy or that twinkle, the monitor hasn't properly grasped the graphics information being sent to it. If the monitor sports an Auto-Adjust feature on its menu, try that. If that doesn't work, turn the monitor off, wait, and then turn it on again.

✦ Some monitors feature a Save option in the menu. Use it to save your favorite settings. A corresponding Recall option restores those settings that you've saved.

✦ Laptop keyboards have function buttons that let you adjust the monitor's brightness and contrast. Beyond that, laptop monitors lack the specific adjustments that desktop monitors have, mostly because the laptop's monitor is dedicated to the laptop and therefore doesn't require any additional configuration.

Figure 6-6:
A typical monitor menu.

Dealing with dead or stuck pixels

A situation unique to LCD monitors is the dead or stuck pixel issue. They're similar problems.

A dead pixel is one with its red, green, or blue element off or "dead." The only way to really find such pixels is to display solid colors on the screen and scour the territory for any "holes" or missing spots.

The sad news is that you cannot fix a dead pixel; it's a manufacturing defect. Your only hope is to find enough dead pixels that void the warranty. Upon inspection of your computer's LCD screen, you find that the manufacturer's warranty allows for a given number of dead pixels. Usually it's fewer than 10.

A stuck pixel is one that stays a certain color despite signals from the display adapter requesting it to change. Unlike a dead pixel, it's possible to correct a stuck pixel: using a diagnostic program, or sometimes something simple like Windows Paint, you can "shock" the stuck pixel back to life by displaying various colors rapidly on the screen. Sometimes that works, sometimes it doesn't.

✦ The higher-priced monitors have less chance of sporting a dead pixel. One of my early LCD monitors has three dead pixels, but I rarely notice them.

✦ Pixels get stuck because they literally remember which colors they're displaying. By rapidly switching colors on the screen, it's possible to unstick the stuck pixel.

✦ A stuck pixel that cannot be unstuck becomes a dead pixel.

Saving the screen

There is no reason to run a screen saver program for its intended purpose: to prevent the perils of phosphor burn-in. Back in the old days, computers were often used for a single task, especially in an office setting. Because the same image was displayed pretty much all the time on the screen, that image burned the CRT's phosphor, making an image visible even when the monitor was turned off.

To help "save" the screen, screen saver software was born.

At first, the screen savers merely blanked the display after a period of inactivity. Later screen savers added graphic images. Today screen savers are mostly toys, though they can also serve a security function by locking the computer after a period of inactivity. But phosphor burn-in is no longer considered a serious computer maintenance issue.

✦ To configure a screen saver in Windows Vista, right-click the desktop and choose Personalize from the pop-up menu. In the Personalization window, click the Screen Saver link to show the Screen Saver Settings dialog box.

✦ To configure a screen saver in Windows XP, right-click the desktop and choose Properties from the shortcut menu. Click the Screen Saver tab in the Display Properties dialog box.

✦ To have the screen saver lock the computer (for security), place a check mark in the box by On Resume, Display Logon Screen (Windows Vista) or On Resume, Password Protect (Windows XP). That option can be found in the Screen Saver Settings or Display Properties dialog box.

✦ Be careful when downloading screen savers from the Internet. Many of the so-called free screen savers can be malware that turns out to be more trouble than it's worth. See Book IV, Chapter 4 for more information on malware.

✦ Primary culprits of the phosphor burn-in peril were Lotus 1-2-3 and WordPerfect (both DOS programs). Although phosphor burn-in was noticeable when the monitor was turned off, it wasn't that noticeable when the program that caused the burn-in was being run. The burn in was terribly noticeable when running other programs.

Saving power

Your computer monitor is most likely energy efficient. That means it has a low-power mode designed to save energy. That mode is activated by a loss of signal from the PC's display adapter. You can confirm the mode in one of two ways:

First, the screen goes blank and a message appears. The message indicates that the signal from the computer is no longer available. The text varies from "Missing signal" to "No input" to any of a variety of terse and confusing messages. (In fact, the message may also appear when you simply disconnect the monitor from the display adapter.)

Second, the monitor's power-on lamp changes from green to amber in color.

The monitor is only a dumb partner in the power-saving scheme. The true mastermind is the operating system, which directs the display adapter to stop sending the monitor a video signal. You can configure your computer to save monitor power based on a period of inactivity. To set that period of inactivity — the sleep timeouts for the monitor — follow these steps:

1. **Open the Power Options icon in the Control Panel.**

2a. **In Windows Vista, choose the link on the left Choose When To Turn Off The Display.**

2b. **In Windows XP, ensure that the Power Schemes tab is selected.**

3. **Use the menu button to set the timeout value for the monitor.**

In Windows Vista, the option is titled Turn Off the Display; in Windows XP it's titled Turn Off Monitor.

4. **Click Save Changes or OK button.**

Optionally close any other windows left hanging open.

I set my monitor to have a 45-minute timeout. (At that point, I'm most likely done.) The screen saver kicks in at 30 minutes.

If you're using a screen saver, it also sports a timeout value. When the monitor's sleep timeout is *less* than the screen saver timeout, you never see the screen saver in action. Therefore, I recommend setting the monitor's sleep timeout to a value several minutes (or hours) greater than the screen saver's timeout.

I set my screen saver to activate after 30 minutes.

✦ If the monitor's power lamp is green and the screen is still blank, you might simply be looking at a blank screen saver image.

✦ The monitor also goes into power-saving mode when the computer is turned off. Though I recommend for true power-savings that you just turn the monitor off as well as the computer.

Adjusting the resolution

Computer monitors display images by lighting up various pixels, or picture elements, on the screen. Those pixels are arranged in a grid, where the number of pixels horizontally and vertically are referred to as the display's *resolution*.

To check or set the display's resolution you need to use either the Display Settings or Display Properties dialog box, an example of which is shown in Figure 6-5.

In Windows Vista, conjure forth the Display Settings dialog box by opening the Personalization icon in the Control Panel, or by right-clicking the desktop and choosing the Personalize command. Choose the Display Settings link in the Personalization window.

In Windows XP, right-click the Desktop and choose Properties to behold the Display Properties dialog box. Click the Settings tab.

Set the resolution by using the slider gizmo: right is higher resolution, left is lower resolution. You're essentially increasing or decreasing the number of pixels displayed, as well as the display's aspect ratio (horizontal to vertical pixels). Use the preview screen to determine how the resolution affects things.

To check the new resolution, click the Apply button. The display changes to reflect the new settings, and you're allowed the option of clicking Yes or No to make the change permanent. If you don't see anything, just wait and the previous settings are restored.

Click OK to confirm the settings and close the dialog box.

+ When the resolution seemingly and without explanation switches to very low (things look comically large on the screen), the problem is most likely a lost or improperly installed video driver. Simply reinstall the current driver; see the section "Updating drivers" later in this chapter.

+ Only a given number of preset resolutions are available. The variety depends on the abilities of the computer's display adapter.

+ Safe mode uses 800-by-600 pixels as its resolution, which is about as low as you want to use Windows.

+ A common resolution is 1024-by-768 pixels.

+ Widescreen monitors with the right display adapter can employ the ultimate 1600-by-1200 resolution. There's also rumor of a 2560-by-1600 resolution, and such a thing makes me lust for technology more than I'm willing to admit.

+ The higher the resolution numbers, the smaller things appear on the screen. When you have trouble seeing the screen, use lower resolutions.

+ Some LCD monitors display only a handful of resolutions well. Using resolutions not recommended by the manufacturer may damage the monitor.

+ If you have two monitors, resolution is set for each of them. Choose the monitor from the list in the dialog box and then make the resolution settings.

+ There's a humongous difference between the display resolution and an image's resolution. An image's resolution is the number of *dots per inch (dpi)* used to render the image. That amount can vary. PC monitors are set at about 96 dots per inch, which is why some images appear small on the screen and others appear huge. See the section "Setting the dpi" later in this chapter.

Changing the icon size

When a lower resolution doesn't help you see the screen, you can also try resizing the desktop icons, as well as the icons in various folders, the Quick Launch toolbar, and the Start menu.

Desktop icons

To resize desktop icons in Windows Vista, right-click the Desktop and choose View⇨Large Icons from the pop-up menu.

In Windows XP, take these steps to show larger icons on the desktop:

1. **Right-click the desktop and choose Properties from the pop-up menu.**
2. **In the Display Properties dialog box, click the Appearance tab.**
3. **Click the Effects button.**
4. **Place a check mark by Use Large Icons.**
5. **Click OK and then click OK again to close the Display Properties dialog box.**

Folder icons

You can change the size of icons in the folder windows only in Windows Vista. For each window, use the Views toolbar button to choose the Large Icons or Extra Large Icons command.

Quick Launch toolbar icons

To change the icon size for the Quick Launch toolbar (or any toolbar on the taskbar), follow these steps:

1. **If necessary, unlock the taskbar: right-click on a blank part of the task-bar and choose Lock The Taskbar from the pop-up menu.**

    You need to remove the check mark by Lock The Taskbar to unlock the taskbar.

2. **Right-click on the toolbar's handle.**

    The handle is located on the left end of the toolbar. (It only shows up when the taskbar is unlocked.)

3. **From the menu, choose View⇨Large Icons.**

4. **Adjust the taskbar's height to properly show the larger icons.**

    Point the mouse at the edge of the taskbar, between the taskbar and the screen. Drag the mouse toward the center of the screen to set the task-bar's height.

5. **Relock the taskbar, if necessary: Right-click on the taskbar and choose Lock The Taskbar.**

Start menu icons

To change the size of the icons on the Start menu, follow these steps:

1. **Right-click the Start button and choose Properties from the pop-up menu.**

2. **Click the Customize button.**

3a. **In Windows Vista, scroll through the list to find the item Use Large Icons; place a check mark by that item.**

3b. **In Windows XP, choose the option Large Icons.**

4. **Click OK and then click OK again to close the Taskbar and Start Menu Properties dialog box.**

Setting the dpi

Dpi refers to dots per inch, and it's a key concept to using computer graphics. Your PC doubtless uses a resolution on the monitor of 96 dpi. That value can be changed to 120 dpi or any dpi value.

Changing the dpi value of your monitor isn't something you need to do; 96 dpi is fine for using a PC. In fact, most programs and Web pages assume that your PC's monitor is set to 96 dpi; that's close to 100 dots per inch. When viewing the screen is difficult, however, selecting 120 dpi works better. And for graphics artists who need a more realistic representation of information on the screen, different dpi resolutions might fix some problems.

To set the dpi in Windows Vista, start with these steps:

1. **Open the Personalization icon in the Control Panel.**

2. **From the list of tasks on the left side of the window, choose Adjust Font Size (DPI).**

3. **Click the Continue button or type in the Administrator's Password when prompted to do so.**

   The DPI Scaling dialog box appears.

4. **Choose either 96 dpi or 120 dpi.**

   When those settings work out fine, you can click the OK button and you're done (though read the notes below for additional information). Otherwise, click the Custom DPI button and continue below with Step 5.

To set the dpi in Windows XP, obey these steps:

1. **Right-click the display and choose Properties from the pop-up menu.**

2. **Click the Settings tab in the Display Properties dialog box.**

3. **Click the Advanced button.**

4. **Choose either 96 dpi or 120 dpi using the drop-down menu.**

You may have to restart the PC to see the results, though if you're done, click the OK button and obey the directions. Otherwise, choose Custom DIP from the drop-down list and continue with Step 5 to set up custom dpi settings.

5. **Use the Custom DPI dialog box to configure the screen's dpi.**

Figure 6-7 illustrates how you can work the dialog box: You can choose a percentage from the drop-down menu, or you can use the mouse to drag the ruler larger. Sadly, you cannot reset the dpi to a value less than 100 percent.

Figure 6-7:
Setting a custom dpi value.

6. **Click the OK button to confirm your settings, or click Cancel if you were just messing around.**

Obey any additional directions given, such as restarting the computer. Oh, and close any other dialog boxes or windows you may have opened.

Windows may have to install or configure new fonts and possibly restart when the dpi is changed.

Setting color depth

The richness of the image on a computer monitor is determined more by the number of colors available as opposed to the number of pixels (the resolution). Lower resolutions with more colors look better than higher resolutions. In fact, most computer games use lower resolutions simply because more colors are available.

Setting the number of colors is done in the Display Settings or Display Properties dialog box — the same location where the resolution is set as described earlier in this chapter (in the section "Adjusting the resolution"). The dialog box has only two settings: Highest (32-bit) and Medium (16-bit). Choose the highest setting available at the preferred resolution for the monitor.

Of course, setting the number of colors doesn't ensure that the screen accurately depicts the colors displayed. Every monitor has variations. You can adjust the way colors are displayed, or *rendered,* with the Windows Color Management tool, covered in the next section.

✦ The number of colors available is often referred to as the *color depth.*

✦ There's a relationship between resolution and colors. Lower resolutions can have more colors; higher resolutions sport fewer colors. The key is video memory. Lots of colors require lots of memory, which leaves less memory available for resolution. Conversely, higher resolutions require more video memory, which leaves less memory available for color depth. It's a twisted graphical circle!

Configuring color management

The idea behind color management isn't to match colors on a computer monitor with colors in the real world. Instead, strive to match colors in a way that satisfies your needs. For example, match the colors on the monitor to the colors produced by a specific printer or other output device. To make that happen, you need to use the Windows Color Management tool.

Messing with the Windows Color Management tool isn't something you mess with casually. My advice is to use it only when you receive instructions on which profiles to select. Such information may be found in a graphics application's reference on in your PC's printer reference.

To use the Color Management tool in Windows Vista, follow these steps:

1. **Open the Control Panel's Personalization icon.**

2. **Choose the Display Settings link.**

   The Display Settings dialog box appears (refer to Figure 6-5).

3. **Click the Advanced Settings button.**

4. **In the display adapter's Properties dialog box click the Color Management tab.**

5. **Click the Color Management button.**

   The Color Management window appears. Yes, it's a very complex place. There's no need wandering about aimlessly.

6. **Choose a hardware device from the Device menu button.**

   Most likely, the PC's monitor and current display adapter are chosen as the device. If you want the display to match the output of a color laser printer available to the computer, choose it from the list.

7. **Place a check mark by the option Use My Settings For This Device.**

8. **Click the Add button to choose a profile.**

   This is the part where it helps to know what you're doing: no additional information is provided for the profiles listed in the Associate Color Profile dialog box.

9. **Select a profile from those listed.**

10. **Click the OK button.**

    The profile is now associated with the device you chose in Step 7.

11. **Repeat Steps 8 through 10 to add additional profiles for the device.**

12. **Click the Close button and then close the other open dialog boxes and windows as necessary.**

Windows XP isn't as sophisticated as Windows Vista when it comes to the Color Management tool. Follow these steps:

1. **Right-click the desktop and choose Properties from the pop-up menu.**

2. **In the Display Properties dialog box, click the Settings tab.**

3. **Click the Advanced button.**

4. **In the monitor and display adapter's Properties dialog box, click the Color Management tab.**

   Unlike Windows Vista, the only device available for configuring is the monitor. You can add a color profile to the monitor, but again it helps to know which profile you need as opposed to just randomly choosing a profile.

5. **Click the Add button.**

6. **Choose a color profile in the Add Profile Association dialog box.**

7. **Click the Add button.**

   The profile is now associated with the device.

8. **Repeat Steps 5 through 7 to add additional profiles.**

   You can highlight a single profile and use the Set As Default button to choose your favorite profile out of several.

9. **Click the OK button when you're done, and optionally close the Display Properties dialog box as well.**

Color profiles are installed by Windows as you add color devices to the computer. For example, when installing a color laser printer, Windows automatically installs the necessary color profiles.

✦ The PC's display adapter may have come with special utilities that set the colors better than the Windows Color Management tool.

✦ The monitor may have color temperature settings in its control panel. See the section "Adjusting the monitor," earlier in this chapter. Check the monitor's menu for a color temperature or other color settings.

Updating drivers

Most video woes can be solved by updating the video driver. The two main companies that develop display adapter technology (ATI and NVIDIA) routinely make new graphics drivers available, ensuring that your PC remains compatible with all the latest graphical software out there.

To manually check for a new driver, visit the display adapter's Properties dialog box, on the Drivers tab:

1. **Right-click the desktop.**

2a. **In Windows Vista, choose Personalize and then click the Display Settings link in the Personalization window.**

2b. **In Windows XP, choose Properties from the pop-up menu; skip to Step 4.**

3. **In Windows Vista, click the Advanced button.**

4. **Click the Properties button in the display adapter's Properties dialog box.**

5. **In Windows Vista, type the administrator's password or click the Continue button when prompted by the User Account Control dialog box.**

   The display adapter's Properties dialog box appears.

6. Click the Driver tab.

Before wasting any time, check the date. Figure 6-8 shows the Driver tab in my computer's display adapter Properties dialog box. The date is old, so it's worth your time to check for an updated driver.

Figure 6-8:
The display
adapter's
Properties
dialog box
— Driver
tab.

7. Click the Update Driver button.

Follow the directions on the screen to find the latest driver for the display adapter; I recommend searching the Internet for a new driver. If nothing is available, you're told so. That's fine; it means you're up-to-date.

You may have to restart Windows to complete the installation of a new video driver.

8. Close any open dialog boxes or windows when you're done.

If you update the driver and — oops! — things are even worse, you can roll back the driver. The easiest way to do this is with System Restore. A prompt for System Restore appears when you first start the PC (refer to Chapter 2, the section titled "The F8 menu"). Or, you can use the Roll Back Driver button in the display adapter Properties dialog box, Driver tab (refer to Figure 6-8).

✦ The best way to ensure that your PC has updated drivers is to use the Windows Update service. Refer to Book II, Chapter 1.

✦ Windows XP suffers from a problem where the current video driver might become "lost." In that case, you need to reinstall a driver already on the computer. After following Step 7 in the preceding step list, simply use the driver already available on the computer's hard drive. That fixes the low-resolution issue.

✦ You can also check for a driver by visiting the developer's Web site and looking for the Support or Drivers link. Confirm which display adapter you have by following the directions outlined earlier in this chapter; see the section "Display adapter info."

✦ Don't forget to check for updated software for a second display adapter, if your PC sports such hardware.

Using the troubleshooting helpers

As you might expect, some troubleshooters are lurking in Windows to assist you with video problems.

In Windows Vista, the troubleshooter can be found by following these steps:

1. **Right-click the desktop and choose Personalize from the shortcut menu.**

2. **Click the Display Settings link in the Personalization window.**

3. **Click Advanced Settings.**

4. **Click the Troubleshoot tab in the display adapter's Properties dialog box.**

5. **Click the Change Settings button, if it's available.**

   Not every display adapter lets you modify the acceleration settings. If your PC's adapter does, click the Continue button (or type the administrator's password), and obey the directions on the screen.

6. **Click OK and close the various open thingies when you're done.**

Windows XP has a bit more interactive video troubleshooter. Here's how to get to it:

1. **Right-click the desktop and choose Properties from the pop-up menu.**

2. **In the Display Properties dialog box, click the Settings tab.**

3. **Click the Troubleshoot button.**

   The Help and Support Center's Video Display Troubleshooter appears.

4. **Answer the questions and work through the troubleshooter to (hopefully) remedy your situation.**

5. **Close the open dialog boxes and windows when you're done.**

Windows Vista doesn't feature a specific Video Display Troubleshooter in its Help system. However, it does contain helpful information on a variety of specific issues. Choose Help and Support from the Start button menu. Then type **video help** into the Help system's text box. The resulting screen lists a few common pickles that may be vexing you.

Chapter 7: Peripheralitis

In This Chapter

- ✔ Understanding change
- ✔ Adjusting the keyboard and mouse
- ✔ Dealing with Sticky Keys
- ✔ Checking audio connections
- ✔ Fixing the silent PC
- ✔ Using the Device Manager
- ✔ Updating device drivers

***P**eripheralitis* ("puh-rif-ur-ell-eye-tis") n. 1. From the word *peripheral*, meaning something outside of the center, and the Greek suffix *-itis*, meaning disease or to forget to place a space between the words *it* and *is*. A computer with peripheralitis is said to have a problem with one of its peripheral devices, some gizmo attached to, but outside of, the computer console. Issues surrounding peripheralitis can be addressed by information covered in this chapter.

General Hardware Troubleshooting

The key to understanding all troubleshooting in a computer is that *change causes problems*.

Change the hardware and you open the door for new hardware issues. The same theory applies to software changes. As long as you can remember what recently changed in a computer, you can narrow down the solutions by eliminating what hasn't changed.

Of course, one thing that can change is that hardware fails. Because a hard drive spins, it wears down bearings. That's change, and fortunately a change you can hear coming. (A hard drive with old bearings squeals like an iron safe being dragged down the street by an inept burglar's getaway car.)

One solid way to confirm that hardware is causing woe is to follow my old adage: When in doubt, swap it out.

A bum keyboard or mouse is easily detected by turning off the computer, removing the suspect device, plugging in a device you know works, and then turning on the computer again. If the problem is gone, simply blame the bum gizmo. Buy a new one, or simply don't return the thing you borrowed.

Because I hear my grandmother telling me that "stealing is wrong," it would probably be best if you bought a replacement for the bad device you swapped out.

+ When swapping out doesn't fix the problem, the problem lies elsewhere. Check the usual suspects: power supply, cable connections, outdated drivers, and robots from Venus, for example.

+ Moving things around is part of the "change" equation I mentioned earlier. My neighbor lost his computer sound after moving the speakers so far back that they disconnected from the console.

+ Also see the section "Your Pal, the Device Manager," later in this chapter. Windows Device Manager is knowledgeable about your PC's hardware and can quickly alert you to any malfunctioning doodads.

+ Chapter 8 covers information on opening the PC's case. Loose cables have been known to happen inside the PC.

Keyboard and Mouse

If you attended computer camp, you probably remember singing songs around the blazing image of a campfire on a computer monitor. The tinny accompaniment of the computer playing tunes on its primitive synthesizer would help you sing merry songs of digital harmony.

One of those computer camp songs was probably about I/O: input and output. That's one of the computer's basic functions, and a vital one at that. For input, you (the human) rely on the keyboard and mouse. When those two items malfunction, the PC becomes stubbornly ignorant of your intent. This section helps you clear up some keyboard and mouse issues.

Troubleshooting basic input dilemmas

Before slamming the mouse into your computer desk or slapping your palms wildly on the keyboard, do some basic troubleshooting.

First, ensure that the computer is turned on. If the tiny power light is illuminated, the computer is on. When the computer's power supply fan is whirring, it is on. If the computer isn't on, refer to Chapter 2 for help.

Second, check the connections. Is everything plugged in? Is it plugged in properly? The old PS/2–style keyboard and mouse connectors look identical, but your keyboard doesn't work when it's plugged into the mouse port, and vice versa.

Do not plug in or unplug the computer keyboard or mouse to a PS/2 connector while the computer is on. Doing so may damage the computer's motherboard. Always turn off the PC before connecting the (old-style) PS/2 keyboard or mouse. This warning doesn't apply to a USB keyboard or a USB mouse.

Third, test the keyboard or mouse for signs of life. For the keyboard, press and release the Caps Lock key. The Caps Lock light should illuminate, or switch off and on as you press the key repeatedly. When the light is active but the keyboard doesn't work, it might be defective. Restart Windows or turn the computer off and on again to confirm whether there's a one-time glitch or the keyboard is deceased.

Optical mice also feature a light, one that's used to read mouse movement. When the light is on, the mouse should function. If the light is on but the mouse isn't working, restart Windows or turn the PC off and then on again. Also consider cleaning the mouse (see Book VI, Chapter 4).

Don't worry when the keyboard or mouse dies. You cannot fix it — just buy a replacement.

Taming the wild mouse

That mouse, that mouse!

It's tracking so bad!

It zaggles, it stalls,

It's driving me mad!

A mouse that doesn't track well on the screen is dirty. Literally. Clean the mouse as described in Book VI, Chapter 4.

When you find the mouse jumping around too much, consider removing the check mark by the Snap To option, officially titled Automatically Move Pointer to the Default Button in a Dialog Box. This option is found in the Mouse Properties dialog box, on the Pointer Options tab, as discussed in the next section.

Making the mouse faster or slower

Speed is a relative thing. For the computer's mouse, you can adjust its speed faster or slower by using the Mouse Properties dialog box. Here's how:

1. **Open the Control Panel's Mouse icon.**

2. **Click the Pointer Options tab in the Mouse Properties dialog box.**

   The Pointer Options tab, illustrated in Figure 7-1, contains a slew of useful tools for dealing with the mouse pointer in Windows.

Figure 7-1:
The Mouse
Properties
dialog
box —
Pointer
Options tab.

3. **Use the slider gizmo below Select a Pointer Speed to throttle the mouse pointer on the screen.**

   Pick a setting faster or slower than where the gizmo is positioned.

4. **Click the Apply button.**

5. **Practice moving the mouse pointer.**

   Gauge the speed.

6. **If necessary, repeat Steps 3 through 5 until you find a speed you like.**

7. **Click OK to confirm the settings.**

   Close the Control Panel window.

The Enhance Pointer Precision option adds a modicum of intelligence to the mouse pointer's speed. When you accelerate the mouse quickly, Windows moves the mouse pointer in a greater leap. When you're moving the mouse slightly, for minute movements, Windows increases the mouse's sensitivity to help you navigate. It's a good feature to have active.

✦ Faster speed works best for larger displays or displays with high resolution. If you find yourself "palming" the mouse to move the pointer from one side of the screen to another, increase the mouse speed.

✦ Some computer mice use a custom Mouse Properties dialog box, different from what's shown in Figure 7-1. In that case, adjusting the mouse speed may take place in a different part of the dialog box, or specific speed tools for the mouse may be available beyond the ones Windows offers.

Making the mouse pointer more visible

The Pointer Options tab in the Mouse Properties dialog box contains a host of options to help you make the mouse pointer more visible. The options are clustered in the aptly named Visibility area (refer to Figure 7-1). Here's a quick review:

Pointer Trails: The Display Pointer Trails option "ghosts" the mouse pointer to form a comet-like tail wherever the mouse wanders. When activated, this features makes it easy to *follow* the mouse pointer on the screen, but not necessarily easier to *find* the mouse pointer.

Mouse Ping: I call this feature *mouse ping,* but it's named Show Location of Pointer When I Press the CTRL Key, where CTRL means *Control.* By activating this feature, you can quickly locate any errant mouse pointer by pressing either Control key on the keyboard. The mouse is zeroed in using a sonar-like (albeit visual) ping from the old *Voyage to the Bottom of the Sea* television series.

Another option for making the mouse more visible is found on the Pointers tab of the Mouse Properties dialog box, as shown in Figure 7-2. The settings you make on the Pointers tab affect how the mouse pointer looks. You can choose a goofy animated pointer, if that pleases you, or for more visibility you can choose a larger mouse pointer or a set of large mouse pointers.

Windows doesn't have just one mouse pointer; it has mouse pointers for specific things that Windows does, and things that you do with the mouse. The list is shown in the dialog box (refer to Figure 7-2).

Figure 7-2:
The Mouse
Properties
dialog
box —
Pointers
tab.

For example, Normal Select is the name of the standard mouse pointer. To choose a larger pointer image, double-click Normal Select in the scrolling list. Use the Browse dialog box that appears to choose a new, larger pointer. The Preview window in the lower-left corner of the Browse dialog box shows you the exact size of the new pointer you select; click the Open button to choose that pointer.

You can select a slew of pointers all at once by using the Scheme button menu. For example, you may find that the Windows Black (Extra Large) scheme works well for your eyeballs. If so, choose it from the list.

Click the Apply button to test your choices.

If you're unhappy, choose the standard mouse pointer schemes from the Scheme button menu: In Windows Vista, choose Windows Aero; in Windows XP, choose Windows Default.

Looking southward

If you're one of the 10 percent of humanity who prefers using its left hand over the right, there's hope: Manufacturers make left-handed computer mice. You can also direct Windows to reverse the role of the main mouse buttons so that left and right buttons are swapped to match your southern-most paw. Follow these steps using either hand:

 1. **Open the Mouse icon in the Control Panel.**

 2. **Click the Buttons tab (if necessary).**

3. **Put a check mark by the option Switch Primary and Secondary Buttons.**

4. **Click OK.**

You can now use your left index finger to click the mouse's right button and get all that good left-click action.

All the manuals, Web pages, computer books, and other documentation on planet Earth assume that the main mouse button is the *left* button. When you switch buttons as described in this section, the main mouse button is the *right* one. Also, when the directions say to right-click, you're doing a *left-click*. Remember that!

Honing the keyboard

The computer keyboard may be just a slab of buttons, all basically innocent little On–Off switches. But you can control a few keyboardy things. Two of them that are most crucial — especially for fussy touch-typists — are the repeat delay and the repeat rate.

Repeat Delay: When you press and hold a key on a computer keyboard, the key eventually repeats itself, spewing out characters across the screen like bullets from a machine gun. The pause between when you press the key and it starts repeating is the *repeat delay*.

Repeat Rate: After pressing and holding down a key on the keyboard, the key starts repeating itself. The speed at which it repeats is the repeat rate, which can be fast or slow.

The best way to understand how the rates work is to mess with them:

1. **Open the Keyboard icon in the Control Panel.**

   The Speed tab, shown in Figure 7-3, is where you set the repeat delay and delay rate values.

2. **Use the sliders beneath Repeat Delay and Repeat Rate to speed things up or down.**

3. **Click the Apply button.**

4. **Click in the text box.**

5. **Press and hold a key on the keyboard to check the rates.**

6. **Repeat Steps 2 through 5 to hone the settings.**

7. **Click OK when things are set up just so.**

   Close the Control Panel window.

Figure 7-3:
Setting the
keyboard's
repeat and
delay rates.

When a key gets stuck, it repeats like crazy, no matter what. A stuck key indicates a mechanical problem with the keyboard, not anything that software can fix. You can try washing the keyboard as described in Book VI, Chapter 4, though buying a new keyboard may be the best solution.

Undoing the Sticky Keys warning

A common problem, especially for idle hands or video game players, is the Sticky Keys warning, shown in Figure 7-4. (The Windows Vista version is shown; the Windows XP version is similar).

Figure 7-4:
Sticky Keys
pesters you.

Sticky Keys is one of the Windows accessibility features, designed for folks who have trouble using a computer keyboard. The feature is activated whenever you press the Shift key five times in a row. It can be unexpected and startling, but it can be switched off.

In Windows Vista, heed these steps:

1. **Click the link Go to the Ease of Access Center to Disable the Keyboard Shortcut.**

    If you already dismissed the Sticky Keys window, follow these substeps:

    a. *Open the Control Panel's Ease of Access Center icon.*

    b. *Click the link Make the Keyboard Easier to Use.*

    c. *Click the link Set Up Sticky Keys.*

2. **Remove the check mark by the option Turn On Sticky Keys When SHIFT Is Pressed Five Times.**

3. **Click the Save button.**

4. **Close the window.**

In Windows XP, follow these steps to disable the Sticky Keys warning:

1. **Click the Settings button in the StickyKeys dialog box.**

    If you've banished the StickyKeys dialog box, open the Control Panel's Accessibility Options icon. Click the Keyboard tab (if necessary) in the Accessibility Options dialog box.

2. **Click the Settings button in the StickyKeys area.**

3. **Remove the check mark by the option Use Shortcut.**

4. **Click the OK button and then click OK to dismiss the Accessibility Options dialog box. (Optional) Close the Control Panel window.**

Sticky Keys helps people use a computer keyboard with only one hand, but it would be sweet if Microsoft turned it *off* as opposed to leaving it on and having it shock people unexpectedly.

Speaking of Trouble

Computers are silent beasts. Blame two things for relating noise to computers. The first thing is Hollywood, where for some reason they believe that text displayed on a computer screen somehow makes noise. Trust me: No one would use a computer if text on the screen made noise as it was displayed.

The second thing to blame is the early teletype machines, which were used as the first computer terminals. (And hence the term *TTY* to describe a computer terminal.) A teletype contained a bell to alert the operator about an incoming message, a priority message, or an error. Early computer terminals came equipped with a tiny speaker for the same reason.

Fast-forward several dozen years and today's computers have not only internal speakers but also an extensive set of external, state-of-the-art, surround sound speakers and a digital sound system to match. This section is where you turn when those speakers suddenly go mute on you.

Testing the speakers

Your PC console has one, internal speaker. That's okay for beeps and boops, but to make sound that scares the neighbors, you want a little more oomph. That means external speakers or headphones.

The easiest way to ensure that noise is coming from the speakers is to use the volume control in the notification area: Click the volume control icon, as shown in Figure 7-5. You should hear an audible *beep* (or other amusing tone) when you click the control as shown in the figure.

Adjust volume

Click to hear something

Figure 7-5:
Testing
the PC's
volume.

Mute

Volume Control in the notification area

Windows Vista features a more thorough way to demonstrate how the speakers are set up, including a stereo test. Follow these steps in Windows Vista:

1. **Right-click the volume icon in the notification area.**

2. **From the pop-up menu, choose Playback Devices.**

The Sound dialog box appears, listing the gizmos on your PC that produce sound.

3. **Select a playback device, such as your PC's speakers.**

4. **Click the Configure button.**

   The Speaker Setup dialog box appears.

5. **Click the Test button.**

   You should hear tones from the left speaker and then the right speaker. (If the right speaker plays first, you have the speakers reversed; swap them.)

   You can continue to work through the Speaker Setup dialog box, if you desire to further configure the computer's speakers.

6. **Close the various dialog boxes; you passed the test.**

When you don't hear a sound, there's a problem. Keep reading in the next section.

✦ You can, of course, use the volume control to set the PC's speaker volume.

✦ To mute the speakers in Windows, click the Mute button in the volume control's pop-up window. In Windows XP, place a check mark by the Mute option.

✦ Headphones don't show up in the Windows Vista Sound dialog box unless you're using USB headphones.

✦ Your PC's sound hardware may have its own icon in the Control Panel, which you can use to test the audio system.

✦ See the later section "Fixing silence" for information on determining whether the speakers are broken.

Connecting the speakers

O, PC! How can I hear you? Let me count the ways!

Internal speaker: Most PCs have a speaker inside the console. It's a cheap, tiny speaker, and you don't want to use it.

Rear speaker jacks: The standard PC setup is to plug a set of stereo speakers into the audio output jacks on the I/O Panel, located on the back of the typical PC.

S/PDIF: High-end audio systems might employ the Sony/Phillips Digital Interconnect Format. It requires special optical cables and equipment used only by serious audiophiles. There are separate S/PDIF connectors: one for input (S/PDIF in) and another for output (S/PDIF out).

DVD speaker jacks: An older PC may require that you connect the speakers to the DVD adapter card instead of to the PC's I/O Panel. A PC without a specific DVD adapter doesn't have this requirement.

Front speaker jacks: For convenience, many PCs duplicate the speaker and microphone jacks on the front of the console. This allows you to easily connect a set of headphones, though not every PC lets you use both the headphones on the front of the console and speakers on the back.

USB speakers: You can plug USB speakers or headphones into any USB jack on the computer.

Traditional audio connectors are color coded on your PC. The three colors used match the purposes of the three connectors, as shown in Table 7-1. Ensure that you plug the speaker into the proper hole! (That's the green hole.)

Table 7-1	PC Sound Jack Color Codes
Color	*Connection*
Black	S/PDIF output
Black	Surround sound left/right
Brown	Surround sound center/subwoofer
Gray	Line-in jack (for audio equipment)
Lime	Speakers or headphone
Pink	S/PDIF input
Red	Microphone
White	S/PDIF input

✦ Obviously, you cannot hear sound from the speakers when you plug them into the microphone jack. Likewise, the microphone may seem undermodulated when it's plugged into the line-in jack.

✦ Speakers require power! Avoid using speakers that need batteries. Instead, use speakers with a power adapter. Speakers can also draw power from a subwoofer, or from the PC's USB port.

✦ A bit beyond the standard stereo speakers are speakers that come with a subwoofer. In that configuration it's usually the subwoofer that connects directly to the console. The stereo speakers then connect to the subwoofer.

✦ At the pinnacle of computer speaker technology is *surround sound*. It involves multiple speakers situated around the computer to create realistic, 3D sound. Setting up such a thing requires a degree in audio engineering, though enthusiastic and motivated computer users can often handle the task.

Fixing silence

The biggest issue with computer sound is not hearing anything. That happens often. The solution is to go through a step-by-step process for eliminating the cause. Here's how I do it:

1. **Test the speakers as described in the section "Testing the speakers," earlier in this chapter.**

The computer merely makes the sound. It's up to the speakers to produce the sound.

2. **Ensure that the speakers are connected to the computer.**

Are the speakers plugged in? Are they plugged into the right jacks? If a subwoofer is connected, is it plugged in? Is it getting power? Is it even working?

Most speakers need power to make noise.

3. **Check to see whether the speaker's volume control is turned up enough or that the speakers aren't muted by some hardware switch.**

4. **If you have another set of speakers, swap them out with the current set to see whether the speakers themselves haven't died and left behind a silent shell.**

5. **Check the Windows volume control (refer to Figure 7-5).**

Is the volume up high enough? Is the volume control muted?

6. **Check the Volume Mixer or Volume Control to ensure that individual audio devices haven't been muted.**

The Volume Mixer or Volume Control allows you to set levels for various sound-generating items in the computer, such as the MIDI player or built-in synthesizer.

To display the Volume Mixer in Windows Vista, choose the Mixer link from the pop-up Volume control, as shown in Figure 7-5.

To display the Volume Control in Windows XP, right-click the Volume icon in the notification area and choose the command Open Volume Control. The Volume Control is shown in Figure 7-6.

Figure 7-6:
The Volume
Control.

Ensure that individual devices haven't been muted; check the buttons at the bottom of the screen. Also confirm that the slider for a device isn't *bottomed out,* where the sound from that device is very low.

Close the volume mixer or volume control when you're done.

7. Check the sound hardware configuration.

Some PCs with speaker jacks on the front and back have to be configured to allow audio input from either place. For example, your PC may allow speakers to be plugged in the rear jacks but not the front jacks at the same time. When your PC has such a configuration, you need to use the special sound software that came with the computer to confirm that all the sound jacks are working as you would expect. (It's not a Windows-specific solution.)

8. Confirm that the sound device is working properly.

Use the Device Manager to confirm whether the sound hardware is hinkey. The Device Manager is covered later in this chapter.

9. Update the audio device drivers.

Updating audio device drivers is also covered under the Device Manager topic, later in this chapter.

If all else fails, check your ears. Are other things making noise in the room? If so, the problem is probably the computer.

Things go wrong in a computer when something changes. If the sound just went out, try to recall what you just changed. That may help lead you to the solution.

✦ If you have trouble listening to an audio CD, the optical drive may have a problem. Some older CD-ROM drives had a separate cable for carrying the audio signal. You might want to open the case to ensure that the cable hasn't become disconnected. See Chapter 8 for details.

✦ Some speakers use both the green audio jack and the USB connector. That's because power is drawn from the USB connection (the audio signal comes from the audio jack). Those speakers are mute when either the audio or USB connection isn't made.

✦ If the computer has never made sound, by all means contact the manufacturer or dealer.

Testing the microphone

For a microphone to work on your computer, it must be plugged into the proper audio jack. Table 7-1 says that's the pink jack. Plugging a microphone into any other audio jack results in less-than-satisfactory results. Well, unless it's a USB microphone, which simply plugs into the USB port.

After plugging in the microphone, it helps to test the thing. Testing works differently between Windows Vista and Windows XP.

To test the microphone in Windows Vista, heed these steps:

1. **Ensure that the microphone is properly connected and stuff.**

2. **Open the Control Panel's Speech Recognition Options icon.**

3. **Choose the link Set Up Microphone.**

   The Microphone Setup Wizard materializes.

4. **Choose the type of microphone you're using: headset, cheap-o desktop microphone, or the "they saw you coming" microphone the guy at the music store sold you.**

5. **Click the Next button, and so on.**

   After seeing a few meaningless screens, you eventually approach the Adjust the Microphone Volume screen — pay dirt.

6. **Speak away.**

   Say: "Enunciation is the prestidigitation of audio infatuation." Or be a wienie and say, "Test, test."

   Watch that green bar go! Basically, by seeing the visual feedback, you confirm that the microphone is working.

7. **Continue working through the wizard or just click Cancel.**

   If you're satisfied with the results, you can bail out on the wizard. Otherwise, keep clicking Next and eventually you arrive at the Finish button.

To confirm that your microphone works in Windows XP, follow these steps:

1. **Plug in the microphone all nice and snug.**

   And stuff.

2. **Open the Control Panel's Sounds and Audio Devices icon.**

3. **Click the Voice tab.**

4. **Click the Test Hardware button.**

   The Sound Hardware Test Wizard appears.

5. **Click the Next button.**

   Hum a jaunty tune while the hardware is tested.

6. **Speak into the microphone to test the volume.**

   The volume meter on the screen should dance up and down as you vocalize.

7. **Click the Next button after confirming that the microphone works.**

8. **Click the Finish button.**

Your computer may not be configured to use the specific microphone jack that your microphone is plugged into. If your PC came with specific audio software, use it to configure the audio jacks to accept microphone input.

✦ Some applications may mute the microphone. Refer to Step 6 in the first set of steps for information on using the Volume Mixer or volume control to unmute the PC's microphone.

✦ You don't want to spend too much or too little on a PC microphone. Cheap microphones don't work well, record poorly, and are annoying to hear for audio chat and on-line communications. Expensive microphones may require a mixer or pre-amp to work properly.

✦ Good microphones can be found in any computer or office supply store.

✦ I use a microphone-headset, which provides both headphones and a microphone. It's perfect for on-line communications and gaming. And I'm not implying that I've been playing computer games when I should have been writing this book. No, sir!

Your Pal, the Device Manager

Windows features a central location for all the hardware in your PC. It's the Device Manager.

The *Device Manager* is like that nerdy buddy you don't want to be seen with yet whose company you desperately need in times of digital peril — like MacGyver, but without a trace of personality or good looks. It's not a secret: The Device Manager merely provides a central location for accessing the various device Properties dialog boxes.

This section covers using the Device Manager as a PC hardware trouble-shooting tool.

Starting the Device Manager

To summon the Device Manager window in Windows Vista, heed these steps:

1. **Open the Control Panel's Device Manager icon.**

2. **Click the Continue button or type the administrator's password to continue.**

   The Device Manager window is shown in Figure 7-7.

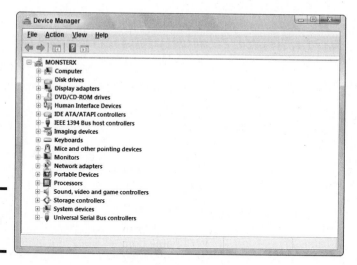

Figure 7-7:
The Device
Manager.

In Windows XP, the steps to summon the Device Manager window are subtly different:

1. **Open the Control Panel's System icon.**

   The keyboard shortcut for the System Properties dialog box is the Win+Break key combination, which is also a punch line somewhere.

2. **Click the Hardware tab in the System Properties dialog box.**

3. **Click the Device Manager button.**

   The Device Manager window in Windows XP looks similar to the one for Windows Vista (refer to Figure 7-7).

The Device Manager window lists all the hardware available to your PC by category. Opening a category lists specific devices, such as the PC's display adapter shown in the Display Adapters category.

To open a category, click the + (plus) button next to the category name. The + button turns into a – (minus) button, which you can then click to close the category.

Double-click a device name to display that device's hardware Properties dialog box.

Close the Device Manager window when you're done.

Finding errant hardware

Compared with other operating systems, Windows is rather forgiving. For the sake of compatibility, Windows tolerates hardware that may not be working properly — hardware that would choke a Linux computer into apoplexy. But rather than be ignorant of the damage, Windows alerts you to the troublesome hardware in the Device Manager.

Open the Device Manager per the instructions from the preceding section. Peruse the list. When you see a small icon flagging a device, or a category is "open" (displaying its devices), there may be trouble.

 In Windows Vista, errant devices are flagged with a yellow-triangle warning icon.

 In Windows XP, errant devices are flagged with a yellow-circle warning icon.

The errant device is shown open beneath its category heading. To see what's wrong (or what Windows believes to be wrong), double-click the device to display its Properties dialog box. In the Device Status area of the dialog box, you read a description of what the problem could be and potentially discover a solution.

Troubleshooting a gizmo in Windows XP

Windows XP features a special Troubleshoot button for devices in the Device Manager window, a button that's curiously lacking in Windows Vista. To access the button, double-click to open a device in the Device Manager window. Click the Troubleshooting button in the dialog box's General tab, as shown in Figure 7-8.

Figure 7-8:
The special
Trouble-
shooting
button in
Windows
XP.

The Troubleshooting button opens a special troubleshooter window for the device, part of the Windows Help System. Follow the directions on the screen to answer questions about problems you're having and view potential solutions.

Updating driver software

One of the most vital things you can do to keep your PC in shape is to ensure that your hardware always has the best, latest software. For many of the computer's gizmos, that means doing a software update. Here's how:

1. **Open the Device Manager window.**

Directions are found earlier in this chapter.

2. **Open the category containing the device.**

For example, Network Adapters for networking hardware.

3. **Double-click to open the device you want to update.**

4. **Click the Driver tab.**

The Driver tab in the device's Properties dialog box, which is beautifully depicted in Figure 7-9, contains several buttons dealing with updating the software that "drives" the device. (Windows XP lacks the Disable button.)

5. **To update a driver, click the Update Driver button.**

6a. **In Windows Vista, choose the option Search Automatically for Updated Driver Software.**

6b. **In Windows XP, choose the option Install the Software Automatically (Recommended) and then click the Next button.**

Windows searches the computer and then the Internet for the latest or most current software to control the device. If a newer drive is found, it's automatically installed and updated; heed any directions given on the screen (such as to restart your computer).

When no new driver is found, you can assume that the driver is up-to-date.

Figure 7-9:
Driver
control.

7. **Close the window when you're done.**

It might be necessary to restart the computer after a software update. You're alerted to whether you need to restart after you close the device's Properties window.

The driver update procedure isn't foolproof. Sometimes, newer drivers are available but not found. In that case, you should go to the manufacturer's Web site to check for new drivers.

If you don't know the manufacturer, use the device name at the top of the Properties dialog box (refer to Figure 7-9) as the search term for the Internet search engine of your choice. Peruse the results for a Web page with Download, Support, or Driver in the title.

Chapter 8: Deep Inside the Computer Case

In This Chapter

✔ Opening the console

✔ Exploring inside your PC

✔ Maintaining basic goodies

✔ Adding an expansion card

✔ Upgrading your PC with more memory

✔ Adding an internal disk drive

*A*fter the trouble is shot, the solution might involve one of the scariest things for any computer owner to do. No, I'm not talking about networking, installing Linux, or letting your 13-year-old computer-genius nephew "check something for you." I'm addressing the issue of opening the computer case and checking things for yourself. That includes the hazards and peril of potentially replacing bum computer parts. It's all covered in this chapter.

Into the Case

Here's one vital piece of information you need to know before you take screwdriver in hand and attempt PC brain surgery: The computer case is the *console*. It's not "the box" or "the case" and it's especially not "the CPU." It's the *console*. Know that, and you're well on your way to computer hardware maintenance success.

Oh, and there's also a few safety issues I should mention, as covered in this section.

Opening the case

Before you can fix things inside the computer console, you must open the case. Here are some steps to take:

1. **Back up the computer's data, if you haven't done so recently.**

You should have a backup copy of your computer's data fresh and available in case the most dreadful thing in the universe happens when you perform computer brain surgery.

2. Set a system restore point in Windows.

See Book II, Chapter 8 for the details.

3. Turn off the computer.

4. Unplug the computer.

This step may seem unimportant because the computer is turned off, right?

Actually, the computer isn't turned off. It's still using power. Look at the PC's rump and you'll probably see the network adapter light blinking. Yep, there's still power a-flowin' inside Mr. PC. Unplug it.

I recommend unplugging the power cord from the computer, not from the wall. If you unplug from the wall, some dutiful person may plug it back in "to help you out." Nope. unplug the cord from the computer. When that's not possible, unplug from the wall and coil up the cord near you. Make snake-hissing noises if anyone trying to help you approaches the cord.

5. Remove the console case cover.

Traditionally, computer cases are screwed shut; you find several screws on the rear of the case. Remove the screws with a screwdriver, though when they're the large-and-knobby type of screw, you can twist them with your thumb and fingers.

If the screws are removable, set them aside and don't lose them.

Some computers lack screws and feature some type of case-release mechanism. You may see a button to press or a bar to lift. The case then slides or lifts open.

After the case cover is released, remove it. Sometimes the whole cover comes sliding off, and at other times you may just be removing a side panel.

6. Behold the computer's guts!

Keep reading in the following section, though the later section "The PC Console Adventure Map" describes where to find various things inside the computer.

Is it dirty inside the console? Computers both blow and suck air, so dust is bound to accumulate. When the dust gets super thick, you can clean it off. Refer to Book VI, Chapter 4 for information on how best to clean the inside of the console.

✦ Video 181 on the DVD offers a demonstration of how to open the computer console.

✦ Refer to Book VI, Chapter 1 for more information on backing up your computer.

◆ Don't forget to close the case when you're done! See the later section "Closing the case."

Grounding yourself

Any electric device plugged into the wall socket commands respect from you, the human. As a soft and mostly water-based biological life form, you're sensitive to mass quantities of electrons. Protection is vital.

The console is designed to keep the scary electronics on the inside, away from your probing fingers and dangling body parts. By unplugging the console, you ensure that the danger is minimized, but only from the console. As a human being, you pose a threat to the computer's electronics in the form of something called electrostatic discharge.

Electrostatic discharge can be a shocking experience. What happens is that the electrical potential between you and whatever you touch is great enough that a spark jumps out. The spark is the electrostatic discharge. It can damage delicate electronic components. That's a bad thing.

To help prevent electrostatic discharge, you must ground yourself.

In addition to having strong moral beliefs and a hardy stalk of ethics, you need to neutralize the electrical potential between yourself and the computer case. To easily accomplish that task, always keep one hand touching the computer's metal casing while you're working. By touching both the casing and whatever doodad you're installing or removing, you reduce the chance of an electrical component-killing electrostatic discharge.

Electrostatic discharge is most likely to happen when it's dry outside. Be extra careful about grounding yourself when the humidity is low.

Closing the case

After meddling with your computer's delicate components, you need to close the case and turn the system back on, the whole time praying to your favorite deity that not only will the sucker work but also the problem will be fixed.

After installing or replacing or checking or whatever prompted you to open the case, follow these general steps to close 'er up:

1. **Ensure that your job is complete.**

Check for any spare parts, screws, wrappers, eyeglasses, or electronic detritus remaining from whatever operation you performed.

Check any cables you might have loosened.

Ensure that every latch, screw, and cover you removed has been properly replaced.

Double-check to confirm that installation was done properly.

2. **Replace the outside case, side, or lid.**

Do you remember how the thing was removed? Whether it slid off or swung up? Sometimes a metal lip or some notches must be aligned to properly position and then slide the case back on. Don't get frustrated! Don't force anything.

3. **Don't screw the lid shut just yet.**

Of course, if the lid lacks screws, do whatever it takes to latch it shut.

4. **Plug in the console.**

5. **Turn on the computer.**

It should come up right away. Refer to sections later in this book for troubleshooting individual hardware upgrades.

6. **If you haven't yet screwed the lid shut, do so after confirming that the computer works just fine.**

The reason I have you wait to screw the thing shut is that the upgrade might not have worked. If you need to go right back into the console, it saves a step by not screwing the thing shut right away.

+ A computer's case must be properly shut for the system to meet radio frequency interference (RFI) standards. These standards, monitored by the FCC in the United States, help keep the electronic noise generated by a computer inside the case from messing with other radio signals.

+ Watch Video 182 to see the author of this book attempt to close a computer case in a proper and dignified manner.

The PC Console Adventure Map

Don't be alarmed, but opening a computer case takes you one step closer to becoming a true computer nerd. In fact, after the fourth or fifth time you open the case, you might find yourself wanting a pocket protector or feeling the urge to visit the back part of a Fry's Electronics store. Such thoughts may paralyze you.

After you've overcome the Geek Factor fear, you'll recognize that maintaining your computer is no more difficult than maintaining your car. In fact, it's better! You rarely, if ever, need to change the oil in your computer. And a memory leak? Keep that bucket in the garage!

Not every computer looks the same inside, but every PC has similar components. Before you rummage around inside the console, get to know the territory. Figure 8-1 shows a typical PC's innards the way you might behold them after removing your PC console's lid.

Power supply   Power cables   Drive bay

Figure 8-1:
A typical
PC's guts.

Motherboard   Data cables

Get to know and identify these major items inside a PC console:

Power supply: The power supply converts the alternating current (AC) from the wall into direct current (DC) inside the computer. The easiest way to find it is to look for the location where the power plug connects to the console (usually on the back). The power supply is right inside the case at that spot.

Cables: The power supply's colorful cables snake from the power supply outward. One or two clusters go to the motherboard, and others go to the disk drives. The majority of them, however, may just hang in space to wait for future internal expansion. In addition to the power cables are various data cables running hither and thither. The smaller your PC, the more the cables obstruct your view of the items inside the console.

Drive bay: Also known as the *disk drive cage*, the drive bay occupies a lot of space inside the console. It contains the hard drive and optical drive, plus it has room to add other drives. The front side of the drive bay is the front of the console, where you can access removable storage.

Motherboard: The motherboard is the main circuitry board dwelling inside the console. It's probably difficult to see, because it can be obscured by cables or the drive bay or both. Figure 8-2 shows a motherboard that has been freed from the confines of its console prison. (It's the same motherboard from Figure 8-1.)

Figure 8-2: A typical motherboard.

The following items are found specifically on the motherboard and illustrated in Figure 8-2:

I/O panel connectors: The I/O panel is where you connect peripherals to the PC, including USB gizmos, the keyboard and mouse, the monitor, and things of that ilk. Sometimes, the I/O panel is right on the motherboard (refer to Figure 8-2), or a cable may connect the motherboard to the I/O panel elsewhere in the console.

Processor cooling fan: You may not see the processor directly. That's because today's processors run very hot, and they require direct cooling. So what you see instead of the processor itself is the tiny heat hat that it wears, which is really a cooling fan (refer to Figure 8-2). Some processors also use an elaborate *heat sink*, which is a metal gizmo shaped like a high-tech flower that helps dissipate the high temperatures.

Processor: The processor rests beneath the cooling fan. You cannot see it unless you remove the fan, though I recommend that you not remove the fan just to see the processor. Trust me: It's there.

Memory banks: A typical PC sports anywhere from 2 to 8 memory banks on the motherboard, or sometimes on a tiny expansion card jutting from the motherboard. Memory banks are always in pairs of two. Essentially, they're tiny expansion slots into which memory cards, or DIMMs, are inserted.

DIMM: Your computer's memory comes on tiny, comb-size expansion cards called DIMMs, for Dual In-line Memory Modules. I cover these DIMMs in detail later in this chapter.

Power supply connector: The motherboard needs power, so a specific connector exists on the motherboard for the power supply.

Data connectors: The motherboard is also home to various places where data cables connect. There may be a place to plug in cables for the disk drives, speaker, I/O panel, console lamps, and other things I can't think of right now.

Clock battery: The clock battery helps the PC keep track of time when the computer is unplugged. It's found somewhere on the motherboard and looks like a large coin. In Figure 8-2, the clock battery is mounted vertically, which makes it difficult to see.

Expansion slots: To help customize your computer, expansion slots allow bonus circuitry in the form of *expansion cards* to be plugged in. The expansion cards can add features such as a new display adapter, more USB ports, fancy audio, wireless networking, and a whole host of options. You may not find the expansion slots inside your PC when expansion cards are plugged into them.

The inside of your computer may look scary. It should! Electronics are intimidating. They command respect. Still, the reason you're using a PC today and not a Commodore 64 is that the PC was designed to be upgradeable. That's part of the PC's success: Anyone with relatively basic knowledge can update, fix, or maintain their computer.

✦ The technology shown in Figures 8-1 and 8-2 is older than most current PCs, though the computer was purchased in 2003 and runs Windows XP. For identifying the major parts, however, the figures are okay. (I'm not ripping apart the computer I use to write this book just to make some illustrations!)

✦ View Video 183 on the DVD to see a visual exploration of the insides of a PC.

✦ Older PCs sport a floppy drive or perhaps even a Zip drive in the drive cage.

✦ PC disk drives come in two *form factors,* or dimensions. A larger size is used by optical drives, which is about 51/4 inches wide. A smaller form factor is used by most hard drives, which is about $3^{11}/_2$ inches wide. You see either different-size drive bays for each type of form factor, or adapters can be used to put the smaller drives into the larger bays.

✦ Sometimes the disk drive cage can be quite extensive. High-end PCs may have room for four or more optical drives and four or more hard drives.

✦ It's not necessary to remove the motherboard from your PC. I don't recommend it. I don't even recommend replacing a motherboard. The motherboard shown in Figure 8-2 was removed merely to show you how it looks.

✦ Another term for the processor is the CPU, or *central processing unit.* Too many people confuse the CPU with the console, so for clarity's sake, I refer to the CPU as "the processor" in this book, and to the console as "that box-thing the computer lives inside of" (which is improper English, but I do that to drive my editor nuts).

✦ In the olden days, the hard drive's face stuck out the front of the PC, just like the optical drive. The blinking hard drive light you saw on a PC from the early 1990s was, in fact, the lamp on the hard drive itself. Today's hard drives, however, are strictly internal beasts. The hard drive interface communicates the blinking light information to the console, which then flashes a hard drive lamp for the human to behold.

Common Problems and Solutions

Some frustrating issues can arrive out of problems that are rather simple to fix. Here's a quick list of some things to look for inside the computer case for general troubleshooting purposes.

Checking for loose cables

Two types of cables are inside the console: power and data. Some gizmos, like disk drives, require both.

To ensure that cables are properly attached, follow these steps:

1. **Follow the steps earlier in this chapter for opening the console.**

2. **Locate where the cable attaches.**

3. **Give the cable a little tug.**

If the cable is loose, it will fall out. If it does, reattach it.

4. **Gently press the cable so that it's snugly attached.**

Cables have two ends. You need to check both ends.

When you find a free cable, one that isn't plugged in anywhere, you need to do some hunting to figure out where it goes. When the cable was plugged into a device, you can guess where it goes by looking in its general vicinity (or remembering which gizmo isn't working).

Cables that connect to the motherboard have multiple issues. Sometimes, you luck out and the cable can plug into only one location and in only one orientation. That's good. When you have multiple opportunities to plug in a cable, it's best not to guess: plugging a cable into the wrong spot may have no ill effects, but then again you could damage the computer by guessing.

If you need to detach a cable while working on the PC, use a pair of colored sticky dots to label both the cable you unplugged and the connector from which you unplugged it. For example, place a blue sticky on the cable end and a blue sticky on the socket. Use different colors for each set of cable ends and connectors. When you're done, you'll know where to reconnect things. Sticky dots can be found at any office supply store.

✦ Cables don't normally pop out by themselves. They can work loose, but they normally don't spring out of their connectors.

✦ Often cables bend and twist, and thanks to mother nature they stay in those positions. You can use the bends and twists to help you locate where cables go and in which orientation they were set originally.

✦ Power cables can often be tough to attach. Sometimes they require a lot of push to seat them all the way in the connector.

✦ Also refer to the section "Reseating expansion cards," later in this chapter, for information on securing a loose expansion card.

Dissipating heat

The biggest issue, and the cause of most console problems, is heat. The computer enjoys a cool environment. Electronics *love* the cold. But all that high-tech madness taking place inside your computer makes for a lot of heat. A major part of the console's design goes toward removing the heat from the computer.

A typical PC has two cooling fans. One fan is atop the processor (refer to Figure 8-2). A second fan is located inside the power supply.

The processor's fan is designed to keep the processor cool, but it just pumps air into the console.

The power supply's fan is designed to draw air out of the console. Air slots on the front of the console draw in (supposedly) cool air from the room. You can easily find the front air slots when you have a dog or cat, because the slots are lined with ample quantities of your pet's hair.

High-end computers offer secondary console fans. You can also purchase upgraded power supplies with better fans, as well as additional fans for the console. The extra fans use the bonus power-supply cables inside the console, and they help circulate the air.

At the extreme end of the console-cooling fixation are various liquid contraptions. The so-called water-cooled computers use liquid (often water) to cool a PC in the same way that water cools a car engine. Usually, you have to buy a specific water-cooled case to get such a feature.

Another heat-dissipating doodad is the traditional heat sink, a piece of metal designed to draw off heat and use the air to keep components cool. Heat sinks aren't as efficient as fans or water cooling.

Upgrade, Replace, Maintain

Your computer was built for expandability. Most of that is conveniently located *outside* the console: Thanks to the ubiquitous USB port, you can instantly attach a number of hardware goodies to your computer — no fuss. But there are options for internal expansion. Not only that, but you may also occasionally need to perform open console surgery on a PC to fix a problem. If so, you've come to the right part of this book.

✦ For tools, you need a medium-size Phillips screwdriver. You might need a small Phillips screwdriver, but that's the most you need. Some computer cases are designed so that you don't really need any tools.

✦ Because I do a lot of upgrading and other electrical work, I have a power screwdriver. You can see me use it on this book's DVD.

✦ One good thing to remember: There's no way you can accidentally plug in anything backward on your PC. All the connectors are *keyed,* which means that you can plug in items in only one way.

✦ Give yourself plenty of time to work on your computer. Don't rush. Have lots of room. If you prefer to work uninterrupted, inform others that you don't want to be disturbed.

✦ Laptops aren't really built for expandability, not like PC desktops are. Refer to Book III for more information on expanding laptop computers.

✦ It took me an hour to add an expansion card to my first computer. That computer wasn't supposed to be upgraded by a user, but I did it anyway. I enjoyed myself so well, and enjoyed not paying someone else to do the work, that I did many upgrades afterward. I even swapped out a CRT monitor tube, which is something I wouldn't recommend — or attempt again.

Buying replacement parts

Gone are the days where you had to search for places that sold computer parts. In the old days, I scoured the back of computer magazines for mail-order places. When you know what you want, it's easy to buy the stuff cheap from a catalog. The Web has replaced that method, though.

The first step to buying replacement parts or upgrades is to know what you want. I leave it up to you to do the research, though I offer some advice in the following sections. Ordering the right part means you don't have to mess with returns or get stuck with something you'll never use. (Visit my Web site for a view of my SCSI adapter collection: `www.wambooli.com/fun/dang/scsi/`.)

The second step is to know where to buy. You have really only two choices left: a real store or the Internet.

Real stores are nice in that you have the opportunity to ask someone a question (count yourself lucky when they know the answer), take the item home right away, and avoid shipping charges — and you have a spot to return the item if it doesn't work.

The Internet is nice because you can find the cheapest prices and a wide variety of vendors. Internet stores also seem to carry more stock than local computer outfits. You do pay for shipping, and you do have to wait for your stuff to arrive. When you need the part in a pinch, that sucks.

The final step is to purchase your stuff with a credit card. I recommend using credit cards because they offer consumers the highest level of protection when it comes to fraud. If you pay cash, you get ripped off. No one pays cash. Check? Same thing. Credit card charges can be reversed if the merchant doesn't fill your order or when you get something you didn't order or that doesn't work. Use a credit card.

Too many dealers are out there for me to recommend specific places to go. If you want recommendations, ask your friends. I like Fry's Electronics. I've bought stuff at Best Buy, Office Max, Office Depot, Staples, and Costco. Online, I use ZipZoomFly.com, shop4tech.com, and the old standby: Amazon.com.

✦ Choose a dealer that's been around a while. It's a plus when the dealer has a real location.

✦ Never buy from a dealer that doesn't have a phone number.

✦ Always, always, always check for the product return policy. Some stuff cannot be returned. Be aware of that before you order. (It's another reason to always order the right item the first time.)

✦ Though too many of my friends swear by them, I don't recommend buying computer parts at a swap meet. Only if the "dealer" is a consistent vendor and has a real-world address or a Web page that's been up for a few years would I trust them. There are just too many stories of junk being sold, or of disreputable people reselling stolen merchandise, for me to feel comfortable with computer swap meets.

Replacing the power supply

If the power supply is dead, it needs replacing. You can have this done by a professional in a white lab coat, or simply note the power supply's product number and search for a replacement unit locally or on the Internet. But the key is knowing the part number. For that, you have to remove the power supply:

1. **Open the computer's case as described earlier in this chapter.**

2. **Lay the computer on its side.**

The open end of the console should be facing up. You don't want to work on the power supply when the console is in a vertical position, because it's more difficult to remove it that way.

3. **Detach all the power cables from all the devices in the console.**

Disconnect power cables from the disk drives, the motherboard, plus any other devices they're attached to.

4. **Remove the power supply screws.**

The screws can be accessed from the back of the console case. Be sure that you're removing the screws that anchor the power supply, not anything else.

Some power supplies use four screws; some use three.

5. **Confirm that nothing is in the power supply's way.**

   Some smaller consoles may have things that need to be removed before the power supply can be freed. I've had to pull out a DVD drive to get a power supply out. I've also had to remove the entire console case to remove a power supply from a PC through the top rather than the side.

6. **Liberate the power supply!**

   When you cannot remove the power supply, you forgot one or more screws.

After the power supply is free, you can search it for its part number or ID. You can search the Internet using that part number, along with the key words *power supply*. Or, you can visit the manufacturer's Web site to order a spare, if that's an option. Most power supplies are fairly standard gizmos.

Consider getting a replacement power supply that packs more wattage or perhaps has extra cooling power. But remember that the replacement must still fit into (or be compatible with) your PC's console.

To install the replacement, follow these steps, which are generally the reverse of the preceding steps, so I've numbered them backward:

6. **Unpack the new power supply.**

   If it came with specific instructions, follow them.

5. **Ensure that the PC case is open and ready to receive the new power supply.**

   If you had to remove anything to get the power supply out, you need to remove those same things to put the new power supply in (unless you just left your PC hanging open in the interim).

4. **Anchor the power supply by screwing it back into the case.**

3. **Reattach all the power cables from all the devices in the console.**

   Every disk drive needs power. The motherboard needs power. Anything else?

2. **Set the computer upright again.**

1. **Close the computer's case as described earlier in this chapter; remember not to tighten the screws until you know that the computer powers up.**

Refer to Video 184 for a visual example of removing and then reinstalling a PC's power supply.

Replacing the clock battery

Computers do keep track of time, but not reliably. A typical computer's clock can be off by as much as several minutes a day, depending on what the computer is doing. The reason for the delay is that the computer's internal clock suffers from a lack of attention.

For example, a busy computer often "borrows" time from the clock. The computer becomes so obsessed with some task that that basic job of updating the PC's ticker just doesn't happen. Those missing seconds add up.

Computers that are connected to the Internet can update the time by using the Internet Time feature in Windows. That fixes those missing minutes every day. But when the computer is turned off, the time is kept ticking by a tiny battery attached to the computer's motherboard. When that battery goes, you see weird start-up messages and potentially other problems.

To fix the clock battery problem, you replace the motherboard's battery: Open the computer's case as described earlier in this chapter. Locate the battery on the motherboard. It's often a lithium battery, one of those coin-size jobs you can buy anywhere that watch or hearing aid batteries are sold.

Be sure to close the computer case when you're done replacing the battery. Directions for both opening and closing a computer's case are offered earlier in this chapter.

 Motherboard batteries last for years. When the battery goes, it's often a sign that the computer is ancient and needs to be replaced. Although you can merely replace the battery, I highly recommend that you consider a new PC eventually.

The Miracle of Expansion Cards

To help add hardware to your console, the PC comes with a set of internal *expansion slots.* You plug *expansion cards* into the slots, adding new abilities and superpowers to your meek and mild computer.

Common expansion card goodies include video adapters, high-end sound cards, networking adapters, port adapters, and more! But this section wasn't written to sell expansion cards, merely to explain how to upgrade your PC using those cards.

Exploring expansion slots

After you know which kind of expansion card you need, the next and most difficult decision is to determine which slot it plugs into on your PC's motherboard. Each of the standards has a bunch of different expansion slot standards and variations.

The two most common slots available on today's PCs are PCI and PCI-express:

PCI: The Peripheral Component Interconnect type of slot is the most popular and widely available expansion slot on today's PCs. It's normally colored white, though often beige is used. The expansion slots shown on the motherboard in Figure 8-2 are standard 32-bit PIC expansion slots. There are also 64-bit versions of the slots, which are longer than those shown in Figure 8-2.

PCI Express: The latest rendition of the PCI standard is PCI Express, which features a different type of slot than the one shown in Figure 8-2. PCI Express slots are generally colored black or dark gray or sometimes even yellow. They also feature a variety of sizes, as illustrated in Figure 8-3.

x1

x4

Figure 8-3: x8
Different
types of PCI
Express
slots. x16

Older expansion standards include the following:

PCI-X: The PCI *Extended* standard was developed to improve upon PCI, but as a standard it was superseded by PCI Express. Some older PCs may still feature the PCI-X slot, which looks like a standard PCI slot but is considerably longer.

 Be careful not to confuse PCI-X with PCI-Express! They're different standards, different slots, and different expansion card types.

AGP: The Accelerated Graphics Port slot was designed specifically to handle high-end graphics adapters. It may still be found on older PCs, but today's systems use PCI Express expansion slots to handle high-end graphics adapters. AGP slots were often colored maroon and had a hinged hook on one end to help anchor the AGP card.

ISA: The original expansion slot for the PC family was ISA, which simply stood for Industry Standard Architecture (because the expansion slot lacked an official and suitably technical-sounding name). It had two varieties: 16-bit and a longer 16-bit version. Older Windows XP systems may still sport an ISA slot, but few (if any) relevant ISA expansion cards are available today.

Sadly, there's no solid way to determine what type of slots are present on your PC's motherboard, let alone whether the slots are available (or empty). The only way to know for certain is to open the case and have a look.

✦ When the PC's motherboard features a variety of slots, and you have a choice, choose a PCI Express expansion card first.

✦ Expansion slots are *keyed*, meaning that the edge connector on the expansion card cannot be plugged in backward. Of course, most expansion cards feature a rear slot mount, which means you have to be really determined to plug an expansion card in backward in the first place!

✦ You can look on the back of your PC and examine the slot covers to determine whether a slot is empty. A blank slot cover, however, may not indicate that an expansion slot is available because some expansion cards may not use the slot cover.

✦ Even though the expansion slots are all standardized, expansion cards come in different lengths. You can find full-length cards, half-size cards, and others. Smaller PC consoles may have room only for smaller expansion cards, or perhaps some of the expansion slots are limited to hosting only shorter expansion cards. Knowing such things before you buy an expansion card will prove a boon to your self-esteem.

✦ PCI-X also featured two sets of voltages for the expansion cards: 5 volts and 3.3 volts. Special notches in the expansion cards prevented the wrong slot from being used, but the differing voltages were still an issue for choosing the proper PCI-X expansion card.

Inserting an expansion card

Expansion cards are almost tinker-toy simple to insert into a computer. Here are my general steps for updating your PC with a new hardware feature via an expansion slot.

These steps assume, of course, that you have bought the proper gizmo you need, that it's compatible with your computer, and that it's of the right expansion slot type for the motherboard:

1. **Study the instructions that came with the expansion card.**

They're more detailed than what's written here, or they may have important notes such as whether to install any needed software and when to install the software (before or after adding the expansion card).

2. **Follow the directions earlier in this book for opening the computer case.**

   Don't forget the part about backing up your data! Don't forget to set a system restore point!

3. **Locate an available expansion slot.**

   Hopefully, you've already done this, or are at least aware of where the open slot is and that it's available and you've further purchased an expansion card designed to fit into said slot.

4. **Remove the slot cover associated with the expansion slot.**

   The slot cover is part of the console, on the back of the PC. It not only anchors the back half of the card, it also provides access for any connectors the card may sacrifice to the outside world. Figure 8-4 illustrates the slot-and-slot-cover relationship.

Figure 8-4:
Expansion slots and expansion slot covers.

The slot cover is anchored in a number of ways. Most commonly, it's single screw on top. You might also find that the entire row of slot covers is held in place by a swinging latch (the latch is opened in Figure 8-4). Some slot covers are punch-out covers and must be twisted or popped out by pressing with your thumb.

Save the screw you removed to take off the expansion slot cover.

5. **Eyeball the expansion slot to ensure that you can easily place the expansion card inside the console.**

Check for any obstructing cables (refer to Figure 8-4) and gently shove them out of the way or disconnect them temporarily, if necessary. You may have to remove another expansion card or perhaps even a disk drive to reach the expansion slot in question.

6. **Remove the expansion card from its protective, antistatic enclosure.**

7. **If the expansion card requires configuration, do so now.**

The manual that came with the expansion card should explain in poor English whether you need to configure it further and how.

8. **Ground yourself.**

9. **Insert the expansion card into the expansion slot.**

Two things help keep the expansion card in place: the slot itself and the slot cover. Gently press the card into the slot. Ease 'er in! Only when the slot cover is flush with the back slot (where it's supposed to be) is the card fully in place.

When the back cover doesn't line up, you most likely removed the wrong slot cover. Go back to Step 4 and find the slot cover properly associated with the given slot.

10. **Check everything.**

Does the expansion card look right? Is the slot cover flush? Don't force anything! If the card isn't inserted properly, you most likely plugged it into the wrong expansion slot.

11. **Reattach any cables you disconnected or reinsert anything you removed to get the card in place.**

12. **Attach the slot cover to the case.**

Use the same screw you removed in Step 4, if need be.

13. **Close the case as described earlier in this chapter.**

14. **Turn on the computer.**

At this point, installation continues but is different depending on whichever device you installed.

Most likely, Windows starts up and instantly recognizes the new hardware. If the drivers weren't already installed, Windows installs them automatically or asks for a disc containing the drivers.

✦ Watch Video 185 on the DVD for a demonstration of how to add a new expansion card to your PC.

✦ You may need to reactivate or validate your copy of Windows after performing a major hardware addition, such as adding a new expansion card. Windows alerts you to this necessity. As long as you have a legitimate copy of Windows, you can easily activate or verify your copy over the Internet.

✦ Discard the old slot cover you removed. There's no need to keep it. I have a drawer full of them. Having a single spare is okay if you ever decide to retire an expansion card, but the odds of that are rare.

✦ Technically, it's not okay to keep a slot uncovered. The computer manufacturer receives its RFI certification based on the case's full design, which includes expansion slot covers. Radio interference generated inside the computer blasts out of an open slot cover.

Updating a display adapter

Adding a new display adapter to your PC works just like adding any expansion card. But beyond the physical installation, I'd like for you to be aware of a few things when performing this type of operation.

When updating a display adapter, you're either removing an adapter card or simply replacing the video adapter supplied by the computer's motherboard. Either way, there's nothing extra you need to do on the hardware side. The computer recognizes the new display adapter when you turn the PC on again.

By the way, turning the computer on again results in a generic, low-resolution display. Don't let that alarm you! Windows doesn't know anything about the new display adapter, so it returns to using the generic, low-end video adapter driver. After you install the new drivers, you can reselect your favorite display resolution.

✦ Yes, by switching to the low-resolution driver, Windows juggles any icons you have pasted to the desktop. You can restore the icons to their previous positions after updating the display adapter software.

✦ There's no need to disable the motherboard's display adapter hardware. You still see it show up in the list of display adapters in the Device Manager (see Chapter 7).

✦ It's possible to install a second display adapter and use two display adapters in Windows. Refer to Chapter 6 for more information on running two monitors.

Removing an expansion card

It's rare, if ever, that you need to remove an expansion card, but it happens. The last card I removed was an internal modem from one PC so that I could install it in another computer.

To remove an expansion card, follow these general steps:

1. **Turn off the computer, and remember to back up your data (if necessary) and set a restore point, all as described earlier in this chapter.**

2. **Open the PC case.**

3. **Locate the expansion card to remove.**

4. **Move any cables or other obstacles out of the way.**

   If necessary, detach cables or remove disk drives. After the procedure is complete, be sure to remember how they were reinstalled.

5. **Free the expansion card's slot cover: Unscrew the screw or release the latch holding the slot cover in place.**

6. **Ensure that no cables are attached to the expansion card or in its way.**

7. **Gently pull out the card.**

   Pinch the card with your fingers and thumb, and gently ease it out. If necessary, rock it from front to back.

8. **Replace the screw or slot cover.**

   If you kept an old slot cover around, put it back over the hole so that the console case is intact.

9. **Close the console as described earlier in this chapter.**

10. **Turn on the computer.**

Windows may alert you to the device's absence. If so, follow whatever directions are given on the screen.

Store the card in a safe place, where it won't be squished, bent, or broken or come into contact with liquid or humans under the age of nine.

As with adding new hardware, when you remove hardware from a PC, you may have to revalidate or reactivate Windows. Do so when prompted after you upgrade and start your PC.

Reseating expansion cards

It's possible, though rare, for an expansion card to wiggle out of its socket. Blame the heat: Turning a computer off and on changes the console's internal temperature. That can have the effect of wiggling an expansion card free of its roost.

To reseat an expansion card, simply press it down firmly but gently into its socket. Ensure that the card's rear bracket is properly attached. (Some consoles use screws, and others may use a hinged bracket to keep the expansion cards in place.)

Your PC Wants More Memory

One of the cheapest and easiest ways to deal with a slow PC is to add more memory. For a computer, more RAM is like the best Christmas ever! This section explains how to upgrade your PC with more memory.

This section refers to memory expansion options using the term DIMM, or Dual In-line Memory Module. Laptops and some older PCs may use different options, such as SIMM, SIP, SODIMM, or others. See Book III for more laptop information.

Understanding memory banks

Your computer's motherboard sports slots into which memory is plugged. I call the slots *memory banks*, simply because I've been trained to use the term by such great television shows as *Star Trek*, *Lost in Space*, and *The Time Tunnel*. In fact, I believe computer science today owes quite a lot to the 1960s television genius of Irwin Allen.

The motherboard shown in Figure 8-2 sports two memory banks. Your PC may have more or less, but what's more important is how those banks are filled with memory; you can't just plug memory into the motherboard willy-nilly.

In Figure 8-5, you see several ways that a motherboard with four memory banks can host two common amounts of memory: 1GB or 2GB. Because DIMMs come in different memory sizes, memory can be set up in a variety of ways inside any PC, as shown in the figure.

There are many reasons for choosing different arrangements of memory in a PC, but the number-one reason is that memory can be expensive. A single 2GB DIMM (refer to F in Figure 8-5) could cost ten times as much as a 256MB DIMM. So, though you probably didn't know it at the time, one reason your PC was offered at a given price was its memory configuration.

Another reason for using, say, two 1GB DIMMs (refer to E in Figure 8-5) rather than four 512MB DIMMs (refer to D in Figure 8-5) to get 2GB of memory is expandability. It's easier to upgrade memory later when memory banks are available.

✦ Some PCs have a pairing requirement. The memory banks are organized in pairs, and each pair must have the same DIMM size. For example, you can have 3GB of memory in a PC with four memory banks. That's two 1GB DIMMs in two slots, and two 512MB DIMMs in the other two slots.

✦ Yes, when you make a poor choice in buying your computer, you may end up throwing away memory to upgrade. If your PC is configured with 1GB of memory (refer to A in Figure 8-5) and you want 2GB of memory total, you have to throw away all the 256MB DIMMs and replace them with a combination of DIMMs (refer to D, E, or F).

Figure 8-5:
Allocating
DIMMs to
memory
banks.

Getting the right DIMM

Not all DIMMs are alike. Things can get confusing when you're picking out a DIMM. Too bad you just can't thump them like you do melons in the grocery store.

First comes *memory type*. There are several common types, as shown in Table 8-1. Consider that to be all technical information, however. Your computer uses only one memory type, and you must pick a DIMM that matches that type. One way to know which type of memory your PC uses is to examine the invoice — if you still have it. Otherwise, other methods are available, as described in the next section.

Table 8-1	PC Memory Types
Type	*Description*
DRAM	The official name of a RAM (Random Access Memory) chip: Dynamic Random Access Memory
DDR	A Double Data Rate RAM chip, also known as DDRRAM, which is an improvement on SDRAM
DDR2	Another implementation of the DDR type of SDRAM chip
DDR3	Yet another implementation of the DDR type of SDRAM chip
EDO	The Extended Data Out RAM chip
FPM	The Fast Page Mode type of DRAM chip
SDRAM	A type of DRAM chip, Synchronous Dynamic Random Access Memory

Second after memory type is the memory chip's *speed*. Oh, I could wax on about memory chip speed and how it ties into this or that technical thing. Unless you really knew a lot about memory, I could probably make it all up and you'd nod your head knowingly, wishing to rush through it and not understand it (despite my making it all up). But like the memory type, the speed isn't something you pick; it's something the PC's designer chose when they built the motherboard. You merely have to ensure that you buy the right memory speed that your computer is designed to accept. Again, look on the invoice or refer to the next section.

Third, and seriously most confusing, is the *type* of DIMM. Not all memory bank slots are created equal. Each slot uses a different number of connectors, or *pins*. Some are 100-pin, some are 184-pin, and others are 200-pin. It varies. To know how many pins the DIMMs need for your PC, you can check the invoice or you can bother to open the PC and count all the connectors. But rather than do that, just refer to the next section.

Yeah, I didn't need to explain all this. It's a bother. But if you ever tried upgrading memory, as I have, and you didn't pay attention to the details, you ended up with a drawer full of DIMMs that you cannot use in any computer. Rather than waste money building a fun yet technologically obscure mobile, it helps to know a little bit about what you're doing.

Adding memory

You must discover two things before you add memory to your PC: how much memory is already in your computer and how many available memory banks it has. After you know that info, it's just a matter of determining which type of DIMM, and how many, you need to bring your PC up to par.

The first step is to figure out how much memory you need. Your PC may only be able to use a specific amount of memory. For example, the PC I'm using to write this book can have only 8GB of RAM, maximum. Right now, it has 2GB. If I needed 4GB, I'd have to buy . . . anyone? Yes! I'd have to buy 2GB more of memory.

The second step is to discover all the quantifications about the DIMMs you need. You can easily pay someone else to do that: Drop off the computer at the shop, and let them fuss over it. But that's probably not why you bought this book.

You can also attempt to discover on your own which type of memory you need. You can open the case and yank out a DIMM. You can stare at it. You can sleep with it under your pillow. But that probably doesn't help you much.

Or, you can find some help and have a computer program determine how much memory is installed in your computer and how best to update. Computer programs can figure this stuff out without the need to open the computer case. After all, programs run inside the computer, where they can see everything.

The program I recommend that you use is on the Internet at Crucial.com, which also, coincidentally, sells computer memory. Visit the Web site. Use the Crucial system scanner tool; follow the directions on the Web page. Eventually, it tells you exactly how to upgrade your PC's memory. My results are shown in Figure 8-6.

Figure 8-6: The Crucial memory-scanner tool.

As you can see in the figure, my PC has 1GB installed using two 512MB DIMMs. It has two open slots. The rest of the figure explains various options for upgrading, including options for keeping the memory and options for removing existing memory. (On my other PCs, I discovered — much to my chagrin — that all the memory banks are full, and I'd have to upgrade to replace memory.)

The third step is to buy the memory. The Crucial Web site not only tells you how much and which type of DIMMs you need but also lets you buy the memory on the spot. It's one reason why I recommend the site. (The other is that Crucial is located in Idaho.)

The final step is to install the memory. Here are the general steps to take:

1. **Open the console as described earlier in this chapter.**

2. **(Optional) Remove any old memory, if necessary.**

   A. *Locate the DIMMs you want to remove.*

   B. *Push the hooks on the ends of the DIMM.*

   By pushing the hooks out and down, you free the DIMM from the slot.

   C. *Pull out the DIMM and gently set it aside.*

   D. *Repeat these substeps for any additional DIMMs you need to remove.*

3. **Push down the clips on both ends of the memory bank slots.**

   See Figure 8-7.

Figure 8-7:
Upgrading a
DIMM.

4. Remove the memory from its protective, antistatic bag.

Avoid touching the metal edge on the DIMM, the part that's inserted into the slot.

If you're removing DIMMs, take the ones you removed and store them in the protective bag that held the new DIMMs.

5. Ground yourself.

6. Line up the DIMM with the slot.

There are notches on the DIMM. There are keys on the slot. They must match to prevent you from accidentally plugging the DIMM in backward. Use Figure 8-7 as your guide.

7. Gently push the DIMM into the slot.

If you're successful, the clips on either end of the DIMM automatically snap into position. Otherwise, lift the clips to complete anchoring the DIMM into its slot.

The clips *must* be in the fully upright and locked position.

8. Repeat Steps 3 through 7 for each DIMM you're installing.

9. Double-check everything!

10. Close the console as described earlier in this chapter.

Trepidatiously turn the computer on. There should be no trouble, no messages, no nothing; the computer instantly recognizes and uses the extra memory. Somewhere in cyberspace, the computer is thanking you.

✦ Refer to Video 186 for a demonstration of installing and removing DIMMs.

✦ DIMMs are clipped into their memory bank slots. Unlike other internal PC expansion options, DIMMs rarely pop out and need reseating. In the olden days, however, when memory chips were manually pushed into sockets, they occasionally wiggled out and required reseating.

More Storage for You!

Beyond giving your PC more memory, another way to be nice to Mr. Computer is to upgrade its storage capacity. You can replace or add internal disk drives.

Right away, I must mention that adding external storage devices to a computer is far, far easier than upgrading them internally. I highly recommend that you choose an external hard drive or optical drive before doing an internal update. But if pressed, you can heed the advice in this section to do an internal upgrade.

Knowing the terms

Internally, there are two types of drives you can add to a computer console: a hard drive and an optical drive. The number of drives, and the type of drives, you add depend on how many disk drive parking spots are in your PC's internal garage.

Disk drives go into the drive bay, which you can find by using Figure 8-1. There must be room for whatever drive you plan on adding to your PC. No room, no internal expansion. When you have one of those small-footprint PCs, or a laptop, then the console probably lacks internal expansion luxury.

Beyond the issue of where it parks, the disk drive connects to the rest of the computer system with two cables. The first is a power cable. The console is probably bristling with extra power cables, enough to fully populate as much storage hardware as it can carry.

The second cable is the data cable. It's one of two types: ATA or SATA.

ATA: The daddy of all hard drive and optical drive connectors is the ATA, which stands for *AT* Attachment. The *AT* came from the IBM PC AT computer, introduced in the 1980s. Yes, it's an old standard. It uses a flat ribbon cable and a boxy 50-pin connector.

SATA: The current and best standard for connecting disk drives inside the console is the SATA, or *Serial ATA*. It fixes some of the annoying issues that are present with the ATA data cable.

As with many hardware upgrades, which standard you use depends on what's inside your computer. But unlike with other internal upgrades, you can determine from the outside what's on the inside: Open the Device Manager as covered in Chapter 7. Open the item titled IDE ATA/ATAPI Controllers. That section lists for you the types of data cables available in the console: IDE or SATA or some other variation.

Even though the Device Manager may cough up information about the drive interface, I highly recommend that you take a peek inside the console to confirm which type is available. When both types are available, I recommend using SATA.

✦ Other names for the ATA data cable include IDE, ATAPI, PATA, and UDMA.

✦ Variations on SATA are *eSATA*, the external version of SATA, and Ultra ATA, which is an older version of the standard.

✦ Some computers may still use the SCSI interface. You can confirm this by viewing the Device Manager (see Chapter 7) and looking under the Storage Controller category. If anything there says *SCSI*, your PC has the

SCSI interface and can expand with those devices as well. SCSI stands for Small Computer Serial Interface, and it's bemusedly pronounced "skuzzy."

+ Having the two data cable standards named ATA and SATA makes room for a slew of computer rhymes, poetry, and song lyrics. I leave it up to you to formulate your own festive literary devices.

Choosing a new hard drive

The number-one thing I look for in a new hard drive is capacity. How much more space will the hard drive give me to store my stuff? Generally speaking, for second internal hard drives, I get a drive that's at least as big as the drive already inside the PC.

Directly related to capacity is cost, of course. The higher the capacity, the more expensive the drive. But rather than look at the bottom line, calculate the storage in terms of dollars per gigabyte.

For example, if a 320GB drive costs $70 and a 500GB drive costs $90, why pay more for the 500GB drive? Because its cost is really 18 cents per gigabyte. The 320GB drive is 21 cents per gigabyte. Yeah, it's pennies, but the better value is in the higher-capacity drive.

Technically, there are a few things you might want to pay attention to in a hard drive. These details are trivial, but I list them here anyway.

Drive speed: Hard drives spin at a certain number of revolutions per minute (rpm). A speed of 7200 rpm is nice, and 10,000 rpm is better.

Buffer: In computer-speak, *buffer* means memory. For a hard drive, a buffer means memory storage on the drive to help speed up operations. A 16MB buffer is very good, and 32MB is better.

Interface: This is either SATA (Serial ATA) or plain ATA, as discussed in the preceding section.

Hard drives may have other technical aspects, but mostly you see them listed online and in stores by capacity, drive speed, buffer size, and interface. (They also have cryptic part numbers.) Some people pay attention to the drive manufacturer. I don't. Yes, you pay more for bigger and faster, for example.

+ When buying a hard drive to upgrade the PC's console, you want an *internal* drive.

✦ The reason the prices are so low on internal drives is that the drive doesn't come with a case, a power supply, or an interface. Also, you're installing things — and troubleshooting — on your own.

✦ Windows cannot access more than 1 terabyte (TB), or 1,000 gigabytes (GB), on a single hard drive. Fortunately, 1TB drives are rare and expensive at this point in history. I assume that when that capacity (and larger) becomes widely available, newer releases of Windows will be able to access such huge storage spaces.

Choosing a new optical drive

A second optical drive may seem excessive, but sometimes it's necessary. For example, you might have a DVD drive and want a DVD-R/RW combo drive. Or, maybe you're a gamer and you like to keep game discs in the drives rather than swap discs all the time. Or, it might be as simple as wanting to replace a dead optical drive.

However you slice it, when there's room you can upgrade the computer with another optical drive. The variety is there.

Optical drives come with two flavors: CD and DVD. You want a DVD. All DVD drives can read CDs, so there's no point in buying a plain CD drive.

The next decision is whether you want to record discs. Although several recording standards exist, most optical drives that record support all the standards. Even so, if you also want to record CDs, you need a combo drive. Be sure to check.

Finally, there's the interface: SATA or ATA, as covered earlier in this chapter.

Remember to buy an internal optical drive. An internal drive is cheaper than an external model, which must be enclosed in a case, supply an interface, and have its own power supply.

What about Blu-Ray?

The current top-of-the-line optical drive standard is Sony's Blu-Ray. A Blu-Ray disc stores twice as much information as a standard DVD, but the drives are expensive. Plus, relatively few software programs are available on Blu-Ray, which means that you're limited to watching Blu-Ray movies on your PC.

My prediction is that Blu-Ray may move in as the replacement for DVDs and CDs, but coming up fast is the solid-state drive, or SSD. Essentially large media cards, the SSDs will most likely become the removable storage media of choice, so I recommend putting off any Blu-Ray upgrades for now unless you're compelled to use that standard.

Installing the drive

To shove a new drive into your computer's case, follow these general steps:

1. **If you're installing a SATA drive, ensure that you have a spare SATA cable handy.**

   SATA drives don't come with cables. You must buy a cable. But before you do, check inside the console. Some console designs feature SATA cables already in place by the locations where SATA drives are to be installed.

2. **Open the case as described earlier in this chapter.**

3. **Locate the empty spot that will accept the new drive.**

4. **Examine how the drive will be inserted.**

   Sometimes, an optical drive must be inserted from the front of the console.

5. **Move things out of the way, if necessary.**

   For example, you may have to remove an expansion card to insert a hard drive. Or, you might have to slide open a cover or other internal hardware to accommodate the drive.

6. **If the drive needs attachments to be inserted, add them to the drive now.**

   Some drives need rails to fit into a drive bay. Sometimes, screws need to be attached to the drive before it's inserted. The screws help position the drive and keep it in place. Some newer systems may use drive caddies: You insert the drive into the caddy and then plug the caddy into the drive bay.

7. **Configure the ATA drive.**

   Some drives have jumpers on the back. You must properly set the jumpers so that the drive is recognized as either Drive 0, which is the first drive on the cable, or Drive 1, which is the second drive. This arrangement is also known as *master-slave,* in which the first drive is the master, and the second drive is the slave. You cannot have two masters or two slaves or else the drives don't work.

   Directions for configuring the jumpers on the drive are found on the top of the drive somewhere. Figure 8-8 shows a typical drive rump, with the ATA connector, jumpers, and power connector. The jumper positions indicated in the figure are most likely different from any drive you might install.

Figure 8-8:
Configuring
jumpers
on an ATA
drive.

Put jumper here
for master drive

Put jumper here
for slave drive

ATA interface   Jumpers   Power

8. **Place the drive into the bay.**

9. **If necessary, anchor the drive.**

Some drives may snap into position, and others may require screws to
anchor the drive. The screws line up with tiny holes on the side of the
drive bay.

10. **Connect the power cable.**

It plugs in only one way.

When you cannot find a power cable that matches the drive's connector,
you need a power cable adapter. These adapters can be found at computer stores (*real* computer stores, not warehouses) or ordered over the
Internet.

11. **Connect the data cable.**

It plugs in only one way. If you're adding an ATA slave drive, you connect it to the middle connector in the 50-pin ribbon cable. SATA cables
plug in only one way — one end on the drive and the other on the
motherboard.

12. **Replace anything you needed to remove.**

For example, reinstall an expansion card, if necessary, or redo whatever
you needed to undo to place the drive into its spot.

13. **Close the case, per the directions offered earlier in this chapter.**

When you turn on the computer, Windows should instantly recognize
the drive, giving it a drive letter and adding it to the list of drives in the
Computer or My Computer window.

+ Video 187 covers installing a new disk drive into a PC.

+ For further information about disk drive configuration, refer to Book VI, Chapter 2. You can reformat the drive, if necessary. Or, you can assign the drive a new letter, which is often needed because the new hard drive may shift all the other drive letters in the computer. That can be bothersome.

+ To help locate the SATA connections on the motherboard, follow the SATA cable from an existing drive. The open connections will be near wherever any existing connections attach.

Book II
Software

Contents at a Glance

Chapter 1: Windows Gone AWOL

In This Chapter

✔ **Repairing broken Windows**

✔ **Working with Windows Update**

✔ **Undoing an update**

✔ **Locating lost files**

✔ **Dealing with missing file error messages**

✔ **Fixing lots of minor annoying issues in Windows**

Your computer, as well as your sanity, relies upon Windows running in a proper and predictable manner. If Windows behaved all the time, this chapter wouldn't be necessary. Because that's not the case, you can turn to this chapter to find ways to fix what ails Windows and get it back in line.

The General Windows Fix

I'm certain that historians 200 years from now will look back upon our culture in awe. (Whether it's respect or disgust remains to be determined.) They will marvel at Windows, the operating system used by more than 80 percent of the humans who are bold enough to use computers. And they will marvel, not at how we could use computers that tend to get weird all of a sudden, but, rather, that the computers were ever normal in the first place.

This section covers the overall situation of Windows going weird — and it does so in a variety of ways. Not only this chapter but also eight other chapters in this book mull over strange things in Windows.

When you truly need to fix Windows, visit Chapter 8. There, you discover why I recommend that you don't reinstall Windows and instead look into System File Checker as a solution.

Restarting Windows

Writing this book is quite a major project for me. A book of this size would be a big deal for any author. During the course of writing this book, I experienced many of the problems this book mentions. I also used one general tried-and-true solution to most of them: Restart Windows.

I'm not saying to log out. I'm not saying to close a few programs. Sometimes, to fix something truly odd in Windows, you must restart the entire computer. When Windows returns, the problem will most likely be gone. I would say, nine times out of ten, the restart-Windows solution works like a charm.

✦ See Book I, Chapter 3 for details on how to restart Windows if you're unfamiliar with the procedure, or if you've never, ever, restarted Windows.

✦ Restarting Windows may fix other programs as well. For example, my Webcam software was acting all screwy and just wouldn't start or recognize the camera. After restarting Windows, however, the problem was mysteriously resolved.

✦ There's no need to restart Windows every so often "just in case."

✦ If you have to restart Windows all the time to fix problems, a better solution probably exists. Refer to Chapter 3 for information on Safe mode to determine whether the problem is specific to Windows. Also see Chapter 4 for information on discovering a memory leak.

Deciphering error codes

There's a difference between an error code and an error message. An error message is something like "The printer is jammed." An error code is something like "Error 20."

Don't fall prey to the folly of trying to understand error codes. Whether you see the error code in Windows or in an application, the code number is useless. In fact, the code number was written by the programmer *for* the programmer. Unless you're being paid to write the program, the error code probably won't help you much.

Sure, you can use the Internet to search for the error code. Sometimes you may find the code listed, along with a definition of what it means. When you're really lucky, you may find a solution. Most of the time, you won't.

Error codes are for the programmer, not the user. If they truly wanted you to know what was going on, they would use an error message rather than an error code.

Peeking at that debug information

Another useless feature offered by many programs is the so-called *debugging information*. It works like this: You see an error message in a dialog box or window. The error message is useless, but you see a button titled Details or More Info. So you click the button and you see something like this:

```
17A7:0000   CD 20 FF 9F 00 9A EE FE-1D F0 4F 03 0B 12 8A 03
17A7:0010   0B 12 17 03 0B 12 41 07-01 01 01 00 02 FF FF FF
17A7:0020   FF FF FF FF FF FF FF FF-FF FF FF FF AF 11 4E 01
AX=0000  BX=0000  CX=0000  DX=0000  SP=FFEE  BP=0000  SI=0000  DI=0000
DS=17A7  ES=17A7  SS=17A7  CS=17A7  IP=0100    NV UP EI PL NZ NA PO NC
```

Yeah, right. That definitely is debugging information. Specifically, it's information about the computer's state when the program crashed. The information is highly detailed and extremely useful — but only to the programmer who wrote the code.

The moral of the story: Unless you want to do the programmer's job and fix what's wrong, there's nothing you can do.

Windows Updates, Doesn't It?

Maybe this update thing is getting out of hand. It's a noble idea: Software is never really "done." Because of its very nature, software programs have bugs that just won't be found — sometimes, for decades. Not only that, but engineers love to add features. It's called *creeping elegance,* and it's something only management can stop.

Regardless of the disease, the symptoms are that your PC's software needs to be updated. The process not only ensures that the computer is running the best possible version of Windows but also provides patches for security holes that may be found. That's important, so like it or not, Windows need updates. This section discusses Windows Update.

Understanding Windows Update

The Windows operating system comes with the feature Windows Update. It uses the Internet to phone home into the Microsoft mother ship and check for any available new files or patches and to relay information about which naughty Web sites you visited. (Just kidding.)

Windows Update was originally found on top of the Start menu, nestled on the main Programs or All Programs menu. Choosing that item whisked you off to the official Windows Update Web page, where you went through a series of convoluted steps to bring the PC's operating system to current status.

You can still visit the Windows Update site to update your computer. I recommend that approach for Windows XP users. Visit

```
http://update.microsoft.com
```

 When you visit this site in Windows Vista, however, you're thrust back into local control, so there's no point to visit the Web page in Windows Vista. Instead, open the Windows Update icon in the Control Panel to perform update operations, review updates, and do things covered in the next few sections.

◆ You don't have to update your computer. If you don't use the Internet and you enjoy your computer in its present state and never plan to upgrade or add anything new, there's no reason to update. Otherwise, I highly recommend running Windows Update, as described in this chapter.

◆ Windows XP features a Security Center icon in the Control Panel. You can open the Security Center icon to view the Security Center window and find therein an Automatic Updates item. There, you can turn Automatic Update off or on, but I still recommend visiting the Windows Update Web site as a more complete way to keep Windows up-to-date.

Configuring updates

Windows Update can be set to run in one of three ways:

◆ **Fully automatic:** Windows downloads and installs critical updates as they appear. You can schedule the updates, but otherwise this is the "blind obedience" choice.

◆ **Semiautomatic:** You're alerted to the updates, and you're given the choice of whether to download them. Updates are installed only when you choose to install them. This option is named "It's my computer, and though I may begrudgingly choose to install the updates, I'll do it on my own damn time."

◆ **Not at all:** Updates are neither checked for nor installed. You can still manually check for and install updates, but Windows Update doesn't do it automatically for you, not even a tiny bit. This option is the one for most hill people.

In Windows Vista, you configure Windows updates by following these steps:

1. **Open the Control Panel's Windows Update icon.**

The Windows Update window appears, as shown in Figure 1-1. Though you can't tell by the picture, the top part of the window is shown in a happy green color. When Windows Update is turned off, the angry red color is used instead.

2. **On the left side of the window, click the Change Settings link.**

3. **Use the Change Settings window to specify how often Windows Update works.**

For example, choose Install Updates Automatically (Recommended) to have the computer do everything for you. If you experience problems updating, or you're just suspicious, choose Download Updates But Let Me Choose Whether to Install Them instead.

When you choose Updates Automatically, be sure to set a time for the updates when the computer will be on and can connect to the Internet.

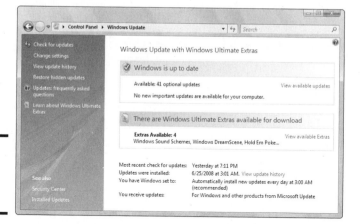

Figure 1-1:
Windows
Update is
happy.

4. **Click OK to confirm the new settings.**

5. **Type the administrator's password or click Continue to proceed.**

    You may close the Windows Update window now, if you're done.

In Windows XP, you turn on Automatic Updates from the Security window; open the Security icon in the Control Panel.

Where is the list of error messages?

At one time, many clock cycles ago, I was fortunate to have the complete list of MS-DOS error code messages. They were printed, single-spaced, on 500 sheets of paper. There were *thousands* of error messages. DOS generated them all.

The list of error messages was interesting, but it was only a list. It didn't mention the cause of the error or how to fix it. Despite the brevity of information, many people wanted to see that list, and I enjoyed showing it off. Man, were those people disappointed!

I don't believe that Microsoft keeps a list of Windows error messages the way it kept the list of MS-DOS error messages. One reason

is most likely that the list by itself is meaningless (or embarrassing). But a larger reason is its sheer mass. It's huge. Even if such a list did exist, why pay someone to maintain it? And if the list is as enormous as it theoretically could be, who would want to go through it and write a solution for every single error message?

To answer the question: No, there's no colossal list of all computer error messages. Rather than think in terms of error message-versus-solution, try to think instead of problem-solving techniques. If you can better understand how the computer works, you can come up with a clever and reusable approach to fixing any problem.

How much updating is enough?

When in doubt, just choose every update, but sometimes it helps to be critical. I prefer to review updates as opposed to automatically installing them all. I recommend always installing security and critical updates. As for optional updates, such as add-ons or bonus files, feel free to deny them at your whim. Especially if you read the update description and discover that it doesn't apply to your situation, there's no need to install the update.

Also, keep in mind that updates don't vanish. When you decline an update, it continues to show up on the list of available updates. If you choose to, you can install that update in the future.

If either of these methods fails to work, you can update manually by visiting the Windows Update Web site. Follow the directions on the site to download whatever software is necessary, and then heed the directions on the screen. My advice is to peruse the updates before you choose one. Not every update is critical or necessary.

+ Windows Update may not install all available updates. Figure 8-1 lists 41 optional updates, plus 4 "extras." Click the appropriate links to view and, optionally, install those updates.

+ I suggest that you choose the weekend for performing Automatic updates. That way, if the computer needs to automatically restart, you don't lose any work documents you may leave open.

+ In Windows Vista, Windows Update may also show driver updates, indicating that new software is available for certain peripherals or hardware components inside your PC. Also refer to Book I, Chapter 7 for information on updating drivers for various gizmos in your computer.

Permitting an update

When you postpone an update for Windows, you're reminded of it. Again and again. Ceaselessly. A notice appears in the notification area, sometimes with a pop-up bubble that says "New updates are available." You'll probably see it each time you log in to Windows. It will tick you off.

To proceed with an update, visit the Windows Update site and install the updates. Sometimes, that's as easy as clicking the annoying balloon tip.

+ Some updates can be installed only by restarting Windows.

+ It's okay to continue using the computer while an update installs. If restarting Windows is necessary, you're alerted. You can choose to restart immediately, have the computer remind you about restarting every so often, or just tell the computer to shut the heck up. But remember to restart eventually.

✦ Yes, selecting the shield icon that appears on the Software Power button in Windows Vista, or the Turn Off button in Windows XP, means that updates will be installed when you turn off the computer.

✦ If you'd rather not install an update when shutting down Windows XP, click the link that says Click Here to Turn Off Without Installing Updates. The link appears in the Shut Down window.

✦ There's no way to disable the pop-up alert "balloon tip" from the notification area. Solutions are mentioned on the Internet, but I've found that they generally don't work.

✦ Naturally, folks who disable Windows Update aren't reminded of anything — not even their birthdays.

Reviewing the updates

Come take a look at what Windows Update has done to your PC! Observe the updates! See what they've done!

In Windows Vista, peruse updates by following these steps:

1. **Open the Windows Update icon in the Control Panel.**

2. **Choose the View Update History link along the left side of the Windows Update window.**

   You see a list of installed updates, plus a handy link titled Troubleshoot Problems with Installing Updates.

3. **Click OK when you're done, because the window is a look-only type of thing.**

In Windows XP, obey these steps:

1. **Open the Add or Remove Programs icon in the Control Panel.**

   The Add or Remove Programs window shows up.

2. **Put a check mark by Show Updates.**

   The list becomes populated with updates; you may have to scroll down a bit to find them.

3. **Close the window when you're done.**

See the following section for information on removing an update.

Undoing an update

If you install a Windows update and it makes things worse, you can easily back up and get your computer back. (If only the family car were so forgiving to Fluffy.)

To uninstall a Windows Vista update, follow these steps:

1. **Open the Programs and Features icon in the Control Panel.**
2. **Choose the link View Installed Updates.**

   All updates installed for your PC are listed, probably categorized by software developer.

   To sort the list by date, choose Details from the Views toolbar button menu, and then click the Installed On column heading.

3. **Choose the update you want to undo.**
4. **Click the Uninstall button that appears on the toolbar.**
5. **Follow the directions provided on the screen.**

   If prompted to restart Windows, do so.

In Windows XP, remove an update by following these steps:

1. **Open the Control Panel's Add or Remove Programs icon.**
2. **Place a check mark by the Show Updates option at the top of the window.**
3. **Choose the update to remove.**

   The update's entry expands to offer more information, including a link titled Click Here for Support Information.

4. **Click the Remove button.**
5. **Follow the directions and steps provided.**

   If necessary, restart Windows when prompted to do so.

The update should be removed successfully and your system restored. When the operation doesn't work, try again in Safe mode. Refer to Chapter 3.

Files Missing and Found

For those times when you experience It Was Just Here syndrome, or any time you're alerted to the absence of something that must be found, turn to this section for answers.

Searching for files

The lesson to be learned when you misplace a file is to keep your files organized in the first place: Create folders. Give the folders names, like categories in a library. Use subfolders. Organize! Organize! Organize! When you forget, use Windows to help you quickly find a file.

In Windows Vista, use the Search box on the Start button menu. Type the information you're looking for. You can type a filename or text that you're looking for inside a file. The results appear right on the Start menu.

Windows XP has a bit more involved form of search than Vista. Here are the steps to take:

1. Choose Search from the Start button menu.

2. In the Search window, choose a category from the left side of the window.

For example, to search for a picture file, choose Pictures, Music, or Video. When you're unsure, choose All Files And Folders.

3. Fill in the dog's balloon, coughing up as much details as you can about the topic you're searching for.

The more details you can offer, the more exact the search.

4. Click the Search button.

The results are displayed in the window.

When the file you're looking for cannot be found, you need to boost your searching skills, as covered in the next section.

You might find a shortcut file rather than the original. Shortcuts may still exist although an original has been deleted. Therefore, search the Recycle Bin next. See the later section "Searching the Recycle Bin."

Really searching for files

The Search command is designed to search only your own files. When you need to search outside your personal area, you need to boost the Search command with more muscle.

In Windows Vista, follow these steps:

1. Press Win+E to summon a Search window.

2. Click the chevron to reveal advanced Search options.

3. From the Location button menu, choose a specific location.

The broadest location is Computer. To search a specific hard drive, choose it from the list.

4. Fill in as much information as you can about the missing file.

5. Put a check by the box labeled Include Non-Indexed, Hidden, and System Files (Might Be Slow).

6. Click the Search button.

In Windows XP, heed these steps:

1. **Press Win+F to conjure forth a Search window.**

2. **Choose the All Files and Folders link.**

3. **Fill in as much information as you can about the file you're searching for.**

4. **From the Look In drop-down list, choose a specific location.**

   To search everywhere, choose the Computer option; otherwise, pick a disk drive or choose Local Hard Drives to search all hard drives inside of or attached to your PC.

 5. **Click the chevron to display More Advanced Options.**

6. **Ensure that a check mark appears by the items Search System Folders, Search Hidden Files and Folders, and Search Subfolders.**

7. **Click the Search button.**

By following these steps, you're directing Windows to look everywhere for the file, including places outside the normal locations where you save your files. Using this technique helps you locate files you might see referenced in error messages or other files you need to access for troubleshooting purposes.

Searching the Recycle Bin

The Recycle Bin isn't normally searched by the Windows Search command. I mean, honestly: How many times have you searched your office trash for your car keys? So I recommend that you take a peek in the trash, er, Recycle Bin whenever the regular version of the Search command comes up empty.

To best search the Recycle Bin, follow these steps:

1. **Open the Recycle Bin icon on the desktop.**

   If the icon isn't available on the desktop, choose Recycle Bin from the Address bar of any Windows Explorer window.

2. **Choose Details from the Views button menu on the toolbar.**

3. **Ensure that the list is sorted by filename.**

   An upward-pointing triangle appears next to the Name column heading. If not, click the Name column heading until you see the triangle. (The upward-pointing triangle indicates an ascending, or A-to-Z, sort.)

4. **Scroll through the list to look for the misplaced, and wrongly deleted, file.**

You can quickly scroll to a specific point in the list by pressing a letter key on the keyboard. For example, to find the file `Secret Plans`, press the S key.

5. **After you find the file, click to select it.**

6. **Take heed of the information in the Original Location column.**

   That information is the pathname to the folder where the file will be restored. That's where you need to look in Step 9.

7a. **In Windows Vista, click the toolbar button Restore This Item.**

7b. **In Windows XP, choose the link Restore This Item from the task panel on the left side of the window.**

8. **Close the Recycle Bin window.**

9. **Open a Windows Explorer window (press Win+E) and navigate to the folder where the file has been restored.**

   I hope you paid attention in Step 6.

If you're unfamiliar with pathnames, treat them like roadmaps that tell you where files are located. You can view Video 211 to see how it's done. Here's an example:

```
C:\Users\Public\Pictures\2009\Vacation\Disney
```

This path directs you to the Disneyland folder: Open drive `C` and then the `Users` folder. Open the `Public` folder and then the subfolders `Pictures`, `2009`, `Vacation`, and, finally, `Disney` to locate the file you just restored.

You cannot search file contents inside the Recycle Bin. Deleted files are compressed by Windows, and there's no way to look inside the file contents unless you first restore the file to its original location.

Really, really searching for files

A truly nerdy way to search for files is ignored in the graphical portion of Windows. By opening a command-prompt window, you can search for files that Windows truly doesn't want you to know are there.

The following steps are technical. Yes, this is a *For Dummies* reference book, but when you really, *really* need to find a file, the method described in the following steps does the job:

1. **From the Start menu, choose All Programs➪Accessories➪Command Prompt.**

2. **Type** CD \ **and press Enter.**

   That's **CD**, a space, and then the backslash character. That command propels you to the root directory (folder) on the main hard drive.

3. **Type** DIR **and a space.**

4. **Type the name of the file you're looking for.**

   For example, if you're looking for the file secret.doc, type **secret.doc**. You can type upper- or lowercase letters.

   When you don't know the full name, replace the part you don't know with an asterisk (which is a wildcard). For example, you type secret* to search for all files beginning with the word *secret*.

   Don't type any spaces, because the command prompt has special ways of dealing with spaces, and this section is not a lesson on using the command prompt. If you must type a space, use the ? (question mark) character instead.

5. **Type another space and then** /S, **a space, and** /P.

   The complete command line to look for the file secret.doc appears like this:

   ```
   dir secret.doc /s /p
   ```

   The /s option directs a search through all folders on the hard drive; the /p option pauses the display after each screen of text. Double-check everything!

6. **Press the Enter key.**

   The results display one screen at a time.

7. **Peruse the screen full of results.**

8. **If you find a file that matches, you can open a Windows Explorer window to display the file's folder.**

   Press Win+E to open a Windows Explorer window. Use the directions from the preceding section to hunt down a file by its pathname, or use Video 211 to help you.

   The pathname is found above the filename in the results. The pathname reads similar to this:

   ```
   Directory of C:\Users\Dang\Documents\Forgotten
   ```

9. **If the file isn't found, press Enter to see the next screen (if necessary).**

   The prompt reads Press any key to continue, but the Enter key is the "any key." Repeat Steps 7 and 8 to review the results.

10. **Type the** EXIT **command to close the Command Prompt window when you're done.**

Yes, this method is not only technical — it's tedious. But the DIR command does a thorough job of scouring the entire hard drive. I've used this method many times, mostly to confirm that a file *doesn't* exist. For finding lost files I created, the steps in the earlier section "Searching for files" always do the trick.

See Video 212, where you can watch me use these same steps at the command prompt to find a lost file.

Adding items to the search index

Today's search commands don't actually search your stuff. Instead, they search an index of your stuff, one that is painstakingly created at another time. That's because it's much quicker to search and index than to search everywhere. Consider this book: It's faster to look up something in the index than to turn every page looking for something. Search indexes work the same way.

For efficiency's sake, a search index doesn't make a note of everything in your computer. But you can direct the Search command to index other locations. So when you find yourself locating lost files outside the normal search locations, it pays to have Windows index those locations to make the search process go faster.

Set the search index in Windows Vista by following these steps:

1. **Open the Indexing Options icon in the Control Panel.**

2. **Click the Modify button in the Indexing Options dialog box.**

3. **Click the Show All Locations button.**

4. **When prompted, press the Continue button or type the administrator's password to continue.**

   A list of locations appears at the top of the Indexed Locations window, shown in Figure 1-2.

5. **Choose a disk drive or folder to add to the index.**

   Browse through the list (refer to Figure 1-2) to find the item you want to index. Placing a check mark in the box by the item adds that folder and all its subfolders and all that content to the index.

   Likewise, to remove an item from the index, remove the check mark by that item.

   The list on the bottom of the Indexed Locations dialog box shows which items are being indexed.

6. **Click OK when you're done adding items to the index.**

7. **Click the Close button to dismiss the Indexing Options dialog box.**

Files selected for indexing

Click to open

Indexed Locations

Change selected locations

☑ 🖳 Offline Files (MonsterX\Dan)
☑ 🖳 Offline Files (MonsterX\Tom Nifty)
☐ ▷ 💾 OldVal (F:)
☐ ▲ 🖴 OS (C:)
☐ ▷ 📁 DELL
☐ ▷ 📁 doctemp
☐ ▷ 📁 Drivers
☐ ▷ 📁 migwiz
☐ ▷ 📁 Program Files
☐ ▷ 📁 ProgramData
☑ ▷ 📁 Users
☐ ▷ 📁 Windows
☐ ▷ 🖴 RECOVERY (D:)

Summary of selected locations

Included Locations	Exclude
🖳 Offline Files (MonsterX\Dan)	
🖳 Offline Files (MonsterX\Tom ...	
📁 Start Menu	
📁 Users	Default

Show all locations   OK   Cancel

Figure 1-2: Adding new items to the indexed locations list.

Indexed locations

Click to add to the index

Windows XP doesn't have as complete a method to adjust indexing. But you should ensure that the indexing service has been activated. Do this:

1. **Press Win+F to summon a Search window.**

2. **From the list of tasks on the left side of the window, choose Change Preferences.**

3. **Choose the link With Indexing Service (for Faster Local Searches).**

4. **Click Yes, Enable Indexing Service.**

5. **Click OK.**

The index is updated automatically by Windows, so you don't notice it happening. You cannot disable the index updating in Windows Vista, nor can you change its update schedule.

+ Avoid the temptation to index *everything* in Windows Vista. When you do, the index becomes useless as its efficiency drops to nil. Index only those folders you frequent to find files.

+ *Offline* files are copies of files that exist elsewhere on the network.

+ Additional search options in Windows Vista can be set in the Folder Options dialog box, on the Search tab. Use the Control Panel to open the Folder Options dialog box.

+ The index is updated by the Windows Search service. See Chapter 2 for more information on services in Windows.

Rebuilding the search index

If you discover that the Search command in Windows Vista is behaving rather ignorantly, you can rebuild the Search command's index. Here's how:

1. **Open the Indexing Options icon in the Control Panel.**

2. **Click the Advanced button in the Indexing Options dialog box.**

3. **Type the administrator's password or click the Continue button to proceed.**

4. **Click the Rebuild button in the Advanced Options dialog box.**

5. **Click the OK button to rebuild the index.**

6. **Close the Indexing Options dialog box.**

The time it takes to rebuild the index depends on how many files are being indexed and how busy the computer is. You can keep the Indexing Options dialog box open to view the progress, though you can still use your computer while files are being indexed.

It's a good idea to rebuild the index after you select new locations to index, as covered in the preceding section.

A file is missing

Often times, it's not you who discovers that a file has gone AWOL. Sometimes, Windows itself notices that files go missing. The missing-file message appears either when Windows starts or when you run specific programs.

The key to fixing the problem is discovering who owns the problem. To draw a line between Windows and your PC's other programs, start-up files, and device drivers, start the computer in Safe mode, as discussed in Chapter 3. When the problem persists in Safe mode, it's most likely Windows' own problem. See Chapter 8 for information on using the System File Checker to recover bits and pieces of Windows.

When the problem lies with other software, you need to turn to the other software itself to find the missing file. For example, if a start-up message indicates that an audio file cannot be found, reinstall your PC's audio software. You can find the software on a disc that came with the PC or from the manufacturer's Web site on the Internet.

A start-up message indicating a missing DLL or other type of file may appear because the program was sloppily uninstalled. The key is to remove the reference to the file in whichever part of Windows is starting the file. This problem tends to happen more in Windows XP than in Windows Vista.

In Windows XP, follow these steps to remove an unwanted start-up file error message:

1. **Take note of the error message.**

For example, if the message is `Unable to locate boogus.dll`, note the name `boogus.dll`.

2. **Press Win+R to bring up the Run dialog box.**

3. **Type msconfig to start the System Configuration Utility.**

4. **Click the SYSTEM.INI tab.**

Windows Vista has no SYSTEM.INI tab, so if you see one, you didn't pay attention to my Windows XP–only admonition at the beginning of these steps.

5. **Peruse the list to look for the name of the missing file.**

6. **When you find the filename that appears in the error message, remove the check mark by that filename.**

By removing the check mark, you direct Windows not to locate the file when it first starts.

7. **Click the WIN.INI tab and repeat Steps 5 and 6 to see whether the filename appears there.**

8. **Click the Startup tab and look for the filename there; repeat Steps 5 and 6 as necessary.**

The filename appears as part of a pathname, as shown in Figure 1-3. Be sure to check the last part of the pathname.

9. **Click OK to close the System Configuration Utility window.**

10. **Choose whether to restart the computer now or later.**

The changes don't take effect until you restart the computer.

Figure 1-3:
Locating
files that no
longer exist.

If the message doesn't appear when you restart Windows, you fixed the problem. When it still appears, you have to check into other solutions, such as reinstalling any recently installed software. Remember to reactivate whatever you disabled in the System Configuration Utility window.

✦ The missing file may also be due to damage to the hard drive. See Book VI, Chapter 2 on disk maintenance. If the hard drive is suspect, though, other errors will occur in addition to a missing file.

✦ When you use the System Configuration Utility to modify a start-up file, you may see a warning displayed when Windows restarts. You can dismiss the warning — be sure to put a check mark in the box so that the warning doesn't appear again.

A Smattering of Annoying Things in Windows

Despite my admonition in this book's Introduction, I shall now devote the following few pages to some items that lie on the border between troubleshooting and annoying. I'm writing this section because I'm a nice guy, not because I tend to go back on my word when writing computer books.

The following items are specific to Windows as a trouble source. If an item isn't listed here, it can probably be found elsewhere in this book.

Blue screen of death

One troublesome item is so loathed that it has its own acronym: BSOD, or Blue Screen of Death. Fortunately, Mr. BSOD isn't as common as he was in years past, but he's still around. Offend Windows in some extreme way and see the BSOD for yourself. If the computer could make a sound at that point, it would be the sound of a gag.

The possible causes of a BSOD are numerous:

✦ Malfunctioning RAM

✦ Overheating

✦ Bad voltage supply

✦ Faulty hardware

✦ Overclocking or other extending system abilities

✦ Poorly written software — specifically, device drivers

✦ Operating system bugs and other types of bugs

In most cases, there's nothing you can do but restart the computer.

Some BSOD error messages you can recover from, such as removing media that is in use by the computer. In that case, you can restore the media to (you hope) remedy the situation.

If possible, you can check the Microsoft Knowledge Base for information about the BSOD. If you see an error number, you can refer to it using the Microsoft Web page; for example:

```
Stop 0x0000001e
```

This line of text might be part of a BSOD message. In that case, visit the Microsoft Knowledge Base at `http://support.microsoft.com` and search for the text **Stop 0x0000001e**.

BSODs are often thought of as a Windows-only thing, but other operating systems and even game consoles use similar techniques. The most humorous examples of the BSOD appear on advertising displays and other terminals. Microsoft engineers once gave a demonstration when the computer malfunctioned and a huge BSOD appeared on the projection screen. Oh, how I laughed.

Silence the sounds

Windows plays a host of musical ditties as you go about your day. Sometimes, those sounds serve as important reminders or warnings. At other times, those sounds annoy the heck out of you. Disabling the sounds can be done without muting the entire sound system. Here's how:

1. **Open the Sound icon or the Sound and Audio Devices icon in the Control Panel.**

The icon is called Sound in Windows Vista, and Sound and Audio Devices in Windows XP.

2. **Click the Sounds tab in the dialog box that appears.**

   You see a list of all the events and activities in Windows that have sounds associated with them, as shown in Figure 1-4.

Figure 1-4:
The Sound dialog box in Windows Vista.

**Book II
Chapter 1**

**Windows Gone
AWOL**

3. **Choose an event to silence.**

   For example, the Windows Logon sound that plays every silly time you log in to Windows.

   If you're unsure of the event but remember the sound, use the Test or Play button in the dialog box to preview the sound for a selected event.

4. **From the Sounds drop-down list, choose (None).**

   Multiple sounds are available from the Sounds drop-down list. The top option, however, is (None), which is blissful silence.

5. **Repeat Steps 3 and 4 as often as necessary.**

6. **Click OK to cement your choices, and close the window.**

7. **(Optional) Close the Control Panel window.**

One sound that may not be obvious is the Windows Startup sound. To disable it in Windows Vista, remove the check mark by the box Play Windows Startup Sound in the Sound dialog box (refer to Figure 1-4). In Windows XP, assign the (None) sound to the item titled Start Windows.

Anchor the taskbar

For several versions of Windows, the taskbar was highly mobile. I suppose that the programmers considered taskbar mobility high on the list of user desires. I mean, Microsoft enjoys throwing way too many options at users. Regardless of the reasons, it was too easy to move the taskbar to any side of the display.

Windows Vista and Windows XP both come with the taskbar locked. It won't move unless you unlock the taskbar.

To unlock the taskbar, right-click a blank part of the taskbar and choose the command Lock the Taskbar. The command has a tiny check mark by it when the taskbar is locked. When the taskbar is unlocked, its appearance changes. Toolbars grow visible "handles," and in Windows XP the taskbar grows a fat upper lip.

Move the taskbar

The taskbar can be moved only when it's unlocked. After it's unlocked, you can drag the taskbar to any edge of the screen: top, left, right, or bottom. Note, however, that most documentation assumes that the taskbar is on the bottom of the screen. That position implies that the Start button is in the lower-left corner and that the notification area is in the lower-right corner.

Some people cannot get the hang of moving the taskbar. If that's you, watch Video 213 to see me demonstrate it onscreen.

Resize the taskbar

The taskbar can be taller or shorter, but you cannot resize the taskbar unless you unlock it first. See the earlier section "Anchor the taskbar" for details.

After the taskbar is unlocked, you can resize it by pointing the mouse at the taskbar's top edge. Drag the mouse in toward the center of the screen to make the taskbar fatter; drag the mouse outward to make it thinner.

Review Video 214 to see a taskbar-resizing demonstration.

Lock the taskbar when you're done setting its size.

The taskbar size is also affected by the size of the icons on the Quick Launch bar. To set those icon sizes, follow these steps:

1. **Unlock the taskbar.**

    Refer to the directions in the section "Anchor the taskbar," earlier in this chapter.

2. **Right-click the Quick Launch bar handle.**

   The handle is the graphical gizmo that appears on the left end of the Quick Launch toolbar.

3. **Choose View⇨Large Icons to set the icons to a larger size, or choose View⇨Small Icons to set the icons to a smaller size.**

4. **Relock the taskbar when you're done.**

Hide the taskbar

I've gotten quite a few e-mails over the years that I can sum up in one panicky sentence:

> Where the heck did the taskbar go!

It's there. The taskbar has two ways of hiding from you. First, the taskbar is going nowhere if you lock it. See the earlier section "Anchor the taskbar" for more information.

Second, the taskbar can be resized to very, very thin — nearly invisible, but only in Windows XP. To find the taskbar, move the mouse to each edge of the screen. The taskbar's presence is noted by the mouse pointer changing to a tiny arrow head. That's your clue: Drag the mouse in toward the center of the screen to resize the taskbar.

Finally, the taskbar has an Auto-hide mode. To enable or disable this mode, follow these steps:

1. **Right-click a blank part of the taskbar.**

   The Taskbar and Start Menu Properties dialog box appears.

2. **Add or remove the check mark by Auto-Hide the Taskbar.**

3. **Click OK.**

In Auto-hide mode, the taskbar appears only when you move the mouse pointer to the bottom of the screen (or whichever screen edge the taskbar is docked to) or when you press the Win key on the keyboard. The taskbar auto-hides whether you locked the taskbar or not.

See all the icons on the Quick Launch bar

Some programs give you the option to add their icons to the Quick Launch bar. Some programs add their icons without letting you know. Eventually, you discover that the Quick Launch bar gets busy, full of icons. A "show more" chevron appears on the Quick Launch bar to help indicate and display the hidden icons, as shown in Figure 1-5.

Figure 1-5:
Quick
Launch bar
bloat.

You have two options for fixing the situation:

✦ **You can remove icons from the Quick Launch bar.** Right-click an icon and choose Delete from the pop-up menu.

You're merely deleting a shortcut, not the original program.

✦ **You can resize the Quick Launch bar.** Here's how:

1. **Unlock the taskbar.**

   See the earlier section "Anchor the taskbar" for details.

2. **Drag the handle to the right of the Quick Launch bar to the right.**

   The handle on the right is the handle for the next toolbar over, usually the taskbar. By sliding the handle to the right, you make the Quick Launch bar longer, allowing more room for the icons.

   Slide the handle over until all the icons appear on the Quick Launch bar and the little chevron thing disappears. Move the handle over a wee bit more, just to be sure.

3. **Relock the taskbar.**

Show the date and time in the notification area

The date-and-time display in the notification area can be turned off or on. Whether you want it missing or visible, follow these steps:

1. **Right-click the taskbar and choose Properties from the pop-up menu.**

   The Taskbar and Start Menu Properties dialog box appears.

2. **In Windows Vista, click the Notification tab, if necessary.**

3. **Add or remove the check mark by the Clock item.**

   In Windows XP, the item is titled Show the Clock.

4. **Click OK.**

The Start Taskbar and Start Menu Properties dialog box in Windows Vista contains options for showing or hiding four items on its Notification Area tab: Clock, Volume, Network, and Power. Alas, in Windows XP, you have to search elsewhere for the Volume, Network, and Power options.

Show the volume control in the notification area

You can view or hide the volume control in the taskbar's notification area. In Windows Vista, refer to the steps from the preceding section for information on showing or hiding the icon. For Windows XP, follow these steps:

1. **Open the Sounds and Audio Devices icon in the Control Panel.**

The Sounds and Audio Devices Properties dialog box appears.

2. **Look for the item Place Volume Icon in the Taskbar on the Volume tab.**

3. **Add or remove the check mark to view or hide the icon.**

4. **Click OK.**

Restore the Show Desktop shortcut on the Quick Launch bar

The Show Desktop icon appears by default on the Quick Launch bar, but there's no handy way to restore it if it's accidentally deleted.

Right away, know that you can always instantly display the desktop by using the Win+D key combination. You don't really need the icon.

Okay. You're desperate. I can respect that. But note that these steps are extremely technical and work only in Windows XP:

1. **Start the Notepad application.**

From the Start menu, choose All Programs⇨Accessories⇨Notepad.

2. **Type the text exactly as shown here:**

```
%HOMEDRIVE%
cd "%USERPROFILE\Application Data\Microsoft\Internet
    Explorer\ Quick Launch"
echo [shell] > "Show Desktop.scf"
echo command=2 >> "Show Desktop.scf"
echo IconFile=explorer.exe,3 >> "Show Desktop.scf"
echo [Taskbar] >> "Show Desktop.scf"
echo command=ToggleDesktop >> "Show Desktop.scf"
```

Yes, this text is very, very technical. But typing this stuff is a lot easier than the 13 other steps you'd need to take to accomplish the same result.

3. **Double-check what you typed.**

Nothing evil happens if you make a mistake, but the solution doesn't work either.

4. **Choose File⇨Save.**

5. **Ensure that you're saving the file in the My Documents folder.**

6. **Type** Make ShowDesktop Icon.bat **as the filename.**

7. **From the Save As Type drop-down list, choose All Files.**

   This step ensures that the file is saved as a batch file, not as a plain-text file. Again, this is important.

8. **Click the Save button.**

By creating the `Make Show Desktop Icon.bat` file, you actually write a program. That program automatically restores the Show Desktop icon to the Quick Launch bar. All you need to do is run the program by opening the Make Show Desktop Icon file in the My Documents folder. If the icon disappears again, simply rerun the program file to re-create it.

Retrieve a window that slid off the screen

It seems like such a simple problem, yet I've received e-mail from readers who were told by tech support people to reinstall Windows to place a window back on the desktop. What a silly, stupid thing to say.

To move a window back on the screen, a window that may have slid off so far that you can't pinch it with the mouse, follow these steps:

1. **Click to select the window.**

2. **Press Alt+spacebar to summon the window's shortcut menu.**

3. **Press M to choose the Move command.**

4. **Use the keyboard's arrow keys to move the window.**

5. **Press Enter when you're done moving the window around.**

See Video 215 for a visual demonstration of recovering a window that woefully slid to one side of the screen.

Windows appear at odd sizes and positions

Windows remembers the size and location of the windows you open. Theoretically, the windows appear at the same size and position as they were when last opened. Theoretically.

When the window doesn't remember its size, you must manually resize it. Use the mouse to drag out the window's edges or corners.

✦ Windows doesn't remember a window's maximized size. When you *maximize* a window, you set its size to be the same as the display.

✦ Sometimes Internet Explorer windows are automatically resized, usually to display advertising.

♦ You can instantly maximize a window by double-clicking the title bar. (Double-clicking the title bar of a maximized window restores it to its previous size and position.)

Change the image viewer

I'll bet that when you open a graphics file, the program you want to use for viewing it isn't the program that opens. That's fine — you can change the image viewer to whichever program you prefer. Here's how:

1. **Locate a graphics file.**

Actually, these steps work for any file type. Technically, you're changing what's known as the *default association*.

2. **Right-click the file and choose Open With⇨Choose Default Program.**

In Windows XP, the command is Open With⇨Choose Program.

3. **Select the program to open the file from the list of programs provided.**

4. **Ensure that a check mark appears by the item Always Use the Selected Program to Open This Kind of File.**

5. **Click OK.**

Folders and icons change position

One reason that you may find folders or icons jumping around in a window is that Windows is automatically sorting them for you. Confirm whether that's true by following these steps:

1. **Right-click in the window (or on the desktop).**

2a. **In Windows Vista, display the View menu.**

2b. **In Windows XP, display the Arrange Icons By menu.**

3. **Ensure that no check mark appears next to the Auto Arrange command.**

4. **If there's a check mark, choose Auto Arrange to remove it.**

Line up icons on the desktop

Maybe you like the desktop icons all lined up in a grid, and maybe you don't. You can make the choice for yourself. Here's how:

1. **Right-click the desktop.**

2a. **In Windows Vista, choose View⇨Align to Grid.**

2b. **In Windows XP, display the Arrange Icons By⇨Align to Grid.**

When the Align to Grid option isn't chosen, the icons rest wherever you put them.

Book II
Chapter 1

Windows Gone
AWOL

Clear the desktop

In Windows Vista, you can hide all the icons on the desktop by following these steps:

1. **Right-click the desktop.**

2. **Choose View⇨Show Desktop Icons.**

Poof! The icons are gone.

Get rid of the Desktop Cleanup Wizard

Recognizing the quandary of icon clutter, Windows XP introduced the Desktop Cleanup Wizard. It was a disappointment. First, it annoyed you to death. Second, it failed to draw the attention of people who truly clutter the desktop with hordes of icons. The wizard was retired and isn't available in Windows Vista.

To disable the Desktop Cleanup Wizard, follow these steps in Windows XP:

1. **Right-click the desktop and choose Properties from the shortcut menu.**

2. **Click the Desktop tab in the Display Properties dialog box.**

3. **Click the Customize Desktop button.**

4. **Remove the check mark by Run Desktop Cleanup Wizard Every 60 Days.**

5. **Click OK to close the Customize Desktop dialog box.**

6. **Click OK to close the Display Properties dialog box.**

Turn off the Documents/Recent Items menu on the Start menu

If you don't like a list of recently opened files appearing on the Start button menu, you can disable the list. Here's how in Windows Vista:

1. **Right-click the Start button and choose Properties from the pop-up menu.**

2. **Remove the check mark by the item Store and Display a List of Recently Opened Files.**

3. **Click OK.**

In Windows XP, follow these steps:

1. **Right-click the Start button and choose Properties from the pop-up menu.**

2. **Click the Customize button.**

3. **In the Customize Start Menu dialog box, click the Advanced tab.**

4. **Remove the check mark by the item List My Most Recently Opened Documents.**

5. **Click the button Clear List.**

6. **Click OK and then click OK again to close the dialog boxes you opened.**

See the Windows Explorer menus in Windows Vista

Windows Vista marks a trend where the program design shies away from menu bars. But the menu bars aren't gone; they're just hidden.

✦ To see a menu bar in a Windows Explorer window, press the F10 key.

✦ You can also press the Alt key to summon the menu bar.

Update a window

Occasionally, files change, especially on network drives or removeable media, and the Windows Explorer window fails to reflect the changes. This isn't a problem in Windows Vista as much as it was a problem in earlier versions of Windows: The solution is simple: Press the F5 key, which is the Refresh command.

Yes, it's the same F5 key you can use to update a Web page. The concept is similar: The page contents have changed, and the Refresh command updates what you see with the actual contents of the folder.

✦ The menu command is View➪Refresh.

✦ The Refresh command works in Windows Vista as well.

Read-only files and folders

Read-only is a file *attribute,* or a characteristic that the operating system assigns to a file. In this case, read-only means that the file can only be opened or read; you cannot delete, change, or rename any file that's been flagged read-only.

To change the read-only attribute, follow these steps:

1. **Right-click the file or folder icon.**

2. **Remove the check mark by the Read Only item in the file's Properties dialog box.**

   The attributes are found at the bottom of the General tab.

3. **Click OK.**

Likewise, you can set the read-only attribute by placing a check mark in the box. This ensures that the file cannot be changed or deleted. Well, it can't be changed or deleted until someone removes the read-only attribute again.

✦ Files and folders that you copy from an optical disc may inherit the read-only status. That's because a CD-ROM or DVD-ROM is a Read-Only (RO) media. After a file is copied from the optical disc, however, you can change its read-only status as described in the steps.

✦ The solid Read-Only check box in Windows Vista refers to the file's or folder's permissions. It may indicate that read-only permissions are set for other users on the same computer. See Book V, Chapter 3 for more information on permissions.

The message "Your activation period has expired" appears

Windows is software, and Microsoft doesn't give it away. To ensure that you're using a copy of Windows that wasn't stolen or illegally reproduced by a disreputable dealer, Windows must be activated to remain functional.

Normally, activation is automatic. It might be done for you by the dealer or if you ordered the PC direct from the factory. It might be done when you initially configure Windows. If not, you're reminded.

You can activate Windows over the Internet or by phoning the telephone number displayed on the screen.

You *must* activate Windows to continue using your computer. There's no work-around. If you don't activate in time, the operating system ceases to function. That's not an error — it's Microsoft protecting its interests.

Icons go missing

As long as you know you haven't deleted the icon, it's probably still where you left it. Sometimes icons overlap. One icon may be hidden behind another. To fix the problem, you can either auto-arrange the icons in the window or align the icons to a grid.

See the earlier section "Folders and icons change position" for information on using Auto Arrange.

See the earlier section "Line up icons on the desktop" for information on aligning icons to a grid. (Those directions there also apply to a window: just right-click in the window rather than on the desktop in Step 1.)

What file is this?

There's a temptation to peek around in a computer. I do it all the time. I even did it when I was new to computers. But there's also a danger.

The danger is that it's a bad thing to delete or change any file you didn't create yourself. Just because you don't understand a file or you feel you can delete the file and don't see any immediately change doesn't mean that the computer is okay. So my first piece of advice is this:

Don't delete any file you didn't yourself create.

Likewise, don't rename, move, or modify any file you didn't create.

To sate your temptations, you may occasionally try to open a file just because you're curious. If the file is a program, the program runs. Generally speaking, any program that can foul up a computer gives you a warning before it starts up the virtual chainsaw. Other files, you may try to open and see a dialog box. But I don't want you to get ahead of yourself.

First thing to note: The reason that the file doesn't open is that your computer lacks the software to open the file. That's a fact. If someone e-mailed you the file, e-mail them back and explain that you cannot open the file. Your situation isn't your own fault; they need to send the file in the proper format.

Second thing to note: Some files aren't worth opening. Don't even try. The file may just be binary code that a human wouldn't understand or appreciate anyway.

When the mood hits you, however, you do have a choice: In Windows XP, you see a dialog box with an Open With button. Click that button. That opens the same type of dialog box displayed immediately by Windows Vista and shown in Figure 1-6.

Figure 1-6:
Windows
Vista is
concerned
about the
file you
opened.

In the dialog box shown in the figure, you can choose the option Use the Web Service to Find the Correct Program, but the odds are good that the search turns up empty. I recommend choosing the section option, Select a Program from a List of Installed Programs. When you do, you see the Open With dialog box, shown in Figure 1-7.

Figure 1-7: The Open With dialog box, Windows Vista flavor.

The Open With dialog box is used to *open* a file *with* a specific program.

The first thing to do is remove the check mark by the option Always Use the Selected Program to Open This Kind of File. When you fail to do so, you perform the process of *file association,* which probably isn't wise to do at this point.

One of the programs listed in the window (refer to Figure 1-7) *might* open the file in a readable state. My suggestion is to try Notepad first. Notepad can easily view text files, and many mystery files are text files.

When Notepad doesn't work, you can try Internet Explorer, which recognizes a wide swath of different programs. If that doesn't work, my heartfelt advice is to give up. Really.

Chapter 2: Programs, Processes, and Services

In This Chapter

✔ Controlling programs in Windows

✔ Viewing processes and services

✔ Stopping something run amok

✔ Dealing with `svchost.exe` and `rundll32.exe`

✔ Halting start-up programs

✔ Understanding blocked start-up programs

*I*n the Mighty Battle of Engineers, the hardware side enjoys blaming the software side for all its woes. With equal gusto, the software side relishes pointing its boney finger of discontent back at the hardware people. As someone in the middle, it's your job not to take sides, but merely to know when to duck. For those times when you do need to venture over to the software side for some troubleshooting, this chapter serves as your guide. Just keep in mind that it's the software you're trying to fix here; hardware is covered in Book I.

What's an Application? What's a Process? What's a Service?

When you get into software troubleshooting in Windows, you discover that the term *software* is too general. Sure, you can use the word *program* to describe files that contain code or computer instructions. But to troubleshoot, you need to know some weird terms, how those weird terms are used, and where to control things. That's what you find in this section.

Don't let the technology baffle you! Although the material can get a bit nerdy, you must constantly remember that you, the human, are in charge of your computer.

Understanding the weird terms

Generally speaking, the kingdom of software includes all computer programs. A computer program is simply a file that contains instructions that tell the computer's hardware to do something. But when it comes time to understand how programs work in Windows, you need to understand three terms:

Application: An application is something that you, the user, start in Windows. Microsoft Word, for example, is an application. Internet Explorer is an application. Even a tiny utility you run is an application. If you started it, Windows calls it an application.

Process: A process is a program that Windows runs, or that runs automatically as part of the start-up process. Unlike applications, which show up on the taskbar and appear as windows on the screen, a process may run invisibly. Some processes, however, appear as tiny icons in the notification area.

Service: A service is a task carried out by either an application or a process. A single process can sponsor multiple services. For example, an antivirus program may run as a process (because it's started automatically), and it may sport several services that monitor your computer for signs of infection.

Basically, applications and processes are the same thing — the only difference is whether you started it or Windows started it. Services can belong to either applications or processes. Pretty much everything is interconnected.

Most people become confused between processes and services. Just remember that a process is a program and a service is what the program does — its task.

To better understand these strange terms, you can visit the Windows Task Manager, as covered in the next section.

Visiting the Task Manager

Windows is a *multitasking* operating system: It can do several things at once. In fact, the typical Windows PC is running about three dozen processes when it's just sitting there. Yes, modern computers are busy pretty much all the time. Most processes sit and wait, but they're in there.

Every program that's running is referred to as a *task;* hence, the term *multitasking.* To view the tasks taking place in your computer, the Task Manager window is used, as shown in Figure 2-1.

To summon the Task Manager in Windows Vista, press Ctrl+Shift+Esc.

To summon the Task Manager in Windows XP, press Ctrl+Alt+Delete.

In the Task Manager window, if necessary, click the Applications tab. The programs listed are programs you started or windows you opened.

Click the Processes tab to display all programs running in Windows, including the applications you opened (shown on the Applications tab) as well as processes being run by Windows itself. (Refer to Figure 2-1 for an illustration of the Processes tab.)

Figure 2-1:
The
Windows
Vista Task
Manager.

There are only a few differences between the Windows Vista and Windows XP versions of the Task Manager. First, on the Processes tab, Windows Vista contains an extra column, Description, which isn't available in Windows XP. Second, Windows Vista also features a Services tab, which Windows XP lacks.

The Task Manager window is special: It floats over every other window on the screen. Even when you click another window or try switching windows (by pressing Alt+Tab), the Task Manager stays on top. You can change this behavior by choosing Options➪Always On Top from the Task Manager's menu bar.

✦ Each window you open in Windows Explorer appears as its own entry in the Task Manager's Applications tab. Likewise, when you have multiple windows open in a single application, such as Excel, each window appears as its own entry. In a way, items on the Applications tab merely echo buttons found on the taskbar.

✦ The only window that doesn't appear in the Application window is the Task Manager itself.

✦ The nerdy way to open the Task Manager is to type **taskmgr** in the Run dialog box. Press Win+R first to summon the Run dialog box.

Understanding the Application/Process relationship

A connection exists between the items on the Task Manager's Applications tab and the items on the Processes tab. The applications are merely superficial; the process actually does the work in Windows. Follow these steps:

1. **Open the Task Manager.**

Refer to the preceding section for directions.

2. **Press Win+E to open a Windows Explorer window.**

Don't worry if you can't see the window behind the Task Manager; this is just a demonstration.

3. **Click the Applications tab in the Task Manager window, if necessary.**

4. **Right-click the Computer or My Computer window item, which represents the Windows Explorer window you opened in Step 2.**

5. **Choose Go to Process from the shortcut menu.**

The Task Manager window switches to the Process tab, highlighting the program `explorer.exe`, which is the name of the Windows Explorer program. Windows Explorer "runs" the Computer or My Computer window that you opened.

6. **Switch back to the Applications tab.**

7. **Click to select the Computer or My Computer window you opened in Step 2.**

8. **Click the End Task button.**

The Computer or My Computer window closes.

The End Task button sends the "you are done" signal to a program, just as though you closed the program's window — same thing.

Viewing the whole mess o' processes

Windows runs a lot of processes. Normally, the Task Manager window displays only the processes that relate to your account in Windows. To see the whole lot of them, including processes that Windows runs but doesn't want you to mess with, do this:

In Windows Vista, click the button Show Processes from All Users. Click the Continue button or type the Administrator's password when prompted.

In Windows XP, place a check mark by the item Show Processes from All Users.

The height of the list of items shown on the Processes tab grows slightly. You see a few more items in the list. Here are some things you can do:

✦ To sort the list by process name, click the Image Name column heading.

✦ Sort the list by the CPU column to find out how much processor time is being used by various processes. In Windows Vista, ensure that the triangle at the top of the CPU column is pointing upward to see the most time-consuming processes listed first.

+ Notice that the System Idle Process might be using a vast amount of the CPU's time — sometimes up to 99 percent. That's normal. Running the System Idle Process is what the computer does when it's not doing anything else. That's probably because the computer doesn't have access to cable television.

+ The process list is also one way you can discover viruses and Trojan horses in your computer. But don't go hunting now. Refer to Book IV, Chapter 4 for directions on how to properly rid your system of nasty programs.

+ Yes, the End Process button is used to kill off a highlighted process. Don't use that button randomly, because it adversely affects your PC.

Enjoying the services

Windows Vista's Task Manager window features a Services tab, something that the Task Manager in Windows Vista lacks. Of course, that doesn't mean that Windows XP lacks services; it only means that you need to look elsewhere to find them.

To view services running on your PC, follow these steps:

1. **Open the Administrative Tools icon in the Control Panel.**

2. **Open the Services icon.**

3. **In Windows Vista, click the Continue button or type the Administrator's password to continue.**

The Services console is shown in Figure 2-2.

4. **Click a service to select it.**

A description of the highlighted service is displayed in the console window (refer to Figure 2-2). Some services can also be started or stopped when they're selected.

Figure 2-2:
The
Services
console.

5. **Double-click a service to view detailed information in its Properties dialog box.**

   The General tab in the service's Properties dialog box has options for starting, stopping, and pausing the service. It also contains a Path to Executable entry, which references the process (program) that's responsible for running the service.

6. **Close the service's Properties dialog box.**

7. **Close the Services window.**

The shortcut to the Services console from the Task Manager in Windows Vista is to click the Services tab and then click the Services button. Type the Administrator's password or click the Continue button — you know the drill.

  ✦ One key issue with services is that your PC probably doesn't need to run all of them. Running unnecessary services only slows down your PC. Chapter 4 discusses which services to disable; disabling services can not only improve performance but also reduce some security risks.

  ✦ In Windows Vista, you can right-click a service shown on the Task Manager's Services tab and choose the Go to Process command to see which process is running that particular service.

Ending a stuck program

In a victory for hardware engineers, it happens often that computer programs die. Of course, the software factions can gleefully point out that when certain software dies, other software can help remedy the situation. (When hardware dies, other hardware often doesn't help.)

A variety of terms are used to describe a program that bit the digital dust: crash, hang, torque, die, and others too foul to mention. The term used in the Task Manager window is Not Responding, as shown so disappointingly in Figure 2-3.

Seeing that *Not Responding* text in the Status column is a surefire bet that the program has achieved an unrecoverable state of existence. You can dispense with the problem as follows:

1. **Summon the Task Manager window (if necessary).**

2. **Click to select the program that isn't responding.**

3. **Click the End Task switch.**

4. **If necessary, click the End Now button, if another dialog box appears.**

5. **Close the Task Manager window.**

Sometimes Windows itself may detect and halt whacked-out programs for you, especially in Windows Vista. You may see a disappointing dialog box like the one shown in Figure 2-4 in that case.

After killing the program, you may be allowed to send an error report back to Microsoft. Whether you do is up to you; sending the report doesn't fix the program, nor does it guarantee that anyone will ever look at the report.

Figure 2-3:
Stuck
programs.

Figure 2-4:
Windows
auto-
matically
killed a
suspect
program.

Halting a process

A process is not something you should randomly stop, especially for the time-honored reason of "I wonder what this does?" Instead, sometimes you're directed to stop a process, or perhaps you're motivated to end a process to troubleshoot problems with your computer. When those needs arise, follow these steps to stifle a process by using the Task Manager:

1. **Summon the Task Manager window as described earlier in this chapter.**

2. **Click the Processes tab.**

3. **Select the process you want to eradicate.**

   It helps if you click the Image Name heading to sort the processes alphabetically.

4. **Click the End Process button.**

   A warning dialog box appears; ending a process isn't to be taken lightly.

5. **Click the End Process button in the Windows Task Manager warning window.**

   The process is slain.

6. **Close the Task Manager window.**

A good example of following these steps is to kill off a program that runs an icon in the notification area. For example, an icon in the notification area might control special display features. You cannot find that program on the Applications tab, but it exists on the Processes tab.

The trick to discovering which process belongs to an icon in the notification area is to somehow get that icon to display a window. For example, right-click the icon to use a Show or Display menu command. After it's open, you can follow these steps in the Task Manager window to locate the given process:

1. **Right-click the application's name in the Application tab.**

2. **Choose Go To Process from the shortcut menu.**

3. **Click the End Process button in the Task Manager window, and then again to confirm the process' demise.**

The process is gone, as is the notification area icon. (Remember that most notification area icons have Exit as a command on their pop-up shortcut menus.)

Randomly killing processes can render your PC inoperable. It's not a Terrible Thing, but you need to restart Windows (or reset the entire PC) to regain control.

Stopping or disabling a service

Windows starts up *way too many* services for your computer. My favorite is the Fax service, which is ridiculous on my PCs because they lack internal modems and cannot fax anything. But sometimes you may be directed to disable or end a service. During those times, refer to these steps for the proper procedure:

1. **Open the Services console.**

   Refer to the section "Enjoying the services," earlier in this chapter, for details.

2. **Double-click the service you want to stop or disable.**

   The service's dialog box appears.

3. **Ensure that the General tab is selected.**

4. **To stop the service, click the Stop button.**

   If the Stop button isn't available (it's *dimmed*), the service hasn't started. Good.

5. **To prevent the service from starting when Windows starts, choose Disable from the drop-down menu next to Startup Type.**

6. **Click OK to confirm the new settings.**

7. **Close the Services console window.**

Book II
Chapter 2

Programs,
Processes, and
Services

It's often not enough to stop a service (refer to Step 4), so you have to disable it as well (refer to Step 5). By disabling the service, you prevent it from restarting. Of course, if you merely need to suspend a service for troubleshooting, don't disable it because it might not be the cause of your misery.

Later sections in this book discuss specific services worthy of stopping or disabling.

Services that rely on other services cannot be stopped willy-nilly. To stop them, you must halt them as Windows starts. That's a job for the System Configuration Utility. Here's what to do:

1. **Press Win+R to bring up the Run dialog box.**

2. **Type MSCONFIG to start the System Configuration Utility.**

3. **In Windows Vista, type the Administrator's password or click the Continue button.**

4. **Click the Services tab.**

5. **Remove the check mark by the service you want to disable.**

   By removing the check mark, you prevent the service from being started the next time Windows starts.

6. **Click OK to close the window.**

7. **Click the Restart button to restart Windows.**

   Or, you can click the Exit without Restart button. Just remember to restart Windows in the future.

Also be sure to check out the section "Using MSCONFIG to set start up stuff," later in this chapter.

Understanding svchost.exe

A process in Windows named svchost.exe is often a source of anxiety and woe among PC troubleshooters. That's probably because the single process svchost.exe is responsible for running a plethora of services in Windows. Yes, a plethora.

The svchost.exe process can run multiple copies (or *instances*) of itself in Windows. Therefore, you may find several svchost.exe entries listed on the Task Manager's Process tab. (You have to show processes from all users in order to see the svchost.exe processes.)

In Windows Vista, you can home in on which services an instance of svchost.exe is controlling by right-clicking a svchost.exe entry and choosing the Go to Service(s) command from the pop-up menu.

To review the full hoard of services run by svchost.exe, you can follow these nerdy command-prompt steps:

1. **Start a command-prompt window.**

From the Start button menu, choose All Programs⇨Accessories⇨Command Prompt.

2. **Type the following command:**

```
tasklist /svc /fi "imagename eq svchost.exe"
```

Type that command exactly as written. Yes, it's nerdy. I said that.

3. **Double-check your typing.**

4. **Press the Enter key.**

Quickly, text spurts onto the command-prompt window. The details show which services are being run by the various instances of svchost.exe, as detailed in Figure 2-5.

You can scroll back through the command-prompt window to review the list or simply resize the window vertically.

5. **Type the** exit **command to close the command-prompt window.**

The information displayed at the command-prompt window is just a quick summary, but it's not the big issue with svchost.exe. No, the big issue is that many of the Bad Guys out there like to name their bad software svchost.exe just to confuse and anger you.

To determine whether svchost.exe, or one of its services, is malware, refer to Book IV, Chapter 4.

```
Image Name                        PID Services
================================ ======== ==============================================
svchost.exe                      824 DcomLaunch, PlugPlay
svchost.exe                      920 RpcSs
svchost.exe                      964 WinDefend
svchost.exe                     1008 Audiosrv, Dhcp, Eventlog, lmhosts, wscsvc
svchost.exe                     1036 AudioEndpointBuilder, CscService, EMDMgmt,
                                     Netman, PcaSvc, SysMain,
                                     TabletInputService, TrkWks, UxSms,
                                     WdiSystemHost, WPDBusEnum, wudfsvc
svchost.exe                     1148 AeLookupSvc, Appinfo, BITS, Browser, gpsvc,
                                     IKEEXT, iphlpsvc, LanmanServer, MMCSS,
                                     ProfSvc, RasMan, Schedule, seclogon, SENS,
                                     ShellHWDetection, Themes, Winmgmt, wuauserv
svchost.exe                     1296 EventSystem, FDResPub, LanmanWorkstation,
                                     netprofm, nsi, SSDPSRV, SstpSvc, upnphost,
                                     W32Time, WebClient
svchost.exe                     1468 CryptSvc, Dnscache, KtmRm, NlaSvc, TapiSrv,
                                     TermService
svchost.exe                     1708 BFE, DPS, MpsSvc
svchost.exe                      196 PolicyAgent
svchost.exe                      812 stisvc
svchost.exe                     2116 WerSvc
svchost.exe                     1260 SDRSVC
```

Figure 2-5: Wonderfully trivial and befuddling information on svc host. exe.

Peeking at that rundll32.exe thing

Another problem child in the Windows pantheon of processes is something called rundll32.exe. Like svchost.exe, it draws a lot of suspicion.

The rundll32.exe program exists to run programs held in DLL files. The DLL is a Dynamic Link Library, a common set of routines used by a number of programs in Windows. To run one of those routines directly, the rundll32.exe program lives up to its name and runs the dll program file.

The problem with rundll32.exe is that it can easily be spoofed by the Bad Guys or run a process that's really malware. Book IV, Chapter 4 has more information on malware and its removal. For now, here's the command you can type at the command prompt to review the list of processes being run by rundll32.exe:

```
tasklist /m /fi "imagename eq rundll32.exe"
```

Refer to the preceding section for information on how to run this command, and substitute the text from Step 2. (It's nearly the same command.) A sample of the command's output is shown in Figure 2-6.

```
Image Name                      PID  Modules
===========================  ========  =============================================
rundll32.exe                     3620  ntdll.dll, kernel32.dll, USER32.dll,
                                       GDI32.dll, ADVAPI32.dll, RPCRT4.dll,
                                       msvcrt.dll, imagehlp.dll, ShimEng.dll,
                                       apphelp.dll, AcLayers.DLL, SHELL32.dll,
                                       SHLWAPI.dll, ole32.dll, OLEAUT32.dll,
                                       USERENV.dll, Secur32.dll, WINSPOOL.DRV,
                                       MPR.dll, IMM32.DLL, MSCTF.dll, LPK.DLL,
                                       USP10.dll, comctl32.dll, NVSVC.DLL,
                                       WTSAPI32.dll, uxtheme.dll, WINSTA.dll,
                                       LVPrcInj.dll, tvtpwm_windows_hook.dll,
                                       tvt_passwordmanager.dll, PSAPI.DLL,
                                       NETAPI32.dll, css_banner.dll, COMCTL32.dll,
                                       csswait.dll, comdlg32.dll,
                                       cssuserdatadispatcher.dll, VERSION.dll,
                                       CRYPT32.dll, MSASN1.dll, WINTRUST.dll,
                                       css_dlgcustompolicy.dll, tvttsp.dll,
                                       tcsrpc.dll, WS2_32.dll, NSI.dll,
                                       rsaenh.dll, tvt_think_res.dll,
                                       css_think_res.dll
```

Figure 2-6:
Processes
being run by
run
dll32.
exe.

As with the svchost.exe program discussed in the preceding section, the information that's displayed only tells you some nerdy things about what the rundll32.exe program is up to. Only when you know which nasty programs to look for can you confirm that rundll32.exe is running them. Book IV, Chapter 4 has the details for you.

+ The rundll32.exe program is merely the messenger. Although it can be abused to run nasty software, or you may occasionally see rundll32.exe in an error message, the program itself is most likely not the problem child. No, it's probably one of the DLLs that rundll32.exe is running that's causing you strife.

+ The original program to run DLL files was named rundll.exe. That was the filename used with Windows 95, 98, and Me editions. Because Windows XP is a 32-bit operating system, the filename was changed to rundll32.exe.

Start-Up Programs

At some point in the start-up process, computer hardware gives way to the software that eventually controls everything. Windows barges in first. As Windows loads, and afterward, more programs are loaded. These include start-up programs you configured to run automatically, such as an antivirus program or a Webcam, and then programs you want to run every time you start Windows, such as an e-mail program or a calendar. To keep things thrilling for you, problems with that software can happen anywhere on the line.

To determine that a start-up software problem is Windows' own doing, you use Safe mode, which is covered in Chapter 3. For disabling other programs during start-up, refer to the following section.

Disabling start-up programs

Lots of programs are started by Windows. These can be device drivers for special hardware, processes run by utilities, or even programs you run each time Windows starts. To determine whether any program is causing a problem, you have to be a PC troubleshooting sleuth.

**Book II
Chapter 2**

The first thing to do is to *pay attention.* Problems with device drivers or processes that load initially are often flagged by start-up error messages. For example, the error message in Figure 2-7 describes the name of a program that's not working. That's a big clue.

Programs, Processes, and Services

Figure 2-7:
A start-up program is having issues.

After you determine which program is causing anguish, you can try to fix it. In Figure 2-7, the keyword is Sonic Focus, which is a trademark and therefore obviously some type of hardware or software program. Another keyword is Intel, found in the window title. My guess is that an audio problem exists — most likely, software related. A quick search of the Internet indicates perhaps a source for new Sonic Focus drivers or perhaps online support.

The second thing to do is to guess. It's not really a bad thing to guess; when the computer doesn't cough up any solid information for you, guessing is the next logical choice. But to be successful, you have to guess methodically.

You guess by systematically disabling various start-up processes or programs, one at a time. Disable, restart, check for the problem. Eventually, you experience a time when the computer starts without the problem. When that happens, you've found the trouble start-up program and can continue to look for support or find an updated version of the file.

The next few sections discuss various ways to disable start-up programs in Windows.

✦ Keeping your computer software up-to-date is one key way to ensure that some problems are avoided. Common problems are addressed by developers, and newer versions of programs with those fixes are made available on a regular basis. (See Chapter 1 for more information on Windows Update.)

✦ Yes, it's tedious to disable the many, many start-up programs in your computer, restart, check, and then reenable. That's the way to do it, though.

Using MSCONFIG to set start-up stuff

Some people refer to it by its proper name, which is the System Configuration Utility. But because you start the program by typing MSCONFIG, I prefer to say it's the MSCONFIG program. What it does is provide a central location for controlling things that happen when you start your computer.

MSCONFIG exists in both Windows Vista and Windows XP. Common tabs in the window for both releases of Windows include the following:

General: This tab contains basic start-up options, including settings to go into Safe mode or to disable certain start-up files.

Services: This tab lists all the services run in Windows, allowing you to disable them. (Services are covered earlier in this chapter.)

Startup: This tab lists all processes started by Windows as well as processes started for your account. (Processes are covered earlier in this chapter.)

Tools: This tab lists shortcuts to handy troubleshooting tools in Windows.

In Windows Vista, MSCONFIG sports the following additional tab, not found in Windows XP:

Boot: This tab controls the operating system start-up process, including the multiple operating system selection menu and other start-up menus and options.

Windows XP lacks the Boot tab but contains tabs for two legacy items from previous versions of Windows:

SYSTEM.INI: This tab lists items found in the old system initialization file used in Windows 95.

WIN.INI: This tab lists items found in the old Windows initialization file, also dating from Windows 95.

Items found on the SYTEM.INI and WIN.INI tabs are start-up items that are included for compatibility purposes with older programs. Few, if any, of your PC start-up problems are caused by settings in SYSTEM.INI or WIN.INI.

You can use MSCONFIG to disable certain start-up items, such as those items causing problems or for troubleshooting. Those items are found on the Startup tab. To bring up the MSCONFIG window, heed these steps:

Book II
Chapter 2

1. **Bring forth the Run dialog box.**

   Press Win+R on the keyboard to summon it forth.

2. **Type** MSCONFIG **and press Enter.**

3. **In Windows Vista, click the Continue button or type the Administrator's password to proceed.**

4. **In the System Configuration Utility window, click the Startup tab.**

   The Startup tab lists all the programs that Windows starts stealthily.

5. **Disable a start-up item by removing its check mark.**

   Unless you know which item is causing the problem, I recommend removing one check mark at a time.

6. **Click the General tab.**

   Note that the start-up selection has changed on the Startup tab. The Startup Selection has changed to Selective Startup, and the option for Load Startup Items is shaded. Those are your clues that the start-up process is no longer the same. It's not bad news; you can reverse your choices easily.

7. **Close the MSCONFIG window.**

8. **I recommend clicking the Restart button to test your changes.**

9. **Wait while the computer restarts.**

   After starting up again, you may see a warning such as the one shown in Figure 2-8. More important, note whether you still have start-up problems or issues with the thing you're troubleshooting. If not, you found the culprit; you're done.

   When problems still prevail, continue:

10. **Start the MSCONFIG utility again.**

    Refer to steps 1 through 3.

11. **Click the Startup tab.**

Figure 2-8:
A friendly
reminder
from
MSCONFIG.

System Configuration Utility

You have used the System Configuration Utility to make changes to the way Windows starts.

The System Configuration Utility is currently in Diagnostic or Selective Startup mode, causing this message to be displayed and the utility to run every time Windows starts.

Choose the Normal Startup mode on the General tab to start Windows normally and undo the changes you made using the System Configuration Utility.

☐ Don't show this message or launch the System Configuration Utility when Windows start

OK

12. **Replace the check mark by the item you previously disabled (in Step 5).**

13. **Set a check mark by the next item you're testing.**

14. **Repeat Steps 7 through 10 to test that next item.**

The idea is to work through all start-up programs until you find the one that's causing you trouble.

After the start-up item is disabled, the computer should start without any problems. I do recommend that you search out the program's developer for an update. Use the program's Startup Item name as displayed on the MSCONFIG window's Startup tab to help you search for a solution on the Internet. (Windows Vista also lists the manufacturer's name, which is a boon to searching for help online.)

By disabling a start-up item, you're placing the PC into selective start-up or diagnostic mode. You may see warnings reminding you about it when you start the computer.

What about looking for start-up programs in the Registry?

The Windows Registry is a central configuration cache of weird and wonderful things. Many users innocently attribute magical and mysterious powers to the Registry. But it's nothing special. Despite that, interest and curiosity persist, often unnecessarily so.

Several locations inside the Registry list start-up programs and processes. You can visit them,

if you like; Chapter 9 deals with the Registry. But there's really no point in wasting your time; the MSCONFIG utility lists all the start-up files you find in the Registry. When you click the Startup tab in the MSCONFIG window, you're looking at a summary of every start-up file that's relevant to your account. There's nowhere else you need to go.

Finding start-up programs for your account

Like many people, you may have configured certain programs to automatically start when you log in to Windows. These start-up items appear on the aptly named Startup menu, found on the All Programs menu.

Many programs automatically put items on the Startup menu for you. You can also copy and paste the items yourself. Be careful to note that the files can be found in *two* locations. Follow these steps to train your brain:

1. **Right-click the Start button.**

2. **Choose the Open command.**

Book II
Chapter 2

A folder window appears, showing the Programs folder. This is your account's private edition of that folder. It lists only those items set up on the computer that are specific to your account.

3. **Open the Programs folder.**

4. **Open the Startup folder.**

Behold the start-up items specific to your account. Well, yes, the folder might be empty. That's because most users don't know any better, and they tend to install programs for everyone. That's the "default," actually.

5. **Close the Startup folder window.**

Now you can find where everyone's start-up programs are located.

6. **Right-click the Start button and choose the Open All Users command.**

7. **Open the Programs folder.**

8. **Open the Startup folder.**

Aye, there's the meat! Shortcut icons in the Startup folder window represent programs automatically started by your computer.

To disable a program, continue with Step 9; otherwise, you're done, so you can close the Startup window.

9. **Select icons for the programs you no longer want started.**

Hold down the Ctrl key while clicking multiple icons to select each one.

Rather than delete the icons, I recommend copying them into a NotStartUp folder.

10. **Press Ctrl+X to cut the icons.**

11. **Press the Backspace key to return to the main Programs folder.**

12. **If necessary, create a new folder and name it** NotStartup.

Here are the steps necessary to create that folder, in case you're rusty in your Windows folder management knowledge:

a. *Choose Organize⇨New Folder or File⇨New⇨Folder.*

b. *In Windows Vista, click the Continue button, and then type the Administrator's password or click Continue to give yourself permission to create the new folder.*

c. *Type the name **NotStartUp** for the new folder and then press Enter.*

d. *Again, click the Continue button in Windows Vista and blah-blah-blah to continue.*

13. **Open the NotStartUp folder.**

14. **Press Ctrl+V to paste in the icons you cut in Step 10.**

You effectively moved the icons from the Startup folder, where they start programs each time you log in, to the NotStartUp folder, where they don't start them each time you log in.

Yes, in Windows Vista, you need to click the Continue button and grant yourself administrative powers to proceed with the pasting operation.

15. **Close the window.**

My reasoning behind creating the NotStartUp folder is that it's good to keep a copy of those files that once lived inside the Startup folder. That way, if you want to restore them at a later date, it's merely a matter of cutting and pasting them from the NotStartup folder back into the Startup folder.

✦ You can also create a NotStartup folder for your own account. Create the new folder in the Programs folder you open by following Steps 1 through 4 in this section.

✦ Like other items on the All Programs menu, the items in the Startup menu are all shortcuts to files dwelling elsewhere on your PC's storage system.

✦ The reasons for all the permissions and Continue buttons in Windows Vista is that by modifying the All Users Startup folder, you're changing things for other users on the computer. Because evil software might try that trick, Windows needs your confirmation to proceed.

✦ Watch Video 221 for an onscreen walk-through of the procedure outlined in this section.

Dealing with blocked start-up programs

Here's one that will bother you until you read this section and figure out what needs fixing. Have you ever seen the `Windows Has Blocked Some Startup Programs` notice, as shown in Figure 2-9?

Figure 2-9:
The
annoying
blocked-
programs
balloon.

⚠ Windows has blocked some startup programs ✕
Windows blocks programs that require permission to run when
Windows starts. Click to view blocked programs.

Try as you can to dismiss the sucker, it won't go away until you deal with the
situation.

Here's how to deal with the situation:

1. **From the Start button menu, choose All Programs⇨ Windows
    Defender.**

    Windows Defender comes standard with Windows Vista, but it's an
    optional upgrade for Windows XP (see Book IV, Chapter 4 for details).

2. **Click the Tools link at the top of the window.**

3. **Choose the Software Explorer tool.**

4. **Ensure that Startup Programs is chosen from the Category drop-
    down list.**

    You see a list of all programs that attempt to start when the computer
    starts, as shown in Figure 2-10. I say "attempt to start" because pro-
    grams of an unknown type can be blocked. That explains the message
    you see when the computer starts (refer to Figure 2-9).

    It's possible to remove or block a program in the list: Simply click the
    Remove or Disable button when the program is selected. Most likely, a
    program that's been blocked appears in the Quarantine area.

5. **Click the Tools link at the top of the window.**

6. **Choose Quarantined Items.**

    If any items are listed, they have been blocked — and most likely for
    good reason.

    You can remove the quarantine by selecting an item and choosing
    the Restore button. But do so only if you're positively certain that the
    blocked program is safe.

7. **Close the Windows Defender window when you're done.**

For more information on Windows Defender, refer to Book IV, Chapter 4. The
program is primarily a spyware removal tool, which is why it's covered in
that chapter.

Other software on your computer might also be blocking certain start-up programs. For example, an anti-spyware or antivirus utility might scan your computer's files for signs of malware. Start-up files can be quarantined or blocked by those utilities as well.

Figure 2-10:
Perusing the start-up programs in Windows Defender.

Chapter 3: The Safe Mode Chapter

In This Chapter

✔ **Starting Safe mode**

✔ **Getting out of Safe mode**

✔ **Diagnosing problems**

✔ **Troubleshooting start-up files**

*I*magine. Microsoft decided to dub it *Safe mode*. I would like to believe that the computer is operating safely all the time, but I don't think the implication here is that normal operation is actually *unsafe mode*. Instead, the Safe mode name implies that the computer can operate in a stable manner when it needs to, specifically for troubleshooting. That's the topic for this chapter.

Safe Mode to the Rescue

It is my wish that you never need to use Safe mode. First of all, it's not fun. It reminds me of the old days of low-resolution graphics and limited abilities. Using Safe mode can also mean that something is terribly wrong, which is seldom amusing. This section describes Safe mode as a troubleshooting tool for those times when you really need it.

✦ Safe mode is available for a number of operating systems, not just Windows. Some portable gizmos, such as MP3 players and cellphones, also feature a Safe mode.

✦ In Mac OS X, Safe mode is called *Safe Boot*. But Apple uses the term *Safe mode* to refer to a computer that has been started with Safe Boot.

✦ Some applications have Safe modes. Microsoft Office applications all feature a safe mode of operation used for troubleshooting. The most common reason for using safe mode in an application is to disable customized features that may not be properly implemented.

Using Safe mode

Safe mode happens in one of three circumstances:

✦ A problem looms in your PC, one that Windows detects at boot time. The computer then automatically starts in Safe mode so that you can deal with the problem.

✦ You direct Windows to start in Safe mode from the F8 menu when the computer first starts up.

✦ You direct Windows to start in Safe mode by using the MSCONFIG utility.

Starting the computer in Safe mode works similarly to the normal start-up process. First you log in, but you may notice that the screen resolution is lower than normal.

Next, you see a start-up splash screen. In Windows Vista, it's the Help page that explains Safe mode. In Windows XP, you see a dialog box explaining that the computer hard-started in Safe mode and blah-blah-blah. Close the Help window or click the Yes button to begin using Safe mode.

When you finally arrive, you see Windows in Safe mode operation, as shown in Figure 3-1. The screen resolution is low because the standard video drivers (often a source of anguish) aren't loaded. The words *Safe mode* appear in all corners of the display.

Safe mode has *three* different modes of operation, which can be set from the F8 start-up menu:

✦ **Safe Mode:** The standard mode of operation. Only the basic processes and services necessary to start Windows are loaded. Some hardware (external drives, audio, power management, and networking) don't work in Safe mode, and the functionality of Windows is limited.

✦ **Safe Mode with Networking:** The same mode as Standard mode, but with networking abilities enabled. Use this mode if you need to access the Internet for any reason.

✦ **Safe Mode with Command Prompt:** The most limited mode, reserved for people who know how to use the command prompt. (It's just like the days of DOS!) This mode is the one to use when the video adapter is acting weird, though you really need to know how to use the command prompt to be effective at troubleshooting.

Later sections in this chapter divulge the details of how to get into Safe mode and how you can use it to resolve issues.

✦ Other messages may appear as you start your computer in Safe mode. For example, you may see a notice that the network is unavailable or network drives were unable to connect.

✦ MSCONFIG is the name I use for the System Configuration Utility. See Chapter 2 for more information, though the utility is also covered in this chapter.

✦ You may notice a bonus administrator login account available in Windows XP when you start the computer in Safe mode. That's the hidden Administrator account, and it's visible only when you start the computer in Safe mode. The password is the same as for the main user account.

✦ In Windows XP, you can click the No button when you see the opening dialog box to do a quick System Restore. That's a good tool to use when Safe mode is encountered unexpectedly. Often, System Restore fixes the problem. See the section "Entering Safe mode unexpectedly." Oh! Here it is:

Entering Safe mode unexpectedly

Safe mode isn't intended to be your computer's main operating mode. When your computer starts in Safe mode automatically or unexpectedly, it's a sign that something is wrong. Do not continue working. Instead, fix the problem.

Often, an error message appears when Safe mode starts out of the blue. Address the issue as described on the screen.

Figure 3-1:
Safe mode.

If you recently updated hardware or software, the appearance of Safe mode most likely indicates a problem. Use System Restore to recover from a software upgrade (see Chapter 8). Shut down the computer and remove the hardware if Safe mode suddenly appears after a hardware upgrade. Restart the computer and if it returns as normal, the software or hardware upgrade was the problem.

✦ Do not use applications in Safe mode! Sure, you can get work done, but don't! Something is wrong with your computer. Fix it.

✦ Don't reinstall any hardware that may have caused Safe mode to appear. Instead, contact the manufacturer for tech support.

✦ Also be sure to check whether MSCONFIG is ordering the computer to restart in Safe mode, as covered in the section "Restarting in Diagnostic Mode with MSCONFIG," later in this chapter.

Getting into Safe mode at boot time

To ensure that the computer starts in Safe mode, you can use the F8 menu, which is covered in Book I, Chapter 2: Just after the computer first starts (or is reset), repeatedly jab the F8 key. Eventually, you see the F8 start-up menu in Text mode.

Choose one of the Safe mode commands from the text menu; refer to the preceding section for definitions of each command, though the top command, Safe Mode, is probably the one you want.

✦ You have to be quick with the F8 key. When you wait too long, Windows starts normally.

✦ If a bootable disc is in the optical drive, wait until the message `Press any key to boot from the CD/DVD` disappears. Then immediately press the F8 key to see the text menu.

Restarting in Diagnostic Mode with MSCONFIG

You can configure Windows to start in Diagnostic mode, which is similar to Safe mode. Diagnostic mode basically works like Safe mode, but it's something you set as a start-up option in Windows. Pay attention to these steps:

1. **Press Win+R to bring up a Run dialog box.**

2. **Type** msconfig **into the box and press the Enter key.**

3. **In Windows Vista, click the Continue button or type the administrator's password.**

4. **Ensure that the General tab is up front in the System Configuration window.**

Figure 3-2 shows the System Configuration Utility, which I call MSCONFIG because everyone else calls it that.

Figure 3-2:
The System
Config-
uration
Utility,
MSCONFIG.

5. **Choose Diagnostic Startup.**

6. **Click OK.**

   The System Configuration dialog box appears.

7. **Click the Restart button.**

   The computer shuts down and immediately restarts in Diagnostic Mode.

   If, in Step 7, you choose to exit without restarting, the computer starts in Diagnostic mode the next time you restart it or turn it back on again.

   As in Safe mode, no extra drivers are loaded in Diagnostic Mode. The screen you see is low resolution because the video drivers aren't loaded. What you have is, just like Safe mode, a good troubleshooting platform. All the same tests and procedures for Safe mode work in Diagnostic mode. In fact, I just call it Safe mode to avoid typing the longer word *diagnostic*.

   ✦ I believe that you'll find the Diagnostic mode troubleshooting method described in this section more reliable than trying to desperately stab at the F8 key during boot time.

   ✦ In Windows Vista, you can start the computer in Safe mode using the MSCONFIG utility: Click the Boot tab and then click to place a check mark by the item Safe Boot. Rather than start in Diagnostic mode, the computer truly starts in Safe mode when you select that option.

   ✦ Refer to Chapter 2 for more information on using MSCONFIG to disable start-up programs.

   ✦ When you make the change described in this section, the computer always starts in Safe mode. The only way to undo that operation is to select the Normal start-up option, as shown in Figure 3-2. Directions are in the next section.

Ending Safe mode

When you're done using Safe mode to troubleshoot, you simply end your Windows session as you normally do: Choose the proper shutdown command from the Start button menu. The computer should restart normally.

When a hardware problem persists, you may find the computer once again starting in Safe mode. That means you have more work do to. Try something else. Use the suggestions in the later section "Safe Mode Troubleshooting" to assist you.

Ending Diagnostic Mode

Just as you used MSCONFIG to direct the computer to start in Diagnostic mode, you must use MSCONFIG to restart the computer normally again. Repeat the steps found in the earlier section "Restarting in Diagnostic Mode with MSCONFIG," though in Step 5 you choose Normal Startup. When the computer restarts, it once again returns to normal operation (well, as long as you resolved whichever issue urged you into Diagnostic mode in the first place).

Safe Mode Troubleshooting

Don't blame Windows! True, some things may be the operating system's fault. Bugs happen. Windows gets updated. But most of the time, the blame for any software woe in your PC can be laid squarely on the shoulders of device drivers. The way to best determine that situation is to use Safe mode. This section tells you how.

Understanding Safe mode

Safe mode tells you one thing best: whether the problem is with Windows. In Safe mode, only Windows itself is loaded: the basic parts of the operating system. Any other software — including device drivers, start-up processes, and other programs — aren't loaded in Safe mode. This leads to one immediate, solid conclusion:

When the computer runs fine in Safe mode, the problem you have is not caused by Windows.

I might add that when the computer performs flawlessly in Safe mode, the problem is also not caused by your computer hardware. No, the problem lies in some program being loaded after Windows itself starts.

Your job in Safe mode is to determine which piece of software is causing the problem and to either update that software or disable it to keep the computer running properly.

✦ When the problem persists in Safe mode, it's most likely a Windows issue. (See Chapter 8 on various ways to repair Windows.)

✦ In some circumstances, a problem that continues in Safe mode isn't caused by Windows. These problems are hardware related. The most common one is overheating. Check the power supply. Other hardware may also be screwing up. (Refer to Book I for various hardware troubleshooting methods and solutions.)

Knowing the three problem sisters

Odds are very good that the problem motivating your PC into using Safe mode was caused by one of three things:

✦ Video

✦ Power management

✦ Networking

These three areas are known as the problem sisters. The problem most likely lies with the software — the *device driver* — used to control the specific hardware. Especially if you just upgraded the hardware or software for any of those three areas, problems can occur that thrust the PC into Safe mode.

The first thing to try is waiting. Just let the computer sit. Or, if possible, try to re-create the situation that caused the computer to crash. If the action can be repeated in Safe mode, the problem lies with Windows, not with the device.

The second thing to try depends on what happened recently. If you just updated software, run System Restore to return the computer to the point *before* the update. Refer to Chapter 8 for more information on System Restore, though be aware that System Restore is an option available on the F8 boot menu (see Book I, Chapter 2).

Finally, check for new software. Use the Device Manager as covered in Book I, Chapter 7. If there's known trouble with the gizmo, its Properties dialog box in the Device Manager tells you so. If not, click the Update Driver button to find a new driver. Also consider contacting the hardware manufacturer to see whether an update is available. (You have to use Safe mode with Networking to access the Internet in Safe mode.)

Disabling start-up files

The most frustrating problems to solve deal with start-up files. You can use Diagnostic mode to help determine which start-up files are causing trouble. The way it works is described in Chapter 2: You systematically disable one start-up process after another using the MSCONFIG utility.

If the problem persists after disabling a start-up process (or the problem gets worse), you disabled the wrong process. Reenable that process, and restart again in Diagnostic mode with the next process disabled.

Yes, it's tedious.

I used this method to determine that my PC's sound software was causing random crashes; the problem wasn't present in Safe mode and ceased to happen after I disabled the sound drivers.

See Chapter 2 for more information on disabling start-up files.

Chapter 4: Putting the Pep Back into the PC

In This Chapter

✔ Know why your PC is slow

✔ Fixing common problems

✔ Improving performance with ReadyBoost

✔ Ensuring proper settings are made

✔ Configuring services for optimal performance

*I*n a memorable commercial from the golden age of television, a rather frumpy-looking man would say, "Sometimes do you feel just plain lousy?" I honestly forget what was being advertised, but what they were selling was an existence full of pep and vigor. In our culture, we seem to admire things that are snappy, upbeat, and full of life. When your computer seems to lack those qualities, turn to this chapter for delousing.

Man, Your PC Is Slow!

Do computers run more slowly over time? The answer is no. Performance can suffer, but electronically, a computer out of the box runs just as fast as the same computer years later. What changes, however, is the computer's *experience*. As Indiana Jones once said, "It's not the years, honey, it's the mileage." This section shows you some tricks to help roll back your PC's odometer.

Understanding slow

Slow is relative, which doesn't explain why Cousin Mike took six attempts to pass the bar exam. No, slow is a measurement of time, and time relies heavily upon human perception.

A modern computer runs many processes and services. Those things take time. Today's software uses a lot of the hardware's capability. That consumes time. You add more software to your computer over time. That takes even more time. Unless you buy the most expensive and powerful computer available — and buy a new computer every six months — things take longer over time.

Although a slow computer can be acceptable, what should be alarming is the onset of *suddenly slow.* I call it the "This damn thing wasn't this slow last week" syndrome. That's a situation that needs to be addressed because it spotlights a problem that you can fix.

✦ Sadly, when your computer is more than five years old and you know it's getting slow, that's just time catching up with it. People e-mail me complaining that their ten-year-old Windows 98 computers are impossibly slow. There's nothing you can do about that, other than buy a new computer. Old computers are slow.

✦ See Chapter 2 for more information on processes and services.

✦ Newer technology is faster than the old stuff; the design, the processor's power, the speed of memory, and the bus — all these combine to make a newer computer definitely faster than your current computer. But over time, that new computer decreases its performance as well.

Testing multiple tasks

It's been written that U.S. President James Garfield could simultaneously write something in Greek with his left hand and in Latin with his right hand. That's *multitasking,* and it's a rare feat for a human being. Most of us have trouble walking while chewing gum. But when it comes to your computer, multitasking is a snap.

Sure, the more programs running at once, the slower they run. But the speed should *not* be noticeable, especially when you switch applications. If it is, your PC may not have enough memory installed. Try this simple test:

1. **Start up a few programs.**

Some programs are memory hogs, especially the larger applications, such as anything in Microsoft Office or Adobe Photoshop, or perhaps a video editing program, such as Windows Movie Maker. Start up some programs and don't close them. You want to have a host of programs running all at once (which Windows easily handles).

2. **Press Ctrl+Esc to switch between each running program.**

Like the Alt+Tab key combo, Ctrl+Esc methodically plods through each program window you have open. Keep pressing Ctrl+Esc to cycle through the clutch of programs you opened.

3. **Observe any delay in the program switching.**

When you experience a delay or you can hear the hard drive crunch away, your PC doesn't have enough memory to properly multitask those applications.

4. **Close any of the applications you don't need.**

What you're experiencing is the computer making up for a lack of RAM. Windows avoids the Out of Memory error message by swapping out chunks of memory to disk storage. That's the delay you experience when switching programs.

There's nothing wrong with chunks of memory being swapped to disk and back. It's a common solution, and it even has a name you've probably heard: *virtual memory*. It's covered in the next section. Keep in mind that virtual memory is really a software workaround for a hardware problem.

To truly resolve the issue, pack your PC with more memory. Refer to Book I, Chapter 8 for information on adding RAM to your computer. A more convenient solution, however, is to use ReadyBoost. See the section "Using ReadyBoost," later in this chapter.

✦ Windows XP requires at least 512MB of memory to function at a minimum level.

✦ Windows Vista requires at least 1GB of memory. I don't recommend buying a Windows Vista computer with less than 2GB of memory installed.

✦ Beyond Windows, the applications you run also require memory. The amount needed is listed on the side of the software box. I advise you use the recommended value as opposed to the minimum suggested value.

Checking virtual memory

Virtual memory is disk storage that's used to supplement the actual memory (RAM) in your PC. As described in the preceding section, when memory resources get low, chunks of memory are quickly written to disk. The memory that's written is then freed for other purposes. Windows manages virtual memory, so it's not something you have to fuss over.

Okay, so you want to fuss over it anyway. Follow these steps:

1. **Press Win+Break to quickly summon the System window or the System Properties dialog box.**

2. **In Windows Vista, click the Advanced System Settings link and then click the Continue button or type the administrator's password to proceed.**

3. **Click the Advanced tab in the System Properties dialog box.**

4. **In the Performance area, click the Settings button.**

The Performance Options dialog box appears.

5. **Click the Advanced tab in the Performance Options dialog box.**

   Information about virtual memory appears near the bottom of the dialog box. The *paging file* is the disk image of your computer's memory. Its size is set by Windows for optimal performance based on your computer's configuration.

   Honestly, you have nothing further to do, but because you really don't believe me, follow Step 6.

6. **Click the Change button.**

   The Virtual Memory dialog box appears, as shown in Figure 4-1. Again, the settings shown in the dialog box are created by Windows; you don't need to change a thing.

7. **Quickly, before the urge to screw things up overwhelms you, click OK and close all open dialog boxes and window.**

   Do it now!

Figure 4-1: You can resist the urge to change virtual memory settings here.

The virtual memory paging file is most likely set to be about 1 percent of your PC's hard drive size. So, if you have a 200GB hard drive, you probably have a 2GB paging file. That's fine; that's what Windows probably set for you. If not, you might be able to improve performance by setting the paging file to be approximately 1 percent of the hard drive's size.

✦ Virtual memory was once an issue in older versions of Windows. People still think it's something they can mess with to improve performance. Although that was once true, it's no longer the case.

✦ In Windows Vista, you must remove the check mark by Automatically Manage Paging File Size for All Drives to set the paging file size.

✦ Having a larger paging file doesn't improve system performance. If you needed a larger paging file, Windows would allocate one for you. Trust me: The system works.

✦ Yes, if you configure the computer with No Paging File (refer to Figure 4-1), you may see those `Out of memory` error messages and experience extremely poor computer performance.

✦ Having a larger paging file doesn't make up for a PC with an insufficient amount of memory. To fix that problem, buy more memory!

Problems That Slow Down Your Computer

Your computer may be getting slow on purpose. It's not your fault. Instead, it's probably the fault of some software you have running — problem software that requires your attention. This section covers the ways to deal with that slowdown-causing software.

Unclogging the spyware

The number-one reason your computer has slowed down over the past several weeks or days is most likely spyware. Hands down, that's the reason.

Without wasting your time, the solution is simple: Install anti-spyware software. For more details, refer to Book IV, Chapter 4.

✦ Don't bother downloading spyware solutions from the Internet. Instead, go to the software store and buy an anti-spyware package. Install it. Use it. (More information is in Book IV.)

✦ Spyware is classified as *malware,* or malicious software. It isn't a virus, but it most likely arrived innocently from the Internet.

Finding a memory leak

Another way bad software can slow down your computer is when that software leaks memory. Don't bother putting a pan below the PC — a memory leak has nothing to do with digital ooze seeping from the console.

Memory leaks happen when a program you run fails to release memory it has used. Normally, when you quit a program, it says to Windows, "I'm done with this memory." Windows then lets other software use that memory. It's kind of like returning a towel to the hamper at a resort swimming pool: A program with a memory leak just keeps taking the towels, and soon there are no towels left for anyone.

You can identify a memory leak by monitoring the computer's resources. When you see resources dwindling over time, it's the sign that a program is leaking memory like some towel-snatching tourist at a summer resort.

To monitor resources, you can use the Task Manager window. The graphs should generally remain steady, as shown in Figure 4-2, especially the Physical Memory Usage History. When that line ramps up slowly over time and you haven't opened any new programs or done anything on the computer, you have a memory leak.

It's not your job to fix the memory leak; only the program developer can address the issue. For your part, you can narrow down which program is leaking memory all over the inside of the computer. As when you diagnose problem programs at start-up, you must use the process of elimination.

The first thing to do is to start the computer, open the proper memory usage monitor window (such as the one shown in Figure 4-2), and watch. Walk away from the computer. Let it sit. If the line doesn't rise over time, the memory leak exists with one of the programs you're running after the computer starts.

Next, you need to open — one by one — the programs you commonly use, keeping the monitor window open. Watch the monitor over time as you use the program. More important, ensure that when you close the program, the memory usage goes down. The most obnoxious memory leaks are caused by programs that don't quite close completely.

Figure 4-2:
Monitoring resources by using the Task Manager in Windows Vista.

Finally, don't run the culprit program again. Look for an update or alternative. If running that program is important, recognize that you most likely need to restart the computer after you run that program. Until the developer fixes the code, that's the best thing you can do.

✦ Windows XP lacks a Physical Memory Usage History graph in the Task Manager window. Instead, it has a Page Memory Usage History graphic, which may or may not indicate a memory leak.

✦ The best way to check for a memory leak is to use the Reliability and Performance Monitor in Windows Vista or the Performance window in Windows XP. (Chapter 7 discusses those useful reporting tools.)

✦ Refer to Chapter 2 for information on diagnosing start-up program problems.

Book II
Chapter 4

Putting the Pep
Back into the PC

Speed Up Your PC

The old joke goes that you can greatly increase your PC's speed by plugging it into a power source with a higher voltage. Although images of a computer blowing up and spewing sparks amuses some people, plugging a PC into a higher-voltage socket doesn't do anything for the computer; either the PC power supply handles it, or the power supply dies. Internally, nothing runs faster. Sorry.

You can, however, try a few things to get a PC up to speed. Refer to the sections earlier in this chapter for solving some slow PC issues. After you get those out of the way, refer to this section for other things you can do.

Performing regular maintenance

Your computer gets sluggish over time, especially the hard drive. To help keep the hard drive spinning light and happy, don't forget regular maintenance — especially a disk defragmentation program.

Both Windows Vista and Windows XP regularly schedule disk maintenance. Most of the time, programs such as ScanDisk and Defrag run automatically. Even so, you might consider getting replacement programs for those utilities. Refer to Book VI, Chapter 3 for information on scheduling tasks.

Using ReadyBoost

Windows Vista users can employ the ReadyBoost tool to improve system performance. ReadyBoost improves system performance by supplementing system memory and disk access with a portion of fast flash memory from a flash drive, such as a USB thumb drive. It's painless and simple, as these steps confirm:

1. **Plug the flash drive into a USB port on your PC.**

Yes, it must be a flash drive that plugs directly into a USB port. For that reason, you cannot use a media card reader with ReadyBoost, even when the media card reader is part of the PC console.

2. **In the AutoPlay dialog box, choose Speed Up My System.**

The flash drive's Properties dialog box appears, as shown in Figure 4-3, with the ReadyBoost tab up front.

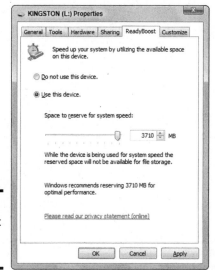

Figure 4-3:
ReadyBoost
is ready to
boost.

3. **Choose the Use This Device option.**

4. **Click OK.**

Your PC immediately starts using the flash drive to improve performance. Supposedly, the best performance increase is noticed in Windows Vista PCs with less than 1GB of RAM. Even so, whether you experience any speed improvements or not, scientists in white lab coats have promised me that ReadyBoost is working.

If the AutoPlay dialog box doesn't appear, you can configure the flash drive manually. Though it probably won't work (the computer isn't that dumb), you can try these steps:

1. **Open the Computer window.**

2. **Click to select the flash drive icon.**

3. **Click the Properties button on the toolbar.**

4. **In the flash drive's Properties dialog box, click the ReadyBoost tab.**

5. **Choose Use This Device.**

   Well, that is, unless it says `This device does not have the required performance characteristics for use in speeding up your system.`

6. **Don't bother clicking the Test Again button.**

7. **Click OK.**

See? I told you so.

✦ ReadyBoost isn't available in Windows XP.

✦ The thumb drive must be removed properly when you're done with it. (See Book I, Chapter 4.)

✦ ReadyBoost can use only as much as 4GB of memory on a flash drive.

✦ The minimum size for a ReadyBoost-compatible flash drive is 256MB.

✦ The best flash drive size to use with ReadyBoost is a flash drive with the same amount of memory as your PC.

✦ Windows Vista technology allows for only one flash drive to be used for ReadyBoost at a time.

✦ Flash memory is designed with a limited number of read/write cycles. Eventually, flash memory wears out. Don't fret about wearing out a thumb drive with ReadyBoost, however; Microsoft estimates it would take about ten years of normal use for a typical thumb drive to be exhausted by ReadyBoost.

Setting the number of CPUs in Windows Vista

Your PC most likely sports a processor that has multiple cores. There are dual core and quad core processors that feature two and four times the power of a regular processor, respectively. Plus, some PCs sport more than one processor. That's a lot of power.

To confirm that all that power is being used by Windows, follow these steps:

1. **Press Win+R to bid come the Run dialog box.**

2. **Type** msconfig **and press Enter.**

3. **Click the Continue button or type the administrator's password.**

4. **In the System Configuration window, click the Boot tab.**

5. **Click the Advanced Options button.**

   The BOOT Advanced Options dialog box appears, as shown in Figure 4-4.

Figure 4-4:
Set the
number of
CPUs here.

6. **Place a check mark by Number of Processors.**

7. **Choose the highest number from the menu button.**

   The highest number is coincidentally the number of processor cores inside your PC.

8. **Click OK to close the BOOT Advanced Options dialog box.**

9. **Click OK to close the System Configuration window.**

10. **Click Restart Now because the changes don't take place until you restart the computer.**

    Or, you can choose Exit without Restart, in which case the changes take place the next time you restart the PC.

The performance boost from setting the proper number of processors may not be noticeable, at least not dramatically. But at least by following these steps, you ensure that Windows is using the PC's hardware better than it did before.

See Video 241 to observe this section's steps in action.

Disabling unnecessary services

A *service* is something that a program does in Windows — specifically, a program that starts automatically when the computer starts. Most services are things that Windows does, and most of those services are things you don't need to have running in your computer.

Table 4-1 lists a bunch of services that you can disable to help improve your computer's performance.

Table 4-1   Services You Can Disable

Service Name	Windows Version	Consequence
Desktop Window Manager Session Manager	Vista	The desktop looks less pretty.
Error Reporting Service	XP	Your computer no longer sends system error reports to Microsoft (which it doesn't do anyway, unless you click the Send Error Report button after an error occurs).
FAX	Vista	You can't send faxes, but if you don't do that anyway, there's no point in wasting resources on this service.
Function Discovery Provider Host	Vista	Windows Media Center doesn't function properly.
Internet Connection Firewall (ICF)	XP	Your system runs faster with this service disabled.
Internet Connection Sharing (ICS)	Both	You cannot share your computer's Internet access with another computer. If you don't know what that means, disable this service.
Messenger	XP	None; this isn't the same as the Windows Messenger program.
Offline Files	Vista	You can't access the offline files, if you're using offline files, and you probably aren't.
Parental Controls	Vista	Parental control features don't work, which is okay if your kids don't use the computer, if you don't have kids, or if you don't act like a child.
Portable Media Serial Interface	XP	You cannot use a Windows Media Player–only MP3 player.
QoS RSVP	XP	A handful of programs that you don't run or that no longer function properly.
Remote Access Connection Manager	Vista	You cannot use dialup virtual private networking (VPN).
Remote Desktop Help Session Manager	XP	NetMeeting users cannot access your PC.

(continued)

Table 4-1 *(continued)*

Service Name	Windows Version	Consequence
Remote Procedure Call (RPC) Locator	Vista	None that I'm aware of.
Remote Registry	Both	You cannot modify your computer's Registry over a network.
Secondary Logon	XP	You cannot use a Limited account, but because most users are administrators in XP, it makes no difference.
Security Center	XP	The security monitor doesn't work, which doesn't affect system security.
Smart Card	Both	You cannot use a smart card to authenticate computer access. This service requires a smart card slot on your computer. (A smart card isn't a memory card.)
Smart Card Removal Policy	Vista	You cannot use a smart card for computer access.
Tablet PC Input Service	Vista	You cannot use a stylus to write on your Tablet PC.
TCP/IP NetBIOS Helper	Both	None, unless you're certain that you're using legacy NetBIOS networking programs. (You probably aren't.)
Telephony	Vista	Your dial-up networking may not work if you disable this service.
Terminal Services	Vista	Remote Desktop, Media Center, and other programs may not work.
Themes	Both	You use Windows in a rather plain, old-fashioned view. Fancy desktop features are disabled (transparency and shadows, for example).
Uninterruptible Power Supply	XP	Your UPS cannot use Windows power management. It still works if you use the UPS's own software to control the power.
WebClient	Vista	The FrontPage Web design program may not work.
Windows Firewall	Vista	The Windows Firewall doesn't run, but if you're using other firewall software or hardware, that's okay.
WMI Performance Adapter	XP	Who knows? Honestly, no one knows what this service does.

To disable a service, follow these steps:

1. **Open the Administrative Tools icon in the Control Panel.**

2. **Open the Services icon.**

3. **In Windows Vista, you need to click the Continue button or type the administrator's password.**

4. **Locate a service to disable.**

   Use Tables 4-1 and 4-2 to help you decide which services to disable.

   It helps if you click the Name column heading to ensure that the services are sorted alphabetically.

5. **Double-click the service to open its Properties dialog box.**

6. **Choose Disabled as the Startup type.**

   By choosing Disabled, you prevent the process from starting when the computer starts.

   Make a note of the service's original state: Automatic or Manual. Just in case you need to reenable the service, it helps to know how it was configured before you changed it.

7. **Click OK to confirm your choice and close the dialog box.**

   When you're concerned about compatibility, or that your computer may work improperly after disabling a service, restart Windows. When the system starts up, try it out for a while to ensure that things are working well. Then continue, or if there's a problem, reenable the service to Automatic or Manual or whatever the previous setting was.

8. **Repeat Steps 4 through 7 as necessary.**

9. **Close the Services window when you're done.**

   You can also, optionally, close the Control Panel window.

If you're the only person using your computer and it's not networked to other computers in your home or office, you can disable even more services. I list them in Table 4-2.

Table 4-2	Network Services to Disable
Service Name	*Windows Version*
ClipBook	XP
Computer Browser	Both
DFS Replication	Vista
Distributed Link Tracking Client	Vista

(continued)

Book II
Chapter 4

Putting the Pep
Back into the PC

Table 4-2 *(continued)*

Service Name	Windows Version
Function Discover Resource Publication	Vista
Link-Layer Topology Discover Mapper	Vista
Net Logon	XP
NetMeeting Remote Desktop Sharing	XP
Network Location Awareness	XP
Peer Network Grouping	Vista
Peer Networking Identity Manager	Vista
Server	Vista
Upload Manager	XP
Windows Remote Management (WS-Management)	Vista
Wired AutoConfig	Vista
Wireless Zero Configuration	XP
WLAN AutoConfig	Vista
Workstation	XP

The services shown in Tables 4-1 and 4-2 aren't complete. There may be other services you can safely disable and that, specifically, would have no negative effect on your PC. It all depends on what you do with your computer.

Of course, the possibility always exists that disabling a service has no effect on the computer and no improvement in performance. That's the case with many services, which is why you don't see more of them listed in Tables 4-1 and 4-2.

✦ Video 242 on the companion DVD shows you how to disable a service in Windows Vista.

✦ If disabling any service causes your PC to run more slowly or some programs to function improperly, reenable that service.

✦ Don't randomly disable services. Some are required for your computer to properly function. If you notice anything odd after disabling a service, reenable it.

✦ See Chapter 2 for more information on services.

Chapter 5: User Accounts

*B*ack in the era of the monotasking PC, a computer really didn't give a darn about who you were. There was one computer, one person, one program. Today, however, one computer can have many people using it and running many programs. Rather than devolve into chaos, computer scientists in white lab coats decided to have everyone and everything properly identify themselves. Thus began the dawn of user accounts, and the need for this chapter to solve problems arising from those accounts.

The User Account

Here's a computer joke for you:

> You: Knock, knock.

> Computer: Logon.

The computer wants to know who you are. Its reasons are many. First and foremost is security. Being able to confirm that you're the user you say you are means that your stuff in the computer is safe. This also explains why various services within the computer also run as "users." For example, look at the Task Manager window, shown in Figure 5-1.

Figure 5-1:
Tasks from
multiple
users.

Various tasks are designated, and programs and processes are running inside the computer. Notice how different items are in the User Name column? Each task is "owned" by a user. Tasks designated SYSTEM are run by Windows itself.

The second reason for having your own user account is to keep your stuff separate from other stuff inside the computer. Specifically, you keep your stuff separate from any other users who may be using the same computer. Not only that, but keeping all your stuff in one spot also makes it easier to back up your documents and settings as well as to transfer them to another computer for an update.

Having separate user accounts is a Good Thing.

✦ It's also important to keep a password on your account, which only helps bolster security and protect your personal files from being spied on by others.

✦ It still surprises me how two people, usually a married couple, both use the same computer yet do *not* keep separate accounts. Especially with e-mail, you should set up a separate account. No, not so that you can cheat on your spouse; it's just to keep your stuff and the other person's stuff separate. It's a sane thing to do.

✦ The computer industry and the illegal drug trade are the only two industries that prominently refer to their consumers as *users*.

Understanding the user profile

Along with your account comes your *user profile.* That's the official name of the folder in which your files and account settings are held in Windows. The name comes from an internal variable used by Windows to help locate your files and settings whenever you're logged in to the computer.

The user profile folder is given the same name as your user account name. So, if you log in as *Betty,* your user profile folder is named `Betty`.

In Windows Vista, the user profile folder is stored on the main hard drive (drive C, usually), in the `Users` folder.

In Windows XP, the user profile folder is stored on the main hard drive, in the `Documents and Settings` folder.

Other necessary folders branch off beneath your user profile folder. Some folders are visible, which is where you keep your stuff. Other folders are hidden, which is where Windows keeps settings and other information.

✦ The user profile folder is created when you first configure your account in Windows.

✦ Additional user profiles are available, one for each user account on the computer. A general purpose user profile is also available, which Windows uses to configure all accounts.

✦ In Windows Vista, a public user profile is available for sharing documents with other users on the same computer. The folder can also be shared over a network (see Book V, Chapter 3).

Configuring your account

You can modify your user profile by opening the User Accounts icon in the Control Panel. Opening that icon displays the User Accounts window, which is different between the versions of Windows.

In Windows Vista, the User Accounts window lets you manage your own account, as shown in Figure 5-2.

In Windows XP, the User Accounts window provides an overview of tasks for all user accounts on the computer. To get to your account, choose its icon at the bottom of the window.

✦ The quick way to see information about your account in Windows Vista is to click the account picture at the top of the Start menu.

✦ Most user account stuff is basic Windows operation, which isn't covered in this book.

Figure 5-2:
The
Windows
Vista User
Accounts
window.

Changing to an administrator-level account

If you tire of typing the administrator's password, you can reset your account level to something higher. Technically, you're resetting your account level from Standard or Limited to Administrator.

Here's how to set your account to Administrator level in Windows Vista:

1. **Open the User Accounts icon in the Control Panel.**

2. **Choose Change Your Account Type.**

3. **Type the administrator's password (for the last time) to continue.**

4. **Choose Administrator.**

5. **Click Change Account Type.**

6. **Close the User Accounts window when you're done.**

In Windows XP, follow these steps for the Administrator account upgrade:

1. **Open the Control Panel's User Accounts icon.**

2. **Click your account's icon, found at the bottom of the window.**

The window changes to display detailed information about your account.

3. **Choose Change My Account Type.**

4. **Choose Computer Administrator.**

5. **Click Change Account Type.**

6. **Close the User Accounts window.**

Yes, I know: Microsoft recommends that you run the computer as a Standard or Limited user. That's a joke. No security advantage exists, and in Windows Vista specifically, using a Limited account adds a level of complexity that is utterly unnecessary for a typical user.

✦ You cannot downgrade your account from Administrator. To do that, you'd have to create a new Standard or Limited account, copy over your files, and then delete your original Administrator account. I don't recommend doing that.

✦ Basically, the only difference between the Standard and Limited accounts is in Windows Vista, where the Standard user often has to type administrator passwords to get things done.

✦ The whole idea behind account levels is to limit access to key computer functions to only authorized users. The history of DOS and then Windows demonstrates that Microsoft doesn't understand how necessary that function is. Rather than have a key, *superuser* account, as with the root account in Unix, you have Standard/Limited and Administrator accounts in Windows. These account types do relatively little to protect the system, though Microsoft continues to move in the right direction.

Deleting a user account

Unused user accounts take up space on the hard drive, but you can easily remove them. For Windows Vista, follow these steps:

1. **Open the User Accounts icon in the Control Panel.**

2. **In Windows Vista, choose Manage Another Account and then type the administrator's password or click the Continue button.**

3. **Choose the account to remove.**

4. **In Windows Vista, choose Delete the Account.**

5. **Click the Delete Files button.**

6. **Click the Delete Account button.**

7. **Close the User Accounts window.**

It's gone.

Also see Book VI, Chapter 2 for information on increasing disk storage space.

Disabling the Guest account

For security reasons, I highly recommend that you remove the Guest account and guest access on your PC. Here's how:

1. **Open the User Accounts icon in the Control Panel.**

2. **In Windows Vista, choose Manage Another Account and then type the administrator's password or click the Continue button.**

If you see that the Guest account is already off, there's nothing else for you do to; go to Step 5.

3. **Choose the Guest account.**

4. **Click the link Turn Off the Guest Account.**

5. **Close the User Accounts window.**

The Guest account is normally off. Even so, I don't recommend that you turn it on to have Cousin Dave or Aunt Wilma use your computer while they visit. Direct anyone wanting to use your computer to buy a laptop computer, and especially to get a copy of my book *Laptops For Dummies* (Wiley Publishing). Thank you.

Finding the secret Administrator account

Your computer has a secret Administrator account that's set up when Windows is first installed. The secret administrator's account is used only for troubleshooting. You see it available in Windows XP when you start the computer in Safe mode. Otherwise, the secret administrator's account appears when you use the Recovery Console or start the computer in Repair mode.

See Chapter 3 for details on Safe mode. See Chapter 8 for more information on repairing Windows.

Changing the Windows XP logon

Windows XP has two types of logon screens. The standard one uses the graphical images, which you click and then (optional) enter a password. A second, more technical prompt is available, as shown in Figure 5-3.

Some say that the technical prompt is more secure. In a way, it's just as secure as putting a padlock on something wrapped in cellophane. Regardless, here's how to change the Windows XP login prompt:

1. **Open the User Accounts icon in the Control Panel.**

2. **Choose Change the Way Users Log On or Off.**

Figure 5-3:
The nerdy
Windows
XP logon.

3. **Remove the check mark by the Use the Welcome Screen option.**

   When the check mark is removed, the nerdy Windows XP logon is used (refer to Figure 5-3).

4. **Click the Apply Options button.**

5. **Close the window.**

The changes take effect the next time you need to log in to Windows.

Avoiding the Windows XP Logon

It's possible to start Windows XP without ever seeing the logon screen or having to enter a password. I don't recommend using your computer that way. Passwords are important. Computer security is important. But if you insist:

1. **Open the User Accounts icon in the Control Panel.**

2. **Choose your account.**

3. **Choose the link Remove My Password.**

4. **Type your account's password.**

5. **Click the Remove Password button.**

6. **Close the User Accounts window.**

The next time you restart the computer, Windows XP immediately displays the desktop.

✦ This trick works only when yours is the only account on the computer.

✦ I don't recommend removing your account password. Not using a password for a computer is a relic from the low-tech, low-security type of computing of the past. If you plan to buy a new computer, you *will* use a password and you *will* log in.

Ode to the Password

Oh, I could rant on and on about how passwords are important and all that jazz. If you appreciate the value of a password, you do. If you don't, if you're one of the millions who casually use the password `password` or something equally silly, skip this section at your own peril.

Creating a strong password

Embrace the password! Don't try to avoid it. Instead, concentrate on creating and using a slew of good, strong passwords. Here are the three requirements your password must meet to make it nice and strong:

+ The password has to be at least eight characters long, and preferably longer.

+ The password must contain a combination of both letters and numbers.

+ The password must contain at least one uppercase letter or one lowercase letter.

Additionally, you should use a separate password for each account you have: Windows, Internet, e-mail, Web pages, and so on. Using the same password for everything means that if you slip up, or have to release that password, you need to change all your accounts.

It's recommended that you change passwords at least once every three months. Although I don't change all my passwords every three months, I do change my online banking and financial passwords often.

To assist you in creating a strong password, this Web site, provided by Microsoft, helps you check whether any given password is strong:

`www.microsoft.com/protect/yourself/password/checker.mspx`

I recommend creating your password by using two common words separated by numbers, or perhaps two common numbers separated by a word. Capitalize one of the letters, and you should be set with a good, strong password.

+ Some passwords can contain characters other than letters and numbers. For example, the Windows logon password can contain just about any symbol you can type on the keyboard.

+ I recommend writing down your password. Nope, not in a computer file. Instead, write down the password somewhere near your computer — in this book, for example. A better location is in a place with other writing, such as a recipe folder or an address book. A password innocuously stuck in the middle of your favorite recipe is obvious to you but not to anyone else.

Changing your account password

To change your account password in Windows, adhere to these steps:

1. **Open the User Accounts icon in the Control Panel.**

2. **In Windows XP, choose your account from the bottom of the window.**

3. **Choose Change Your Password.**

    It's titled Change My Password in Windows XP.

4. **Type your current password.**

5. **Type the new password.**

6. **Type the new password again to confirm that you can, indeed, type the same thing twice.**

7. **Enter a password hint.**

    It isn't secure to make the hint the same as the password or to place the password into the hint text.

8. **Click the Change Password button.**

9. **Close the User Accounts window.**

Book II
Chapter 5

User Accounts

You probably use passwords all over the place in your computer and on the Internet. The methods for changing those passwords vary. For programs on your computer, such as your e-mail program, use that program's Options or Setup window to configure the e-mail account password.

Recovering your password

Honestly, forget it: If you lose your password, you're screwed. Write down the password if you tend to forget it. Refer to the section "Creating a strong password," earlier in this chapter. A password is something you should never lose.

Windows Vista offers a tool where you can create a Password Reset disk, though it's really a thumb drive. Although it doesn't recover your password, it does let you reset it, which lets you back into your account. Here's the lowdown for creating the Password Reset disk:

1. **Plug the USB thumb drive into your PC console.**

    It can be any USB drive, or even a media card. Attach it now. Do it! Don't delay!

2. **If an AutoPlay dialog box appears, dismiss it.**

3. **Open the User Accounts icon in the Control Panel.**

4. **Choose Create a Password Reset Disk.**

It's one of the tasks listed on the left side of the window. If you don't see it, you're using Windows XP and you haven't really read this entire section now, have you?

5. **Click the Next button to proceed through the wizard.**

6. **Choose the storage device for the gizmo you inserted in Step 1.**

7. **Click the Next button.**

8. **Type your current password.**

9. **Click Next.**

10. **Click Next.**

11. **Click Finish.**

12. **You can safely remove the gizmo you inserted back in Step 1, if need be.**

See Book I, Chapter 4 for mass storage-device removal instructions.

See Video 251 Where I walk through creating a Password Reset disk.

Windows creates a teensy file on the USB device. The file is named `userkey.psw`. It helps you only when you need to use the Password Reset disk, as you would when following these steps:

1. **Try logging in to Windows.**

The logon prompt is where you use the Password Reset disk.

2. **Choose the link Reset Password.**

3. **Ensure that the Password Reset disk is attached to the computer.**

4. **Click the Next button.**

5. **Choose the drive containing the media used for the Password Reset disk.**

6. **Type a new password.**

7. **Type the new password again.**

8. **Click Next.**

9. **Click Finish.**

10. **Log in to Windows.**

11. **Don't forget the new password.**

I strongly recommend creating a new Password Reset disk immediately, just in case.

+ Biggest password tip of this chapter: Don't forget your password.

+ The biggest problem with typing passwords is when you accidentally have the Caps Lock key on. Fortunately, Windows reminds you when Caps Lock is set.

+ You must create a new Password Reset disk when you change your password in Windows. Just repeat the steps in this section, though after Step 9 you may be required to confirm that you're overwriting the original password backup information.

+ You can use the Password Reset disk for anything in addition to holding the password. For example, on my PC, I also use the Password Reset disk as my ReadyBoost drive. (See Chapter 4 for more information on ReadyBoost.)

+ You might be able to recover information from your account by using the Windows Recovery Console, as covered in Chapter 8. You may not be able to recover all your files or restore the password, but it's one thing to try.

+ Avoid using those password-cracking utilities found on the Internet. Sure, some of them really work; Windows isn't that secure with how passwords are stored. But many password-recovery tools are Trojan horses that will damage your computer or, at minimum, recover a password and then share it with thousands of hackers across the globe. Caveats abundant.

+ See Book IV, Chapter 4 for more information about computer Trojan horses.

Book II
Chapter 5

User Accounts

Protecting folders with a password

You have no way in Windows to password-protect a folder or an individual file. In fact, there's no way to do that in Unix, either. Some older computer operating systems had that feature, and I know darn well that many people want and ask for such a feature, but it's not available.

The closest thing to password-protecting a file or folder is to compress that folder. In Windows XP, you can assign a password to a compressed folder (or zip file archive). Windows Vista lacks password protection on its compressed folders.

Third-party utilities might be able to apply password protection to your files, but I have nothing to recommend.

The Windows Vista User Account Control

The author would like you to read this paragraph. Cancel or Allow?

Ha-ha. That was a Windows Vista joke. This section, in fact, is about one of the biggest Windows jokes: the User Account Control, which I want to abbreviate as UAC because *User Account Control* takes too long to type.

 The UAC is Windows Vista's attempt to ratchet up security. Anytime you click a link or button flagged with the Windows security logo (see the margin), you should expect a UAC to appear. When one appears that's unexpected, you choose Cancel or Deny because it might be a sign that something is trying to compromise your computer's security.

For an Administrator, the UAC looks like Figure 5-4. When you use a Standard account, however, the UAC looks like Figure 5-5.

Figure 5-4:
The Administrator's
UAC.

Figure 5-5:
A Standard
user's UAC.

There are also various flavors of UAC. Don't bother licking the screen — Table 5-1 lists the variety.

Table 5-1	UAC Levels
Level	*What It Means*
Red	A program has been blocked and cannot run. You may even see an option to run the program, but with a strict warning against doing so. This UAC, the most serious one, is colored red with a red alert shield.
Blue-Green	You're about to change something that affects all users on the system. Generally speaking, it's okay to proceed.
Orange Exclamation Point	A nontrusted application is attempting to control the computer. It's only Windows that assumes the application is "nontrusted." If you trust the program, it's okay to proceed.
Orange Question Mark	A program on the Internet wants to run a program or somehow access your computer. This warning is less serious than the Orange Exclamation Point. You may see this warning, for example, when you open a PDF on a Web page or try to view a document using Microsoft Word or Notepad.
Silver	Windows recognizes the program's publisher and is simply asking you to proceed. This less serious but still necessary UAC is basically the safe version of the Orange Exclamation Point warning.

Book II
Chapter 5

User Accounts

Try to avoid the temptation to blindly proceed through any UAC.

A UAC should be expected. It should somehow relate to something you're doing in Windows or on the Internet. When you don't expect a UAC is when you can safely cancel the operation.

Disabling the UAC

Here's something I don't recommend that you do: Disable the UAC warnings. Yeah, yeah: They're annoying. You don't like them. But after you configure Windows to your liking, they shouldn't show up that often. In fact, as long as you remember that whenever you see the shield icon, you should also expect a UAC warning, they shouldn't surprise you.

Regardless, you're probably still reading for a reason. Here are the steps:

1. **Open the User Accounts icon in the Control Panel.**

2. **Choose Turn User Account Control On or Off.**

3. **Type the administrator's password or click the Continue button.**

   Whoa! You were expecting that, right?

4. Remove the check mark by the option Use User Account Control (UAC) to Help Protect Your Computer.

5. Click OK.

6. Click the Restart Now button.

   Your computer restarts.

When the computer starts up again, *things will be different.* Passwords entered automatically for you will no longer show up. You may see other things that are unusual. Those are the consequences of disabling the UAC. If you like that, cool. If not, repeat these steps, but in Step 4, put the check mark back.

Disabling UAC Secure Desktop mode

The UAC tends to dominate the desktop. It not only beeps — it also places the screen into Secure Desktop mode: The screen goes dark and, in fact, no other program can use the display until you dismiss the UAC. Here's how to disable that feature:

1. Open the Administrative Tools icon in the Control Panel.

2. Open the Local Security Policy icon.

3. Click the Continue button or type the administrator's password to proceed.

4. On the left side of the window, open the Local Policies folder.

5. Choose the Security Options folder.

   A list of settings is shown on the right side of the window.

6. Double-click the setting titled User Account Control: Switch to Secure Desktop When Prompting for Elevation.

7. Choose Disabled.

8. Click OK.

9. Close the Local Security Policy window and the Administrative Tools window.

Disabling Secure Desktop mode doesn't reduce the level of security for the UAC. In fact, it merely allows you to see the UAC without the desktop dimming. Other programs can still access the screen, such as a screen capture utility, but that's not considered a security exploit, at least not at the time this book goes to press.

Changing the UAC beep

The noise that a UAC makes is called the Windows User Account Control, and the file that makes that sound is named `Windows User Account Control.wav`. To change that sound, you need to modify the Windows Registry. It's technical. Proceed with caution:

1. **Locate or create a new sound file to use for the UAC beep.**

   For example, a file like `burp.wav` is ideal. Save this file in the Music folder for your account. (That's where I save my sound files.)

2. **Open the Control Panel's Sound icon.**

3. **Click the Sounds tab in the Sound dialog box.**

4. **Select the Windows User Account Control item from the scrolling list.**

5. **Click the Browse Button.**

6. **Use the Browse dialog box to locate the sound you created or saved in Step 1.**

   For example, browse to your account's Music folder.

7. **Select the sound you want to use to replace the UAC warning sound.**

8. **Click the Open button.**

   Back in the Sound dialog box, the sound you chose is now assigned as the UAC "beep."

9. **Click the Test button to confirm your sound selection.**

   The sound should play and satisfy your sense of appropriateness to the UAC.

10. **Click OK to dismiss the Sound dialog box, and close the Control Panel window.**

The new sound file replaces the old one. Now when a UAC warning appears, your special sound, not the traditional sound, plays.

✦ I recommend using WAV files for the replacement sound.

✦ You can find a copy of the `burp.wav` file on my Web page. Go to

   `www.wambooli.com/help/troubleshooting`

Chapter 6: Unexpected Application Situations

In This Chapter

✔ Installing software

✔ Solving installation problems

✔ Removing software

✔ Cleaning up bloatware

✔ Associating and reassociating file types

✔ Dealing with older software

✔ Fixing a program

✔ Changing a program's privileges

A complete book could probably be written on troubleshooting every single program that's out there. I could easily write a chapter on each application in Microsoft Office. Stir in Photoshop, Quicken, and a host of others, and you see what I mean. Rather than write an entire library of books, I decided to capture the essence of application troubleshooting in this chapter.

Installation Issues

I doubt if there's ever been a computer that didn't need any extra software installed. Okay, some servers and dedicated computers are sold with all their programs fully installed. But for mere mortals such as you and I, installing software is part of the game. Turn to this section when the game runs afoul.

Adding new software

Shoving a new program into your computer is super cinchy — well, as long as the program was purchased at a store or somehow comes on an optical disc. In that case, shove the disc into the computer and wait. Eventually, the installation program pops up on the screen. Heed the directions. You're done.

✦ Do read the directions that came with the software. Especially for adding software with new hardware, you must know whether to add the hardware before or after installing the software. That's important.

✦ Sometimes, installing new software requires you to restart Windows; sometimes, it doesn't.

✦ Software downloaded from the Internet is installed the same way as software found on a disc. For details and help with downloaded software, see Book IV, Chapter 5.

✦ Inserting the optical disc doesn't automatically install the program, you need to manually motivate it. See the section "The program doesn't install" in Book I, Chapter 4.

Dealing with installation problems

When a program doesn't install properly, the first thing you need to know is this: *It's not your fault.*

When the error is a missing file, it's not your fault. When the disc cannot be read, it's not your fault. Keep in mind that you're not a software developer. It's not your job to track down missing files or repair defective discs.

So what do you do?

Before getting frustrated, try doing the installation again. Just start over. Reread the directions that came with the software. Confirm that you have everything you need. Then restart Windows, and proceed as before, but perhaps this time pay real attention to the messages during installation.

Sometimes, it's necessary to uninstall the program before you reinstall it. Refer to the section "Uninstalling software," later in this chapter.

To finally and formally resolve the situation, follow the money. Who did you pay for the software? Contact the software store or software developer for assistance. They owe it to you. (Of course, visiting the developer's Web site may provide you with an instant clue because you're probably not the only one experiencing the problem.)

Be sure to check the software box for updates and notices, usually found on one of those sheets of paper you're quick to throw away. I missed one such sheet when I tried to install a program and got very frustrated. When I phoned the developer, the message I heard while on hold reminded me to look through the software box for the sheet.

Resolving Windows Vista compatibility issues with your program

Microsoft maintains a database of software that doesn't really like Windows Vista. When you attempt to install such a program, you receive a warning such as the one shown in Figure 6-1.

Figure 6-1:
This
program's
got issues.

**Book II
Chapter 6**

Unexpected
Application
Situations

If you click the Show Details button, you may see a potential solution. The details are shown in Figure 6-1, and they explain that an update for Macromedia Flash might be required before installing the program. Otherwise, you can click the button Check for Solutions Online to see what's up. Don't expect happy news, however.

My advice is to *not* install the program. Check with the publisher for an update.

Banish the Unwanted

Perhaps the primary reason most people remove software from their computers is to make room on their hard drives. But even when hard drive space isn't a concern, you should feel free to evict any unwanted or seldom-used software on your computer. This section explains the details.

Uninstalling software

You don't just yank a program from the hard drive. That's bad. It's the old way to do things. Software is installed *all over,* so to remove it, you need to follow these specific directions for Windows Vista:

1. **Open the Programs and Features icon in the Control Panel.**

2. **Select the program you want to remove.**

3. **Click the Uninstall button on the toolbar.**

4. **Heed the directions on the screen.**

Follow these directions for Windows XP:

1. **Open the Add or Remove Programs icon in the Control Panel.**

2. **Select the program you want to remove.**

3. **Click the Change/Remove button that appears to the right of the selected item.**

4. **Heed the directions on the screen.**

Generally speaking, you want to remove the program — all of it. It's okay to leave some of the data files. For example, for a game, it's okay to leave your high score or character profiles, just in case you ever reinstall the game and don't want to earn all your achievements over again.

+ Do not just remove programs. Do not delete them manually.

+ Refer to the section "Dealing with phantom removed programs," later in this chapter, for information on programs you remove yet continue to be shown as installed.

+ The Programs and Features window (Windows Vista) or the Add or Remove Programs window (Windows XP) lists all the software installed on your PC. Anything not listed there is probably a virus or spyware. See Book IV, Chapter 4 for information on removing spyware.

+ A stubborn program may require manual deletion, but I don't recommend it. Generally speaking, only spyware is completely stubborn about being removed.

+ If you haven't yet installed a program but you downloaded an EXE or ZIP file from the Internet, feel free to delete it. Also see Book IV, Chapter 5 for information on downloading software.

+ Deleting a program's shortcut icon doesn't delete the program. Shortcut icons are found on the desktop, on the Start menu, on the Quick Launch bar, and elsewhere in Windows.

+ Other software you installed in your computer includes Windows Updates. See Chapter 1 for information on removing them.

Pruning Windows programs

Windows is technically an operating system. Despite that, it comes with lots of software, including some utilities, simple applications such as Write and Paint, and games. Removing those programs is done differently between Windows Vista and Windows XP.

In Windows Vista, follow these steps:

1. **Open the Programs and Features icon in the Control Panel.**

2. **Choose the link on the left titled Turn Windows Features On or Off.**

3. **Type the Administrator's password or click the Continue button to proceed.**

The Windows Features dialog box appears, as shown in Figure 6-2.

Figure 6-2:
Removing
Windows
components
in Windows
Vista.

4. **Remove the check marks by any items to uninstall those Windows features.**

   Some items in the list have subitems, which you view by clicking the plus signs (+). When only a few of the subitems are chosen, the check boxes are filled in solid (refer to Figure 6-2).

5. **Click OK.**

   It takes a while, but eventually the items are uninstalled.

6. **Close the Programs and Features window.**

In Windows XP, obey these directions:

1. **Open the Add or Remove Programs icon in the Control Panel.**

2. **Click the icon on the left titled Add/Remove Windows Components.**

   The Windows Components Wizard window appears.

3. **To uninstall a component, remove the check mark by that component.**

   Keep an eye out for that Details button. When it's highlighted, click it, and you can see various subitems. For example, choose the Accessories and Utilities item and then click the Details button. Choose Games and then click Details. Only at the lowest level can you remove individual programs (such as Minesweeper) and Windows components.

4. **Click the Next button to proceed with removing the component.**

5. **Click the Finish button when you're done.**

6. **Close the Control Panel window.**

System Restore and unexpected uninstallation

Sometimes, a System Restore operation has the unintended consequences of messing up a program that you recently installed. The net effect is that a program may appear to be installed but is missing some vital files that were "unhooked" by the System Restore operation.

Because you probably ran System Restore to recover from a disaster, I don't recommend undoing the System Restore. Instead, what you need to do is reinstall the program that's screwing up. Doing so reconnects those items that System Restore disconnected.

Notice that some programs are missing from the list. Microsoft hides a few of its installed programs from you, preventing them from showing up on the list. Unless you want to get technical, in which case you can read the nearby sidebar, "Remove WordPad from Windows XP," I recommend not concerning yourself with items you're unable to remove from Windows.

✦ If Windows cannot fully remove a component, you're warned. There's nothing more you can do in that situation; Windows tries its best to remove the component, but portions may still remain.

✦ Don't disable a Windows feature if you're unfamiliar with it. For example, you may think, ".NET? What's that? I don't need it!" But you do. Otherwise you may find parts of Windows not working properly and end up having to reinstall the feature.

✦ I don't recommend that you remove the Notepad text editor. All operating systems need a basic text editor.

Removing bloatware

In the early days of the PC, the computer came with an operating system preinstalled, but nothing else. Well, the BASIC programming language was available. It was provided so that you could write your own software. I'm glad that those days are over.

Despite the fact that most people buy software and install it on their computers right away (or even have the software preinstalled), someone over in Marketing determined that it was a crime that PCs didn't come with more software, especially demo versions and advertising. It was a crime that required immediate justice.

Eventually, bonus software crept into the basic PC configuration. The programs accumulated into what is now known as bloatware. Basically, *bloatware* is any software preinstalled or available on your PC that you don't want. You're free to remove that software at any time, which generally frees up disk space and potentially speeds up your computer.

Remove WordPad from Windows XP

This information is technical! To unhide WordPad from Windows XP's Add/Remove Programs window, follow these steps carefully:

1. Start a command prompt window: choose Start⇨All Programs⇨Accessories⇨ Command Prompt.

2. Type **cd \Windows\Inf** and press Enter.

3. Type **notepad sysoc.inf** and press Enter.

   The Notepad window opens with the SYSOC.INF document present.

4. Locate the line that begins `MSWordPad=`.

5. Near the end of that line, delete the word `EDIT`. Keep the commas before and after it. On my computer, the line looks like this:

   ```
   MSWordPad=ocgen.dll,ocEntry,wordpad.
             inf,,7
   ```

6. Choose File⇨Save.

7. Close Notepad.

8. Type **exit** to close the Command Prompt window.

You now find WordPad listed in the Windows components you can remove (beneath Accessories and Utilities and then Accessories), as covered in the earlier section "Pruning Windows programs."

**Book II
Chapter 6**

**Unexpected
Application
Situations**

Removing bloatware is done just like uninstalling any PC software: Refer to the section "Uninstalling software," earlier in this chapter.

✦ Some bloatware arrives uninstalled. For example, online Internet services generally avail themselves through install icons in a special folder or on the Start menu. Just delete them if you don't plan on using them.

✦ Do be careful! Some of the bonus software on your PC might seem to be bloatware, but it isn't. Things such as custom utilities or BIOS upgrade tools for your PC or laptop may be required. Other items, such as error reporting programs or manufacturer advertising, aren't needed.

✦ To help you determine which manufacturer bloatware you need or don't need, disable programs before you uninstall them. (Refer to Chapter 2 for information on disabling programs.)

✦ No, you don't have to live with the antivirus software preinstalled on your PC. You can remove it, but I would recommend doing so only after any "free" or prepaid term has been completed.

Dealing with phantom removed programs

The situation isn't as common as it once was, but due to sloppy installation programs, some software refuses to leave the list of installed programs. Despite your efforts to remove it, and even if the program no longer exists on your PC, its name continues to show up in the list.

Before hurling the keyboard into the monitor, take one last stab at a technical way of solving the problem. Follow these steps *only* when a program has been removed but its name remains in the list of installed programs:

1. **Just in case, set a System Restore point and back up the Registry.**

   Refer to Chapter 8 for information on System Restore; see Chapter 9 for information on backing up the Registry.

2. **Follow the directions in the earlier section "Uninstalling software" for bringing forth the window that lists installed programs on your PC.**

3. **Make a note of the name of the program that appears in the list that shouldn't appear in the list.**

4. **Press Win+R to bring forth the Run dialog box.**

5. **Type** regedit **into the box and click the OK button.**

   The Registry Editor window appears.

6. **In Windows Vista, type the Administrator's password or click the Continue button.**

7. **Press Ctrl+F to bring up the Find dialog box.**

8. **In the Find dialog box, type the exact text of the program's name —
   the program that says it's installed but isn't.**

9. **Click the Find Next button.**

   The Registry is scoured for the matching text. Most likely, it's found in the HKEY_CLASSES_ROOT\Installer part of the Registry.

10. **Press the Tab key to select the folder containing the Product Name key.**

    The folder is given a complex number as a name. This number is Microsoft's way of making the Registry user hostile.

11. **Press the Delete key to remove the item.**

12. **Click the Yes button to confirm the deletion.**

13. **Press the F3 key and repeat steps 10 through 12 to remove any additional entries, if found.**

14. **When no more entries are found, you may close the Registry Editor window.**

See Chapter 9 for more information on the Registry Editor as well as the Windows Registry.

Cleaning up the crud

It's most disappointing after removing software to see a message along the lines of `Some elements of the program were not removed`. Ugh. Thanks for the letdown, Mr. Computer. Imagine trying to pull something like that on your mom when you were a kid, "Mom, I finished vacuuming my room, but some parts of the floor remain unvacuumed."

Some programs don't uninstall all their pieces because they might be used by other programs. That's only polite. After all, when you're done eating, you don't remove the salt, pepper, butter, catsup, and other items from the table when others might still be using them.

My advice: Don't sweat it. The program is gone and that's what you wanted.

The Good and Evil of File Association

File association is the operating system magic that makes an icon look the way it does. The icon takes on its appearance because the operating system believes that the icon *belongs* to a program. That scheme works well, for the most part. When it doesn't, turn to this section for desperate assistance.

Understanding file association

There's more to opening an icon than double-clicking the mouse.

Each and every icon is really a file. A file is merely a chunk of information stored on disk. Boring. But the last part of the file's name, the *filename extension,* is used by Windows to identify the file. That filename extension clues Windows in to the file's *type.*

The file type tells Windows how to open that file, which program to use to display the file's contents, whether the file is a program, or whether the file doesn't really belong to anything. The official term for all this nonsense is *file association.*

For example, the file named `My plans to kayak the storm drain.doc` has the filename extension `.doc`, short for *doc*ument. On your computer, `.doc` files are associated with a word processor, such as Microsoft Word. The association means that the file's icon looks like a Word document icon and that opening the file opens the file inside Microsoft Word. That's how file association works.

✦ Windows keeps track of dozens of filename extensions, noting which programs open those files.

✦ The filename extension is the final part of a filename. It begins with a period and is followed by one or more characters. Most extensions are three or four characters long.

✦ Files without extensions cannot be associated with any program. Likewise, not every extension is known to Windows. See the later section "Creating an association for unassociated files."

✦ A file may appear to not have an extension, but it's there. See the section "Hiding or showing file extensions."

✦ File association can be overridden manually. So you can choose, on the fly, another program to open a file. Or, you can change the file association permanently, as discussed in this section.

✦ One major problem with filename association is that installing a new program may reassociate existing files on your computer. For example, programs opened by Paint may suddenly be opened by Photoshop Elements. To prevent that, most programs ask before they make the reassociation. If not, you can reassign files to associate with any program; see the section "Changing file association (the easy way)," later in this chapter.

✦ File association based on filename extensions isn't a good system. It's relatively easy to change a filename's extension, which changes the association without changing the file's contents. That can cause trouble, which is why you're warned in Windows when you attempt to rename or change a file's extension.

Hiding or showing file extensions

As it comes out of the box, Windows is loath to display filename extensions. Typically, only unassociated files reveal their extensions. Otherwise, when you peer into a folder window, you don't see the extensions for files that are associated with programs.

Because I'm more of a technical-minded person, I prefer to see all the filename extensions. To direct Windows to be more forthcoming about filename extensions, heed these steps:

1. **Open the Folder Options icon in the Control Panel.**

2. **Click the View tab in the Folder Options dialog box.**

3. **Remove the check mark by the item Hide Extensions for Known File Types.**

4. **Click OK.**

5. **Close the Control Panel window.**

The filename extensions are now displayed in each folder window. That makes it easier to see, but it also adds another dimension to the filename: You now see the extension as you save and open files.

Don't change a file extension when you use the Save As dialog box to save something to disk.

Reviewing associations in Windows Vista

In Windows Vista, you can easily review all file associations on your PC. Open the Default Programs icon in the Control Panel and choose the link Associate a File Type or Protocol with a Program. After a spell, a list appears in a window, as shown in Figure 6-3. The list is populated with all known filename extensions on your computer, along with descriptions and their associated programs.

Figure 6-3:
Filename
associations
in Windows
Vista.

You can use the Set Associations window to change which programs open a file type. Here are the quick steps:

1. **Select the extension or file type description you want to change.**

   For example, .bmp represents a Windows Paint file.

2. **Click the Change Program button.**

   The notorious Open With window appears. It lists programs recommended for opening the file type — programs that are known to be compatible.

3. **Choose the proper program from the list.**

   For .bmp files, I prefer that they open in Paint, not in the Windows Photo Gallery or Picture Viewer.

If the program you want to use isn't listed, you can employ the Browse button to hunt it down. Be careful! You must be certain that the program you browse to opens the file. Don't make me wag my finger at you!

4. **Click OK.**

   The file type is reassociated.

5. **Close the Set Associations window when you're done.**

There are other ways to change associations, as covered in the next few sections.

Opening a file with a different program

When you want to open an icon using a specific program, you need to take advantage of the Open With command. It's simple:

1. **Right-click the icon you want to open.**

2. **From the shortcut menu, choose the Open With submenu.**

   Figure 6-4 illustrates the Open With submenu.

3. **Choose the program to open the file.**

   The file opens in that program.

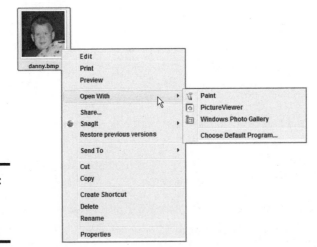

Figure 6-4: The Open With submenu.

If the program you want to use isn't on the Open With submenu, choose the last command on that submenu, either Choose Default Program or Choose Program. You can then browse for a program to use for opening the file.

TECHNICAL STUFF

Associations at the command prompt

Windows maintains two lists to do the file association tango. The first list, the file association list, contains filename extensions and their related file types. The second list, the file type list, links file types to the programs that open those files. Such a system may seem like a lot of work, but it's not.

For example, consider that HTM and HTML are both filename extensions for Web pages. Their file type is `htmlfile`. So you have:

```
.htm=htmlfile
.html=htmlfile
```

The file type `htmlfile` is associated with the Web browser, such as Internet Explorer:

```
htmlfile="C:\Program Files\
   Internet Explorer\iexplore.
   exe"
```

By associating both filename extensions with the `htmlfile` file type, you make it easy for the computer to reassign that file type to another Web browser; only the `htmlfile` entry needs to be changed. Otherwise,

Windows would have to pluck out each and every file extension that might be opened by a Web browser. So the dual lists save some time.

To review file associations at the command prompt, the `assoc` command is used. Typing `assoc` at the command prompt lists all file associations — the filename extension followed by the type. To see the type for a specific extension, type `assoc` followed by that extension. (The extension must start with a period.)

To see which programs are associated with a file type, use the `ftype` command. Typing `ftype` alone displays all file types and their programs. Following `ftype` with a file type shows which program opens that type.

You can also use `assoc` and `ftype` to create or reassign file types and associations, though it's a technical booger way beyond the scope of this book; you need to know about pathnames and the exact locations of programs, which is a bother. Instead, use the methods for file association that are described in the main text.

Unexpected
Application
Situations

REMEMBER

Remember to remove the check mark by the item Always Use the Selected Program to Open This Kind of File! If you fail to remove that item, the association is changed for all files of the same type, forever.

✦ It's also possible to open any icon by using drag-and-drop. The only limitation is that you need to see both the icon you're opening and the icon for the program file. Just drag one icon onto the other, and the file opens using that program. (That's one reason I keep an icon for the Notepad text editor on the desktop, because many text files can be quickly opened and viewed by dragging and dropping them into Notepad.)

TIP

✦ You can use the Open or Preview button on the toolbar in Windows Vista to choose a program for opening a file, or to change file associations.

Changing file association (the easy way)

To reassociate any file with a new program, follow these steps:

1. **Right-click the icon representing the file type you want to reassociate.**

2. **From the shortcut menu, choose the Open With submenu and then choose either Choose Default Program or Choose Program.**

   An Open With dialog box appears.

3. **Choose the program to open the file.**

4. **Ensure that a check mark appears by the item Always Use the Selected Program to Open This Kind of File.**

5. **Click OK.**

All files of the type represented by the icon you clicked in Step 1 are now reassociated with the program you selected.

Dealing with unknown file types

Attempting to open an unassociated file causes Windows to get all flustered, and maybe even wet itself. But rather than show actual embarrassment, Windows displays a warning dialog box, shown in Figures 6-5 and 6-6 for Windows Vista and Windows XP, respectively.

Figure 6-5: An unknown file type is encountered in Windows Vista.

Figure 6-6: Windows XP is bereft of ideas about a file type.

Here's what you do:

1. **Click Cancel.**

I'm serious. If the file isn't associated with anything, your computer cannot open it. If you received the file as an e-mail attachment, reply to the message and request that the sender resend the attachment in a common file format. That's all you can do.

You can try to search the Web for the file by choosing that option (if it's presented). That action might lead you to a Web site where you can download, say, the Microsoft PowerPoint reader or perhaps a version of Adobe's Acrobat Reader. Mostly, searching the Web doesn't work. Give up.

The option Select a Program from a List of Installed Programs (Windows Vista) or Open With (Windows XP) displays the standard Open With type of dialog box, where you can attempt to make an association. I don't recommend doing that.

Creating an association for unassociated files

Some files don't belong to any program. They're plastered with a generic icon, as shown in the margin. Such icons aren't intended to be opened by mere mortal computer users.

If you're desperate to try an association or you know that file has a weird name or no extension, you can give it a try. Here's what I do in Windows Vista:

1. **Double-click the nettlesome icon.**

Yes, you may have tried this. The annoying dialog box shown in Figure 6-5 shows up; ignore my advice from the preceding section.

2. **Choose Select a Program from a List of Installed Programs.**

3. **Click OK.**

4. **Pick a program from the list.**

No help from me here, though if you're just stabbing in the dark, the Notepad program is generally a good choice.

5. **Remove the check mark by Always Use the Selected Program to Open This Kind of File.**

You don't want to make a permanent file association.

6. **Click OK.**

In Windows XP, I generally obey these steps:

1. **Double-click the vexatious icon.**
2. **Click the Open With button.**
3. **Choose Select The Program from a List.**
4. **Click OK.**
5. **Select a program.**

   I don't recommend that you pull a best guess here. My advice is to choose Notepad and cross your fingers.

6. **Ensure that no mark appears by the item Always Use the Selected Program to Open This Kind of File.**
7. **Click OK.**

If you're lucky, the file was a text file and you see its contents. If you're unlucky, the file is gibberish, containing random bits of text or just unrecognizable junk. That's okay; it was worth a try.

Close the Notepad window when you're done.

Yes, it might be worth it to choose the option for checking the Web, but don't count on any miracles happening.

Common Problems and Solutions

After all my years in troubleshooting, I know that's there's a clutch of common questions regarding applications. Without getting overly specific and prattling on for far too many pages, in this section I give you some solutions for common software problems that I've experienced over the years.

Running older software

Microsoft tries hard to keep the current version of Windows compatible with older versions. In fact, one reason that Windows Vista is so slow is that it takes great pains to ensure that older software still runs. Hopefully, that goes off without a hitch. If not, you can try a few tricks to get older software to run. The first one is to follow these steps:

1. **Right-click the program's icon.**

   It can be the program itself or a shortcut icon. But if you choose a shortcut icon, the effect takes place only when you start the program by using that shortcut.

2. **Choose Properties from the pop-up menu.**

3. **Click the Compatibility tab.**

   You see compatibility options, as shown in Figure 6-7.

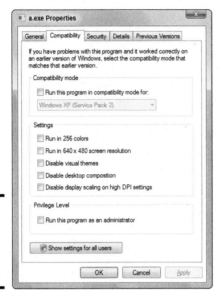

Figure 6-7:
Forcing a
program
to be
compatible.

4. **Place a check mark by the top item, Run This Program in Compatibility Mode For.**

5. **Choose a Windows version from the drop-down list.**

6. **Set other options.**

   For example, some older games may require that you set the monitor to 256 colors.

7. **Click OK.**

When you try running the program, Windows loads older versions of its files to make a good try at being compatible. It may work, it may not. What matters more than what Windows does is how the software behaves; older Windows programs were notorious for being less than compatible, even with older versions of Windows!

Yes, at some point you should just give up. Some older software, especially DOS programs or applications for Windows 95, are just not compatible with today's version of Windows.

Repairing a program

Some programs have built-in repair features. Just as you can repair Windows (covered in Chapter 8), you can often repair programs installed on your computer.

The first place to check is the Help menu. Often, a Diagnose or Repair command can be found lurking there.

 You can also try opening the Control Panel's Programs and Features icon (Windows Vista) or the Add/Remove Programs icon (Windows XP). After selecting a faulty program, click the Change button. In Windows Vista, a Repair button may even be available (on the toolbar).

When repairing a program doesn't work, your last resort is simply to reinstall it. The installation program may recognize that you're reinstalling and attempt a fix. It may even ask you to uninstall the program before it's reinstalled. That's okay: Reinstalling a program doesn't erase your files. It may just fix the problem.

Opening a Word document in an oddball format

In one Word *feature* (I won't call it a bug), the Open dialog box remembers the file format you chose the last time you opened a file. Most of the time, the Open dialog box's memory isn't an issue. That's because you open Word documents. But when you choose to open a file as plain text or in another format, you may experience a problem.

When you open a Word document and notice that the formatting is strange, or perhaps that Word tells you something is wrong with the document, immediately close that document. Summon the Open command again and note the File Type option at the bottom of the Open dialog box. Ensure that the file type matches the type of file you're opening. That usually fixes the problem.

For more information on troubleshooting Word, refer to my book *Word For Dummies* (Wiley Publishing), which contains an entire chapter on fixing Word and your documents.

Eliminating personalized menus

Some versions of Microsoft Office had the *personalized menus* feature. Rather than use reliable, consistent menus, Office would hide seldom used menu items. The result was a shorter menu, but one that was frustrating because some commands were missing.

I recommend that you disable the personalized menu feature in Microsoft Office versions 2000, 2002, and 2003. Here are the general steps:

1. **Choose Tools⇨Customize.**

2. **In the Customize dialog box, remove the check mark by the item Menus Show Recently Used Commands First.**

3. **Click the Close button.**

The menus should now display all the commands.

Getting rid of recently opened file lists

Even though that file may be gone, deleted, and dead with no possibility of recovery, its name still stubbornly appears in one of those recently-opened-files menus. For some reason, that problem annoys folks more than anything else!

The official name for that list of recent files is the *MRU list.* MRU stands for *m*ost *r*ecently *u*sed, and Windows has a lot of MRU lists.

The easiest way to purge the list is to set the number of entries to zero and then reset the number of entries to whatever it was before. For example, in Office 2007, the general steps to follow are these:

1. **From the Office Button menu, click the Options button.**

It says Word Options in Word, Excel Options in Excel, and so on.

2. **Choose the Advanced item on the left side of the Options window.**

3. **Under the Display heading, set the number of recent documents to zero.**

4. **Click OK.**

5. **Repeat steps 1 through 4 and set the number of recent documents back to 17, or whatever it was before you zeroed it out.**

6. **Click OK.**

Although this action effectively eliminates the list, it isn't picky. To be picky, you have to get technical and use the Registry Editor to find and eliminate specific filenames from the MRUs. Here are the steps to take:

1. **Make a note of the filename you want to purge from an MRU.**

2. **Press Win+R to summon the Run dialog box.**

3. **Type** regedit **and press Enter.**

4. **In Windows Vista, type the Administrator's password or click the Continue button.**

The Registry Editor runs.

5. **Press Ctrl+F to summon a Find dialog box.**

6. **Type in the Find box the filename you want to purge, and press Enter.**

   The Registry is searched for that filename.

7. **When the filename is found, delete that entry from the Registry: Highlight the filename on the right side of the window and press the Delete key.**

8. **Close the Registry window.**

The change doesn't appear until you restart the application that listed the missing file.

If the text isn't found, it's probably listed in the Registry using its full pathname and not just the filename. To aid your search, you can look for MRU lists in the Registry locations shown in Table 6-1.

Table 6-1	Registry Places to Find MRU Lists
Application	*Registry Location*
Kodak Imaging	HKEY_CURRENT_USER\Software\Kodak\Imaging\ Recent File List
Media Player	HKEY_CURRENT_USER\Software\Microsoft\MediaPlayer\ Player\RcentFileList
Microsoft Office	HKEY_CURRENT_USER\Software\Microsoft\Office*version*\ *application*\File MRU
	HKEY_CURRENT_USER\Software\Microsoft\Office*version*\ *application*\Recent Files
Paint	HKEY_CURRENT_USER\Software\Microsoft\Widnows\ CurrentVersion\Applets\Paint\Recent File List
Photoshop Elements	HKEY_CURRENT_USER\Software\Adobe\Photoshop Elements*version*\Common\settings\Elements MRU
Run dialog box	HKEY_CURRENT_USER\Software\Microsoft\Windows\ CurrentVersion\Explorer\RunMRU
WordPad	HKEY_CURRENT_USER\Software\Microsoft\Windows\ CurrentVersion\Applets\Wordpad\Recent File List

Also see Book IV, Chapter 1 for information on removing AutoComplete entries that may embarrass you when typing Web page addresses.

The Registry Editor is also covered in Chapter 9.

Running a program with elevated permissions in Windows Vista

Sometimes, you need to run a program as Administrator in Windows Vista. Running a program as Administrator means that the program has more access to the computer when it runs: It has *elevated privileges.* Yeah, that sounds weird, but it's often something necessary that you need to do in Windows Vista to ensure that some programs run properly.

To run a program with elevated privileges, follow these steps:

1. **Right-click the program or shortcut icon.**

2. **Choose the Run As Administrator command from the shortcut menu.**

    You see a User Account Control (UAC) warning appear.

3. **Type the Administrator's password or click the Continue button.**

    The program then runs with elevated privileges.

Book II
Chapter 6

To make the change permanent and have the program always run under elevated privileges, follow these steps:

1. **Right-click the program or shortcut icon.**

2. **Choose Properties from the shortcut menu.**

3. **Click the Compatibility tab in the program's Properties dialog box.**

4. **Put a check mark by the item Run This Program As an Administrator.**

5. **Click OK.**

Each time you run that program or open its shortcut icon, you're prompted with a UAC warning; type the Administrator's password or click the Continue button to run the program.

 Programs flagged for elevated privileges appear with the shield icon superimposed on their regular icon. That shield icon is your reminder that you need to click the Allow button or type the Administrator's password to use the program at the elevated level.

There's no need to slap every program with elevated privileges. I did this only two times. The first was to run an Administrator command prompt, which is occasionally necessary for troubleshooting. The second was to run an Internet communications program. The program needs to access the keyboard no matter which other program I'm running. To get that keyboard access, it requires elevated privileges.

Chapter 7: Reporting for Duty

In This Chapter

✔ Culling information from Mr. PC

✔ Checking recent logs and events

✔ Finding specific events

✔ Discovering problems in Windows Vista

✔ Using diagnostics

A sk children why they did something, and they say, "I don't know." Ask children when they did something, and they don't remember. Unless your computer is possessed by a small child or it's really goofing up, it dutifully reports to you its current condition, what it did in the past, when it did it, what it believes to be wrong, and lots of other information. That data is kept in various reports and logs. Reviewing that information helps you understand what's going on in your PC, and definitely aids in the troubleshooting process. This chapter explains it all.

The Joys of System Resources

Information is organized data. Without organization, data can be accurate, but not necessarily useful. For example, ask a doctor what's under your skin. The doctor could reply, "Meat." It would be accurate but useless information. This section helps you appreciate the difference between the meat in your computer and the specifics that really make it work.

Understanding resources

Basically, *resources* are bits and pieces of computer hardware that help the computer to do its thing. That thing, of course, is I/O, or input and output, which is basic computer-science stuff.

Resources include memory, disk storage, network access, processor power, and so on. When your program needs more memory or needs to access the Internet, it makes a request to the operating system. Windows then tries to fulfill the request and provide the software that the resources requested. If not, a severe hissy fit ensues, and you'll find using your computer difficult.

Although Windows does try to make the best of things, computer resources are finite. Your PC has only so much memory. The operating system does the best it can with what's available, but resources may run low. When that happens, the computer slows down — or stops. That's why monitoring resources is a necessary part of troubleshooting.

Getting system information

I remember back in the bad old days of computers, an installation program had the audacity to ask me whether my PC had a color monitor. It did, but I found the question offensive. After all, the installation program was running inside the computer — couldn't it just check for itself to see whether a color monitor was installed?

Of course, it could! The computer knows itself. Each time the PC starts, it takes inventory of its hardware. The operating system knows that information, not only when the computer starts but also as you add or remove components. You can see that information for yourself by using the System Information tool.

To start the System Information tool, from the Start menu choose All Programs⇨Accessories⇨System Tools⇨System Information. The System Information window opens, as shown in Figure 7-1. You see a quick summary of nerdy details about your computer, such as the type of processor installed, total memory, Windows version, and other technical tidbits.

To see specific information, choose a category from the left side of the window. The information is detailed and, by itself, useless. But when you need that specific information, you know where to find it.

Figure 7-1:
The System
Information
tool.

The information shown by the System Information tool is static. It's just a report. For more dynamic information, you need to use one of the Windows resource monitors, covered in the next section.

TIP

TECHNICAL STUFF

◆ The final entry in the System Information window, beneath the heading Software Environment, is Windows Error Reporting. It's a quick way to review recent mishaps in your computer. Also refer to the "Reviewing events" section, later in this chapter, for information on the Event Viewer.

◆ There's also a command you can type at the command prompt for getting system information. The command is `systeminfo`, though if you want to use it, I recommend that you type the following line:

```
systeminfo | more
```

Follow `systeminfo` with the pipe character and then the word `more`. That command pumps the output through the `more` filter, which pages each screen of information. (Yes, this information is technical, which is why that icon is in the margin one paragraph back.)

Monitoring system resources

Although there's little you can do about system resources, you can monitor their consumption. The easiest way to do so is from the Task Manager window, on the Performance tab, as shown in Figure 7-2.

Figure 7-2:
The system resources in the Task Manager.

Book II
Chapter 7

Reporting for Duty

Summon the Task Manager by pressing Ctrl+Shift+Esc in Windows Vista; in Windows XP, press Ctrl+Alt+Delete. Click the Performance tab to view some simple resource information.

In Figure 7-2, and on your computer's display, you see CPU and memory usage. (Windows XP displays page file usage, which is similar.) Information listed at the bottom of the window details other vital stats.

To see more detailed information, you can summon a resource monitor window. Follow these steps:

1. **Open the Administrative Tools icon in the Control Panel.**

2a. **In Windows Vista, open the Reliability and Performance Monitor icon; click the Continue button or type the administrator's password when prompted.**

2b. **In Windows XP, open the Performance icon.**

Windows XP has a rather limited display in its Performance window, shown in Figure 7-3. To view a similar window in Windows XP, choose Performance Monitor from the Reliability and Performance Monitor window.

You can add or remove items to monitor by clicking the toolbar's Add button (the giant plus sign). The new items appear as a new line on the chart, allowing you to review that resource. But that's about it for Windows XP; skip ahead to Step 5.

Figure 7-3:
The Windows XP Performance window.

3. **In Windows Vista, choose the item Reliability and Performance from the left side of the window.**

   The main display in the Reliability and Performance Monitor window is shown in Figure 7-4. It lists lots of graphical information about basic resources: CPU, disk, network, memory, and more!

   To see more information for a specific resource, click the downward-pointing arrow button to reveal the details.

4. **From the left side of the Reliability and Performance Monitor window, choose Reliability Monitor.**

   Perhaps the most interesting item to check is the Reliability Monitor in Windows Vista, shown in Figure 7-5. It lists events that have occurred in the computer that may affect overall performance and reliability.

   Figure 7-5 shows a graph detailing the system's reliability. To see details about an event, click the icon. As shown in the figure, you see details about what occurred. It's a great way to spot troublesome software that may require updating or disabling.

5. **Close the window when you're done.**

   One of the key things you can do with the resource information is to track down a memory leak (see Chapter 4).

Figure 7-4:
The Windows Vista resource overview.

Book II
Chapter 7

Reporting for Duty

Figure 7-5:
The
Windows
Vista
Reliability
Monitor.

What Has Gone On Here?

Sophisticated operating systems keep track of all the details in *log files*. Just about anything that goes on in the computer — from a user logging in (get it?) to programs crashing to routine scheduled tasks — is noted in a log somewhere. Because Windows has recently joined the ranks of sophisticated operating systems, it, too, keeps detailed logs. This section discusses where to find those logs, how to review them, and what to do with the information found in the logs.

Reviewing events

The first place to check for your PC's recent activities and happenings is the Event Viewer. As you may have come to suspect, the Windows Vista version is more complete and informative than the Windows XP version, so I discuss Windows XP first.

In either version of Windows, follow these steps:

1. **Open the Control Panel's Administrative Tools icon.**

   I almost wrote *Administrative Toes*. Ha! That would be funny.

2. **Open the Event Viewer icon.**

3. **In Windows Vista, click the Continue button or type the administrator's password to get beyond the UAC warning.**

4. Also in Windows Vista, choose the Windows Logs item on the left side of the Event Viewer console window.

Finally, both versions of Windows display the same type of information, as shown in Figure 7-6. In Windows XP, only the list of events is shown; Windows Vista shows more detailed information.

Figure 7-6:
Information
shown
in the
Windows XP
Event
Viewer.

Table 7-1 describes event categories. Not every event is a nasty one; most are informational, which means that something happened and was noted in the log. All event types are listed in Table 7-2.

Table 7-1			Event Categories
Log	*Windows Vista*	*Windows XP*	*Type of Events Monitored*
Application	X	X	Third-party programs; anything that's not Windows itself
Forwarded Events	X		Events on network computers (with a subscription set up in order to see these types of events)
Internet Explorer		X	Problems with Internet Explorer
Security	X	X	Logon/logoff events, file deletions, and events pertaining to resources
Setup	X	X	Events relating to application setup and configuration
System	X	X	Things that go on with Windows itself, such as start-up events and device driver failure.

Table 7-2	Event Types
Type	*Description*
Error	Something bad happened, such as a service failed or data was lost.
Failure Audit	Something was attempted that didn't work, such as an illegal login or an attempt by a non-administrator to access administrator-level features.
Information	Something happened successfully.
Success Audit	Something was attempted and worked out, such as logging in to a remote PC; the opposite of a failure audit.
Warning	An event occurred that's worth noting, but it's not specifically an error.

5. Double-click an event to view its details.

In Windows Vista, you can either double-click or just click as the details are shown in the bottom center of the Event Viewer window.

6. Close the Event Viewer window when you're done.

Yes, some of the details shown in the Event Viewer window are technical. Heck, some are downright boring. Later sections in this chapter describe how you can filter events to better see only those things that interest you.

Using the Windows Vista Event Viewer

Windows Vista employs a more richly detailed event viewer that goes beyond what's available in Windows XP. Follow steps 1 through 3 in the preceding section to conjure up the Event Viewer window.

The key difference between the Event Viewer in Windows Vista and the Windows XP version is the Overview and Summary portion, shown in Figure 7-7. (It's the main screen.) For example, from the figure, you see that there were five errors in the past 24 hours. It's easy to expand the Error category by clicking the plus sign (+) before the Error heading to expand that section and quickly review the error events; double-click an event to see the fine details.

By double-clicking an error event, you create a custom view. Essentially, you make an event filter (covered in the next section) that shows information about the error or another event.

Figure 7-8 shows the details of one of the errors shown in Figure 7-7. As you can see by the message, it's an ACPI BIOS error message. (ACPI is the Advanced Configuration and Power Interface, or the computer's power management hardware.) The message explains that I would contact the system vendor for an update. (In this case, it would mean looking for an ACPI BIOS update from Dell Computer.)

Generally speaking, the Event Viewer in Windows Vista is more thorough and detailed than its predecessor in Windows XP.

Figure 7-7:
The Windows Vista Event Viewer.

Figure 7-8:
Error details in the Windows Vista Event Viewer.

Filtering and searching events

The true power of reviewing an event log is to be able to quickly filter out the information you need. Most of the log entries are rather mundane events. That's okay when you just want to confirm that something is happening that should happen. But the key to reviewing logs for troubleshooting is to look for pesky events. To help in your search, you need to employ a filter.

A filter is nothing more than a search through the logs. It's more like a database search-and-sort than a file search; you specify the event type, time, and other information. Then, using the Power Of The Computer, you can quickly see relevant events.

Windows Vista has more powerful event filters. Here's how to use them:

1. **Bring up the Event Viewer window.**

   Directions are found earlier in this chapter, in the section "Reviewing events" (Steps 1 through 3).

2. **From the list of actions on the right side of the window, choose Filter Current Log.**

   The Custom View Properties dialog box appears, as shown in Figure 7-9.

   You can make the report permanent by choosing the Create Custom View link instead of Filter Current Log in this step. The rest of the steps in this section remain the same, but the filter you create is saved under the Custom Views folder on the left side of the window.

3. **Choose a timeframe from the Logged button.**

4. **Select the event levels you want to view by checking boxes.**

5. **Choose By Log and then select specific logs from the drop-down list, or, if you have a device to monitor, choose By Source and then select the device or driver from the list.**

6. **Choose other items as necessary, though unless you really know the details, there's little need to fill in the rest of the dialog box information.**

7. **Click OK.**

8. **Peruse the results.**

   Any logged events that match your filter are displayed.

In Windows XP, you can sift through the events in a specific category by following these steps:

1. **Summon the Event Viewer window.**

   See steps 1 and 2 from the section "Reviewing events," earlier in this chapter.

2. **Right-click an event category.**

   For example, pick System.

3. **Choose Properties from the shortcut menu.**

4. **On the category's Properties menu, click the Filter tab.**

   The Filter part of the dialog box, shown in Figure 7-10, lets you sift and sort through the events.

5. **Choose the type of events you want to view.**

   Place a check mark by each event type you want to monitor.

6. **Select a source.**

   Choosing a source works best when you want to monitor a specific source or you suspect a certain piece of hardware or device driver to be causing trouble.

7. **Select a category.**

8. **The item's event ID, user, and computer can generally be left blank.**

9. **Use the From and To settings to narrow the timeframe, if necessary.**

10. **Click OK.**

    The results are displayed in the center portion of the Event Viewer window.

Figure 7-9:
Filtering events in Windows Vista.

Application Properties

General **Filter**

Event types

☐ Information   ☐ Success audit
☑ Warning   ☑ Failure audit
☑ Error

Event source: (All)

Category: (All)

Event ID:

User:

Computer:

From: Events On   ▾   8/ 5/2008 ▾   12:00:00 AM ⬍

To: Events On   ▾   8/ 5/2008 ▾   9:26:30 AM   ⬍

Restore Defaults

[OK]   [Cancel]   [Apply]

Figure 7-10:
Filtering
events in
Windows
XP.

If no matching events show up, no events of the types specified have occurred. That might be good news because it means that no events relating to whatever concerned you have taken place. But if you want to be a stickler, consider broadening your search to find those events. Or, you can just forgo filtering and review the logs manually.

See Video 271 for a visual walkthrough of the steps outlined in this section.

Finding logs

You find logs mostly in a forest. But that's not the subject here. Nope, when you talk about logs in a computer, you talk about *information*.

The Event Viewer is basically a tool that collects information from various logs and places that information in a central place. The log files themselves exist elsewhere in Windows and are maintained and updated as your computer treads through its day.

Most of the vital logs have their information displayed by the Event Viewer. Many log files, however, dot the PC's hard drive. Most of them are found in the `Windows` folder. Some might inhabit the root directory of the boot drive (usually drive `C`). Others are found all over.

Two files you might concern yourself with are the boot log files. These files are created when you specify boot logging as a start-up option. The files are named either `ntbtlog.txt` or `bootlog.txt`, depending on how old your PC is. These files, found in the `Windows` folder, list the success or failure of various pieces of Windows as it's loaded into memory from disk.

You can enable or disable boot logging by using the MSCONFIG utility in Windows Vista. Here's how:

1. **Press Win+R to summon the Run dialog box.**
2. **Type** msconfig **and press Enter.**
3. **Type the administrator's password or click the Continue button.**
4. **Click the Boot tab.**
5. **Place a check mark by the item Boot Log.**
6. **Click OK.**
7. **Click the Restart button to restart now. Otherwise, click Exit without Restart.**

   The logging doesn't take effect until you restart Windows, and there's no reason to do so immediately unless you *really* want to see the boot log.

In Windows XP, you must enable boot logging by editing a text file, boot. ini, on disk. That's nerdy, and the file boot.ini may not exist on your computer. Instead, I recommend pressing the F8 key when Windows first starts (see Book I, Chapter 2) and choosing the item Enable Boot Logging.

The boot log is overwritten each time you start Windows. And it's produced only when you turn the option on.

What can you do with the boot log? You can check for the failed installation of certain pieces of Windows or device drivers. The drivers or files are obviously flagged in the log. Because you know the filename, you can then either disable it from loading or look for an update. (Also see Chapter 8, on repairing Windows.)

+ Also see Book I, Chapter 2 for more information on PC start-up issues.

+ Activating the boot log in Windows Vista means that you configured your PC for a custom start-up. If that bothers you, disable the boot log after you cull whatever useful information you need from the boot log file; repeat the steps from this section, but in Step 5, remove the check mark.

+ Traditionally, computer logs are all text files. They may have the filename extension log, or they may use txt.

+ You can search for log files using the Windows Search command, covered in Chapter 1. Simply look for files named *log* anywhere on the hard drive, including system, hidden, and non-indexed locations.

+ In Windows Vista, log files are plain text, but the text is organized using the XML, or Extensible Markup Language. *XML* is merely a way to organize information, and although XML files are readable as text, to get the most from the information, you should use an XML reader, such as the Event Viewer program.

✦ If you find the file `boot.ini` on your Windows XP computer, you can enable boot logging by modifying the file. Open it in Notepad and look for the line that contains this text:

```
Windows="Windows XP
```

(That's only a portion of the line; in the file, it's longer). Add the text `/bootlog` to the end of that line. Save the file. When you restart Windows, boot logging takes place automatically.

Problems and Solutions for Windows Vista

Nope, wise guy — the problem isn't Windows Vista, and the solution isn't to downgrade to Windows XP. Consider the Problem Reports and Solutions tool, available in Windows Vista, as a godsend, not a punch line. It's a helpful utility for troubleshooting your PC.

Open the Problem Reports and Solutions icon in the Control Panel to see the Problem Reports and Solutions window, shown in Figure 7-11. That's where the troubleshooting happens.

Figure 7-11: The Problem Reports and Solutions window.

Reviewing problems and solutions

The first thing to do in the Problem Reports and Solutions window is to review any pending solutions or current problems. If there are no solutions or problems to report, you see the text `No Solutions Found`; otherwise, current solutions and problems are displayed.

For example, on my screen (refer to Figure 7-11), I see an update for DirectX as well as problems about the game Half Life 2, which I rarely play because I spend most of my days writing computer books. Regardless, clicking a link displays a solution window with suggestions on what do to. Mostly, you see a Web page link or perhaps the name of the program's publisher, and the rest of the solution is something you need to pursue.

Some solutions listed are the results of problems you checked on, as discussed in the next section.

Checking on new solutions

Just to ensure that everything is up to snuff, click the link on the left, Check for New Solutions. Windows reviews various issues that are logged for your computer.

If you're prompted to send information to Microsoft, click the Send Information button. It may help.

Finally, when any solutions are found, you see them listed in the window. Click a solution to see the advice that's offered. Oftentimes, you find a link to a Web site where new drivers can be downloaded or where you can review the issue on a support page.

Perusing recent issues

To review recent problem reports, on the left side of the Problem Reports and Solutions window, click the link View Problem History. The list you see works like a mini-log of issues with certain programs.

To see more details on a certain issue, double-click that item in the list. Such a report is shown in Figure 7-12. The report may list things you can do or try to remedy the situation.

Figure 7-12:
Details from
a problem
report.

Be sure to close the Problem Reports and Solutions window when you're done using it.

Diagnostics

Contrary to popular belief, a diagnostic isn't someone who doesn't believe in two gods. Nope, a *diagnostic* is a computer tool you can use to help diagnose (get it?) something that happened in your PC. This section details your options.

Understanding diagnostics

Next to the terms *plasma inducer* and *phase inhibiter, diagnostic* was one of the most common terms used in the old TV series *Star Trek: The Next Generation.* But unlike those other terms, *diagnostic* is a real word that applies to a real computer tool you can use for troubleshooting.

A diagnostic comes in two flavors: Report and Check.

A report type of diagnostic simply inventories what's available. For example, the System Information window, covered elsewhere in this chapter, is an inventory type of diagnostic report. Its value lies in telling you what's up with the computer. Oftentimes, an internal hardware conflict or a malfunctioning device is obvious on this type of diagnostic report.

The check type of diagnostic is to computer hardware what a physical examination is to a human being: The hardware is tested. For a video display, it might mean that colors are displayed and various graphics modes reviewed. For a hard drive, information may be written to and read from the hard drive repeatedly to ensure reliability. That type of testing is a check type of diagnostic.

On *Star Trek,* of course, there were various diagnostic "levels." Supposedly, the Level 1 diagnostic was the most intense, apparently forcing such introspective self-examination that the starship itself struggled with the process. The Level 3 diagnostic was more casual. All that is silliness compared to the realistic diagnostics you can perform on your PC for troubleshooting purposes.

Diagnosing DirectX

Microsoft introduced DirectX in the 1990s to help game programmers better use the PC's hardware muscle. The results were good: Today, the PC remains a superior gaming platform. By allowing game programmers access to components such as memory, video, sound, and input devices, DirectX has proven to be a success.

You can use the DirectX Diagnostic Tool to check not only on how the DirectX system is working but also on problems with video, sound, and other basic PC components. Here's how:

1. **Press Win+R to bring forth the Run dialog box.**

2. **Type** dxdiag **and press Enter.**

3. **If prompted, click the Yes button to confirm that you want to proceed.**

   Behold the DirectX Diagnostic Tool as it peruses your PC's system, as shown in Figure 7-13. Wait until it's done before you proceed.

4. **Click the Next Page button to view information about each different part of your PC, those various things controlled by the DirectX software.**

   Check the Notes section, at the bottom of the window, to see whether any problems are reported.

5. **Close the DirectX Diagnostic Tool window when you're done.**

   Click the Exit button.

Your PC most likely has the best version of DirectX for whatever software you use. The only time you need a DirectX update is when you install new software that requires it. For example, when installing a new game, you may be prompted to upgrade to the latest version of DirectX. Do so at that time.

DirectX is smart enough that an older version cannot overwrite a more current version.

DirectX versions 10 and later are available only for Windows Vista, not for Windows XP.

Figure 7-13:
The DirectX
Diagnostic
Tool.

Using the Memory Diagnostic Tool

Shockingly enough, Windows Vista comes with a Memory Diagnostic Tool, and it's one of those memory-testing diagnostics, not just a diagnostic that says "You have this much memory." Here's how to use the Memory Diagnostic Tool:

1. **Save everything.**

Your computer is restarted by the memory diagnostic procedure, so save your stuff, close windows, and get ready for a restart.

2. **Open the Administrative Tools icon in the Control Panel.**

3. **Open the Memory Diagnostic Tool icon.**

4. **Click the Continue button or type the administrator's password to continue.**

5. **In the Windows Memory Diagnostic Tool window, choose the option Restart Now and Check for Problems.**

Wait until the computer restarts. When it does, the Memory Diagnostic Tool screen appears almost immediately. Wait while memory is checked thoroughly. Don't get bored; the display entertains you.

When the test is over, the PC restarts again.

6. **Log in to Windows as you normally do.**

The test results are displayed from a pop-up bubble in the notification area.

Because the Memory Diagnostic Tool is a serious diagnostic, I don't recommend using it unless you suspect your PC of falling victim to memory issues, such as random errors, system crashes, and other weird activities. (Well, seeing how "weird" is typical for a computer, look for activities weirder than normal.)

Windows cannot properly detect such malfunctions on its own because Windows itself must dwell in the same foul RAM that's causing the problem. But the Memory Diagnostic Tool can get to the bottom of the situation as it starts up as its own operating system.

If problems are detected, the only true solution is to find and replace the bad memory. That can be a pain in the butt, unless you just want to replace *all* the memory in your PC. And, as long as you're going to do that, you might as well buy your computer even more memory than it had.

Doing a hardware diagnostic

Windows doesn't come with specific hardware diagnostic tools. Even so, when you add new hardware to your PC or it's installed by the manufacturer, diagnostic tools or programs may be available.

For example, the PC's display adapter software may include a diagnostic tool: Look for the adapter name, such as ATI or Nvidia, on the Start menu's All Programs submenu. Or, you might find the diagnostic tool accessible from the notification area: Right-click the manufacturer's icon and choose the diagnostic tool from the pop-up menu.

Likewise, the network adapter may have its own diagnostic tool or a suite of tools available. The only way to know for certain is to look. (Also see Book V for information on troubleshooting networking issues.)

If you own a utility suite, such as Norton Utilities, you may find hard drive diagnostic tools as well as other utilities for checking various PC components. (Check out Book VI, Chapter 2 for things you can do in Windows to maintain the PC's disk drives.)

✦ Yes, using one of the many hardware diagnostic tools can be time-consuming.

✦ Video diagnostics can be something to behold: The colors are fascinating. Watching the display adapter change between various text and graphics modes can be fun to watch. But mostly the diagnostic does repeated tests that don't have any effect on the display.

✦ The best diagnostics usually come on bootable discs. That's because, in order to truly ensure that the hardware is being examined, the program must have direct access to the PC's guts. You can't do that through Windows. Even so, few diagnostic tools available to the general public take the boot disc approach. Only professional diagnostic tools come on boot discs. Even then, few PC technicians use them because it's just cheaper to replace parts than it is to do a true, deep level of troubleshooting.

Chapter 8: Recovery Options

In This Chapter

✔ **Working with System Restore**

✔ **Recovering previous versions**

✔ **Using the System File Checker**

✔ **Starting the Recovery Console**

✔ **Repairing a master boot record**

✔ **Using a recovery disc**

✔ **Determining whether to reinstall Windows**

Supposedly, a sign above the vestibule to Hell reads, "Abandon hope all ye who enter here." Or, the sign might be found above the DMV building. I'm not certain which. Perhaps both are the same place. Regardless, when Windows starts, it doesn't display a similar message, though MS-DOS once did (in invisible text, no less). Despite the fact that you may feel hopeless when Windows is broken, you have many ways to fix, recover, and repair the PC's operating system. The methods various are in this chapter discussed.

Restore the System, Restore Your Sanity

The best and first trick you should try when Windows goes awry is a restart. Simple. Effective. Works most of the time.

When restarting Windows fails to cure the PC's ills, the next instant cure you should try is *System Restore*. It's a tool that's been around since Windows 98, where it was tucked away in a command line utility. But, starting with Windows XP, System Restore gained full graphical popularity as a way to recover common goofs from making wrong settings or improperly installed software or hardware. This section explains how to use System Restore.

✦ System Restore isn't a miracle worker. For example, it cannot restore files you deleted. For that job, see the section "Files Missing and Found" in Chapter 1. Also refer to the section "Windows Vista Time Travel," later in this chapter.

✦ When disk space runs tight, you can create more room by removing old restore point data. Refer to Book VI, Chapter 2 for information on Disk Cleanup.

✦ The best way to restore your system is to use Backup. I'm serious. See Book VI, Chapter 1.

Using System Restore

It happened. Something weird. A driver made things worse. The hardware update conflicts with something, and now *two* things don't work. Or, perhaps your 13-year-old "computer genius" nephew decided to trick out your PC. Regardless of the foul, you want to recover your PC to The Way Things Were.

Follow these steps to use System Restore in Windows Vista:

1. **Save all your stuff.**

The System Restore operation restarts your computer. Save your files, close your programs. Do it now.

2. **From the Start button menu, choose All Programs⇨Accessories⇨ System Tools⇨System Restore.**

3. **Click Continue button or type the administrator's password.**

System Restore's main window appears.

4. **Click the Next button.**

A list of recent restore points appears, as shown in Figure 8-1. The most recent restore point is selected, which is most likely the one you want.

If you don't see the recent restore points, as shown in the figure, and instead see another screen, choose the Recommended Restore option.

5. **Click the Next button.**

A screen detailing which hard drives to restore is shown. Again, the one you need is most likely already selected, so there's nothing else to do.

6. **Click the Next button.**

7. **Click the Finish button.**

8. **Click Yes to restart Windows.**

Wait while Windows restarts.

Follow these steps to use System Restore in Windows XP:

1. **Save everything.**

Because System Restore restarts your computer, I recommend that you save files, close open programs, and get ready for a restart.

2. **From the Start button menu, choose All Programs⇨Accessories⇨ System Tools⇨System Restore.**

   You see the main System Restore window, which is boring, so I don't illustrate it here.

3. **Choose the option Restore My Computer to an Earlier Time.**

4. **Click the Next button.**

5. **Choose a restore point from the cute calendar-like thing.**

   The most recent date is chosen by default, and I recommend using it unless you already tried it and experienced problems.

6. **Click the Next button.**

7. **Read the scary warning.**

   Ooo! Scary! Red text! They must be *serious* this time! Just kidding: You're good to go.

8. **Click the Next button.**

   It should be called the Finish button because it's the last step: System Restore does its magic. Windows restarts itself.

After you log in again, you need to wait a bit more. Eventually, you see a confirmation message explaining that Windows has been restored: In Windows Vista, you see (after a seemingly endless amount of time) a dialog box explaining how the System Restore operation went; click the Close button. In Windows XP, you see a window that details what happened; click OK to close that window.

Figure 8-1:
System
Restore in
Windows
Vista.

When should you reinstall Windows?

Short answer: *Never.*

I'm serious. Most problems in Windows can be fixed. This chapter tells you how to address what I would say are 98 percent of the major issues that most too-busy tech support people and amateur computer consultants would say requires a major reinstallation of your PC's operating system. Before you succumb to their good-natured yet ill-informed suggestions, consider a few points of my own:

Most problems in Windows can be fixed. This chapter covers some marvelous tools you can use to help recover, restore, and return Windows to an operable state. *Remember:* The reason most tech support people claim that reinstalling Windows is a solution is because their motivation is to get you off the phone and not truly address your problem. Sad but true.

There's no need to reinstall Windows to "refresh" the computer. Some wag once said that it's a "good idea" to reinstall Windows to keep the computer fresh — or some such nonsense. Well, I say poppycock! Computers are constantly changing beasts. If you reinstall Windows, you also have to spend lots of time online reloading updates and patches. The benefits are nil, especially given that disk tools exist to remove the problems that reinstalling Windows supposedly solves.

The only time you really need to reinstall Windows is when the operating system has been horribly damaged. For example, some doofus might delete a given number of files in the Windows folder, or perhaps a computer virus or corrupt program deletes a swath of files necessary to Windows. That kind of damage can only be fixed by reinstalling Windows.

Avoid the temptation. Shun those who claim otherwise. A computer's operating system is its soul, and rarely do you have a need or a reason to replace the thing, especially for trivial or passing reasons. Trust me.

Any problems you were trying to fix should be fixed. If they're not, continue reading other sections in this chapter for additional solutions.

✦ Restoring the system is also a start-up option, as described in Book I, Chapter 2. Choose the option Last Known Good Configuration, which is more or less the last system restore point.

✦ You can also perform System Restore in Safe mode. That's a good choice, especially when the computer is unusable otherwise. See Chapter 3 on Safe mode.

Restoring to a specific date and time

Windows naturally chooses the most recent System Restore point, which is generally a safe bet. Sometimes, you may want a less recent restore point. For example, when I managed to botch a system upgrade *and* a software addition, I needed to restore my computer to a point several days earlier.

To restore to an earlier point for Windows Vista, refer to the steps in the preceding section. After Step 4, choose the proper restore date. To restore to an earlier time, place a check mark by the option Show Restore Points Older Than 5 Days. Complete the rest of the steps.

In Windows XP, follow the steps in the preceding section, but in Step 5 choose an earlier restore point from the cute calendar-like thing. Then work through the rest of the steps.

✦ Choosing an older restore point increases the likelihood that the restore won't be successful. If possible, you can try to incrementally restore by choosing a more recent restore point and then running System Restore again with an increasingly older restore point.

✦ When you restore to an older restore point, you remove software and hardware updates installed in the "between time." That means some programs and certain hardware won't work and will require reinstallation after the system restore operation is complete.

Setting a restore point

System Restore points are set automatically in Windows Vista, usually just after midnight (assuming that you're up that late or leave the PC on all the time). They're also set before you install any new software, as part of the Setup program. But, for other times, and for Windows XP all the time, you must set a manual restore point.

For example, just before installing new hardware or perhaps before you take a stab at configuring wireless networking for the first time, manually set a restore point.

Here's how to set a restore point in Windows Vista:

1. **From the Start button menu, choose All Programs⇨Accessories⇨System Tools⇨System Restore.**

2. **Click the Continue button or type the administrator's password.**

System Restore's main window appears.

3. **Click the Open System Protection link.**

The System Properties dialog box opens, displaying the System Protection tab.

4. **Click the Create button.**

5. **Type a name for the restore point.**

   Don't disappoint me and type **restore point.** That's silly. Be descriptive. Tell your future self why you created the restore point: "Installing New Hardware," "Messing with the Network," and "Updating Video Driver" are all good descriptions for a restore point.

6. **Click the Create button.**

7. **Click the OK button to dismiss the System Protection informative dialog box.**

8. **Close the System Properties dialog box.**

Setting a restore point is done by following these steps in Windows XP:

1. **From the Start button menu, choose All Programs➪Accessories➪System Tools➪System Restore.**

   You see the main System Restore window, which is boring, so I don't illustrate it here.

2. **Choose the option Create a Restore Point.**

3. **Click the Next button.**

4. **Type a descriptive name.**

   Use your writing skills to create a name that reflects the reason for creating the restore point. Examples include About to Do Something Utterly Foolish, My Cousin Ralph Is Visiting, and I Do Everything I Read in a Computer Book.

5. **Click the Create button.**

   The restore point is created and described in scary, bold, red text.

6. **Click the Close button.**

After creating the restore point, proceed with whatever modifications you plan on making to your computer. You now have peace of mind, knowing that a restore point looms in the past, in case you need it.

✦ You must manually set restore points in Windows XP!

✦ You can review the schedule for automatic restore points in Windows Vista by visiting the Task Scheduler. (See Book VI, Chapter 3.)

✦ My challenge in writing this section was to use the phrase *peace of mind* (which I just heard on the television). I succeeded.

Undoing a System Restore

Windows XP sports an undo feature for System Restore, allowing you to gracefully back out of a restore operation. Supposedly, that means that the System Restore process made things worse. I don't know. Whatever the reason, Microsoft saw fit to not include the feature in Windows Vista.

Meanwhile, to undo a recent System Restore operation in Windows XP, heed these steps:

1. **Save your stuff!**

   The undo operation restarts your computer. Save now. Close open programs.

2. **Start System Restore: From the Start button menu, choose All Programs⇨Accessories⇨System Tools⇨System Restore.**

3. **Choose the option Undo My Last Restoration.**

4. **Click the Next button.**

   Scary! Red! Text!

5. **Click the Next button, which, honestly, should be relabeled the Undo button.**

   Windows undoes the System Restore operation. Your computer restarts. You log in.

6. **Click the OK button in the System Restore window after the computer restarts.**

   You can then use the computer as it was before you shamefully attempted to use System Restore.

Obviously, the sooner you can undo after using System Restore, the better.

Disabling System Restore

Some people believe that System Restore is a security risk. For example, you could effectively restore a virus with System Restore, or System Restore could be taken over by hostile software. In Windows Vista, System Restore also maintains information about nonsystem files that may contain data you don't want others to access. Regardless of the reasons, you can disable System Restore.

To turn off System Restore in Windows Vista, heed these steps:

1. **Press Win+Break to quickly summon the System window.**

   The Break key is the same key as Pause, though Win+Break has a more devious sound to it than Win+Pause.

2. **Choose the link System Protection on the left side of the window.**

3. **Type the administrator's password or click Continue.**

4. **Remove the check mark by all disk drives in the Automatic Restore Points portion of the dialog box.**

5. **After being shocked by the warning dialog box, click the button Turn System Restore Off.**

6. **Click OK and then close the System window.**

To stop System Restore in Windows XP, follow these steps:

1. **Press Win+Break to bring forth the System dialog box.**

2. **Click the System Restore tab.**

3. **Click the check box by the option Turn Off System Restore.**

4. **Click OK.**

5. **Click the Yes button to confirm that you want System Restore turned off.**

Turning on System Restore is done by repeating the steps: For Windows Vista, in Step 4 place a check mark by each hard drive you want to monitor for System Restore; in Windows Vista, remove the check mark by the option Turn Off System Restore in Step 3.

If you're going to disable System Restore, please back up your data. (See Book VI, Chapter 1.)

Windows Vista Time Travel

A new feature I call *previous versions* was introduced in Windows Vista. It uses System Restore technology to rescue older versions of a file. For example, if you massively change a file, or the file (or folder) is overwritten, it can be restored by using the previous versions feature. Here's how:

1. **Right-click the file or folder.**

2. **Choose Restore Previous Versions from the shortcut menu.**

   The file or folder's Properties dialog box appears, with the Previous Versions tab up front, as shown in Figure 8-2.

   When no previous versions exist, you see the message There Are No Previous Versions Available. That's it. You're done: Go to Step 5. Otherwise, you see a list of older copies of the file.

Figure 8-2:
Previous
versions
of a file.

3. **Choose a previous version from the list.**

   Ideally, you should select the most recent version, though if you're after an ancient version of the file or folder, you can pluck that out from the list instead.

4a. **Click the Open button to open the file and review its contents.**

   The Open button is best used when you just want to peek. In fact, I've used the Open button to open a file, copy a swath of text (or an image), and then close the file without ever restoring it.

4b. **Click the Copy button to copy the file or folder to a specific location in your PC's storage system.**

   The Copy option is useful when you don't want to overwrite the existing version of the file.

4c. **Click the Restore button to overwrite the existing file or folder with the previous version; click the Restore button in the warning dialog box to confirm this choice. Click OK.**

5. **Close the file or folder's Properties dialog box when you're done.**

It's right about here that you would expect the author to rant about how Backup is a better option than relying on the previous versions feature. It is. But, the previous versions feature also uses Windows Backup. In fact, you see in Figure 8-2 how the location for some of the older file versions is given as Backup. That's because recent backups are checked for previous versions of files. Indeed, the previous versions feature provides a quick shortcut to the Restore operation for file backup.

✦ See Book VI, Chapter 1 for more information on Backup.

✦ The previous versions feature isn't a substitute for recovering a file from the Recycle Bin; if you deleted a file, you need to recover it from the Recycle Bin.

✦ The Recycle Bin doesn't contain older versions of files, nor can it help you restore a file that's been overwritten with new data. Only the previous versions feature can bring back a file that's been changed.

✦ The previous versions feature works only when System Restore is active in Windows Vista. (The previous versions information is kept as part of a restore point.) If you disabled System Restore, you cannot use previous versions. (See the section "Disabling System Restore," earlier in this chapter.)

✦ You cannot use the previous versions feature for Windows files or for your programs. To recover bad Windows files, see the next section. For bad program files, reinstall the program.

✦ To restore previous versions of files that have been renamed, use the previous versions feature on the folder containing that file. Click the Open button to open the folder's previous version, and then copy the old file from the folder to its new location.

✦ To disable the previous versions feature, you simply turn off System Restore. (See the section "Disabling System Restore," earlier in this chapter.)

The System File Checker

One of the most useful yet overlooked tools in Windows is the *System File Checker*, fondly known by its initials, *SFC*.

You can use the powerful SFC tool to ensure the integrity of the Windows operating system as well as to effectively restore broken parts of Windows without having to completely reinstall the operating system. Is SFC not the Windows-fixer-upper tool you've been waiting for?

✦ SFC may prompt for the Windows disc, which is either the disc you used to install or upgrade Windows or the system recovery disk provided by your computer manufacturer. Have that disc handy!

✦ When SFC cannot fix the problem, you should try additional recovery options, as described in the section "Windows Recovery," later in this chapter.

Running SFC in Windows Vista

The System File Checker (SFC) is a command line utility in Windows Vista. Furthermore, you have to start an administrator command prompt to run SFC and have it do its magic.

Before heading into the operation, be aware that running SFC takes time. It's not a quick-check-before-you-do-something-important type of operation.

Here are the steps to take to scan and repair Windows Vista using SFC:

1. **Save all your stuff and close any other programs you're running.**

SFC isn't a light or casual utility. It does major repair. Don't blow it by losing information in an open program window. Save now!

2. **From the Start menu, choose All Programs⇨Accessories.**

3. **Right-click the Command Prompt menu item.**

4. **From the pop-up menu, choose Run As Administrator.**

5. **Click the Continue button or type the administrator's password.**

The Command Prompt window appears on the screen.

You run SFC by typing **sfc** at the command prompt, but don't do it yet. You can type various options after SFC that let it do its magic. Table 8-1 lists each of them, but the key one to use is /scannow.

6. **Type** sfc /scannow **and press the Enter key.**

You see text:

```
Beginning system scan. This process takes some time.

Beginning verification phase of system scan.
Verification 26% complete.
```

7. **Wait.**

SFC fixes what it can. Mostly, it plods through and displays the results, something like this:

```
Verification 100% complete.
```

What you see after that depends on the results of the operation. When nothing is wrong, you see this text:

```
Windows Resource Protection didn't find any integrity
    violations.
```

When problems have been found and repaired, you see this:

```
Windows Resource Protection found corrupt files and
    successfully repaired them. Details are included in
    the CBS.Log windir\Logs\CBS\CBS.log. For example C:\
    Windows\Logs\CBS\CBS.log
```

When things go awry, you see this text message:

```
Windows Resource Protection found corrupt files but was
    unable to fix some of them. Details are included in
    the CBS.Log windir\Logs\CBS\CBS.log. For example C:\
    Windows\Logs\CBS\CBS.log
```

Don't fret: Your PC is most likely fine. See the next section for information on the cbs.log file.

If you're prompted to insert the Windows disc, do so. Corrupt files must be replaced by fresh ones.

8. Close the Command Prompt window.

You've done the best you can. Hopefully, by running SFC, you thumped Windows back into shape. If not, keep reading the later section "Windows Recovery" to see what else you can do.

Table 8-1	Windows Vista SFC command options
Option	*What It Does*
/offbootdir	Specifies the location of boot files when they cannot be found on the current PC
/offwindir	Specifies the location of Windows files when they cannot be found on the current PC
/scanfile	Scans and (optional) repairs or replaces the named file
/scannow	Scans all Windows operating system files, repairing or replacing any that are defective or the wrong version
/verifyfile	Scans the named file but doesn't replace the file
/verifyonly	Scans all Windows operating system files but doesn't repair or replace any bad files and saves information in a long, huge log file

Reviewing the cbs.log file in Windows Vista

The SFC utility keeps track of its actions in a log file named after a major American television network. Don't bother reviewing the log; it's massive. On my PC, the file ended up being 39MB. Massive.

Obviously, the entire log isn't what you want to read, unless you really need the sleep. The idea is to find out which files couldn't be repaired. To do that, you can follow these steps:

1. **From the Start menu, choose All Programs⇨Accessories.**

2. **Right-click the Notepad menu item.**

3. **Choose Run As Administrator from the pop-up menu.**

You must run Notepad as an administrator to access a log file located beneath the Windows folder.

4. **Type the administrator's password or click the Continue button.**

5. **Choose File⇨Open.**

6. **In the File Name box, type** %windir%\logs\cbs\cbs.log

As you type, a drop-down list of matching folders and files appears, which is your clue that you're doing it correctly.

Don't type a period after the word *log!* You're typing a filename, not a sentence.

7. **Click the Open button.**

The log file cbs.log appears in Notepad — though it may take some time to load because the sucker is huge.

Yes! The log contents are complex. No need to fuss:

8. **Choose Edit⇨Find to summon the Find dialog box.**

9. **Type the text** cannot repair **into the box and click the Find Next button.**

You see a log entry highlighted in the Notepad window, telling you which file SFC wasn't able to fix and why. The filename appears in double quotes along with a lot of gobbledygook about what's wrong.

10. **Click the Find Next button to look for the next file in the list that SFC couldn't fix.**

Or, you can dismiss the Find dialog box and press the F3 key as the keyboard shortcut for the Find Next command.

11. **Close Notepad.**

What do logs tell you? Well, not much. If SFC cannot fix the file, there may be nothing further you can do — other than repair Windows, as discussed later in this chapter.

You might also try searching the Microsoft Knowledge Base for information about the filename. Visit http://support.microsoft.com and type the name of the file that befuddles SFC.

Running SFC in Windows XP

Windows XP comes with the command line utility SFC, or System File Checker. You can use SFC to check for corrupt or missing Windows files and have them instantly fixed or replaced. It's a miracle!

Follow these steps to run SFC on your Windows XP computer:

1. **Close open windows and save your stuff.**

   I recommend saving things because SFC may necessitate restarting your computer. In any case, it's always a good idea not to be working on your computer while you're troubleshooting.

2. **Pop up the Start button menu and choose All Programs⇨ Accessories⇨Command Prompt.**

   A lovely Command Prompt window appears.

   The System File Checker runs when you type sfc at the command prompt, followed by one of six options. Those options make SFC do its thing, so at least one of them is required. All options are described in Table 8-2. The option you use is /scannow.

3. **Type** sfc /scannow **and press the Enter key.**

   A graphical window appears, monitoring the System File Checker's progress.

   You may be prompted to insert the Windows disc. Do so!

4. **Wait.**

   When everything is okay, you don't see anything; the graphical window disappears and you're left at the Command Prompt window.

5. **Close the Command Prompt window.**

The System File Checker can do only so much. If it fails, I recommend that you use more drastic means to repair Windows, as covered in the aptly named section "Windows Recovery," next.

Table 8-2	Windows XP SFC Command Options
Option	*What It Does*
/cachesize	Sets the size of the cache used by SFC for storing backups of system files
/purgecache	Removes backups of Windows system files, which is something you don't want to do
/revert	Undoes the boot scanning activated by the /scanboot switch

Option	What It Does
/scanboot	Directs SFC to perform a (time-consuming) System File Check each time you start Windows
/scanonce	Directs SFC to scan all system files the next time you restart Windows
/scannow	Scans all Windows operating system files, repairing or replacing any that are defective or the wrong version

Windows Recovery

Having ample recovery options for Windows isn't a dismal admission that Windows is worthy of having them. Believe me, back in the Cro-Magnon days of computing, I yearned for a recovery disc or special mode for repairing the operating system. You should consider yourself fortunate. This section explains the various available options.

Understanding the recovery console

One of the most useful tools for fixing problems in Windows is the *recovery console.* It's a nerdy thing. Unlike Windows with its graphical glory, the recovery console is a text-mode operating system. It's similar to the old MS-DOS. Indeed, many of your old favorite DOS commands can be used in the recovery console, making it popular with nostalgic nerds.

The recovery console isn't DOS, however. It's a tool used to troubleshoot your computer. It's either run from a recovery partition on your PC's hard drive or started from any Windows or system recovery disc. Later sections in this chapter explain the methods.

Table 8-3 lists some recovery console commands of note. I don't have the space here to go into complete details; documenting the recovery console and doing it well would take an entire book unto itself.

Table 8-3		Recovery Console Commands
Command	Windows	What It Does
bcdedit	Vista	Boot configuration editor, used in Windows Vista rather than the older `bootcfg` utility
bmrui	Vista	Runs Windows PC Complete Restore (can also be run from the System Recovery Options menu; see Figure 8-4, later in this chapter)

(continued)

Table 8-3 *(continued)*

Command	Windows	What It Does
bootcfg	XP	Edits the `boot.ini` file, used to set start-up and other configuration options for older PCs
bootrec	Vista	System start-up and repair utility
chkdsk	Vista, XP	Checks a volume for errors and repairs them if it can
exit	Vista, XP	Closes the recovery console window in Windows Vista and restarts the PC for Windows XP
fixboot	XP	Re-creates the boot sector on a specific drive
fixmbr	XP	Writes a new master boot record on the named device
format	XP	Formats a disk drive, preparing it for use
mbr	Vista	Starts graphical utility to manage the master boot record
recover	Vista	Reads information from a troublesome disk
reg	Vista, XP	Lets you edit the Registry
sfc	Vista	Runs the System File Checker, covered earlier in this chapter

In addition to the commands available for Windows repair, all standard prompt commands and utilities are available in the recovery console. These include tools for file manipulation, such as `copy` and `ren`, the network configuration tool `net`, and commands for general system management.

The following sections describe how to start the recovery console for your version of Windows.

✦ The recovery console is just one of many tools available for repairing Windows.

✦ Yeah, you probably don't have any "old favorite" DOS commands, either.

✦ You can run and manage any Windows computer using the command prompt alone. Most of the technical setup and configuration of your PC was most likely done by a command prompt script at the factory.

✦ Of course, all this command prompt stuff is *nerdy*. One reason that most technicians don't bother with the recovery console is that it's just faster and cheaper to reinstall Windows. (See the later sidebar "When Should You Reinstall Windows?")

✦ On the subject of reinstalling Windows: *Don't.* You do not have to reinstall Windows to fix minor problems.

Starting the recovery console in Windows XP

To start the recovery console in Windows XP, follow these steps:

1. **Stick a Windows disc in the optical drive.**

Yes, you need a Windows installation disc to make this procedure work. The system recovery disc might also work.

2. **Restart the computer.**

3. **Ensure that the system attempts to start from the Windows installation disc.**

You must boot from the optical drive; press Enter when you see the prompt `Press any key to boot from optical drive` (or whatever the message says).

4. **Proceed with the "installation" of Windows.**

Trust me: Just follow along with the directions on the screen. You're not really installing Windows, but you must complete the initial steps to get where you need to go.

5. **When prompted, choose the option to start the recovery console.**

For example, the prompt may say to press the **R** key to start the recovery console, similar to what's shown in Figure 8-3. Do so.

Book II
Chapter 8

Recovery Options

```
Windows XP Professional Setup
==============================

  Welcome to Setup

  This portion of the Setup program prepares Microsoft(R)
  Windows(R) XP to run on your computer.


     •  To set up Windows XP now, press ENTER.

     •  To repair a Windows XP installation using
        Recovery Console, press R.

     •  To quit Setup without installing Windows XP, press F3.
```

Figure 8-3:
One way
to start the
recovery
console.

6. **Select a Windows installation, if prompted.**

The Windows installation may be the only one. If you fail to select a Windows installation and, for example, just press Enter, Windows cancels the operation and you have to start over.

7. **If prompted, type the administrator's password.**

Finally, you should see the text-mode command prompt, which looks something like this:

```
C:\WINDOWS>
```

You're ready to work.

8. **When you're done, type** exit **to restart your computer.**

The `exit` command closes the recovery console and reboots the PC. If it doesn't, press Ctrl+Alt+Delete to restart the computer.

The Recovery Console is a command prompt window, in text mode. If you don't see a console window, choose whatever option is available to present you with a command prompt or Recovery Console window. If you still don't see a text-mode Recovery Console, you have to restart the computer and begin these steps again.

✦ You should also look into starting the computer by using a recovery partition, as discussed in the section "Booting into a recovery partition," later in this chapter. The Recovery partition might also have a Recovery Console option.

✦ The `exit` command restarts the computer only when using the Windows XP version of the recovery console.

✦ See Book I, Chapter 2 for more information on your PC's start-up options.

Getting to the recovery console in Windows Vista

The recovery console in Windows Vista (which is graphical as opposed to XP's command prompt) is available from either the F8 start-up menu or any Windows installation or recovery disc. Here are the steps to take for starting the recovery console from the F8 boot menu:

1. **Restart the computer.**

2. **After the start-up message appears, press the F8 key.**

You must press F8 before Windows starts. See Book I, Chapter 2 for some helpful hints.

3. Choose the option Repair Your Computer.

At this point, your computer may start up a custom recovery program, such as the Rescue and Recovery tool available on Lenovo PCs. If so, you should attempt to access the Recovery Console using that utility, or refer to the second set of steps in this section.

4. Click the Next button.

You may be prompted to choose a keyboard layout and language. There's usually no need to change those options.

5. Choose your username.

If you know the administrator password, you can choose Administrator. The password should be the same as on your own user account, though it may not be.

Select only an account that has administrator access.

6. Type your password and click OK.

A window appears on the screen, listing several repair and recovery options and tools, as shown in Figure 8-4. Your PC may not have these same options. For example, Dell Factory Image Restore appears only on Dell computers. (On other computers, you may find an option titled Recovery Manager, which is pretty much the same thing.)

Book II
Chapter 8

Recovery Options

Figure 8-4:
Windows
Vista
System
Recovery
Options.

7. **Choose the option Command Prompt.**

   A command prompt window opens. You're now ready to use Recovery Console commands. Refer to the next section.

8. **When you're done using the command prompt, close its window.**

9. **Choose the option Restart from the System Recovery Options window.**

   The computer restarts.

In some cases, the preceding steps may not get you to the recovery console. You may instead find a special recovery program or another utility. Don't give up! It's still possible to access the Recovery Console by using a Windows installation or update disc or the recovery disc that came with your computer. Follow these steps:

1. **Insert the Windows or system recovery disc into your PC's optical drive.**

2. **Restart the computer.**

3. **Choose the option to boot from the CD or DVD.**

   Refer to Book I, Chapter 2 to set up this option, if it's not available.

4. **Work your way through the installation process until you find the option Repair Your Computer.**

   Don't worry: Nothing is changed on your computer until you choose to reinstall Windows. But you're not doing that.

5. **Press the R key to choose the option Repair Your Computer.**

6. **If prompted, don't choose to repair any start-up or boot issues or errors.**

   You can return to fix any errors later.

7. **Choose the Windows Vista installation from the list.**

8. **Click the Next button.**

   The System Recovery Options window appears (refer to Figure 8-4).

9. **Choose the Command Prompt option.**

   Say hello to the Recovery Console.

10. **When you're done using the command prompt, close its window.**

11. **Choose the option Restart from the System Recovery Options window.**

    The computer restarts.

The recovery console isn't a friendly place. Go there only when you know what you're doing or when you're following directions, such as those provided in this book.

Fixing the master boot record

One useful and often necessary thing you can do in the Recovery Console is to fix a corrupt or damaged master boot record (MBR). Chapters 1 and 2 in Book I discuss how the MBR plays a role in starting your PC and what happens when it's damaged. Recovery is entirely possible if you can access the Recovery Console and you know which command to type for your version of Windows.

In Windows Vista, type the following command at the Recovery Console prompt:

```
BOOTREC /FIXMBR
```

Type the command exactly as written: BOOTREC, a space, a forward slash, and then FIXMBR *not* followed by a period. Press Enter.

In Windows XP, you use the following command to fix the master boot record at the Recovery Console prompt:

```
FIXMBR
```

Press the Enter key, and then press Y and Enter to confirm.

For either version of Windows, the command works instantly. You see another command prompt displayed. Type exit to quit the command prompt, and then restart the PC if it doesn't restart automatically.

When the computer restarts, whatever problems afflicted the MBR should be gone. For example, if you were removing a boot manager program, it no longer appears when the PC first starts.

There's no danger involved in fixing the MBR; if it wasn't damaged, it doesn't screw anything up.

Book II
Chapter 8

Recovery Options

Booting into a recovery partition

PC manufacturers now often partition a computer's primary hard drive into two volumes. Drive C is the computer's main hard drive, the one on which Windows is installed. A second, smaller drive D is created on the same physical hard drive. It's given the name *Recovery,* and it can be used to help rebuild, restore, re-create, or just troubleshoot Windows problems.

Figure 8-5 illustrates a typical Computer window found in Windows Vista. You see that there are two hard drives, C and D, with drive D labeled Recovery. To use that drive for starting the computer and troubleshooting, you need to access the computer's Boot menu.

Figure 8-5:
The
Recovery
drive, found
in the
Computer
window.

A prompt describing which key to press for accessing the Boot menu appears when the computer first starts; see Book I, Chapter 2 for the details. On some computers, it's the F10 key, though on my Dell computer, it's F12.

When the Boot menu appears, notice that one of the options presented is to boot into the recovery volume. Choose that option to start and use the recovery volume.

What happens when you start the Recovery partition depends on the computer manufacturer. You may see a custom operating system loosely based on Windows but geared toward troubleshooting and maintenance. Sometimes, you may see the System Recovery Options window (refer to Figure 8-4). The tools you find available can be used to help you fix the main Windows volume (drive C), access special utilities, or even restore the PC from a backup.

✦ Another way to use the Recovery partition is to choose the Repair Your Computer option from the F8 boot menu, described earlier in this chapter. (See the section "Getting to the recovery console in Windows Vista.")

✦ Some computers may feature a special button, such as the ThinkVantage button on Lenovo laptops, that boots the computer into the recovery volume.

✦ Not every PC has a recovery volume. In that case, I recommend that you use a recovery disc, as mentioned in the next section.

Using a recovery disc

Welcome to the Drastic Measures Department. Here at the DMD, the object is to fix things by wiping them out and then rebuilding them. Have a problem with your plumbing? The easy DMD solution is to level your home and rebuild it from scratch, just the way it was the first day you moved in. Problem solved! Ditto for your computer!

Most PCs sold today come with a recovery disc, or a set of discs. The purpose of those discs is to let you restore your computer to the same condition it was in when you bought it. As far as a recovery solution goes, it is indeed *drastic*. Basically, it works like this:

1. **Insert the recovery disc into your PC's optical drive.**

2. **Restart the computer (or turn it on).**

3. **Boot from the optical disc.**

4. **Obey the directions on the screen for restoring your PC.**

When you're done, the PC exists just as it did when you first bought it. Windows is restored, as is any additional software that came with your computer (though some software might not be included on the main recovery disc).

**Book II
Chapter 8**

Recovery Options

✦ The recovery disc works best only for fixing *software* problems — specifically, massive damage to the Windows operating system. It's ideal for recovery after a virus or other malware is found.

✦ The recovery disc doesn't work to fix hardware problems. If the hard drive is kaput, the recovery disc doesn't help you. It *does* help if you buy and install a replacement hard drive. See Book I, Chapter 8.

✦ Before using a recovery disc, consider running the System File Checker (SFC), as covered earlier in this chapter.

✦ A recovery disc is also part of a backup-restore operation. After recovering the computer to its pristine state, restore your backup files. That recovers your computer fully, bringing it back to the state it was in when the last backup was performed.

✦ Sometimes, you must use several discs to restore your PC. First, you restore Windows. Then you need to use subsequent discs to install drivers for your PC's hardware.

✦ Don't forget about updates! After you restore your computer, immediately use Windows Update to install all necessary updates. You may need to install updates in a series, which can take some time. See Chapter 1.

✦ See Book VI, Chapter 1 for information on Backup and Restore.

✦ See Book IV, Chapter 4 for more information on malware.

Reinstalling Windows

Just as you can reinstall any software program, you can reinstall Windows. It's a relatively easy operation: Start your computer with a Windows disc, either a system recovery disc or any Windows disc. Obey the directions on the screen to install Windows.

If you have a backup disc handy, you don't need to reinstall Windows: Simply restore the data from the backup. You might have to start the computer with the Windows installation disc and then choose an option to run the Restore program. For example, the System Recovery Options window (refer to Figure 8-4) contains an item for running System Restore; see the earlier section "Getting to the recovery console in Windows Vista," for more information on opening that window.

Chapter 9: Registry Fixes

In This Chapter

✓ **Appreciating the Registry**

✓ **Editing the Registry**

✓ **Creating a backup of the Registry**

✓ **Adding a new Registry key or value**

✓ **Searching the Registry**

✓ **Cleaning the Registry**

*W*indows stores all its important information, settings, choices, options, preferences, and the combination to Bill Gates's secret vault in a giant repository called the *Registry*. It's supposed to be a place that mere mortal users fear to tread, yet by hanging out that digital No Trespassing sign, Microsoft sparked legions of curious PC users to prod, probe, and ponder the Registry's mysterious depths. This chapter exists to sate your Registry curiosity, by answering necessary questions and providing tips on keeping that forbidden place safe and solid.

Behold the Registry

In the merry old Land of Oz, Windows is the Wizard. It works its magic mostly behind the scenes, projecting a false image to those who dare to confront it. But if Toto were to pull back the curtain a tad, you would behold the wonders that make Windows work. One of those wonders is the Windows Registry. It's a central part of the operating system's personality. This section explains, first in black and white and later in full Technicolor, how the Registry fits into the PC troubleshooting picture.

The Registry doesn't hold secrets. Settings made in the Registry can just as easily be viewed or changed using Windows itself. A few items hidden in the Registry, however, require you to delve into its depths. Just don't expect anything to overwhelm or thrill you.

Understanding the Registry

The Registry contains information used by Windows and your programs. It helps the operating system manage the computer, it helps programs use the computer's resources, and it provides a location for keeping custom settings you make in both Windows and your programs.

For example, when you change the Windows desktop, the changes are kept in the Registry. When you see a list of recently opened files, that list is kept in the Registry. And, changes you make to the status bar in Word, yep, they're kept in the Registry, too.

The Registry is essentially a database. Its information is stored on disk for the most part, though *dynamic* information also exists in the computer's memory. (That dynamic information concerns the computer's hardware and operating state.) All the information is organized using a structure similar to folders in the file storage system.

The top level of the Registry contains *hives,* each of which starts with the curious word HKEY. Table 9-1 describes the visible hives in the Registry. (The Registry has other hives that are used internally and not of significance, despite your disbelief. Honestly, you should get it out of your head that secret things dwell in the Registry!)

TECHNICAL STUFF

Needless historical Registry information

The Registry has been around since the early days of Windows, but it took on prominence only in Windows 2000 and later. It was created to solve the problem of having too many configuration files.

Back in the early days of Windows, programs used text files to load their options, settings, and other memorable information, such as the high scores for Minesweeper. Those files had the extension .ini and were called "innie" files, though ini was short for initialization.

The problem was that Windows soon grew cluttered with multiple ini files. The two main ini files that governed Windows, system. ini and win.ini, soon grew cumbersome and unwieldy. Programs abused those files. Problems erupted. Civilization almost collapsed.

As a solution, Microsoft created the Registry. It did so with two goals.

The first goal was to create a central repository for vital system and program information. The Registry would have rules, and programs would have to follow specific guidelines to modify or create entries in the Registry.

The second goal, honestly, was to make the Registry a foreboding and inhospitable place. The reason was to keep casual users from poking around and messing things up. On that front, Microsoft failed miserably: The Registry is a source of curiosity for many users who believe that it holds hidden secrets.

Table 9-1		**Registry Hives**
Name	*Abbreviation*	*Contents*
HKEY_CLASSES_ROOT	HKCR	Information used by programs for file association and for sharing information.
HKEY_CURRENT_USER	HKCU	Settings and configuration for the current user.
HKEY_LOCAL_MACHINE	HKLM	Settings and configuration for all users.
HKEY_USERS	HKU	Settings and configuration for each user on the computer; the information in HKCU is copied from this hive when the user logs in.
HKEY_CURRENT_CONFIG	N/A	Hardware information about the PC's resources and configuration.

Book II
Chapter 9

Registry Fixes

Beneath the hives are folders, or *keys.* Keys can also have *subkeys,* just as folders have subfolders. The name of the game is organization.

Keys contain *values.* Each value has a name and data. Unlike the old `ini` files, the data can be something other than text, including numeric values and binary information. You can find several values in a single key, or a key can be empty or just contain subkeys.

As with files and folders, values stored in the Registry are found by following a *pathname* that gives the location of a specific key or value. For example, the following pathname to the key gives the location where Adobe Acrobat Reader 8.0 is installed on the computer:

```
HKCU\Software\Adobe\Acrobat Reader\8.0\InstallPath
```

I used the abbreviation HKCU above for `HKEY_CURRENT_USER`. That's followed by the subkeys Software, Adobe, Acrobat Reader, 8.0, and, finally, InstallPath. In the InstallPath key is a value that holds data in the form of text. The text is the pathname for the storage system location where Acrobat Reader 8.0 is installed.

Keys, like pathnames to files, can get long. Sometimes, it's necessary to wrap a key name that's too long to fit on a single line, such as

```
HKCU\Software\Microsoft\Windows\CurrentVersion\Explorer\
    VisualEffects\CursorShadow
```

This key contains a binary value that determines whether Windows displays a shadow on the mouse pointer. The line is too long to fit on the page, so it wraps.

Incidentally, that CursorShadow key helps demonstrate a point I will continue to drive home: You can easily turn the mouse pointer shadow on or off by using the Mouse Properties dialog box, on the Pointers tab. You don't have to delve into the Registry, nor is there any advantage to doing so.

✦ To view or modify the Registry, the Registry Editor program is used, as covered in the next section.

✦ Some keys may be empty, though they still contain a *Default* value. That's because all keys must contain a value or a subkey.

✦ The Registry concept exists in all modern computer operating systems. In Unix, for example, custom settings are kept in the /etc directory. In Mac OS X, settings are kept in a Library folder.

Using the Registry Editor

To view, modify, or create information in the Registry, you use the *Registry Editor* program. It's also known by its filename, regedit.

To run the Registry Editor, follow these steps:

1. **Press Win+R to summon the Run dialog box.**

2. **Type** regedit **and press Enter.**

3. **In Windows Vista, type the administrator's password or click Continue.**

Behold the Registry Editor window on the screen, shown in Figure 9-1.

Figure 9-1:
The Registry Editor.

The Registry Editor window works a lot like Windows Explorer does for navigating folders on the PC's storage system: Open a key, or click the triangle next to it, to display that key's contents. Values appear on the right side of the window, as shown in Figure 9-1.

A pathname appears on the Registry Editor window status bar (at the bottom of the window), which helps you better determine which key is selected.

4. **Close the Registry Editor window when you're done.**

The next several sections describe various things you can do in the Registry Editor.

All the information organized into keys and values is vitally important to Windows. Don't experiment with the Registry, by modifying values to see what happens. Doing so can have adverse effects on your computer.

✦ Nerds like me also point out that you can run the Registry Editor by popping up the Start menu and typing **regedit** in the Search box. Then click the Registry Editor icon that appears on the menu. That doesn't work, however, on every PC.

✦ It's possible to explore the Registry, to view things, to waste time there. But don't view the Registry as a playground or an opportunity to learn more about your computer. Use the Registry only when you need to, such as when directed to do something by documentation or technical support people.

✦ Once upon a time, the program `regedit32` was used to edit the Registry. That's no longer the case. A program named `regedit32` still exists in Windows, but it merely runs the regular Registry Editor program, `regedit`.

Backing up the Registry

A healthy thing that any sane user does before messing with the Registry is to back it up. Back up! Back up! Back up! I shan't be sick of screaming that mantra!

Follow these steps to back up the Registry:

1. **Summon the Registry Editor, as described earlier in this chapter.**

2. **Choose File➪Export.**

   The Export Registry File window appears. It's basically a specialized version of the typical Save As dialog box.

3. **Choose a location for the backup.**

   Windows automatically selects the System32 folder beneath the Windows folder. Saving the backup there works, but I recommend that you instead choose your User Profile (or "home") folder instead, or save to an external device, like a media card.

4. **Type a name for the backup.**

   I name the backup based on the reason for backing up — for example, `Removing files from MRU lists`.

5. **Click the Save button to save.**

6. **Proceed with whatever you plan on doing in the Registry.**

7. **Close the Registry Editor window when you're done.**

To restore a Registry backup, choose File➪Import in the Registry Editor.

A backup of the Registry is made when you set a restore point in Windows. In fact, a quick way to restore the Registry is simply to run System Restore. But, like backing up the Registry, you need to ensure that you set a restore point before you modify the Registry. (See Chapter 8 for more information on System Restore.)

Modifying the Registry

You can do three things to modify the Registry:

✦ Add a new key.

✦ Add a new value.

✦ Rename a key or value.

✦ Change an existing value.

✦ Delete a key or value.

I strongly recommend that you take any of these actions only upon direction from a higher authority. The Registry isn't a playground or a place to experiment — even on your spouse's laptop.

Here are the general steps you take to modify the Registry:

1. **Start the Registry Editor.**

   Refer to the directions found earlier in this chapter.

2. **Back up the Registry.**

   See the section "Backing up the Registry," just before this section.

3. **Open the key containing the item you want to modify.**

   The higher authority tells you the key's pathname. For example:

   ```
   HKCU\Software\Microsoft\Windows\CurrentVersion\
      Explorer\Advanced
   ```

   Start at the top level, the hive. Then open successive folders until you find the key you're looking for. The key just mentioned contains numerous settings for Windows.

4. **To create a new key, follow these substeps:**

   a. *Choose Edit⇨New⇨Key from the menu.*

   The new key appears, with its name (New Key #1) selected for editing.

   b. *Type the key's name and press Enter.*

   The key is created, but it's empty; it contains no values. The next step is probably to create a value for the key.

5. **To create a new value, follow these substeps:**

   a. *Choose Edit⇨New.*

   b. *Select the data type from the New menu.*

   The higher authority you're referencing should specify which data type to choose. After you choose the data type, the new value appears in the key. Its name is selected, ready for renaming.

   c. *Type the value's name.*

   Creating a value doesn't set the value's data. (Well, actually, it sets the data to zero.) See Step 7 to set a value.

6. **To rename a key or value, follow these substeps:**

   a. *Select the key or value to rename.*

   b. *Press the F2 key.*

   F2 is the Rename keyboard shortcut in Windows.

   c. *Type the new name and press Enter.*

7. **To change a value, follow these substeps:**

   a. *Double-click the value to summon an editing dialog box.*

   The Edit dialog box that appears is customized for the type of data the value stores. Sometimes, it's a simple numeric value or string, as shown in Figure 9-2, but the Edit window can be quite complex when editing raw binary data. Again, the Registry isn't a place to tread lightly.

   b. *Type the new data.*

   c. *Click OK.*

Book II
Chapter 9

Registry Fixes

Figure 9-2:
Editing a
value in the
Registry.

8. **To delete a key or value, follow these substeps:**

 a. *Select the key or value.*

 b. *Press the Delete key on the keyboard.*

  Deleting a key deletes all the key's values and all the subkeys and all their values.

 c. *Click the Yes button to confirm.*

9. **Close the Registry Editor window when you're done.**

The changes you make to the Registry may or may not take effect right away. Sometimes, you need to restart Windows to test the changes.

✦ See Table 9-1 for a list of common abbreviations used to describe the Registry hives.

✦ The Registry Editor window remembers which keys were open the last time it was used. Because of that, you may have to scroll to the top part of the left pane and close the top-level hives to better get around the various keys.

✦ You must be precise when creating or renaming a key or value! A misnamed key or value may not harm Windows, but then again it doesn't have any effect whatsoever.

✦ I don't consider Web pages or advice from an Internet chat room a "higher authority" for modifying the Registry.

✦ Only when you can confirm directions from two separate sources on the Internet should you consider following those directions to modify the Registry. Even then, be sure to check that the two sources aren't just duplicate copies of the same information.

✦ One of the best sources for Registry information is the Microsoft support site: http://support.microsoft.com.

Finding stuff in the Registry

Occasionally, you don't know where something exists in the Registry, but you know that it exists. In those instances, you need to summon the power of the Registry Editor's Find command to help you locate the text or information tidbit you desire. Here's how:

1. **Start the Registry Editor.**

 Refer to directions found elsewhere in this chapter.

2. **Back up the Registry.**

 "Oh, but I'm just finding something." Sure you are. Back up anyway. Directions are found earlier in this chapter, in the section "Backing up the Registry."

TIP

Test your Registry-editing prowess

If you're desiring to mess with the Registry, here's a tip for you: You can add to the Registry a value that suppresses the balloon tips that pop up from the notification area in Windows Vista. This value is one of those rare ones that cannot be set from within Windows itself; only by editing the Registry can you fix that annoying issue. Follow these steps:

1. Open the Registry Editor.

2. Navigate to this key:

```
HKCU\Software\Microsoft\
    Windows\CurrentVersion\
    Explorer\Advanced
```

3. Choose Edit⇨New⇨DWORD (32-Bit) value.

4. Name the new value **EnableBalloonTips**.

That's it. Because the data for the value is automatically created at zero, the Balloon Tips feature is disabled. To enable it, you reset the value to 1 or just delete the value.

**Book II
Chapter 9**

Registry Fixes

3. **Scroll to the top of the left side of the window and click the word** *Computer.*

   By selecting Computer, you ensure that your search starts at the beginning of the Registry.

4. **Press Ctrl+F.**

   The Find dialog box appears, as shown in Figure 9-3.

Figure 9-3:
Use the Find dialog box to locate tidbits in the Registry.

   Enter the text you want to find — for example, the name of a file that appears in a most recently used (MRU) list.

5. **Click the Find Next button.**

6. **Review the key or value to ensure that it's the one you're looking for.**

   Depending on how detailed you were, some false positives might occur in the search.

7. **Click the Find Next button, if necessary, to locate the next tidbit in the Registry.**

8. **Do whatever task needs completing when you find what you're looking for.**

9. **Close the Registry Editor window when you're done.**

Indeed, the Registry is huge. Sometimes it can take a long time to search it. Yet that's why the Find command exists.

✦ I generally close the Find dialog box after the first find result. You don't have to close the dialog box, but it does get in the way.

✦ You can press the F3 key to repeat the last Find command. The F3 shortcut is handy because it lets you repeat a search without reopening the Find dialog box.

Registry Cleaning

Oh, how many times do I need to say that you don't really need to mess with the Registry? I shouldn't even bother repeating myself, but I do. To bring the message home, I'd like to address the issue of cleaning the Registry. In a word: Don't.

Sure, some third-party utilities claim that they can somehow miraculously scour the Registry and remove redundant entries and unused keys and values or purge the Registry of nasty things. Although that statement might be true, it's probably not. Therefore, I don't recommend using a Registry cleaner or even attempting to do so on your own.

✦ Many of those free Registry cleaners that you download from the Internet are really spyware. They serve only to slow down your computer, making the problem worse.

✦ Some free Registry cleaners are Trojan horses.

✦ Honestly, it would be impossible for any third-party program to know which Registry keys are useless and whether they can be deleted. To assume that any program would know that information is ridiculous.

✦ Cleaning the Registry may do more damage than good.

✦ No evidence exists that any Registry-cleaning utility provides any improvement in performance.

✦ I can, however, recommend anti-spyware programs or other utilities that purge spyware and other nasty programs from the Registry. Those programs know what to look for and, therefore, actually do something useful. (See Book IV, Chapter 4 for more information.)

Book III
Laptops

The 5th Wave — By Rich Tennant

"Hurry, Stuart! The power bar's almost on zero!"

Contents at a Glance

Chapter 1: Laptop Asleep, Laptop Awake, Laptop Dead

In This Chapter

✔ Dealing with start-up problems

✔ Fixing a snoozing laptop

✔ Controlling what happens when you close the lid

✔ Understanding hybrid sleep

✔ Dealing with hibernation

✔ Fixing the power management system

✔ Checking the battery

✔ Setting battery alerts

✔ Keeping the battery happy

A laptop computer lives a carefree existence, untethered by the wires that bind its desktop cousin. Although it can do everything a desktop computer can do, and suffers the same slings and arrows of outrageous misfortune, laptops have their own, special quirks. Most of those quirks involve the laptop's amazing ability to run on its own power, which is this chapter's subject.

Laptop Start-Up Issues

Perhaps the number-one issue that vexes laptop owners is the problem of turning on a laptop and experiencing the dread of nothing happening. Nothing. No power. No blinking lights. Nada. This section addresses those start-up issues.

✦ Computers, even laptops, suffer problems when there's a change. Did you add or change anything recently, hardware or software? Did you drop or damage the laptop? Or, perhaps the machine is suffering from the greatest change of all: time. Old laptops fail.

✦ The abbreviation *AC* is used in this section. It stands for *alternating current*, the type of power that comes from a wall socket. This is opposed to the direct current (DC) supplied by a laptop's battery.

✦ Also see Book I, Chapter 2 for general start-up issues.

Laptop just won't start

There are several phases of "just won't start" when it comes to a laptop. The problem with not being able to start is compounded because a laptop has two power sources: When AC isn't available, electricity is drawn from the laptop's battery. So you know immediately that when the laptop doesn't turn on right away, you have a power supply issue.

+ If the laptop appears dead, there's a power supply issue. Check to ensure that the laptop is plugged in.

+ Check to ensure that the battery is properly installed.

+ Try removing the battery to run the laptop just from the AC power. If that works, you may have a defective battery that needs replacing.

+ If you have a second battery, use it instead.

+ Check the power brick on the AC cord. Is it the right adapter for your laptop? Other portable devices may have similar-looking adapters, but unless they match the volts and amps for your laptop, the laptop won't work. (Not that this has ever happened to me.)

+ Volts and Amps would be great team names. Imagine them playing each other. It would be electric.

+ When the laptop's power lamp is on, it shows that the laptop has some sign of life. It means that the laptop's hardware is recognizing that it has power. The problem could then lie with the laptop's hardware, not with the power supply.

+ When your laptop has separate lamps for the AC power and battery, you can check both to see where the problem lies. If the AC lamp lights but not the battery, there's a battery issue. When the battery lamp is lit but the AC lamp remains dark, the AC power brick might be dead or the AC power from the wall could be messed up, or you might have a connection issue.

+ If you consider yourself to be technically proficient, you can try testing some hardware. For example, if the laptop has removable disk drives, check to ensure that they're properly connected: With the laptop's power off, take out the drives and put them back in again. Ditto for the PC's memory card: Turn off the laptop, remove the memory, and then put it back.

+ Laptops don't start when they're broken. I'm not being flip, either: Laptop hardware can fail. Failed electronics are covered by most laptop warranties. You need to get support by contacting the laptop manufacturer.

Why you need a laptop warranty

In my book *Laptops For Dummies* (Wiley Publishing), I recommend buying at least a three-year warranty on a laptop. No, you're not paying to pad the manufacturer's bottom line; you're simply taking out insurance on a product you need.

Long-term warranties are necessary for a laptop because of their miniaturized nature. It's not that the manufacturers need Oompa Loompas to fix the little gizmos, it's that, unlike desktop PCs, laptop components cannot easily be replaced or repaired. To fix a problem with your laptop's wireless connection, for example,

the entire motherboard may need to be replaced. That ain't cheap.

If you can afford a warranty longer than three years, buy one. Many manufacturers offer long-term warranties. I buy five-year warranties for my laptops, as long as I plan to use them for that length of time.

You do not, however, need to buy an extended service plan. Those are sold by the dealer, and they don't provide extra coverage of laptop hardware. If you sleep better at night with an extended service plan, buy one. But, for most people, buying at least a three-year warranty serves them well.

Laptop is slow to start

Time issues are subject to perception, so the question of "slow" is always relative. Windows Vista, for example, is notorious for looking like it finished starting up but in fact has several more seconds of gyrations to complete before you can smoothly use the laptop.

The finger of slow-start blame can be pointed equally at hardware and software. Alas, there's little you can do for hardware problems other than return the laptop to the shop.

On the software, side, I recommend that you check the system for spyware or other nasty software. See Book IV, Chapter 4 for more information. Also consider defragging the hard drive, as covered in Book VI, Chapter 2.

You have control over how much the laptop does when it starts. Running a host of start-up programs — instant messaging, Webcams, the Windows Vista Sidebar, as well as other utilities — add time to the computer's start-up process. Most of those programs can be started as you need them. Consider reconfiguring that software not to start automatically when the laptop starts.

Laptop won't wake up

A wakeup problem isn't really a start-up problem, but is, rather, a failure of the laptop's power management system. The situation arises when you put the laptop to sleep (in Stand By mode) or hibernate it. When you go to rouse the laptop, nothing happens.

First, try screaming at the laptop. Loudly say "Get up!" I've found, surprisingly, that this method doesn't work.

Second, try pressing the Ctrl key on the laptop. That should rouse it out of Sleep mode. I assume, however, that you probably tried that one already.

When pressing a key on the keyboard doesn't work, press and hold the laptop's Power button until the system turns off. After it's off, restart the laptop. Of course, that fixes the symptoms but not the disease.

To fix the laptop-won't-wake-up disease, you need to confirm that the laptop is using the most current version of the power management software. See the section "Updating power drivers," later in this chapter.

- ✦ Try not to scream "Get up" in public libraries. I will not explain further why I believe this to be a bad idea.

- ✦ The laptop won't wake up when it's on battery power and the batteries are low or drained dry.

- ✦ The laptop's power lamps should be on when the laptop is in Sleep mode. If the lamps are off, the laptop has been turned off.

- ✦ A laptop's power lamps are often on when the laptop is plugged in. That simply means that, duh, the laptop is plugged in. Unplugging the laptop should cause the lights to turn off.

Check the display

Sometimes, the power lamps are lit but the laptop still appears to be dead or sleeping. As long the power lamps are up, there may still be hope.

First, just as with a crashed desktop, press the Caps Lock key. The Caps Lock lamp on the laptop should blink on and off as you press the key. If so, the laptop is functioning, but the display may have a problem.

Second, check the display's brightness settings. If it's turned down too much, the screen will be dark, especially in a bright room. In that same vein, know that LCD displays don't work well outside or in direct sunlight. Some displays may not be backlit and may not show up at all in low light.

Third, look at the screen closely to ensure that it's not working.

Finally, plug an external monitor into the laptop's monitor port. Today's laptops are designed to instantly recognize and use those external monitors, though you may have to press a special Fn (Function) key combination to make sure. If the external monitor works, the problem is with the laptop's display only, not with the laptop's display adapter or other internal hardware.

Sadly, you cannot go to the store and buy another "laptop monitor." Because the laptop and monitor are the same thing, fixing the monitor (or the display adapter) involves replacing major laptop components. You must return the laptop to the dealer for repair.

Laptop starts and then turns off

As on a desktop PC, a laptop that starts up and shuts down right away has a hardware issue. You can try starting in Safe mode (see Book II, Chapter 3) to see whether the problem continues. If so, it's hardware.

✦ Is the laptop too hot? Heat and electronics do not mix! Consider getting a cooling pad for your laptop as a solution.

✦ Also refer to the section "Problems with Restarting" found in Book I, Chapter 3.

Laptop turns off and then immediately starts

Sometimes, a laptop demonstrates its disdain for being turned off by refusing to turn itself off. There are two causes: human error and power management problems.

Before blaming the hardware, try to remember whether you chose the Shutdown command or the Sleep command. If you chose Sleep instead, it might explain why the laptop is turning on again.

Sometimes a laptop restarts when it's installing updates. If so, try shutting it down again.

If the laptop continually restarts, it's a problem with the power management hardware. Take the laptop into the shop.

Laptop won't stay asleep

Unlike small children, a laptop must obey you when you send it to Sleep mode. But keep in mind that a computer does wake up when you press a key or move the mouse. I've even found that pounding the table next to a sensitive mouse can jar it enough to wake a PC. So, no table pounding!

When the mouse or touch pad is overly sensitive, you can check the system's BIOS settings to see whether you can disable the mouse from waking the computer. See Book I, Chapter 2 for information on checking into the computer's BIOS settings. Note, however, that not every laptop has settings for Sleep mode that monitor the mouse (or keyboard).

You might consider checking the BIOS settings to ensure that the laptop isn't waking up because of network activity.

Before sending the laptop into the shop

Coming in first in the category of painful departures, only second to sending a child off to college, is sending your laptop away for fixin' at the factory. Time for some comfort food! But before you indulge, I recommend doing several things — if possible.

Back up the laptop. Your data is important to you. Your data is *not* important to the factory that fixes your laptop. Back up your stuff before sending any computer away if you can possibly do so. This process may involve removing the hard drive and connecting it to a PC or another laptop by using an external hard drive case to pull off the data. See Book VI, Chapter 1.

Document the problem. It helps the people fixing your laptop to know as much about the situation as possible. For example, is the problem predictably repeatable? Double-check what you're doing to ensure that an easy or overlooked fix isn't available.

Contact text support. Sure, let them have fun with it. Maybe they can help you, but most likely they'll give you a case number and authorize a warranty fix.

Put the laptop in its original packaging. In my book *PCs For Dummies* (Wiley Publishing, again), I recommend keeping all your original computer boxes. Shipping the laptop in its original box is necessary for returns. It's also good to have when you move or otherwise need to store the laptop long-term.

When you're ready to send off the laptop, send it by following whatever directions you're given. Many manufacturers have Web pages that help you track the laptop's progress and diagnosis. Don't expect any miracles, though: the factory will probably merely confirm that the laptop is broken, swap out the parts, and then send it back to you. Or, it may send you another laptop as a replacement. It all depends on the warranty.

What Happens When You Close the Lid

I don't have any hard data, but my guess is that a laptop computer gets started and stopped more often than a desktop computer. It's the lid. Because you can close the lid on a laptop, you can quickly pick it up and be on the road. Closing the lid, however, raises an important point: what happens when you do close your laptop's lid? To find out, follow these steps:

1. **Open the Control Panel's Power Options icon.**

2a. **In Windows Vista, click the link that says Choose What Closing the Lid Does.**

2b. **In Windows XP, click the Advanced tab.**

You see a screen that shows options for the laptop's Power button, Sleep button, and lid. Figure 1-1 shows the Windows Vista version of the available settings.

Figure 1-1:
Power options for closing the laptop's lid.

3. **Choose a power option for the lid.**

Your choices are

Do nothing: Closing the laptop's lid does nothing; when the laptop is on, it stays on.

Hibernate: The laptop goes into Hibernation mode, saving the contents of memory and then turning off the system.

Shut down: The laptop turns itself off.

Sleep/Stand By: The laptop goes into a special low-power state.

4. **(Optional) Set the lid's function for times when the laptop is plugged in or running from battery power.**

5. **Click the Save Changes or OK button.**

When I'm on the road, I prefer to have my laptops go into Hibernation mode when I shut the lid. That way, I'm not losing battery power. (I generally shut the lid when I'm done working.) At home, the laptops turn themselves off when I shut the lid.

✦ If nothing happens when you close the laptop's lid, Do Nothing is probably the selected option. To change that predicament, follow the preceding set of steps.

✦ If you put the laptop into Sleep mode when you shut the lid, be mindful that it drains the battery over time. Sleep mode is fine for short durations, and the laptop recovers quickly from being in Sleep mode. But if you close the lid, put the laptop into Sleep mode, and then stick it in your case, the battery drains over time. Nothing is more disappointing than opening your laptop on the road and finding the battery dead.

✦ Windows Vista uses the term *sleep*; Windows XP uses the term *Stand By*. Both refer to what's commonly called *Sleep mode*.

✦ I've not seen a laptop with a separate Sleep button in a few years, but some desktop PCs still have that option.

✦ Windows XP lacks separate Power button settings for times when the laptop is plugged in.

✦ Similar power options exist for desktop PCs, but not the "close the lid" options, for obvious reasons.

✦ The Do Nothing option might seem useless for closing the laptop's lid, but it can come in handy. For example, when using the laptop with an external monitor or keyboard, having it do nothing when you close the lid means that you can keep using the computer while keeping it in a smaller location.

Power Management Issues

The laptop's power management hardware is one of the Three Sisters of Despair when it comes to computer problems. Officially known as the Advanced Configuration and Power Interface (ACPI), it's the hardware and software specification that allows your computer to go into Sleep mode, hibernate, manage power consumption, and shut itself off. This section explores potential ways to deal with power management problems.

✦ The other two sisters in the Despair trio are the display adapter and networking hardware.

✦ See Book I, Chapter 6 for information on troubleshooting PC display issues.

✦ Refer to Book V for network troubleshooting.

✦ You can see my books *Laptops For Dummies* (Wiley Publishing) or *PCs For Dummies* (also Wiley) for an explanation of the various computer power-saving options. If you can't decide which to buy, buy both.

✦ See my book *Laptops For Dummies* for information on customizing a power plan for your laptop.

Explaining Windows Vista hybrid sleep

Microsoft introduced a new power management concept for Windows Vista. Called *hybrid sleep*, it confuses the bejeebers out of many power-management-conscious computer users. Allow me to explain.

Hybrid sleep is neither hibernation nor Sleep mode (called Stand By under Windows XP). Nope, it's *both*.

Sill confused? Sorry.

In hybrid sleep, the computer is placed into Sleep mode. No big deal. Additionally, however, information in memory is saved to disk — just like in hibernation. The advantage is that you can easily rouse the computer from hybrid sleep just as you can from Sleep mode. But, if the power goes out or the laptop's battery drains, information is saved to disk, just like in hibernation. So it's a combination of both modes.

Hybrid sleep must be enabled for you to use it. Here's how to enable hybrid sleep, or to confirm that it's active:

1. **Open the Control Panel's Power Options icon.**

   The Power Options window appears.

2. **Beneath your selected power plan, click the link that says Change Plan Settings.**

3. **Click the link Change Advanced Power Settings.**

   The Power Options dialog box appears, as shown in Figure 1-2.

Figure 1-2: Turning on hybrid sleep.

4. Click the plus sign (+) by the word *Sleep*.

5. Click the plus sign (+) by the phrase *Allow Hybrid Sleep*.

6. To allow hybrid sleep when the laptop is on battery power, click the word *Off* to display a menu button, and then choose the word *On* from the menu.

7. To allow hybrid sleep when the laptop is plugged in, click the word *Off* to display a menu button, and then choose the word *On* from the menu.

8. Click OK to close the Edit Plan Settings window.

If you want to not use hybrid sleep and just stick with sleep and hibernation modes, disable hybrid sleep by setting the Allow Hybrid Sleep options to Off in Steps 6 and 7.

Finding hibernation in Windows Vista

You may notice the Hibernation command missing from the Start menu's Shutdown menu, tearfully depicted in Figure 1-3.

Figure 1-3:
Wo liegt die *hibernation* Befehl?

Start menu power button

Hibernation missing

Shutdown menu

Don't freak. The Hibernation command is gone because hybrid sleep has been activated. To see Hibernation back on the Shutdown menu, turn off hybrid sleep, as described in the preceding section.

You can also set the function of the software's Power button (also refer to Figure 3-3 in Book I, Chapter 3) to place the laptop into hibernation. Here's how:

1. **Open the Control Panel's Power Options icon.**
2. **Click the link that says Change Plan Settings, found beneath the selected power plan.**
3. **Choose Change Advanced Power Settings.**
4. **In the Power Options dialog box, click the plus sign (+) to open the section under Power Buttons and Lid.**
5. **Click the plus sign (+) by the Start Menu Power Button option.**

   Two options are beneath the Start Menu Power Button item: one for setting the button's function on battery power and the other for when the laptop is plugged into the wall.

6. **Choose Hibernate for both options.**

   Clicking the setting for an option displays a drop-down menu from which you can choose Hibernate.

7. **Click OK. Close the Edit Plan Settings window.**

Of course, you could also choose Sleep or Shutdown for the Start menu Power button, but the point of this exercise is to make the Hibernate option available.

Speeding up hibernation

Sometimes, getting into Hibernation mode can be time-consuming. Be patient. The laptop will get there, but you can pull one trick to try accelerating the process: Defragment the hard drive.

Because hibernation copies information from disk to memory, it pays to keep the hard drive maintained. By defragmenting the drive, you ensure that ample space is available to quickly copy swaths of memory to disk. That helps expedite not only hibernation shut down but also start-up.

**Book III
Chapter 1**

**Laptop Asleep,
Laptop Awake,
Laptop Dead**

✦ Refer to Book VI, Chapter 2 for more information on defragmenting the hard drive.

✦ The laptop's hard drive light (also known as the "moon" light) may flicker as the system goes into hibernation. That's normal. Expect to see the lamp lit until the system turns itself off. That means it's okay to close the lid and put the laptop away: it eventually turns itself off.

Testing the power management hardware

There's no direct way to confirm that you have a booboo in the computer's power management software. Even when you do, the result is the same: You have to turn the laptop over to the manufacturer (or wherever) to get it fixed. Even on a desktop PC, the power management hardware is part of the motherboard and not something you can fix, like replacing a Lego brick.

The good news: The laptop's ACPI hardware has its own BIOS. That means that, like other BIOSs in the system, it does its own testing and diagnostics when you first start the machine. So the first place to look for power management hardware trouble is the PC's start-up screen, where you may find various power management, or ACPI, start-up error messages.

Another way to test the power management hardware is to use the System Information utility. Because some laptop manufacturers poorly implement the ACPI standard, there may be conflicts that the System Information utility would detect. Follow these steps:

1. **From the Start menu, choose All Programs⇨Accessories⇨System Tools⇨System Information.**

2. **Click the plus sign (+) to expand the Hardware Resources list on the left side of the System Information window.**

3. **Choose Conflicts/Sharing.**

   You see a list of items displayed, as shown in Figure 1-4.

Figure 1-4: Scanning for potential power-management hardware trouble.

The items in the list are both conflicts *and* sharing. What you probably see, as shown in Figure 1-4, are shared hardware resources, which aren't a problem. But:

4. **Scan the list for any mention of power management hardware — specifically, the acronym ACPI.**

Finding something wrong with the ACPI hardware merely confirms your suspicion. Again, there's no way to fix the problem, especially by using the System Information window.

5. **Close the System Information window.**

Hardware issues, especially IRQ conflicts, aren't as prevalent in today's laptop hardware as they once were, and then primarily with PC desktops loaded with expansion cards. Even so, checking the System Information display may explain why you're having power management issues.

For example, if the power management hardware is being shared with an internal modem, you may notice power management issues when the modem is being used. That's the type of conflict the System Information window would highlight. Resolving the issue involves reconfiguring the conflicting hardware, which might be possible in the BIOS/Setup program.

✦ Refer to Book 1, Chapter 1 for more information on the PC's start-up process. The details described in that chapter apply equally to desktop and laptop computers.

✦ It's difficult to troubleshoot power management issues in Safe mode. That's because the power management software isn't loaded in Safe mode, which means that even if the power management hardware is broken, there's no way to test it. See Book II, Chapter 3 for more information on Safe mode.

✦ The System Information window is covered in Book II, Chapter 7. See the section "Getting system information."

Updating power drivers

Most often, power management issues are resolved by obtaining the latest version of your laptop's ACPI power management software, or *device driver*. Ensuring that you have the latest version is something you should check; the Windows Update program may not look for new power management software for you.

The easy way to check for new power management software is to follow these steps in Windows Vista:

1. **Open the Device Manager icon in the Control Panel.**

2. **Type the administrator's password or click the Continue button.**

3. **Open the System Devices branch to display the items beneath that heading.**

4. **Right-click the item Microsoft ACPI-Compliant System.**

5. **Choose the item Update Driver from the shortcut menu.**

6. **Follow the directions on-screen.**

   In some cases, the driver may claim to be up-to-date — but don't give up yet; skip to the section after the following steps for Windows XP.

In Windows XP, obey these steps:

1. **Press Win+Break to quickly summon the System dialog box.**

2. **Click the Hardware tab.**

3. **Click the Device Manager button.**

4. **Open the System Devices item by clicking the plus sign (+).**

5. **Right-click Microsoft ACPI-Compliant System.**

6. **Choose the shortcut menu item Update Driver.**

7. **Heed the instructions on-screen.**

You might also try repeating these directions, but use the item titled Microsoft ACPI-Compliant Embedded Controller in Step 5. (Indeed, you can choose any of the items with ACPI in them if one seems to be the source of trouble, such as the ACPI Lid item when you're having issues with the laptop not sleeping when you close the lid.)

The automatic method described in these steps may not work. In that case, you must visit the laptop manufacturer's Web site. Search the Support section for your PC's make and model for any new power management drivers.

✦ Some Web sites offer a scanning utility that can confirm whether the laptop's software is up-to-date. Use those tools!

✦ Do not remove any of the ACPI entries, because doing so may disable some of your laptop's power management features, such as the ability to sleep the laptop by pressing the Power button. Also, it is a *real pain* to reinstall those features after they've been removed.

✦ See Book II, Chapter 1 for more information on Windows Update.

✦ See Book I, Chapter 7 for a discussion of the Device Manager.

A Battery of Issues

The key to unlocking the door of laptop freedom is the battery. You must care for the laptop's battery with loving affection. This section has some tips and suggestions.

Monitoring battery life

Your laptop may be fortunate enough to provide you with *two* battery meters, and perhaps more. You're the lucky one, indeed. Imagine a car with two fuel gauges.

No, a car with two fuel gauges doesn't work the same. Unless the car has two gas tanks, having two fuel gauges is obsessive and sad. No, laptops are special.

The first battery meter is found on the laptop's case, along with other fancy lamps: power, hard drive, Caps Lock, Num Lock, and wireless activity, for example. The lamp may be solid, or it might fade over time or change colors. Although such a thing is handy, it's only for show. You need more information, which is why Windows provides you with a second software battery meter.

The second battery meter is found in Windows, in the notification area, shown in Figure 1-5. The tiny icon appears in two ways: one when the laptop is plugged in or charging and another when the battery is being used. In the latter case, the icon drains as the battery is used.

Figure 1-5:
The battery
meter.

By pointing the mouse at the battery meter, a pop-up balloon appears, detailing battery life, as shown in Figure 1-5. In Windows Vista, you can click the icon to see even more information.

The battery meter is supposed to show up in the notification area on all Windows laptops. If you don't see it, you can twist some arms to get it to show up.

In Windows Vista, follow these steps to show the battery icon in the notification area:

1. **Open the Taskbar and Start Menu icon in the Control Panel.**

2. **Click the Notification Area tab.**

3. **Place a check mark by the Power Icon item.**

4. **Click OK.**

In Windows XP, obey these directions to make the notification area (well, system tray) battery icon to appear:

1. **Open the Control Panel's Power Options icon.**

2. **Click the Advanced tab.**

3. **Place a check mark by the item Always Show icon on the Taskbar.**

4. **Click OK.**

Your laptop may feature, in addition to the hardware battery meter and the teensy battery icon in the notification area, a third meter. Some laptops feature a manufacturer's battery meter. It might be a toolbar, an extra notification area icon, or another tool or feature.

- ✦ If you're a fan of the Windows Vista Sidebar, various battery power gadgets are available.

- ✦ Good meters show both battery percentage remaining as well as time remaining.

- ✦ The battery time remaining is an estimate. Don't bet the bank on it.

- ✦ The battery meter lies. Generally, the meter skews toward being full more than it shows a steady decline representing the battery's true power. So don't be surprised when the battery power drops quickly as it gets low; when the meter claims you have 15 minutes left, you probably have more like 7 minutes until the laptop runs out of juice.

Setting low battery warnings

Windows can be configured to assault you with various low battery warnings. Furthermore, you can configure Windows to automatically hibernate or shut down your laptop when the battery gets *way* too low.

In Windows Vista, follow these nimble directions to set the low-battery-power warnings:

1. **Open the Power Options icon in the Control Panel.**

2. **Beneath the selected power plan, click the link Change Plan Settings.**

3. **Click the link Change Advanced Power Settings.**

   The Power Options dialog box shows up.

4. **Click the plus sign (+) by Battery.**

   There are five items for consideration, each with settings available for when the laptop is plugged in or on battery power. These are the items, in chronological order:

Low Battery Notification: Turns on a warning for when the battery power gets low, as set by the Low Battery Level item.

Low Battery Level: Determines at which percentage the Low Battery Notification warning appears. The value is set as a percentage of battery life.

Low Battery Action: Specifies what happens when the battery reaches the Low Battery Level warning. Options are Do Nothing, Hibernate, Sleep, and Shut Down.

Critical Battery Level: Determines at which percentage the critical battery action takes place. Values are set as a percentage of battery life and must be lower than the Low Battery Level values.

Critical Battery Action: Specifies what happens when the battery reaches the percentage set by the Critical Battery Level. Options for On Battery are Hibernate, Sleep, and Shutdown. The additional option of Do Nothing is available for when the laptop is plugged in.

5. **Set the values for the various warnings, levels, and actions.**

6. **Click OK and (optional) close the Edit Plan Settings window.**

In Windows XP, obey these directions to set various battery warnings:

1. **Open the Control Panel's Power Options icon.**

2. **Click the Alarms tab.**

3. **Place a check mark by the item Activate Low Battery Alarm When Power Level Reaches.**

4. **Use the slider to set the battery percentage level for the Low Battery Alarm.**

   Ten percent seems like a good level.

5. **Click the Alarm Actions button.**

6. **Choose what happens when the alarm kicks in.**

   For example, set a Sound Alarm or Display Message. Add an action, such as Hibernate, Sleep, or Shut Down.

7. **Click OK to close the Alarm Actions dialog box.**

8. **Repeat Steps 3 through 7 for the Critical Battery Alarm.**

9. **Click OK to close the Power Options Properties dialog box.**

The visual warnings you specify appear as shown in Figure 1-6. Obey them!

Figure 1-6:
A low-
battery-
power
warning.

It might make no sense to have options for low and critical battery levels when the laptop is plugged in, but consider what happens when the battery is charging: If you plug in a laptop when the battery is low, and the Plugged In setting for Critical Battery Action were set to Shut Down, the laptop would turn itself off even when it's plugged in.

Swapping batteries

Unlike flashlights, toys, and television remotes, laptops don't share a common battery size and shape. They may in the future (let's hope), but for now: Nope. So, although you cannot swap batteries with another laptop user (unless they have *exactly* the same kind of battery), you can buy your laptop a second battery and use that battery to prolong battery life.

Whether your laptop came with two batteries or you purchased one after the fact, swapping batteries works simply:

1. **Charge the spare battery.**

   No point in swapping in a dead battery.

2. **Save all your stuff before the swap.**

3. **Have the spare battery at hand.**

4. **Eject the laptop's battery.**

5. **Insert the spare.**

6. **Continue working.**

Your laptop has the ability to keep itself alive while the batteries are being swapped. As long as you do so immediately, you should be able to remove the battery and replace it with no interruption in computing (though the screen may go blank).

   ✦ Use a Sharpie to label your batteries. Name them A and B or Fred and Ethel. That way, you don't mistakenly swap in the same battery. Avoid using tape or anything sticky to label a battery, because the sticky stuff is adversely affected by the battery's heat.

✦ If you discover that your laptop cannot survive the swapping, shut down or hibernate the laptop first. After swapping batteries, turn the laptop on again.

✦ Laptop batteries are charged in the laptop. After charging the first battery in the laptop, remove it and charge the second.

✦ Some laptops come with an external battery charger. If so, use it. Some companies may have a rack charger for a whole host of batteries. If you're obsessive, you can buy one for your house. Put it in the "sewing room" that no one uses.

✦ Be sure to store the extra battery properly. I put mine into a Ziploc bag and then into my laptop case.

✦ I hope that the nice people at Glad see my Ziploc plug in this book and send me a whole crate of Ziploc bags.

✦ As this book goes to press, keep in mind that you aren't allowed to pack spare laptop batteries in your checked luggage, only in your carry-on baggage. Furthermore, the Transportation Security Administration (TSA) prefers that you cover the spare battery's terminals with electrical tape and store the battery in a clear plastic bag.

Prolonging battery life

There are many things you can do to get the most from your laptop's battery. Aside from not turning on your laptop, here are my suggestions for prolonging the laptop's battery life:

✦ Craft yourself a viable power management program in Windows. See *Laptops For Dummies* (Wiley Publishing) for steps and suggestions.

✦ Turn down the laptop monitor's brightness when it's using battery power. Some laptops do this automatically as part of the power management system.

✦ Create a power plan that spins down the laptop's hard drive after a few minutes of use.

✦ Avoid using the optical drive while on battery power. While watching a movie on your laptop, the power drains faster than normal.

✦ Mute the speakers.

✦ Avoid accessing the network while on battery power.

✦ Disabling the wireless networking adapter also saves power.

✦ Try to use the laptop's modem only when connected to a power source. Modems drain battery power, and usually when you're near a phone jack, you find a wall socket nearby. Use it.

+ Battery usage statistics are calculated under ideal circumstances. Though your laptop manufacturer may boast that the battery lasts for a full three hours, expect less.

Maintaining the battery

Your laptop's battery isn't immortal. No, I'm not referring to its ongoing ability to drain as you use it, but, rather, to its demise over time. Eventually, even the smartest smart battery becomes useless.

There's nothing extra you need to do to maintain a laptop's battery. You don't even need to remove it regularly to clean the terminals. Except on laptops where I have two batteries available, I don't think that I've ever removed a battery from my laptops.

Bottom line: Maintaining the laptop's battery is easy.

+ When you're storing a laptop for a long time (say, more than a month), remove the battery and store it separately. That way, if the battery leaks, it doesn't wreck the laptop.

+ When storing a battery, put it in a dry location where it won't be disturbed or come into contact with metal.

+ A battery not used or stored for a period of time loses its charge. Blame the planet Earth for that. (I hear a lawsuit is in the works.)

+ Do not throw away old batteries! Always dispose of a computer battery properly, according to the hazardous waste regulations for your locality.

+ Never drop a laptop battery, get it wet, open it, or place it in a fire.

+ Generally speaking, don't do anything to the battery that an intoxicated person would do, especially just before they would say, "Hey, check this out."

+ Don't manually drain a battery by shorting it. For example, don't connect the battery terminals by using a wire. That causes fires.

+ Keep the battery's temperature even. Avoid situations where the battery may get too hot or too cold. Like Goldilocks, your laptop battery likes temperatures that are *just right*.

Chapter 2: A More Usable Laptop

In This Chapter

✓ **Creating a laptop base station**

✓ **Choosing devices for a stationary laptop**

✓ **Keeping the laptop cool**

✓ **Making the screen larger**

✓ **Typing with the On-Screen Keyboard**

My guess is that laptops will continue to get lighter and more powerful and will last longer away from a power source. Even so, they'll probably remain about the same size. That's because human eyeballs, fingers, and laps aren't getting any smaller. (Hardly!) To help you deal with the laptop computer's unique constraints, this chapter offers some suggestions for making the laptop a more usable gizmo.

A Home for the Laptop

The laptop may be a merry wanderer of the night, but eventually it comes home to roost. Just where does it roost? This section is about creating that useful place for your laptop.

Making the laptop feel at home

When you're out on the road all the time, you might settle on keeping the laptop in its case when you're home. That works. It's handy. I've done it, snaking the power cord out of the case and into a handy wall socket. But, for many of us road warriors, the laptop shares a place of prominence when it returns home or to the office. Do your laptop a favor and make that laptop lounging location feel like home.

✦ I recommend that you have a home for your laptop — a place to put it for recharging, connecting to the local network, and perhaps even adding some big-boy desktop toys.

✦ As with a desktop computer, make your laptop's home in a sturdy, well-ventilated place. Maybe have a vase of flowers nearby to add some cheer.

✦ Keep the laptop out of the sun or where it might get too hot.

✦ If the laptop must be in the sun, do not apply sunscreen to the laptop.

✦ If you're using a security device to anchor the laptop, find a home for your laptop near something permanent to which you can attach the security cable.

✦ Even though the laptop is anchored with a security cable, you still need to protect your laptop's data. Use a password on your account! (Students in college dormitories seem to forget this point.)

✦ Allow plenty of room around the laptop's home for adding external devices, as described in the next section.

✦ Although you can use a laptop on a coffee table or kitchen table or anywhere in your home, these locations do not make a good permanent place for Mr. Laptop. Think *dedicated* laptop home.

✦ When the laptop gets home after an arduous journey, offer it some cookies or a beer. When the laptop refuses, ask whether you can have the snacks and beverages yourself. Most laptops will concede.

Selecting devices for the laptop

Of the many types of gizmos you can buy for your laptop, I like to lump them into two categories: portable and stationary. The difference between the two categories has to do with bulk and power requirements. Not only that, but some devices are also better suited for a laptop's permanent abode.

The portable devices are those gizmos you take with you on the road. My book *Laptops For Dummies* (Wiley Publishing) lists a slew of such devices. For the laptop at home, you need to consider some devices that are not only less portable but can also boost the laptop's potential at a single location. Here's a rundown of some gizmos to consider:

Monitor: All laptops feature a handy way to connect an external monitor. Normally, the connection is used for a video projector to make presentations. But it's still possible to connect a normal, stand-alone PC monitor.

Full-size keyboard: I must confess that PC laptops sport nice keyboards that serve the device well. As a typing snob, I enjoy the larger PC keyboard, with its roomier layout and separate numeric keypad. Honestly, giving a laptop a full-size keyboard at its home location gives you the best of both desktop and portable PC worlds.

Mouse: I believe that all laptops, portable or stationary, benefit from having a real mouse. Some smaller-than-normal wireless mice prove ideal for road use. Back home, however, having a good, palm-size mouse with a wide assortment of buttons and an ominous, glowing LED is better.

Printer: I suppose that if your laptop is your only computer, connecting a printer to it when you get home is good. The printer may be an optional item, however: For most folks, accessing a printer is done through the network. As long as the laptop is connected to a network at home (either wired or wireless), you can access and use any printer available on the network.

External storage: As a huge fan of backups, I recommend getting your laptop a hefty external hard drive for its at-home base. Furthermore, if you have a lighter laptop (a "subnotebook") without an optical drive, get your laptop a nice optical drive for its at-home resting place.

Powered USB hub: Most external gizmos you add to your laptop are USB devices. Just plug them into the laptop's USB port — until you run out of laptop USB ports. In that case, set up a powered USB hub. By *powered,* I mean that the hub plugs into the wall. A powered USB hub accepts a wider variety of devices than the portable, nonpowered USB hubs.

Arranging these goodies works just like setting up a desktop PC, but you leave everything in place awaiting the arrival of the laptop. Yeah, it's kind of like a shrine awaiting an idol. When the laptop arrives, plug, plug, plug everything in and you're ready to go. Well, *stay.* Okay, you know what I mean.

✦ A great way to set up a laptop shrine is to perch the thing atop a tiny riser or shelf. That way, the laptop's screen is at eyeball height when you work. People who fix bad backs and necks tell me that having a computer monitor at eyeball height is ideal.

✦ Getting an external optical drive is a must for a laptop without an optical drive, especially for installing software.

✦ Obviously, if your laptop has a wide-screen monitor (as many of them do), there would be no need to connect an external monitor. That is, unless you want to use two monitors at a time. See the section "That second-monitor thing" in Book I, Chapter 6.

✦ If all you need is a numeric keypad, you can forgo a separate, full-size keyboard and just get a numeric keypad. Many of them are USB-powered and highly portable.

✦ You need a USB keyboard to expand your laptop. Nearly all keyboards sold today are USB, though if you plan on saving money and using an older PS/2-connection keyboard, get an adapter so that you can plug the thing into one of your laptop's USB ports.

✦ You can also add a desktop scanner to the list of stationary items, though I found some nifty portable scanners that are worth looking into. Not only are some of them light and skinny, but they also run off the laptop's USB port. That makes them helpful for a swift scan when on the road.

✦ Newer laptops come with a Mini-VGA connector, which is smaller than the standard VGA monitor jack. The Mini-VGA has the advantage of being able to communicate with more optical devices, though you need to keep a stock of adapters to hook up that variety.

Book III
Chapter 2

A More Usable Laptop

Using a port replicator or docking station

A laptop sits and works just fine by itself. But two types of electronic nest are available, into which your at-home laptop can potentially perch: a docking station and the port replicator. They're different expansion options, yet easily confused.

The port replicator: A *port replicator* is merely a gadget that allows your laptop to connect to additional peripherals. What it does is replicate the available ports on a standard PC. So, where your laptop may be missing extra USB ports, an old-style printer port, or even an IEEE port, you add those items by attaching the port replicator.

The docking station: A docking station is more sophisticated than a mere port replicator. You place your laptop into the device, like docking a ship. Permanently attached to the docking station are various grown-up, PC desktop gizmos, such as the monitor, keyboard, printer, and other vital yet nonportable peripherals.

Having the docking station allows you to quickly turn your on-the-road laptop into a desktop PC. Sadly, not every laptop has the option of getting a port replicator or docking station or both. Because laptops are nonstandard, the port replicator or docking station must be provided by the manufacturer and cannot be purchased generically.

✦ Traditional port replicators are rapidly becoming obsolete. Older PC hardware connectors, such as the serial port, printer port, and older keyboard and mouse ports, are being replaced by USB counterparts. With a USB hub, you can probably connect 90 percent or more of your devices these days without the need for a port replicator.

✦ Some newer port replicators simply provide your laptop with additional USB ports and perhaps an IEEE or Mini-VGA attachment.

✦ The port replicator may not work unless the laptop is plugged in.

✦ Some port replicators are portable, which means that you can take them with the laptop. But because many port replicators may not work while the laptop is on battery power, it makes them more of a stationary addition.

✦ A docking station or port replicator may also contain cooling fans for the laptop. If not, see the next section on obtaining a cooling pad for your laptop.

Cooling Mr. Laptop

A lot of hardware problems are due to heat, and nothing turns up the heat like a laptop. Therefore, I suggest that you bless your laptop with a breath of fresh air by getting it a cooling pad, such as the one shown in Figure 2-1.

Figure 2-1:
A typical
laptop
cooling pad.

The cooling pad makes an ideal placemat on which to set your laptop. Even better, most cooling pads are USB-powered, which means they work by plugging into a USB port. That makes the thing portable — a bonus.

Laptops get hot because of their size. A smaller case makes it more difficult to keep hardware cool. Furthermore, the laptop's process just oozes heat. Although the laptop is designed to deal with the heat, using a cooling pad makes things better. It may also prolong the laptop's life by keeping the electronics at a more even temperature.

Handy Laptop Utilities

Portable computing has always had its drawbacks. As mentioned earlier in this chapter, a keyboard can be only so small before human fingers cannot use it. Some laptops feature lovely wide-screen monitors, but at a trade-off to battery life and weight. Where compromises can't be made, there are software solutions. They come in the form of utilities that help make using your laptop a tad bit easier.

✦ The Magnifier and On-Screen Keyboard utilities described in this section are part of the Windows Vista Ease of Access tools. They're not available in Windows XP.

TIP

✦ Your laptop manufacturer may provide you with other, specific tools in addition to those listed here. To find them, summon the Windows Mobility Center by pressing the Win+X shortcut. Any available bonus utilities appear in the bottom part of the Windows Mobility Center window.

Magnifying the screen

Windows Vista features the Ease of Access program Magnifier, shown in Figure 2-2. It has two parts: a control window where you can set various options and the main magnifier window.

Magnifier window

Figure 2-2:
The Magnifier in action.

Control window

The magnifier window is what you use to better see a portion of the display. It follows the action, either the mouse pointer or the location where you're typing. That part of the screen appears as much as 16 times larger, which can make using a small laptop screen more bearable.

To start the Magnifier, from the Start menu, choose All Programs⇨ Accessories⇨Ease of Access⇨Magnifier. The screen blinks and blanks for a second, and then you see the two windows (refer to Figure 2-2). (Or, if you've used the Magnifier before, the control window may not appear.)

To use the Magnifier, first make settings in the control window. Then minimize the control window to better use the magnifier window.

To summon the control window again, click the Magnifier button on the taskbar.

Closing the magnifier window closes the Magnifier program.

✦ The magnifier window remains on top of all other windows, allowing you to see what you're doing, but in a larger size.

✦ I recommend undocking the magnifier window. To do so, remove the check mark by the Docked option in the control window. Then you can resize and move the magnifier window just as you can mess with any window on the display.

✦ You cannot move the magnifier window when it's docked, but you can make it wider or taller.

✦ You can increase the magnification size by choosing a new value from the Scale Factor button in the control window.

Using the On-Screen Keyboard

Unless you have one of those aircraft-carrier-size laptops with a wide screen, your portable puppy probably lacks a full-size keyboard. For most purposes, you can get by with a laptop standard keyboard just fine; there's an embedded numeric keypad, plus smaller keys ring the main typewriter keys along with an Fn key for doing various and useful things.

At those times when you're desperate for a full-size keyboard, however, you can summon the On-Screen Keyboard utility, fondly called the OSK and shown in Figure 2-3.

Figure 2-3:
The
On-Screen
Keyboard.

The OSK gives you mouse-pointer access to full-size keyboard luxury right there on your laptop's screen. Because it's really an Ease of Access tool, it's not a rapid or sneaky way of doing things. Nope, it's just a handy alternative.

To view the On-Screen Keyboard, choose All Programs⇨Accessories⇨Ease of Access⇨On-Screen Keyboard from the Start menu. The On-Screen Keyboard window shows up, floating atop all other windows on the screen (refer to Figure 2-3).

Use the On-Screen Keyboard by plucking out keys with the mouse pointer. Clicking a shift key (Shift, Alt, or Ctrl) locks the key for one keystroke. So, "typing" Ctrl+S, for example, is done by clicking either Ctrl key and then clicking the S.

You can still use the laptop's keyboard while you use the On-Screen Keyboard. In fact, you can press and hold a shift key on the laptop's keyboard to affect the OSK display.

+ You can view a smaller version of the OSK by choosing Keyboard⇨Standard Keyboard from its menu.

+ To ensure that the OSK window always stays on top of other windows, choose Settings⇨Always On Top.

+ Tablet PCs feature a special input mode using something called the Input Panel. For more details on using it, as well as on using a stylus for input directly on the tablet screen, see my book *Laptops For Dummies* (Wiley Publishing).

+ In the battle of I Must Be the Top Windows on the Screen, the Magnifier kicks the On-Screen Keyboard's butt. You can bring the OSK forward, however, by clicking its window. But hovering the mouse pointer outside the OSK window pops the magnifier window up front again.

Chapter 3: Out on the Road

In This Chapter

✔ **Finding the perfect laptop bag**

✔ **Putting stuff into the laptop bag**

✔ **Checking things before you go**

✔ **Breezing through airport security**

✔ **Using your laptop on a plane**

I've met them, but I'm not one of them. They are those few, but not insignificant, laptop owners who seldom (if ever) take their laptops on the road. No, please don't shake your head and mutter, "It's a cryin' shame." There is strength in being different. Although going on the road with your laptop is a dogged necessity for some, many of us escape with a laptop for the sheer pleasure of it. This chapter helps you on the road, whether it's for sweaty toil or a sweet scone in a trendy latté bar.

The Elsewhere Laptop

It's entirely possible to disconnect your laptop from the wired world and go merrily prancing out the door with it. Well, maybe not *prancing*. The notion is that portable computing involves several degrees of freedom.

There have been a few times that I quickly yanked my laptop from its home office perch and went out on the road. Few times, indeed. Most often, before you leave, a few things are worthy of preparation. Those things are covered in this section.

Choosing a proper laptop bag

I highly recommend that you find a dedicated case or bag for your laptop. It *needs* one. Nothing fancy, nothing expensive. The variety is out there, and most backpacks and briefcases these days are designed to accommodate a laptop computer.

Ensure that you get a laptop bag that comfortably fits the laptop. The last thing you want is your laptop bouncing around inside an empty space. Worse, you don't want to waste space and weight for filler foam and pads. Likewise, avoid a case where the laptop fits too snugly; your future laptop may be smaller or larger and when you plan ahead, you can continue to use the same laptop bag.

Find a case that has room for the laptop's power brick and various cables, portable goodies, plus a smattering of office supplies. But don't go too big! The ideal laptop case size is something that fits easily beneath an airline seat.

Finally, look for protection. The case should be soft enough that minor abuse won't damage the laptop. I prefer zippers on the case because the laptop is less likely to slide out or be damaged by snaps.

✦ My favorite laptop case is a soft Eddie Bauer briefcase. Second to that is a standard, though rugged, backpack. The backpack is nice for those trips when I need a lot of accessories that don't fit into the Eddie Bauer case. Also, I can hoist the backpack over my shoulders, which keeps my hands free: one for the coffee and another for the airline ticket.

✦ The manufacturer's case may not be your best choice. I'm not saying that it's a bad choice, just that you should review other options and decide for yourself.

✦ Avoid any laptop case that has the manufacturer's name or the word *Laptop* emblazoned on the outside. A backpack with a laptop inside is just another backpack, but a laptop case with the bold word *Laptop* or *Dell* on it is a target for thieves.

Packing the laptop bag

In addition to the laptop itself, there are a few things you want to put into the laptop bag. Here's a list of stuff to consider:

✦ Power brick and cord

✦ Spare battery

✦ Ethernet cable

✦ Portable mouse

✦ Headphones

✦ Lock or cable

✦ Screen wipes

✦ Phone cord, if you plan on using the laptop's modem

✦ Media (thumb drives, media card reader, and optical discs, for example)

✦ PC Cards you plan to use

I listed the portable mouse here, but it shouldn't be the only USB gizmo you toss into the bag. The variety of small, portable USB devices is almost endless, so consider putting a few of your favorites into the laptop bag.

Additionally, have a smattering of office supplies in your laptop bag. You know: pens, paper, sticky notes, paper clips, highlighters, stress toys, or anything else you'd find handy while you use the computer.

If you have a video projector, you can pack it in your laptop case or use its own case. (I put my video projector in my checked luggage when I travel.)

Checking stuff before you leave

With your laptop, go on the road boldly, but be prepared. Here's a checklist of things to peruse before you leave:

+ Back up. See Book VI, Chapter 1.

+ Charge the battery.

+ Charge the spare battery.

+ Check with the Windows Update service to ensure that you have the latest updates. Install those updates before you leave. See Book II, Chapter 1.

+ Synchronize files between the desktop and laptop, if necessary. Refer to my book *Laptops For Dummies* (Wiley Publishing) for the details.

+ Ensure that you have copies of necessary passwords, either in your head or "hidden in plain sight" in your laptop bag.

+ If you're travelling overseas, remember a power adapter.

TIP

Regarding Windows Update, it's important that you not allow the laptop to automatically install updates when you're on the road, or anywhere on the go. Especially with Windows Vista, updates install when you shut down the laptop. That not only keeps the laptop on longer than expected, but it can also screw things up if the power goes out in the middle of an update.

After installing any available Windows updates, I recommend that you reset the Windows Update options. Select the setting that has updates checked but not downloaded or installed. By doing so, you prevent surprise updates.

When you return from the road, or whenever you're in a place where you have a solid Internet connection and a power supply, you can install updates. Allow yourself plenty of time because some updates tend to take a few minutes to download, and perhaps a restart or two.

See Book II, Chapter 1 for details on how to configure Windows Update.

Resuming life after you travel

After returning your laptop to its home (covered in Chapter 2), you have a few things to accomplish. The two main things you need to do are to charge the laptop again and re-sync your files.

Charging the laptop is easy: Plug it in.

Re-syncing files can be a rather complex issue. In fact, I believe that Windows makes it more complex than necessary, whether you're using the older Briefcase application or the newer Windows Vista Sync program. There are, however, other alternatives, as discussed at the end of this section.

One thing you might want to avoid after coming home is reconnecting to the network if the laptop is coming out of hibernation. Because the laptop was hibernated, it retains its previous network connection settings. For a wireless network, no issues should crop up. But, for a wired network, your laptop may still cling to its previous IP address. That can wreak havoc with the current network. Disconnect the laptop from the network, restart it, and then reconnect.

✦ The topic of synchronizing files between desktop and laptop computers is covered in depth in my book *Laptops For Dummies* (Wiley Publishing).

✦ I prefer not to use the crazy Windows synchronization schemes. Instead, I use the network to copy to the laptop any files I need, and then I copy them all back when I'm done.

✦ Projects that I keep bouncing between laptop and desktop find a good home on a thumb drive instead. That way, I don't need to worry about synchronization, though I do remember to back up the thumb drive from time to time.

✦ Let me rant on synchronization some more: One thing Windows doesn't synchronize is your e-mail folder. To resolve that conundrum, I recommend leaving your e-mail on the server when you're on the road. See Book IV, Chapter 3 for details.

✦ To fix the IP issue, do not connect your laptop to a wired network when you first bring it back home or to the office — specifically, when rousing the laptop from hibernation. Instead, shut down the laptop, connect the network, and then start up the laptop again. That should resolve any network conflicts.

✦ See Book V for network troubleshooting.

Life in the Air

I always get a teeny thrill when I whip out my laptop above the 10,000-foot level in an airplane. I get an even bigger thrill when I actually get work done and don't end up playing Spider Solitaire the whole time. This section has some tips on using your laptop whilst travelling aloft. Sadly, it doesn't feature any suggestions that will motivate you toward working instead of playing or watching a movie on your laptop.

Getting through security

I suppose that the airport security people somehow got wind that laptop PCs, just like all computers, will *crash*. That alarmed the security people. They innocently don't know anything about technology, so it would be easy to believe that laptop computers are a security threat. Whatever. I'm not going to debate the government here (as much as I'm tempted).

Airport security is a fact of life. Well, unless your life is *really* good, in which case you fly an executive jet and there is no security. Then again, you probably have a well-dressed minion toting your laptop and a paid tech staff to advise you. So I don't waste time with you, especially because you're probably not even reading this book anyway. For the rest of us, the laptop presents a special issue at airport security.

Laptops must dwell in their own bin. To be x-rayed, the laptop must be placed in a bin by itself (though I also put my cell phone in the same bin). Put your shoes, laptop bag, keys, coat, hand grenades, and other personal items in a separate bin.

Laptops must be x-rayed. The x-ray machine will not harm the laptop, nor will it "erase" any digital memory cards.

Grab your laptop from the bin *first* when you exit the metal detector. Place it immediately back into your laptop bag. Then gather up your phone, keys, and other items. You don't want someone pilfering your laptop while you're desperately struggling to put on your shoes at the security gate.

As this book goes to press, the Transportation Security Administration (TSA) is allowing laptops to go through the x-ray machines in their own bags, as long as the bags meet certain criteria. How do you know? The bag says so when you buy it. If the bag doesn't say it's approved, it's not. Simple.

- ✦ Send your laptop through the x-ray machine last. First, send your luggage, shoes, coat, and other items. Then send the laptop through last, and in its own bin. That way, you can gather your things and then be ready for the laptop when it arrives on the exit side of the security area.

✦ The key to getting through security is to *pay attention*. Don't chat it up with others, and don't be distracted. Focus on the immediate task, and the short, annoying experience and suspension of your Fourth Amendment rights will soon be over.

✦ A laptop goes in a separate bin because it helps the security people identify the laptop as a laptop. It also helps you better keep track of it.

✦ The bins used by the TSA in the United States remind me of the old *bus tubs* I used when I was a busboy at a restaurant long, long ago.

✦ Typically, the TSA-approved bags are flat, either a pouch or sleeve design, or a folding flat bag. The bags lack pockets, and the TSA prefers that nothing else be in the bag but the laptop, which in my opinion makes for a lousy laptop bag. Even then, security may ask that you remove the laptop from the TSA-approved bag if it cannot get a clear image on the scanner.

✦ Way back when laptops weren't as commonplace, the airport security people required that you open and turn on the laptop. That was to prove that it was a laptop and not an empty laptop case filled with C4 explosives. I remember opening a laptop at airport security in the early 1990s and discovering that its battery was dead. The security guy waved me through, anyway. The fool.

Storing the laptop

Earlier in this chapter, I recommended getting a laptop bag. If you're going to travel by air, I must *insist* that you get a laptop bag. Furthermore, I'm making this admonishment:

Do not put your laptop in checked luggage.

The risk of putting your laptop in checked luggage is not that it might be stolen. Although that's always a possibility, the odds are greater that your laptop will be damaged in checked luggage. Rough handling and the weight of other bags can crack the screen. Spilled liquids can render your laptop useless. Nope, it's just better to put the laptop in its own bag.

Once onboard, put the laptop bag under the seat in front of you. Placing the laptop bag at your feet gives you quick access to the laptop and all the goodies in your laptop bag; you don't have to stand up or have others move when you need to retrieve or store the laptop.

✦ Keep the laptop bag with you. Do not lose sight of it. (You know that I'm serious here because I wrote *do not* instead of the friendlier *don't*.)

✦ Obviously, it helps when you plan to use your laptop on an airplane that you don't get a bulkhead seat. Those seats don't have storage beneath the seat in front of them because there is no seat in front of them.

✦ Don't ask the pilot if you can store the laptop under his seat.

✦ Never put the laptop in the seatback pocket. You will forget it. Plus, who knows what gloopy evil lurks in the seatback pocket?

Using your laptop in the air

The most important thing you need to do when using your laptop in the air is to *disable the wireless network*.Often times, that's as easy as sliding the wireless networking switch to the Off position.

When your laptop lacks a wireless networking hardware switch, you have to disable the wireless networking software. I recommend that you do so before you get on the plane, but I've had to make that switch in the air and lived to tell about it, so I assume that you'll be given a little slack as well, if you forget.

To disable wireless networking in Windows Vista, follow these steps:

1. **Press Win+X to summon the Windows Mobility Center.**

The Windows Mobility Center window appears, as shown in Figure 3-1.

2. **Click the button in the upper-right corner, Turn Wireless Off.**

3. **Close the window.**

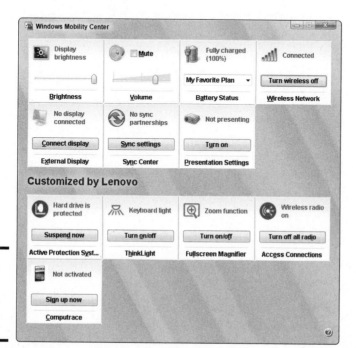

Figure 3-1: The Windows Mobility Center.

In Windows XP, you have to follow a different set of steps when there's no hardware wireless switch:

1. **Open the Control Panel's Network Connections icon.**

2. **Right-click the wireless network connection.**

3. **Choose Disable from the shortcut menu.**

4. **Close the Network Connections window.**

After you're certain that the wireless networking hardware has been disabled, it's time to work! Using your laptop in the air works just like using it anywhere, though it's less comfortable and the milieu sucks.

+ Use your laptop only when the flight crew announces that it's okay to do so. Likewise, when they tell you to shut down the laptop, don't hesitate.

+ You most likely want to reenable the wireless networking hardware after you're back in civilization. To do so, flip the hardware switch. If you used the software method described in this section, repeat the preceding set of steps but choose Turn Wireless On in Step 2 for Windows Vista, or Enable in Step 3 for Windows XP.

+ Some laptops feature an airplane mode. Use it.

+ I recommend getting a window seat if you plan to use your laptop aloft. The main reason: You have control over the window shades. When it's too bright outside, it makes seeing the laptop screen impossible.

+ You can buy screen filters that prevent other passengers on the plane from peering into the laptop screen. Get one.

+ If you're lucky, the airplane cabin feature EmPower, which allows you to plug in your laptop and use it without sacrificing battery life. You need to get an EmPower adapter to make the connection work.

+ If your laptop doesn't have a wireless networking hardware switch, peruse the keyboard for a special key combination that disables the wireless network. For example, on a Lenovo laptop, the key combination is Fn+F5.

+ The keyboard combination to disable the wireless networking adapter on Lenovo laptops is Fn+F5.

+ Pay heed to those low-battery-power warnings! Even when your laptop is fully charged, it will poop out eventually. See Chapter 1 for more information on setting battery warnings and timeouts.

Chapter 4: Laptop Maintenance

In This Chapter

✓ **Cleaning the laptop case**

✓ **Cleaning the screen**

✓ **Cleaning the keyboard**

✓ **Understanding laptop hardware upgrades**

*J*ust as there are two parts of a computer's personality, there are two types of maintenance on a computer: hardware and software. The software side rules the hardware side, and, indeed, there's more you can do maintenance-wise with software than with hardware. For software maintenance, I recommend reading Book VI, which applies to all PCs, including laptops and tablets. For maintaining your laptop's hardware, you have this chapter.

A Sparkling Laptop

All computers require cleaning, and laptops even more so. That's because you end up handling a laptop more than you do a normal computer. A laptop can also wind up in exotic environments, so it can suffer from gunk and debris that would make a mere desktop computer blanch. Cleaning the thing involves more care than putting your laptop in the dishwasher (which I don't recommend). Instead, follow the handy, helpful cleaning advice in this section.

Making the case beautiful again

Here are the ingredients for maintaining your laptop case:

Sponge: Any household sponge will do, especially the kind my kids call a SpongeBob sponge.

Cleaning liquid: Mix one part standard dishwashing detergent with five parts water.

Lint-free cloth: This item can be found anywhere that cleaning supplies are sold.

Cotton swabs: You can use the standard Q-tip, though I prefer medical swabs because they're better made and wrapped a little tighter).

Cleaning is a standard operation:

1. **Turn off the laptop.**

   Don't clean a laptop while it's on. In fact, unplug it. Here, let me make that a step:

2. **Unplug the laptop.**

   There.

3. **Mix the cleaning liquid.**

4. **Soak the sponge in the cleaning liquid.**

5. **Wring out the sponge until it's dry.**

6. **Gently wipe down the laptop's case.**

7. **Use the swab to get into the nooks and crannies.**

   Do not insert the swab into any ports, jacks, or holes on the laptop. There's no need to clean inside of those places.

8. **Finish the job by wiping the case again with the lint-free cloth.**

   Use the cloth to sop up any excess moisture.

Now prepare to take your laptop on the road again and get it dirty all over!

Unlike desktop PCs, laptops are designed to be out in the wild. You may notice that your laptop's case has a more rugged feel to it than a standard desktop computer. That's a good thing. Indeed, you probably don't need to clean your laptop unless it's *really* dirty. Then again, everyone's idea of *really dirty* is different. I remember disagreeing with my mother on that point many times when I was younger.

✦ The laptop case is the *outside*. on the inside, where the thing hinges, you find the keyboard and screen. Cleaning those items is covered in the following two sections.

✦ Okay, I lied. You can also use the sponge and swabs to help clean up the touch pad. It lives near the keyboard.

✦ Medical swabs can be found at any pharmacy or medical supply store.

✦ Isopropyl, or "rubbing," alcohol makes a good cleaning liquid. But *do not* use it to clean the monitor.

✦ Avoid using any detergent that contains strong chemicals, such as ammonia or bleach.

✦ Don't ever get any liquid inside the laptop!

> ✦ Check out Video 341 to see me go through the steps of cleaning a laptop case.

Washing the screen

Things are better since the mayor cleaned up the downtown coffee bistros. I remember when smelly bums from the street used to walk in. They'd just start cleaning everyone's laptops with these filthy rags. Guilt would obligate you to pass the helpful hobo a dollar or your "spare change" and then thank him. You'd smile, wait for him to leave, and then clean the screen all over. Thankfully, those days are over.

When you feel like cleaning the laptop screen, you have three options (in addition to waiting for a vagrant to do it for you):

Use a lint-free cloth to dry-clean the screen. All laptops use LCD monitors. Those monitors are *very* fussy about liquids. A lint-free cloth helps get the dust off the screen and can also help remove finger smudges and some (but not all) sneeze globs.

Use a damp sponge to wipe the screen. Use only water to make the sponge damp. Definitely wring out all the moisture from the sponge before you wipe the screen. Rub gently, lovingly.

Get an LCD monitor cleaning kit. By getting a cleaning kit, perhaps the best option, you receive a lint-free cloth as well as a package containing a damp towelette moistened with official LCD monitor-cleaning solution. I use and recommend the Klear Screen brand:

```
www.klearscreen.com
```

As with cleaning the case, you should turn off the laptop and even unplug it before you clean the monitor. In fact, it's easier to see what you're cleaning when the screen is off.

After the screen is clean, let it dry before you close the lid or use the laptop again.

Unlike cleaning the case (see the preceding section), you'll most likely end up cleaning the laptop's monitor more often. I do. So don't believe that you're becoming obsessive or turning into your own mother just because you clean the laptop's monitor more often than you clean the case.

> ✦ Never ever, under any circumstances, use alcohol or ammonia cleaners on an LCD screen. Just don't.

**Book III
Chapter 4**

Laptop Maintenance

+ Tablet PCs require more screen cleaning than standard desktops. That's because you touch the screen more often when using the laptop in tablet mode.

+ The monitor should be completely dry before you close the laptop's lid.

+ Yes, for some extra cash, you can dress down and wander the cafés and clean laptops. Remember not to shower for several days before attempting this task. I cannot, however, recommend being a laptop-screen-cleaning tramp as a way to pay for college.

+ Refer to Video 342 to watch how I clean my laptop's monitor.

Kleaning the keyboard

The best way to clean the laptop's keyboard is by using a small, portable vacuum. Using the vacuum's tiniest attachment, gently suck the hair, scone flakes, and crud from between the laptop's keys. *Thwoop!*

To clean the laptop's key caps, turn off the laptop and then use a pencil eraser to rub off the crud and build-up. Afterward, use the vacuum again to clean out any eraser stubble and crud between the cracks.

+ I don't recommend using a can of compressed air to clean a laptop's (or desktop PC's) keyboard. The air may clear away the debris, but it may also blow it deeper into the laptop. After the gunk is inside, there's no way to clean it out.

+ Unlike on a desktop PC keyboard, you do not wash a laptop keyboard by using liquid. In fact, if you spill anything into a laptop keyboard, you're pretty much screwed. I pray that you followed my advice (in *Laptops For Dummies*) and originally purchased a nice warranty for your laptop.

+ Watch Video 343 to witness the author deftly cleaning a laptop keyboard.

Hardware Upgrades

You just can't upgrade laptop hardware the same way you can upgrade a desktop PC. That's one reason why we're not all using laptops exclusively these days.

The desktop PC system is built on upgradeable, swappable, easy-to-replace-and-fix parts. That aspect of the PC's design was the key to its success back when it first came out, and continues to be one of the best reasons to buy a PC desktop today. For laptops, there are three ways to upgrade the hardware:

Not at all: Some laptops are entirely shut out of the hardware upgrade path. For those systems, the laptop is a closed box. You can get a new battery. You can add USB gizmos and PC Cards. But you cannot upgrade any other hardware.

Limited, factory upgrades: A few laptops allow upgrades, but those are limited to the manufacturer's whim. For example, your laptop may have a swappable drive bay, where you can add an extra hard drive, optical drive, or media card reader. But that additional hardware is available only from the manufacturer. You can't just go into a big-box store and buy a new hard drive, as you can with a desktop.

Slightly flexible upgrades: Finally, a smattering of laptops have both upgradeable memory and permanent storage options. Some even allow for a new video card to be installed. But those laptops are few and generally not as portable or lightweight.

Bottom line: You have to look into your own laptop's potential for hardware upgrades to see what's available and how the upgrade works.

+ Most people don't buy laptops to upgrade them. When buying a laptop, I recommend that you buy *all* you need.

+ My best advice for any hardware upgrade — when one is possible — is to add more memory. Windows Vista, for example, needs 2GB RAM minimum. If you're working with graphics on your laptop, more memory helps tremendously.

+ I recommend buying laptop memory from Crucial (www.crucial.com.). Its Web site features a memory configuration utility that you can use to determine how much RAM is installed in your laptop and that tells you which type of memory and how much more you can install.

+ Some types of laptop hard drives are standard and can be removed easily by using a tiny screwdriver and some patience. I've ordered spare hard drives for my laptops and haven't had any trouble swapping them out. (For my book *Laptops For Dummies,* 2nd Edition, I swapped two hard drives: one with Windows Vista and the other with Windows XP.)

+ If you plan to buy a larger-capacity hard drive for your laptop, ensure that you have a set of system recovery discs. You need those discs in order to reinstall your laptop's operating system and control software after initializing the new drive. Furthermore, you need a backup from which to reinstall your personal files and programs.

+ It's possible to add external storage to your laptop. One of those Western Digital MyBook external hard drives makes for a useful home-location addition to any laptop, especially for backing up.

Book IV

Internet

SOMEWHERE IN THE CITY, SASQUATCH, BIGFOOT AND ELVIS SPEND ANOTHER WARY NIGHT.

"Look—all I'm saying is every time they come out with a new browser with an improved search function, it's just a matter of time."

Contents at a Glance

Chapter 1: Internet Malaise

In This Chapter

- ✔ Checking the Internet connection
- ✔ Setting timeout values
- ✔ Dealing with call waiting
- ✔ Confirming that the Internet is out there
- ✔ Selecting primary Internet programs
- ✔ Cleaning up history
- ✔ Eating cookies
- ✔ Fixing AutoComplete's memory

Suppose that Al Gore didn't invent the Internet. Upon reflection, I believe that the Internet was invented by the ancient Greek gods. That's because, like many of the gods' gifts, the Internet can be both a blessing and a curse.

The gods may have had personal flaws, but they most definitely excelled at making things arduous for mankind just as it looked like things were going great. You've probably experienced such misfortune yourself, especially when you take on the Internet. Although this chapter isn't an epic poem on mankind being knocked down a notch for its technical hubris, you will find the information here useful for dealing with basic Internet woe and strife.

Problems Getting (and Staying) Online

Sometimes the Internet seems like the high-wire act at a circus. Despite any skills you may have, your balance depends not so much on your skill as it does on other factors you cannot control. I mean, who would perform a high-wire act when, at any time, the wire itself may vanish? That's the kind of struggle the typical Internet user faces. The answers to those common Internet connection problems are covered in this section.

Before proceeding, don't troubleshoot something that isn't there. This book isn't about setting up an Internet connection for the first time. If you've never connected to the Internet, you have nothing to troubleshoot. Instead, get your system set up and then get on the Internet. Your Internet service provider (ISP) should be your primary source of assistance.

Testing broadband Internet

At the dawn of the 21st century, connecting to the Internet seems to be routine. Being on the Internet all the time is more or less the norm: always on, always available, generally high-speed. Well, until something goes wrong.

When you experience problems getting or staying online, check these items:

Confirm that there's power. When the power goes out, the Internet goes out.

Check other signals. If you're using cable Internet access, check the cable TV. If the TV signal is out, there's a problem with the cable system. On a DSL connection, check the phone line: No dial tone means no Internet.

Check the modem. Broadband modems, illustrated in Figure 1-1, feature several pretty lights that do more than just look impressive.

Figure 1-1:
Typical
broadband
modem
lights.

Power

Online

Signal (send/receive)

Activity

Printer / Other

Table 1-1 explains what the lights could mean and how they factor into checking the Internet connection. Not all modems have the variety of lights listed, but the lights are there for a reason: They help you troubleshoot the Internet connection.

Table 1-1	Broadband Modem Lights
Lamp Name	*What the Lamp Means When It's Lit*
Power	The modem is receiving power and operating normally.
Online	The modem is connected to the service, but not necessarily on the Internet.
Signal	The modem is sending information to, and receiving it from, the Internet.
Send	The modem is sending information to the Internet.
Receive	The modem is receiving information from the internet.
Activity	(Flashing) The modem is sending communications to, or receiving it from, the computer or local network.
Status	The modem is working or has issues. This lamp may change color, depending on the modem's condition or connection.

The variety of lamps on a broadband modem is endless. My cable modem, for example, features a USB lamp that flashes whenever the USB port is being used (for a printer or a network disk drive).

First, check the power light. Is the modem turned on? Check the power connection from the modem to the wall socket. No power means no Internet.

Second, check the modem's signal or receive lights. When that light is off, blinking, or colored red or orange, there's a problem with the Internet connection. Specifically, a signal isn't being broadcast. You can phone your ISP for assistance, but I recommend instead that you wait a few seconds to see whether the problem clears itself.

Disable the standby or loopback. Some modems feature a diagnostic switch, which could be labeled Standby or Loopback. Ensure that it's in the proper position for the modem to communicate.

Check physical connections. Is the modem connected to a router? Is the router plugged in and functioning? Are the network connections working? Can your computer access other computers on the local network? Can you *ping* the router? (See the later section "Checking to see whether the Internet is really out there" for more information on ping.)

Restart the modem. Turn the modem off, and turn it on again. If the modem lacks a power switch, unplug it and plug it back in. Restarting the modem is perhaps the most common trick for getting a broadband connection back up and running. In fact, you may want to perform the official, desperate modem-restart steps:

1. **Unplug the modem.**

2. **Wait 30 seconds.**

3. **Plug the modem back in.**

After performing these desperate steps, proceed with the following suggestions:

Restart the computer. The problem might be with your computer, and the generic trick for fixing just about any computer problem is to restart the PC.

Restart the network. The modem may be fine. Your computer might be fine. The problem may lie in the network betwixt the two. See Book V for more information about restarting the network.

If the problem continues, perhaps the modem needs replacing. If you're renting the broadband modem, have your ISP bring out a replacement for you. Otherwise, you have to buy a new one (or borrow one) to see whether the modem has gone hinkey.

✦ Also refer to the section "Checking to see whether the Internet is really out there," later in this chapter.

✦ Checking connections may also involve checking outside your home or office. Usually, the ISP (cable or phone company) can test the line all the way up to your modem. That should determine whether the problem is the ISP's or yours.

✦ The broadband connection relies heavily on computer networking to function properly. When the local network connection is down, you cannot access the Internet. See Book V for more information on network troubleshooting.

✦ *Broadband* is a generic term that describes cable, DSL, satellite, and other high-speed connections to the Internet.

Checking dialup connections

Well, say hello to the 20th century. Using a dialup connection is slow, and I hope that you recognize that it's the antique way to access the Internet. Still, my Uncle Herb claims that coffee heated in a saucepan stays hot longer than coffee zapped in a microwave. ("Takes the same time, too," Herb wants me to add.) That's quaint, but there's nothing charming about a dialup Internet connection.

I know: You may have no choice about using dialup. You might not have broadband out where you live. Or, you don't see the point in spending extra money for broadband (or a microwave oven). Or, you don't use the Internet that much anyway (or drink coffee). Fine. That doesn't mean that the dialup connection won't be without problems.

The first place to look when you have dialup connection conundrums is on the Connections tab in the Internet Options dialog box, shown in Figure 1-2. Here's how to get there:

Figure 1-2:
Checking
dialup
settings.

1. **Open the Control Panel's Internet Options icon.**

2. **Click the Connections tab.**

3. **Select the dialup connection from the list.**

In Figure 1-2, it's named Booga, which isn't my ISP but is one of my favorite made-up names (next to Wambooli).

4. **Choose a new setting for the dialup connection (if necessary).**

You choose from three settings:

Never Dial a Connection. Choose this option if you don't want your computer to automatically dial into the Internet.

Dial Whenever a Network Connection Is Not Present. This standard option is the one you select to be prompted whenever an Internet connection is requested by a program on your PC.

Always Dial My Default Connection. This option may seem like the best one, but it's not. Do not choose this option.

5. **Click OK.**

6. **Close the Control Panel window.**

The number-one dialup issue is dialing up at seemingly random times. Choosing the option Never Dial a Connection (refer to Step 4 in the preceding step list) solves that annoying issue. Of course, you may need to manually connect to the Internet in that case. If so, refer to the later section "Dialing in manually" for the details.

✦ Contrary to what it says, the Never Dial a Connection option doesn't mean that you'll never be connected to the Internet. It should be renamed Never *Automatically* Dial a Connection.

✦ When you don't hear a dial tone when the modem starts to connect, there's most likely a problem with the phone system.

✦ Also check the phone cable to ensure that it's plugged in at both ends.

✦ Some options in various e-mail programs allow dialing into the Internet — or not. See Chapter 3 for details.

Remembering your dialup Internet password

Why tire of continually typing your Internet password when you can have the computer remember it for you? Here's how:

1. **Open the Control Panel's Internet Options icon.**

2. **Click the Connections tab.**

3. **Select the dialup connection from the list.**

4. **Click the Settings button.**

A Settings dialog box for the dialup connection appears.

5. **Type your Internet username.**

6. **Type your password.**

7. **Click OK.**

8. **Click OK to close the Internet Options dialog box.**

By typing your username and password, you allow Windows to supply them automatically when you summon a dialup connection.

✦ Your Internet username and password are most likely different from your other usernames and passwords, such as the ones you use to log in to Windows or collect your e-mail.

✦ Passwords are a fact of life in the modern computer. See Book II, Chapter 5 for more information and suggestions about using and keeping passwords on your PC.

Dialing in manually

When starting an Internet program doesn't automatically connect you to the Internet, you need to manually summon a connection. The procedure is different between Windows Vista and Windows XP.

In Windows Vista, follow these easy steps:

1. **From the Start menu, choose Connect To.**
2. **Choose your ISP's connection icon from the list in the Connect to a Network window.**
3. **Click the Connect button.**
4. **If prompted, enter your username and password.**
5. **Click the Dial button.**

    Wait until the modem connects you and you're online.

In Windows XP, follow these convoluted and complex steps:

1. **From the Start menu, choose Network Connections.**
2. **Double-click to open your ISP's connection icon.**
3. **Click the Dial button.**

    Wait until the modem makes the connection, and then you're online.

When I first used a modem (way before the Internet existed), I had to dial a phone myself. After waiting for the answering modem to wail, turning on my PC's external modem, and hanging up the phone, I was online. The modem communicated at 300 bits per second (bps), which is slow enough that anyone can read the text as it comes in. Today's dialup modems are more than 150 times faster than that. Speed is relative.

Dialing randomly

As long as you can hear the modem, you may notice that it occasionally decides — with no apparent motivation — to dial up the Internet. It may happen at random times, or it may be predictable, such as when you first log in to Windows.

Nothing that happens in a computer is truly random, so there has to be some program somewhere trying to phone up the Internet for some reason, legitimate or not. My general advice is to click the Cancel button. If you're lucky, you may see a message displayed that can help you identify the disgruntled program, and, hopefully, configure it to either not dial in to the Internet or at least understand why it tries to do so.

✦ If you're not prompted, or do not see a Cancel button, when the PC dials into the Internet, change the dialup settings. See the earlier section "Checking dialup connections" for information.

✦ Most of today's Help programs, such as those for Windows or Microsoft Office, rely on the Internet to supply relevant information. When you click the Help button, or press the F1 key, you may experience the computer trying to connect to the Internet.

✦ A common reason for the seemingly random dialups is that Windows confuses the Internet with your local network. For example, Windows may dial into the Internet when you try using a network printer or accessing a network computer. Sadly, there's nothing you can do about that; the computer is just being dumb.

Dealing with dialup timeouts

An annoying and preventable reason for being disconnected from the Internet is that your dialup account has *timed out.* The dropped line can happen for two reasons.

First, noise on the line can drop the connection. It can be as simple as someone else picking up a phone extension or as complex as sunspots. Poor-quality phone lines cause frequently dropped connections. The biggest culprit, however, is call waiting. (See the later section "Disabling call waiting" for information.)

Second, *you* timed out. Both the PC and the ISP monitor the Internet connection. When your connection fails to send any information after a set amount of time, the connection is dropped. That's because it's assumed that you left the computer, fell asleep, or perhaps were even shot from behind by a jealous lover.

To prevent a timeout disconnection, review the timeout settings in Windows. Three of them are buried in two separate locations. Here's how to find the lot:

1. **Open the Phone and Modem Options icon in the Control Panel.**

   If you see a Location Information window displayed, the modem hasn't yet been configured for your computer. Configure the modem by setting a location, and then start these steps over. Refer to my book *PCs For Dummies* (Wiley Publishing) for details on setting up and using a modem.

2. **Click the Modems tab.**

3. **If necessary, select the PC's modem from the list.**

4. **Click the Properties button.**

5. **If you're using Windows XP, skip to Step 8.**

6. **In Windows Vista, click the Change Settings button on the General tab.**

7. **In Windows Vista, click the Continue button or type the administrator's password to continue.**

8. **Click the Advanced tab in the modem's Properties dialog box.**

9. **Click the Change Default Preferences button.**

10. **Set the modem's timeout values in the modem's Default Preferences dialog box.**

The dialog box you see, shown in Figure 1-3, contains some generic settings for the modem — stuff you might not otherwise give a rip about. But one item in particular is the Disconnect a Call If Idle for More Than value. That setting controls the modem's maximum timeout value; after that period of inactivity, the modem disconnects.

Figure 1-3:
Setting the modem's timeout values.

Place a check mark by the item Disconnect a Call If Idle for More Than and select a timeout value.

There's no way to set an "unlimited" timeout. The maximum value is 42 minutes.

11. **Click OK to lock in the new timeout for the modem, and keep clicking OK to close the various dialog boxes you opened.**

Meanwhile, back in the Control Panel, you can begin the steps for setting the second timeout value:

12. **Open the Internet Options icon in the Control Panel.**

13. **Click the Connections tab in the Internet Options dialog box.**

14. **Select the dialup connection from the list.**

15. **Click the Settings button.**

16. **Click the Properties button.**

17. **Click the Options tab in the ISP's Properties dialog box.**

18. **Use the menu button to set the value for Idle Time Before Hanging Up.**

    Your choices are limited to those present on the menu.

19. **Click OK.**

    But you're not done yet.

20. **Click the Advanced button.**

    The final timeout setting is made in the Advanced Dial-Up dialog box, shown in Figure 1-4.

Figure 1-4:
The final timeout setting.

21. **Place a check mark by the item Disconnect If Idle For XX Minutes.**

22. **Set the number of minutes to have an automatic disconnect.**

23. **Click OK.**

24. **Close the other dialog boxes by clicking OK until you're out of dialog boxes with OK buttons.**

25. **Close the Control Panel window.**

Indeed, there appears to be an abundance of locations where you can set timeout values for a dialup account. Perhaps one of them was set too low, which explains why you unexpectedly disconnected from the Internet.

Your ISP can also drop your connection when it detects that your dialup connection has been idle for too long. You have to check with the ISP to see what that timeout value is.

Disabling call waiting

One of the most abrupt and preventable ways to get knocked offline is by the call waiting signal. It's the bane of dialup Internet users.

You may want call waiting on. After all, you have that service for a reason. But being kicked offline is annoying. Therefore, the phone company allows you to stifle the call waiting feature on a per-call basis: You just dial a special code before making a call. That code suspends the call waiting feature for the duration of the call. Because your computer's modem works like a telephone, you can have it "dial" the call waiting suspension code for you. Follow these steps:

1. **Open the Control Panel's Phone and Modem Options icon.**

2. **Click the Dialing Rules tab.**

3. **Choose your current location from the list.**

   The setting to disable call waiting is available only when you set up a location. If you don't have a location set up, click the New button to create one.

4. **Click the Edit button.**

   The Edit Location dialog box shows up.

5. **Place a check mark by the item To Disable Call Waiting, Dial.**

6. **Choose the proper code to disable call waiting from the menu button.**

   If the code you need to dial isn't listed, type it in.

7. **Click OK to close the Edit Location dialog box.**

   You can also close the Phone and Modems Options dialog box and the Control Panel window.

You have better alternatives than disabling call waiting. If you prefer to have call waiting as a feature while you're using the modem, you can look into some specialized software. For example, AOL users can use the AOL Call Alert feature. The following Web sites describe services you can consider if you really hold the call waiting service dear:

```
www.buzzme.com
www.callwave.com
```

Because dialup Internet access is on the wane, these services may no longer be offered in the future; these two Web sites may change.

Internet Troubleshooting Tools

Troubleshooting the Internet is a big task, so my initial advice is not to bother with it. After all, highly paid black-belt nerds work for the major communications companies already, and it's their job to troubleshoot the Internet. Let them. On your end, you can choose from a smattering of general network tools to determine whether an Internet problem lies locally or far away. This section tells you how.

✦ The information in this section is general to the Internet. For specific help on the Web, see Chapter 2. E-mail miseries are ameliorated in Chapter 3.

✦ Most of these tips and tricks are technical in nature. They arise from basic networking and the early, text-only days of the Internet. Because of that, many of the tools run in a Command Prompt window. Scary.

Checking to see whether the Internet is really out there

The Internet's immediate ancestor was built to survive a nuclear attack. So, in theory (because there hasn't been a nuclear attack — yet), the Internet is always with us. The question is, however, whether the Internet is available to your computer.

You may have a solid Internet connection. The modem's lights indicate that everything is sending and receiving hunky and dory. But something leads you to believe that the Internet is not "up": The game you're playing may not respond. Web pages may not come up. E-mail refuses to be sent. Although the problem may not be something you can fix, it's something you can check by using the ping command.

Ping stands for *packet Internet groper*. The program sends a chunk of information (the packet) to a network address. The computer at that address echoes the packet back. The ping command then reports information about the packet sent and received, such as the total length of time taken by the round trip.

You can use ping to confirm that a specific domain or IP address on the Internet is up and available. Follow these steps:

1. **From the Start menu, choose All Programs⇨Accessories⇨Command Prompt.**

A Command Prompt window appears.

2. **Type** ping wambooli.com **and press the Enter key.**

   The word `ping` is followed by a space and then the name of a server or an IP address. In this example, I'm using `wambooli.com`, which is my own Web site. In practice, you can use the name of any domain or server on the Internet, such as `yahoo.com`, `google.com`, or `microsoft.com`.

   You should see output similar to the output shown in Figure 1-5.

3. **Type** exit **to close the Command Prompt window.**

Figure 1-5:
The ping command confirms that the Internet is up and available.

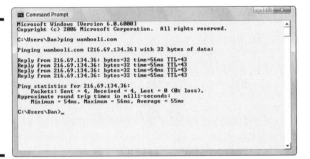

```
Command Prompt

Microsoft Windows [Version 6.0.6000]
Copyright (c) 2006 Microsoft Corporation.  All rights reserved.

C:\Users\Dan>ping wambooli.com

Pinging wambooli.com [216.69.134.36] with 32 bytes of data:

Reply from 216.69.134.36: bytes=32 time=56ms TTL=43
Reply from 216.69.134.36: bytes=32 time=55ms TTL=43
Reply from 216.69.134.36: bytes=32 time=54ms TTL=43
Reply from 216.69.134.36: bytes=32 time=55ms TTL=43

Ping statistics for 216.69.134.36:
    Packets: Sent = 4, Received = 4, Lost = 0 (0% loss),
Approximate round trip times in milli-seconds:
    Minimum = 54ms, Maximum = 56ms, Average = 55ms

C:\Users\Dan>_
```

When the ping command is successful, the Internet is up. Specifically, it means that the domain or IP address you typed is accessible. You should see results such as those shown in Figure 1-5. The information displayed indicates a successful, round-trip ping adventure.

When ping isn't successful, it could mean any number of things.

When you see the response `Destination host unreachable`, the Web site or domain isn't available, or "up," on the Internet. That message may also mean that the Internet isn't available. So, despite your having an Internet connection, something else that's out there on the Internet is preventing you from accessing information. (Think "backhoe.")

The message `Request Timed Out` means that the host is out there but cannot be reached. It's probably busy, although the message may also indicate that some or all of the Internet isn't available.

In all cases, there's really nothing you can do; the ping command merely confirms whether the Internet is reachable. When ping reports that something isn't available, you can just sit and wait, knowing that the problem isn't related to your equipment.

✦ The backhoe is the natural enemy of the Internet.

**Book IV
Chapter 1**

Internet Malaise

✦ *Domain* is short for a *fully qualified domain name*. It's the official name of a computer or network on the Internet. The domain includes the host-name, such as `wambooli` or `yahoo` or `google`, followed by a top-level domain like `com`, `net`, or `edu`. The domain is simply a word related to an IP address. It's easier to use the Internet by typing a domain rather than a long, complex, easy-to-forget number.

✦ You can also use ping to troubleshoot the local-area network in your home or office. See Book V for more on network troubleshooting.

✦ The IP address for most — but not all — routers is `192.168.0.1` or `10.0.0.1`. Try pinging them to ensure that your router isn't having the issue.

✦ Just because the ping command is successful doesn't mean that a Web site is available. The Web server on a domain could be down or busy, in which case ping reports that everything is fine even though your Web browser is still unable to view that site. My advice is to try again later.

✦ There's a condition when ping falsely reports that a Web site that isn't available appears to be available. Some ISPs redirect bad domain requests to a special search page. So rather than see an "unknown Web page" message in a Web browser or a `Destination host unreachable` message from the ping command, you see the ISP's redirection page instead.

✦ The term *ping* is often used as a noun in online computer gaming. It refers to the speed at which a connection is made by a remote server. High pings are bad, indicating a slow connection (or long-distance connection). Low pings are best.

✦ Beyond gaming, ping time is also used to determine which servers are closest to your location. For example, when given the choice of multiple servers for downloading a file, choose the server that reports a fast ping time. To determine the fastest ping time, it's necessary to ping each server and note its average ping time.

✦ Ping is also used in Internet denial of service (DOS) attacks. A vast number of infected or compromised computers send a huge number of ping requests to a specific server on the Internet, which effectively shuts down all other traffic to that server.

✦ The ping command was named after the sound made by a submarine sonar. Later, the term *packet internet groper* was retrofitted to make ping an acronym. The result of using this method is commonly called a *backronym*.

Confirming that an Internet location exists

Visiting some locations on the Internet for the first time is like trying to find an address in an unknown part of town: You can easily get lost and, worse, you might be in the wrong location, looking for an address that doesn't exist. With a computer, however, you can easily confirm a few things before you give up.

The first thing to try when you're told that a Web site or another Internet location doesn't exist is to check your typing. Especially for those `Web page 404` errors, which tell you that a Web page doesn't exist, odds are pretty good that you incorrectly typed the address. (You may also have clicked a bad link, but there's nothing you can do to fix that.)

The second thing to try is to reload. In Internet Explorer, press the F5 key to refresh the page. Reloading a Web page gives the Internet a second chance to send you that same information. It's amazing how often the reload trick works — especially for missing pictures or Web pages that suffer from ugly formatting.

Finally, you can use the ping command to confirm that the Web site's domain exists. But note that you can ping only a Web site's domain, not an individual Web page. For example, the Web site `http://sports.espn.go.com/nhl/index` is part of the domain `go.com`. You would need to ping `go.com` to see whether the site is accessible. Refer to the preceding section for details.

✦ The Refresh command for most Web browsers is the Ctrl+R key combination. There's also, most likely, a Refresh shortcut button on the browser's toolbar.

✦ The Refresh command is also used to order a new version of a Web page. Because many Web pages are updated frequently, by refreshing you always see the most recent version of the page.

✦ Well, actually, when the Web site is `http://sports.espn.go.com`, you can ping `go.com` or `sports.espn.go.com`. But you cannot ping `sports.espn.go.com/nhl/index` because it's an "unknown host."

Choose Your Internet Programs

There's more than one way to skin a cat, but save kitty for a moment and recognize that there's also more than one way to browse the Internet or pick up your e-mail. You may have several e-mail programs on your computer, plus a browser or two. You can let each of them fight it out for your favors, or you can advanced to a more civilized state and pick your top programs in a calm and less brutal manner.

To specify which programs are set up in Windows Vista, follow these steps:

1. **Open the Default Programs icon in the Control Panel.**

2. **Choose Set Your Default Programs.**

It probably should read Set the Computer's Default Programs because you, a human, don't have any default programs. You see the Set Your Default Programs window, shown in Figure 1-6. Though the list doesn't specifically contain Internet programs, you will find Internet programs in the list.

Figure 1-6:
Choose the
computer's
Internet
programs
here.

3. **Choose from the list the program you want to use as your Web browser.**

   One example is Firefox, shown in Figure 1-6.

4. **Choose the option Set This Program As Default.**

5. **Repeat Steps 3 and 4 for your e-mail program.**

6. **Click OK.**

In Windows XP, follow these steps to set the programs used for Internet access:

1. **Open the Control Panel's Internet Options icon.**

2. **Click the Programs tab.**

3. **Choose an e-mail program from the E-Mail drop-down list.**

4. **Add the check mark by the item Internet Explorer Should Check to See Whether It Is the Default Browser.**

   The option is at the bottom of the dialog box. When the option is selected, Internet Explorer begs you to make it the default Web browser when it starts. That allows you to switch browsers, but only between Internet Explorer and another Web browser.

5. **Click OK.**

6. **Close the Control Panel window.**

Whenever you install new Internet software, such as a new e-mail program or Web browser, it typically asks whether you want that program to be the "default." Answering Yes at that time sets the new software as the main program. There's no need to go through the preceding set of steps.

✦ Not every program may make the list. For example, Google's new Web browser, Google Chrome, didn't appear on the list when I first installed it. That's generally okay, because running the program for the first time lets you select it as your default Web browser (as just described).

✦ Internet Explorer is the preferred Web browser in Windows. Sometimes it runs because Windows wants it to run, regardless of which browser you set up as the default Web browser.

✦ Yes, it's silly that Windows XP lacks a better way to choose a default Web browser. Various lawyers agree with you, but because Microsoft will no longer support Windows XP at some later date, the well-advised solution is to get a new PC running Windows Vista.

✦ Some programs, such as Internet Explorer, incessantly ask whether you want them to be the defaults every dang doodle time they run, even after you specify another program as the default.

Binary Breadcrumbs

Hither, thither, and yon, where you've been on the Internet isn't a secret. Like seeing a car driving a dusty road miles away, a plume of digital dust lingers behind your every online movement. Always.

Keeping track of where you've been on the information superhighway is billed as a "feature" of the Internet programs you use. It's designed to help you get back to where you once were, to quickly recall places or things you typed. But such a feature can also be a security risk, not to mention that it holds a potential for embarrassment. This section tells you how to cover your online tracks.

Revising history

All Web browser programs come with a History feature. It details the Web sites and pages you visited, usually for the past week or two. That way, you can quickly return to where you once were, but others using the computer can also view a trail guide of your Internet travels. When you go somewhere that you would rather not have others know about, you need to practice some good old historical revision.

**Book IV
Chapter 1**

Internet Malaise

For Internet Explorer versions 7 and later, follow these steps to prune the history list:

1. **Choose Tools⇨Delete Browsing History.**

The Delete Browsing History dialog box appears, as shown in Figure 1-7. Obviously, this dialog box plays a key role in deleting digital history.

2. **Click the Delete History button.**

Delete Browsing History

Temporary Internet Files
Copies of webpages, images, and media that are saved for faster viewing. [Delete files...]

Cookies
Files stored on your computer by websites to save preferences such as login information. [Delete cookies...]

History
List of websites you have visited. [Delete history...]

Form data
Saved information that you have typed into forms. [Delete forms...]

Passwords
Passwords that are automatically filled in when you log on to a website you've previously visited. [Delete passwords...]

About deleting browsing history   [Delete all...]   [Close]

Figure 1-7:
The Delete
Browsing
History
dialog box.

3. **Click Yes to confirm that you want to remove all records of the places you've visited.**

4. **Click the Close button to close the Delete Browsing History dialog box.**

5. **Click OK to close the Internet Options dialog box.**

If you'd rather just dispense with history altogether, you can disable it as a feature by following these steps:

1. **Choose Tools⇨Internet Options.**

2. **Click the Settings button in the Browsing History area of the dialog box's General tab.**

3. **Set the Number of Days to Keep Pages in History to zero.**

    The option is at the bottom of the Temporary Internet Files and History Settings dialog box.

4. **Click OK.**

5. **Click OK to close the Internet Options dialog box.**

Keep in mind that the History feature continues to track recent Web sites, even when you disable it. Setting the Number of Days to Keep Pages in History value to zero merely erases the history list every day, not every second.

If you desire simply to pluck out specific unwanted remnants of where you've been, follow these steps:

1. **Press Ctrl+H to summon the History window in Internet Explorer.**

    The Web page history is categorized by day, Web site, and, finally, Web page.

2. **Right-click a day, Web site, or Web page to remove from the History list.**

3. **Choose the Delete command from the shortcut menu.**

4. **Click the Yes button to confirm the deletion.**

    And the offending entry is gone.

You have to repeat all these steps to delete additional entries; after you delete an entry, the History panel/window/thing closes.

You can use the preceding technique to clear out the history when you set the Number of Days to Keep Pages in History to zero, as described earlier. Simply delete the items you don't want to keep, and know that the rest of history will be zapped at the end of the day anyway.

✦   To clear the history for Internet Explorer 6 and earlier, click the Clear History button found on the General tab of the Internet Options dialog box.

✦   To set the Number of Days to Keep Pages in History option in Internet Explorer 6, open the Internet Options dialog box and set the value on the General tab.

✦   In the Firefox Web browser, you can remove what's called "personal information" by using the Clear Private Data command: Choose Tools⇨Clear Private Data to summon the Clear Private Data dialog box. Choose which items to remove and then click the Clear Private Data Now button.

Removing cookies

I'm not one to believe that Web page cookies are evil, but I recognize that a lot of people prefer to lose their cookies as they travel the Internet. Here's how to purge those digital biscuits in Internet Explorer:

1. **Choose Tools⇨Delete Browsing History.**

    The Delete Browsing History dialog box shows up (refer to Figure 1-7).

2. **Click the Delete Cookies button.**

3. **Click the Yes button.**

4. **Close the dialog boxes you opened.**

The steps for deleting cookies are different for Internet Explorer 6 and earlier: Skip Step 2 (in the preceding list) and click the Delete Cookies button found on the General tab of the Internet Options dialog box. Click the OK button to confirm deleting the cookies.

Sadly, there's no way to delete specific cookies in Internet Explorer; you're given only an all-or-nothing choice. You can, however, remove individual cookies — if you can find the secret location where they're stored.

In Windows Vista, here's where the cookies are hidden:

```
%USERPROFILE%\AppData\Roaming\Microsoft\Windows\Cookies
```

In Windows XP, the Cookies folder is found here:

```
%USERPROFILE%\Cookies
```

To see the Cookies folder, summon a Windows Explorer window (Press Win+E) and type one of these pathnames. Press Enter and you see the contents of the Cookies folder, as shown in Figure 1-8.

Figure 1-8:
The secret Cookies folder in Windows Vista.

Cookies are given names based on your Windows username, followed by the @ sign and then the name of the Web site that planted the cookie on your computer.

You can view the cookie's content by double-clicking any Cookie icon; cookie files are text files. The content isn't really useful, however, it consists mostly of numbers that have meaning only to the Web site that created the cookie.

Delete a single cookie the way you would delete any file: Select the icon and press the Delete key on the keyboard.

+ Cookies are re-created when you visit the same Web site again.

+ You can disable cookies altogether in Internet Explorer, but by doing so, you render some Web pages useless. My advice is to not bother with disabling cookies.

Purging temporary files

As you surf the Web, your Web browser picks up all sorts of stuff. Primarily, it collects media — pictures, sounds, videos — but also other information you see on any Web page. All those items are known collectively as *temporary files*. You might also hear it referred to as the *cache*.

Normally, there's no reason to worry about temporary files. They exist to help Web pages you frequent load faster. But the temporary files also serve as a digital fingerprint of places you visit. To remove those remnants, you can purge your computer of temporary files. Here's how:

1. **Choose Tools⇨Delete Browsing History.**

The Delete Browsing History dialog box pops up (refer to Figure 1-7).

2. **Click the Delete Files button.**

3. **Click the Yes button to confirm.**

4. **Click the Close button to dismiss the Delete Browsing History dialog box, and then close the Internet Options dialog box. (Click OK.)**

In Internet Explorer 6, follow these steps:

1. **Open the Internet Options icon in the Control Panel.**

2. **Click the Delete Files button.**

3. **Place a check mark by the option Delete All Offline Content.**

4. **Click OK.**

5. **Click OK to close the Internet Options dialog box.**

The files you deleted accumulate again as you revisit Web pages. It's nothing you can prevent — temporary files are part of the Web browsing process. But you can delete those files every so often.

✦ Yep, anytime you see porn on a Web page, even if you visited the site "accidentally," a copy of that image is retained on your PC as a temporary file. That is, until you delete the temporary files.

✦ You can also delete temporary files by using the Disk Cleanup utility. See Book VI, Chapter 2 for more information.

✦ There's a way to eliminate temporary files. You can configure the Web browser to not display any media files. That means you see only text when you visit a Web page — no graphics, sounds, videos, or other files. On some Web sites, you can still view the information because most of it is text. But making such a change renders a number of popular Web sites unreadable. To suppress the media display in Internet Explorer, click the Advanced tab in the Internet Options dialog box and remove all check marks under the Multimedia heading.

Dealing with AutoComplete

The AutoComplete feature is the handy tool that quickly summons stuff you previously typed, saving you from spending time typing it all over again. Whenever you type a Web page address or fill in a form, AutoComplete displays a list of options or previously typed text. The feature is a blessing, but it can also be a curse — especially when things you don't want others to see keep popping up on the screen.

To utterly disable AutoComplete, follow these steps:

1. **Open the Internet Options icon in the Control Panel.**

2. **Click the Content tab.**

3. **Click the Settings button in the AutoComplete area.**

For Internet Explorer 6, click the AutoComplete button.

4. **Remove all check marks to utterly disable AutoComplete.**

Or, you can be selective and remove the check marks just by the items that bug you, such as Web Addresses to remove those previously typed Web page addresses that keep popping up on the Address bar.

In Internet Explorer 6, you can also click the Clear Forms and Clear Passwords button at this time. Doing so removes any stored information that AutoComplete has collected. Follow through with Step 5 and you're done.

5. **Click OK.**

You can stop here, if you like. But I wouldn't: Purging items from AutoComplete's memory takes another approach. With the Internet Options dialog box still open, continue with these steps:

6. **Click the Delete History button.**

   The handy Delete Browsing History dialog box again shows its sunny countenance (refer to Figure 1-7).

7. **Click the Delete Forms button to purge AutoComplete information from Web page forms.**

8. **Click the Yes button to confirm.**

9. **Click the Delete Passwords button.**

10. **Click the Yes button to confirm.**

11. **Click the Close button.**

12. **Click OK to close the Internet Options dialog box.**

If you want to further check that items have been properly purged from the AutoComplete repository, get technical and peruse the Registry for those entries. See Book II, Chapter 9 for information on searching the Registry — but be aware that a search works only when you know the text of the AutoComplete item you want to remove. For URLs, look in the following Registry key:

```
HKCU\Software\Microsoft\internet Explorer\TypedURLs
```

Watch Video 411 to see a demonstration of how to purge AutoComplete information on your Windows Vista PC.

Contending with e-mail AutoComplete

Just when you think that you've fled the AutoComplete maze of despair, along comes another AutoComplete monster to devour you. This time, the AutoComplete beast resides in your e-mail program. It serves up previously typed e-mail addresses. Although I see that as a feature, I recognize that others may find it a pestilent hex. Here's how to stop the thing:

1. **Open Windows Mail or Outlook Express.**

   The programs share similar options at similar locations, so these steps work with both.

2. **Choose Tools⇨Options from the menu.**

3. **Click the Send tab in the Options dialog box.**

4. **Remove the check mark by Automatically Complete E-Mail Addresses When Composing.**

5. **Click OK.**

You're now free to peruse a life unfettered by textual reminders of your wayward past. Well, at least on the computer.

Chapter 2: Woes on the Web

In This Chapter

- ✔ Setting up toolbars
- ✔ Fixing Internet Explorer
- ✔ Working offline
- ✔ Dealing with ActiveX
- ✔ Fixing pop-up problems
- ✔ Adjusting a Web page's display
- ✔ Printing problems
- ✔ Resurrecting missing pictures

Spiders have it good. No doubt they relish the thought of a bug in their webs. Humans are not spiders, but, daily, millions of humans traverse the electronic Web of the Internet, prowling for information. When things get too sticky, or when you come across unwelcome bugs, consider dipping into this chapter for some helpful advice.

✦ Many Web woes are caused by malware or evil software. That's a big category, so it gets its own chapter; see Chapter 4. Go there for information on malware as well as phishing attacks.

✦ Files are also downloaded from the Internet, which may seem to you like a Web page issue, but it's really a file transfer issue. Therefore, it's covered in Chapter 5.

Internet Explorer Hates Your Guts

Microsoft decided to name its official Web browser Internet Explorer. Back in the early days, I enjoyed calling it Internet Exploder. Oh, such mirth makes me tingle. But after seven iterations, Internet Explorer continues to be the bane of many Web surfers. This chapter covers some common issues in Internet Explorer and how to deal with them.

✦ Internet Explorer isn't your only Web browsing choice. A popular alternative is the Firefox Web browser, which has features and powers far beyond anything Microsoft is capable of creating. Grab a free copy of the Firefox Web browser at `mozilla.com`.

✦ I don't cover Firefox specifically in this book. After all, this isn't a Web browser troubleshooting book. Where appropriate, I do mention some things that Firefox is capable of doing.

✦ As this book goes to press, Microsoft is testing a new version of Internet Explorer. Any updates to this book for Internet Explorer version 8 can be found on this book's support Web site:

    www.wambooli.com/help/troubleshooting

Showing the menu bar

After the menu bar enjoyed a good 20 years as a computing paradigm, Microsoft decided to dispense with it in many of its programs. For the purposes of this section, the menu bar has apparently vanished from Internet Explorer. But not really.

To see the good ol' familiar menu bar in Internet Explorer, press the F10 key.

Indeed, the F10 key is an *old* paradigm itself. Pressing F10 in Windows programs selects the menu bar, which reveals menu bar shortcut keys in a traditional sense or reveals the entire menu in a modern sense.

Alas, the F10 menu bar trick is only temporary. To see the menu bar full-time in Internet Explorer, choose the Menu Bar command from the Tools button on the toolbar.

Managing toolbars

The dawn of the 21st century also saw the dawn of the overabundance of Internet Explorer toolbars. Microsoft slaps one on, called the Windows Live toolbar. There's an endless cornucopia of Google Desktop toolbars. Developers are creating Internet Explorer toolbars more rapidly than teenagers are creating MySpace pages, and with similar reckless abandon.

You don't need all those toolbars. They add clutter to the Web browser window. Plus, they add features you probably never use. It's your computer — you be the boss!

Manage the toolbars in Internet Explorer by following these steps:

1. **From the Tools button on the toolbar, choose Tools⇨Toolbars.**

The Toolbars submenu appears. Active toolbars appear with a check mark by their names, as shown in Figure 2-1.

2. **Choose a checked toolbar from the submenu to remove it.**

3. **Repeat Steps 1 and 2 until Internet Explorer is purged of all unwanted toolbars.**

Figure 2-1:
Where the
toolbar
controls
lurk.

Removing the check mark by a toolbar doesn't uninstall that toolbar. You
can reactivate the toolbar at any time by choosing the toolbar from the
Toolbars submenu.

The Links bar is another toolbar you can remove, though I prefer keeping
it active as a bookmarks menu. The status bar is also useful because it provides information about the Web page you're viewing (or trying to view).

To dispense with all toolbars and enjoy a wonderful, full-screen Web browsing experience, press the F11 key. That key activates the Full Screen command (shown in Figure 2-1, beneath the Tools button menu). In Full Screen
mode, almost *everything* that's a part of the Internet Explorer window van-
ishes (except for the status bar). Press F11 again to return to Normal view.

To uninstall a toolbar, you need to remove the program that set the thing up
in the first place. See Book II, Chapter 6 for details.

Dealing with add-ons

An *add-on* is a supplemental program designed to enhance your Web browsing experience.

Wow. That's good. I should write ad copy. But because you're not buying
anything here, let me explain in a friendlier manner: An *add-on* is a tiny program attached to Internet Explorer, like adding chrome to a car. The add-on
serves to run special Web page features, like animation or video or other
must-see elements on a Web page. Without the add-on, those items don't
function, or else you see text begging you to install the add-on.

You manage add-ons by clicking the Tools button in Internet Explorer 7. From the Tools button menu, choose Manage Add-Ons➪Enable or Disable Add-Ons. You see the Manage Add-Ons dialog box, shown in Figure 2-2. It displays which add-ons are loaded and whether they're enabled or disabled.

Figure 2-2:
The Manage
Add-Ons
dialog box.

To disable an add-on that's bugging you or causing Internet Explorer to crash, select it from the list in the Manage Add-Ons window and click the Disable option. Likewise, to reenable the add-on (in case it isn't the cause of your Web page troubles), select it and choose the Enable command.

Click OK to close the Manage Add-Ons window.

✦ To hunt for additional add-ons in Internet Explorer, from the Tools button, choose Manage Add-Ons➪Find More Add-Ons. Doing so whisks you off to a Web site gallery where you can choose additional add-ons.

✦ I recommend installing add-ons. Most of them add favor to the Web pages you visit and are required for that "enhanced Web browsing experience." Besides, you now know how to remove those add-ons and controls if they displease you.

✦ You can also manage add-ons by opening the Internet Options icon in the Control Panel. In the Internet Options dialog box, click the Programs tab and then click the button Manage Add-Ons.

+ You can temporarily disable all add-ons in Internet Explorer, which comes in handy for troubleshooting. To do so, from the Start menu, choose All Programs⇨Accessories⇨System Tools⇨Internet Explorer (No Add-Ons).

+ In Internet Explorer 6, choose Tools⇨Manage Add-Ons to see the Manage Add-Ons window.

+ In Firefox, choose Tools⇨Add-Ons to find and manage add-ons.

+ Also see the later section "Secret Ingredient: Active X."

Resetting Internet Explorer

Just as restarting your computer often fixes minor software ills, you can attempt to repair Internet Explorer by performing a software reset. Here's how:

1. **Open the Internet Options icon in the Control Panel.**

2. **Click the Advanced tab.**

3. **Click the Reset button.**

   The Reset Internet Explorer Settings dialog box appears. It's not an entertaining read.

4. **Click the Reset button in the Reset Internet Explorer Settings dialog box.**

   Purge! Purge! Purge!

5. **Click the Close button.**

You have to close Internet Explorer, in case an Internet Explorer window is open.

After you restart Internet Explorer, all the add-ons and customization you completed are removed. The home page is also reset to whatever it was when you first set up your PC (such as to the manufacturer's Web site or whichever MSN or Windows Live site Microsoft is pushing).

+ Resetting Internet Explorer doesn't remove any of your bookmarks. But if you added a custom toolbar or reset the home page, you need to reconfigure those settings after resetting.

+ Internet Explorer can also be repaired by running the System File Checker. See Book II, Chapter 8.

+ I don't recommend repairing or attempting to fix older versions of Internet Explorer. Instead, upgrade. See the next section.

**Book IV
Chapter 2**

Woes on the Web

Upgrading Internet Explorer

One of the most fundamental ways to fix Internet Explorer is to upgrade it. The newer version offers features you probably want or need, plus, it fixes a lot of the bugs and security flaws of the previous edition. (The preceding sentence is eternally true for all versions of Internet Explorer, past and future.)

In fact, I recommend upgrading Internet Explorer to the latest version even when you aren't having issues with the program.

Internet Explorer upgrades are obtained simply. First, the Windows Update process installs any newer versions of Internet Explorer that are available. Second, an automatic check is done every time Internet Explorer starts. If a newer release of the program is available, you're immediately whisked to an update Web site (even when your home page is set elsewhere).

Manual updates for Internet Explorer can be obtained at the Microsoft Web site:

`www.microsoft.com/windows/downloads/ie/getitnow.mspx`

See Book II, Chapter 1 for more information on Windows Updates.

Understanding the "work offline" thing

A menu item curious to many users is Work Offline. It's on the Tools button menu in Internet Explorer, but might also dwell on the File menu in other Internet applications. It shouldn't be a mystery: Choosing that option tells the program not to access the Internet. Indeed, you work offline when you choose that command.

If you attempt to do something on the Internet or the Web page you're viewing tries to fetch new information, you see a warning such as the one shown in Figure 2-3. Click the Connect button to disable the Work Offline setting and reconnect to the Internet. Or, click Stay Offline to continue to have the program ignore the Internet.

Figure 2-3:
The re-
connection
warning.

To disable Work Offline mode and return to normal, choose the command again.

✦ Choosing the Work Offline command doesn't disconnect the computer from the Internet.

✦ I use Work Offline mode when I'm reading Web pages on an airplane. I save the Web pages before I leave and then choose the Work Offline command so that I'm not constantly bothered by the PC's vain attempts to contact the Internet while I read.

Secret Ingredient: ActiveX

The letter *X* is so cool that our culture would be lost without it. Phonetically, it's useless. As long as there's a *K* and an *S* in the alphabet, *X* remains a mystery. Indeed, *X* itself often refers to an unknown value. It's that mystique that lends the *X* to so many wickedly awesome things. Could *ActiveX* be one of them? This section explains.

Understanding ActiveX

I'm certain that there's a lot of technical mumbo jumbo I could explain about ActiveX, but the purpose of this book isn't to cure insomnia. Simply put, ActiveX is a software technology — a computer program to help other programs. What ActiveX does is to create wee little programs that work on a Web browser — specifically, Internet Explorer.

Anytime you visit a Web page that shows a video or plays a game or lets you use a text editor, you're probably seeing an ActiveX *control*. The ActiveX program is sent from the Web page to your computer, and the program "runs" in Internet Explorer.

There was some concern a few years back about ActiveX being a bad thing. A security flaw in the way ActiveX was run years ago allowed the Bad Guys to send viruses and other nasty software to your computer. Those issues have since been addressed.

✦ Controlling ActiveX is covered in the next two sections.

✦ There's no relationship between ActiveX and other Microsoft technologies using the word *Active*: Active Desktop or Active Directory, and so on. Microsoft just enjoys using the word *active* to describe things.

✦ Likewise, the technology DirectX has no relationship to ActiveX. Apparently, Microsoft also enjoys sticking the letter X to the end of certain words. (See Book II, Chapter 7 for a tiny tidbit on DirectX.)

✦ Web browsers other than Internet Explorer use Java and other network software technologies instead of ActiveX.

Book IV Chapter 2

Woes on the Web

Restricting ActiveX controls

Internet Explorer automatically installs ActiveX controls from the Web sites you visit. If you prefer a higher level of security, you can restrict that access. Follow these steps:

1. **Open the Internet Options icon in the Control Panel.**

2. **Click the Security tab.**

3. **Choose Internet from the list of zones.**

4. **Click the Custom Level button.**

The Security Settings – Internet Zone dialog box appears, as shown in Figure 2-4.

Figure 2-4:
Control ActiveX in this dialog box.

5. **Scroll down to the section titled ActiveX Controls and Plug-Ins.**

The items organized in the Active X section deal with how Internet Explorer deals with various ActiveX situations on the Internet. Each option has two or more settings:

Enable: The ActiveX feature works automatically.

Disable: The ActiveX feature isn't allowed.

Prompt: You see a warning whenever an ActiveX control is being sent to your computer. At that time, you can choose whether to allow it.

Administrator Approved: A User Account Control warning appears when the ActiveX control tries to run.

The items in the list are set up tightly as far as security is concerned: Digitally signed and approved ActiveX controls are allowed, and you're prompted for almost everything else. Questionable ActiveX controls are disabled. However, I do recommend the change in Step 6.

6. **Beneath the entry Run ActiveX Controls and Plug-Ins, choose Prompt.**

7. **Click OK to close the Security Settings – Internet Zone dialog box.**

8. **Click Yes to confirm the changes you made.**

    If you haven't made any changes, the Warning dialog box doesn't appear.

9. **Click OK to close the Internet Options dialog box, and you can close the Control Panel window as well.**

By making the change I suggest in Step 6, you add a higher level of security to your Web browsing. But you also add a level of annoyance: the ActiveX control warning, shown in Figure 2-5. As you'll soon discover, the Web pages you use are crawling with ActiveX controls.

Figure 2-5:
The ActiveX
warning.

There are two solutions. The less secure one is to change the Run ActiveX Controls and Plug-Ins setting back to Enable from Prompt. That works. A more secure setting, however, is to simply add to your list of Trusted Sites the Web sites you visit and trust. I explain how that's done later in this chapter, in the section "Adding a Web site to your trusted zone."

Removing ActiveX controls

When an ActiveX control comes floating in, it pretty much becomes part of your computer, attaching itself to Internet Explorer like a tick on an Alabama hound dog. In the old days, there was no way to remove that ActiveX tick. Now you can disable or remove an installed ActiveX control by following these steps:

1. **Open Internet Explorer.**

2. **From the Tools button menu, choose Manage Add-Ons⇨Enable or Disable Add-Ons.**

    The Manage Add-Ons dialog box comes into view (refer to Figure 2-2).

3. **From the drop-down menu, choose Add-Ons That Run without Requiring Permission.**

4. **Peruse the list for ActiveX controls to disable.**

   Which ones? That's the question! Immediately, any ActiveX control you see that has no publisher (the Publisher column is empty) deserves scrutiny. Otherwise, don't delete anything unless you know that it's suspect.

   You can delete an ActiveX control when it's selected and the Delete button is available (undimmed).

5. **Click OK when you're done.**

You have several ways to determine whether an ActiveX control is deleterious. First, don't panic: There are a lot of ActiveX controls, and only a handful of them are twisted. Second, many of the antivirus and anti-spyware utilities automatically seek out and disable bad ActiveX controls for you. Beyond that, you should be alerted to the presence of an ActiveX control that needs to be removed by a source that tells you what to disable or delete. Above all: Don't guess!

✦ I don't recommend randomly deleting ActiveX controls.

✦ Despite what I said in the preceding bullet, when you delete or disable an ActiveX control, if you need it, you'll find it downloaded into Internet Explorer the next time it's called for. (Well, unless you changed settings according to the preceding section and are prompted for downloading ActiveX controls.)

✦ You might also look for ActiveX controls to remove from the Programs or Add/Remove Programs icons in the Control Panel. See Book II, Chapter 6 for details.

What's Up, Pop?

Advertising is as old as mankind. Indeed, were not the original cave paintings a way for Og to communicate to everyone else that he killed a beast in a most deft and stunning manner? As mankind has progressed, advertising has grown more effective to the point that the Ogs in marketing figured out how to sell you stuff by popping up a special Web browser window. It has been dubbed the *pop-up*, and people hate it. This section explains how it works and what you can do about it.

Understanding pop-ups

The problem isn't as bad as it once was. Back, say, ten years ago or more, online advertisers virtually throttled Web page viewers with an onslaught of pop-up advertising windows. Opening a single Web page would often produce a flurry of three or more additional windows, each of which contained an advertisement. It was annoying.

Pop-up windows are created in several ways. Primarily, it's the JavaScript programming language that's responsible. JavaScript is built into every Web browser. One of its features is that it allows for one Web page window to spawn another window. Or four.

Advertisers took advantage of the spawning feature to display a new window boasting about their product every time you visited a certain Web page. The window would *pop up* over or under the window you were viewing — hence the term *pop-up* to describe them.

Eventually, the situation got out of hand. Pop-ups ceased to be effective advertising and became irritating almost to the point where a negative backlash occurred. Legitimate advertisers stopped using pop-ups, and the questionable pharmaceutical dealers and porn peddlers took over. Fortunately, browser developers responded swiftly by allowing the JavaScript pop-up window feature to be disabled.

The bottom line is that pop-ups are still out there, but not as pervasively or as perversely as in days gone by. Like many Web browsers, Internet Explorer has an anti-pop-up tool you can use, described in the next section.

✦ One of the most insidious pop-up schemes was the *mouse trap*. When a pop-up advertising window appeared, you would click to close it. But by closing the window, another one opened in its place. Sometimes, two windows would open every time you closed one window.

✦ Technically, a window that pops up behind the Web page you're viewing is a *pop-under* window. It's still a pop-up.

✦ I should mention that many of the early pop-up windows featured unpleasant, hard-core pornographic images.

✦ The pop-up problem was worse years ago because Internet Explorer was directly wired into the Windows operating system; you could not "quit" Internet Explorer. That meant, for many users, that their desktops were eventually overwhelmed with pop-up windows, requiring them to restart their computers (often by forcing a shutdown) to get rid of them.

Dealing with pop-ups

Internet Explorer is configured to block all pop-up windows; the pop-up blocker feature is *on*. When a Web page tries to sneak in a pop-up window, a warning is displayed just below the tabs and toolbar, as shown in Figure 2-6.

Book IV
Chapter 2

Woes on the Web

Figure 2-6:
A pop-up
looms.

When you click the warning (shown in Figure 2-6), a menu appears. Here are your choices:

Temporarily Allow Pop-Ups: Lets the pop-up sneak on through, but only because you gave it permission.

Always Allow Pop-Ups for This Site: Lets you grant permission for the Web site (and all pages on that site) to toss pop-up windows your way.

Settings: Displays a submenu that allows you to change how Internet Explorer reacts to pop-ups.

More Information: Displays a Help window about pop-ups.

I generally ignore the warning myself by clicking the X on the right end to close the thing. In fact, if you tire of the warning and just don't want to be bothered or you don't mind the warning but hate the beep, or both, you can control the pop-up blocker's settings. To do so, from the Tools button menu, choose Pop-Up Blocker⇨Pop-Up Blocker Settings. You see the Pop-up Blocker Settings window, shown in Figure 2-7.

Figure 2-7:
Controlling the Internet Explorer pop-up blocker.

You can use the Pop-up Blocker Settings window to manually add sites for the pop-up blocker to ignore (though I prefer to add each site individually as I encounter them). Most important for me is the option Play a Sound When a Pop-Up Is Blocked. I don't like random beeps, so I turn that option off.

Incidentally, the Pop-Up Blocker Settings window is where you can remove any Web sites you accidentally added to the Do Not Block list: Choose a site from the list of Allowed Sites and then click the Remove button.

Click the Close button when you're done messing around with the Pop-Up Blocker Settings window.

✦ You can turn the pop-up blocker on or off by choosing the proper command from the Tools button menu's Pop-Up Blocker submenu.

✦ Pop-ups aren't always ads, of course. Some Web sites use pop-ups to display information.

✦ At the Custom-level settings, pop-up windows are allowed whenever you click a button or link to display the pop-up.

✦ If you set the Filter Level in the Pop-Up Blocker Settings window to High (refer to Figure 2-7), all pop-ups are blocked, no matter what.

✦ There's a new type of pop-up that isn't the traditional type, but it can be just as annoying. It's a Flash pop-up, which sometimes looks like a pop-up window, but at other times appears to seamlessly float over the top of a Web page. (The Internet Movie Database, at `imdb.com`, features some annoying examples.) Internet Explorer's pop-up blocker doesn't block those Flash windows. The only way to block them is to disable the Flash ActiveX component, but that would also make many videos, media, and games cease to function on the Internet.

Web Page Hell

The list is practically endless when it comes to generic Web page mayhem. Things are better than they once were; today's Web browsers are truly sophisticated beasts that can usually handle even the most unruly Web sites. When they don't, turn to this section for assistance.

Adding a Web site to your trusted zone

When you ratchet up Internet security (such as disabling ActiveX components, as discussed earlier in this chapter), you might find your once pleasant and speedy Web browsing experience plagued with speed bumps. There's a way to fix that, and to ensure that you're not bothered with ActiveX or other warnings for Web sites you trust. Follow these steps:

1. Browse a site you can trust.

For example, go to any Web page you visit frequently, but also one where you see warnings about security, such as ActiveX controls.

2. **From the Tools menu button, choose Internet Options.**

3. **In the Internet Options dialog box, click the Security tab.**

4. **Choose the big green check mark: Trusted Sites.**

5. **Click the Sites button.**

   You discover the Trusted Sites dialog box, shown in Figure 2-8. The Web site you're visiting is shown by the Add button.

Figure 2-8:
The Trusted
Sites
dialog box.

6. **Remove the check mark by the option Require Server Verification (https:) for All Sites in This Zone.**

   When you forget to uncheck this option and you add a non-`https` site, a rude warning dialog box appears.

7. **Click the Add button.**

   The Web site is added to the list.

8. **Click Close.**

9. **Click OK to send off the Internet Options dialog box.**

Adding a site you frequent to your trusted zone helps expedite things that happen on that Web site, without having to compromise overall Internet security.

✦ You don't need to add individual pages within the site; add only the root part of the site. For example, adding `www.microsoft.com` provides for all Web pages within the `microsoft.com` domain to be trusted.

✦ You may still be prompted for ActiveX alerts when you add a Web site to the trusted zone. Those alerts may be coming not from the Web site directly but, rather, from frames or links to online advertising.

✦ Web sites whose addresses begin with `https` are secure Web sites, verified by a verification process. Such sites ensure that the information you send is encrypted and cannot be lifted by a bad guy en route. That doesn't imply that an `http` (no *S*) site is insecure, but rather that it's possible to trust a normal site that doesn't need the extra verification.

Fixing weirdly sized windows

Weird-size windows are more appropriately an issue with Windows, not with the Web browser. The problem seems to surface often in a Web browser, probably because that program opens more windows than other programs do.

Some Web pages automatically resize windows: The Web page opens and suddenly fills the entire screen. There's nothing you can do to prevent that from happening (other than not visiting the Web site). All you can do is to resize the window after it opens.

Because Windows remembers the size and position of previous windows you opened, you may experience new Web pages opening in odd-size windows. To fix the problem, manually resize the window.

✦ To manually resize a window, use the mouse to move the window's edges. You can grab the top or bottom edge of a window to make it taller or more squat. You can grab the left or right edge of a window to make it wider or thinner. You can grab a window's corner to resize the window in two directions at one time.

✦ Resized windows are most apparent when you have a nice, roomy, wide-screen monitor. The newly resized window enlarges to cover the entire screen, but it's not maximized.

✦ Maximizing a window isn't the same as resizing it. When you maximize the window, you do not reset the window's size and position on the desktop.

Looking bigger (smaller)

Zoom can mean something that goes really fast. But it can also mean to move in closer, such as with a camera's zoom lens. The latter definition is the name of a command featured in just about every program. The Zoom command is used to make what you see appear smaller or larger on the screen.

In Internet Explorer, you can zoom an entire Web page, making its contents larger or smaller: From the page menu, choose Zoom and then choose a zoom size from the submenu.

When it's merely the text size that needs adjusting, you can use the Text Size submenu, also found on the Page button menu.

✦ The keyboard shortcut to zoom into a Web page is Ctrl++ (the plus key).

✦ The keyboard shortcut to zoom out of a Web page is Ctrl+– (the minus key).

✦ You can also zoom an image by pressing the Ctrl key and using the wheel button on the mouse: Ctrl+scroll up zooms in; Ctrl+scroll down zooms back out.

Printing a Web page

The mechanics of printing a Web page work like printing any document in any application: Choose the Print command from the File menu, work the Print dialog box, and then print, blah-blah-blah — you know the drill. Assuming that the printer is connected and ready to go, the Web page should print. But that *is* an assumption.

My first mistake is assuming that the Print command is on the File menu. Internet Explorer doesn't have a File menu, but it does have a Print button on its toolbar. Clicking the button prints the Web page, or you can display a menu, as shown in Figure 2-9, that shows more printing options.

Figure 2-9:
The Print
toolbar
button's
menu.

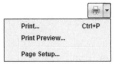

Print...	Ctrl+P
Print Preview...	
Page Setup...	

My second mistake is to assume that you can fit all the content of a single Web page on a single sheet of paper. You can! But often, Internet Explorer shrinks the content to fit a page. Here's how to fix that:

1. **From the Print button on the toolbar, choose the Print Preview command.**

The Print Preview window opens, as shown in Figure 2-10. The window not only helps you prevent wasting paper but also assists you in ensuring that you print the Web page exactly the way you want.

2. **Select the proper page orientation.**

Some Web pages look better on paper when they're printed in landscape orientation. Again, the Print Preview window helps you to determine whether landscape is a better choice before you print anything.

Print

Portrait orientation

Landscape orientation   Change print size

Margin adjuster

Figure 2-10:
The Print
Preview
window
for Internet
Explorer 7.

Margin adjusters   Page viewing controls

3. **Set the proper zoom or shrink value using the Change Print Size menu.**

As you choose a size, use the preview image to determine whether it looks good.

**Book IV
Chapter 2**

Woes on the Web

4. **Click the Print button to bring up the Print dialog box.**

5. **Work the options in the Print dialog box.**

Some examples are number of copies and which pages to print.

6. **Click the Print button to print the Web page.**

In an amazing twist of technology, a once electronic Web page is now inked onto a sheet of paper. Be sure to amaze your friends with such a thing.

✦ Clicking the Print button on the toolbar instantly prints the Web page. To work the Print dialog box, choose Print from the Print button's menu or press Ctrl+P.

- ✦ A single Web page prints out to several printed pages.
- ✦ To print only part of a Web page, select that part with the mouse. Then press Ctrl+P and in the Print dialog box, choose Selection. Click the Print button to print only the selected portion of the Web page.
- ✦ Only one part of a Web page can be selected at a time.
- ✦ Sometimes, text fails to show up when you select the Shrink to Fit option. That's a "feature" of the Web page. Simply choose another size from the Change Print Size menu.

- ✦ You can print an image on a Web page by right-clicking the image and choosing Print Picture from the shortcut menu. This trick comes in handy when the image doesn't print with the rest of the Web page.
- ✦ For printer troubleshooting, see Book I, Chapter 5.

Disabling JavaScript error messages

It isn't your job to fix a broken Web page. You may feel like it's your job. I guess that's because the Web page error message, like other computer error messages, appears on the screen and blares at you. It makes you assume that it's your problem and that you must deal with it. But, for a Web page, it's not your problem. Further, there's nothing you can do about it.

A specific error message case comes with the *JavaScript* programming language. What JavaScript does is help automate and format Web pages. You'll probably never deal with JavaScript, other than to use it on a Web page. But you may, occasionally, see something like what's shown in Figure 2-11.

Figure 2-11:
The Web page screwed up, not you.

Figure 2-11 features warning message. The warning is for the programmer, which can be seen when you click the Show Details button. (Don't bother.) Instead, remove the check mark by the item Always Display the Message When a Page Contains Errors.

To ensure that errors don't appear in the future, follow these steps in Internet Explorer:

1. **Choose the command Internet Options from the bottom of the Tools button menu.**

2. **Click the Advanced tab in the Internet Options dialog box.**

   There are three items to check in the list, all found beneath the Browsing heading.

3. **Place a check mark by the item Disable Script Debugging (Internet Explorer).**

4. **Place a check mark by the item Disable Script Debugging (Other).**

5. **Remove the check mark by the item Display a Notification about Every Script Error.**

6. **Click OK to close the Internet Options dialog box.**

Suppressing the error message doesn't remove the error from the page. The error is still there. But it's up to the programmer or Web page designer, not you, to fix the problem.

Dealing with missing pictures

The World Wide Web is here today because it was the first and best method for accessing information on the Internet, both text and graphics. Still, it's those graphics that have bothered Internet users since the early days. It's not the graphical images themselves (though some of those can be annoying), but rather when the images fail to show up.

A missing picture on a Web page is replaced by a placeholder, as shown in Figure 2-12. (Different Web browsers use different missing-picture icons. Internet Explorer uses the red X in a box, as shown in the figure.)

Figure 2-12: One thousand words missing.

> **Our Vacation at Nude City**
>
> ☒

Book IV
Chapter 2

Woes on the Web

The first trick to try getting the picture to appear is to refresh the Web page: Press F5 or Ctrl+R. Refreshing loads a new Web page from the Internet, which may pick up an image that the Web server was too slow to send in the first place.

The second trick is to right-click the missing-image icon and choose the Show Picture command. Sometimes that method works, but only when you configure Internet Explorer *not* to display images, which brings up the third trick:

Ensure that Internet Explorer is configured to display images. Follow these steps:

1. **From the Tools button menu, choose Internet Options.**
2. **In the Internet Options dialog box, click the Advanced tab.**
3. **Scroll down to the Multimedia heading and ensure that a check mark appears by the item Show Pictures.**
4. **Click OK.**

Some users disable pictures on Web pages, which greatly increases the speeds at which Web pages load. But it also means that you have to manually load the images when you want to see them (refer to Trick 2). By completing the preceding steps, you ensure that the images are loaded.

When these tricks fail, it's simply a problem with the Web site; the image file isn't present or the code that lists the image's filename is wrong. There's nothing you can do about that.

Chapter 3: E-Mail Postage Due

In This Chapter

✔ **Knowing how e-mail works**

✔ **Struggling with a draft**

✔ **Working in the trash**

✔ **Dealing with repeated messages**

✔ **Fixing e-mail program quirks**

✔ **Blocking and unblocking messages**

✔ **Using junk mail filters**

✔ **Avoiding large e-mail attachments**

1 was looking back the other day in a tattered old book, *Mail For Dummies*, published in 1934. It had such interesting chapters as "Thank-You Notes," "Proper Salutations," and "Stamps." The troubleshooting information was fairly limited, covering topics like folding stationery, knowing when it's okay to use pencil, and picking which side of the stamp to lick. With today's electronic mail, there are no more stamps, but there are certainly some troublesome topics to lick. This chapter seals the envelope on those issues without your having to use your tongue.

✦ There's no single e-mail program, though e-mail works pretty much the same for all e-mail programs. Wherever possible, I keep the information in this chapter generic.

✦ This chapter assumes that you already set up and configured your e-mail program and that it has worked in the past. If you need help getting your e-mail, my best advice is to contact your Internet service provider (ISP) for assistance.

✦ A big hurdle for e-mail users to clear is the topic of e-mail attachments. Because that process falls under the topic of file transfer, it's covered in Chapter 5.

✦ Your PC may be blessed with multiple e-mail programs. To determine which one is used as the primary program, see the section "Choose Your Internet Programs" in Chapter 1.

Message for You, Sir!

Electronic mail, or e-mail, predates the Internet. Computers back in the early 1960s were often caught sending each other mail, some of it quite salacious. Eventually, the computer operators learned how the trick worked and e-mail was born. E-mail is now the number one reason that people use the Internet. This section covers the basics of e-mail so that you can better understand what it is that you're troubleshooting.

Understanding e-mail

There are many parallels between e-mail and traditional postal mail. The biggest difference is in speed, which is why regular mail is referred to as *snail mail*. (The snail has long been a beloved mascot of the U.S. Postal Service.) Otherwise, the similarities between e-mail and mail are numerous.

Figure 3-1 illustrates the basic e-mail-sending concept. A message is composed on a computer using an e-mail program: a *client*. The e-mail program combines the text you wrote (the *body*) with the recipient, subject, date, and time (the *header*).

Figure 3-1: The illustration of how e-mail works.

Your e-mail program (the client) then sends the message off to an e-mail server by using the *Simple Message Transfer Protocol*, or SMTP. The e-mail server is basically a program running on another computer. For most people, that computer is located at your Internet service provider, or ISP.

At the server, the message is dissected and the recipients culled from the message's To, Cc, and Bcc fields in the header. The SMTP server then finds the host computer for the recipients. For example, if the message is being sent to `billg@microsoft.com`, the server looks up `microsoft.com` and sends the message off to that computer.

For a few nanoseconds, the message hops around the Internet as it makes the connection to the destination computer.

At the destination computer, another SMTP server fetches the message and stuffs it into a mailbox for the intended user. There, it sits and waits until the user logs in to collect his mail. But the mailbox on the server isn't the same thing as the inbox in your PC's mail program.

The recipient's mail program collects new messages from his ISP's server. The mail program uses the Post Office Protocol (POP) to fetch the message. POP is used instead of SMTP because the e-mail message is no longer being sent on the Internet; it has arrived. All the POP does is fetch the message waiting on the server and transfer it back to the user's computer and his e-mail program.

After the mail messages are on the recipient's computer, they're stored in a database. Secretly, all e-mail programs are database programs. After your messages are received, they exist in various mailboxes organized by your e-mail program: Inbox, Deleted Items, and Junk, for example. Messages can be read, forwarded, deleted, and so on, which is all basic e-mail program stuff.

✦ The e-mail methods described in this section don't apply to Web-based e-mail. They also don't apply to e-mail systems at large organizations, such as Lotus Notes or Microsoft Exchange.

✦ In addition to POP is the Internet Message Access Protocol (IMAP) method of reading e-mail. Unlike POP, IMAP doesn't delete messages from the user's mailbox on the server until the user deletes the message. IMAP is often preferred by Web-based e-mail programs, such as Gmail and Hotmail.

✦ All e-mail is plain text — all of it. When you write a message, the message itself is text, the technical *header* information is plain text, and even the formatting you apply is plain text. If you attach a file, the file is converted to plain text and sent with the message.

**Book IV
Chapter 3**

E-Mail Postage Due

✦ Your e-mail is stored on the ISP's computer until you pick it up. Unless you retrieve those messages, your mailbox on the ISP's mail server continues to fill up until it's so bloated that no more messages can be received.

✦ Most ISPs limit the size of your mailbox to 5MB or 10MB of storage.

✦ When your mailbox gets full, the ISP *bounces* any new e-mail you might receive. The message is returned to the sending SMTP computer, but the sender may not receive a notice that the message has bounced.

✦ To fix a full mailbox, you must *read your mail!*

✦ After you pick up your mail from the server, the messages are deleted from your personal mailbox on the server. When that's not done, your e-mail client continues to pick up the same e-mail messages repeatedly. That's why you sometimes receive multiple copies of the same message. Also see the section "Leaving mail on the server," just next in this chapter.

✦ The ISP keeps an archive of the mail arriving in your mailbox. E-mail is legally *discoverable*, which means that in a lawsuit, either side can ask for and get all the messages you sent and received. E-mail is *not* private.

✦ E-mail's lack of privacy is why I highly recommend that you never send sensitive information (bank account numbers, credit card numbers, or Social Security numbers) via e-mail.

✦ Locally, your e-mail program puts your mail into mailboxes or mail folders. Those folders work like the folders in Windows, but the mail messages in the folders aren't stored as individual files. Instead, each mailbox or folder in your mail program is a single text file on disk. See the later section "Trashing a message" for reasons why it's important to know how e-mail messages are stored on your computer.

Leaving mail on the server

In the standard e-mail scheme of things, whenever your e-mail program goes to pick up new mail, the mail is sent to your computer and then deleted from the server. There is, however, an option that lets you elect to *not* delete the message from the server. Here's how to set up that option in Windows Mail and Outlook Express:

1. **Choose Tools⇨Accounts from the menu.**

2. **Choose your mail account from the list.**

   In Outlook Express, you can click the Mail tab to see only your mail accounts.

3. **Click the Properties button.**

4. **Click the Advanced tab in the mail server's Properties dialog box.**

   The settings for leaving mail on the server are kept in the bottom part of the Advanced tab, as shown in Figure 3-2.

Figure 3-2:
Settings
for leaving
mail on the
server.

5. **Place a check mark by the option Leave a Copy of Messages On Server to prevent your e-mail from being deleted after you receive it.**

   Yes, the mail stays on the server. When you check your mail again, the same messages can be received again — and again and again.

   When you keep getting the same e-mail over and over, you should *disable* this option.

6. **If you want to have the messages removed after a number of days, place a check mark by the item Remove from Server after X Days, and then enter the number of days.**

   You can enter values from 1 through 100 in the Days box.

7. **If instead you want the messages removed when you delete them locally, place a check mark by the item Remove from Server When Deleted from 'Deleted Items.'**

   I believe this option to be the best one, which I explain in a few paragraphs.

8. **Click OK to confirm the settings and close the dialog box.**

If you're using Microsoft Outlook, follow these steps in Outlook 2007 to leave messages on the server:

1. **Choose Tools⇨Account Settings.**

   In older versions of Outlook, the command is E-Mail Accounts.

**Book IV
Chapter 3**

E-Mail Postage Due

2. **Choose your e-mail account in the Account Settings dialog box.**

   In older versions of Outlook, choose the option View or Change Existing E-Mail Accounts and then click the Next button.

3. **Click the Change button.**

   The Change E-Mail Account window opens.

4. **Click the More Settings button.**

5. **Click the Advanced tab in the Internet E-Mail Settings dialog box.**

6. **Proceed with Steps 5 through 7 in the previous set of steps.**

   The settings and commands are the same at this point.

7. **Click OK and then close the various open dialog boxes and such.**

The reason for leaving mail on the server is simple: You can pick it up again. Indeed, when you keep picking up the same e-mail over and over, you probably have the option set to leave the mail on the server. But for most folks, leaving mail on the server is done on purpose.

Suppose that you're on the road with your laptop. You don't have time to answer e-mail, but you want to read it. Further, there's no coordination with e-mail between your desktop and laptop computers. The solution is to leave the messages on the server. That way, you can reply to e-mail that requires an immediate response, but you can also recollect those messages when you return to the desktop PC. (This scheme works only when the desktop PC is configured *not* to leave messages on the server.)

✦ It's common for laptop computers, cellphones that get e-mail, and other portable devices to be configured so that they leave mail on the server.

✦ In the Thunderbird e-mail client, you can leave messages on the server by choosing Tools⇨Account Settings. In the left pane of the Account Settings dialog box, choose Server Settings. You find the option Leave Messages On Server toward the middle of the window, on the right side.

General E-Mail Melancholy

For the most part, your e-mail experiences should be pleasant and unremarkable, for the most part. For those other parts, turn to this section for help on what to do.

Dealing with drafts

Most e-mail clients feature folders into which you can stuff your e-mail messages. There are folders named Inbox, Outbox, Sent, Deleted Items or Trash, Junk, and Drafts. It's the Drafts mailbox that seems to vex too many users. Don't let it.

A *draft* is simply an e-mail message you haven't yet sent. That's not the same thing as an e-mail *waiting* to be sent. Nope, it's an e-mail message that you close by choosing File⇨Save or closing the window instead of clicking the Send button. That act places the message into the Drafts folder.

You have three choices for dealing with messages in the Drafts folder:

Do nothing. This option is always a favorite, especially for elected officials.

Open the message and send it. It's a simple solution: You open the message (double-click it in the Drafts folder), review it, edit it, and touch it up, and then click the Send button to zip the e-mail along its merry way.

Delete the message. Click to select the message and then drag it to the Deleted Items or Trash mailbox.

That's how to deal with your drafts.

✦ Sometimes, the Drafts folder doesn't show up until you create a draft e-mail to put in it.

✦ Messages can "suddenly appear" in the Drafts folder when you forget to send a message or you close the message window without sending. That happens. In fact, even I am surprised to find messages in my Drafts folder when I was double-dog certain that I sent them.

Trashing a message

Deleting an e-mail message is a simple affair: In most e-mail programs, you simply drag the message into the Deleted Items or Trash folder. Done.

The Deleted Items or Trash mail folder works like all other folders in your e-mail program: It stores messages. The messages sit in the folder and aren't actually deleted until you direct the program to purge them. You have several options for purging messages:

Not at all: This option leads to the Deleted Items or Trash folder growing very large and eventually your e-mail program becoming sluggish as it deals with the bulk.

Delete messages after a given amount of time: I like this option. I prefer setting the delete interval to one month. That way, I can fish for something urgent that I might have accidentally deleted and still be able to find it.

Delete messages when you close the mail program: This option still allows you to rescue missives from the Deleted Items or Trash folder, but only until you close the e-mail program.

Delete at once! This option doesn't allow any recovery for deleted mail — vicious, satisfying, and permanent.

Here's how you can adjust the Deleted Items folder's behavior in Windows Mail and Outlook Express:

1. **Choose Tools⇨Options.**

2a. **In Windows Mail, click the Advanced tab in the Options dialog box and then click the Maintenance button.**

2b. **In Outlook Express, click the Maintenance tab in the Options dialog box.**

3. **Place a check mark by the item Empty Messages from 'Deleted Items' Folder On Exit.**

By placing the check mark there, you ensure that the mail program purges all your deleted messages when you exit. Otherwise, the messages are retained.

4. **Click the OK or Close button, and close any other open dialog boxes.**

In Microsoft Outlook, you can control the Deleted Items folder behavior by following these steps:

1. **Choose Tools⇨Options from the menu.**

2. **In the Options dialog box, click the Other tab.**

3. **Place a check mark by the item Empty the Deleted Items Folder Upon Exiting to have that folder purged when you close Outlook.**

4. **Click OK.**

If you're using Thunderbird as your e-mail client, follow these steps to control the Trash folder's behavior:

1. **Right-click the Trash folder and choose Properties from the shortcut menu.**

2. **In the Folder Properties dialog box, click the Retention Policy tab.**

3. **Choose one of the delete options presented.**

I prefer the option Delete Messages more than 30 days old, shown in Figure 3-3.

Folder Properties

| General Information | Retention Policy |

To save disk space, old messages can be permanently deleted

☐ Use server *d*efaults

○ Don't delete *a*ny messages

○ Delete all but the last [   ] messages

● Delete *m*essages more than [30] days old

☐ Always delete *r*ead messages

[OK]   [Cancel]

Figure 3-3:
Trash folder
options
in the
Thunderbird
e-mail
program.

4. Click OK to confirm your choices and close the Folder Properties settings dialog box.

You can always purge an individual message from the Deleted Items or Trash folders by opening that folder, selecting the message, and then deleting it.

The Deleted Items or Trash folder works like every other e-mail message folder. It's not a real folder, but is actually a long text file database stored on your PC. When you purge a message from the Deleted Items or Trash folder, or when you empty that mailbox folder, the deleted messages are gone for good!

In Windows Mail and Outlook Express, you can instantly purge the Deleted Items folder by choosing Edit⇨Empty 'Deleted Items' Folder.

Multiple message mayhem

Suppose that you don't use Windows Mail or its ancestor, Outlook Express. One day, in your e-mail inbox, you see a series of messages from the same person. They have titles like the ones shown in Figure 3-4. Opening the messages reveals garbage. What can you do, what can you do?

The cause of this problem is that the person sending the mail has configured an option in Windows Mail or Outlook Express to split apart long messages. There are only two things you can do:

		From	Subject	Received
Inbox		Al Gore	Please keep it between us!	9/16/2009 6:09 AM
Outbox		B Rodriguez	I hear you have some pix?	9/16/2009 6:12 AM
		Paris Hilton	What you wanted agnph.jpg [1/6]	9/16/2009 4:21 PM
Sent		Paris Hilton	What you wanted agnph.jpg [2/6]	9/16/2009 4:21 PM
Drafts		Paris Hilton	What you wanted agnph.jpg [3/6]	9/16/2009 4:21 PM
		Paris Hilton	What you wanted agnph.jpg [4/6]	9/16/2009 4:21 PM
Junk		Paris Hilton	What you wanted agnph.jpg [5/6]	9/16/2009 4:21 PM
Trash		Paris Hilton	What you wanted agnph.jpg [6/6]	9/16/2009 4:21 PM
		Dan's Editor	Why aren't you working?	9/17/2009 8:24 AM

Figure 3-4:
Weird,
multiple
messages.

First, go back in time and use Windows Mail or Outlook Express as your e-mail program. Those programs automatically reassemble split-apart message attachments. That's the easy solution, but because the author of *Time Travel For Dummies* is taking way too long to complete that title, I offer an alternative solution:

Second, tell the person sending the message to reconfigure the mail program *not* to split apart long messages and to resend the message. To do that, instruct that person to go out and buy a copy of this book and follow these steps in Windows Mail or Outlook Express:

1. **Choose Tools⇨Accounts.**

2. **Choose your e-mail account from the list.**

   In Outlook Express, you can click the Mail tab and then choose your e-mail account, because that screen is less cluttered.

3. **Click the Properties button.**

4. **Click the Advanced tab in your mail server's Properties dialog box.**

5. **Remove the check mark by the item Break Apart Messages Larger than X KB.**

6. **Click OK and then click the Close button to dismiss the Internet Accounts dialog box.**

Ensure that the sender goes out and gets his own copy of this book. Don't loan this book to anyone, especially people who break apart long messages.

Repairing hyperlinks in Outlook Express

A problem that plagued users of Outlook Express for generations was the bad hyperlink conundrum. Most sophisticated e-mail programs display as a clickable link any text that looks like a Web page or e-mail address in an e-mail message. It's magic! But sometimes Outlook Express loses the magic.

To remedy the situation, and to try to restore links to your e-mail message in Outlook Express running Windows XP, follow these technical steps:

1. **Open the Folder Options icon in the Control Panel.**

2. **Click the File Types tab.**

3. **Select (NONE) URL: HyperText Transfer Protocol in the list of registered file types.**

Figure 3-5 illustrates what you're looking for.

Figure 3-5: Finding the proper item on the File Types tab in the Folder Options dialog box.

4. **Click the Advanced button.**

The Edit File Type dialog box appears.

5. **Click the Edit button.**

6. **If you don't see the word *open* in the Action dialog box, type it in there.**

   Type **open** (no period).

7. **Confirm that the Application Used to Perform Action text box contains the text `"C:\Program Files\Internet Explorer\iexplore.exe" -nohome`**

   If the text box doesn't contain that text, type it exactly as written:

   ```
   "C:\Program Files\Internet Explorer\iexplore.exe" -nohome
   ```

   The final option is a hyphen followed immediately by the "word" nohome (there's no space between the two).

8. **Place a check mark by the option Use DDE.**

9. **Ensure that the text `"%1",,-1,0,,,,` is written in the DDE Message box.**

   If the text isn't written, type it. Here's how it looks:

   ```
   "%1",,-1,0,,,,
   ```

   That's `%1` in double quotes, followed by two commas, and then `-1`, a comma, zero, and four commas. The text must be typed exactly as shown.

10. **Ensure that the text `IExplore` is typed in the Application box.**

11. **Check to confirm that the DDE Application Not Running box is left blank.**

12. **Click OK.**

    No, you're not done yet. You need to confirm that a second item has also been set properly and then fix it, if necessary.

13. **Back in the Folder Properties dialog box, on the File Types tab, choose (NONE) URL: HyperText Transfer Protocol with Privacy from the Registered File Types list.**

    It's the item just below (NONE) URL: HyperText Transfer Protocol (refer to Figure 3-5).

14. **Repeat Steps 4 through 12 exactly.**

15. **Click OK to close the Folder Options dialog box.**

If there are still problems, repeat these steps, but modify Step 7. First, try changing the first part of the text to `%programfiles%`, like this:

```
"%programfiles%\Internet Explorer\iexplore.exe" -nohome
```

If it still doesn't work, add the text %1 to the end of the command. Here's how the command should look:

```
"%programfiles%\Internet Explorer\iexplore.exe" -nohome %1
```

Fixing that e-mail disconnection urge

The Windows Mail e-mail program may disconnect a dialup Internet connection after it receives e-mail. It's a problem inherited from the old Outlook Express program: After the program checks for available e-mail, it hangs up the modem. The hang-up occurs even when you're online doing something else. Here's how to fix it:

1. Start Windows Mail or Outlook Express.

The solution in this set of steps works in both programs.

2. Choose Tools⇨Options from the menu.

3. Click the Connection tab in the Options dialog box.

4. Remove the check mark by the option Hang Up after Sending and Receiving.

5. Click OK.

That should fix the problem. If not, you can take some additional steps:

1. Choose Tools⇨Options from the e-mail program's menu.

2. If necessary, click the General tab.

The General tab in the Options dialog box is shown in Figure 3-6.

3. Remove the check mark by the option Check for New Messages Every xx Minutes.

4. Choose Do Not Connect from the menu button titled If My Computer Is Not Connected at This Time.

5. Click OK.

By making the changes in the last set of steps, you ensure that the mail program doesn't automatically check for messages and, hopefully, doesn't disconnect you from the Internet.

✦ By disabling the e-mail program's automatic e-mail checking, you must manually check for new mail. It's an easy thing to do: Click the Send/Receive button from the mail program's toolbar to check for new messages.

✦ The Send/Receive toolbar button may be labeled Send/Recv in earlier versions of Outlook Express.

Figure 3-6:
Connection
options are
set here.

"Why doesn't the address book work?"

A common e-mail question I get, mostly from Outlook users, is that something is amiss with their address books. Names can't be recalled or used, and nothing seems to work correctly. Sadly, the problem isn't anything you can fix.

Outlook works best when it's on a network with something called Microsoft Exchange Server. That program (running on a main computer, or *server*) is responsible for controlling address book and contact information. You should consider it as the "rest of Outlook."

For a small-office or home setup, it's impractical, not to mention expensive, to set up an exchange server. A better solution, and my suggestion for you, is to use an e-mail program other than Outlook.

"I can't read your message!"

When e-mail arrives in an unreadable state, you must first recognize this simple fact: *It's not your fault*. Your e-mail program can only deal with what it receives, and though you use that program to read incoming mail, the program did not compose or format that mail. How could it?

If the message is all gibberish, one of two things has happened. The first is that the e-mail was sent using foreign language characters that your PC cannot display. Most of those messages are usually foreign language spam. (I get Russian language spam all the time.)

The second type of message is a formatted message. For example, the text may be very small or very large. You may see bright-pink text on a blue background. Animated goobers may be dancing or winking at you. That's all formatted text, similar to the way a Web page is formatted.

The solution to the formatted-text problem is to ask the sender to resend the message using *plain text*, not formatted text.

When e-mail is sent using plain text, it's received in plain text. Your e-mail program has no trouble displaying such a message; the font size is fine and it has no foreign characters or gibberish — well, unless the person is just writing nonsense, and even *that,* you cannot control!

✦ In Outlook 2007, you create a new message in plain text by clicking the Options tab and clicking the Plain Text button in the Format area.

✦ In Windows Mail, Outlook Express, and older versions of Outlook, you compose a message in plain text by choosing Format➪Plain Text from the New Message window.

✦ In Thunderbird, choose Options➪Format➪Plain Text Only in the Compose window to create an e-mail using only plain text.

✦ For small text in an e-mail message, you can try zooming the e-mail message in the window by using the View➪Text Size submenu.

Unable to send e-mail

A problem you sometimes encounter on the road is an inability to properly send e-mail. You may receive a validation error message from the e-mail server or encounter a problem with the recipient's names not being recognized as valid. Welcome to life on the road.

The problem with your e-mail is most likely that you're trying to send it using your home SMTP server and, when you're on the road, you're using another SMTP server that doesn't appreciate your laptop's settings.

A possible solution is to fuss with the mail program's SMTP server settings and try to figure out the outgoing mail's proper SMTP server settings. But I can instantly recommend that you not bother with this process in a hotel or wireless hotspot (such as an airport or café).

The solution I use is to pick up my e-mail in the standard way, but to send the e-mail out using Hotmail, Yahoo Mail, Gmail, or one of the other Web-based mail services. Those services don't seem to have a problem with my laptop's location. You can also contact your ISP to see whether it has Web-based e-mail service.

The worst-case scenario is that you cannot even send e-mail. Although it may be the "worst case," it's not the end of the world. Remember that phone calls also work for communications and that most serious stuff can generally wait until you have a good connection that appreciates your e-mail.

E-Mail You Don't Want

Everyone loves getting e-mail, but they don't love all the e-mail. Though the problem of spam or junk e-mail isn't quite as obnoxious as it has been in years past, there are still unwanted messages that beach themselves like so much digital jetsam. This section describes how you can deal with those messages.

Blocking senders

The good news about bad news is that it seems to consistently come from the same sources. Whether it's unwanted e-mail, spam, junk mail, or perhaps a persistent relative or acquaintance who won't stop sending you "cute" stuff, most e-mail programs have an easy way to block them.

Perhaps the best, quickest way to deal with unwanted e-mail is to use your e-mail program's feature to place a message recipient on a Block Senders list. It's an easy thing to do, though the method varies depending on the e-mail program.

In Windows Mail, follow these steps:

1. **Choose the message you want to block.**

Sadly, the message has to float into your inbox before you can block it.

2. **Choose Message⇨Junk E-Mail⇨Add Sender to Blocked Senders List.**

3. **Click OK.**

The messages from that sender are purged from the inbox.

In Outlook Express, follow these steps:

1. **Click to select the message you want to block.**

2. **Choose Message⇨Block Sender.**

   A message window appears, telling you that the sender has been placed in the infamous Blocked Senders list. Certain doom awaits any subsequent messages from that person's account.

3. **Click the Yes button to purge all that sender's e-mail from the inbox.**

   If you don't click Yes, the message still sits there in the Inbox, taunting you.

Now feel free to read your e-mail without being bothered by the sender. Then again, it probably won't be the last time you need to block a sender.

When your e-mail program lacks a Block Sender feature, you have to use the feature that filters e-mail or creates a mail rule. Simply create a rule that identifies the sender, or the sender's domain, and then redirect any message from that user into the Deleted Items or Trash folder. See the later section "Junking e-mail" for information.

Unblocking senders

The Blocked Senders tool was a welcome addition to Outlook Express and then to Windows Mail. It worked! Sometimes it worked too well. The biggest problem people had with it was blocking people they didn't mean to block. Oops.

Here's how to unblock an accidentally blocked sender in Windows Mail:

1. **Choose Tools⇨Junk E-Mail Options.**

2. **Click the Blocked Senders tab.**

3. **Select the user you want to unblock.**

   Users are listed only by their e-mail address, so it helps to know their address.

4. **Click the Remove button.**

   Yeah, the button should read Stop Blocking or something similar, but Microsoft doesn't ask for my input.

5. **Click OK.**

In Outlook Express, you can unblock a sender by following these steps:

1. **Choose Tools⇨Message Rules⇨Blocked Senders List.**

2. **Select the user you want to unblock in the Message Rules dialog box.**

3. **Click the Remove button.**

4. **Click OK.**

Removing someone from the Blocked Senders list doesn't automatically restore any of their blocked messages. To find those, you need to dig through the junk mail or Deleted Items folders.

Junking e-mail

Junk filters are relatively new on the e-mail scene. They use formidable logic and magical incantations to identify the telltale signs of spam. Or, you can train them to identify e-mail you don't want. It all depends on how your e-mail program implements the junk mail filter.

In Windows Mail, follow these steps to configure automatic junk-mail options:

1. **Choose Tools⇨Junk E-Mail Options.**

   The Junk E-Mail Options dialog box appears, as shown in Figure 3-7. The Options tab, shown in the figure, is where you make the primary settings. Other tabs are more specific, including information about blocked senders (see the preceding two sections.)

Figure 3-7: Setting junk mail options in Windows Mail.

2. **Choose a level for filtering junk mail.**

   There are four settings, as described on-screen.

3. **Click OK.**

Some e-mail programs use a "mark as junk" approach to identifying junk e-mail. The idea is that you can train the e-mail program to identify suspect e-mail. Over time, the program instantly recognizes what you don't like and automatically transfers it into the Junk mail folder.

For example, in Thunderbird, you can click the Junk button on the toolbar to flag a message as junk. The message is instantly placed into the Junk folder, and the program examines the message sender and subject. As you continue to flag messages as junk, Thunderbird learns. Other e-mail programs work in a similar way, where you train the program to identify what you believe to be Junk e-mail.

✦ Junk mail filters aren't fool-proof. Odds are good that a junk e-mail filter will capture some legitimate messages and falsely determine them to be junk.

✦ I recommend routinely checking the Junk mailbox or mail folder to determine whether real mail is inside. If so, you can remove the messages, and I also recommend toning down the junk mail filter's aggressiveness.

✦ Which is better — using a junk mail filter or training your e-mail program? It's pretty much a draw. Most of the programs you can train, such as Thunderbird, have options to untrain or reset the training. You also have options to mark a message as "not junk," which further refines the training.

Creating a junk mail filter

Nearly all e-mail programs feature a standard message-filtering system. You use that system to organize your e-mail, such as by transferring business messages into a Work mailbox, but you can also use those filters to help fight spam.

A junk mail filter works simply: Identify junk e-mail by its sender or Subject line, and then either delete the message or move it into a Junk mailbox. Here's how to implement such a thing in Windows Mail or Outlook Express:

1. **Click to select the junk mail.**

2. **Choose Message⇨Create Rule From Message.**

The New Mail Rule dialog box appears, as shown in Figure 3-8. There are four parts of the dialog box, just as there are four steps to creating a mail rule. Start in Area 1.

Figure 3-8:
Creating a
junk mail
rule.

3. **To filter a message by subject, choose Where the Subject Line Contains Specific Words; to filter a message by sender, choose Where the From Line Contains People.**

   Suppose that you keep receiving e-mail from a certain outfit that tries to connect you with old friends from high school . Because the won't unsubscribe you, you decide to filter their messages. The best way to do that is to filter by the From line. On the other hand, if you want to remove messages with the words *oil change* in them, filter by subject.

   Next comes the action, set in Area 2.

4. **Select the Move It to the Specified Folder check box.**

   Or, if you want to be vicious, you can choose Delete It. But the idea here is to filter junk, not just delete it outright.

   In Area 3, you refine the rules by choosing specific parameters. (I find this process backward, but it's the way Windows Mail does things.)

5. **In Area 3, Rule Description, click the specified link to replace that text with the name of a specific folder.**

   A Move dialog box appears, listing the mailbox folders used by your e-mail program. If you don't see them, click the plus sign (+) by the item Local Folders.

6. **Choose the Junk E-Mail folder from the list in the Move box.**

   If you don't see the Junk E-Mail folder there, click the New Folder button to create it. Name the new folder **Junk E-Mail**; click OK to create it.

7. **Click OK.**

8. **In the Name of the Rule box, type a descriptive name for the rule.**

   For example, type Annoying High School Contact Junk Mail Rule for filtering e-mail from a Web site that promotes contacting old friends but has no way to unsubscribe from the service.

9. **Click OK to create the rule.**

10. **Click OK to confirm that you know that you created the rule.**

Creating the rule doesn't instantly filter the Inbox in Windows Mail; you still have to manually drag a junk message to the Junk E-Mail folder. But any new mail that arrives will fall victim to your mail rule, helping keep such messages out of the inbox.

✦ You might consider not using the full message subject, as shown in Area 3, Rule Description. Sometimes, setting the subject to include only a keyword, like *porn* or *mortgage,* is enough to filter out the unwanted. See the next section for information on editing and refining your message rule.

✦ The idea behind junking a message instead of deleting it is to ensure that you can rescue it out of the Junk E-Mail folder *false positives.* Those messages are flagged as junk but may not be junk. When you delete a potential junk message, you run the risk of having it purged from the Deleted Items folder before you have a chance to review it.

✦ Check the Junk E-Mail folder from time to time to ensure that your rules are doing their job. If not, edit the rule! See the next section.

✦ In the Thunderbird e-mail program, chose Tools⇨Message Filters to create a message filter.

Editing a junk mail rule

Rules may need refining from time to time, which probably explains why the U.S. Tax Code runs some 60,000 pages. New rules are necessary for unwanted e-mail; they not only make the junk mail filters more powerful but also help them rule out false positives. On the other hand, adding rules to the Tax Code merely keeps accountants and lawyers employed.

To edit or customize a rule in Windows Mail or Outlook Express, follow these steps:

1. **Choose Tools⇨Message Rules⇨Mail.**

   The Message Rules dialog box appears, as shown in Figure 3-9.

2. **Choose the rule to edit from the list on the Mail Rules tab of the Message Rules dialog box.**

3. **Click the Modify button.**

    You can add new conditions to the rule in Area 1, Select the Conditions for Your Rule. Mostly, however, you can edit by choosing a link in Area 3, Rule Description.

    For example, if the subject is too long or detailed, click that link and edit the Subject line to be more concise.

    If the From part of the rule is too specific, edit it. Back in the early days of the Internet, I once blocked all e-mail from the service Juno. Although there were legitimate Juno users, most of them were spam accounts. So rather than add rules for individual Juno accounts, I just filtered everything from Juno.

4. **Click the OK button when you're done making modifications.**

Filters are executed in order, from the top down, in the Message Rules dialog box. Some rules may not be executed because earlier rules take priority. Therefore, to fix the situation, you can select a specific rule and use the Move Up or Move Down arrows to adjust the sequence.

Deleting a mail rule

Sometimes, mail rules become old and unused. I know that in the Eudora e-mail program, for example, rules that are no longer used are flagged with a cute dinosaur icon. Windows Mail, and its prehistoric ancestor Outlook Express, don't provide any feedback on which rules are being used, but you still can disable or delete a rule.

To disable a rule in Windows Mail or Outlook Express, follow these quick steps:

1. **Choose Tools⇨Message Rules⇨Mail.**

   The Message Rules dialog box appears (refer to Figure 3-9).

2. **Remove the check mark by the rule you want to disable.**

3. **Click OK.**

To reenable a rule, simply replace the check mark in Step 2. Otherwise, when you confirm that the rule isn't needed and the junk mail it was trying to filter has stopped, you can delete the rule by following these steps:

1. **Choose Tools⇨Message Rules⇨Mail.**

2. **Select the rule to delete.**

3. **Click the Remove button.**

4. **Click OK.**

I don't recommend deleting a rule until you disable it first. It's far easier to reenable a rule than it is to re-create it.

Skipping e-mail over a certain size

The last chapter in the book of unwanted e-mail dwells on the subject of huge e-mail attachments. I hate them. What a huge e-mail attachment tells me is that someone hasn't read my books. They either are unaware that it's easier to send a link to a Web page, video, or sound or they just don't know how to resize and properly send pictures as an e-mail attachment. *Enough with them!*

To deal with my frustration, I practice yoga. But in the electronics world, I deal with large e-mail attachments by creating an e-mail filter to merrily skip over them. Here's how to configure Windows Mail and Outlook Express not to download large e-mail messages:

1. **Choose Tools⇨Message Rules⇨Mail.**

   The Message Rules dialog box saunters onto the display (refer to Figure 3-9).

2. **Click the New button.**

   The New Mail Rule dialog box appears (refer to Figure 3-8). Because a message wasn't selected, the dialog box is blank.

3. **In the first area, Conditions, place a check mark by the item When the Message Size Is More than Size.**

   You have to scroll down to find that option. And, no, that option doesn't make literal sense, but you're replacing the second word `size` with a specific value in Step 5.

4. **In the second area, Actions, choose the option Delete It from the Server.**

5. **In the Rule Description area, choose the word `size` to replace it with a specific size value.**

   The Set size dialog box appears. When I had dialup Internet, I set the size to 500KB. For my faster connection, I set the size to 3000KB, or 3MB.

6. **Click OK to close the Set Size dialog box.**

7. **In the Name of the Rule box, type** Filter Out Large Messages.

8. **Click OK to create the rule.**

9. **Use the Move Up button to place the rule at the top of the list in the Message Rules dialog box.**

   You want the Filter Out Large Messages rule to come first; otherwise, the message might be downloaded to your computer, which isn't what you want.

10. **Click OK to close the Message Rules dialog box.**

See Video 431 for a demonstration of filtering large e-mails.

When a large message comes in, you won't know about it; the message just never arrives in the inbox. That also implies that the person who sent it will never know that the message wasn't received.

✦ Do not choose the option Do Not Download It from the Server (Step 4). If you do, the message continues to dwell in your mailbox on the server, taking up space and potentially leading to a full mailbox. That's a Bad Thing.

✦ The size limit on an e-mail attachment depends on your ISP's mailbox limits. That limit can be as little as 5MB or even unlimited. Most ISPs use a 10MB limit. Contact your ISP to see what the limit is.

✦ Don't be part of the problem: Try not to send your friends large e-mail messages.

✦ Instead of trying to send huge file attachments in e-mail, consider burning an optical disc and sending it in the regular mail.

✦ A more effective way of sending videos or other large files is to send a Web page link instead. For example, a video link to YouTube or some other video Web site takes up only one line of text compared to the megabytes required for the video itself.

✦ Other e-mail programs have better options for denying large messages on the server. For example, Eudora prompts you when a large message arrives, displaying the message size and the sender's e-mail address. You can then decide whether to download the message or just delete it from the server.

Chapter 4: Wicked Software

In This Chapter

✔ **Ridding your PC of malware**

✔ **Protecting against viruses**

✔ **Avoiding a phishing scam**

✔ **Clearing your PC of spyware**

✔ **Using a firewall**

✔ **Preventing Internet nasties**

By the pricking of my thumbs,
Something wicked this way comes.
Open, locks,
Whoever knocks!

— *Macbeth,* Act IV, Scene 1

*L*ike the murderous thane, there are evil plots afoot to dethrone you from the seat of power before your PC. Indeed, one of the easiest ways that wicked software oozes into your computer is by opening locks. Sometimes, the software picks the locks by itself, but most often it's you, the user, who lets in the software. It's kind of like inviting a vampire into your home: Once you do, he makes himself right at home and soon you're dead — or just down a few quarts. This chapter covers software of the wicked kind.

Malicious + Software = Malware

The Internet isn't responsible for evil software, though I placed this chapter in the bosom of the Internet minibook. No, the Internet is merely the delivery system. Software of the wicked bent has been around computers since the steam-powered age. This section explains what you need to know.

Understanding malware

I suppose that people grew tired of using the terms *virus* or *Trojan* to refer to evil software. There was also a big issue about what was a virus and what was a *worm*. It got messy. Nerds extremely dislike using an incorrect term. So somewhere along the line, someone glued together the terms *malicious* and *software* and came up with *malware*.

Malware has always been a computer category, even if the term is new. Programmers often wrote self-destruct programs that would either quickly remove items from their own computers or destroy an employer's computer system in the event that the programmer was fired. With the dawn of the Internet, a distribution system became available for sending such evil programs out into the ether. It proved wildly successful.

As far as you're concerned, malware exists and you must take extra steps to fight it. Believe it or not, the first step is *not* to buy a security utility. That's Step Three. The first two steps require more effort on your part.

The first, best thing you can do to protect yourself from malware is to *learn more about your computer*. Honestly, you can't tell when something is wrong when you're unable to determine exactly what "right" is.

The second thing you can do is to not be a fool. Malware succeeds by preying on human weakness. The most successful computer virus works despite every effort by software developers to stop it. That's because you cannot program the human brain; people do things they shouldn't do because of social engineering.

Put simply, *social engineering* is the art of making people do things that they otherwise wouldn't. For example, you're fooled into opening an e-mail attachment because the message claims that it contains a compromising picture of a celebrity or an embarrassing video of a politician. Despite the warnings, you open the attachment. Your computer is infected. The Bad Guys win.

The final thing you can do to protect yourself from the malware tsunami is to use software tools to ensure that your computer hasn't been compromised, and to repair any damage done. These tools include an antivirus program, anti-spyware, a firewall, plus a smattering of other utilities. Windows provides a smattering of its own tools. Or, you can choose to buy everything at once in an Internet security software suite.

Finding malware

There's no need to find malware; it will find you. That's the motivation behind the sick freaks who produce malware. Knowing that, know also that malware will enter your computer in one of three ways:

As a download from a Web page: If you have the latest version of your Web browser, you're alerted to any download from a Web page to your computer. In other words, you must *invite* the program into your realm. If the program is malware, in it comes.

Malware malcontents

Phishing: The phishing scam masquerades as a legitimate Web site or link to a site, but what it's really trying to do is "fish" for information. By fooling you into thinking that you're visiting your bank or a shopping or government Web site, the scam gets you to divulge personal or financial information, which the Bad Guys then exploit.

Spyware: Like the name says, spyware monitors your movements on the Internet, sending information back to a central computer that then targets you with advertising. That sounds okay, but the category has broadened to include programs you download to your computer that monitor your activities to the point that your computer slows down to a useless state. Further, the spyware itself becomes nearly impossible to remove.

Trojan horse: The Trojan program is malware that masquerades as a legitimate program. The program may have a real function, but it carries ulterior motives. Trojans can delete data, compromise security, relay spam or porn, and otherwise infect your computer.

Virus: Like its living counterpart, a computer virus infects your computer, taking control over some or all of its functions. The virus destroys data or looks for things like passwords, credit card numbers, or other sensitive data. That information is often sent to another computer. A virus can also "own" your computer, turning it into a zombie box on the Internet. The *zombie box* is used to relay spam e-mail or pornography, or to coordinate attacks against Web sites on the Internet.

Worm: Officially, a worm is a virus that replicates itself over a network. Worms often arrive via e-mail, peruse your address book, and then send a copy of themselves to others in your address book, masquerading the message as though it's from you. Worms are used to deliver viruses, or the worm itself could be a virus, because the terms are interchangeable.

As an e-mail attachment: Malware arriving as an e-mail attachment is the same bad stuff that comes from a Web page. The difference is primarily social engineering: The malware is most likely disguised as a message from a friend or has some other tempting aspect that indulges you to open it.

As a file on infected removable media: Originally the most popular method for malware distribution, inserting a strange disc or other media into your PC's storage system is still a way to give your computer a virus. The disc offers something enticing — a free game or software. The worst scenario is when you're required to start your PC with the disc. Bad, bad, bad.

Antivirus software can help identify malware as it arrives on your PC, but don't let it be your crutch. Just be vigilant. Remember: Even antivirus programs can be fooled. In fact, all the major viral infections of the past dozen or so years managed to slip by the antivirus programs that were then widely in use.

✦ The key to getting malware to work is social engineering. In the case of a Web page link, the Web page may direct you to ignore warnings from Windows or to disable your antivirus software to continue.

✦ If the Web site looks fishy, or it's offering something that cannot possibly be true, it's probably not a good idea to download any of its files. See Chapter 5 for more information on downloading.

✦ If a file downloads automatically and you didn't request it, do not open the file. Delete it at once.

✦ If a pornography Web site downloads a "video viewer," it's a virus.

✦ If the e-mail says to disable your antivirus program before opening the attachment, don't.

✦ It's common to get malware from chat rooms. Some (bogus) user comes into the chat room and coughs up a Web page link to malware, often with an enticing but wrong description of what you find when you click the link. Don't click the link.

✦ Sometimes, programs can be sent directly from an online chat room. Whatever you do, however you're tempted, do not click the link or open the file.

Protecting your PC

There exists something called *PC survival time*. It's the average length of time an unprotected Windows computer spends on the Internet before malware takes over and controls the entire system. The current PC survival time is about 16 minutes.

Your PC doesn't have to fall prey to the PC survival-time challenge. As long as you know what to do, your computer can last for months on the Internet with no problems whatsoever. But you must take steps to protect the system from the Bad Guys.

Windows features a central location for protecting your PC — the Windows Security Center, shown in Figure 4-1. It provides an information summary of your PC's security state, plus quick access to the vital items you need in order to keep your PC safe.

Firewall: The firewall is designed to protect your PC from unwanted network traffic moving both into and from your computer. See the later section "Life Behind the Firewall" for more information.

Automatic Updating: Keeping your copy of Windows up-to-date ensures that any known threats are being dealt with. Indeed, after the firewall, the most common reason for the PC's short survival time on the Internet is that many users don't update their software. See Book II, Chapter 1 for more information on updating Windows.

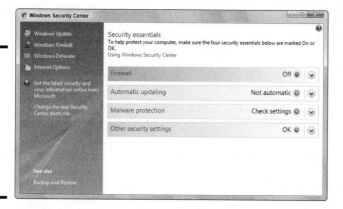

Figure 4-1:
The
Windows
Vista
version
of the
Windows
Security
Center.

Malware Protection: The general category of malware protection includes services that defend your computer against viruses and spyware. For virus protection, see the section "When Mr. Virus Comes Calling," next in this chapter. Spyware and other software nasties can be fought by using the program Windows Defender. See the section "I Spy, with My Little Eye," later in this chapter.

Other Security Settings: The most generic category in the Windows Security Center covers two topics: Internet security settings (see Chapter 2 in this minibook) and the Windows Vista User Account Control (covered in Book II, Chapter 5).

 To open the Windows Security Center window, open the Control Panel and then double-click to open the Security Center icon. The settings you see may look different from what's shown in Figure 4-1; your options may appear green, yellow, or red, depending on the settings.

Windows XP sports a different version of the Security Center that replaces the Malware Protection and Other Security Settings areas with a single area titled Virus Protection.

The Windows Firewall window mostly serves as a gateway to other, specific locations in Windows. Various sections in the rest of this chapter discuss how you can use those locations to help protect your PC.

✦ The PC survival time is so short primarily because the computers that are tested are *not* behind a *firewall*. The firewall protects you from a great majority of the Internet attacks. See the section "Life Behind the Firewall," later in this chapter.

✦ The Windows Security Center is available only after you update your copy of Windows XP to the latest release or service package (SP2 or SP3).

When Mr. Virus Comes Calling

The first computer virus was created back in the 1970s. Curiously enough, the second computer virus was created to track down and delete copies of the first computer virus. As the personal computer revolution caught fire in the mid-1980s, computer viruses broke out all over. It was the perfect storm of people who failed to understand their computer, pirated software, and human weakness.

Viruses continue to thrive, and the need to fight them is still present. Unlike in the early days, however, today's computers offer a better line of protection against the viral scourge. This section explains the details.

Inoculating your computer

To properly fight viruses, you should get an antivirus program. That's because Windows itself doesn't come with antivirus software. If your PC came with antivirus software, it was most likely a trial version. Still, because Windows lacks a specific antivirus utility, the antivirus information in this chapter is generic and applies to all antivirus programs.

The antivirus program you choose should have two modes of operation:

Interactive: In this mode, the program lurks in the background and monitors the computer's activity. Specifically, the interactive mode looks for a virus coming in from the Internet (a download or an e-mail attachment) or delivered on removable media.

Scan: In this mode, the antivirus program probes all parts of the computer's memory and storage system, looking for signs of infection. You can direct the program to scan your PC at any time, though traditionally an antivirus program scans the computer when it first starts.

When a virus or sign of infection is found, the antivirus software alerts you to its presence. The virus may be destroyed or the file quarantined for later examination. Either way, whatever operation the virus was set out to perform is thwarted.

✦ It's possible to be vigilant and avoid using antivirus software. But that big, looming monster called Doubt plays a role in how you use your computer. Nasty software exists. Even if you don't run an interactive antivirus program, I highly recommend that you use antivirus software to scan your computer routinely for signs of infection.

✦ Antivirus software requires frequent updating. Normally, you subscribe to the antivirus developer's Web site, allowing downloads of new virus definitions and protection information. Only by keeping your antivirus software up-to-date do you ensure that your computer can battle new and malevolent threats.

The quarantine conundrum

Often when your antivirus software finds a sign of infection, it places the suspect file into quarantine. Some people are confused by the quarantine concept, so I thought I'd explain it a bit.

The normal way to deal with an infected file is for the antivirus software to ruthlessly delete it. That's good. In fact, the antivirus software may not only ruthlessly delete the infected file but also obliterate it so that no portion of the file exists anywhere on your PC's storage system. That's a good thing. But what happens if the file wasn't really infected and, worse, you really need that file? That's why the concept of quarantine was created.

A quarantined file isn't deleted. It shows signs of infection, but by being in quarantine, the file has no opportunity to infect your computer. It's safe. If the file can be fixed and the infection removed, the file can be removed from quarantine and put back into service. Or, if the file was falsely identified as being infected, it can be removed from quarantine and reused right away.

Generally speaking, I keep files in quarantine for a few weeks or longer. Every so often, I review the list of files in quarantine and then just have them rubbed out. I figure, after that long of a time, that I didn't need the file anyway, so they can go away and not be missed.

♦ Yes, those subscriptions cost money. But consider that the cost is far less than the cost of taking your computer into the shop to have a professional rid your system of infection and restore your data.

♦ It's possible to run more than one antivirus program at a time. In fact, having two antivirus programs is a great way to boost your PC's security. For example, you can run Norton or McAfee's antivirus software as your primary protection. Then, every so often, run a secondary program to perform a scan-only; that secondary program may find things that the first program misses.

♦ If you choose to run two antivirus programs at once, place only one into Interactive mode. Running two antivirus programs in Interactive mode doesn't help fight viruses and instead merely slows down your computer.

♦ Avoid using Web-based antivirus scans, because most of them are malware, either spyware or Trojan horses. It's okay to download an antivirus program from a legitimate developer on the Web, but I don't recommend using any antivirus software that runs from a Web page.

Disabling antivirus software

Sometimes an installation program requests that you disable your antivirus software. The reason is that the antivirus software has difficulty determining whether the program you're installing is a legitimate program or perhaps a virus taking roost in your PC's storage system.

As long as you purchase software in a store or download it from a reputable site on the Internet, it's safe to install the thing. To disable your antivirus software, locate its icon in the notification area on the taskbar. Right-click that icon and choose the option to disable or exit the program.

✦ Disable your antivirus program only when installing new programs. If you downloaded those programs from the Internet, ensure that they're from a reputable source. See Chapter 5 for more information on determining what a reputable source is.

✦ After installing the software, reenable the antivirus software. In fact, it might even be a good idea to restart your PC at that point; by restarting, you ensure that the computer is scanned for new infections and that the antivirus software starts up as it should.

✦ Never disable the antivirus software when you don't expect anything to be installed or when you're prompted to do so by a Web site or e-mail message.

✦ At times, legitimate software has been shipped from the developer with a virus lurking on the disc. Those times are extremely rare, however, and if you subscribe to an antivirus update service, you're alerted to such infected discs almost immediately.

Hook, Line, and Stinker

Not everyone can write computer software. Fewer still can manufacture a clever virus, such as one that would rush out to your computer, find your passwords, PINs, and bank account numbers. But some ambitious people get all that information without writing a line of code. Their technique is called *phishing*, and this section tells you all about the scam.

Understanding the phishing scam

The phishing scam is so deceptively simple that you would think for a moment it could never work. Often, it starts with a phony e-mail message. The message looks like it's from your bank, the government, an online retailer, or some outfit you would do business with. It may have graphics that look official. If may even have a disclaimer or security alert in the message.

The message requests information and implies a sense of urgency. Something bad will happen if you don't reply to the e-mail or visit a Web site. Part of your duty is to supply sensitive information: account numbers, Social Security information, credit card numbers, personal identification numbers, mother's maiden name, or passwords, for example.

You've already won!

Though not officially phishing, another popular e-mail scam involves prize money or other free loot that you're somehow spontaneously entitled to. Often called the Nigerian Scam, 419 fraud, or the Foreign Lottery scam, it's generically known as the *advanced-fee fraud*.

The scam works like this: You get an e-mail alerting you that money is coming. You won a foreign lottery, or perhaps some big wig needs help transferring money into the United States. All you need to do is forward some cash to help with processing, pay taxes, or release something from impound. Or perhaps the scam artist merely wants your bank account number.

None of it is true.

Again, social engineering is to blame for the advanced-fee fraud. With the lure of getting something for nothing, the gullible and greedy follow along with these scams and lose millions of dollars annually to the Bad Guys. Nothing is free. And if they claim that it's free but requires money up front, it's still not free.

The worst news is that only common sense helps you fight this type of scam. A phishing filter doesn't matter. When you get an e-mail saying "You've won," you most likely have not. Delete the message.

First, a word of reassuring advice: Nothing legitimate ever gets passed through e-mail. Your bank may e-mail you, but if there's a problem with your account, someone will definitely phone or send you a regular letter — not an e-mail message.

Second, tools available in both the Web browser and e-mail program can help you quickly identify a phishing scam. The next few sections describe how.

The phishing scam works because of social engineering. It's much easier to believe that something bad will happen if you don't do anything than it is to simply ignore what is basically a cleverly disguised scam.

Fighting phishing in Internet Explorer

Like most modern Web browsers, Internet Explorer features an anti-phishing filter. The filter is used to flag known phishing Web sites as well as to report suspect sites. If you obeyed your computer, the filter is probably on already. Just to be certain, follow these steps:

1. **Choose Tools⇨Phishing Filter⇨Turn On Automatic Website Checking.**

If you see Turn Off Automatic Website Checking, the anti-phishing filter is on already; there's nothing else for you to do.

2. In the Microsoft Phishing Filter window, choose Turn On Automatic Phishing Filter (Recommended).

3. Click OK.

After the phishing filter is on, it flags suspect Web pages for you automatically. The Address bar turns red in Internet Explorer, and you see a message displayed, as shown in Figure 4-2. My advice: Choose the option Click Here to Close This Webpage.

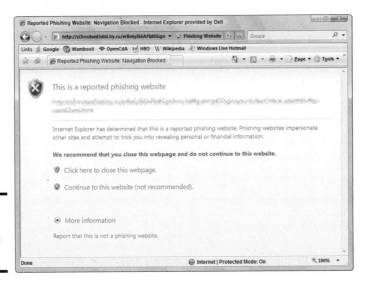

Figure 4-2:
A phishing
Web site is
found.

When you encounter a Web site you suspect of phishing but it's not flagged, you can test it and report it.

To test a Web site, choose Tools⇨Phishing Filter⇨Check This Web Site. You see an information dialog box asking you to confirm the Web site address and to ensure that it was what you were suspecting. Click OK to dismiss the dialog box.

If the Web site looks bad and wasn't reported, you can report it yourself: choose Tools⇨Phishing Filter⇨Report This Website. Information about the site is sent to Microsoft. If it's confirmed that the Web site is a phishing site, the site address is added to several lists and Web browsers using phishing filters are blocked from accessing the site.

Avoiding evil e-mail

Most phishing scams begin with an e-mail message. That's how they got me once: I had just bought something on eBay when a phishing scam mail came in. It looked like it was from eBay, so I replied and almost filled in the entire form when I noticed that I wasn't on an eBay Web site. Things have since changed, and your e-mail program most likely provides protection against e-mail phishing scams.

To confirm that Windows Mail is configured to protect you against phishing scams, follow these steps:

1. **Choose Tools➪Junk E-Mail Options.**

2. **In the Junk E-Mail Options dialog box, click the Phishing tab.**

3. **Ensure that a check mark appears by the item Protect My Inbox from Messages with Potential Phishing Links.**

4. **Click OK.**

When a potential phishing e-mail message comes in, such as one that contains a misleading Web page link, you're alerted before the message ever roosts in the Inbox. The warning dialog box is shown in Figure 4-3. Simply click the Close button.

Figure 4-3: A phishing e-mail has arrived.

By clicking the Close button, you instantly stuff the suspect message into the Junk E-Mail folder in Windows Mail. Whew.

I Spy, with My Little Eye

Look! Inside your PC! It's a virus! It's a Trojan! It's a worm! Nope. It's *spyware*, yet a new type of malware, vicious and invasive. This section discusses what spyware is, what it does, and how to squish it.

Understanding spyware

How would you like to use your computer while, the entire time, people are sitting behind you, looking over your shoulder and watching what you do on the Internet? Hundreds of people are watching you. Not only that, but you also cannot get any of them to leave. If you can picture that, you understand the evil concept of spyware.

It all started out innocently enough: Spyware was designed to help customize advertising on the Internet. Based on which Web pages you visited, advertising was targeted specifically for you. That sounds good. But that fresh concept quickly turned sour.

Several flavors of malware all fall under the category of spyware:

Tracking: The most innocent form of spyware is merely a tracking cookie placed by a Web site on your computer. The cookie is really little more than a text file, though it's read by various Web sites as you plod through your Internet activities. This type of spyware can easily be removed by deleting all your Internet cookies, described in Chapter 1.

Adware: As its name implies, adware is advertising software. It may not even be spyware, but, rather, software that features ads to support the program's development. Examples include free toolbars and screen savers that may have a legitimate function but also display advertising and just may also monitor Internet use or scan your e-mail.

Piggyback: The worst spyware is the piggyback program. The spyware attaches itself to another program and may reset your Web home page, redirect Web site requests, flood your screen with advertising at random times, and perform other irritating acts. The worst thing is that the piggyback software is nearly impossible to remove. Indeed, the software agreement that many users innocently agree to states that the program cannot and will not be removed from their computers.

Though spyware is malware, it's not considered a virus. That's because spyware doesn't self-replicate and most of it is acquired voluntarily. Yes, it's true: Most people *invite* spyware into their computers. Irritating programs are downloaded willingly; they promise a service or claim to do something clever. Then they prove to be the piggyback type of spyware that cannot be uninstalled.

The insidious part is that spyware multiplies. Unless you keep an eye on things, the amount of spyware in your loaded PC grows larger and larger. You may not lose data, but the PC slows to a crawl because of all the spyware programs clogging the arteries.

Because spyware isn't considered to be viral, most antivirus programs don't scan for, detect, or remove spyware. To combat the scourge, use specific anti-spyware software, such as Windows Defender.

- ✦ An example of adware that isn't software is the free version of the Eudora e-mail program. The program features sponsored advertising, which helps support the program's development and allows a copy to be given away at no cost.

- ✦ Some antivirus programs are bundled with anti-spyware utilities as part of an Internet security suite.

- ✦ Most free spyware scanners simply remove Internet tracking cookies. They don't perform a complete evaluation of your computer system for spyware infection.

- ✦ Some spyware programs steal credit card numbers. They fly under the banner of making your online purchases easier by storing all your payment information for you. Wrong! If you value your financial security, credit card information should never be stored anywhere.

- ✦ Avoid free or Web-page-based anti-spyware programs. They are often spyware themselves. The only spyware programs I trust are Windows Defender and anything they sell in a box at the software store.

Getting Windows Defender

One of the best ways to fight spyware is to use the Windows Defender program. It comes standard with Windows Vista, but if you have Windows XP, you may need to get it as an update.

First, check to ensure that Windows Defender isn't already installed; it's found as a command on the Start button's All Programs menu. If it's not there, download the program by following these steps:

1. **Browse to the following Web site:**

     www.microsoft.com/windows/products/winfamily/defender

2. **Click the big, fun Get It Now button.**

    Microsoft may change its Web page design, so if you don't see the big, fun Get It Now button, look for some other clue on how to download the program.

3. **Follow the directions on-screen to continue with the download.**

   (See Chapter 5 for more general information on downloading and installing programs from the Internet.)

4. **After Windows Defender has been downloaded, work through the Installation Wizard for Windows Defender.**

5. **When prompted, click to use the recommended settings, and opt for a complete installation.**

Windows Defender immediately begins scanning your computer. Continue reading in the next section.

Using Windows Defender

Windows own spyware-fighting utility is Windows Defender. Windows Defender not only scans your system for spyware, but it can also help you remove stubborn piggyback programs.

 Start Windows Defender by choosing the Windows Defender item from the Start button menu's All Programs menu. In Windows Vista, you can also find a Windows Defender icon in the Control Panel.

After starting the program, you see the Windows Defender main screen, shown in Figure 4-4.

Figure 4-4:
Windows
Defender.

Hopefully, the screen you see looks a lot like Figure 4-4, where you see the message that your computer is running normally. If not, you can choose from several options to remedy the situation:

Always Allow: As long as you recognize and allow the program, Windows Defender remembers the software and flags it as okay. You're no longer bothered by the warning. The program name then appears in the Allowed Items list.

Ignore: Windows Defender gives the item a pass, allowing it to run or be installed on your computer. But the next time the program runs, you see the same warning again.

Quarantine: The item in question is placed into a special area on disk; it's not running and not in risk of harming your computer. The software remains in quarantine until you unquarantine the program or delete it.

Remove: Windows Defender obliterates the program, rubbing it out of existence. Smoldering bits puff out the back side of your PC.

Choose your option, and Windows Defender deals with the suspect program appropriately.

Windows Defender may also pop up a warning while you're using the Internet in what's called *real-time protection*. The Windows Defender Warning dialog box alerts you to the presence of known spyware. There are several alert levels for the programs that are found:

Not Yet Classified: The program is most likely okay. Many programs are unknown to the various spyware databases and therefore are "not yet classified." If you recognize the program, let it be. If you don't recognize the program, such as you did not mean to install it or don't know where it came from, remove it.

Low: The program is probably not evil, but you don't want it anyway. If the program was installed without your knowledge, remove it. Otherwise, check the publisher or source.

Medium: A medium-level program may compromise your PC's security or collect sensitive data. Review the details and decide whether to remove it, especially when you don't recognize the publisher.

High: Remove the software.

Severe: Definitely remove the software.

Click the appropriate button, Remove All or Ignore, to deal with the items that are found. Remember that if you don't recognize the publisher or you're not trying to install new software, *remove it!*

✦ See the section "Exploring software," later in this chapter, for information on how the "Not Yet Classified" message is also used to reference installed programs on your PC.

✦ Windows Defender is set up to work all the time. To disable it, refer to the next section.

✦ You can remove a program from the Allowed Items list if you discover later that it is indeed spyware. To do so, choose Tools and then choose Allowed Items from the Tools and Settings window.

✦ Review items held in quarantine by choosing Tools from the Windows Defender window and then clicking the Quarantined Items link. You can then select an item and click the Remove or Restore buttons to deal with it.

✦ It's okay to run multiple spyware checking programs, though I don't do so myself. As long as I have and trust a spyware program, such as Windows Defender, I don't see a need to add more programs to my PC or run more utilities that may slow down the system.

Scanning for spyware in Windows Defender

For the most part, Windows Defender runs automatically. You can perform a quick scan at any time by clicking the Scan button.

To perform a more rigorous scan, click the arrow next to the Scan button. From the menu, choose the Full Scan option. It goes into far more detail, but it also takes longer to complete. I recommend using it only when you suspect spyware to be bothering you.

Scheduling Windows Defender

To schedule when and how Windows Defender runs, follow these steps:

1. **Click the Tools link at the top of the Windows Defender window.**

The Tools and Settings part of the Windows Defender window appears. It lists many powerful utilities for helping pluck nasty software from your PC.

2. **Choose the Options link.**

The Options page appears.

3. **Ensure that there's a check mark by the item Automatically Scan My Computer.**

When this option is unchecked, Windows Defender is turned off. I don't recommend turning it off.

4. **Choose a frequency, either daily or a specific day of the week.**

   Daily is best.

5. **Pick a time.**

   Specify a time when the computer will be on (either running or in Sleep mode). Windows Defender doesn't wake the computer up from hibernation. See Book I, Chapter 3 for more hibernation information.

6. **Choose the type of scan, either Quick or Full.**

7. **Review other settings in the window.**

   There are too many to list here, and none is incorrectly set by default.

8. **Click the Save button.**

9. **In Windows Vista, type the administrator's password or click the Continue button.**

A key to the success of running any malware utility is to keep it updated. Windows Defender is no exception. Updates for Windows Defender are automatically installed on your computer — if you have Automatic Updates configured that way. If you don't, you might want to reconsider your automatic update strategy. See Book II, Chapter 1.

Exploring software

One of the most amazing tools in the Windows Defender tool chest is Software Explorer. You can use Software Explorer to examine programs that are started or running on your PC to check their legitimacy and potentially halt spyware.

To see Software Explorer, choose Tools from the Windows Defender home page and then click the link for Software Explorer. You see Software Explorer, shown in Figure 4-5, listing the startup programs for your version of Windows.

Programs listed by name (see Figure) and whether they fall under the category of Permitted or Not Yet Classified.

Don't let a program that's Not Yet Classified freak you out! That label simply means that the program isn't in the spyware database. As long as you recognize the program, or it looks like something that should belong on the computer, don't remove or disable it.

When you see a program that looks suspect, or is flagged as such, you can disable or remove it: Select the program and then click the Remove button to delete it, or click the Disable button to merely prevent the program from starting up.

Figure 4-5:
Windows
Defender
examines
startup
programs.

✦ In Windows Vista, you must first click the Show for All Users button to enable the Remove and Disable buttons; enter the administrator's password or click the Continue button after clicking the Show for All Users button.

✦ By disabling a program, you start Windows in a special diagnostic mode, similar to what can be done using the MSCONFIG tool. See Chapter 2 in Book II for more information on disabling startup programs.

Life Behind the Firewall

I don't expect you to use your computer without using the Internet. I tried that once: I had a PC set up that I wanted to keep *pure*. The thing wasn't connected to the Internet and I wouldn't play any games on that system or run any software other than Microsoft Word. That scheme lasted all of about 20 minutes.

It's tough to be a part of the universe while not connected to it. One way to make that connection safer is to use a *firewall*. This section explains the details.

Understanding firewalls

Consider the Internet a hole through which wonderful things can travel both to and fro. You send information to the internet, but more often gobs of information flow in from the Internet, all coming through that tiny hole you call your Internet connection.

The problem with the hole through which the Internet flows is that it's wide open. There's no guard, no monitor, not even a doorbell. That's because the Internet was designed by very trusting people, mostly scientists and researchers who appreciated the unfettered, free-flowing nature of information. The fools.

The Bad Guys soon learned that the Internet was a highway with no traffic rules. Like any eager opportunist, the Bad Guys were soon wandering unwelcomed, poking, prodding, and pilfering information as well as planting viruses and other toxic software. Obviously, a highway patrol was needed.

To help monitor the hole through which Internet information flows, software designers borrowed a concept from the construction industry: the firewall.

In construction, firewalls are rated by how long they take to burn through. A one-hour firewall theoretically will stand for one hour before the flames lick into the next room. Computer firewalls work in a similar manner, though, the idea is to keep the bad guys out permanently, not just after a given amount of persistence.

What the firewall does is to monitor both incoming and outgoing Internet traffic. When a firewall is properly configured, only the information you request from the Internet is allowed in. Outgoing information can also be filtered.

When information you didn't request comes in, the firewall instantly squishes it, blocking the doors and windows, so to speak. Likewise, when information tries to sneak out, you can be queried about whether it's okay for that information to be sent.

Generally speaking, the firewall prompts you with Allow or Deny types of messages. If you don't want something coming in, you can choose to deny it by blocking it temporarily or permanently. The firewall can also learn from your choices so that after a few times, you aren't bothered with the warnings.

Bottom line: To help keep your computer system secure, you need a firewall.

✦ The first line of defense against Internet-spawned malware should be a firewall.

✦ A firewall should be a priority for broadband Internet users. Those high-speed connections are coveted by the bad guys, who need the connection speed and storage that your compromised PC offers.

✦ Two types of firewall are available for your computer: hardware and software.

✦ A *hardware* firewall is an electronic gizmo installed between the broadband modem and your computer. It's often included as part of the router. (See Book V, Chapter 1 for basic information on a network router.) A hardware router monitors all incoming and outgoing Internet traffic. It's a far more robust solution than a software firewall.

Book IV Chapter 4

Wicked Software

✦ A software firewall is a program running on your PC that monitors only the Internet traffic entering and leaving your computer.

✦ Dialup Internet users aren't at risk as greatly as broadband Internet users, but I do recommend using a software firewall for dialup Internet access.

Setting up a router with a firewall

The best solution for broadband Internet users is to set up a hardware firewall. Most wired and wireless routers sold today feature such a hardware firewall. That's good news. The better news is that the firewall is most likely configured perfectly for you; there's really little left to do.

Chapter 1 in Book V offers some basic router information, including information on how the thing is set up. Without my repeating too much of that information here, you access the router using the PC's Web browser. Figure 4-6 shows my router's firewall configuration screen, which is set similar to the way most routers deal with firewalls.

Figure 4-6: A router's firewall setup screen.

At its simplest level, the hardware firewall is an On-Off type of affair. Some routers may feature an advanced firewall where you can add rules and such, but in most cases the rules are straightforward: Don't allow in any Internet traffic that wasn't specifically requested by a computer on the network. That rule pretty much blocks all the Bad Guys from getting through.

✦ When you have a hardware firewall, you don't need to use a second, software firewall.

✦ You can test your computer's firewall by visiting the Gibson Research Web site and using their Shield's Up program. Visit:

> www.grc.com

Using the Windows Firewall

Windows comes with a firewall called, remarkably, Windows Firewall. To access it, open the Windows Firewall icon found in the Control Panel. You see the main Windows Firewall window, which is boring, so I don't show it here.

The Windows Firewall window features two options: one for turning the firewall on and the other for turning it off. When the Windows Firewall is on, it monitors all network traffic coming into and going out from your PC. Any suspect information, such as information you didn't request, is blocked automatically.

Sometimes, the Windows Firewall prompts you when it encounters something smelly. A firewall warning appears, and you're given three options:

Ask Me Later: Access is blocked, but only once. If the same request comes through again, you see the warning again.

Keep Blocking: Access is blocked and continues to be blocked.

Unblock: Access is allowed. Choose this option when you recognize the program making the request and everything is okay. Pat Windows Firewall on the head for being diligent.

Always choose the Keep Blocking option when you don't recognize the program or service making the request.

✦ Other software firewalls that are out there are better and more thorough than the Windows Firewall. I have none that I can recommend offhand, though if you have purchased an Internet security suite, you may find a software firewall included.

✦ If you use dialup networking, I highly recommend using a software firewall like the Windows Firewall.

✦ You don't need to use the Windows Firewall, or any software firewall, when your computer sits on a network behind a hardware firewall. (See the preceding section). Running redundant firewalls doesn't keep your PC any safer, but it does unnecessarily slow down the system.

**Book IV
Chapter 4**

Wicked Software

✦ Software firewalls are often a cause of network woe; they often prevent you from accessing other computers on your network. See Chapter 3 in Book V for more peer-to-peer networking information.

✦ The Windows Firewall warnings aren't the same as the Windows Vista User Account Control (UAC) warnings. See Chapter 5 in Book II for more information on UAC warnings.

Disabling the Windows Firewall

To disable the Windows Firewall, follow these steps:

1. **Open the Control Panel's Windows Firewall icon.**
2. **If you're using Windows XP, skip to Step 5.**
3. **Click the Change Settings link in the Windows Firewall window.**
4. **Type the administrator's password or click the Continue button.**
5. **Choose Off in the Windows Firewall Settings dialog box.**
6. **Click OK.**
7. **Close the Windows Firewall window.**

When you disable the Windows firewall, the Windows Security center screen reports that "something is wrong" (refer to Figure 4-1). You may also find yourself bothered by its attempts to remedy the situation (such as with pop-up reminders from the notification area). That's okay: If you have a hardware firewall, you don't need to run the Windows Firewall, or any other software firewall, on top of it.

Disabling Windows Remote Assistance

Windows comes with an option to allow someone else on the Internet or a local network to access your computer. It can be done to share files, but primarily the feature exists to let someone somewhere help you fix your PC. The feature is *Windows Remote Assistance.*

For some reason, the Windows Remote Assistance feature is activated on just about every PC. I recommend turning it off because it presents a serious security risk.

Here's how to disable Windows Remote Assistance in Windows Vista:

1. **Press Win+Break to quickly summon the System window.**
2. **From the list of links on the left, choose Remote Settings.**

3. **Type the administrator's password or click the Continue button.**

4. **Remove the check mark by the item Allow Remote Assistance Connection to This Computer.**

5. **Choose the Remote Desktop option Don't Allow Connections to This Computer.**

6. **Click OK.**

7. **Close the System window.**

In Windows XP, follow these steps to disable Remote Assistance:

1. **Conjure forth the System dialog box by pressing the Win+Break key combination.**

2. **Click the Remote tab in the System Properties dialog box.**

3. **Remove the check mark from the item Allow Remote Assistance Invitations to Be Sent from This Computer.**

4. **If available, also remove the check mark from the option Allow Users to Connect Remotely to This Computer.**

5. **Click OK.**

If you do need over-the-Internet help in the future, you can reenable Remote Assistance: repeat these steps, but add the check mark in Step 4 for Windows Vista or in Step 3 for Windows XP. Also in Windows Vista, you can enable the Remote Desktop settings if you want to allow that feature.

You must respond to a request for assistance to use Windows Remote Assistance. Responding opens up your computer for remote access — but because you responded, the access is permitted through a firewall. In other words, a firewall doesn't protect you from unwanted "assistance."

Chapter 5: The File Transfer Chapter

In This Chapter

- ✓ Understanding files
- ✓ Knowing what *download* means
- ✓ Getting images from a Web site
- ✓ Installing a program from the Web
- ✓ Sending a picture via e-mail
- ✓ Dealing with e-mail attachments
- ✓ Using FTP
- ✓ Saving an FTP site
- ✓ Working with file permissions

*F*orget about all the pornography — what the Internet is really all about is information. Storing information. Sending information. Receiving information. That information exists elsewhere, anywhere, and everywhere in the form of a file. Therefore, the whole arena of "file transfer" is essentially what the Internet is all about. Files hither. Files thither. Files yon. This chapter covers all of that (though not as much on the files yon as files hither and thither).

What Is a File?

Before you can understand *file transfer*, you need to appreciate the entire concept of a computer file. I'm continually surprised at how many people who use computers, and who are generally smart, really don't know what a file is. Because of that, they never really get their arms around the notion of file transfer. So let me explain.

Computers store information in chunks called *files*. The file is the container. Although the information in a file is all those ones and zeroes you read about in computer folklore, the information itself is useful stuff. Files contain your programs, the documents you create, pictures, music, video — anything and everything you save on your computer. No matter what it is, it's stored in a file.

To help make files useful, the operating system slaps various attributes on the file. That helps the operating system deal with the files, but it also aids you in discovering which files are which. To help you connect with this process, open and view the Documents or My Documents folder on your computer; you can choose that folder from the Start menu. The Documents folder on my computer is shown in Figure 5-1.

Figure 5-1:
Looking at
files.

A folder window normally lists files by their icons and names, plus additional information. The additional information that's displayed depends on the view you choose. In Figure 5-1, I chose Details view. On your PC, choose Details from the Views toolbar button or menu.

There are five basic attributes to recognize for a file:

Name: The filename is given when the file is created or saved to disk. Files can also be renamed after they're created. The filename is the number-one file attribute.

Type: All files have a type, which identifies either the program that created the file or the category to which the file belongs. The file type is tied directly to the last part of the filename, the filename extension.

Icon: The icon helps identify the file in the graphical environment of Windows. The icon shown is directly related to the file type.

Size: The file's size is measured in bytes, which may seem like a complex computer concept, but it's not: A single byte is merely one character. So a 24-letter signature stored in a file is 24 bytes in size. Complex information, such as images, sound, or video requires more storage than plain text. Regardless, the size of a file, measured in bytes, is another important file attribute.

Date: The operating system records the date and time when a file is saved, making that information part of the file's attributes. Further, the operating system also records the date a file was last opened as well as the date a file was last modified. In Windows, the modification date is shown in the standard folder window (refer to Figure 5-1).

Every file has these basic attributes. Files have additional attributes as well, such as the read-only attribute, hidden file attribute, and a host of others (including some secret stuff they don't even tell to Bill Gates). But the basic file attributes are things you should know.

Above all, here's an important point to remember:

Everything you create on the computer is stored in a file.

When you use a program such as WordPerfect to create a document, that document is saved as a file on disk. The document isn't "in" WordPerfect. The document is a file.

After the file is created, you can copy it to another folder or storage device on your computer, or you can copy that file to a location on the Internet or send the file to another person as an e-mail attachment. That's the essence of the file, and that's why it's important to understand what a file is before you understand what file transfer is all about.

✦ Programs are files, just like the documents you create or music you play. The difference is that programs contain instructions that tell the computer what to do.

✦ You can change the number of columns displayed in a folder (in Details view) by dragging the column headings left or right. You can add or remove columns by right-clicking a column header and choosing the column types to add or remove from the shortcut menu.

✦ Yes, both the type and icon file attributes are directly tied to the file's name.

✦ The file's name is its most important attribute. That's why I urge readers of my other books to save their stuff to disk using short, descriptive filenames.

✦ Refer to Chapter 6 in Book II for more information on how file types tie into the filename extension and how the weak concept of file association can lead to weird things happening on your PC.

✦ Because files have sizes measured in the thousands and millions of bytes, abbreviations are used. KB represents *kilobytes,* or increments of 1,000 bytes. MB represents *megabytes*, or increments of 1 million bytes.

✦ See my book *PCs For Dummies* (Wiley Publishing) for more information on the concept of bytes in relation to file size and computer storage.

✦ A *shortcut file* is also a file, though a tiny one. The shortcut file itself merely contains a reference to another file elsewhere on the PC's storage system. So the shortcut file *is* a file, but when you open it, you're really opening the referenced file.

✦ See Book II, Chapter 1 for information on finding files lost in your PC's storage system.

✦ See Chapter 4 in Book I for information on your PC's storage system, where the files dwell.

The Art of Downloading

On your computer's storage system, you work with files by creating, copying, moving, renaming, or deleting them. That's all basic file management stuff. But to work with a file on a network or on the Internet, you need to use a new term. That term is *download,* and it's the topic for this section.

Downloading the right term

I find it amusing when technical terms are used by people who don't understand the terms. A good example is the word *downloading.* What is *downloading?*

If you were to hear the brie-and-chardonnay crowd talk about downloading, you would believe that *download* is defined as any type of file transfer; sending information to any computer is a download. They say, "I'll download this to your computer" or "Download that to me." It's an incorrect use of the term, but it amuses me, so I don't bother correcting them.

The term *download* refers to transferring information from another computer into your computer. Originally, the term applied to receiving a file from a server or a mighty computer out on the Internet. I'd always imagine that computer up on a hill with my computer at the bottom of the computer. That helped me remember that downloading meant receiving a file.

The companion term to download is *upload*, though it's not as abused as download. To upload a file is to send something from your computer to another computer. That's it. Figure 5-2 illustrates the concept.

✦ Download = Receive from the Internet

✦ Upload = Send to the Internet

✦ When you don't know whether you're downloading or uploading a file, you're merely doing a *file transfer.*

Figure 5-2:
The
illustrated
concept
of down-
loading.

Internet
computer

You

✦ You don't download or upload when you copy files on your own computer's storage system. For example, saving a file to an optical disc
doesn't imply that you're "downloading" the file (though the term may
be used regardless).

✦ Some sticklers out there claim that copying a file between two computers on a network isn't the same concept as downloading. No, to the
purists, you download only when you fetch a file from a server, either
locally or (most often) on the Internet.

✦ Sending a file as an e-mail attachment is neither downloading nor
uploading.

✦ Of course, when you're using the server or you're sending a file to a friend
on the Internet, you're downloading the file into their computer. That's
kind of a weird exception to the download/upload scheme of things, but
then again, you could merely say that you're "transferring files" and not
have to worry about any nerds snickering behind your back.

Grabbing an image from a Web page

Technically, it is considered a download to snag an image from a Web page. Here's the simple process:

1. **Right-click the image.**

2. **Choose the command Save Picture As.**

3. **Use the Save Picture dialog box to find a location to save the picture.**

   (Optional) You can rename the picture as it's saved to your computer's storage system.

4. **Click the Save button.**

The image now exists as a file on your computer.

You can also drag the image from the Web page window out onto the desktop or into any open folder window. (You might be prompted to click Yes or No to ensure that dragging the image is okay, which it should be.)

✦ Windows Vista prefers to save images in the Pictures folder, which is My Pictures in Windows XP. If you want to get more organized, you can use subfolders within the Pictures folder.

✦ Some images cannot be saved to disk. These images are protected from being copied or they're somehow created or displayed in a manner that makes copying impossible.

✦ Don't bother saving the image if you plan only to e-mail it. Instead, choose the command E-Mail Picture from the menu instead of Save Picture As (refer to Step 2).

✦ It's okay to copy and use images from the Internet, but keep in mind that many of those images are copyrighted. Under the fair-use laws, you can keep a picture for your own purposes, but you cannot reuse, sell, or otherwise profit from the images.

Downloading a program from a Web site

I'll bet nearly half the software on your computer was downloaded from a Web site. Some of it's free stuff, some may be driver updates, and some might be programs you are trying out or have purchased online. The rest, of course, is probably stuff you stole. Or maybe not; I shan't judge you.

Downloading a program works like this:

1. **Click the link that says to download the file.**

   It may be a button or link or a graphical image.

   If prompted, choose the EXE, or executable, file option. Your second choice should be a ZIP file (Compressed Folder).

2. **Click the security warning at the top of the window (below the tabs), and choose the menu item Download File.**

   Older versions of Internet Explorer don't have a security warning.

   The File Download dialog box appears, as shown in Figure 5-3.

Figure 5-3: The File Download dialog box.

3. **Click the Save button.**

   You can, if you like, click the Open button (named Run in older versions of Internet Explorer). The difference is that Save keeps the download on your PC, allowing you to reinstall the program later without having to download it again. The Open (or Run) option downloads the file but doesn't save it for reuse later.

4. **Click the Save button in the Save As dialog box.**

   I recommend saving the program into your account's Downloads folder in Windows XP. If you're using Windows XP, you can create a Downloads folder in the My Documents folder, and save the file there.

   If the name provided in the Save As dialog box is obscure, feel free to change it to something more memorable.

5. **Wait as the download progresses.**

After the download, a number of things could happen. They all depend on what type of file you received.

If you downloaded an EXE file, simply click the Run button in the dialog box that appears, which begins installation. Follow the directions on the screen.

If you downloaded a ZIP file, you need to open the ZIP file to continue installation. Follow these steps:

1. **Click the Open button, if one is available after the download is finished.**

2. **In Windows Vista, click the Allow button to allow the Web site to open a folder on your PC.**

    The Web site isn't really opening the folder; you are.

    If there's no Open button, open the Downloads folder window and then open the Compressed Folder (ZIP) icon.

3. **In Windows Vista, click the toolbar button Extract All Files; in Windows XP, click the link on the left side of the window, Extract All Files.**

4. **Work through the Extraction Wizard.**

    In Windows Vista, click the Extract button. In Windows XP, click the Next button repeatedly until it turns into the Finished button and then click that button.

    When Windows is done extracting the files, you should see them in a folder window.

5. **Double-click to run the Install or Setup program.**

    If you don't see the Install or Setup program, open the Install, Setup, or Bin folder, or just open the only folder visible on-screen. Eventually, you find an Install icon or a Setup icon.

    If you still cannot find an Install program or a Setup program, open any file named readme. That file contains instructions for getting started, or at least more information on what to do next.

6. **Follow the directions as the installation program runs.**

    At this point, you're running the setup program; the file is being installed on your computer.

Sometimes, a download is really a *stub*, or another program loader. By running the stub, you download an even larger file from a remote server. In that case, continue following the directions on the screen that work through the setup procedure.

When the program is fully installed, it should work like any other program you installed from a disc: The program's name and icon appear on the Start button's All Programs menu, and perhaps even an annoying icon or a dozen appear on the desktop or on the Quick Launch bar.

✦ Sometimes, you may be presented with a series of links to download the file. These links are to various *mirror sites*, which are simply other locations on the Internet that have the same program for downloading. The idea is to pick a mirror site near you. That way, the download proceeds faster than if you choose a server located halfway around the world. Also, some sites may be busy, in which case choosing another mirror site results in a faster download.

✦ Program files listed on Web sites often include the version numbers in their names. For example, version 5.6 is the sixth release of the fifth version. It's one release later than version 5.5.

✦ Typically, multiple versions of a program are made available. You can choose the most recent version or an older version that might be more stable.

✦ Prerelease, or *beta*, versions of programs are available. Don't download them unless you really need the software or feel like providing the developer with troubleshooting information.

✦ Some programs also come with their source code, which means that the files used to create the program are included. These files often use the abbreviation SRC somewhere in the name.

✦ You don't need to download the SRC version of a program.

✦ Unless you truly need (and recognize) alternative download file formats, don't bother: Archives (GZ, TAR) are for other operating systems or those with special extraction utilities.

✦ Programs can also be received by FTP. See the section "FTP Trouble," later in this chapter.

✦ As with other installed software, you remove a program downloaded from the Internet by using the techniques covered in Chapter 6 of Book II.

**Book IV
Chapter 5**

**The File Transfer
Chapter**

E-Mail Attachment Irritants

Yet another way e-mail becomes desirable is as a file transfer program. In fact, the last time I printed a book and sent it into a publisher was in 1987. For a while, some publishers flirted with FTP servers. But now all the stuff I write — including every chapter in this book — is sent by e-mail. This section explains how all that works and what to do when things go wrong.

E-mailing a file

One of the simplest e-mail operations you can perform is to send someone a file. It works like this:

1. **Compose the message.**

The primary thing you're doing is sending e-mail. An e-mail message has one or more recipients, a subject line, and an actual message.

2. **Click the Attach button on the toolbar.**

The Attach button commonly sports a paperclip icon, such as the example from Outlook Express, shown in the margin. There may also be a File⇨Attach command, though choosing that command seems like a lot of work compared to using the toolbar button.

3. **Use the dialog box to search out the file to attach to the message.**

The dialog box is similar to the standard Open dialog box found in any application. Use the dialog box's controls to look for the storage media, folder, and eventually the file you want to send.

It's important to understand the whole folder concept to be able to quickly locate files you want to attach to an e-mail message. I recommend my book *PCs For Dummies* (Wiley Publishing) to help you organize files on your computer.

4. **After the file is found, click the Open or Attach button to attach it.**

5. **Repeat Steps 2 through 4 to attach additional files.**

6. **Send your message.**

In most e-mail programs, you simply click the Send button and off the message goes, attachment in tow.

It may take longer to send the message than normal, depending on the size of the attachment. Delivery is nearly instantaneous, though keep in mind that it might take some time for the recipient to pick up her e-mail.

✦ Avoid sending any e-mail attachment larger than 10MB. Most online mailboxes are capped at 10MB. If you send a larger message, it's rejected by the recipient's mail server.

✦ See Chapter 3 for more information on general e-mail troubleshooting.

✦ File attachments grow. Sending a 1MB file may result in the e-mail message being 1.4MB. That's because the file attachment is converted into plain text by your e-mail program. (All e-mail is plain text.) The recipient's e-mail program converts the attachment back into its original format after the recipient opens or saves the attachment to disk.

✦ Rather than send larger files through e-mail, burn them to an optical disc and place that disk in the regular mail. Yes, it's slower to send a file by *snail mail,* but it's a waste of time and Internet storage to e-mail files that might be rejected for being too large.

✦ An easier way to send multiple files is to first place the files into a compressed folder (or ZIP file archive). After they're there, you can send all the files as that single compressed folder. Of course, the recipient has to deal with the compressed folder, which is an extra step. If that person has trouble, just recommend one of my books.

✦ Not only does a compressed folder contain multiple files, it also takes up less space than sending the files individually.

✦ Avoid using the Insert⇨Picture command in Windows Mail or Outlook Express. That command *embeds* an image into your e-mail message; it doesn't attach the picture. To attach a picture, use the steps described in this section. Otherwise, the recipient cannot save the image to disk.

✦ In older versions of Outlook, the command to attach a file is Insert⇨File.

✦ Do not send shortcuts! Send the original file. If you send a shortcut, the recipient gets only a tiny file stub that's utterly useless.

✦ Try to send the generic version of a document file; don't send documents created in Office 2007 or in WordPerfect, because not everyone has those files. The generic document file format is RTF, or Rich Text Format. You can also save the document using the HTML format, which can be read by anyone using a computer with a Web browser.

✦ Avoid sending programs. Most antivirus utilities automatically assume that a program attachment is a virus. The program file may make it, but the recipient most likely will delete it. To avoid that, send *two* messages. In the first one, explain that the next message contains a program attachment and it's legitimate. Then follow up with the e-mail message containing the attachment.

E-mailing a photo

The most common thing to e-mail is a photo and the easiest way to do that is overlooked by far too many people. Follow these steps to e-mail a picture file the easy way:

1. **Open the folder containing the image you want to e-mail.**

Ha! Fooled you. I'll bet you were thinking that you needed to be in your e-mail program for this task. Nope.

2. **Right-click the image file to send.**

3. **Choose Send To⇨Mail Recipient from the shortcut menu.**

   An image-size-adjustment dialog box appears. The one used in Windows Vista is shown in Figure 5-4; in Windows XP, the dialog box offers only two choices: Make All My Pictures Smaller or Keep the Original Sizes.

Figure 5-4:
Adjusting
the image
size before
sending.

4. **Choose a size for the image and then click the Attach button.**

   The button is labeled OK in Windows XP.

5. **If prompted, choose an e-mail profile.**

   The e-mail profile is no longer used in Windows Vista, because you should really be using separate user accounts for your e-mail, not a single account on the computer with multiple e-mail accounts.

   Your e-mail program starts, creating a new message with the image file automatically attached. Depending on the program, the Subject line may reflect the attachment and the message body may contain information about the attachment and a warning about computer viruses.

6. **Type the recipient's address.**

7. **Edit the Subject line, in case the one that's automatically used seems vague and meaningless.**

8. **Type the message body.**

   Feel free to edit any text placed automatically in the body by Windows.

9. **Click the Send button.**

   There's no need to close your e-mail program after sending; only the New Message window appears; then the message is sent and you're back to doing whatever distracts you from getting real work done.

The method described in these steps helps address the biggest issue with sending photos: sending them in a convenient size.

Of course, another way to send a smaller-size image is to use an image editing program to reset the image's size. Then again, going through those steps either alters the image's original size or you wind up with two copies of the same image on your PC: one small for e-mail and the larger, original copy. That's why I recommend following the steps in this section.

✦ You can right-click any file icon to send it, similar to the way you send an image as described in this section.

✦ Although it's possible to make a large image smaller, it's not quite as easy to make a small image larger. If the image is already small, making it larger just makes it fuzzy.

✦ Store your digital photographs in a large format. The larger file format is a must for image editing. Also, larger picture files print better than smaller ones that might be better suited for attaching to an e-mail message.

Choosing the right graphics file format

Beyond file size, discussed in the preceding section, another important factor to note when sending an image is to send it in the proper graphics file format.

Not all graphics files use the same format. As computer graphics have evolved and various image editors developed, a slew of image file formats have come and gone. Some are well suited for sending e-mail, and some are better suited for image editing.

The best formats for sending e-mail photo attachments are JPG and PNG. These are also the most common formats, and those widely used on the Web. The images look good, and the file size is small.

Among the worst formats for sending e-mail photo attachments are TIFF and BMP. Those are graphics file formats, but the file size is *huge*. In addition to those file formats, the graphics file formats native to image editing software, such as the PSD format used by Adobe Photoshop, are inappropriate to send unless the recipient asks for such file formats and also has the software to open and edit those images.

To convert a TIFF, BMP, PSD, or other graphics file into the JPG or PNG format, use image editing software. Open the file and then use the File⇨ Export or File⇨Save As commands to save the file using another graphics file format. Further, if you have the skills, consider resizing the image before you save it in the new file format.

✦ JPG is also written JPEG.

✦ The GIF image format is also small, but has limited resolution for photographs. PNG is a better choice.

✦ TIFF images are used primarily in applications. Although you can e-mail them, unless the recipient requires the file in TIFF format, you're wasting time.

Receiving an attachment

More than receiving e-mail, it seems people love getting e-mail *attachments*. That's my guess. It's based on the fact that so many people send me e-mail attachments. They send pictures, music, videos, and PowerPoint presentations — all to amuse, inform, or outrage.

A good chunk of the e-mail you receive will likely have attachments tagging along. Depending on your e-mail program, you may see the attachments right in the message: The images appear, and perhaps even the videos show up in their own windows, where you can watch them, right in the message.

To save the attachments, follow these general steps:

1. **Select the message or open the message in its own window.**

Double-click a message in the Inbox to open it in its own window.

2. **Choose File⇨Save Attachments from the menu.**

The command may be subtly different, depending on your e-mail program, but generally it's found on the File menu.

3. **Use the Save As dialog box to find a location for the file.**

You may not see a Save As dialog box. In Windows Mail, for example, there's a Save Attachment dialog box. It chooses to place all attachments in the Documents folder, though you can use the Browse button to change that folder location.

4. **Click the Save button to save the attachment.**

The most important thing to do is follow Step 3 closely: Remember where you saved the attachment. The biggest problem with receiving attachments is that people forget where they put them.

To solve the attachment dilemma, I create a special folder for my e-mail attachments. Inside my Documents folder, I create a subfolder named `E-Mail Attachments` or just `Attachments`. I place all attachments in that folder initially. Later, I may copy the attachments to other, more appropriate folders. But by placing all the attachments in the same folder, I always know where to find them.

✦ You don't have to open an e-mail attachment.

✦ It isn't your job to be able to open the e-mail attachment. If you cannot open the thing and Windows reports that it cannot open the file or find the proper program to open it, reply to the sender. Have that person resend the document in a common file format.

✦ If you're not expecting an e-mail attachment, do not open it.

✦ You're never required to open an e-mail attachment; there's no legal liability for failing to do so. Serious stuff arrives through the real mail, not e-mail.

✦ It may also be possible to save a file attachment by clicking an attachment icon in the message window. Again, all e-mail programs handle attachments differently.

✦ Compressed folders or ZIP archives sent as attachments require a bit more work: You must first save the ZIP attachment. Then you need to open the ZIP archive or compressed folder and extract its contents.

✦ It's common for some folks to send out PowerPoint presentation files. You need to have the Microsoft PowerPoint program to view those files. When you don't have PowerPoint, you can download a free PowerPoint viewer from Microsoft's Web site: Visit `microsoft.com` and type **PowerPoint viewer** in the Search box.

✦ Some types of images sent in an e-mail message cannot be saved. These are typically embedded images, which are part of the message itself and not really an e-mail attachment. The only way to save those images is to reply to the sender and request that the images be attached. (What the person is doing is using the Insert⇨Picture or Insert⇨Image command instead of Insert⇨File Attach or File⇨Attach.)

✦ Your PC's antivirus software may add a few steps to the attachment retrieval process. That's a good thing; it's wise to be wary.

FTP Trouble

The oldest and perhaps best way to fling files between two remote computers is to use something ancient and potentially cryptic called *FTP*. This section discusses the to's and fro's of FTP.

Understanding FTP

FTP is one of those wonderful computer terms that's both a noun and a verb.

As a noun, FTP takes on its formal expansion to *File Transfer Protocol*. That's the name for a method of sending files, but also the name of the program that actually sends the files. Usage example: "Log in to my FTP server to pick up those files."

As a verb, *FTP* means to send or receive files. A proper replacement is the word *send* or *fetch*. Usage example: "FTP that to me."

Originally, FTP was developed to send and receive files in the old text-based computers and networks of the pre-graphical era of computers (before the mid-1980s). Unlike on your own computer, you have to use FTP to access a remote computer on the network to *get* or receive files, or to *put* or send files.

FTP existed as one of the original programs for accessing information on the Internet, long before HTTP became popular for accessing Web pages. As such, your PC's Web browser, as well as the Windows Explorer program that displays files on your computer, can be used to access FTP servers to get or put files from places remote.

✦ FTP stands for File Transfer Protocol.

✦ The term *get* is used in FTP to refer to receiving files.

✦ The term *put* is used in FTP to refer to sending files.

✦ In the modern context, using FTP in Windows is similar to opening a Windows Explorer window for a remote folder on a network computer. The next section explains the details.

✦ A computer on the Internet that offers FTP access is said to be an *FTP host* or *FTP server*.

✦ You're required to enter a username and password to access an FTP server, just like logging in to your own computer.

✦ Various public FTP servers don't require you to have an account for access. Occasionally, you may have to log in to such servers. Often, the account name is `guest` and the password is either `please` or `pass-word`. Sometimes you're required to give your e-mail address as the account name and then you can type anything for the password.

✦ Web pages are uploaded to the Internet by using FTP. The Web page files are created on your own computer and then sent to the ISP's Web server using FTP, either by itself or as part of the Web page creation program. FTP can also be used to access any "Web space" or Internet storage your ISP offers.

✦ Windows comes with a text-based version of the FTP program, similar to the one originally found on the old Unix computers that dominated the Internet back in the early days. I don't bother covering the text-based FTP program in this book because the book is overdue already and, though it tempts me, I don't like angering my editor.

Accessing an FTP server in Windows Explorer

The first step to accessing an FTP server is to know its name. Like a Web page, FTP servers on the Internet sport a unique *Universal Resource Locator,* or *URL.* It's that text thing you type into a Web browser's Address bar.

Obviously, you know where you're headed in your FTP journey — personal Web space, corporate file repository, or software download page. In that case, you have the name of the FTP server — the URL — already. For purposes of this exercise, I'm using the Free Software Foundation's GNU FTP server: ftp.gnu.org. To access that FTP server, follow these steps:

1. Open a Windows Explorer window; press Win+E.

You can use either Windows Explorer, which displays folder windows, or Internet Explorer. Because FTP involves working with files, I chose Windows Explorer.

2. Click to select the Address bar.

If the Address bar isn't visible in Windows XP, choose View⇨ Address Bar.

3. Type the FTP site's address.

In this example, type **ftp://ftp.gnu.org**.

4. Press Enter.

The GNU FTP server is open to the public using anonymous access. Most FTP servers, however, are password-protected. See the next section for more information.

In a second, you see the window populated with folders and files, just as though you were looking at storage on your own PC, as shown in Figure 5-5. Keep in mind, however, that you're using a remote computer on the Internet.

As an example, I show you how to download the Emacs text editor from the GNU FTP site.

5. Open the GNU folder.

6. Open the Emacs folder.

7. Open the Windows folder.

You're now in the location where the files to install Emacs on your computer are located.

Figure 5-5:
An FTP
server
folder.

8. **Select the icon emacs-xxxxx-i386.zip.**

   The *xxxxx* is replaced by a version number. Otherwise, the icon represents the current version of the Emacs text editor.

9. **Press Ctrl+C to copy the file.**

10. **Press Ctrl+N to summon a new Windows Explorer folder window.**

    If you're using Internet Explorer instead of Windows Explorer, a new Internet Explorer window appears instead. That's okay, but what you really need is a folder window, not a Web page.

11. **In the new window, browse to your Downloads folder.**

    Windows Vista comes with a Downloads folder, found in your account's primary folder (the User Profile folder). In Windows XP, you have to create a Downloads folder if you haven't done so already.

12. **Press Ctrl+V to copy the file to the Downloads folder window.**

    It takes a few moments to copy the file because, technically, you're *downloading* it from the Internet.

    Once the file is copied, it exists on your own computer. You can open the icon to continue installation, or you can feel free to delete it if you really don't want to use the Emacs text editor.

13. **You can close the Downloads folder window.**

14. **Close the FTP server window to disconnect from the FTP server.**

    You can also break the connection by simply closing the FTP server window.

You work with an FTP server folder just like any other folder on your own computer. The three common activities are browse, get, and put.

Browse: To open a folder, double-click that folder icon. It takes a bit longer to open the folder because you're working remotely over the Internet.

Get: To copy a file from the FTP server (to *download* it), choose the file and press Ctrl+C on the keyboard. Open a folder on your own PC and press Ctrl+V to paste. The file is then copied from the FTP server to your own PC.

Put: To copy a file to the FTP server (to *upload* it), choose the file on your own PC and press Ctrl+C. Click in the FTP server window and press Ctrl+V to paste, thus copying the file to the FTP server.

These techniques work on all FTP servers, including the one for your own, personal Web space on the Internet, though that FTP server (like many others) sports a login option. See the next section.

✦ A public FTP server allows you to copy files from that server, but you cannot copy files *to* the server. For that, you need higher access; see the next section.

✦ You can also drag to copy files between your computer and an FTP server. Both folder windows must be open and visible for the file-drag operation to work.

✦ When dragging files between a local folder and FTP server folder window, you're always *copying* the files, not moving them.

✦ You may be denied access to any part of an FTP server, whether the server is public or not.

✦ *URL* stands for Universal Resource Locator. It's used in a Web browser to identify a place to find stuff on the Internet. The most popular URL is `http` for locating Web pages. There's also the `mailto` URL for sending e-mail. `ftp` is also a URL, as is the ancient `gopher` URL, which is no longer used.

✦ You may be given a specific FTP URL, similar to a Web page URL. It all works the same; type the full FTP server URL to log in to the server and use the specific folder.

✦ I've been informed that the major ISPs no longer offer personal Web space. Regardless, you'll probably use a Web page creation program to build your own, personal Web site, not the raw FTP, as demonstrated in this chapter.

Accessing a password-protected FTP site

You don't want just anyone waltzing into your PC on the Internet and uploading a few megabytes of porn and viruses. To prevent that, most FTP sites have password protection. Accessing them works the same as described in the preceding section. After Step 4, however, you see a password prompt similar to the one shown in Figure 5-6.

Figure 5-6:
An FTP
site logon
prompt.

Type your FTP account username and password. Click Log On to connect to the site.

After you log in to a password-protected site, you can get or put files just like using a public FTP server: Copy and paste files just as you do in Windows.

One issue you encounter with password-protected FTP sites is that they have timeout values set. After several minutes of inactivity, you're logged off the FTP server; in Windows, the FTP server window is replaced with the Computer window. That's your clue that you're logged off.

✦ Windows automatically remembers the username you typed to access the password-protected FTP server. The name appears in the Log On As dialog box the next time you connect to the server.

✦ If you place a check mark by the option Save Password, Windows also remembers your FTP server password.

✦ Obviously, remembering your password is part of the FTP process; don't forget it!

✦ Automatic logouts from FTP servers are part of the system security process. Even if you could, I don't recommend resetting the FTP server timeout value to anything longer than a few minutes.

Remembering an FTP site for future access

Windows allows you to save FTP sites you frequent, which saves time when accessing the same FTP site repeatedly. To save an FTP site, follow these steps:

1a. **In Windows Vista, open the Computer window.**

1b. **In Windows XP, open the My Network Places window.**

You can open either window by choosing Computer or My Network Places from the Start menu or from the Address Bar in any Windows Explorer window.

2a. **In Windows Vista, right-click in the Computer window and choose Add a Network Location from the shortcut menu.**

2b. **In Windows XP, choose Add a Network Place from the left side of the window.**

A wizard opens to help you add the FTP site to your computer's favorite place for remembering FTP sites: the Computer window in Windows Vista or the My Network Places window in Windows XP.

3. **Click the Next button.**

4. **Select the option Choose a Custom Network Location.**

5. **Click the Next button.**

6. **Type the FTP server address into the text box.**

Type the full name, including the `ftp://` part.

7. **Click the Next button.**

8. **If you're accessing an anonymous (public) FTP server, keep the check mark by Log On Anonymously and skip to Step 10. Otherwise, remove the check mark.**

9. **Enter your username into the User Name box.**

10. **Click the Next button.**

11. **(Optional) Type a name for the FTP server.**

For example, type **Work Server** or **Picture Uploads**. The name appears in the My Computer window, under the FTP server's icon.

12. **Click the Next button.**

13. **Click the Finish button to connect to the FTP server and finish the wizard.**

After you complete the wizard, the FTP server opens in its own window. If you need to log in with a password, you're prompted (refer to Figure 5-6).

 After the FTP server is added, you can quickly access it by opening its icon. In Windows Vista, the icon appears in the Computer window. In Windows XP, you find the icon in the My Network Places window.

Setting file permissions

When uploading to the Internet, there are certain attributes for files stored on an FTP server that you might consider setting. These include Read, Write, and Execute permissions for your own account as well as others who may visit the FTP site. By not setting the proper permissions, you may prevent access to the files by other users or inadvertently allow unknown users access to your stuff.

To set permissions for a file, follow these steps:

1. Open the FTP server and browse to the folder containing the file you want to modify.

You can also modify a folder itself.

2. Right-click the file icon and choose Properties from the shortcut menu.

You see the FTP Properties dialog box, shown in Figure 5-7.

Figure 5-7:
The FTP Properties dialog box.

The dialog box shows you details about the file and gives you the ability to change the file's permissions. There are three permission settings:

Read: Files can be opened or copied from the server.

Write: Files can be changed. For a folder, Write access means that files can be added to the folder.

Execute: Files can run, like programs. Folders can be opened.

These permissions are set for three different types of users:

Owner: The person who created the file or folder — you or whoever created the folder on a public server.

Group: Used to apply permissions to a whole mess of people, such as a guest or public group

All Users: Everyone

3. **Set the permissions as necessary.**

   For example, to allow only your own account to access the file, set the Read and Write permissions for only the Owner. To let others access the file but not change it, set their Read permission, but don't set the Write permission.

4. **Click OK.**

The file or folder's attributes are now changed.

You can repeat these steps for other files in your FTP folder that require special permissions.

✦ Generally speaking, the attributes are properly set for you. Normally, a file is set with Read and Write permissions for the Owner and then Read permissions for the Group and All Users.

✦ It's silly to not give a file any access. At minimum, your own files should have both Read and Write access for the Owner.

✦ All folders require Execute access if you're to open them. Normally, the Execute attribute is set for all users automatically.

✦ Beyond folders, don't set the Execute attribute unless you know that it needs to be done; having executable files on an FTP server can be a security risk.

Book V
Networking

Open the computer window

Open a Web browser

Nifty links

Open the network window

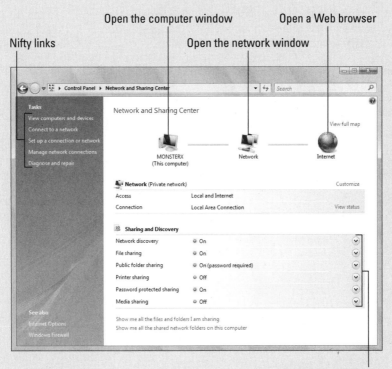

Local network settings

Contents at a Glance

Chapter 1: Network Hardware Help

In This Chapter

✔ Configuring a basic network

✔ Dealing with router problems

✔ Checking network connections

✔ Testing the PC's network adapter

✔ Restarting the modem

✔ Fixing the entire network

Some people are born to network, and others have networking thrust upon them. I assume that you're in the latter class. Where once the computer network was the domain (sic) of nerds and engineers, anyone with a home computer and high-speed Internet connection is suddenly plunged into the mysterious world of networking. This chapter explains what can go wrong with the hardware part of that world.

✦ Like all things in a computer, networking is composed of two parts. There's the hardware part, covered in this chapter, and then there's the software part. See Chapter 2 for all that wonderful software information.

✦ The information here assumes that the network is set up and running. You might have done it, or someone else might have done it. But it's your job to fix things.

✦ This book covers only the basic type of PC networking, commonly known as *peer-to-peer* networking. I do not cover file servers, local domains, or other, larger types of networks. In those situations, a hired hand often deals with and fixes networking problems for you.

The Network Big Picture

To better understand the whole world of networking, you need to get the *big picture*. Know the terms. Experiment with the jargon. Read this section.

Understanding networking

Networking is about communications and the sharing of resources. Along with sunny days in May and free cake, communications and sharing are possibly the best things in the world. But cake isn't free, and it rains in May, so don't believe everything that you read.

The story of networking is about the desire of yesterday's protonerds to get information out of one computer and into another computer. Oh, I suppose they started with just two computers. But then the guy with the third computer got jealous and soon, well, *everyone* wanted in on this networking gig.

Information being sent and received among various computers smacks of communications, and that's the basis of a computer network. It all happens in such a manner that information destined for one computer arrives at that computer intact and accurate, and the sending computer knows that the information was received.

The result of the communications is not that the computers start up a 1-900 cyberfriends chat line. No, the computers are more interested in the sharing of *resources*. For your PC, there are several resources to be shared on a computer network:

Mass storage: Hard drives, optical drives, and other types of storage can be shared and used by others on the network. Networking provides a solution whereby you don't need to copy files to removable media and walk them between computers — the "sneakernet."

Media files: Another resource you can share between PCs on a network is your music, picture, and video files. The Windows Media Player, as well as Apple's iTunes and other media jukeboxes, can be accessed and their media libraries shared over a simple computer network.

Printers: There's no need for each PC on the network to have its own printer when you can have one key printer on the network. Everyone can then use Larry's nice color printer, even though it's in Larry's office and he's overly possessive of his stuff.

Modems: A single modem can be shared by everyone on the network. In fact, high-speed modems must connect to your computer by using the network interface.

That's pretty much the networking philosophy. The methods by which computers are networked, however, became standardized in the early 1990s, at just about the same time the Internet exploded on the scene. Conveniently, the Internet is also a network, so the world is starting to make sense.

The protocols and methods for networking are referred to as *Ethernet*. That's the networking standard used by the Internet and by all local networks. Before that time, computer networks could use a number of different networking schemes, both hardware and software. But with Ethernet, pretty much all computer networking has become standard.

✦ Mass storage resources consist of folders you can access on other computers. Additionally, there can be stand-alone network hard drives, up for grabs by anyone using the network.

✦ Windows Media Player version 11 and later has the ability to share your media files with other PCs running copies of Windows Media Player. A teensy icon in the notification area alerts you to the presence of other PCs sharing their Windows Media Player libraries.

✦ Only those folders you elect to share are available for others to use on the network. There's also a level of security provided by password protection as well as read-only access. See Chapter 3 for the details.

✦ Even when you have only one computer and a broadband modem, you technically have a network set up. Don't deny it! Embrace it!

Discovering network hardware

In the beginning, there was the wire. And it was good. But communications doesn't live by wires alone.

To make the network work, you need some basic hardware components. Nothing is too outrageously expensive, but some things have outrageous names attached to them. Knowing what the names refer to is important to understanding the big network picture:

NIC: The first part of the network dwells inside your PC, either as part of the motherboard's circuitry or an expansion card. It's a *NIC,* or "nick." NIC stands for Network Interface Card, though I've also seen it defined as Network Information Card. Regardless, just say "NIC" and you'll be fine.

The NIC most likely does some technical and confusing things that I don't bother describing here. It's controlled by Windows and a special NIC software driver. But most importantly, the NIC is where you plug in the network cable.

Ethernet cable: Named after the protocol for networking, a cable is required in order to connect your PC to other PCs on the network. That standard is referred to as *Ethernet cable*, but it has a technical name: *CAT 5,* for Category 5, not kitty cat 5.

Every computer on the network must have a NIC with an Ethernet cable attached. That cable doesn't go to other computers (they aren't daisy-chained, which was a popular but older way to network PCs). Instead, the computers and their Ethernet cables all tether directly to a central location, or *hub*. On a typical PC network, that hub is a *router*.

Router. The router not only manages traffic on your network, it also coordinates larger network traffic, such as information coming in from and going out to the Internet. Most routers also have the smarts to deal with USB devices, like printers and hard drives.

The router is a big deal in your computer network. Therefore, specific information on routers is covered in the later section "You Say Rooter, I Say Router."

Broadband modem: The final piece of the network for most common setups is a broadband modem. It communicates with the router, so really it's just another shared resource on the network. The modem is your local-area network's gateway to the Internet, which is the world's computer network.

When it comes to the NIC and router, there's a speed issue. Ethernet can run at speeds of 10Mbps (megabits per second), 100Mbps, or 1Gbps (gigabits per second). The faster, the better.

Only older, antique Ethernet networks ran at 10Mbps. Today, 100Mbps is common, though the 1Gbps, or *Gigabit Ethernet,* connections are preferred. But if you want to have a network that runs at that speed, the NIC and router and any additional network devices must all be Gigabit Ethernet.

A typical small-office or home-office network setup is shown in Figure 1-1. As shown in the figure, the center of the operation is the router. It connects to three computer systems: two desktops, and one laptop PC.

Assume that each PC has a NIC (not shown in the figure). The cable goes from the PC to the router.

The router has some USB ports, and Figure 1-1 illustrates the router connected to a printer and hard drive.

The router is also connected to a broadband modem. As on PCs, the modem is connected to the router by using an Ethernet cable. The modem is also plugged into a phone line or cable line or connected to a satellite dish. That's how the modem talks with the Internet.

Not shown in Figure 1-1 is the myriad of power supply cables. Routers and cable modems, plus printers and hard drives, all require power. That makes for a heck of a mess.

Figure 1-1:
A primitive
type of
local-area
network.

✦ Your computer network is a *LAN*, or local-area network.

✦ This LAN is your LAN, this LAN is my LAN.

✦ Stand by your LAN.

✦ Know your network! Know what the parts are called. Know where to connect the cables at each end. Check the router connections. The more you know how your network looks now, when it's working, the better you can fix it later, when it's not working.

✦ The NIC's presence is evident by the networking cable jack on the back of your computer or the side of a laptop. The jack is often called an *RJ-45*, though that's not its official designation.

✦ Even wireless networking uses a NIC. In that case, you don't plug anything in the NIC as it sends and receives its information wirelessly. That's why they named it a "wireless" NIC.

✦ Another way to create a network is to use a simple device called a *hub*. It's basically a box into which you plug Ethernet cables so that your computers can chat with each other. Hubs are electronically stupid, so I don't recommend getting a hub.

✦ Hub is also a generic term applied to any location where network information is coordinated — for example, a wireless hub, which is really a router.

✦ One step up from a hub (and a step down from the router) is the switch. Switches are a bit better at managing network traffic and are often used to expand the number of Ethernet ports available on a network, as covered elsewhere in this chapter.

+ The Ethernet cable features the same connections on either end. There's no way to plug the cable in backward.

+ Like Penn & Teller, networking cable is also referred to as *twisted pair.* That provides for the cable's two-way communications and also explains how you cannot plug in an Ethernet cable backward. But it doesn't explain why an Ethernet cable is incapable of magic and is bereft of sardonic wit.

+ It doesn't matter where you plug an Ethernet cable into the hub, switch, or router. Some older hubs, however, may have a special *uplink* connector, which is used to connect that hub to another hub or switch. See the section "Adding more Ethernet ports to the router," later in this chapter

+ Both the NIC and the hub/switch/router have status lights that blink when data is being transmitted over the network. These lights flicker — sometimes often. It's nothing bad.

+ Gigabit Ethernet gizmos are often labeled *GbE* or sometimes *1 GigE.*

+ It's possible to connect a broadband modem directly to your PC's NIC. Don't. I could list several reasons why such a configuration is a Bad Thing, but the number-one reason is security: Your PC would be wide open to Internet attack in such a setup.

+ Creating and configuring your own home or small-office network is easy. You can even buy starter kits. I recommend hiding the cables as best you can. Try to avoid situations where someone can trip over them or they become snarled in a viper nest of other cables and power cords.

+ If you plan to run network cable through the ceiling or through ducts, get *planar* cable, which is designed for such purposes.

+ This is the last bullet point.

Putting a printer on the network

A network printer is any printer "up for grabs" on the network. Officially, it's a *shared* printer. That can be a printer connected to a PC on the network, where the computer operator has elected to share that printer, making it available for anyone else on the network to use. Or, it can be a printer directly connected to the network.

It might seem odd to have a printer out there, all by its lonesome, connected to the Internet. It happens. There are two ways it can happen.

First, you can add a USB printer directly to the network's router, if the router features a USB connection. After connecting the printer, access the router's control program to complete its setup. See the section "Configuring the router," later in this chapter, for information on accessing the router's control program.

The IEEE 1394 network connection

The IEEE 1394 interface, also known as *FireWire* or *iLink*, is used primarily to connect high-speed devices to your computer. The most popular devices are digital video cameras, though there are also high-speed scanners and external IEEE 1394 drives. Although IEEE 1394 is common on Macintosh computers, it remains an oddity on most PCs. It's seldom found on PC laptops.

As a high-speed communications device, the IEEE 1394 interface can also be used for networking. When you have two PCs with IEEE 1394 connectors, and as long as they're not far apart, you can cable them together and

configure the two as a tiny network. Because the IEEE 1394 interface runs at 400Mbps (or even 800Mbps), it's a faster connection than 100Mbps Ethernet.

Sadly, the IEEE 1394 network connection isn't ideal. Besides being able to connect only two PCs at a time, Microsoft dropped IEEE1394 networking abilities from Windows Vista. You can still configure an IEEE 1394 network in Windows XP, and you may see an icon representing the IEEE 1394 "network" adapter in the Network Connections window. My advice is to forego IEEE 1394 as a serious alternative to the standard Ethernet network.

Second, you can add a printer directly to the network, if the printer has an Ethernet port. Simply connect the printer to the network and turn it on. Sadly, you must use Windows to hunt for the printer before you can use it on your PC. I call it a manual network connection.

After the printer is turned on and connected to the network, you can direct your PC to use the printer by following these steps in Windows Vista:

1. **Open the Control Panel's Printers icon.**

2. **Click the Add a Printer toolbar button.**

   The Add Printer window appears.

3. **Choose the option Add a Network, Wireless or Bluetooth Printer.**

4. **Rather than wait for the inevitable, choose the option The Printer That I Want Isn't Listed.**

5. **Ensure that the option Add a Printer Using a TCP/IP Address or Hostname is selected.**

6. **Click the Next button.**

7. **Type the printer's IP Address into the Hostname or IP Address box.**

   You can often find the IP address by printing the printer's configuration; check the printer's documentation to find out how to use the printer's control panel to cough up its current configuration, including the IP address.

8. **(Optional) Enter the port name, if you know what it is.**

9. **Click the Next button.**

10. **Continue with the printer setup.**

   I have to be vague at this point because Windows may recognize the printer, in which case setup continues rather quickly. Otherwise, you need to choose the printer make and model from the list.

In Windows XP, follow these steps to set up a sole, lonely network printer:

1. **Open the Printers and Faxes icon in the Control Panel.**

2. **Choose Add a Printer.**

   The link is on the left side of the window.

3. **Click the Next button.**

4. **Choose the option A Network Printer or a Printer Attached to Another Computer, and click the Next button.**

5. **Choose the option Connect to This Printer, which is the second option.**

6. **Type the printer's IP address into the text box.**

   The IP address should be available from the printer, either on its control panel or by printing the printer's information sheet.

7. **Continue with the printer's setup.**

   At this point, the setup can change, depending on how Windows recognizes the printer. As long as contact is made with the printer over the network, you can figure out the rest of the steps.

When you're done setting up the printer, print a test page. It confirms that the printer is connected and working.

✦ There's no need to make the network printer your PC's *default* printer — unless it's Larry's printer and, well, we all remember how possessive he is.

✦ Obviously, there's no need to configure a network printer when it shows up automatically in the Printers window.

✦ If the printer is connected to the network by using one of those tiny printer server dongles, you probably need to configure the printer by using the software that came with the printer server dongle. That configuration program either allows the printer to be used on the network, on your PC, or it provides you with the IP address you can use for the steps in this section.

✦ You might also be able to get the printer's IP address from the router's configuration program. See the section "Configuring the router," later in this chapter, for information on accessing the configuration program. The printer's IP address is listed along with the IP addresses assigned to all devices connected to the router.

✦ The printer should set its IP address by using DHCP. You don't need to know what that means, but it's important to make that setting if you're given a choice.

✦ Network printers can also be added by plugging the printer directly into the network. As long as the printer features an Ethernet connection, you can plug it into the router directly. Such a printer may not show up immediately.

Adding a network hard drive

As with network printers, putting a hard drive up for grabs on the network is done primarily by sharing folders on your computer with other computers on the network. But it's possible to connect a hard drive directly to the network — a hard drive that doesn't have a computer attached. That can happen in one of two ways.

First, you can connect an external USB hard drive to a router that features USB ports. Plug the hard drive into the wall and then connect it to the router. The hard drive may be instantly recognized, or it might require additional configuration. See the section "Configuring the router," later in this chapter, for information on accessing a router's configuration program.

The second method to connect a hard drive is directly. This method works only when the hard drive features its own Ethernet port: Simply plug the hard drive into its power supply, plug the hard drive into the router with an Ethernet cable, and you're done. The hard drive appears in the Network window along with other drives shared on the network.

✦ See Chapter 2 for more information on where you can view and access network hard drives in Windows.

✦ In Windows XP, networked hard drives appear in the My Network Places window.

✦ Not all external hard drives feature an Ethernet port. None of the cheap ones does.

You Say Rooter, I Say Router

The heart in your computer network's circulatory system is the *router*. Yes, you need a router. Especially when you plan to use a broadband modem, a router is a must-have item. This section explains how the router fits into your networking picture and how to deal with minor router despair.

✦ Router rhymes with "powder."

✦ Don't say "rooter" unless you live in the U.K.

✦ In Australia or Canada, either pronunciation is acceptable: "rooter" or "router."

Understanding the router

If you've been around high-speed Internet or have had a small network installed at your home or office for a while, you know that you have a router, but you probably don't know what the router does or why it's needed. In a normal *For Dummies* book, I'd simply say "Live with it," but this isn't a normal *For Dummies* book.

Technically, what you have in your home or office (refer to Figure 1-1) is a *gateway,* not a router. It's a tiny computer that manages the local network traffic, sending bits and bytes between any computers connected. It also may manage a hard drive or printer.

On the other end, the router acts as your network's gateway, presenting all local network traffic to the Internet as a single front. It further provides defense against probing attacks from the Internet, mostly by ignoring them with a firewall.

Do you need a router? Theoretically, no: You can hook up your PC directly to the broadband modem and be online. In such a configuration, you would need an extremely robust software firewall and a lot of Internet security software. Even so, the setup may not work because some broadband modems require a router to be present or else they cannot communicate. Regardless, though you may not need a router, you *want* one.

✦ There are wired routers and wireless routers. There are also combination wired/wireless routers. Indeed, most wireless routers also sport a standard Ethernet cable connection.

✦ See Book IV, Chapter 4 for more information on firewalls.

Connecting the router

Though it be a technical beast, a router isn't that difficult to set up. In fact, after it's set up, you rarely, if ever, have to reconfigure or mess with the router. They're solid little gizmos.

On the hardware side, the router features connections on its rump, as shown in Figure 1-2. Defer to the directions that came with the router for specifics on how things are set up, but generally the Ethernet cables from your PCs hook into the LAN connectors. A single connector is designated for the broadband modem, which also plugs into the router using an Ethernet cable.

Figure 1-2: Connectors on a typical router.

Some routers have On-Off switches, but mostly you just plug the thing into the wall socket to turn it on. There's no need to turn off the router unless you're troubleshooting the network or you plan on not using the network for an extended period; most folks leave their broadband modems and routers on all the time.

One important item to find on the router is its reset switch. It's probably located on the back of the router (refer to Figure 1-2). The reset switch is most likely recessed. See the later section "Resetting the router" to find out how and when to use the reset switch.

The front of the router is less interesting than the back. The front features a few lamps that flicker as traffic flows into and out of the router, plus perhaps a status light or three. Ho-hum.

✦ You must properly plug the modem's cable into the router. Don't connect the modem into any Ethernet plug other than the one designated for the modem or for the Internet.

✦ Wireless routers have similar connectors to the wired router (refer to Figure 1-2), with the addition of one or more antennas.

✦ Not all routers feature the connections shown in Figure 1-2. Some lack the USB connectors. That's okay: It's possible to connect a printer or hard drive to the router by using an Ethernet cable, as discussed later in this chapter.

✦ Plug the modem into the Internet or Modem jack on the router.

Configuring the router

Routers, like all computer gizmos, have both hardware and software setup. After connecting the router, the next step is to configure it. Primarily, and for security reasons, the most important thing is to set an administrator password for the router.

You connect to the router by using Internet Explorer (or your favorite alternative Web browser). Follow these general steps:

1. Connect the router.

Refer to the preceding section for tips on the hardware connection.

2. Start up Internet Explorer or your favorite alternative Web browser.

The computer you're using must be connected to the router.

3. Type the router's address into the Web browser's address bar.

The address looks something like `http://192.168.0.1` or possibly `http://10.0.0.1`. The quick-start guide for the router gives you the proper address.

When you're successful, you see the router's login screen, similar to the one shown in Figure 1-3.

If you cannot connect to the router, restart your PC and try again.

4. If necessary, log in to the router.

You may have the preset administrator's password supplied in the documentation, or maybe no password is set yet.

After you're "in" the router, you continue to use your Web browser to set various options. The two most important are setting the administrator's password and enabling the firewall.

5. Change the router's administrator password.

Please O please, pick a nice, strong password. Especially for a wireless router, you don't want to pick something obvious or easy that the hackers or neighborhood kids will figure out.

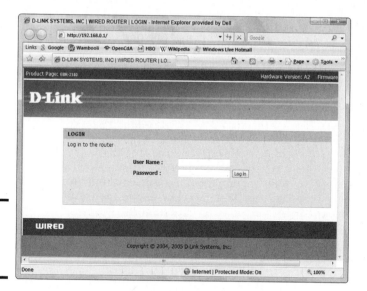

Figure 1-3:
A router's
login
screen.

6. **Ensure that the router's firewall is active.**

It most likely is active, but check just in case. Use the router's
Web-based interface in your PC's Web browser to navigate to the
firewall option screen.

7. **When you're done, close the Web browser window.**

You may see a logout option; if so, log out before you close the window.

The router remembers its settings, so there's no need to reconfigure it after
a power outage. After it's set up, you'll probably never need to mess with it
again.

And now, the shortcut. There's a quick way to connect to your router, by
skipping Steps 1 through 3 in the preceding set of steps, but the trick works
only in Windows Vista:

1. **Open the Network window.**

You can choose Network from the Start menu or from the Address bar in
any Windows Explorer window.

2. **Double-click to open the router's icon in the Network window.**

By opening the router's icon in the Network window, you immediately open
a Web browser window where you can log in and begin messing with the
router.

- ✦ Write down the router's password! Do not rely on it being in a computer.

- ✦ You can access the router from any computer on the network — if you log in with the proper password.

- ✦ If you forget the password, you can reset the router. See the next section.

Resetting the router

Perhaps the best general solution for a stupid router is to reset it. To do so, stick a bent paper clip into the Reset hole, using Figure 1-2 as your guide. Press and hold the paper clip. Release. That should restart the router, erasing its settings and placing it into the condition it was in when you first set things up.

After resetting it, you need to set the router's administrator password and review other settings, such as the firewall.

- ✦ Sometimes, you need to have the router turned on for it to reset, and sometimes the reset works whether the router is on or off.

- ✦ You might also consider restarting the entire network to fix a router issue. See the section "Restarting the entire network," later in this chapter.

Pinging the router

The first test you need to make for a router is to *ping* it, or send it a signal that proves not only that the router is there but also that your computer is connected to the router and that all communications are taking place in a friendly manner.

To send the router a friendly ping, follow these steps:

1. **From the Start menu, choose All Programs⇨Accessories⇨Command Prompt.**

A Command Prompt window opens.

2. **To discover the router's address, type** ipconfig **and press Enter.**

The ipconfig command coughs up some information about your PC's current network configuration. You see information that includes something like this:

```
IPv4 Address. . . . . . . . . . . . : 192.168.0.103
Subnet Mask . . . . . . . . . . . : 255.255.255.0
Default Gateway . . . . . . . . . : 192.168.0.1
```

The *IPv4 address* is your PC's IP address on the local network. That address is assigned by the router using something called DHCP, discussed in Chapter 2.

The *subnet mask* is a type of filter that helps PCs on the network better see each other. (And I'm sticking with that explanation for now.)

The *default gateway* is the IP address of the router. Make a note of it.

If you see the message media disconnected, check both ends of the Ethernet cable.

3. **Type the command** ping, **a space, and then the IP address of the router, or default gateway; press Enter.**

   For example, using the output shown in Step 2, the command is

   ```
   ping 192.168.0.1
   ```

   After pressing the Enter key, the ping command attempts to send four packets of information to the router, which should echo those results to you. You see something like this:

   ```
   Pinging 192.168.0.1 with 32 bytes of data:
   Reply from 192.168.0.1: bytes=32 time<1ms TTL=127
   Reply from 192.168.0.1: bytes=32 time<1ms TTL=127
   Reply from 192.168.0.1: bytes=32 time<1ms TTL=127
   Reply from 192.168.0.1: bytes=32 time<1ms TTL=127

   Ping statistics for 192.168.0.1:
       Packets: Sent = 4, Received = 4, Lost = 0 (0%
       loss),
   Approximate round trip times in milli-seconds:
       Minimum = 0ms, Maximum = 0ms, Average = 0ms
   ```

   The information is technical, but not complex. The key is that you want to see a mess of data, as shown in the previous example. When you see the text Destination host unreachable or Request timed out, that's when the PC has trouble communicating with the router.

4. **Type** exit **and press Enter to close the Command Prompt window.**

Are there problems? There may not look like any, but first confirm that the gateway address given in Step 2 is the same as the router's address. If not, the PC is most likely just pinging itself in Step 3. That works, but it's not the same as communicating with the router.

When the router is unreachable, you probably need to turn off the router and then turn it on again. Because most routers lack a Power button, that means you need to unplug it and then plug it back in. After the power is back on, try repeating these steps to see whether you can ping the router.

If the router remains unreachable, you need to restart the entire network, as described in the section "Restarting the entire network," later in this chapter.

✦ Yes, routers can go bad. I've seen a few of them spoil in my day. The last router I had died and needed to be replaced. Fortunately, a replacement router won't break you financially. Routers are cheap.

✦ Well, *gateways* are cheap. The real routers, used by the big boys, are *not* cheap.

✦ The `ipconfig` command's output in Windows Vista lists some `Tunnel adapter` information. Feel free to ignore it.

✦ The router is really a *gateway*, which is why the results of the `ipconfig` command list its address as Default Gateway.

✦ IP stands for Internet Protocol. See Chapter 2 for more information on the IP address.

✦ See Book IV, Chapter 1 for more information on using the `ping` command.

Adding more Ethernet ports to the router

Soon you may discover that the router has run out of Ethernet ports. There's your computer, another computer, perhaps a network hard drive, a printer, and then — oops! You're out of Ethernet sockets.

The solution is to add more Ethernet sockets. How you do that is to buy something called a *switch* which allows you to plug in more Ethernet cables, and attach that switch to the router. An illustration of the result is shown in Figure 1-4.

The operation is simple: First, buy a switch that matches the speed of the router and your PC's NIC cards. For example, if they're 1-gigabit Ethernet cards, buy a 1-gigabit Ethernet switch.

Second, plug in the switch. All switches need a power supply.

Third, connect the switch to the router. Some switches have a special connector for this task, labeled an Uplink connector. Quite a few switches, however, are "smart switches" that feature automatic uplink abilities. That means you can connect them to the router by using any available Ethernet socket.

Finally, plug the Ethernet cables from the various PCs on the network into the switch.

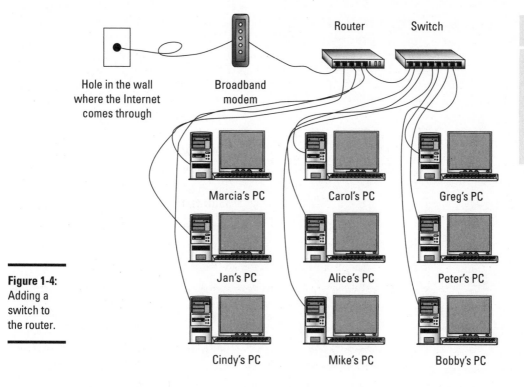

Figure 1-4:
Adding a
switch to
the router.

The result is that you can connect all the network gizmos you need to connect.

✦ Don't worry about order or sequence or anything; the switch is smart, but the router is smarter. All computers connected to either the router or the switch are on the same network.

✦ If the switch loses power, the computers connected to the switch lose their network connections.

✦ Granted, not everyone will have all the computers illustrated in Figure 1-4. But there's a possibility that you'll run out of Ethernet ports on your router.

✦ Buy a switch with many more Ethernet ports than you need. To drive this point home, I can tell you that I have an 8-port Fast Ethernet switch for sale right now on eBay. If I can sell it, it will offset the cost of the 16-port Fast Ethernet switch I just bought recently.

✦ Refer to the section "Restarting the entire network," later in this chapter, for information on getting a stubborn switch to work.

General Network Troubleshooting

Most of the network troubleshooting you do involves configuring a PC to talk with the network. That's a software duty, so those issues are covered in Chapter 2 of this minibook. Everything else is most likely a hardware networking problem. Those issues are addressed in this section.

Inspecting the NIC

Whether old St. NIC is part of your PC's motherboard circuitry or attached as an expansion card, you can sneak a peek at its status by using the Device Manager.

In Windows Vista, follow these steps to check on the NIC's hardware:

1. **Open the Device Manager icon in the Control Panel.**

2. **Type the administrator's password or click the Continue button.**

3. **Click the [+] plus sign by the Network Adapters item to expand that area and view all network adapters installed on your PC.**

   There's most likely only one.

4. **Double-click the Network Adapter entry to display your PC's network adapter's Properties dialog box.**

   The General tab in the Properties dialog box lists the device status. Any problems detected by Windows appear in that message box. Otherwise, the message reads, "This device is working properly."

5. **Click the Resources tab in the Properties dialog box.**

6. **Check the Conflicting Device List.**

   You should see no conflicts listed. If not, the source of the conflicts must be resolved. Generally, it would mean removing whatever other device is conflicting with the NIC or reconfiguring that device. See the sidebar "Device conflicts," later in this chapter, for details.

7. **Click OK to close the Properties dialog box.**

8. **Close the Device Manager window as well as the Control Panel.**

Follow these steps to check on the NIC's hardware in your Windows XP computer:

1. **Press Win+Break to quickly summon the System Properties dialog box.**

2. **Click the Hardware tab.**

3. **Click the Device Manager button.**

   The Device Manager window appears.

4. **Expand the Network Adapters area by clicking the [+] plus sign icon.**

   You see a list of all network adapters installed in your PC.

5. **Double-click a network adapter entry.**

   The adapter's Properties dialog box appears. On the General tab, you see the device status. It should say, "This device is working properly." If not, any specific problems are noted.

6. **Click the Resources tab.**

7. **Review the Conflicting Device List.**

   No conflicts should be listed. When they are, you need to resolve them by looking at the source of the conflict. Refer to the sidebar "Device conflicts" for information.

8. **Click the OK button to close the Properties dialog box.**

9. **Close the Device Manager and the Control Panel windows.**

The first solution for fixing a bad NIC is first to view the suggestions listed in the Properties dialog box. When those suggestions aren't helpful, one alternative is to use another NIC.

If you have a NIC on an expansion card, simply remove the old one and install a new one. See Book I, Chapter 8 for information on replacing expansion cards.

When the NIC is on the motherboard, your alternative is simply to install a second NIC as an expansion card.

For a laptop, get a USB NIC, either wired or wireless, when the laptop's NIC fails.

✦ You will probably know when the NIC isn't working properly before you even open its Properties dialog box. That's because bum devices are flagged with a yellow icon in the Device Manager.

✦ When you're having network adapter problems in Windows XP, click the Troubleshoot button (after Step 5) to run the NIC Troubleshooter.

✦ If your PC came with a NIC diagnostic tool, using it, obviously, would be a better option for checking on the NIC as well as testing the NIC's condition. Check the Start button's All Programs menu. Look for a folder (submenu) specific to the NIC manufacturer, such as Intel, Netlink, or Linksys.

✦ Yes, it's possible to have multiple network adapters in a PC. For example, a laptop computer would have both wired and wireless NICs. When you have multiple NICs, you can repeat the steps in this section to review any problems or conflicts with each of the adapters.

✦ To disable a NIC, open its Properties dialog box by following the directions listed in this section. In Windows Vista, use the Disable button on the Driver tab; in Windows XP, choose Disable from the drop-down menu at the bottom of the General tab. By disabling the device, you ensure that Windows doesn't use it and instead uses another NIC that functions properly.

Upgrading the NIC's driver

The software that controls the network hardware — specifically, the NIC — is a *driver*. Very rarely do you need to update this software. In fact, a routine or security update is included with the standard Windows Update, as described in Book II, Chapter 1.

To specifically update a NIC driver, obey these steps:

1. **Set a system restore point.**

   See Book II, Chapter 8 for more information.

2. **Follow the steps in the preceding section to open the PC's NIC Properties dialog box.**

   There are separate sets of directions for Windows Vista and Windows XP.

3. **In the NIC Properties dialog box, click the Driver tab.**

4. **Click the Update Driver button.**

5. **Follow the directions on-screen to search the Internet, or use the Windows Update service to find the best or most current driver.**

6. **In Windows XP, choose to install the software automatically.**

   What happens next depends on whether you need a new driver.

   If the driver is up-to-date, you see a message explaining as much. Otherwise, a newer driver is downloaded from the Internet and installed on your PC.

7. **Close the NIC Properties dialog box as well as any other open windows when you're done.**

Device conflicts

Device conflicts arose more often in earlier PCs because of their limited expansion options. A network adapter, for example, had to be assigned memory space as well as something called an IRQ. The PC has a limited number of IRQs. To fix the conflict, you had to re-assign the IRQ of the conflicting device, which involved some hardware marksmanship. On today's PCs, such hardware conflicts are rare.

To deal with a hardware conflict, you must reset the IRQ on one of the two conflicting devices. Or, you can remove one of the devices. My suggestion is to see which devices can be replaced by a comparable USB device. USB devices don't have the conflicts that IRQ gizmos do.

It might be necessary to restart your computer; do so if prompted.

✦ When the new driver doesn't fix the problem, my next suggestion is to replace the NIC.

✦ If problems occur, restore the system: Restart the computer, and, if you can, run System Restore and choose the most recent restore point.

✦ Updating the NIC driver may solve some problems. But mostly, when you have NIC problems, you should do a hardware analysis as described in the preceding section.

Disconnecting from the network

You can disconnect from the network in a hardware or software fashion.

Hardware-wise, simply unplug the Ethernet cable from the PC. Poof — the Internet is gone. A small warning bubble may appear in the notification area, as shown in Figure 1-5. That's also your visual clue that the network has connection issues.

Figure 1-5:
A dis-
connected
cable!

> ⓘ **Local Area Connection** ✕
> A network cable is unplugged.

The solution to the problem is to reconnect the cable. Check both ends.

Normally, an Ethernet cable shouldn't become accidentally unplugged. When it does, it means that the cable's end is broken. Get a replacement.

Reconnecting to the network is simple: Plug the Ethernet cable back into the PC. There's nothing else you need to do. Windows instantly recognizes the network connection, as shown in Figure 1-6.

Figure 1-6:
A recon-
nected
cable!

> ⓘ **Local Area Connection is now connected** ⊠
> Speed: 100.0 Mbps

Cables can also go bad, in which case the cable may appear to be plugged in but no signal is coming through the cable. In that case, check the lights on the NIC or router. The lights should routinely blink as network traffic is sent and received. When the light isn't on or turns yellow rather than green, it could indicate a connection problem. Replace the cable.

✦ You can also disconnect the PC's Ethernet cable from the router (or switch). I don't recommend that approach, however; unless you're using a different-colored Ethernet cable for each PC, it's difficult to determine exactly what you're disconnecting.

✦ Software-wise, you can disconnect from the Internet by using Windows. See Chapter 2 for the details.

✦ It's more common to disconnect from a wireless network than from a wired network. The common way to do that on a laptop is simply to shut the laptop's lid, but see Chapter 4 for more wireless information.

Resetting the broadband modem

Occasionally, you may lose your connection to the Internet. The local network is okay: You can still access network printers and hard drives just fine. But the Internet is unreachable.

The first things to check are the lights on the modem: Is the modem getting a signal? If not, the problem is with your Internet service provider (ISP).

Next, turn the modem off and then on again. By *cycling* the modem's power in this way, you can often wake it up and it reconnects to the Internet. (An e-mail pal of mine who works for an ISP's tech-support center says that the power cycling solution fixes about 90 percent of broadband modem problems.)

When turning the modem off and on doesn't work, you have my permission to phone up your ISP for tech support.

Restarting the entire network

The ultimate network fix is to restart the entire network. It's a simple thing to do — not a regular activity or routine maintenance — but a general cure-all for many network ills. The procedure works like this:

1. **Turn everything off.**

   Computers. Printers. Hard drives. Modems. Switches. Routers. Hubs. If it's connected to the network, you turn it off.

2. **Turn on the broadband modem and wait for it to start properly.**

   It takes a few moments for the modem to find a signal and chat it up with the Internet. When all the modem's status lights are on and the modem is happy, you can move on to the next step.

3. **Turn on the router.**

   Again, wait for the router to start up and get happy.

4. **If you have a switch connected to the router (refer to Figure 1-4), turn it on next.**

5. **Turn on a computer connected to the network.**

   Let the computer start up as normal. Observe network errors, if any.

6. **Log in to the computer and connect to the Internet.**

   When you can get on the Internet, the network is up and working properly. The network has been reset.

7. **Repeat Steps 5 and 6 for each computer on the network.**

8. **Start up any network printers or hard drives.**

Throughout these steps, observe any problems. When you find a problem, you find the problem hardware. Replace that hardware.

For example, I had a bum switch on my office network. Only by restarting the entire network did I locate the bad switch and replace it.

Working through these steps is necessary only when you're having trouble with the network. There's no need to restart your network every few months or so. Yes, some people do so anyway. If it makes you feel better about the network, restart it every few months or so. Otherwise, if the network is behaving normally, there's no need to restart it.

✦ There's no need to unplug the Ethernet cables when you restart the net-work. However, if a problem occurs with a specific device, disconnect it so that the rest of the network can operate properly.

✦ If the network remains unreachable, the problem is with one of the components — most likely, the router. If you still cannot ping the router after restarting the network, replace the router.

Chapter 2: The Soft Side of Networking

In This Chapter

✔ Searching out network places in Windows

✔ Determining your PC's IP address

✔ Fixing IP address troubles

✔ Working with DHCP

✔ Diagnosing and repairing the network

✔ Disconnecting the network

Your computer network is not the cables or blinky-light things or anything you can pick up and angrily throw out a window. Network hardware is no more a network than an MP3 player is music. Although the network hardware makes the network possible, networking itself takes place only when there's software to control things. The software side of networking troubleshooting is covered in this chapter.

Where Is the Network?

The path to fixing the computer network begins with a click or two of the mouse. Sounds like fun, right? But where exactly do you click the mouse? Before you set out on the network troubleshooting journey, you need a map. The map is provided in this section.

Finding network locations in Windows Vista

There are multiple places in Windows Vista where you can dig up network information. Here are the various windows, wizards, and places with which to concern yourself:

✦ Connect to a Network

✦ Manage Network Connections

✦ Network

✦ Network and Sharing Center

✦ Network Map

✦ Notification area

✦ Network Connections

✦ System

Each of these locations has something to do with networking on your PC — specifically, the software side of networking. You should know how to open each window and recognize what can be done in each one in regard to troubleshooting the network.

Networking and Sharing Center window

Of the horde of networking places, the most central location is the Network and Sharing Center, shown in Figure 2-1. From that window, you can open just about any other networking location in Windows.

Open the computer window   Open a Web browser

Nifty links   Open the network window

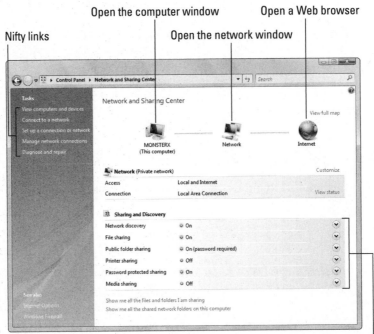

Figure 2-1:
The
Network
and Sharing
Center
window.

Local network settings

 To get to the Network and Sharing Center window, open the Network and Sharing Center icon in the Control Panel.

The list of tasks on the left side of the window lead you to other, exciting networking locations in Windows. The Sharing and Discovery area near the bottom of the window controls various peer-to-peer networking features.

✦ A network disconnection is indicated in the Network and Sharing Center window by a red X appearing over the lines between your computer and the Network icon, or between the Network icon and the Internet. When you click that red X, a network troubleshooter runs to help diagnose the problem.

✦ By clicking the Customize link (on the right side of the Network and Sharing Center window), you can give your local-area network a name other than Network.

✦ You can also display the Network and Sharing Center window by clicking the Network and Sharing Center toolbar button in the Network window.

System window

Though it's not listed on the fast track of networking tasks in the Network and Sharing Center window (refer to Figure 2-1), the System window contains a few key items of interest for creating a small peer-to-peer network. Primarily, that window is where you specify the computer and network names.

To visit the System window, open the System icon in the Control Panel. The area of concern with regard to networking is found in the Computer Name, Domain, and Workgroup Settings area, as shown in Figure 2-2.

Figure 2-2: Networky things in the System window.

You change the items in the Computer Name, Domain, and Workgroup Settings area by clicking the Change Settings link on the right side of the window. For more details, refer to Chapter 3.

Quickly summon the System window by pressing the Win+Break keyboard shortcut.

Network window

Honestly, the Network window has little to do with managing the network. The window is named correctly, but rather than show you network controls on your computer, the Network window displays a list of computers and network devices available *on* the network, as shown in Figure 2-3.

Figure 2-3:
The
Network
window.

To open the Network window, choose Network from the Start menu, open the Network icon on the desktop, or choose Network from the drop-down Address Bar list in any Windows Explorer window. You can also type **Network** on the Address Bar to visit the Network window.

Not much network hardware troubleshooting gets done in the Network window, but it does help you "see" other computers in a peer-to-peer work-group. Troubleshooting the workgroup, such as when computers should shoot up in the window but don't, is covered in Chapter 4.

✦ You can click the Network and Sharing Center button on the Network window's toolbar to get to the Network and Sharing Center's window.

✦ You can log in to the router by opening its icon in the Network window.

✦ A variation on the Network Window is the Network Map, covered in the next section.

✦ If I had my choice, I'd rename the Network window to Local Network and then rename the Network and Sharing Center window to Networking. Oh, I know: It's all about *me*. . . .

Network Map

A curious invention provided with Windows Vista is the Network Map window, shown in Figure 2-4. It provides a detailed look at how Windows assumes that the network is physically laid out. Yeah, it's a guess, but it's interesting to look at.

Figure 2-4:
The
Network
Map
window.

To view the Network Map window, open the Network and Sharing Center window and click the link View Full Map (refer to Figure 2-1).

The Network Map window may not place all computers on the network into the map. In Figure 2-4, the computer Dugan is in Sleep mode, and the NetDriveAlpha network hard drive is connected directly to the network.

Windows XP computers can appear in the map, but only when they're running special software that makes them visible in the map. The software is Link Layer Topology Discovery (LLTD), and it can be installed on your Windows XP PC by grabbing the LLTD update on the Windows support Web site:

```
http://support.microsoft.com/kb/922120
```

Click the Download link in the middle of this Web page to install LLTD. Having the update installed doesn't do anything else for the Windows XP computer other than make it show up in a Windows Vista Network Map window.

✦ The map doesn't show a computer on the network unless the Network Discovery item is turned on. See Chapter 3 for details.

✦ The map isn't visible when you're using a public network, such as in a cybercafé.

✦ Software firewalls may also prevent a PC from appearing on the map.

✦ PCs running antique versions of Windows (earlier than Windows XP or Windows 2000) don't show up on the map.

✦ Figure 2-4 shows my PCs connected to a switch and then to the router, which is properly labeled Gateway in the Network Map window. I use a switch because the router has only four Ethernet ports and I have more than four PCs or devices connected.

Notification area

Nestled among the teeny icons that pock the notification area (or taskbar, on the far right side) is an infinitesimal icon representing the local network. When the network is on and connected to the Internet, it appears as shown in Figure 2-5.

Figure 2-5:
The Network icon in the notification area.

Pointing the mouse at the Network icon in the notification area displays a brief pop-up window explaining the current connection status. Clicking the Network icon displays a larger pop-up (refer to Figure 2-5). Right-clicking the icon displays a pop-up menu, from which you can choose a host of networking options.

Mostly, the Network icon shows you that the network is running, and the globe part of the icon means that the local network is connected to the Internet.

To ensure that the Network icon shows up in the notification area, follow these steps:

1. **Open the Taskbar and Start Menu icon in the Control Panel.**

The Taskbar and Start Menu Properties dialog box appears.

   2. **Click the Notification Area tab.**

   3. **Ensure that a check mark appears by the Network item.**

   4. **Click OK.**

The Network icon always shows up in the notification area, even when other
icons may be hidden.

Network Connections window

The most technical place to visit in the Network Land of Wonder is the
Network Connections window, shown in Figure 2-6. The window lists each
network adapter connected to your PC, as well as dialup adapters you may
have, such as the one shown in the figure (which is a laptop PC).

Figure 2-6:
Network
connections
are listed
here.

To view the Network Connections window, choose the link Manage Network
Connections from the list of tasks in the Network and Sharing Center window
(refer to Figure 2-1).

Immediately, the Network Connections window alerts you to the presence of
a disconnected network (refer to Figure 2-6). It even mentions the cause as
"cable unplugged." Very tope.

By opening a connection icon, you can check the connection specifically.

Connect to a Network Wizard

Windows is designed to instantly recognize a network anytime you plug an Ethernet cable into the PC. Well, there are details to be attended to, which are covered in Chapter 3. But you can't connect to all networks by plugging in a cable. Those other networks require the Connect to Network Wizard.

To see the Connect to Network Wizard, choose Connect To from the Start menu. You can also choose the link Connect to a Network, found on the left side of the Network and Sharing Center Window (refer to Figure 2-1).

The Connect to Network window lists available dialup connections as well as various wireless networks available to the computer. It doesn't help you set up a network. That's done in the Setup Network Connections Wizard, covered in the next section.

Setup Network Connections Wizard

Yes, Windows Vista has *another* location for networking nonsense. It's the Set Up a Connection or Network window, shown in Figure 2-7. The window is the first step in a wizard that lets you connect to the Internet, a wireless network, a virtual private network (VPN), or any other computer with a modem.

Figure 2-7:
The Set Up a Connection or Network window.

To access the Set Up a Connection or Network window, choose the link labeled Set Up a Connection or Network from the left side of the Network and Sharing Center window (refer to Figure 2-1). A description of working through the steps to set up a peer-to-peer network is offered in Chapter 3.

Finding network locations in Windows XP

If you thought that Windows XP kept all its networking settings and information in only two locations, you're woefully wrong. Windows XP features a multitude of windows, dialog boxes, and wizards for gathering and setting network information. Here's the list:

✦ My Network Places

✦ Network Connection Properties dialog box

✦ Network Connections window

✦ Network Setup Wizard

✦ Notification area

✦ System Properties dialog box

Each of these locations has something to do with networking on your PC — specifically, the software side of networking. You should know how to open each window and what can be done in each window in regard to troubleshooting the network.

Network Connections window

The start of the Windows XP network software journey begins in the Network Connections window, shown in Figure 2-8. In that window, you find an icon for each network or dialup connection. If you have wired and wireless NICs on your PC or laptop, you see separate icons for those connections as well.

Figure 2-8:
The
Network
Connections
window.

To open the Network Connections window, open the Network Connections icon in the Control Panel. You can also display the Network Connections window by right-clicking the Network icon in the notification area. See the section "Notification area," later in this chapter.

Network Connection Properties dialog box

Specific network setup information is linked to the icons that appear in the Network Connections window. Each network connection features its own Properties dialog box, such as the one shown in Figure 2-9. That's the location where network settings are made regarding file sharing, as well as other configuration stuff.

Figure 2-9:
A network connec-
tion's
Properties
dialog box.

To see a connection's Properties dialog box, follow these steps:

1. **Open the Network Connections icon in the Control Panel.**

2. **Right-click a connection icon.**

3. **Choose Properties from the shortcut menu.**

There are different connection Properties dialog boxes for each network connection. On a laptop, for example, there are separate dialog boxes for the wired and wireless connections.

My Network Places

It's not really a network configuration place, but the My Network Places window shows you shared folders that are available to your computers on the network, as shown in Figure 2-10.

Figure 2-10:
The My Network Places window.

By choosing the link View Workgroup Computers, you can see the list of computers available on the peer-to-peer network, similar to the Windows Vista Network window (refer to Figure 2-3).

Various links on the left side of the My Network Places window display other important networking locations. For example, the link Set Up a Home or Small Office Network helps you configure a new network connection. The link Set Up a Wireless Network for a Home or Small Office gets you started with a wireless network.

Notification area

One of those tiny icons dwelling in the notification area is a networking icon. I call it the Network icon. It indicates the presence of a network connection, but that's about it.

What's magical about the Network icon in the notification area is that when you double-click the icon, you see the Local Area Connection Status dialog box, shown in Figure 2-11. That window also appears when you open a connection icon from the Network Connections window (refer to Figure 2-8).

Figure 2-11:
The
network's
Connection
window.

To ensure that the Network icon shows up in the notification area, follow these steps:

1. **Open the Network Connections icon in the Control Panel.**

2. **Right-click a network connection icon.**

3. **Choose Properties from the shortcut menu.**

4. **In the network connection's Properties dialog box, ensure that a check mark appears by the item Show Icon in Notification Area When Connected.**

5. **Click OK.**

6. **Close the Network Connections window.**

You need to repeat these steps for any extra connection icons appearing in the Network Connections window (refer to Figure 2-8). That way, a little Networking icon appears in the notification area for each of your network connections.

Network Setup Wizard

To connect to a wireless network, or to configure a wired network, you can use the Network Setup Wizard. It's accessed by opening the Network Setup Wizard icon in the Control Panel.

You work the Network Setup Wizard like you work any wizard: Answer questions and click the Next button as necessary. I don't find myself using it that much, but I'm mentioning it here because the Windows XP list is lame when compared to the Windows Vista list of networking places.

System Properties dialog box

Though it's called the System window, information is buried there that deals with networking names — specifically, your computer's network name as well as the name of the peer-to-peer workgroup you might join. That information is kept on the Computer Name tab in the System Properties dialog box, shown in Figure 2-12.

Figure 2-12:
The System
Properties
dialog box
and its
Computer
Name tab.

To view the system Properties dialog box, open the System icon in the Control Panel. The quick-and-dirty way to open the System Properties dialog box is to press the Win+Break key combination. Then click the Computer Name tab and you're there.

IP Gone Wrong

I've discovered that anyone even remotely exposed to the Internet or computer networking recognizes the acronym IP. They don't know what it is, and maybe not even what it stands for, but they recognize that it plays a role in computer networking. This section explains why IP is important to your computer network and what to do with IP problems.

Understanding the IP address

IP is an acronym for Internet Protocol. It's used to describe a set of methods and procedures for sending and receiving information. It's nerdy stuff, not worthy of your attention here.

What is worth noting is that IP is sometimes followed by the word *address*. In that context, an IP address is something assigned to every computer on an Ethernet network. Like the street address for your home, an IP address identifies network computers. It helps traffic flow between computers because each one has its own IP address.

An IP address is formatted as a series of four values separated by periods:

```
192.168.0.1
```

Each value ranges from 0 through 255.

Each period is just a period.

For your home or office network, the IP address is most likely assigned by the router using something called DHCP (covered later in this chapter). The router keeps track of each computer's NIC and maps an IP address to that NIC every time that computer joins the network. In the end, all computers have a unique IP address, and the world is safe for local networking.

✦ The IP address assigned to your PC on a network is a *local* address. Similar IP addresses are used on the Internet to identify domains and other resources. Those are Internet IP addresses, separate from your local address.

✦ The router is assigned an IP address by your Internet service provider (ISP). That IP address is an Internet IP address. It's shared by all PCs on your network.

✦ Local IP addresses start with `192.168` and `10.0`.

✦ The IP addresses discussed in this section are IPv4 addresses. Because there's a limit on the number of unique IP addresses, a second standard, IPv6, has been established. The IPv6 standard allows for many more addresses, which will help accommodate growth of the Internet.

✦ If the router doesn't assign an IP address, one must be configured manually.

✦ No two computers on the network can have the same IP address.

✦ IP is often prefixed by the acronym TCP, as in *TCP/IP*. The TCP part stands for Transfer Control Protocol. It's simply a set of rules for transmitting information on a network. Technically, TCP/IP refers to the methods and engineering as opposed to a specific address or value.

Checking your PC's IP address

When your computer is on an Ethernet network, it has an IP address. If it doesn't, there are problems, covered later in this chapter. For now, the task is to find your PC's IP address.

To check the IP address assigned to your computer, follow these steps in Windows Vista:

1. Open the Network and Sharing Center icon in the Control Panel.

2. On the right side of the window, click the View Status link.

A dialog box appears, listing some brief information about the network connection. But that's not good enough!

3. Click the Details button.

You find the PC's IP address listed as IPv4 IP Address in the Network Connection Details dialog box.

4. Click the Close button and close the Network and Sharing Center window.

In Windows XP, follow these steps to discover the IP address assigned to your PC:

1. Open the Control Panel's Network Connections icon.

2. Open the icon representing your PC's network connection.

When there's more than one icon, just pick the main one.

3. In the Status dialog box, click the Support tab.

The Connection Status area lists the IP address.

4. Click the Close button.

Each network connection has its own IP address. So a laptop PC that has both wireless and wired network adapters features two IP addresses when both adapters are connected to a network. You need to repeat the steps in this section for each network icon to check the IP address for each connection.

Understanding DHCP

Back in the early days, IP addresses were set up manually. I'm old enough to remember doing that. I had to configure each PC on my network with its own IP address, unique from all the other computers. I even wrote the IP address on each PC's monitor. I was proud of myself, but was forgetting one tiny fact: Computers exist to make life easier. Why punish yourself by assigning IP addresses when the computer can do it for you?

On a modern Ethernet network, with a robust router as overseer, IP addresses are assigned to each PC as it joins the network. The process, which is automatic, is referred to as Dynamic Host Configuration Protocol, or *DHCP*.

There's really nothing to set up: Your router's configuration program most likely contains a page that directs the router to use DHCP to set IP addresses. You can turn the option off, but there's no reason to do so.

✦ When your computer isn't connected to a network, its DCHP client program assigns a random IP address to the computer. That IP address is useless because the PC isn't connected to a network. But the random IP address confuses some users because it appears as though the computer has a legitimate IP address. It does not.

✦ The best way to test a network connection is to ping the router. See Chapter 1.

✦ Also see Chapter 1 for more information on the router's configuration program.

✦ You can configure the router to specify which range of IP addresses to use. Again, there's no reason to change the DHCP settings for a small home or office network.

Resolving an IP conflict

An IP conflict means that another computer on the same network is using the same IP address as your computer. For example, both PCs may have the address 192.168.0.104 (which seems to be a troublesome IP address for my own computer network). Obviously, such a situation cannot stand.

The first thing to do is to run the Repair and Diagnose options, as covered later in this chapter, in the section "Repairing the network." If that doesn't work, try the old standby of restarting the computer with the conflict.

The final thing you can try is to determine which computer is the problem child: Check the IP address of all PCs on the network to see which one is assigned the duplicate IP. If you can, turn off that PC or disconnect it from the network. Restart the computer (or reconnect it to the network) to see whether that technique can fix the issue.

Renewing the DHCP lease

The router is configured to let your PC have its IP address for only a given amount of time. After that time expires, the DHCP server must renew your use of the assigned IP address. The action is called *renewing the DHCP lease*.

The DHCP lease is renewed automatically, one would hope. If not, you can try to renew it by diagnosing and repairing the network connection, as described in the section "Repairing the network," later in this chapter.

You can force a renewal by using the Command Prompt window. Follow these steps:

1. From the Start menu, choose All Programs➪Accessories➪Command Prompt.

2. At the command prompt, type ipconfig /renew **and press the Enter key.**

3. Close the Command Prompt window.

The command `ipconfig /renew` forces all network adapters on your PC to immediately request a new DHCP list from the server (the router).

Manually assigning an IP address

If you want to "go rogue," you can configure your PC to use its own IP address, DHCP be damned. Here's how to do that in Windows Vista:

1. Open the Network and Sharing Center icon in the Control Panel.

2. On the right side of the window, click the View Status link.

3. In the Status dialog box, click the Properties button.

4. Type the administrator's password or click the Continue button.

A Properties dialog box for the connection appears. It lists the various protocols and services being used by the connection, as shown in Figure 2-13.

Figure 2-13:
Protocols
and
services
used by a
network
connection
in Windows
Vista.

5. **Select the service titled Internet Protocol Version 4 (TCP/IPv4).**

6. **Click the Properties button.**

    The dialog box labeled Internet Protocol Version 4 (TCP/IPv4) Properties appears.

7. **Choose the option Use the Following IP Address.**

8. **Type the IP address.**

    At this point, it becomes important that you know what you're doing. Seriously. Typing an improper IP address, or one that's out of range, means that your computer cannot use the network.

9. **Type a subnet mask.**

    For a local-area network, the value is usually 255.255.255.0, but then again, I'm assuming that you know what to type as a mask.

10. **Type the default gateway address.**

    The default gateway address is the IP address for the network's router.

    Because DHCP also obtains the address for the DNS server, which helps your computer find addresses on the Internet, you need to manually list those addresses as well.

11. **Type the address of the preferred DNS server.**

    This value is obtained from your ISP.

12. **Type the address for the alternate DNS server.**

13. **Click OK to close the Internet Protocol Version 4 (TCP/IPv4) Properties dialog box.**

14. **Close the other open dialog boxes and windows.**

In Windows XP, follow these steps to manually set an IP address on your computer:

1. **Open the Control Panel's Network Connections icon.**

2. **Open the icon representing your PC's network connection.**

3. **Click the Properties button in the Status dialog box.**

4. **From the list of items, choose Internet Protocol (TCP/IP).**

5. **Click the Properties button.**

    The Internet Protocol (TCP/IP) Properties dialog box appears.

6. **Choose Use the Following IP Address.**

7. **Type the IP address for your computer.**

   Well, officially, you're typing an IP address for the network adapter, but it's kinda the same thing.

   Don't randomly type an address. You need to type a value that's useful for accessing the network. Obviously, if you don't know what you're doing here, don't choose to manually assign an IP address.

8. **Type a subnet mask.**

   The value used on a local network is commonly `255.255.255.0`, but it can be different, such as `255.255.255.127`.

9. **Type the default gateway address.**

   The default gateway is the router, so type the router's address.

10. **Type the address for the preferred DNS server.**

    The address should be obtained from your ISP. It's used to help your computer find Web pages and other addresses on the Internet.

11. **Type the address for the alternate DNS server.**

    The alternate DNS server's IP address is something that your ISP provides.

12. **Click OK to confirm the settings.**

13. **Close all other open dialog boxes and windows.**

Yes, it's kind of an ordeal to manually configure an IP address. The complex process underscores why DHCP was necessary and how it became popular.

Network Troubleshooting

As long as the network hardware is connected and the router, switches, and NICs have their lights blinking in a pleasing manner, your next stab at troubleshooting the network is to take a good look at the software that drives the hardware. This section covers various software tricks for network troubleshooting.

✦ Refer to Chapter 1 for information on network hardware troubleshooting.

✦ Any network troubleshooting involving accessing other PCs on a network is covered in Chapter 3, which deals with peer-to-peer networking.

Repairing the network

Lurking in various places around the numerous networking windows and dialog boxes are certain Repair links and buttons. Your first stab at resolving a network oddity is to grasp one of those Repair options to see whether using it helps. Here's the rundown on where to look:

Network icon: Right-click the Network icon in the notification area and choose Diagnose and Repair from the pop-up menu.

Network and Sharing Center window (Windows Vista): Click the link Diagnose and Repair, found on the left side of the window.

Local Area Connection Status dialog box: In Windows Vista, click the Diagnose button. In Windows XP, click the Support tab and then click the Repair button.

Network Connections window: Choose a network connection icon in the window, and then click the Diagnose This Connection button on the toolbar (Windows Vista), or click the link on the left side of the window, Repair This Connection (Windows XP).

No matter how you get there, the results are the same: Windows looks at the network connection and attempts to resolve some issues. For example, it may renew an expired DHCP lease or it might explain that another computer on the network is "bogarting" your PC's IP address.

If everything is okay, simply click the Close button and get on with your computer day.

 ✦ There may be other locations where you can access the standard Diagnose and Repair utilities. Generally speaking, they all do the same thing described in this section.

 ✦ Windows: 1,000 different ways to do one thing wrong.

Using the Windows XP Network Troubleshooter

Windows XP features a Network Troubleshooting Wizard, which includes a swath of useful diagnostic tools as well as some tests.

To run the Network Troubleshooting Wizard, open the Control Panel's Network Connections icon. In the Network Connections window, choose the task on the left, under the See Also heading, titled Network Troubleshooter. You see a Help window, as shown in Figure 2-14.

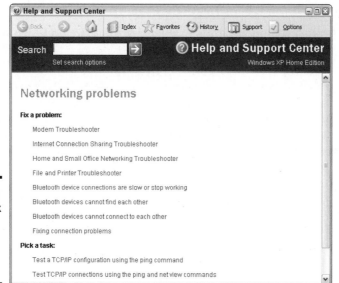

Figure 2-14:
The network
trouble-
shooter in
Windows
XP.

The item of primary interest to you is probably the third one down, Home
and Small Office Networking Troubleshooter. Choosing that item displays a
multiple-choice review of common problems and potential solutions.

The two links near the bottom of the Help system window (refer to Figure 2-14)
might appear interesting, but they're merely directions for using the ping
command, covered in Chapter 1.

Close the troubleshooting wizard when you're done working through its
steps.

Disconnecting from the network

The last final and fatal move you can make is to simply disconnect the PC
from the network. You can do this physically, or you can break the
connection by using software.

Here's how to disable an Ethernet connection in Windows Vista:

1. **Open the Network and Sharing Center icon in the Control Panel.**

2. **On the right side of the window, choose View Status.**

3. Click the Disable button in the connection's Status dialog box.

4. Type the administrator's password or click the Continue button.

5. Close the Network and Sharing Center window.

Follow these steps in Windows XP to disable the network connection:

1. Open the Control Panel's Network Connections icon.

2. Double-click to open the icon representing the PC's Ethernet connection.

3. Click the Disable button.

The disconnection is instant. In Windows Vista, you see the red X marking the line between your PC and the network or Internet. In Windows Vista, the connection icon appears dimmed with the text *Disabled.*

To reconnect to the network in Windows Vista, click the red X icon between your computer and the Internet (or Network) icon in the Network and Sharing Center window. When you see the option Enable the Network Adapter, click it.

To reconnect in Windows XP, double-click to open the disabled-connection icon in the Network Connections window.

Chapter 3: Peer-to-Peer Networking

In This Chapter

✔ Using a peer-to-peer workgroup

✔ Enabling file and printer sharing

✔ Sharing folders and printers

✔ Setting network access for your folders

✔ Searching for shared folders

✔ Setting up a private network

✔ Making the firewall network-happy

✔ Checking out who's using your PC's folders

*I*n such an environment of sharing this and sharing that, doesn't it make sense that all computers on the network should be friends? They are, of course! To prove it, the type of simple network setup you probably have in your home or office is called a *peer-to-peer* network. It's not a bully overlord client-server type of network. No, rather than have one computer in charge, everyone is in charge. They share. They live in peace. It's a simple, happy life — until something goes wrong and you need to read this chapter.

Once Upon a Time, There Was This Workgroup

The peer-to-peer network happens because all computers on the network are the same: They're peers. In Soviet Russia, the term was сеть товарищи, network comrades. No one is in charge! Not even the KGB! All computers work happily together in one workgroup. This section discusses that concept.

Understanding the workgroup

When your PC joins a peer-to-peer network, it becomes part of a workgroup. The *workgroup* is simply a group of computers using the same Ethernet network. There has to be a hub, which can be merely a switch or a router. The computers don't necessarily need to be connected to the Internet — just to each other.

The workgroup can be the entire network — all the computers connected — as shown in Figure 3-1. That's the most common setup for home or small office networks.

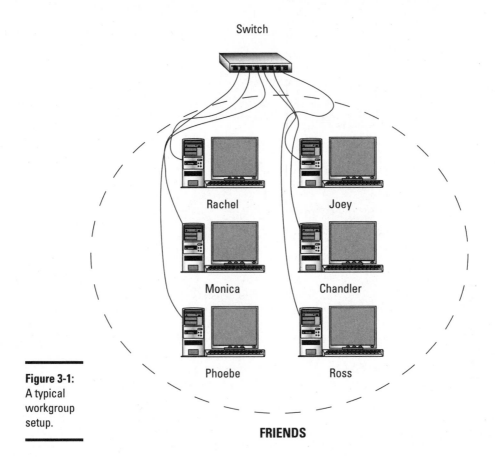

Switch

Rachel

Joey

Monica

Chandler

Phoebe

Ross

FRIENDS

Figure 3-1:
A typical
workgroup
setup.

The workgroup can also be a collection of computers on the same network, as shown in Figure 3-1.

The key to creating a workgroup is simply to assign computers on the network the same workgroup name. So in Figure 3-1, all computers are configured to use the workgroup FRIENDS simply because that's the workgroup name set by each computer. In Figure 3-2, half the computers are in the GALS workgroup; the rest are in the GUYS workgroup.

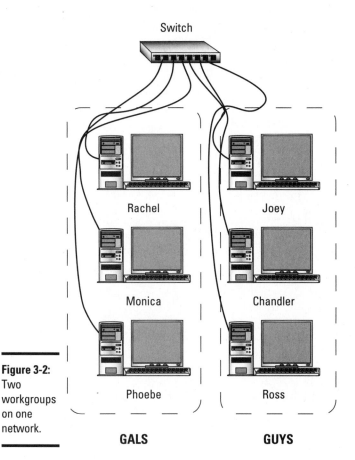

Figure 3-2:
Two
workgroups
on one
network.

There's no reason to split up a small network into workgroups (refer to Figure 3-2). In fact, I highly recommend that all computers on your network use the same workgroup name because it makes accessing the computers easier, especially in Windows XP. There's no advantage to having separate workgroups; no security is provided. Multiple workgroups are simply an option for classifying computers on a larger network.

✦ The workgroup name is a software thing. Setting a workgroup name has no effect on the network hardware; for example, the router couldn't care less about the workgroup name.

✦ The workgroup name has no effect on a network IP address.

✦ All computers on the network must belong to a workgroup.

✦ Other, non-peer-to-peer networks may have other hierarchies, or forms of organization, other than a workgroup, or they may feature a concept similar to the workgroup. Who knows? I don't cover that setup in this book.

Creating a workgroup

There's no magic to creating a workgroup. Out of the box, Windows assigns your PC to a workgroup named WORKGROUP, or possibly MSHOME. You can stick with those names. In fact, that's probably what you're doing now on your computer. Or, you can change the names of the workgroup. Here's how:

1. **Open the System icon in the Control Panel.**

   Or, as an alternative, you can press the Win+Break key combination.

2a. **In Windows Vista, click the Change Settings link in the Computer Name area, and then type the administrator's password or click the Continue button.**

2b. **In Windows XP, click the Computer Name tab in the System dialog box.**

   The System Properties dialog box lists the computer's description, its name, and the workgroup name.

3. **Click the Change button.**

   Another dialog box appears.

4. **Type a new Workgroup name.**

   In Windows Vista, you may need to choose the Workgroup option first.

   Workgroup names should contain only letters and possibly some numbers. The name cannot contain any spaces, and Windows converts the name into ALL CAPS no matter what you type.

5. **Click OK.**

   After a few seconds, you see a dialog box welcoming you to the workgroup.

6. **Click OK.**

   Windows begs you to restart your PC, which is necessary for the computer to *really* join the workgroup.

7. **Click OK to dismiss the dialog box.**

8. **Restart your computer.**

After your computer is restarted, it belongs to the new workgroup. That affects networking on your PC as far as which network computers show up in the Network window. That topic is covered in the next section.

✦ Ensure that all computers connected to the network use the same workgroup name.

✦ To join a workgroup, enter the workgroup's name as described in this section.

✦ If you have trouble joining a workgroup, check the name; it must be spelled exactly.

✦ MSHOME is "em es home," or *Microsoft home* network.

✦ There's no reason to change the workgroup name from WORKGROUP or MSHOME, though I do it anyway. More important than resetting the workgroup name is to ensure that your network is properly identified as public or private. See the section "Checking the network privacy in Windows Vista," later in this chapter.

✦ Despite my recommendation in the preceding bullet point, I change the network name for my laptop. That's because it's more difficult to find a laptop on a different workgroup in Windows Vista, especially at a public wireless hotspot.

Browsing the workgroup in Windows Vista

When it comes to workgroup names, Windows Vista really doesn't give a darn. That's because, regardless of how you set it up, all computers on the network appear in the Windows Vista Network window. Even those computers with a different workgroup name show up. So much for workgroup name recognition.

Well, not so fast.

Windows Vista doesn't organize the workgroup computers like Windows XP does (as described in the next section). The workgroup ID is there; just click a computer icon in the Network window, and the bottom portion of the window displays the workgroup name, as shown in Figure 3-3.

Figure 3-3:
Network computers organized by workgroup.

To see the workgroups, you need to organize the window to display computer icons in workgroup categories (refer to Figure 3-3). To make that happen, right-click in the window and choose Group By⇨Workgroup from the shortcut menu.

To restore Normal view, right-click in the window and choose Group By⇨None.

If you don't see the information at the bottom of the window (refer to Figure 3-3), use the Organize button on the toolbar: Choose Layout⇨Details Pane.

Browsing the workgroup in Windows XP

Windows XP follows the workgroup paradigm a little more seriously than Windows Vista does. When you open the My Network Places window, you first see a listing of network folders and perhaps some Internet locations. That's handy for accessing resources on the network, but it doesn't show you workgroup information.

To see the computers in the workgroup, choose the link View Workgroup Computers from the list of network tasks on the left side of the My Network Places window. The window changes to show only the computers assigned to your PC's workgroup; you see the workgroup name shown on the Address bar.

 To see all workgroups on the network, click the Up button on the toolbar. You see any additional workgroups on the network, as shown in Figure 3-4. To browse those workgroups, open their icon and you see the list of computers and other resources available.

Figure 3-4: Workgroups available on the network (Windows XP).

If you click the Up button one more time, you see a window describing the entire network named, ironically, Entire Network. The icon titled Entire Windows Network represents the peer-to-peer network your PC uses.

Don't fret over the hierarchy of the network-and-workgroup structure as presented in Windows XP. The bottom line is that you can easily access shared folders within the My Network Places window, regardless of in which workgroup those computers reside.

Everybody Share

The key issue with having a network is sharing resources: folders, modems, and printers, for example. Of the lot, the primary resource to share between computers in a peer-to-peer network is the folder. That's the topic of this section.

Making sharing possible in Windows Vista

Before you run amok with sharing, you must ensure that Windows has a favorable attitude toward offering up the computer's precious resources. In Windows Vista, enabling (or disabling) sharing on the network is done in the Network and Sharing Center window, shown in Figure 3-5. To see that window, open the Network and Sharing Center icon in the Control Panel.

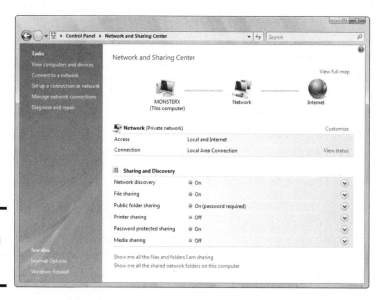

Figure 3-5:
Set sharing options here.

You set options in the Sharing and Discovery portion of the Network and Sharing Center window by clicking the Show More arrow next to each of the six sharing categories. For each item, there are two settings: one to turn the item on and another to turn the item off. An Apply button confirms your choice, also displaying a User Account Control (UAC) dialog box for you to confirm Administrator permission to make the change.

Here's how to set the items to allow your computer to share its resources on the network:

Network Discovery: Choose the option Turn On Network Discovery. This action ensures that your computer will find other PCs on the network as well as find printers and shared folders. It also lets other computers on the network find your PC.

File Sharing: Choose the option Turn On File Sharing if you plan to share folders on your PC with other computers on the network.

Public Folder Sharing: Choose the option Turn On Sharing So That Anyone with Network Access Can Open Files. The second option allows full access. The third option (and this item is the only one with three options) disables Public folder sharing. Essentially, this item is a shortcut that allows you to share the Public folder without messing directly with its sharing and permissions options.

Printer Sharing: Choose the option Turn On Printer Sharing if you have a printer directly connected to your PC and you want to share it on the network.

Password Protected Sharing: Choose the option turn On Password Protected Sharing to ensure that only those with an account on your computer can access files. I recommend that setting for security reasons.

Media Sharing: Click the Change button to control media sharing with the Windows Media Player. I generally leave this option off because I'm an iTunes person.

Setting the options as described in this section merely confirms that you have sharing set up. Additional steps include joining a workgroup and ensuring that the network hardware and software is all connected and good to go. See Chapters 1 and 2 for additional instructions.

Making sharing possible in Windows XP

To configure sharing for folders and printers on your Windows XP computer, you must customize the network connection. That's normally done when you first set up the computer for networking. But it can also be accomplished by following these steps:

1. **Open the Network Connections icon in the Control Panel.**

2. **Right-click your computer's network connection icon.**

There should be only one icon for the main Ethernet connection, though laptop computers will have two — one for the wired and another for the wireless connections. Yes, that means you need to repeat these steps for both types of connection.

3. **Choose Properties from the shortcut menu.**

4. **In the connection's Properties dialog box, ensure that a service titled File and Printer Sharing For Microsoft Networks is listed.**

If there is, great. Ensure that a check mark appears by that option (which turns the option on), and you're done. Skip to Step 10. Otherwise, continue:

5. **Click the Install button to summon the Network Component Type dialog box.**

6. **Choose Service.**

7. **Click the Add button.**

8. **From the list in the Select Network Services dialog box, choose File and Printer Sharing for Microsoft Networks.**

9. **Click OK.**

10. **Click the Close button in the connection's Properties dialog box.**

If you're prompted to restart the PC after completing these steps, do so. Otherwise, your computer is all set up to share folders and a printer.

Sharing your PC's printer

To share a printer attached to your PC with other computers on the network, follow these steps:

1. **Open the Printers icon in the Control Panel.**

In Windows XP, the icon is named Printers and Faxes.

2. **Right-click the printer's icon.**

3. **Choose Sharing from the pop-up menu.**

4. **In Windows Vista, click the button Change Sharing Options, and then type the administrator's password or click the Continue button.**

Because you're sharing one of the computer's hardware resources, and it affects all users on the computer, you need administrator access to share the printer.

5. **Choose the option Share This Printer.**

6. **(Optional) Type a share name.**

   Be descriptive. The name Possessive Larry's Color Laser is a good description, as is Mom's Inkjet in the Den.

7. **Click OK to share the printer.**

 Shared printers sport a tag on their icon in the Printers window. In Windows Vista, the icon looks like a man and woman, or what I call the *sharing buddies* tag, as shown in the margin. In Windows XP, the tag is the *serving hand* that appears under the icon.

✦ Some types of printers, such as PDF printers or Fax printers, cannot be shared on the network. Windows bluntly tells you so when you make the attempt.

✦ Shared printers are available only when the computer they're attached to is turned on.

✦ You cannot print on a shared printer when the computer it's attached to is in Sleep mode or Stand By mode. Likewise, because Hibernation turns a computer off, you cannot use the printer attached to a hibernating PC.

✦ You can print to any printer directly attached to the network, though that printer must be turned on as well. See Chapter 1 for information on attaching a printer directly to the network.

Sharing a folder

The key to accessing information on a network is to share folders between computers. After a folder is shared, any other user on the network can access it, using its files just like any folder on their own computer. That's the gist of it.

To share a folder in Windows Vista, follow these steps:

1. **Right-click the folder you want to share.**

   You have to see the folder, not be "in" the folder.

2. **Choose Properties from the shortcut menu.**

   Yeah, I know: a Sharing command is on the shortcut menu. That type of sharing refers to sharing the folder between users on the same computer, not on the network.

3. **Click the Sharing tab in the folder's Properties dialog box.**

4. **Click the Advanced Sharing button.**

5. **Type the administrator's password or click the Continue button.**

   The Advanced Sharing dialog box appears, as shown in Figure 3-6.

Figure 3-6:
The
Advanced
Sharing
dialog box,
where the
real sharing
takes place.

6. **Place a check mark by the option Share This Folder.**

7. **If necessary, type a more descriptive share name.**

   The folder's name already appears in the Shared name box. Additionally, when other users see this folder available on the network, they also see your computer's name after the folder's name.

8. **Click OK to close the Advanced Sharing dialog box, and then click the Close button to discharge the folder's Properties dialog box.**

You share a folder in Windows XP by obeying these steps:

1. **Find the folder you want to share.**

2. **Right-click the folder's icon.**

3. **Choose Sharing and Security from the shortcut menu.**

   The folder's Properties dialog box appears with the Sharing tab up front.

4. **Choose the option Share the Folder on the Network.**

5. **(Optional) Type a share name.**

   Windows automatically sets the share name to the folder name. Although the folder name might make sense on your PC, you may need something more descriptive for network users.

6. **Click OK to share the folder.**

After the folder is shared, it appears with a tag on its icon. In Windows Vista, the tag is the *sharing buddies*, shown in the margin. Windows XP uses the *serving hand* tag.

Other computers can access the shared folder on your computer. At this point, they have read-only access, which means that they can open files or copy them from your PC, but they cannot add files to the folder, delete files already in the folder, or modify the folder. See the section "Setting shared folder permissions," a little later in this chapter, for more details on how to modify access to a shared folder.

+ No, you cannot share individual files — only folders.

+ Because a compressed folder is really a file, you cannot share it unless it's inside a shared folder.

+ Share a folder within your personal area, or your "home" folder. Do not share any other folder, such as one in the Program Files or Windows folders.

+ Do not share your account folder. Doing so is a security risk.

+ Although technically you can share an entire hard drive by sharing its root folder, don't. Sharing an entire drive is a security risk because it gives everyone on the network access to everything on that drive.

+ Sharing a folder doesn't allow someone on the Internet to use that folder on your PC. Sharing works only with computers on the local network.

Setting shared folder permissions

Any little kid knows the difference between sharing and giving. How many times in your own life do you remember saying, "You said you only wanted to *look* at it, not take it"? The same type of playground logic applies to sharing folders on a network: Unless you explicitly say so, other users can only look at your files, not modify them, delete them, or add to their numbers.

Bottom line: It's not a bug or even PC trouble when you cannot copy a file into a shared folder; it's *permissions*.

To set folder permissions for a shared folder in Windows Vista, heed these steps:

1. **Right-click a shared folder icon.**

Shared folders appear with the sharing buddies tag on them.

2. **Choose Properties from the shortcut menu.**

3. **In the folder's Properties dialog box, click the Sharing tab.**

4. **Click the Advanced Sharing button.**

5. **Click the Continue button or type the administrator's password.**

The Advanced Sharing dialog box shows up

6. **Click the Permissions button.**

The shared folder's Permissions dialog box appears. You see a list of users who can access the folder, coupled with a set of access privileges at the bottom of the dialog box.

7. **Select a group or username.**

You can add individual usernames or categories by clicking the Add button. The Everyone group means that anyone and everyone on the network gets access.

8. **Set the permissions for the selected group or user.**

There are three types of permissions:

Full Control: Gives a user the same control over the folder as your account has.

Change: Lets a user change files, but not add any new ones or create folders.

Read: Lets a user open files and copy files from the folder.

For each permission, you can choose either Allow or Deny. Choosing neither option means that the user gets the same permissions as his account has for your computer.

9. **Click OK to close the Permissions dialog box.**

10. **Click OK to close the Advanced Sharing dialog box.**

11. **Click OK to close the folder's Properties dialog box.**

In Windows XP, follow these directions to set folder permissions:

1. **Right-click the shared folder icon and choose Sharing and Security from the shortcut menu.**

2. **Place a check mark in the box Allow Network Users to Change My Files.**

3. **Click OK.**

Yes, Windows XP has a far easier game of it when it comes to setting folder permissions. But then again, keep in mind that Windows Vista is the more secure operating system.

I recommend that you consider sharing the Public folder on your computer, making it "up for grabs" to any other user on the network. That way, you can easily make files available by copying them to the Public folder. That avoids complications that arise when sharing individual folders.

✦ If you add more specific users or groups in Windows Vista (refer to Step 8 in the preceding set of steps for Windows Vista), you must select each group individually and set permissions for that user or group.

✦ Having multiple users and groups in a shared folder is often a source of woe. When you have trouble accessing a shared folder on a Windows Vista PC, it's most likely because individual users, as opposed to groups, are selected for sharing.

✦ Setting file permissions can get quite technical in Windows Vista. You can not only share files on a network but also share folders with other users on the same PC.

Managing multiple shares in Windows Vista

It's possible in Windows Vista to set multiple names for a shared folder. The reason has to do with file permissions: Say that you want everyone to have read-only access but you want yourself to have full access on your own computer from elsewhere on the network. That's entirely possible in Windows Vista, if you follow these steps:

1. **Right-click a shared folder icon and choose Properties from the shortcut menu.**

2. **In the folder's Properties dialog box, click the Sharing tab.**

3. **Click the Advanced Sharing button, and then type the administrator's password or click the Continue button.**

4. **Click the Add button to create a new share name.**

The New Share dialog box appears.

5. **Type a unique share name for the folder.**

I typically use the folder's original name followed by the word *Private*, which means that the folder is fully accessible only by me.

6. **(Optional) Type a description.**

7. **Click the Permissions button to set the shared folder's permissions under the new name.**

The Permissions dialog box appears for the shared folder's new name.

8. **Select Everyone from the list and click the Remove button.**

Remove from the list any other users you don't want on the new share, and repeat this step as necessary.

9. **Click the Add button.**

The befuddling Select Users or Groups dialog box appears, as shown in Figure 3-7. The key to using this dialog box is to get the user or group names, called *object names*, perfectly correct. It's not easy.

Figure 3-7:
Adding specific users for folder sharing.

10. **Type your username into the box labeled Enter the Object Names to Select.**

For example, I log in to my computer with the username Dan, so I type **Dan** into the box.

11. **Click the Check Names button.**

The Check Names button magically converts the username you type into the official object name format that Windows Vista desires.

If you see a Name Not Found dialog box after clicking the Check Names button, you improperly entered the username. Click the Cancel button and try again.

12. **Click OK to confirm the name you typed in the Select Users or Groups dialog box.**

13. **Set the proper permissions for the user.**

For my own "Private" access, I put check marks in the Allow column for all three levels: Full Control, Change, and Read.

14. **Click OK.**

15. **Click OK in the New Share dialog box.**

16. **Click OK to close the Advanced Sharing dialog box.**

17. **Click OK to close the shared folder's Properties dialog box.**

The folder now shows up on other network computers' Network or My Network Places windows with two icons representing the same folder. Each icon represents a different type of access.

By creating a second level of access for shared folders, you ensure that folks on the network can have limited access while those who share accounts on your computer can have more access.

The whole issue of accounts, groups, and access levels is a complex one in Windows Vista. There are many levels of permissions and groups and such that a casual PC user can be easily confused. Couple that with the Windows Vista notion that file sharing can also happen between users on the same computer, and then the entire topic makes for one whopping headache. My advice is to stick with the types of sharing and permissions offered in this chapter. That should save you on your annual aspirin bill.

Accessing shared folders

Finding and using shared folders on the network happens either from Windows Explorer or within an Open or Save As dialog box. Still, considering that an Open or Save As dialog box is basically just a little Windows Explorer window, it's all the same thing regardless.

The methods for accessing a shared folder differ between Windows Vista and Windows XP.

In Windows Vista, open the Network window or choose Network from the Address bar in an Open or Save As dialog box. Open the icon representing a computer on the network. If necessary, log in to that computer by using the Connect To dialog box. Then open the shared folder that appears in the list.

In Windows XP, open the My Network Places window or choose My Network Places from the Address bar in any Windows Explorer, Open, or Save As dialog box. The list of shared folders for all computers on the network appears in the window, as shown in Figure 3-8. Just open the icon of the folder you want to use.

As in Windows Vista, you may be prompted to provide login information to access the shared folder. Type your username and password to get proper access to the folder. Yes, that often means that you need to have an account on the shared computer, or you need to know the username and password of an account on that computer.

✦ A Browse dialog box is essentially the same thing as the Open dialog box.

✦ Shared folders are available only when the computer sharing the folder is turned on and not in either Sleep mode or Stand By mode.

Figure 3-8:
Shared
folders on
the network
in Windows
XP.

Discovering which folders you're sharing

Windows Vista has two features that clue you in to not only which folders are
being shared on the computer but also which shared folders on the network
your computer is using. Both tools are found at the bottom of the Network
and Sharing Center window (refer to Figure 3-5). They're described next:

Show Me All the Files and Folders I Am Sharing: Choosing this link displays
a Search Results window that lists all the folders you're sharing with others
on your PC. These are folders that other users on your computer can access
when they log in. They are *not* network shared folders.

Show Me All the Shared Network Folders on This Computer: Choosing this
link displays the Network window listing all the folders that your PC is sharing
on the network. These aren't necessarily folders in use by other computers.
(For that information, see the section "Finding out who else is using your
computer," later in this chapter.)

Unsharing a folder

To stop sharing a folder, repeat the steps from the section "Sharing a folder,"
earlier in this chapter, and uncheck the option Share This Folder (Windows
Vista) or Share This Folder on the Network (Windows XP). That effectively
"unshares" the folder.

What is a domain?

The term *domain* is often tossed around when referring to computer networking. Indeed, you often see options for setting a domain name or prefix for your network in Windows. You might think that it's an option you need to set, but it's not.

A domain type of network relies on a central computer or server to rule over the rest of the network. It's not democratic, like the peer-to-peer type of network hat most Windows users have in their homes or small offices. When you work on a larger, domain-type of network, a central computer is responsible for your files and programs. In fact, you can log in to any computer in the domain to work on your stuff because files aren't stored on the PC you're using.

Bottom line: If you have a domain type of network, someone is probably being paid to maintain and troubleshoot it for you. Don't sweat it.

If someone else on the network is using the shared folder as you unshare it, you see a warning dialog box. It's always a good idea to ensure that the other user is done sharing before you cut them off; if that person is changing a file, then by halting sharing, you could damage the file. Then again, if the other user is doing so without permission, the file has already been damaged.

Workgroup Woes

Life is good on the network. I enjoy it. Moving files back and forth is a breeze. In fact, the images you see in this book were sent over the network from my test computer to my writing computer. Everything worked smoothly. When things failed to move smoothly, I took notes and then wrote this section on general workgroup woes.

Checking the network privacy in Windows Vista

Windows Vista doesn't let you create just any old peer-to-peer workgroup. Nope, it lets you configure a workgroup to be either public or private. That may seem like a silly question, but it's not: A public network requires more security. After all, the network is in public. Who knows where those other people's laptops have been?

A private network, however, is most likely the kind of network you have in your home or small office. The network isn't (or shouldn't be) visited by random folks driving by or stopping in for a quick porn download.

In Windows Vista, you can check whether the network you're using is public or private and then reset the network type for your computer. Follow these steps:

1. **Open the Control Panel's Network and Sharing Center icon.**

   Right away, next to the Network heading in the middle of the window, you see whether the network you're connected to is a public network or private network. In Figure 3-5, you see that my own network is a private network. Good.

2. **Click the Customize link.**

   The Set Network Location Wizard appears, as shown in Figure 3-9.

Figure 3-9:
Setting the
network
type.

3. **Choose Public if the network is in a public location or in a situation where anyone can join the network. Choose Private when you control the entire network and only computers you know of are connected.**

   Generally speaking, when in doubt, assume that you're using a public network. A hotel room connection, for example, is public. Cybercafé? Public. The wireless network at your friend's apartment? Public.

4. **Name your network or assign a new icon.**

   This step is optional.

   Those settings are more for fun than for network security.

5. **Click the Next button.**

6. **Type the administrator's password or click the Continue button.**

   Changing the network type is a security issue; you don't want a random program or virus making the change for you.

7. **Click the Close button.**

The changes you make don't affect the entire network. After all, if you just joined a wireless network in a cybercafé, why would your computer be allowed to lord it over all other computers on the network? No, the public/private thing merely tells Windows Vista how to treat the network.

Reaching unreachable PCs

Perhaps the biggest problem with a peer-to-peer network is to find that a computer has suddenly gone missing. Worse, the whole network might be gone! The situation is almost as teeth-gnashing as a missing Web page, but it's more frustrating because *you* might be the one responsible because it's your network. What to do, what to do. . . .

Here are some things to check for finding wayward network PCs:

✦ Check to ensure that the PC is turned on. A computer that's turned off cannot be accessed — don't let that surprise you!

✦ Computers that are hibernating, in Stand By mode or Sleep mode cannot be accessed on the network.

✦ Likewise, a shared printer connected to a snoozing PC cannot be used.

✦ Conversely, you can use a computer that is on but no one is logged in to.

✦ You can, however, access a computer where only the monitor is sleeping.

✦ Check the firewall on your PC to ensure that local network traffic is allowed. (See the next section.)

✦ Check the workgroup name. The computer may not show up in the workgroup window, specifically on Windows XP, when it's using a different workgroup name.

✦ Confirm that the computer's user hasn't discontinued sharing that folder.

✦ Check the other computer to ensure that it doesn't have an IP conflict.

✦ Check a Windows Vista PC to ensure that all the sharing options are properly set in the Network and Sharing Center window. (See the section "Making sharing possible in Windows Vista," earlier in this chapter.)

If all these solutions fail, consider restarting your PC. And if *that* fails, restart the network. See Chapter 2 for information on restarting your local-area network.

Allowing local traffic through the Windows firewall

Perhaps the number-one reason why computers don't communicate with each other on a peer-to-peer network is a software firewall. The firewall can prevent your PC from accessing other computers as well as prevent those computers from accessing your PC. Either way, it's frustrating.

To fix the problem, you need to ensure that all local network traffic is allowed through the firewall. Because specific programs aren't accessing the firewall, you probably need to make the change manually. Here's how to check or change the local network traffic setting in the Windows Firewall:

1. **Open the Windows Firewall icon in the Control Panel.**

2. **In Windows Vista, click the Change Settings link and then type the administrator's password or click the Continue button.**

3. **Click the Exceptions tab in the Windows Firewall Settings dialog box.**

   The Windows XP version of the dialog box is titled Windows Firewall.

4. **Ensure that a check mark appears by the item File and Printer Sharing.**

   By enabling that exception, you ensure that all local traffic flows through the network without being blocked.

5. **Click OK and close any other open windows.**

These steps are specific to the Windows Firewall. If you're using another software firewall, take similar steps to ensure that local network traffic — specifically, file and printer sharing — isn't being blocked.

You don't need a software firewall when the network's router sports a good hardware firewall. See Chapter 1 for more information on router configuration.

Getting at multiple networks

Windows features a Bridge Connections command, which allows you to access two separate networks on a single PC. For example, if you have a laptop computer with both wired and wireless connections *and* you're using both, you can bridge those connections so that your laptop can access computers on both networks.

Yes, such a situation might be rare. But Windows lets you do it.

To bridge connections, follow these steps:

1. Open the Network Connections window.

In Windows Vista, open the Network and Sharing Center icon in the Control Panel, and then click the link Manage Network Connections, found on the left side of the window.

In Windows XP, open the Network Connections icon in the Control Panel.

2. Select the network connections to bridge.

To select more than one connection at a time, press and hold the Ctrl key as you click each one.

3. Right-click the selected icons and choose the Bridge Connections command.

4. In Windows Vista, click the Continue button or type the administrator's password, if you're prompted to do so.

5. Dismiss the confirmation dialog box, if one appears.

There are a few times when this trick doesn't work. Windows doesn't, for example, bridge a connection between a local network and the Internet, which would be a security risk. Bridging also doesn't work when you're using Internet Connection Sharing, which is a way of sharing your PC's Internet connection directly with another PC by hooking the two computers together with an Ethernet cable.

To break up a network bridge, open the Network Connections window, right-click the bridge, and choose Delete from the shortcut menu.

Finding out who else is using your computer

The question is, who else on the network is using my PC? What other computers on the local network are peeking into my folders? You may not know, but your computer does. Want to know the answer? Follow these steps:

1. From the Start menu, choose All Programs⇨Accessories⇨Command Prompt.

A Command Prompt window opens.

2. **Type** netstat **and press the Enter key.**

The netstat command displays network statistics. In its basic form (what you typed), current local connections to your computer are displayed. You see something like this if another computer is using one of your PC's shared folders:

```
Active Connections

    Proto   Local Address           Foreign Address
      State
    TCP     192.168.0.103:139       192.168.0.101:60172
    ESTABLISHED
    TCP     [fe80::e1fe:4a18:c135:883f%8]:445
    MonsterX:50209          ESTABLISHED
```

The output is, admittedly, technical. (You should expect no less from the command prompt.) What you're looking for is the other computer's network name, such as MonsterX, as shown in the code example.

3. **Type** exit **and press Enter to close the Command Prompt window.**

If you cannot determine another computer's name from the netstat command output, you need to pay attention to the IP addresses. You have to cross-check the IP address displayed with that of other computers on the network, which can be a pain. But that's the only other way to use the command.

✦ The output also doesn't explain exactly which folder the other computer is using. In fact, the other computer may not even be using a folder. It could be using a printer or accessing something else. The mystery of it all!

✦ The netstat command can also be used to determine which Internet connections are active on your computer. Type **netstat -a** to see the list, which can be quite extensive.

✦ See Chapter 2 for information on discovering a PC's IP address.

Chapter 4: Networking Unplugged

*O*to be wild and free, to live a life untethered by obligations, duties, wires. It's the dream of all computer users, or any cleaning lady who's looked behind a computer desk. The wild and free networking dream can become a reality, not only for laptops but desktop PCs as well. The solution is commonly called *wireless networking*. This chapter was born to help you deal with wireless networking and its tribulations.

Unwired Networking Basics

Perhaps you're one of the rare people who finds networking easy. Don't laugh: Networking isn't a constant source of trouble after the network has been configured. But that's often the case only for wired networking. With wireless networking, configuration seems to be an ongoing ordeal, especially if you're out in the real world and roaming wireless networks.

To help get your wireless networking bearings, I offer this section on the basics of wireless network.

Setting up a wireless network

There are two types of wireless networks: *infrastructure* and *ad hoc*. The infrastructure network is most likely the type of wireless setup you have in your home or office. It's laid out similarly to a wired network, but (surprisingly) without wires, as shown in Figure 4-1.

Internet   Broadband modem   Wireless router   Network printer   Network hard drive

Figure 4-1: A typical wireless network setup.

Carter's PC   Lillian's PC   Hawthorn's laptop

The basic wireless, peer-to-peer network consists of these components:

Wireless router: The heart of the wireless network is the wireless router. Like a wire-based network, the hub is a central location that all computers connect to, providing the computers with network access.

The wireless hubs available today also serve as routers. Well, officially, wireless hubs are gateways, not routers, but they're called routers. They're also called access points, so get used to that term as well.

Despite the nomenclature confusion, all you need to know is that the hub/router/access point is a smart little beast that helps manage wireless connections as well as helps connect your wireless network to the Internet.

Wire-based connections: Almost every wireless router I've seen has one or more standard, wire-based Ethernet ports. One port is used to connect the router to a broadband modem. Other Ethernet ports might be also available, allowing you to connect standard wire-based networking to the wireless hub, as shown in Figure 4-1.

Wireless NIC: To make your PC talk to the wireless router, the PC needs a wireless network information card, or NIC. A laptop comes with a wireless NIC standard, but for a desktop PC, you have to get a wireless NIC as an option. It's installed internally as an expansion card, or you can use one of the various plug-in USB wireless NICs.

That's pretty much it for the infrastructure type of wireless network.

The ad hoc type of wireless network is basically a group of wireless computers connecting with each other. There's no central hub or router in an ad hoc network. Instead, each computer can directly access the other computers' files and shared resources. There may or may not be any Internet access, but that's not the point of the ad hoc network.

As long as you have all the hardware, you can quickly set up any wireless network. But that's only the hardware. The software side presents additional challenges, as covered later in this chapter.

✦ One of the beauties of a wireless network is that you can mix in wired components as needed. If you need more Ethernet ports, for example, simply add a switch to the wireless router. See Chapter 1 for more information on switches.

✦ Despite the wireless nature of wireless networking, you still need an Ethernet cable (a wire) to connect a wireless router to a broadband modem.

✦ Another advantage of a wireless network is that it's portable. It's far easier to pull up stakes with a wireless network than to pack up all the bits and pieces of a wired network. If you live in an apartment, that makes a wireless setup a good option.

✦ See Figure 1-2 (in Chapter 1 of this minibook) for an illustration of a wired router, which has similar connections and features to a wireless router.

✦ The term *access point* is often abbreviated AP. Don't be puzzled when you see the words *wireless AP* — it simply refers to the access point, not the Associated Press.

✦ A wireless network is often called a *WLAN*, for wireless local-area network.

✦ Ad hoc networks are often used by computer gamers to gather in a single location and play games with each other.

✦ See Chapter 1 for basic network hardware information.

✦ See Chapter 3 for information on peer-to-peer networks.

Using the proper wireless network standard

If you're familiar with written music, you're probably used to seeing a lot of Italian. If you're familiar with computers, you're probably used to seeing a lot of numbers. One of them, 802.11, deals with wireless networking. Specifically, all the gizmos on your wireless network must adhere to the 802.11 wireless networking standard.

The number 802.11 refers to the methods and protocols used to send network information without wires. But the number 802.11 isn't enough; a tiny letter suffix also determines which revision of the 802.11 standard is being used:

802.11n: The most current wireless networking standard. It can communicate with all the older standards. If you can, ensure that all your wireless networking equipment uses the 802.11n standard.

802.11g: The second most popular wireless networking standard, but one notch older than 802.11n (despite the missing letters *h* through *m*). The 802.11g wireless networking devices can communicate with the other 802.11 standards, but they don't use all the nifty new 802.11n features. Specifically, 802.11g gear lacks the range of 802.11n stuff.

802.11b: The oldest popular wireless networking standard. Although it can talk with the truly ancient 802.11a equipment, it can also communicate with 802.11g or 802.11n wireless hardware.

802.11a: The original wireless standard; not good for much any more.

To see which type of wireless NIC is installed in your computer, follow these steps:

1. **Press the Win+Break key combination to open the System window (in Windows Vista) or System Properties dialog box (in Windows XP).**

2a. **In Windows Vista, click the link on the left titled Device Manager and then type the administrator's password or click the Continue button.**

2b. **In Windows XP, click the Hardware tab and then click the Device Manager button.**

3. **In the Device Manager window, expand the area titled Network Adapters.**

   You most likely see two network adapters, as shown in Figure 4-2. One entry represents the wired Ethernet adapter (NIC); the other, the wireless.

   One way to gauge the adapter type is by looking at its name. In Figure 4-2, the adapter's name ends with 4695AGN, which implies that the NIC might adhere to the wireless networking standards 802.11a, 802.11g, and 802.11n. But you can dig deeper:

4. **Open the wireless networking adapter item.**

   The adapter's Properties dialog box appears.

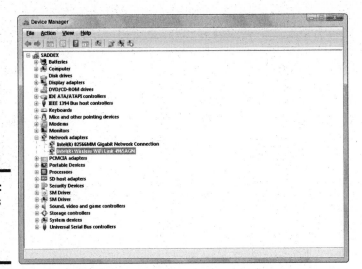

Figure 4-2:
A wireless
NIC in the
Device
Manager.

5. **Click the Advanced tab.**

   If you have an 802.11n compatible adapter, you see a couple of entries
   for 802.11n settings. They confirm that the adapter is 802.11n compatible,
   which means that it can also talk with older 802.11g as well as 802.11b
   wireless networking hardware.

6. **Click the Cancel button to close the adapter's Properties dialog box.**

7. **Close the Device Manager window and any other open windows.**

All your wireless network devices should be of the same standard, especially
if you want to get the most performance from the wireless network.
Although you can mix up the lot, such as an 802.11n hub with 802.11g NICs,
things still work — although you're not getting all the 802.11n goodness from
your 802.11g adapters.

When you're having trouble connecting an older PC or laptop to the wireless
network, it's probably using an older wireless standard. Replace it with a
newer NIC.

✦ Say "eight-oh-two-eleven." Say it any other way and your geeky friends
   will never take you seriously.

✦ If any of your computers is using an 802.11b NIC, I highly recommend
   replacing it with an 802.11n model or getting an 802.11n USB adapter.

✦ Yes, some letters are missing. I'm sure that there was an 802.11c standard, and who can forget that 802.11j standard? Although they probably had datasheets and prototypes, those standards were released or made widely available to the public.

Configuring the wireless base station

Setting up a wireless base station works similarly to configuring a router for a wired network. See the section in Chapter 1 about configuring the router for a general overview.

Connecting to the router is done by setting it up according to the manual. Next, access the router by using a Web browser on your computer. (The computer can be connected to the router wirelessly or connected directly using an Ethernet cable.)

To access the wireless base station's configuration menu, start a Web browser on the computer connected to the base station. In the Web browser's Address bar, type the router's IP address, such as

```
http://192.168.1.1
```

The exact address is found in the router manual. You're prompted for a username and password; that information is also in the manual.

There are probably a lot of things you can set up; a configuration tool may walk you through the basics. For security's sake, ensure that the following items are all set when you configure the wireless router:

Change the base station's administrator password: Set a new password for accessing the base station's configuration program. Too many people forget to do this part, so their wireless hub has the password *netlink* or something similar. That's too easy for the bad guys to figure out, so set a good, strong password for the base station!

Set the network name or SSID: The SSID, or service set identifier, is basically the wireless network's name. It's not the workgroup name, which can be set separately. Instead, it's the name that people see when they look to join the wireless network. Change the name to something unique — something other than *Linksys* or whatever name is preset for the router.

Suppress the SSID: It's more secure not to broadcast the SSID, so if you have the option to suppress it from being broadcast, consider setting this option. When the name is suppressed, the access point is still known; only by typing the proper name, though, can someone access the network.

Password-protect access: To join the wireless network, you want users to supply a password. Set a good one.

Set up a firewall: Ensure that the wireless router has its firewall settings activated. Nothing protects your computers from the nasties of the Internet like a good, solid hardware firewall.

The items listed here represent only a small taste of the vast assortment of settings and options for a wireless network — another reason why many people find wireless network setup to be a pain in the rump.

✦ Additionally, you can restrict access to only a limited set of computers, as described in the later section "Restricting access to your wireless network."

✦ When the wireless router setup goes haywire, you can restore the router's factory settings by punching its Reset button. Found on the back of the router, the Reset button requires that you insert a bent paper clip or similar implement of destruction to push it.

✦ For wireless security, you want to use a password on your network and the WPA-/WPA2-level security. WPA, or Wi-Fi Protected Access, is a replacement for the older WEP standard. You might also see the term *PSK,* which refers to a *pre-shared key,* a common security method for wireless networks.

✦ The wireless network's WPA/WPA2 password is anywhere from 8 to 64 characters long. After you set it, *write it down.* The password for my office's wireless network is 28 characters long, including upper- and lowercase letters, numbers, and symbols. Yes, I wrote it down.

✦ Set a nice, tough password for your wireless network. You can configure Windows to remember the password so that you don't have to type it every time you turn on the computer. But you also don't want something that one of the Bad Guys can easily guess.

✦ I used to suppress my wireless hub's SSID, but I don't do it any more. Instead, I use MAC address filtering to help restrict access. See the section "Restricting access to your wireless network," later in this chapter.

✦ My favorite local SSID is named `This Is My Network Keep Off.`

Connecting base stations

Yeah, they lied. The box probably said that your wireless router has a range of 300 feet. Perhaps that's true on the moon, but obstacles on this planet easily interfere with a wireless network signal — obstacles such as wood and brick and especially metal. If you look around right now, you can probably see lots of wood and brick or metal. That stuff is hindering the wireless signal.

If all your wireless computers are in one room, a single wireless base station works just fine. But when you have dreams of darting around your house using a laptop or having that game machine in the den access the wireless network, you're probably better served by using a second wireless base station.

The secret to using multiple base stations is to bridge the connections so that all your wireless hubs are part of the same network. This concept is called creating a *wireless distribution system (WDS)*, as shown in Figure 4-3.

To make WDS happen, the wireless router must have WDS capability. You can confirm it by reading it on the box or by checking the router's configuration program for a WDS settings page.

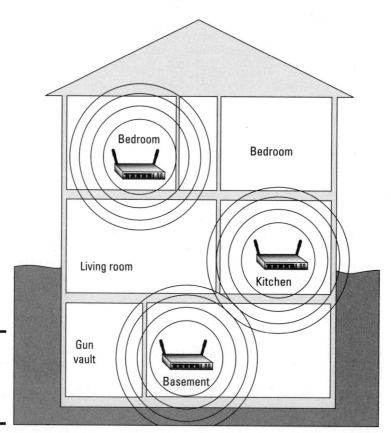

Figure 4-3:
Connecting
base
stations
with WDS.

With both WDS-capable wireless routers in range, you configure the first router (the one connected to the Internet) as the WDS main router, and the second as a WDS remote. Activating WDS for both routers spreads out the wireless network, giving you more access points but keeping all wireless connections on the same network.

You can even add a third WDS access point by setting up a third router as another WDS remote. It all depends on the router's signal strength and the area being covered.

✦ Creating a WDS depends on the abilities of the wireless routers. All the routers involved must be able to be configured for a WDS. When there's no WDS setup page for the router's configuration, you cannot create a WDS.

✦ The wireless router's WDS configuration may require you to manually enter the other router's MAC address. Find the MAC address by contacting the router using your PC's Web browser; or, sometimes the manufacturer prints the MAC address on the bottom of the router.

✦ The wireless routers should all be of the same type, such as 802.11g.

✦ You might have to configure all the wireless routers in a WDS to use the same network channel, such as Channel 1 or Channel 11.

✦ Some wireless routers can bridge to only one other router, and some can do "multipoint" bridging to create a larger WDS.

✦ Setting up a WDS for multiple wireless routers isn't the same thing as using the Bridge Connections command in Windows. By bridging a wired and wireless network connection on a laptop, for example, you allow network access to both networks. See the section in Chapter 3 about getting at multiple networks.

✦ By using WDS, you can have one wireless router connected to the Internet and then other wireless routers around your home or office that help distribute that connection to all the computers.

Restricting access to your wireless network

One major weakness of wireless networking is security. Your best move is to apply a good, solid network password, as described in the section "Configuring the wireless base station," earlier in this chapter. A better option is to restrict access to only those computers known to the wireless router or base station. That way, only computers you authorize can use the network, even when the network password is known.

How the technique works depends on the router. It may be called a wireless MAC filter, MAC address filter, network filter, or restricted MAC access. The idea is to supply the router with a list of MAC addresses. That works because each wireless NIC has a unique MAC address. The result is that only those PCs whose MAC addresses are known can access the wireless network.

After enabling MAC address filtering for your router, you need to enter the list of MAC addresses from the PCs that use that network. The method for obtaining that information is different between Windows Vista and Windows XP.

In Windows Vista, follow these steps to discover your PC's wireless NIC's MAC address:

1. **Open the Control Panel's Network and Sharing Center icon.**

2. **Click the Manage Network Connections link in the Network and Sharing Center window.**

   The Network Connections window appears. Each network connection, wired or wireless, appears as an icon in the window.

3. **Select the Wireless Network Connection icon.**

4. **Click the View Status of This Connection toolbar button.**

   You may need to click the Show More chevrons at the right end of the toolbar to see the View Status of This Connection button.

5. **In the Wireless Network Connection Status dialog box, click the Details button.**

   The MAC address, titled Physical Address, appears in the Property column.

6. **Close the various dialog boxes and windows.**

Follow these steps to discover the wireless NIC's MAC address in Windows XP:

1. **Open the Network Connections icon in the Control Panel.**

2. **Open the Wireless Network Connection icon.**

3. **Click the Support tab in the connection's Status window.**

4. **Click the Details button.**

   Lots of information is listed in the Details dialog box, including the MAC address, which is listed in the Property column as Physical Address.

5. **Close the various windows and dialog boxes.**

Most routers have the ability to determine the MAC address for the PC you're using to access the router. A button lets you copy the MAC address instantly. Use it. Otherwise, you have to enter the MAC addresses manually. It's a pain, but I believe that the payoff is worth it, for security reasons.

✦ All NICs have a unique MAC address.

✦ MAC stands for Media Access Control. It's a Scottish thing.

✦ The MAC address is a series of six values separated by hyphens. The values include the numbers 0 through 9 and letters *A* through *F.*

Resetting a base station

As with a wired router, you reset the wireless base station by locating its teensy, tiny Reset switch, found somewhere on the back of the unit. Use a bent paperclip to push the Reset switch in, wait a sec, and then release it.

By resetting the base station, you revert it to its factory presets. Those presets include the default password and configuration, essentially turning the thing into another stupid wireless router. So, after you reset the router, be sure to reconfigure it to the settings you want.

When the Hook-Up Gets Hung Up

As a human being, you're unable to see into that portion of the electro-magnetic spectrum where wireless networks flit and hum. I'm certain that the wireless signals would prove an awesome sight, probably all purple and bubbly. But you'll never see it — only your PC can. Assuming that a wireless network is out there somewhere, and that your PC can see it, the next step is to connect to it. This section describes how that happens, or doesn't happen, and what to do about it.

Enabling the wireless NIC

The biggest problem with connecting to a wireless network is that you don't have your computer's wireless NIC activated. There are two places to look.

 First, check for an external switch on a laptop computer that turns wireless networking on or off. You may find a tiny wireless NIC icon next to the switch, similar to the one shown in the margin. Place that switch into the On or active position.

Second, confirm that the wireless NIC has been activated in Windows. Often times, the NIC is disabled, especially when traveling by air, and there's no external wireless NIC switch.

To confirm that Windows has enabled the wireless NIC, follow these steps in Windows Vista:

1. **Open the Control Panel's Network and Sharing Center icon.**

   The Network and Sharing Center window appears.

2. **Click the link Manage Network Connections.**

3. **Confirm that the Wireless Network Connection icon in the Network Connections Window is enabled.**

   If so, you're done. Skip to Step 6. Otherwise, you need to enable the connection.

4. **Right-click the Wireless Network Connection icon and choose Enable from the shortcut menu.**

5. **Type the administrator's password or click the Continue button.**

   The adapter is enabled.

6. **Close the various dialog boxes and windows.**

In Windows XP, obey these steps to check your PC's wireless NIC:

1. **Open the Network Connections icon in the Control Panel.**

2. **Confirm that the Wireless Network Connection icon is enabled.**

   If the icon sports the text *Enabled,* you're done. Skip to Step 4.

3. **Right-click the Wireless Network Connection icon and choose Enable from the shortcut menu.**

4. **Close the Network Connections window.**

After you enable the wireless NIC, your computer may instantly connect to one of its recognized networks. If not, you need to proceed with a manual connection, as described in the later section, "But I can't find the network!"

+ Do not enable a wireless NIC on an airplane unless you're told by flight personnel that it's okay to do so.

+ The wireless switch might also be labeled Airplane Mode.

Finding a wireless network

There are at least two ways to seek out a wireless network. The first is the common way, which is to use Windows. Boring. The second is to use any custom software that came with the wireless NIC. The custom software doesn't work better at finding the signal, but often it displays the signals it found in a better, sexier way than the traditional Windows method does.

In Windows Vista, connect to a wireless network by choosing the Connect To command from the Start button menu. A Connect to Network window appears, as shown in Figure 4-4, from which you can choose a wireless network.

Figure 4-4:
Available
wireless
networks
seen by
Windows
Vista.

In Windows XP, you need to access the Wireless Network Connection icon in the Network Connections window: Open the Network Connections icon in the Control Panel and then right-click the Wireless Network Connection icon. Choose the command View Available Wireless Connections from the shortcut menu.

Accessing the custom wireless network connection software that came with your PC's wireless NIC depends on that software, so I can't be specific here. On my laptop, for example, I right-click a teeny icon in the notification area. Eventually, after wading through some weird dialog boxes, I can see a fancy connection window, shown in Figure 4-5. It not only shows available wireless networks but also graphically shows the network's signal strength.

Figure 4-5:
A custom
wireless
network
access
program.

After choosing a network, the next step is to enter a password for access, unless the network is already known to your computer and the password has been saved or the network doesn't use a password.

After you're connected, you see a wireless connection icon appear in the notification area. You can point the mouse at that icon to check the connection's status.

✦ See the later section "Managing wireless connections" for more information about saved wireless connections.

✦ In Windows Vista, you must also specify whether the network is public or private. Refer to Chapter 3, the section about checking network privacy in Windows Vista, for more information on the public/private question.

✦ Some of those passwords can be long and tedious to type, especially in Windows XP, where you have to type it twice.

✦ Yes, some networks have no passwords. That makes access easier, but it's also less secure, just like keeping all the doors to your house unlocked and open.

✦ If you're using an unsecured network, definitely employ a software firewall. See Book IV, Chapter 4.

✦ Public wireless hot spots often lack passwords. You might be required to "log in" by providing your e-mail address or some form of temporary ID.

✦ In Windows Vista, always set to Public, not Private, any wireless network that you use outside your home or office. That helps boost general wireless security.

✦ Windows Vista also assaults you with various User Account Control (UAC) warnings as you connect to wireless networks. Type the administrator's password or click the Continue button to proceed.

"But I can't find the network!"

Boy, wireless networks would sure work better if there were a more substantial way to connect to them. Say, something like *wires?* But I jest. The first problem you encounter when trying to make the wireless network connection is finding the network.

First of all, have patience. Not all wireless networks show up at first blush. Remember that the signal is affected by physical objects around you: walls, bookcases, large partitions made from lead, and depleted uranium slugs. Those things readily block the wireless signal.

Next, move around. Sometimes, moving the laptop just a few feet in one direction improves signal reception. Remember that if you cannot see the wireless hub directly, odds are good that you won't get a solid signal.

In Windows Vista, click the Refresh button found in the upper-right portion of the Connect to Network window (refer to Figure 4-4). Keep clicking that button to have the wireless NIC rescan for network availability.

Some wireless networks don't send out their SSIDs. Although the wireless NIC still picks up the signal, no name is given for the access point. You have to supply the name. Of course, I'm assuming that you know the SSID already. After you know it, from either the network administrator or a stained piece of paper given to you by the tattooed, pierced guy who makes your coffee, you must use that information to tell Windows how to find the wireless network. Here's how to do that in Windows Vista:

1. **Pop up the Start button menu and choose Connect To.**

2. **Click the link Set Up a Connection or Network.**

    It's at the bottom of the window (refer to Figure 4-4).

3. **Choose Manually Connect to a Wireless Network and click the Next button.**

    A window appears with various fill-in-the-blanks items, helping you hone down which wireless network you desire to connect to.

4. **Type the SSID into the Network Name box.**

5. **Select Security Type from the button menu.**

6. **If the Encryption Type button becomes enabled, click it.**

    The encryption type is based on the security type.

7. **Type the security key or passphrase.**

    I prefer putting a check mark in the Display Characters check box so that I can double-check my typing.

8. **Click the Next button.**

   If all goes well, Windows presents the network as ready for a connection.

9. **Choose the option Connect To.**

   And . . . you're only half done. Now you need to use the Connect To command from the Start button menu to actually connect to the network.

In Windows XP, supply the SSID by following these steps:

1. **Open the Network Connections icon in the Control Panel.**

2. **Right-click the Wireless Network Connection icon.**

3. **Choose Properties from the shortcut menu.**

4. **Click the Wireless Networks tab in the Wireless Network Connection Properties dialog box.**

5. **Click the Add button.**

   It's found near the bottom of the dialog box.

6. **Type the SSID into the Network Name (SSID) text box in the Wireless Network Properties dialog box.**

7. **If required, type the Network Key — twice.**

8. **Click OK.**

   You're not connected at this point, but the network should now show up in the list of available networks. Connect to the network as you normally would.

Another cause of a dropped connection may be a timeout. For example, some for-pay wireless services give you only a limited amount of access time. After that time expires, you're no longer connected or you may see the Pay Up home page rather than the Internet.

Finally, the connection problem may simply be that the password is incorrect. A dialog box warns you about it, but keep in mind that any wireless network passwords you stored in your PC might be changed by the various networks you access. In fact, I purposely don't memorize the wireless password at the coffee shop I frequent in town because they keep changing it.

✦ You can check the connection strength by pointing the mouse at the wee connection icon in the notification area.

✦ In Windows Vista, the wireless connection strength is also displayed beneath the network's information area in the Network and Connection Sharing window.

✦ You can install various wireless networking gadgets for the Windows Vista Sidebar. Most display wireless network's name, signal strength, and IP address.

✦ Third-party utilities can also be used to gauge signal strength, such as the wireless networking tool shown earlier, in Figure 4-5. Various *war driver* utilities, used to find wireless signals, can also be used to discover signal strength. The popular NetStumbler program can be downloaded here:

```
http://www.netstumbler.com/
```

Managing wireless connections

Windows Vista has a little black book. But unlike former dates, the black book helps you keep track of all the wireless networks your computer has gone out with. You can see the whole list of 'em by opening the Control Panel's Network and Sharing Center icon and clicking the Manage Wireless Networks link. When you do, the Manage Wireless Networks window appears, as shown in Figure 4-6.

Figure 4-6:
The wireless networking black book in Windows Vista.

The Manage Wireless Networks window displays a list of wireless networks you accessed in the past. By keeping track of those connections, Windows Vista makes it easier for your computer (okay, your laptop) to recognize and instantly connect to those networks when they're within range. It saves time.

If you have trouble connecting to one of the networks, you can enter updated information as your computer tries to make the connection. For example, you can enter a new password if the old one is rejected or has expired.

You can change any saved wireless connection by double-clicking its icon in the Manage Wireless Networks window. In the connection's Properties dialog box, click the Security tab to type the new password.

If you'd rather not have a connection made automatically, double-click the connection icon and in its Properties dialog box, remove the check mark by the Connect Automatically When This Network Is in Range option.

To set a priority for the connections, use the Move Up or Move Down buttons on the toolbar: Select a network connection icon in the window, and then use Move Up to make that connection a higher priority. Or, use the Move Down button to lower the connection's priority.

Windows ensures that the computer first connects to the higher-priority networks. Well, that is unless you turned off that option in the connection's Properties dialog box. (The setting is titled Connect to a More Preferred Network If Available.)

Close the Manage Wireless Networks window when you're done messing around.

+ Even when you don't remember choosing to save a wireless network connection, don't be surprised to see it in the list.

+ Removing an item from the list is easy: Select the wireless network connection icon and click the Remove (green minus sign) toolbar button.

+ I recommend removing older connections. For example, after a road trip, I just remove all the various icons for the hotel networks I connected to.

Book VI

Maintenance

The 5th Wave   By Rich Tennant

"How's the defragmentation coming?"

Contents at a Glance

Chapter 1: Backup, Backup, Backup

Sad is the PC user who is resigned to losing her stuff. Documents and reports, lost. Music, lost. Vacations, photos, and videos gone forever. It doesn't have to be that way. Thanks to the useful tool *backup*, you can keep the precious data on your PC safe and easily recoverable. By creating a backup copy, or *archive*, of your stuff, you avoid many of the pratfalls and issues that so many other tools and utilities must remedy. I pray that you join the ranks of the PC backup fanatics and take the first step of reading this chapter.

That Emergency Copy

Nothing is better than having a good collection of stuff on a computer: work, play, music, video, pictures, e-mail — an electronic image of your digital life. Well, actually, there's something better: having a *second copy* of all that stuff. I'm shocked at how many people fail to make a second, safety copy. Read this section to learn more.

Understanding backup

It's one of the old ones, perhaps the most ancient of computer utilities. It's commonly called *backup*, though it's had other names, such as the curious *tar*. The purpose is a vital one: to ensure that you have a second copy, or even multiple copies, of your data. Sounds good, right? Yet few people bother and end up paying the price later.

You can make a safety copy, or backup, of your computer files in two ways:

Manual copy: To back up your files, simply duplicate them on removeable media: an optical disc or media card. You use the standard file copying methods in Windows to copy the files. It's simple. Time-consuming, but simple. I do it all the time.

Backup program: Employ a backup program. The program does basically the same thing as copying files. The advantage is that it automates and simplifies the process. Plus, the program adds features such as scheduling, the ability to manage backup *sets*, and the power to quickly restore files from the backup.

No matter how you back up, the result is the same: You have a second copy of your files. You can use that copy to restore files you accidentally deleted, recover files irreparably changed, or restore portions of your system damaged by a virus or hardware disaster. Backup is good news.

And now, for the bad news:

Too many people don't back up. In the olden days, people didn't back up because it was a chore. I remember backing up one of my early PC's hard drives to a set of about 40 floppy disks. Shuffling those disks in and out was a nightmare. That's why few people bothered back then.

Today's backup programs take advantage of high-capacity optical discs, media cards, external hard drives, and network storage. There's no more disk-swapping. (Well, there can be, when you use optical discs.) External storage is cheap and plentiful. Backup programs are widely available, and a good backup program comes with Windows Vista. Despite all that, the bad news remains that few people back up.

Worse: People who don't back up seem somehow resigned to the fact that all computer data is temporary. It need not be.

There's no reason in the digital age not to keep with you copies of your digital life — pictures, videos, music, and documents — forever. You will never lose that stuff, if you use backup and stick with a regular backup schedule. It's not that difficult.

✦ The process of backing up files is referred to as *archiving*. A backup copy of a file is also known as an *archive*.

✦ The key to being successful with backing up your files is to place them on removable media, which is a type of storage different from the computer's internal hard drive. Remember that the hard drive is the first location for storing files on your computer. To keep the backup copy safe, it should be on another storage media. That way, if your PC has a hardware problem, your files exist safely elsewhere.

✦ Removable media or an external hard drive (which is really another form or removeable media) is best for your file backups. That's because you can store the removable media elsewhere, such as in a fire safe.

✦ Yes, I strongly recommend storing your backup copies in a fire safe. You can find a small, portable fire safe for your data at most office supply stores.

✦ A small, portable fire safe isn't available on this book's companion DVD.

✦ Backup programs can be run automatically. You never forget to back up when you schedule the backup program to run every day and make that safety copy of your stuff.

✦ Backup programs remember which files have been backed up and which files have been created or modified since the last backup. You can take advantage of that situation by directing the backup program to archive only those files that are newly created or have been modified since the last backup operation.

✦ The clutch of files that's backed up is referred to as a *backup set*. Backup programs can manage multiple backup sets.

✦ Backup programs feature a restore utility that allows you to easily recover files that have been backed up. The files can be restored individually, or the computer's entire file system can be rebuilt using the archived copy.

✦ A *full backup* is an archive copy of all the files on your computer's main hard drive.

✦ A *personal backup* is an archive copy of all your user files on the computer's main hard drive. It doesn't include program files or the Windows operating system.

✦ An *incremental backup* is the official name of a backup set that includes only those files created or modified since the last backup.

✦ An *image backup* copies information directly from the computer's hard drive at a very low level. It's a backup copy, but merely of raw data and not separate files.

✦ The tar utility still exists in the Unix operating system. It means *t*ape *ar*chive and relates to copies made to a tape backup machine often connected to early Unix systems. The tar utility is still used, mostly to create archive files similar to compressed folders (ZIP files) in Windows. Tar archives often use the filename extension `tar` or `tar.gz` for compressed archives.

Making that backup copy

You don't need to run a backup program to make a backup. In fact, anytime you copy a file, you're essentially making a backup; the duplicate file is a safety copy of the original. However, to be a true backup, the copy must exist on an external storage device or media.

The following steps demonstrate how you can manually create a backup copy of one or more files. These steps work for any version of Windows, and you can use them whether or not your computer has a backup program. To complete these steps, you need an external storage device, such as a media card or USB thumb drive:

1. **Open the folder containing the files you want to back up.**

If you're backing up a folder, that folder's *parent* folder must be visible. For example, to back up my Work folder, I need to be able to see the Documents folder, which is where the Work folder lives.

I don't recommend backing up your personal, or *home,* folder using the file-copy method. That's because your personal folder is probably larger than any storage media you have. If it isn't, that's swell. If it is, however, you'll run out of room on the backup media and won't know about it until it's too late (which is another reason to use a real backup program rather than just copy over files).

2. **Click to select the files or folders you want to back up.**

To select more than one icon at a time, press and hold the Ctrl key as you click each icon.

3. **Press Ctrl+C to copy the files.**

The Ctrl+C key places the list of files (or a single file) into the Windows Clipboard, where they sit happily until you paste them into another folder, which completes the entire copy operation.

4. **Insert or attach the removable media to your PC.**

For example, plug in the USB thumb drive or stick a media card into your PC's media card reader. If the removable storage device is already attached, you're set to go.

You can also use an optical disc as the removable storage media. Ensure that the disc has been inserted and prepared by Windows for use as a data disc.

5. **Open the Computer window.**

In Windows XP, it's the My Computer window. The window lists all storage devices attached to your PC, similar to what's shown in Figure 1-1. One of them should represent the storage media you're copying the files to.

6. **Open the icon representing the removable media.**

Which one is it? The answer depends on the type of media and on how the drive letters are assigned. In Figure 1-1, for example, the USB thumb drive is given letter *G.* That's the one I'm using.

Figure 1-1:
Removable media in the Computer window (in Windows Vista).

7. **Create a new folder for the backup: Right-click in the media's window and choose New⇨Folder from the shortcut menu.**

Sure, you could just copy the files over, but you find life easier to deal with if you create a special backup folder.

8. **Name the folder to reflect the backup contents and today's date.**

I name my work backups using something like `work.2009-06-01.bak`. That's the name `work` for the content, and then the date, and then the word `bak` for backup. This book's backup folder files are named `TroubleAIO.2009-10-10.bak` and so on, depending on the backup date.

9. **Open the folder.**

10. **Press Ctrl+V to paste in the files, which effectively copies them from your PC's hard drive to the backup media.**

11. **Properly eject the media and keep it in a safe place, such as in a fire safe.**

I admit that most people don't put the backup media into a safe place. Even I just keep the media card sticking out of the front of my PC's console, looking like a tiny diving board.

For backups to be effective, you must keep making them. These steps aren't something you follow once and consider yourself finished. Backing up is like doing the laundry: There are always new dirty clothes that need washing. So, just like you're never really done doing the laundry (unless you wash your clothes naked), you should back up on a regular schedule to catch those new or modified files.

How often is enough? Once a day seems about right for people serious about their data. That's another reason to consider a real backup program instead of merely copying and pasting files.

✦ I use both a real backup program, and I copy and paste files. I'm very serious about backing up my stuff.

✦ The keyboard shortcut to copy a file is Ctrl+C, and then press Ctrl+V to "paste" the file copy into a destination folder.

✦ There are about a jillion other ways to copy files in Windows. Anytime you see a book on Windows that's thicker than your fist, it probably lists every last way to copy a file.

✦ The steps in this section work differently if you use an optical disc. The optical disc must be prepared, and then the files must be burned to the disc and, finally, the disc ejected.

✦ In Windows Vista, use the Live File System to create your backup discs. See my book *PCs For Dummies* (Wiley Publishing) for details.

✦ True, you don't need to include the current date in a filename because Windows slaps a creation date on every file it creates. I add dates to filenames anyway because the date stamp on old files doesn't always survive the transfer to newer computers or media. By putting the date in the filename, I ensure that I always know the backup date.

✦ Another advantage to placing the date in a backup filename is that you can use Windows to easily sort the file list. As long as you use the same format, such as year-month-date, the files are sorted chronologically.

✦ When you're adept with wildcards, you can use them to match groups of backup files by their names or dates. For example, `work.*.bak` matches all my work folders on the backup media.

✦ Then again, using a real backup program allows you to manage all that information automatically. It's your call.

✦ If you forget to properly name a folder, click to select it and press the F2 key. Type the new folder's name.

✦ Another, valid way to back up is to place all your file duplicates into a compressed folder. If you recall from elsewhere in this book, a compressed folder is also a ZIP file, which is also an *archive*. The advantage of using a compressed folder for your file-copy backups is that it takes up less space on the backup disk. See my book *Find Gold in Windows Vista* (Wiley Publishing) for more information on compressed folders.

Using a backup program

Far simpler than copying files is to run a backup program. The benefits are many, as discussed throughout this program.

Windows Vista comes with the backup program Windows Backup. It's available in all versions of Windows Vista.

Windows Vista Business Edition and Windows Vista Ultimate come with the backup program Complete PC Backup. Unlike the standard Windows Backup program, Complete PC Backup copies all files from your computer to external media. It's ideal for completely restoring your computer system.

Windows XP also comes with a backup program, though it might not have been installed on your PC. You may be able to locate the program by looking in the special folder ValueAdd. You can look for that folder on your PC's start-up hard drive or drive C or on the Windows XP distribution CD. Open the Msft folder inside ValueAdd, and then open the NTBackup folder. Run the NTBackup program, NTBackup.msi, to install the Windows Backup Utility in Windows XP.

Numerous third-party backup programs are also available. Among those I can recommend are Norton Ghost, EMC Retrospect, and Roxio Backup MyPC.

✦ I'm just guessing at the name Windows Backup for the backup program that comes with Windows Vista. That's because I don't see the words *Windows Backup* on any of the dialog boxes, windows, or wizards used by the backup program.

✦ Several programs can also back up. For example, Microsoft Word can be configured to automatically create a backup copy of any old document you modify. The Quicken money-management program also urges you to create a backup copy of your financial stuff about every third time you close the program.

The Computer Backs Up for You

There's no need to fuss over backup. As long as you configure the backup program properly, things should run just fine. This section explains how to set things up for automatic, reliable backups on your PC.

✦ Also see the later section "The Complete PC Backup" for information on backing up your entire PC using certain editions of Windows Vista.

✦ The information in this section can be applied to any backup program, including the Windows Backup Utility in Windows XP. The steps listed in this section, however, are specific to the backup program that comes with Windows Vista. (It comes with all editions of Windows Vista except for Windows Vista Home Basic.)

Getting an external hard drive

The best way to back up in Windows is to get an external hard drive. Forget about using optical discs; they're not large enough, and managing multiple disc sets is a pain. Forget digital media because the capacity is too low. Instead, invest in an external USB hard drive, such as the popular MyBook series of drives from Western Digital.

All the external hard drives I purchased recently require no extra setup on the software side; after plugging in the drive, it pops right up in the Computer window, and I'm ready to use the thing.

Okay, well, some programs may be preinstalled on the hard drive. In fact, the hard drive may have an *autorun* setting, in which case some configuration program may appear when you first turn on the drive. Whatever.

✦ Get an external hard drive that has a capacity at or greater than the capacity of your PC's internal hard drive.

✦ If you can afford it, get the largest-capacity external hard drive.

✦ Another advantage of an external hard drive is that you can easily detach it and put it into a fire safe.

✦ For more information on external hard drives, see Book I, Chapter 4.

✦ Feel free to delete any bonus programs that came with the external hard drive.

✦ Remember that it's *your* hard drive. If you don't plan to use the "free" programs that came with the drive, don't. Delete them. Delete anything you don't want on the external hard drive. You need the storage space more than you need those programs.

✦ Okay, I lied. If you plan to use Complete PC Backup, you probably need to convert the external drive's format. Information is provided in the section "Setting up an external hard drive for Complete PC Backup," later in this chapter.

Finding the backup program in Windows Vista

Buried somewhere in the myriad files that comprise a complex operating system like Windows Vista must exist a single backup program. Good luck finding it. In fact, don't bother. Instead, concentrate on getting to know on the two locations in Windows Vista where backup (and restore) operations are configured and performed: the Backup Status and Configuration window and the Backup and Restore Center.

Backup and Restore Center. Open the Control Panel's Backup and Restore Center icon to view the Backup and Restore Center window, shown in Figure 1-2. The window lists information about recent backups and allows you to back up your computer or restore files.

Figure 1-2:
The Backup and Restore Center window.

Backup Status and Configuration. The Backup Status and Configuration window is shown in Figure 1-3. To open that window, from the Start button menu, choose All Programs⇨Accessories⇨System Tools⇨Backup Status and Configuration. The window you see looks similar to the one shown in Figure 1-3.

Why are there two locations? I don't know. It's confusing. That's because there's lots of overlap, which means that you can do the same things in both windows. Yes, it's dumb and redundant. But then again, it's Windows, which is why those "I'm a Mac and I'm a PC" TV commercials are so darn funny.

✦ When your version of Windows lacks the Complete PC Backup program, Figures 1-2 and 1-3 look different. The buttons Back Up Computer and Restore Computer, plus the areas they're in, are missing from the Backup and Restore Center window (refer to Figure 1-2). In Figure 1-3, the Complete PC Backup button-thing is missing from the left side of the window.

Figure 1-3:
The Backup
Status and
Configur-
ation
window.

+ Of the two locations, I use the Backup Status and Configuration window more often.

+ Two or three large buttons are on the left side of the Backup Status and Configuration window. The top one is Backup, which causes backup options to appear in the window. The second button is Restore, which deals with restoring files to your computer from a backup. See the section "Files from Days of Yore," later in this chapter, for information on restoring files.

+ A third button that appears on the left side of the Backup Status and Configuration window is Complete PC Backup. See the later section "The Complete PC Backup" for more information.

+ You can quickly jump from the Backup and Restore Center to the Backup Status and Configuration window by clicking the Change Settings link beneath the Back Up Files button.

+ Windows also features, in the notification area, an itsy-bitsy icon that appears when a backup is overdue. Clicking that icon opens the Backup Status and Configuration window. Or, is it the Backup and Restore Center window? Oh, it doesn't matter. . . .

Configuring (and making your first) backup

The first backup you make with Windows Backup is different from the rest of them, mostly because that first-time operation also configures the backup software. The following steps walk you through the process and assume that you're backing up to an external hard drive that's always connected to your PC:

1. **From the Start button menu, choose All Programs⇨Accessories⇨ System Tools⇨Backup Status and Configuration Open the Backup Status.**

This step opens the Backup Status and Configuration window, though if you haven't used Backup, you see a different window than the one shown earlier, in Figure 1-2.

2. **Click the button Set Up Automatic File Backup.**

It looks like a link, but it's really a button — a big button.

3. **Type the administrator's password or click the Continue button.**

The computer desperately looks for backup devices. These include the following backup destinations:

> **Hard Drive:** The best choice, though I recommend selecting an *external* hard drive. Although an internal hard drive works, you should choose a separate physical hard drive inside the computer, not a partition.

> **Optical Drive (CD or DVD):** An okay choice, though if you have more information to back up than can fit on a single optical disc, you'll swap discs. That also means automatic backups require extra preparatory work.

> **Network Drive:** Works only when the computer is connected to a server type of network. That explains why a shared network hard drive doesn't appear on the list.

4. **Choose the option Hard Disk.**

5. **Select the external hard drive from the drop-down menu.**

6. **Click the Next button.**

When your PC has more than one internal hard drive or disk partition, you may be prompted to select those additional disks for backup. I don't recommend doing that unless you keep important files on those drives, such as images, music, or important documents.

7. **Choose any extra disk drives to back up, if prompted.**

8. **Click the Next button.**

The next step is to choose which types of files you want to back up. Rather than fuss over that decision, I recommend backing up *all* your personal information; keep all options selected.

9. **Click the Next button.**

10. **Set a backup schedule.**

Use the gizmos in the window to set a regular backup schedule. The type and variety of available gizmos depends on whether you select Daily, Weekly, or Monthly from the top, How Often, menu button.

How often you back up depends on how often you use the computer and the nature of the information it holds. For example, in an office situation, I recommend backing up daily, right after work. At home, I work every day, so I back up every day. For my kid's game computers, I have the backup program run once a week.

11. **Click the Save Settings and Start Backup button.**

Because the next thing you should do after setting up the backup program is to back up your computer, the steps are combined.

Feel free to do something else while the backup proceeds. A typical backup can take anywhere from a few minutes to several hours, depending on how much stuff is being backed up. Browse the Web, check your e-mail, play Spider Solitaire — you get the idea.

When the backup is completed, a pop-up balloon from the notification area alerts you (unless that feature has been disabled).

12. **Click the Close button to dismiss the Back-Up Files window.**

13. **Close the Backup Status and Configuration window.**

Now count yourself lucky, for several reasons:

First, you just backed up your computer. A second, safety copy of your personal files exists, allowing you to recover them if unwelcome fates befall you.

Second, the computer is backing up to an external hard drive that will always be there and (hopefully) take a long time to fill up. You don't need to set things up or remember to do this or that in preparation.

Third, you set up automatic backups to take place. As long as the computer is on (or sleeping) when that time rolls around, the computer is backed up.

Now you can use your computer with confidence. Files are regularly being updated on the backup disk. They can swiftly and accurately be recovered if anything bad ever happens, when anything bad ever happens.

✦ To recover files from a backup disk, see the section "Files from Days of Yore," later in this chapter.

✦ You can also set the backup configuration by clicking the Change Settings link in the Backup and Restore Center window.

+ Though it would make sense to back up your PC to a standard, shared network hard drive, that option works only when you're using a computer network that's more sophisticated than the standard peer-to-peer networks that are popular in homes and small offices.

+ Yes, your computer must be on when the backup takes place. The computer can be in Stand By or Sleep mode. That's okay; Windows wakes up the computer and runs the backup. But an automatic backup doesn't run when the computer is turned off or in Hibernation mode (which means that it's turned off).

+ Backing up your data consumes some computer resources. Be sure to schedule a backup for when you're not doing anything else, especially something processor-intensive on the computer, such as editing video, working with images, or playing a sophisticated computer game (full-screen with action).

+ Even if you employ a nifty, full-time backup program, you can still manually copy files. I do. I routinely back up my stuff to a media card or even to the same external drive I use with the Windows Backup program. You can never be too safe with backing up files. (Okay, but don't obsess over it.)

+ Unlike other backup programs, you cannot use the Windows Backup program in Windows Vista to back up a single file or folder or clutch of files and folders.

+ Each time you back up your files, the Windows Backup program creates a new, unique *backup set* on the external hard drive. Those sets are maintained like a database for use by the Restore portion of the Backup program. That way, not only can older files be recovered, but older *versions* of those files can be recovered as well.

Confirming that the backup worked

When you do things correctly, your computer is backed up all the time automatically. But how do you know? To confirm that the backup took place, open either of the two backup windows: Backup Status and Configuration or Backup and Restore Center (refer to Figures 1-2 and 1-3).

As usual, I prefer viewing the Backup Status and Configuration window (refer to Figure 1-3). Ensure that the Back Up Files button is selected (in the upper-right part of the window), and then read the information in the Backup Status area. It not only lists the last successful backup but also describes when the next scheduled backup takes place.

When an automatic backup doesn't take place, a warning pops up from the notification area. You can click that icon to open the Backup Status and Configuration window or right-click the icon to choose Backup Now and immediately run the backup procedure.

+ To open the Backup and Restore Center window, open the Control Panel's Backup and Restore Center icon.

+ To view the Backup Status and Configuration window, choose All Programs⇨Accessories⇨System Tools⇨Backup Status and Configuration.

Making an immediate backup

Do you have moments of brilliance? Perhaps a burst of productivity? I do. Sometimes I seem to just churn out a lot of work in a short amount of time. When that happens, I want to make doubly sure that I have a backup copy of my stuff. I call it an *immediate* backup.

Sometimes I make an immediate backup by simply copying a file or folder to a media card. That works. But when I end up doing work all over the computer, the only way to ensure that I catch everything is to simply usurp the scheduled backup and run an instant, immediate backup. Here's how:

1. **From the Start menu, choose All Programs⇨Accessories⇨System Tools⇨Backup Status and Configuration.**

2. **Ensure that the Back Up Files button is chosen from the left side of the Backup Status and Configuration window.**

3. **Click the Backup Up Now button.**

4. **Type the administrator's password or click the Continue button.**

    Windows starts running the backup program. While it runs, you're free to do something else, which I recommend because backing up files takes time.

5. **Click the Close button when the backup is done, and then close the Backup Status and Configuration window.**

There's no need to do an immediate backup if your computer's backup schedule is tight — say, once a day. But on those PCs where backup is a weekly or monthly routine, I recommend making an immediate backup once in a while, just to be safe.

An immediate backup can also start by clicking the Back Up Files button in the Backup and Restore Center window.

Modifying the backup routine

If you originally configured the backup properly, there's no need to modify things. Then again, I suppose that they wouldn't have a way to modify the backup routine if people always guessed the proper ways to do things in the first place.

There are a number of reasons to modify the computer's backup routine:

✦ You want to back up more often.

✦ You want to choose a different set of files to back up.

✦ You added another internal hard drive and need to back it up.

✦ You need to reset the time to later in the day because the backup routine is causing your PC to lag while you're playing *Call of Duty* online.

✦ You just bought a newer, larger external hard drive to write off as a tax expense, and you need to start using it.

✦ Other reasons I cannot think of right now.

To "recajigger" the backup routine, follow these steps:

1. **From the Start menu, choose All Programs➪Accessories➪System Tools➪Backup Status and Configuration.**

2. **Ensure that the Back Up Now button is chosen from the left side of the Backup Status and Configuration window.**

3. **Click the big Change Backup Settings button.**

4. **When prompted by the User Account Control (UAC) warning, click the Continue button or type the administrator's password to proceed.**

5. **Work through the wizard to reset whatever backup options need resetting.**

The complete walk-through of steps is the same as described in the section "Configuring (and making your first) backup," earlier in this chapter. Specifically, you repeat Steps 4 through 11 in that section.

6. **Sit back and watch the backup proceed.**

No, you cannot change the settings without starting an immediate backup. The settings have been changed, and it's a good idea to back up often anyway.

7. **Click the Close button when the backup is complete.**

8. **Close the Backup Status and Configuration window.**

Also see the earlier section "Confirming that the backup worked" for information on how you can ensure later that the backup has taken place according to your wishes.

Stopping a backup in progress

Though I can't really make up any reasons to stop a backup, you can halt one by clicking the Stop Backup button. That button appears in either the Backup Status and Configuration window or the Backup and Restore Center window while a backup is taking place.

There's nothing wrong with stopping a backup; it doesn't destroy any data that's already on the backup hard drive. Stopping the backup does, however, prevent the backup program from making copies of all the files in need of backing up.

✦ You can't resume a stopped backup, but you can make an immediate backup to make up for the stopped backup. See the earlier section "Making an immediate backup."

✦ Okay, I can think of one reason to stop a backup: Once I noticed that my PC was running slowly. I discovered that the backup program was running, so I stopped it to see whether the backup program was the cause. (It wasn't, but after restarting the computer, things ran faster, and I did an immediate backup.)

Disabling the backup program

You have no way to postpone a backup, but you can turn off the backup program, essentially disabling automatic backup. Follow these steps:

1. **Open the Backup Status and Configuration window: From the Start menu, choose All Programs⇨Accessories⇨System Tools⇨Backup Status and Configuration.**

2. **Ensure that the big Back Up Files button is selected on the left side of the window.**

3. **Click the Turn Off button, found at the bottom of the window.**

   A User Account Control (UAC) warning dialog box rudely awakens you.

4. **Click the Continue button or type the administrator's password.**

   Automatic backups are stopped.

5. **Close the Backup Status and Configuration window.**

You can easily resume the backup schedule again by clicking the Turn On button, which conveniently replaces the Turn Off button in Step 3.

✦ Backup programs don't run when you turn them off.

✦ Turning off the backup program is one way to suppress the constant pop-up messages about missing the backup. For example, on my laptop, I turn off the backup program when I'm on the road because I'm away from the external backup drive. Upon returning home, I turn on backup again.

Files from Days of Yore

Backup files are nice to have, but they don't do any good unless it's possible to fish out one or more files from time to time, or even — in the worst-case scenario — when you lose all your files. In that case, you rely on Backup's lesser-used but wonderfully opposite program, Restore. This section explains how to use Restore.

✦ Most of the information here is specific to the Backup program that comes with Windows Vista. The Windows XP backup program has a similar restore option, as do the various third-party backup programs.

✦ I refer to the restore procedure as a "restore program," "restore operation," or sometimes just "restore." It's not a different program from the Windows Backup utility — just a different part of the same program.

✦ Unlike the backup program, there's no need to configure Restore.

✦ The restore operation works best when you have a recent file backup. Back up your files! Do it often.

✦ You can also restore files from a manual backup or file copy. The operation works the same as creating the manual backup: Look on the backup media for the file you want, and then copy it back to the computer's primary storage device, the hard drive.

✦ Yea verily, even when you have a backup file, you don't get everything back. All the files created or modified since the last backup are lost. But that's better than the alternative of losing them all.

Restoring something from the last backup

The beauty of having a backup set of files is that you can recover a file, either long lost, destroyed, or just a previous version of something you once had. So, although you cannot use the backup sets to restore your misspent youth, you can perform the following steps in Windows Vista to restore a file from a backup set:

1. **From the Start menu, choose All Programs⇨Accessories⇨System Tools⇨Backup Status and Configuration.**

2. **Click the Restore Files button on the left side of the window.**

   You see the Restore Files portion of the window, shown in Figure 1-4. (If you're a Standard user, the two buttons are flipped; the Restore Files button appears on top.)

Figure 1-4: The Backup Status and Configura- tion, Restore window.

3. **Click the Restore Files button.**

   You're next asked how to restore files. You have two choices:

   Files from the latest backup: The file you restore is the most recent version of the file that's backed up. Most often, this choice is the one you want.

   Files from an older backup: Use this option only when you want to recover an older version of a file, as discussed in the next section.

4. **Choose the option Files from the Latest Backup.**

5. **Click the Next button.**

   You use the next screen, similar to the one shown in Figure 1-5, to build a collection of files to recover.

   The next step is to pick which files or folders you need to recover.

Figure 1-5:
Choose files
to restore
here.

6. **Add files and folders to be recovered.**

You can use three buttons on the right side of the screen (refer to Figure 1-5) to add files to the list.

Add Files: Click this button to browse for individual files to restore. An Add Files to Restore window appears, similar to the standard Open/Browse dialog box. You can select multiple files by dragging over their icons or by using the Ctrl+click method.

Add Folders: To restore an entire folder — and all the files and folders in that folder — click the Add Folders button. Use the Add Folder to Restore dialog box to choose one or more folders to add to the list. You can add only one folder a time, so when you need to recover more than one folder, you have to repeat Step 6 and click the Add Folders button for each folder to add.

Search: Click the Search button to summon a Search for Files to Restore window, where you can use the standard Windows Search command to locate the files you want to restore.

Keep adding the files you want to restore. If you need to restore only a single file, just restore that file. Don't feel pressured to restore a bunch of them just because the program gives you that ability.

7. **Click the Next button.**

   You need to choose where to restore the file or files. You have two options:

   In the original location: The files and folders you selected are placed back on the hard drive in the same folder where Backup found them. Most of the time, this option is the one you choose, especially for file recovery.

   In the following location: You get to select in which folder to place the restored files. This option is best for recovering an older version of a file where you don't want to overwrite the current version.

8. **Click the Start Restore button.**

   The files are restored.

9. **Click the Finish button.**

10. **Close the Backup Status and Configuration window.**

The only kink in the hose happens when you attempt to restore a backed-up file, and the same file still exists on the hard drive. A warning message appears, as shown in Figure 1-6.

Figure 1-6:
Restoring a file that already exists.

You have three options:

Copy and Replace: The backup file replaces the existing file. This option is most likely the one you want, unless you want to keep both versions of the file. In that case, choose the option Copy and Keep Both Files.

Don't Copy: The file isn't restored. Choosing this option basically undoes the restore operation for that single file.

Copy, but Keep Both Files: The file is restored but given a new name. Both files exist in the same folder: the current one and the restored copy with a number in parentheses after its name.

If you have any doubt, please choose the option Don't Copy. You can always try to restore the file later, but you don't want to lose something unexpectedly.

✦ You can also start the restore operation in the Backup and Restore Center window by clicking the Restore Files button.

✦ The files you restore aren't removed from the backup set. If the need arises, you can restore them again.

✦ The Ctrl+click method of selecting multiple files works by holding down the Ctrl key as you click the file's icons.

✦ Recovering a deleted file from the Recycle Bin is easier than recovering a file from a backup.

✦ See Book II, Chapter 8 for information on the Previous Versions command in Windows Vista.

Restoring from an older backup

Unless otherwise directed to do so, the restore operation looks for only the most recently backed-up file. But what about older files? What if you have a file that's evolved and you need to recover an earlier version? Maybe you want both the earlier version and the current version. Windows Backup can handle that.

To scour older backup sets, follow the steps presented in the preceding section. At Step 4, however, choose the option Files from an Older Backup. After clicking the Next button, you see a list of recent backup sets, as shown in Figure 1-7.

Figure 1-7:
Search for
an earlier
backup to
restore.

To see even older backup sets, put a check mark by the option Show Backups Older than 30 Days (refer to Figure 1-7).

Choose a date and time in the window. The dates march back through time as long as you've been backing up your computer (though older backup sets are purged as the backup media gets full).

After choosing a date, click the Next button. At that point, the restore operation proceeds as described in the preceding section, in Step 6 and Figure 1-5.

Be sure that you choose the option Copy But Keep Both Files when restoring the older version, when you do want to keep both files.

Restoring all your personal files

The restore operation works simply for restoring files or folders that get smooshed or seemingly vanish overnight. You can also restore *all* your personal files if anything nasty ever befalls them. The steps work the same as for restoring any file or folder, but you must take care to find the right folder. Follow these steps:

1. **Click the button Restore Files on the left side of the Backup Status and Configuration window.**

From the Start menu, choose All Programs➪Accessories➪System Tools➪Backup Status and Configuration to open the window.

2. **Click the Restore Files button.**

3. **Choose the option Files from the Latest Backup.**

   I'm assuming that you want the most recent version of the file, which makes sense.

4. **Click the Next button.**

   The key to restoring your personal files is to choose your account's personal folder.

5. **Click the button Add Folders.**

   The Add Folder to Restore window appears.

6. **From the Address Bar, choose Users.**

   The Users folder is "one folder up" from your account folder.

   You may have to click the angle-brackets thing (<<) at the start of the Address bar to display a drop-down folder menu. From that menu, you can choose the Users folder.

7. **Click to select your account folder from the list.**

   Your account folder has the same name as your account in Windows. On my PC, the folder is named Dan.

8. **Click the Next button and continue to restore the files.**

   Follow through with Step 7 and onward in the section "Restoring something from the last backup," earlier in this chapter.

Don't worry when you're prompted to overwrite files. It's okay to keep the existing ones (if any) and just restore the files that have been missing since the last backup.

+ This type of restore operation doesn't recover all files on your computer. For that operation, see the section "The Complete PC Backup," later in this chapter.

+ It's possible to recover all your PC's files even when your version of Windows lacks the Complete PC Backup. You can start by reinstalling Windows and then reinstalling your program files. After that, use Restore to recover your personal files as described in this section. The process isn't perfect, and it's time consuming, but it works.

Using the Advanced Restore option

An option in the Backup Status and Configuration, Restore panel is titled Advanced Restore. Just to make it more intimidating, it's flagged with the Windows Vista security shield icon. Scary.

The Advanced Restore option does what the description claims in the window: It allows you to restore files backed up by other users on your PC. So, obviously, if you're the only one using your computer, there's no need to mess with that option.

The Advanced Restore option also lets you recover files backed up by Windows Backup and saved on another hard drive. For example, you might have backed up files from another PC and then attached its external backup drive to your computer. If so, you can use the Advanced Restore option to restore files from that backup disk — even though those files never existed on your own computer.

So, although it's not that scary, the Advanced Restore option is something you have available, in case the need arises.

The Complete PC Backup

Suppose that the worst possible thing happens, and I'm not talking about that dream coming true where you're naked in public. I'm talking about that dreaded day when you lose everything on your computer: your files, music, pictures, videos, programs, all that pornography, Windows — everything. Yes, even your great American novel. Such a day of woe, but it need not be when you use the Complete PC Backup, as described in this section.

✦ Complete PC Backup is a feature found only in Windows Vista Business, Windows Vista Enterprise, and Windows Vista Ultimate editions.

✦ Yes, if you have the Home Premium version of Windows Vista, you don't have Complete PC Backup. (Reread the preceding check mark.)

✦ The odd thing about dreaming that you're naked in public is that no one else in the dream seems to mind that you're naked. That's because the dream isn't really about being *nude*; rather, it's about being exposed, or vulnerable. Roll that in your cigar and smoke it, Dr. Freud!

Understanding Complete PC Backup

The Complete PC Backup program is different from the regular backup program. Unlike the automatic backup, which is a file copying and archiving utility, the Complete PC Backup program is a disk imaging program. That sounds cool — and it is.

A *disk imaging* program doesn't copy individual files to a backup disk. Instead, it copies the raw information from a hard drive — specifically, the main drive partition on your PC. That's where Windows, your programs, and all your personal files and other information are stored. All that stuff is compressed and copied to an external hard drive.

Unlike when you use a regular backup, you have no way to pluck out individual files or folders from a disk image backup. Still, that's not the reason behind Complete PC Backup. No, the reason you use it is to fully restore your computer's hard drive in case of a disaster. The restore recovers everything: Windows, program files, and all your personal information. Ta-da! You get your computer back.

You access the Complete PC Backup program from the standard backup locations in Windows: the Backup and Restore Center window (refer to Figure 1-2) or the Backup Status and Configuration window (refer to Figure 1-3). Both locations launch the same program, though I prefer (as usual) to use the Backup Status and Configuration window.

Setting up an external hard drive for Complete PC Backup

To use an external hard drive for the Complete PC Backup, you must ensure that the drive is formatted with the NT File System, or NTFS. Because most external hard drives come formatted using the FAT32 standard, it means that the drive must be converted.

The conversion operation is technical, but not that difficult to work through. Here are the steps:

1. **Open the Computer window and make a note of the external hard drive letter and its volume label.**

   In Figure 1-1, earlier in this chapter, you can see that the external hard drive is named My Book and is given drive letter J. You need to know that drive letter.

   The drive's volume label is a smidgen of text used to identify the media by name. It's not used for much in Windows, except for instances that involve formatting or conversion. In the Computer window, the volume label name appears before the drive letter. For drive J, the label is My Book.

2. **Close the Computer window.**

   The next step is to open an administrator Command Prompt window.

3. **From the Start menu, choose All Programs⇨Accessories and then right-click the Command Prompt icon.**

4. **Choose the command Run As Administrator from the pop-up menu.**

   The Administrator Command Prompt window opens and displays a command prompt.

5. **Click the Continue button or type the administrator password to continue.**

6. **Type the command** convert D: /fs:ntfs, **but replace D with your PC's external drive letter.**

    For example, on my PC, the external drive letter is J, so I type this command:

    ```
    convert j: /fs:ntfs
    ```

    Double-check your typing! A colon appears after the drive letter followed by a space. A colon appears between `fs` and `ntfs`.

7. **Press Enter.**

    If you see the message `Drive is already NTFS`, you're fine; skip to Step 10. Also, confirm that you typed the proper drive letter in Step 6.

    You're prompted for the drive's volume label:

    ```
    The type of the file system is FAT32.
    Enter current volume label for drive J:
    ```

    To cancel the operation at this point, press Ctrl+C.

8. **Type the drive's volume label.**

    You can always reopen the Computer window, if you forget what the label was, but because you made a note of it in Step 1, you won't have to.

9. **Press Enter.**

    Windows converts the drive's internal structure to the NTFS format. Again, none of the drive's files is erased.

    The process can take several minutes, depending on the drive's capacity. You see some information displayed on the screen as you wait.

    When the operation has been completed, you see the text `Conversion complete` and then another command prompt.

10. **Type** exit **and press Enter to close the Administrator Command Prompt window.**

To confirm that the drive has been converted, open the Computer window and select the external drive's icon. The bottom part of the window, the Details Pane, should describe the file system as NTFS. (If the Details pane doesn't show up, choose Layout⇨Details Pane from the Organize button menu.)

✦ Converting the drive to NTFS doesn't really change how you can use the drive. As far as you're concerned, the drive still shows up and holds files just like before. Internally, however, Windows is using the drive more efficiently.

✦ Most operating systems now available understand the NTFS format and can use an NTFS hard drive just as well as they can use a FAT32 hard drive.

✦ Converting the drive is *not* the same as reformatting the drive. The reformat operation erases the drive's contents.

✦ Also see the section "Getting an external hard drive," earlier in this chapter.

✦ If you attempt to use Complete PC Backup with a non-NTFS external hard drive, you're suitably thumped with a warning. Better convert the drive before that happens.

**Book VI
Chapter 1**

Backup, Backup,
Backup

Backing up your entire computer

I recommend running Complete PC Backup on your PC. Doing so is in addition to having a regular backup schedule, as described elsewhere in this chapter. Here's how to pull off the Complete PC Backup operation:

1. **Open the Backup Status and Configuration window.**

Choose All Programs⇨Accessories⇨System Tools⇨Backup Status and Configuration from the Start button's menu.

2. **Ensure that the big button Complete PC Backup is selected on the left side of the window.**

The Backup Status and Configuration window appears, as shown in Figure 1-8.

Figure 1-8:
The Complete PC Backup is done here.

3. **Click the button Create a Backup Now.**

4. **Type the administrator's password or click the Continue button.**

5. **Choose the option On a Hard Drive.**

   Trust me: You *do not want* to use optical discs. The Complete PC Backup operation takes a zillion of them.

6. **Select the external, NTFS-formatted hard drive from the menu button.**

   If the disk doesn't have enough room, you're warned; choose another disk or work in Windows to remove excess files from the disk.

7. **Click the Next button.**

8. **If necessary, choose any additional disk drives or partitions in your computer for backing up, and click the Next button.**

   A summary screen appears, listing which disks will be backed up and how much space will be used.

   If you already ran Complete PC Backup, you see a message describing how only newer information will be added to the backup; unlike in a traditional backup, a new backup set isn't created when you run Complete PC Backup a second time.

9. **Click the Start Backup button.**

10. **Do something else while the program runs.**

    Actually, the backup may not take that long. An image backup doesn't consume as much time as a file-by-file backup.

    You can continue to use your computer while the Complete PC Backup is running. Browse the Web. Write a letter. Play a game of Spider Solitaire.

    When the backup is complete, you see the message `The Backup Completed Successfully`.

11. **Click the Close button and then close the Backup Status and Configuration window.**

Unlike in a regular backup, you have no need to refresh the Complete PC Backup often. In fact, the thing cannot be scheduled; you can only run Complete PC Backup manually. But continue to make regular backups as described earlier in this chapter. Those backups keep your own files current, which is more important than keeping a full image of the PC's hard drive.

You can run the Complete PC Backup again, and I recommend doing so every six months or thereabouts. When you run the Complete PC Backup again, it makes a note of only the changed items on your PC, so it keeps the image backup fresh and also avoids eating up a whole lot of disk space.

Beyond a couple of times a year, there's really no reason to run the program more often.

◆ You can also start a Complete PC Backup operation by clicking the Back Up Computer button in the Backup and Restore Center window.

◆ The Complete PC Backup can be done whether or not you turned on the regular PC backup. See the section "Disabling the backup program," elsewhere in this chapter.

◆ The backup image is placed on the external hard drive in a folder named WindowsImageBackup. It's separate from any folders used with the standard backup program.

Restoring your entire computer

If you're astute, you probably noticed that the Backup Status and Configuration window (refer to Figure 1-8), lacks an option to do a restore operation for Complete PC Backup. There's no Restore button. I mention this because I wasn't astute and really didn't notice that the button was missing until just a moment ago. That's probably because I've never really needed to restore my entire PC. (Not yet, anyway — knock on wood.)

A Restore Computer button can be found in the Backup and Restore Center window (refer to Figure 1-2). But clicking that button is useless; a warning dialog box appears when you click the button. The warning basically says this:

Using the Complete PC Backup restore operation is designed only for disaster recover. As such, it can be run only by starting your computer with a recovery disc or booting into a RECOVERY hard disk partition. For details, refer to Book II, Chapter 8. Use the System Recovery Options menu to choose Windows Complete PC Restore, and then follow the directions on-screen.

◆ The recovery option isn't something to use casually. For example, it would be silly to run the Complete PC Backup restore procedure simply to recover a lost file. Instead, use the Backup program as described in the section "Files from Days of Yore," found earlier in this chapter.

◆ Recovering your hard drive with the Complete PC Backup program erases the computer's hard drive.

Chapter 2: Pampering the Hard Drive

In This Chapter

- ✔ Grabbing more disk space
- ✔ Cleaning up the hard drive
- ✔ Using compression
- ✔ Working with disk tools
- ✔ Setting a new drive letter
- ✔ Assigning a drive to a folder
- ✔ Formatting media
- ✔ Creating a new volume
- ✔ Making a hard drive larger

The PC's hard drive is a robust little dude. Hearty and reliable, it stores the stuff that makes your computer *your* computer. It's your PC's personality. It's the primary storage device, where your precious files are stored. Obviously, taking care of that hard drive should be a top priority. This chapter explains what you can do.

Free Up Some Disk Space

This section is sponsored by the word *capacity*. It's a great word, especially when applied to mass storage on a computer. The more capacity you have, the more room for storing your stuff. Not just programs and your documents, but also massive files, such as your music collection or videos. You need the storage space! This section explains how you can deal with dwindling room on the hard drive, which is the number-one hard drive problem.

- ✦ One of the easiest ways to increase disk storage is to add another hard drive to your PC. Refer to Book I, Chapter 4.

- ✦ In Windows Vista, you can increase disk storage by extending a volume. See the section "Extending a volume," near the end of this chapter.

Looking at the storage situation

Forget files, folders, and whatnot. I'm writing about *bulk* here. The stuff you create and collect on your PC's hard drive — the primary storage device — can grow to colossal proportions. Yet while all that stuff accumulates, the hard drive itself doesn't change from its original capacity. It's like a closet: You can keep buying new clothes, but that doesn't make the closet any larger.

The hard drive is the PC's primary storage device. It's home to three vital items:

✦ The computer's operating system, Windows.

✦ The software — programs and applications — that let you do things with your computer.

✦ Your stuff: files, documents, media, and other things you create or collect.

The ideal situation is to have a hard drive that boasts a capacity to deal with all three things, not only for now but also for as long as you plan to own your computer. Most people, sadly, aren't that forward-thinking. Not only that, but the casual computer buyer also doesn't have a clue to how much storage is enough. So they buy less than they need.

Before you have a conniption fit over disk storage, you should first check on how the hard drive is doing. How much space is being used? How much space is available? How soon before you run out? Those questions can be answered by following these steps:

1. **Open the Computer window.**

In Windows XP, it's called My Computer.

2. **Right-click the main hard drive icon and choose Properties from the shortcut menu.**

On the General tab, shown in Figure 2-1, you see detailed information about disk usage as well as the handy purple pie chart, illustrating disk usage.

3. **Close the disk's Properties dialog box when you're done looking.**

4. **Close the Computer/My Computer window.**

The more purple you see in the disk size pie chart, the better. (Purple is the Free Space chunk of the pie.) The smaller the purple slice is, the more it means you're due for a disk capacity solution. Your options are to remove files, compress files, or compress the entire disk to recover some space. Another solution is to buy a second hard drive. The most complex solution is to replace the hard drive, but that can be quite technical.

Figure 2-1:
Hmmm.
Disk pie.

The rest of this section describes methods for increasing disk capacity.

At what point do you worry? I'd say when capacity reaches 90 percent, it's a good time to start seriously cleaning up a hard drive. Even before that, however, it's a good idea to prune away things you don't need.

✦ When hard drive storage (free space) ever falls below a certain percentage, Windows displays a warning message. If you see that message, I highly recommend that you act immediately.

✦ The term *hard drive* applies to the PC's primary storage device. It's known on most PCs as drive C, though it could be some other drive letter or you could have multiple hard drives inside your PC. In the future, the PC's primary storage device might be a solid-state drive (SSD), but the drive letter, as well as the problems of not having enough storage, will linger.

✦ Dwindling disk capacity is an old issue — almost as old as having hard drives in PCs.

✦ Back in the late 1980s, software solutions were devised to deal with full hard drives. The software compressed files on the hard drive on the fly, allowing for more room. But the software solution avoids the real issue, which is having a larger hard drive in the first place.

✦ See the sections "Using file compression" and "Compressing every dang doodle file on a hard drive," elsewhere in this chapter, for more information on creating room on a hard drive by using software solutions.

✦ As this book goes to press, the typical PC is sold with a hard drive capacity of about 300GB. That's fine for most usage, though more is always better.

✦ See my book *PCs For Dummies* (Wiley Publishing) for a better understanding of what a gigabyte (GB) is, as well as more information on how storage capacity is measured.

✦ Perhaps the best solution for dealing with the storage situation is a hardware one: Get another hard drive, either an internal or external model. More importantly, *use* that hard drive. See the sections "Moving your program files," later in this chapter.

✦ Another storage space solution is to remove software you don't use. See Book II, Chapter 6 for information on uninstalling software in Windows.

✦ Ironically, the pie chart is used to show capacity on all mass storage formats, including media cards that don't use a round disk for storage.

✦ Optical discs are always shown as being full. That's because they're read-only. When you're burning a new optical disc, the software you use to burn the disc reports how much space is available.

Things that gobble storage space

Back in the old days, it was computer software that grabbed the biggest chunk of disk space. Programs developed in the late 1990s often asked whether you wanted to install the entire thing on the hard drive or keep portions of the program on a CD. The culprits are now your own files — specifically, media files.

Video: The most space-consuming file you can add to your computer is a movie. Feature films eat up several gigabytes. Even regular video files are very large; a 2-minute video can be 30MB or more.

Music: Expect to use about 1MB of disk storage for each minute of music you store on your PC.

Pictures: Image files can be small, such as those you find on the Internet or exchange by e-mail. But raw image files — those you want to keep so that you can print a 4-by-5 enlargement (or larger) — they occupy several megabytes of storage.

Programs: A typical program uses about 20MB or so of disk storage, though some computer games can use gigabytes of storage. But that value is *static:* After you install the program, it doesn't continue to consume more space. The documents you create in the program use space, but the size of the program itself doesn't grow.

Documents: The documents you create on your computer take up the least amount of space. A word processing document uses maybe 100K or so, which is 0.1MB — just a slice of disk storage.

You can estimate how much disk storage you need on your PC. There's a formula I use to calculate it, though it doesn't help to know the formula after you buy the hard drive. Generally speaking, the average size of about 300GB is good enough for most uses. If space concerns you or you plan to produce videos or music, get a higher-capacity hard drive — 500GB or larger.

Removing large files

Where's that big fish? No, not a fish. A *whale*. Where are the whales located in the ocean that is your PC's hard drive? I mean, *big* files. Have you ever done a large-file search? Not a comprehensive search, but a search for large files? If you've never done such a search and disk capacity is running low, now is the time.

Obey these steps in Windows Vista to find some whale-size files:

1. **Press Win+F to summon a Search Results window.**

2. **Click the Advanced Search button.**

3. **From the Location button, choose Indexed Locations if it's not already chosen.**

4. **From the Size KB button menu, choose Is Greater Than.**

5. **Type 5000 in the Add a File Size text box.**

You're looking for files larger than 5MB.

6. **Click the Search button.**

Windows scours the hard drive for files larger than 5MB. There are a bunch of them. Of course, Windows doesn't sort them for you; plus, it doesn't even list the file sizes in the Search Results window.

7. **Ensure that Details is chosen from the Views toolbar button menu.**

8. **Right-click any column heading in the list of found files.**

9. **From the shortcut menu, choose Size.**

You're adding the Size column to the list of details.

10. **Locate the Size column and drag it to the right, just after the Date Modified column.**

Refer to Video 621 on the companion DVD for details on how to work the last four steps in this list.

11. **Click the Size heading until the list of files is sorted from largest to smallest.**

It may take two clicks to do it. The results I see on my PC are shown in Figure 2-2.

12. **Peruse the list.**

If you're like me, you see a file you downloaded or created ages ago — something you needed once but don't need any more. If so, great: You can delete or archive the file.

To delete a file, select it and then press the Delete key on the keyboard.

To archive a file, select it and press Ctrl+X to cut it. Then open a folder window on an external drive or a media card, and move the file to that drive by pressing the Ctrl+V key.

13. **Close the Search Results window when you're done.**

In Windows XP, heed these steps to go whale-size file watching:

1. **Press Win+F to bring up the Search Results window.**

2. **Click the link on the left side of the window: All Files and Folders.**

3. **From the Look In drop-down menu, choose My Documents.**

4. **Click the chevron to expand the What Size Is It area.**

5. **Choose Specify Size (in KB).**

6. **Choose At Least.**

7. **Type 5000 in the Size text box.**

You're directing the Search command to scout out files larger than 5MB.

8. **Click the Search button.**

Windows looks through your stuff, trying to find files you created or collected that are larger than 5MB. The files are listed in the Search Results window.

To sort the files from largest to smallest, click the Size heading.

9. **Peruse the list.**

What are you looking for? Large and largely forgotten files. If you don't recognize the file, delete it. If you recognize it and don't need it, delete it.

To delete a file, select it and then press the Delete key on the keyboard.

You can also archive the file by moving it from the hard drive to an external hard drive, burning it to an optical disc, or moving it to a media card.

10. **Close the Search Results window when you're done.**

I use the term *archiving* to simply imply moving a file from the main hard drive, the one running out of room, to another hard drive, optical disc, or media card. The notion is that you still want the file but don't necessarily need to have it handy.

✦ You can hone the search for large files by specifying specific file types. For example, specify the filename `*.wmf` to look for all Windows Media Files (videos) on the hard drive. Additional large file formats are shown in Table 2-1, in the Type column.

✦ View the Search Results window in Details view. Choose Details from the Views toolbar button in Windows Vista; in Windows XP, choose View⇨Details from the menu.

✦ If you delete the file, it merely moves to the Recycle Bin. There really isn't mush disk storage space savings — until you empty the Recycle Bin.

✦ You can press Shift+Delete to instantly delete a file and recover the disk space used by the file. The Shift+Delete operation isn't reversible, however. Use it with care.

✦ I prefer that you *archive* program files as opposed to delete them outright.

✦ To move a file, you cut and paste it. Cut it from its current folder window or select it from the Search Results window by pressing Ctrl+X. Then open the window where you want to move the file, and press Ctrl+V to complete the operation.

✦ You may find some compressed folders when perusing the list. Be careful! You want to confirm the compressed folder's contents before you whisk it off into oblivion.

✦ If you're using the Windows Media Center to record live TV, you should peruse the list of recorded shows to see whether any require deleting. Recorded TV takes up a *lot* of disk space. To delete a recorded TV show in the Windows Media Center, choose Recorded TV from the TV + Movies menu, select a recorded show, and choose Delete from the list of buttons that appears. Click Yes to confirm the deletion.

✦ Music files can be removed from the Windows Media Player by right-clicking the music file's icon and choosing Delete from the pop-up menu.

Table 2-1	Filename Extensions for Large Files	
Filename Wildcard	**File Type**	**Description**
*.AVI	Audio Video Interleave	QuickTime or Real Player media format
*.BMP	Bitmap Graphics	Windows Paint document, also used by Windows for wallpaper
*.EXE	Executable	A program file (delete carefully!)
*.MOV	Quicktime Movie	Apple QuickTime movie format; video files
*.MP3	MPEG Audio	Music or sound file
*.PDF	Portable Document Format	Adobe Acrobat document
*.WAV	Windows Sound	Music or sound file
*.WMA	Windows Media Audio	Windows Media Player sound file
*.WMF	Windows Media File	Windows Media Player media format; videos
*.WMV	Windows Media Video	Windows Media Player video file
*.ZIP	Compressed Folder	ZIP file archive (delete carefully!)

Using Disk Cleanup

A handy way to remove lots of files you don't need on a hard drive is to employ the aptly named Disk Cleanup tool. What Disk Cleanup does is locate files that can easily be removed to free up some disk space, especially files that may not be obvious to you, such as temporary files used by Windows or when browsing the Internet.

To run Disk Cleanup in Windows Vista, follow these steps:

1. **From the Start button menu, choose All Programs⇨Accessories⇨ System Tools⇨Disk Cleanup.**

2. **Choose the option My Files Only.**

 I recommend that you start with your own files first. If that doesn't remove enough files, repeat these steps and choose the option Files from All Users on This Computer.

3. **If prompted, choose the hard drive to clean up.**

 I recommend cleaning the computer's main hard drive, C, first.

4. **In the Disk Cleanup dialog box, check marks by all the items you want to remove.**

The dialog box is shown in Figure 2-3. It's okay to place check marks by *all* items. Those things wouldn't be listed if they were crucial to the computer's operation.

Figure 2-3:
The Disk
Cleanup
dialog box.

There's one exception, however: Hibernation File Cleaner. Do not remove that item if you use hibernation on your computer.

5. **Click OK.**

You're not quite there yet.

6. **Click the Delete Files button to begin the cleanup process.**

Wait while the disk is being cleaned. When the process has been completed, the window goes away.

You run Disk Cleanup in Windows XP by adhering to these steps:

1. **From the Start button menu, choose All Programs⇨Accessories⇨ System Tools⇨Disk Cleanup.**

2. **In the Disk Cleanup dialog box, click the More Options tab.**

The Disk Cleanup dialog box's More Options tab lists additional items worthy of cleanup. Three buttons are labeled Clean Up, which take you to various other locations in Windows:

Windows Components: Clicking the Clean Up button here opens the Windows Components Wizard window, where you can remove (or add) various pieces of Windows. You can also display the Windows Components Wizard by opening the Add/Remove Programs icon and clicking the button Add/Remove Windows Components on the left side of that window.

Installed Programs: Clicking the Clean Up button here opens the Add/Remove Programs window, which can also be opened from the Control Panel.

System Restore: Clicking the Clean Up button by this option displays a Yes/No dialog box. Click the Yes button to remove all but the most recent restore point, which is a safe move.

3. Click the Disk Cleanup tab.

4. Place check marks by all items you want to remove.

You can select an item beforehand to read its description. There's really nothing in there to be concerned about; the Disk Cleanup program doesn't present you with options that would damage your computer or its performance — at least not on the Disk Cleanup tab.

5. Click the OK button.

A Yes/No dialog box appears.

6. Click the Yes button to begin the cleanup process.

Windows removes the files you specified. When it's finished, the window goes away. You're done.

Because there's no final report, I recommend that you check the hard drive's size to see any improvement in the storage situation. Refer to the steps in the section "Looking at the storage situation," earlier in this chapter.

✦ You can also access the Disk Cleanup utility from a disk drive's Properties dialog box by clicking the Disk Cleanup button on the General tab. See Figure 2-1.

✦ See Book II, Chapter 8 for more information on System Restore.

Moving your program files

I'm often asked whether it's possible to move program files from the primary hard drive, C, to either a secondary internal hard drive or an external hard drive. It's a good question, but one that has a complex answer.

First, and most importantly, you cannot simply move a program file. In Windows, programs aren't single files. Often, they're not even found in a single folder, but rather in dozens of places on the hard drive. The file locations are referenced throughout Windows, which means that moving any of them would cause the program to fail. A simple file-move operation will be unsuccessful.

Second, I recommend using a second, internal hard drive as your PC's supplemental disk storage. The problem with external hard drives is that it might get its drive letter suddenly reassigned when you add new media to the PC. That would be bad. An internal hard drive, on the other hand, has a solid, reliable drive letter.

Finally, the way to move a program file is to uninstall it and then reinstall it on the secondary hard drive. That's it.

You need to uninstall the program because most software doesn't let itself be installed twice on the same computer. Besides, the idea is to clean up disk space, and the original installation must be removed.

After uninstalling the program, reinstall it. Set the location for the software to be installed as the secondary drive. Often, to set the location, you must complete a customized, or "advanced," installation. Choosing that option allows you to specify where the file is installed, and you can select the second hard drive as the file's destination.

To keep your computer organized, I recommend creating a Program Files folder on the secondary hard drive. Install the programs in that folder.

After setting up the program on the new hard drive, it should run as it did before. Nothing is lost, and as a bonus, you free up some disk space.

✦ This trick works only when you remember to install all new software on the secondary drive. So, the next time you run an installation program, remember to choose the secondary hard drive as its location or destination.

✦ If you have problems registering the reinstalled program, contact its developer. When you purchased the program, you bought the right to install it on your computer. Some program licenses prohibit reinstalling the same program, which is disappointing. But in most cases, reinstalling shouldn't be an issue.

✦ It helps if you reinstall the largest programs onto the secondary drive. You can discover how big programs are by opening the Control Panel's Programs and Features icon in Windows Vista; in Windows XP, open the Control Panel's Add or Remove Programs icon. The software installed on your computer is listed in the window that appears, along with the program's bulk specified in megabytes (MB).

✦ Uninstalling a program doesn't erase the data files created by that program. So, if you have documents or images or other files you made, uninstalling the program doesn't delete them.

✦ Some programs even retain their setting information after they're uninstalled. That means that reinstalling the program instantly gives you back any custom settings or options you already configured. In a way, reinstalling the same program, but on a different drive, is like performing an upgrade.

✦ See Book II, Chapter 6 for more information on installing and removing programs on your PC.

Using file compression

Windows comes with a feature I call *blue file compression*. It's an on-the-fly type of compression that stores files on a disk in a smaller size. When you open the file, it's decompressed to its original size. So, as a user, you don't notice the compression in any way other than that your files consume less disk space.

Oh, and I call it blue file compression because the compressed files are listed in the folder window with blue text instead of black. Here's how to blue-compress a file:

1. **Right-click the file or folder icon to compress.**

When you compress a folder, you compress all files and folders held in that folder. It's a simple way to compress a slew of files all at once.

2. **Choose Properties from the shortcut menu.**

3. **On the General tab of the Properties dialog box, click the Advanced button.**

The Advanced Attributes dialog box appears, as shown in Figure 2-4.

Figure 2-4:
The
Advanced
Attributes
dialog box,
Windows
XP version.

4. **Place a check mark by the option Compress Contents to Save Disk Space.**

5. **Click OK, and then click OK again to dismiss the Properties dialog box.**

You see the name of the file or folder displayed in blue text when it's compressed. Beyond that, there aren't really any changes; the file can still be manipulated or opened as it was before. It does, however, take up less space on disk.

✦ Also see the following sidebar, "Compression isn't always the answer."

✦ To remove compression from a file, repeat these preceding steps, but in Step 4 remove the check mark.

✦ There's an option in the Windows XP version of the Disk Cleanup program to compress seldom-used files. That's another way to automatically reduce the file size of those documents and whatnot that you seldom use. I recommend it. See the section "Using Disk Cleanup," earlier in this chapter.

✦ The encryption attribute (see Figure 2-4) is available only on NTFS-formatted hard drives. See Chapter 1, the section "Setting up an external hard drive for Complete PC Backup," for information on the NTFS format.

✦ You can also archive files into a compressed folder, which takes up less space. In fact, for seldom used files, I recommend creating a compressed folder and moving the files into it. Although that method compresses the files, keep in mind that you cannot open a file stored in a compressed folder, nor does the Windows Search command find files (or their contents) inside a compressed folder.

Book VI
Chapter 2

Pampering the
Hard Drive

Compression isn't always the answer

Digital compression works because a file has a lot of redundant information in it — lots of bytes and chunks that repeat over and over. Compression software takes advantage of that situation by removing those repeating chunks of code. Using magic I can't begin to explain (or understand), a file that once sucked up 1MB of disk space can suddenly consume only 64KB or so. That's a lot of savings.

Compression, however, isn't a magic lozenge for curing a cramped hard drive. That's because only certain files compress well.

For example, text files can be smooshed down to become really small. Windows Bitmap files (BMP) compress well. Most of the files on your hard drive, however, are probably already in a compressed state. Therefore, they don't benefit from any additional compression. In fact, by compressing them, you might make your computer run slower because of all the overhead required to decompress the file on the fly.

Compressing every dang doodle file on a hard drive

Windows offers a single command that sifts through every file on a hard drive and applies the compression attribute to them. The result is that the entire hard drive is compressed and takes up less space. This strategy isn't a surefire solution to a cramped hard drive, but it can be done.

To compress an entire hard drive, follow these steps, though I recommend that you read through this entire section before you begin:

1. **Open the Computer window in Windows Vista; in Windows XP, open the My Computer window.**

2. **Right-click a hard drive icon and choose Properties from the shortcut menu.**

3. **Place a check mark by the item Compress This Drive to Save Disk Space.**

4. **Click the Apply button.**

5. **Ensure that the second option is selected in the Confirm Attribute Changes dialog box: Apply Changes to Drive X:, Subfolders and Files.**

6. **Click OK.**

7. **In Windows Vista, click the Continue button and then type the administrator's password or click Continue (again) to continue (again).**

   Doubtless, during this process, you encounter some file errors. If so, click the Ignore All button. Files get busy and are in use by other processes, for example. There's no way to compress them all.

8. **Wait.**

   It takes a long time to assign the compression attribute to all files on the hard drive. On my test hard drive, with 48GB worth of files, Windows is reporting that compression will take 12 hours to complete. Definitely, this is an overnight operation. (See? I told you to read this section before diving in.)

   If you grow weary, you can always click the Cancel button and resume later.

9. **Close the drive's Properties window.**

   No confirmation dialog box appears when the operation is over, which is kind of a letdown.

To confirm that the files on the drive have been compressed, open the drive icon and view the files; you discover that the files are compressed and sport blue filenames. You also note that some folders are compressed and others are left alone. That's okay; it's the best that this type of compression can offer.

The kicker, however, is to discover whether any disk storage savings have resulted. To view that information, open the drive's Properties dialog box and take a look. (Specific steps are offered in the section "Looking at the storage situation," earlier in this chapter.)

✦ **Blue file compression works on the fly.** Windows decompresses files when you access them, and then it recompresses those files when you save them back to disk.

✦ Even though Windows may compress a file, it doesn't necessarily mean that the file will occupy less disk space. That's because not all files compress well. See the earlier sidebar "Compression isn't always the answer."

✦ The type of disk compression covered in this section isn't the same thing as the old DoubleSpace program that came with earlier versions of Windows.

✦ To decompress the drive, repeat the preceding steps but remove the check mark in Step 3.

Disk Drive Tools

When I was so very young, I thought that the yellow Oil light on my car's dashboard was the friendly reminder that the oil needed changing. After the car's engine seized, I recognized my error. As my friend Brad says, maintain your toys, and you'll have them forever. Those who practice regular maintenance enjoy the blessings of keeping their possessions in good shape. The PC's hard drive, with all its precious data, is no exception. This section explains how to keep that spinning gizmo of digital goodness in tiptop shape.

✦ Most computer maintenance is done automatically in Windows Vista. Even so, you should consider manually running the programs discussed in this section, or at least becoming familiar with them.

✦ Just in case maintenance doesn't happen automatically, you can use task scheduling in Windows to set up automatic maintenance. See Chapter 3.

Understanding fragmentation

Don't believe the doomsayers: Fragmentation is natural and accepted. All storage media have some level of fragmentation. It's related to how information is stored by the operating system and, honestly, it's beneficial. It's too much fragmentation that does you in.

Fragmentation can be a tough subject to comprehend. Most people who use a computer don't even understand the concept of a file. To grasp the concept of fragmentation, which is really *file* fragmentation, you have to accept that everything stored on a computer media is stored as files.

Files are stored on storage media, such as the main hard drive. The fragmentation part occurs when the file isn't stored as a single chunk of information on the disk. Instead, the file is split: Part of it may be stored in one spot on the hard drive, and another part of the file might be stored elsewhere. The file isn't damaged because the operating system knows where to find it. But the file is *fragmented* or, as the nerds say, *noncontiguous*.

To help you form a picture of how file fragmentation works, think of your PC's hard drive as a parking lot surrounding a large municipal stadium. Figure 2-5 illustrates this concept; note that the stadium isn't drawn to scale and it has far too few parking spaces.

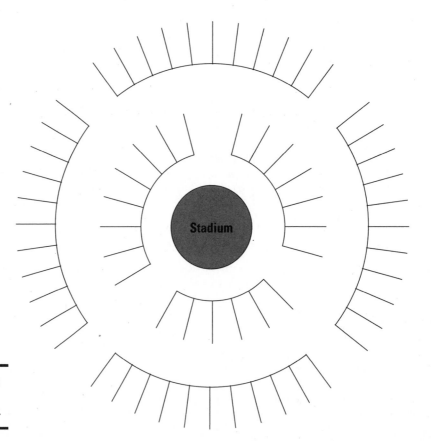

Figure 2-5:
A stadium
parking lot.

A parking lot is basically asphalt. For the parking lot to function, it must be painted with spaces, as shown in Figure 2-5. A similar thing happens to a disk's surface, though the surface material is some form of magnetic oxide, not asphalt. The painting of "parking spaces" on a disk is called *formatting*.

Both painted parking spaces and disk formatting are similar concepts: Without parking spaces or disk formatting, cars and files wouldn't know where to go. Chaos would ensue.

Now pretend that it's an hour before game time. The parking lot is beginning to fill. Cars come in one side of the parking lot and are directed by cheerful parking lot employees in orange tunics to fill the empty spaces in an orderly manner. Each car is parked next to another car, as illustrated in Figure 2-6.

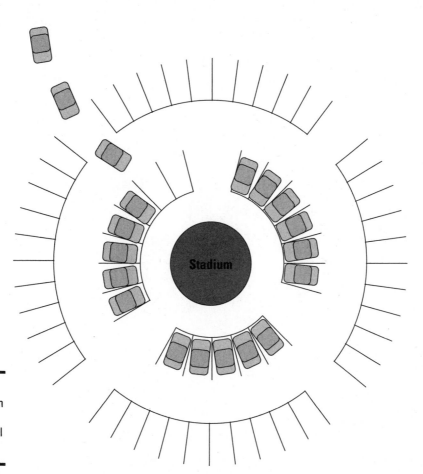

Figure 2-6:
The stadium parking lot begins to fill with cars.

Your PC's hard drive fills will files in a manner similar to the way the stadium parking lot fills with files: Files are placed on the media one after the other, just like the cars illustrated in Figure 2-6.

The stadium parking lot and your PC's hard drive fill up sequentially. But the hard drive doesn't stay that way for long. On your computer, you probably delete a file now and then, or you uninstall a program. Windows itself creates and deletes temporary files all the time. If that situation were duplicated in the stadium parking lot, the picture would resemble Figure 2-7. There are empty parking spaces where cars have left because the home team is losing 52-3, and people are leaving in droves.

Is the parking lot in Figure 2-7 full? Of course not. Plenty of spaces are available. But if the cheerful parking lot attendants in orange tunics continue to fill the parking lot sequentially, they may report that the parking lot is full — despite parking spaces still being available.

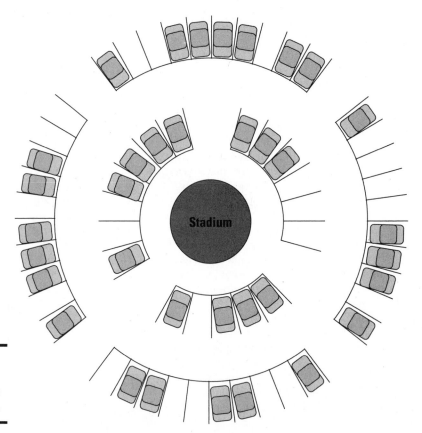

Figure 2-7:
Spaces
open up as
cars leave.

That same kind of nonsense can happen on your computer. If the operating system continues to fill the disk sequentially, you might see a hard drive with half its storage space available, yet the operating system reports that it has no room for any more files. Obviously, such a situation would tick you off.

To make the best use of the storage space available, the operating system begins to split up, or *fragment,* new files stored on the hard drive. So, when a new file is added to the hard drive, the operating system fits it into the available empty space. If the file fits, great. If the file doesn't fit, the operating system splits the file into smaller chunks that do fit. That's *fragmentation*.

A fragmented file isn't damaged; the operating system merely reassembles the file's pieces into a single whole when the file is accessed. So information isn't lost. A tad more overhead is involved, however, in reassembling a file's fragments.

Problems arise when files are overly fragmented. As you continue to use the hard drive, more and more files are split up to take advantage of the available space. More fragments equals more overhead to reassemble the files when they're loaded or saved. The result from all that overhead is sluggish disk performance.

The solution to the fragmentation problem is to use a defragmentation, or *defrag*, utility.

A defragmentation utility does two things:

Attempts to put all files stored on disk into nonfragmented chunks: Using the parking lot example, the cheerful parking lot attendants in the orange tunics rearrange the cars so that all cars in a tailgate party are parked together.

Removes the empty spaces between the files: Files on disk are reordered, just like emptying the stadium parking lot and reparking all the cars so that it has no empty spaces. In real life, that would be a waste of time, but because the computer can automate the task, it happens quickly and efficiently. And no one complains.

Some defragmentation utilities may even do a third task: Relocate important and frequently accessed files to the start of the disk. Such a feature greatly improves disk performance.

The moral of this story is that fragmentation is a good and necessary thing. To keep your PC's hard drive working at maximum efficiency, it should be regularly defragmented.

Book VI Chapter 2

Pampering the Hard Drive

+ Defragmentation utilities appeared early on in the PC's life, at just about the time hard drives were becoming popular. (Before hard drives, PC users stored information on floppy disks.)

+ The speed improvement from running those early defragmentation utilities was stunningly dramatic. Early tools, like the Mace Utilities, PC Tools, and Norton Utilities, sold defragmentation programs as a miracle cure for a sluggish PC.

+ The PC's hard drive *always* contains some fragmentation. That's just the nature of the business of storing files on a disk. Too much fragmentation, however, leads to sluggish performance. Regular hard drive maintenance must include some type of disk defragmentation.

Finding the disk tools

Windows keeps its disk maintenance utilities in one handy place, nestled in a disk drive's Properties dialog box, on the Tools tab, as shown in Figure 2-8. Well, not all the tools: Disk Cleanup is found on the General tab in the Properties dialog box; see the section "Using Disk Cleanup," earlier in this chapter.

Figure 2-8:
Media
maintenance
options.

You need to visit the Tools tab to perform some routine disk maintenance, as covered elsewhere in this chapter. Here's how to get there:

1. **Open the Computer window to peruse storage devices attached to your PC.**

The window it titled My Computer in Windows XP.

2. **Right-click a disk drive icon, such as the hard drive, C.**

Because you use drive C more than any other drive, it's most likely due for a defragmentation.

3. **Choose Properties from the shortcut menu.**

The media's Properties dialog box appears.

4. **Click the Tools tab in the Properties dialog box.**

If there's no Tools tab, the media cannot be defragmented. Otherwise, you see disk maintenance options, as shown in Figure 2-8.

Error-checking: Runs a utility that checks the disk for errors. See the section "Checking the disk," later in this chapter.

Defragmentation: Starts the Defrag utility, covered in the next section.

Backup: Available only when Windows Backup has been installed on the PC. Refer to Chapter 1.

5. **Choose a button to run a specific disk utility.**

Running the error-checking or defragmentation utilities in Windows Vista requires that you type the administrator's password or click the Continue button to proceed. That's because those operations affect all users on the computer.

Refer to the following sections for information on how to run the individual disk utilities.

Defragmenting a hard drive

If you haven't defragmented your PC's hard drive in a while (or ever), you're in for a treat. A freshly defragmented hard drive makes your computer seem brand-new (but without that out-of-the-box smell).

To defrag the hard drive, or any media, in Windows Vista, follow these steps:

1. **Open the media's Properties dialog box and, on the Tools tab, click the Defragment Now button.**

Steps describing how to open the Tools tab are listed in the preceding section.

2. **Type the administrator's password or click the Continue button.**

Windows Vista is equipped to automatically defrag the computer's hard drive. Rather than see a defragment screen, you see a dialog box, shown in Figure 2-9.

Figure 2-9:
The Disk Defragmenter window in Windows Vista.

The dialog box lets you customize the schedule, customize the Defragmenter utility, or just defragment anyway. Honestly, if the schedule is to your liking, there's nothing left to do. But that's probably not why you're reading this section.

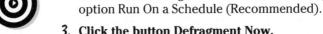

If scheduled defragmentation isn't enabled, place a check mark by the option Run On a Schedule (Recommended).

3. **Click the button Defragment Now.**

4. **Choose the media to defragment.**

Windows automatically chooses all media that is attached to your PC and can be defragmented. If you just want to fragment the main hard drive, deselect the rest of the media.

5. **Click OK.**

Windows begins defragmenting the drive. Unlike viewing the glorious windows of Defrag programs past (see Figure 2-10), you just get to stare at a tiny spinning loop while the media is defragmented.

It's okay to use your computer while it's being defragmented.

When the operation is complete, the spinning loop gizmo goes away. You see the Last Run item in the Disk Defragmenter window (refer to Figure 2-9), updated to reflect the recently completed operation.

6. **Close the Disk Defragmenter window.**

7. **Close the disk's Properties dialog box as well as the Computer window.**

To run the Defragmentation utility in Windows XP, follow these steps:

1. **From the My Computer window, right-click the media's icon and choose Properties from the shortcut menu.**

2. **In the media's Properties dialog box, select the Tools tab.**

3. **Click the Defragment Now button.**

The Disk Defragmentation window appears, similar to the one shown in Figure 2-10.

Book VI
Chapter 2

Pampering the Hard Drive

Figure 2-10:
Disk defrag-
mentation
in Windows
XP.

4. **Click the Analyze button.**

Windows performs a scan of the drive, providing visual feedback about the fragmentation situation, which is shown in Figure 2-10.

You can click the View Report button to see a list of fragmented files and the number of fragments. Some files have hundreds of fragments. One file on my PC was reported to have 123,784 fragments. (I should win a prize for that.) Click the Close button to dismiss the Analysis Report window.

5. **Click the Defragment button.**

   Depending on how large the disk is and how long it's been since it was first fragmented, defragmentation can take several hours. Be prepared to wait.

6. **Click the Close button when the operation is complete.**

7. **Close the Disk Defragmenter window.**

8. **You can also close the disk's Properties dialog box and the My Computer window.**

You may not notice any drastic improvement in disk performance, especially when the hard drive is frequently defragmented. But if you just defragmented your PC's hard drive for the first time, prepare to be stunned.

✦ You cannot defragment a network drive.

✦ Do not defragment a media card or flash drive. Those drives have a limited number of "writes" available to them. That is, the media can support data being written to it a finite number of times. That number can be huge, but it's a real number; after reaching that number, the media becomes useless. By not defragmenting a media card or flash drive, you avoid accelerating that deadline.

✦ Optical drives cannot be defragmented. Though, honestly, I don't believe that optical drives can even become fragmented in the first place.

✦ Even after running the Defragmentation utility, file fragments remain on the hard drive. That's just the nature of disk storage. Please don't obsess and run the defragmentation utilities over and over, trying to get a perfectly defragmented hard drive.

✦ Look on the DVD for some third-party defragmentation utilities that have more to offer than the standard defragmentation program that comes with Windows.

✦ See Chapter 3 for more information on the Task Scheduler and how to automatically schedule disk maintenance on your PC.

✦ Also see Book II, Chapter 4 for information on speeding up a slow PC.

Checking the disk

The disk checking tool in Windows has its roots in the old DOS utility chkdsk, which is pronounced "check disk." That old program could fix some disk problems, but most users treated it like a lucky charm, running it whenever the computer did anything unexpected and hoping that chkdsk did some sort of magic. We haven't really come that far.

You can still check the disk in Windows. The modern Check Disk program still seeks out errors on storage media, fixes them if it can, and does other routine household disk chores.

To run Check Disk, follow these steps:

1. **Open the Computer window.**

2. **Right-click the icon for the media storage gizmo you want to check.**

3. **Choose Properties from the shortcut menu.**

4. **In the Properties dialog box, click the Tools tab.**

5. **Click the Check Now button.**

6. **Type the administrator's password or click the Continue button.**

The Check Disk dialog box appears, similar to the one shown in Figure 2-11.

Figure 2-11: It's not impressive, but it's useful.

7. **Ensure that a check mark appears by the option Automatically Fix File System Errors.**

8. **To do a more thorough check, place a check mark in the box next to Scan for and Attempt Recovery of Bad Sectors.**

There's no reason to choose that option when you're not experiencing any disk trouble.

9. **Click the Start button.**

10. **If you see a warning regarding checking a disk in use, click the button Schedule Disk Check in Windows Vista or click the Yes button in Windows XP.**

By scheduling a disk check, you place a one-time task into the Windows Task Scheduler, which runs later when you're not using the specified disk drive. Often, that's as far as you get in this operation, especially when you attempt to check drive C, the PC's main hard drive.

If you choose to schedule a disk check, the operation is over. The disk check takes place the next time you start Windows, so there's really nothing else to do for now. Skip to Step 12.

11. **Click the Close button in the Checking Disk dialog box.**

Hopefully, no problems were found. If they were, the dialog box explains what to do. Or not.

12. **Close the storage device's Properties dialog box.**

13. **(Optional) Close the Computer window.**

If you had to schedule a disk check, the operation takes place when you restart Windows.

If anything awry is discovered, it's fixed automatically. That's why you checked the Automatically Fix File System Errors box.

✦ Certain disk utilities are more thorough than Check Disk. Or, at least they seem to be more thorough. Honestly, if the hard drive is malfunctioning, it's probably a hardware issue. Software cannot fix hardware problems, but it can avoid them. Check Disk quarantines unusable portions of a hard drive, but it cannot repair them.

✦ Generally speaking, bad sectors and disk errors are a sign that a hard drive needs replacing. They increase dramatically over time, especially when the disk is more than five years old. See Book I, Chapter 4 for more information.

✦ Check Disk is good at cleaning up *lost* files, or file fragments that exist on storage media but don't belong to any specific file. These *missing clusters* can hinder disk performance. Check Disk eliminates them automatically.

✦ The number-one cause of a missing cluster is an improper shutdown.

✦ The Check Disk routine runs automatically each time your computer recovers from a bad shutdown. For example, if you just turn off the computer without properly shutting down, Windows is smart enough to run Check Disk automatically the next time the computer starts.

✦ For a while, the Check Disk program was renamed ScanDisk. That name was retired after Windows 95.

✦ Even though the program is now called Check Disk, and its command line counterpart is chkdsk, it isn't the same program as the original DOS chkdsk.

Media Manipulation Mania

You can do a few advanced things with the storage media on your PC — specifically, the hard drives. These aren't regular, everyday type of activities but, rather, are nuts-and-bolts, deep-tissue types of things. The bad news is that the overall topic is technical. The good news is that Windows gives you an amazing array of tools. This section explains what the tools are and how to use them.

✦ Few people bother working with a disk drive at an advanced level because they don't know that they can. Even so, the activities described in this section aren't things you do regularly.

✦ The information in this section is technical. I make a lot of assumptions. If you need a review, see Book I, Chapter 4 for some basic terms, descriptions, and explanations. I assume that you know what all the basic disk terms mean, such as *partition*, *format*, and *volume*.

✦ Be careful when you work with hard drives on a technical level! You can easily and irreparably damage a hard drive, losing data stored on the drive. That's a bad thing, which is why Chapter 1 covers backing up your data.

Opening the Disk Management Console

The *Disk Management Console* is a special location in Windows where you can manage your PC's storage devices. Rather than repeat the steps for opening the Disk Management Console, I list them here for your referencing pleasure.

To open the Disk Management Console, follow these steps:

1. **Open the Control Panel's Administrative Tools icon.**

2. **In the Administrative Tools window, open the Computer Management icon.**

3. **In Windows Vista, click Continue or type the administrator's password.**

   The Computer Management window appears. It contains various *consoles*, which are kind of like mini-windows that use a specific format for displaying and controlling information.

4. **On the left side of the window, choose Disk Management.**

   It's underneath the Storage heading.

When you open the Disk Management item in the Computer Management window, you see the Disk Management Console. You can flip over to Figure 4-2 in Book I if you need to see an illustration. Otherwise, the following sections deal with various fun and useful things you can do in the Disk Management Console.

Changing drive letters

The stars may be fixed in the heavens, but your PC's disk drive letters aren't fixed in the computer's universe. It's possible to change the letter assigned to a storage device. The question remains: Why would you want to?

I like to keep my external drive letters consistent. Back in the old days, I assigned the CD-ROM drive the letter *R* and the DVD drive the letter *V*. That way, if I modified the PC by adding another internal drive, the optical drive letters weren't rearranged, which would often be the source of anguish.

I don't recommend merely changing a drive letter "just because," though! Randomly reassigning drive letters can lead to unimaginable woe, especially if a program is installed on a drive and you change that drive's letter. End of warning.

Here's how to assign a storage device a new drive letter:

1. **Ensure that you're not using the drive.**

By *using,* I mean that no files are open on that drive and no programs are being run from the drive; not even folder windows from the drive are open. You can still change the drive letter when you ignore my device, but odds are good that things won't go smoothly for you.

2. **Open the Disk Management console.**

Specific steps are provided in the preceding section.

3. **Right-click the storage media you want to modify.**

The storage media are listed by drive letter in the upper-center part of the window.

4. **Choose the command Change Drive Letter or Paths from the shortcut menu.**

A Change Drive Letter or Paths dialog box appears. It sports the icon and letter for the drive you selected, and it lists any associated drive letters and pathnames.

5. **Click the Change button.**

The Add Drive letter or Path dialog box appears, as shown in Figure 2-12.

Figure 2-12: Disk drive descriptors are manipulated here.

A warning dialog box appears if you attempt to change the system drive, such as drive C, or the drive where Windows is installed. Click OK and then Cancel, and then choose another drive.

6. **Choose a new drive letter from the drop-down list.**

   Only drive letters not currently used by other devices or network drives are available. Due to the limitations of the Latin alphabet, only 26 drive letters are available.

7. **Click OK.**

   An important warning appears. Some programs rely on consistent drive letters. For example, older software may always insist that the optical drive have the same letter now as it did when the program was installed. Changing the drive letter means that the program cannot find itself and will then refuse to run.

8. **Click Yes to confirm that you read the warning.**

   The drive is instantly assigned a new letter. Further, a new window opens, displaying the drive's contents.

9. **Close the window that opened.**

10. **Close the Computer Management (Disk Management) window.**

To reset the drive letter, just repeat these steps. You can assign and reassign drive letters all the do-dah day.

See Video 622 for an onscreen demonstration of changing a drive letter.

✦ Review Book I, Chapter 4 for information on how drive letters are assigned as the computer starts.

✦ I don't recommend that you change the drive letter on any internal drive. This includes all internal hard drives, optical drives, and any memory card readers you might have installed. Doing so may screw up previously installed programs.

◆ The drive used by Windows is known as the *system drive*. Its drive letter cannot be reassigned while Windows is running, nor is there really any reason to do so.

◆ Other operating systems do not use the Windows method of assigning drive letters to storage volumes. Instead, on those operating systems, the entire file system exists as a single entity; there's only one root folder. Any drives added to the system are mounted or joined to a folder and they become part of the single file system. Perhaps a future version of Windows will take advantage of such a file system structure, and we'll see the end of the drive letter.

Joining a disk drive to a folder

It may seem silly, but it's not: You can secretly disguise storage media as folders. It makes no sense until you see how useful it can be.

Consider that your hard drive is getting full. You added a second hard drive to create more room, but you keep forgetting to use that hard drive. What if you could take that entire hard drive and turn it into a folder on drive C? That way, it would be easier to reference, access, and use the hard drive's contents.

To map a storage device to a folder, follow these steps:

1. **Open the Disk Management console.**

Specific steps are provided in the section "Opening the Disk Management Console," earlier in this chapter.

2. **Right-click the icon representing the storage device you want to map to a folder.**

3. **Choose the command Change Drive Letter or Path from the shortcut menu.**

4. **Click the Add button.**

The Change Drive Letter or Paths dialog box appears (refer to Figure 2-12).

5. **Click the Browse button.**

The Browse for Drive Path dialog box appears. It's not totally unfriendly, but it assumes that you know where things are on the hard drive. Here's some helpful info:

• Your personal folder is in the Users folder in Windows Vista.

• In Windows XP, your personal folder is found in the Documents and Settings folder.

• Your personal folder has the same name as your account name.

6. **Use the Browse for Drive Path dialog box to locate the mounting point for the drive.**

7. **If you already set up an empty folder as the mounting point, skip to Step 9.**

8. **Click the New Folder button and create a new, empty folder.**

   The empty folder serves as the location where Windows will mount the disk drive or storage media.

9. **Click OK to set the folder you selected.**

   Back in the Change Drive Letter and Paths dialog box (refer to Figure 2-12), you see the full, technical pathname to the folder that's listed.

10. **Click OK.**

The disk drive or storage media is now linked to the folder you specified. When you open that folder, you see the contents of the storage media's root folder displayed, but the pathname on the Address bar reflects the new folder you created.

You can add multiple mounting points for a single drive letter. Simply repeat the steps in this section to map the drive to another folder. A single hard drive, for example, can be mapped into several locations.

To dismount the storage media from its linked folder, repeat Steps 1 through 3. In the Change Drive letter and Paths dialog box, select a pathname and click the Remove button. Click the Yes button to confirm.

✦ Removing a disk drive's mounting point from a folder doesn't delete the folder. In fact, you can use that empty folder again to reattach the disk drive or storage media in the first place.

✦ The storage media can still be accessed from its drive letter just as before; mounting the drive (or whatever storage media) in a folder doesn't erase the drive from the Computer/My Computer window.

✦ The old word for attaching a disk drive to a folder was *join*. DOS featured a `join` command. In Windows Vista, the term is *junction*.

Formatting a volume

Once upon a time, disk formatting was a regular computer chore. That's because floppy disks were all the rage and, as I often wrote, "Disks must be formatted before you can use them." PC users were intimate with (or intimidated by) the `format` command. Those were the days, and good riddance.

The only time you format something now is when you're preparing an optical disc. Even then, it's not a true format; the disc is formatted as you write to it. Hard drives come preformatted for your use and enjoyment. Floppy disks, well, God bless you if you still use them.

Disks must be formatted before they can hold data. Think of the format as painting parking spaces, just like the stadium parking lot example discussed in the earlier section "Understanding fragmentation" and illustrated in Figures 2-5, 2-6, and 2-7.

To review disk formats, open the Disk Management console, as described in the section "Opening the Disk Management Console," earlier in this chapter. The top-center portion of the window lists various storage devices attached to your PC. The File System column lists the formatting method for the media. Common formats are described in Table 2-2.

Table 2-2	Media File Systems and Formats	
File System	*Meaning*	*Description*
CDFS	Compact Disc File System	Also known as ISO 9660, the most popular optical disc format.
exFAT	Extended File Allocation Table	Also known as FAT64, designed by Microsoft for use with media cards and flash drives.
FAT	File Access Table	The original disk format used for storing files on the PC eons ago. Had many limitations.
FAT32	File Access Table, 32-bit	An updated version of the FAT that allowed access to larger hard drives. Still popular today because the FAT32 is recognized by many operating systems. Not as useful as NTFS, however.
HPFS	High Performance File System	Developed for OS/2 and still used on PCs, though not as popular as NTFS.
NTFS	File System for Windows NT	The current and best disk format.
UDF	Universal Disk Format	A replacement for ISO 9660, used by DVDs. Also called ISO/IEC 13346.

Because all media comes preformatted, there's never a need to initially format storage media on a PC. You may, however, find the need to reformat media. One reason to do so is to erase all the information previously stored on the media. Another reason may be to make the drive compatible with another computer, such as reformatting an NTFS volume to FAT. Beyond that, honestly, I cannot think of any real reason to reformat media. Regardless, here are the steps to do so:

1. **Open the Disk Management Console, as described earlier in this chapter.**

   See the section "Opening the Disk Management Console."

2. **Right-click the media you want to format.**

   You can click an icon at the top or bottom of the window.

3. **Choose Format from the shortcut menu.**

   The Format command is dimmed for media you cannot format, such as an optical disk. You also cannot format the media that's running Windows, such as drive C.

   The Format dialog box appears, as shown in Figure 2-13.

Figure 2-13:
The Format
dialog box.

4. **Type a volume label.**

   The *volume label* is merely a name that helps you to identify the media.

5. **Choose a format for the drive.**

   Refer to Table 2-2.

   The rest of the options in the Format dialog box don't need to be adjusted unless you're directed to do so by a higher authority.

6. **Click the OK button to display a suitable warning.**

   A suitable warning appears, reminding you that formatting is a drastic step and erasing any data stored on the media.

7. **Click the OK button to begin the formatting process.**

8. **If Windows detects that the volume is being used, click the No button.**

   Media is used when files are open, folder windows are open, or programs are accessing the drive or media card. If you're certain that nothing is accessing the card, click the Yes button to proceed with the format.

   You can watch the formatting progress in the Disk Management Console; see the Status column for the media being formatted.

Wipe out your data

No one wants to throw out a hard drive, at least no one who values their data. Even if you reformat a hard drive, or any media, clever people can still read the information that was once stored there. As such, a security issue arises over information stored on old hard drives.

One solution that many folks rely on are the *disk wiping* utilities. A few of them are out there. Rather than merely reformat a drive, random information is written and rewritten over and over. The result is that the random information obscures enough of the previous information written to the disk so that, supposedly, nothing

can be recovered. (Such utilities are also available for erasing individual files.)

The problem with such utilities is that they don't work. They make the user feel good, but anyone with a solid knowledge of data recovery tells you that latent data is always available on the disk. In fact, one man I know has made a good living recovering data from damaged hard drives. He tells me that only an intense furnace can destroy data. I do not, therefore, recommend placing your old hard drives into an oven.

Formatting takes time. The larger the volume, the longer it takes.

9. **Close the Disk Management console when you're done.**

Freshly formatted (or reformatted) media is ready for use. The media will be empty, though Windows creates the root folder. At that point, you're free to use the storage device as you see fit.

✦ The volume label is applied to the media, not to the drive. So, you can apply a label to a removeable media card, which changes the card's volume label but doesn't change the name of all media you read.

✦ There's no way to unformat a drive.

✦ Just as you can repaint a parking lot, you can also reformat storage media. Doing so, however, erases all the information previously stored on the disk. Reformat storage media only if you truly need to.

✦ Honestly, the information isn't utterly destroyed when storage media is reformatted. Computer experts can recover information from a disk that's been reformatted.

✦ For information on seriously erasing media data, see the following sidebar, "Wipe out your data."

✦ Windows Vista sports the Convert utility, which changes the disk format to NTFS for certain types of storage media. The Convert utility doesn't reformat the drive, so no information is deleted. See Chapter 1 for more information.

✦ PC users were intimidated by the `format` command because they often typed only `format` to set up a floppy drive. But because the `format` command formatted whichever drive was being used, the result was often that the hard drive was reformatted. Even various warning prompts proved ineffective at stopping such accidental reformats. The `format` command was subsequently modified so that a drive letter had to be specified.

Messing with Volumes in Windows Vista

This section has nothing to do with sound on the computer. No, the term *volume* dates back to the early days of the computer. Just as a book can be a volume, mass storage on your PC can be a volume. Indeed, Book I, Chapter 4 discusses a lot of the hard drive nomenclature, and much of it is rooted in those murky old days of the PC, where the folklore was rich and the grooming habits poor.

Windows Vista features a slick array of hard drive manipulation tools once found exclusively in the domain of third-party disk management utilities. These tools let you create partitions, shrink partitions, and expand drives to make them larger. This section explains the details.

✦ I might suggest a refresher from Book I, Chapter 4 to get up to speed on the terms *partition* and *volume*.

✦ The techniques covered in this section apply only to hard drives.

✦ You cannot mess with the *system drive*, the hard drive from which Windows was started.

✦ Windows doesn't let you manipulate a drive that's in use. A drive is considered in use when its main window or a folder window is open, when a file on the drive is being accessed, or when a program is running from the driver or accessing the drive.

✦ In the olden days, many of the activities described in this section were accomplished by using the `fdisk` utility. But even `fdisk` didn't have the power to shrink or expand a hard drive.

Repartitioning a drive

The art of repartitioning involves several steps in Windows Vista. The drive must first be *shrunk*. Windows uses any free space on the drive to create a new partition, which is called a *volume*. The original hard drive retains all its files, but its overall capacity gets smaller.

The second step is to create a new volume using the space made available by shrinking the drive. The volume can be created in the Disk Management Console for use by Windows, or you can use another operating system's installation routine to find and then deal with the empty, or *unallocated,* volume.

To repartition the drive, heed the steps provided in the next section, "Shrinking a volume." Then follow through with the section after that, "Making use of unallocated drive space."

+ A single physical hard drive can be divided into multiple volumes, or *partitions.*

+ All hard drives feature one main volume. In most cases, that volume consists of the entire hard drive.

+ You can also repartition a drive by deleting its volume outright. That destroys any information stored on the drive, but it's another way to repartition. See the later section "Unallocating a volume."

+ Before moving on, I do not recommend repartitioning a hard drive. The only reason I can think of for doing so is to install a second operating system. Even then, most operating systems you install come with software that does the repartitioning for you. That makes a lot of the tools Windows provides redundant. Despite that, I feel compelled to write about it anyway.

Shrinking a volume

Shrinking a volume takes advantage of a hard drive that isn't using all its space. For example, you can have a 200GB hard drive and use only 50GB of that space. If so, the drive can be shrunk to, say, 100GB. That makes the remaining 100GB of disk storage available for use as another volume, such as another disk drive in Windows.

To shrink a volume in Windows Vista, follow these steps:

1. **First, clean up some of the crap.**

   To get the most space available, consider removing some unused files for the drive. Empty the Recycle Bin. And, perform other actions to ensure that you're not wasting space on the drive. See the section "Free Up Some Disk Space," at the beginning of this chapter, for some tips.

2. **Open the Disk Management Console.**

   Directions are found earlier in this chapter, in the section aptly titled "Opening the Disk Management Console."

3. **Right-click a volume.**

It cannot be the system volume, such as drive C, or a media card, flash drive, or optical drive. It must be a hard drive.

4. **Choose Shrink Volume from the shortcut menu.**

   Windows examines the volume to see how well it can be shrunk. Then it displays the Shrink dialog box, shown in Figure 2-14, where you can set the size of the new partition.

Figure 2-14: Shrinking a volume.

> **Shrink F:**
>
> Total size before shrink in MB: `114471`
>
> Size of available shrink space in MB: `23086`
>
> Enter the amount of space to shrink in MB: `23086`
>
> Total size after shrink in MB: `91385`
>
> Size of available shrink space can be restricted if snapshots or pagefiles are enabled on the volume.
>
> [Shrink]   [Cancel]

5. **Set the amount of disk space to release.**

   Use the text box by the item Enter the Amount of Space to Shrink in MB to set the new volume size. In Figure 2-14, the amount listed is 23086, or just over 23GB of storage. That's also the maximum amount that can be shrunk; you can set the value lower, but not higher.

   Set the size to what you need. Don't restrict the existing volume too much, or else it may fill up and cause other problems.

6. **Click the Shrink button to reduce the drive's size.**

   The computer busies itself with shrinking the volume. When the operation has been completed, you see the new Unallocated volume appear in the same slot as the current drive in the Disk Management Console. Figure 2-15 shows a before-and-after comparison of my test drive F, which I shrunk by 10,000MB.

After shrinking an existing volume, a new volume has been created, as shown in Figure 2-15 and as you can see in the Disk Management Console. Because the volume is unallocated, it's not available for use, at least not in a way that's recognizable to Windows. (Some Linux volumes might show up as unallocated.)

✦ The next section discusses what you can do with an unallocated volume.

✦ When a single physical hard drive sports unallocated drive space, you can take advantage of it to make the hard drive larger. See the section "Extending a volume," later in this chapter.

Before shrinking

🖥 **Disk 1**
Basic
111.79GB
Online

(F:)
111.79 GB NTFS
Healthy (Active, Primary Partition)

Figure 2-15:
The before-
and-after
effects
of drive
shrinking.

After shrinking

🖥 **Disk 1**
Basic
111.79GB
Online

(F:)
102.02 GB NTFS
Healthy (Active, Primary Partition)

9.77 GB
Unallocated

Existing volume   New volume

Making use of unallocated drive space

To make the unallocated portion of a hard drive useful, you must create a new volume, one that's recognized by Windows. You can create three types of volumes:

Simple: This is a typical hard drive; a simple volume is the type of hard drive that most PC users have in Windows. If you're shrinking a volume to create a new logical drive, such as a new drive F (or something), this option is the one you want.

Spanned: A spanned volume combines two or more unallocated volumes, even on separate physical hard drives, creating a new drive. That new drive combines all the space of the various unallocated volumes into a single volume. Obviously, this option works only when more than one unallocated chunk of disk storage is available.

Striped: Striped volumes are used to improve disk performance by spreading information between multiple disks. The net result is that several drives are used to quickly access information, which makes all disk operations faster. You need two or more unallocated chunks of disk space to set up a striped volume.

If you're using the new volume to install another operating system on the PC, do not create another volume in Windows. Just leave the volume unallocated, and let the other operating system's installation program do its thing with the drive.

To allocate the unallocated space as a usable hard drive in Windows, follow these steps:

1. **Right-click the unallocated volume in the Disk Management Console.**

2. **Choose New Simple Volume from the shortcut menu.**

   The New Simple Volume Wizard appears.

3. **Click the Next button.**

4. **Set the size of the new volume by using the Simple Volume Size in MB text box.**

   The size is already preset to equal the entire disk capacity, which is what I recommend. If you need to set it to a smaller size, do so. The remaining space on the drive continues to be unallocated.

5. **Click the Next button.**

   Windows lets you assign the drive a letter, or you can mount the drive on an NTFS volume as a folder. Or, you can do neither, depending on how you fill in the wizard.

6. **(Optional) Choose a letter for the new volume.**

   My advice is to use the letter that's provided.

7. **Click the Next button.**

8. **Ensure that the option Format This Volume with the Following Settings is chosen.**

9. **Ensure that the NTFS format is chosen.**

10. **Click the Next button.**

    A summary screen appears. Looks good.

11. **Click the Finish button to create the new volume.**

    Windows prepares the disk by formatting it, laying down the tracks (or parking spaces) for the files. The amount of time taken to complete the operation depends on the size of the volume. Larger disk drives take longer to format.

    The display in the Disk Management Console shows the drive being formatted; you can watch the progress in the Status column at the top-center of the window. The drive isn't assigned its new letter until after it's formatted.

12. **When the operation is complete, you can close the Disk Management Console.**

The newly created disk drive appears in the Computer window along with the other host of drives. It's immediately available for use.

Don't be disappointed if the new volume shows up with less capacity than you wanted. The missing bytes are overhead, used by the drive.

Unallocating a volume

When you unallocate a volume in the Disk Management Console, you're not only removing it from the storage media roster, you're also deleting all its data. In fact, the command used isn't "unallocate" or "de-allocate" but rather *delete*. After a volume is deleted, it's gone. Its status in the Disk Management Console window returns to Unallocated.

By unallocating a volume, you destroy all the data on that drive. There's no way to recover folders or files from a drive that's been unallocated. Proceed with these steps at your own peril:

1. **Open the Disk Management Console window.**

   Refer to the directions in the section "Opening the Disk Management Console," earlier in this chapter.

2. **Right-click the volume you want to unallocate.**

   It cannot be the system volume, from which Windows was started, or any volume that is in use, has files open, or has programs running, or is accessing the drive.

3. **Choose the Delete command from the shortcut menu.**

   The title of the command is Delete, but it doesn't destroy the physical hard drive. Instead, it merely removes the reference to the disk drive partition from the operating system's view, and it unlinks the partition from the drive's master boot record. (See Book 1, Chapter 4 for more information on the master boot record.)

4. **Click the Yes button in the suitable warning dialog box.**

   Another warning may appear if Windows believes the volume to still be in use.

5. **If you're certain that the volume isn't in use, click the Yes button to proceed.**

That's it. The volume is instantly deleted, and its status in the Disk Management Console window is demoted to unallocated.

The unallocated portion (all or a part) of a disk drive cannot be used by Windows. You can do three things with that chunk of disk space:

Reallocate the space. You can reallocate the partition by setting it up as another drive in Windows. Refer to the preceding section, "Making use of unallocated drive space."

Extend the volume. It's possible to use unallocated space on an existing hard drive to increase that existing drive's capacity. The steps are presented in the next section.

Use the partition for another operating system. By not doing anything, you keep the unused space available for some other operating system, such as Linux. The installation program for that operating system prepares the volume for use.

You can always choose to do nothing, of course. In fact, some unallocated chunks of disk space may already be shown in the Disk Management Console for your PC. That's fine. Sometimes, a chunk of disk is too small to use for anything, anyway. If that's the case, though, consider extending the volume, as described in the next section, "Extending a volume."

Extending a volume

Sometimes, an extra chunk of storage exists on a hard drive. For example, in Figure 2-15, you see a 9.77GB chunk of unused disk space, unallocated for drive F. You can use that unallocated portion of disk space to make a drive's main volume larger.

What may not be obvious is that you can use any chunk of unallocated storage on any drive to make any other drive larger. You can even combine unused chunks from several hard drives to increase the storage capacity of a single drive. To make any or all of that happen, follow these steps:

1. **Open the Disk Management console window.**

2. **Right-click the volume you want to extend.**

The volume can be extended only when it dwells on a hard drive not currently in use and where an unallocated portion of storage is available somewhere else on the computer.

3. **Choose the command Extend Volume.**

The Extend Volume Wizard opens.

4. **Click the Next button.**

The next screen of the wizard allows you to select chunks of unallocated space on hard disks in your PC.

5. **Choose the chunks of unallocated space to add to the existing drive.**

Any unallocated space on the current drive (the one you're extending) already shows up in the Selected column (on the right side of the
window). Any additional unallocated space on other drives shows up in
the Available column. Use the Add or Remove buttons to choose which
unallocated volumes to use.

If the Next button isn't available, the value specified by Select the
Amount of Space in MB is too high. Set it to something lower.

6. **Click the Next button.**

7. **Click the Finish button.**

As if by magic, the size of the drive instantly increases, by grabbing up
all the unallocated portions.

8. **Close the Disk Management Console window.**

The drive is now living large and ready for use.

Chapter 3: On Schedule

In This Chapter

- Finding where tasks live in Windows
- Creating your own tasks
- Doing a task test run
- Stopping a task
- Modifying a task
- Reviewing a task log
- Suspending a task
- Destroying a task

*B*etter than maintenance is regular maintenance. Most humans would agree, but regular maintenance remains a concept that few people embrace. For example, as a human, you probably rely upon subtle hints to remind you to perform various maintenance tasks, such as that one pair of "wash day" clothes, a pile of dirty dishes in the sink, or a funny smell emitting from the refrigerator. The computer, on the other hand, needs no hints. It has an internal clock. Plus, computers love doing repetitive, mundane tasks. Put the two together and you have the concept of *scheduled tasks*, where computer maintenance happens automatically. This chapter describes how it works.

Windows Vista Task Scheduler

Unlike its predecessors, Windows Vista sports a feature-rich task scheduler called, amazingly, the *Task Scheduler*. The Task Scheduler shows you all the tasks scheduled in Windows Vista, tasks you create yourself as well as various top-secret system tasks. You can take advantage of that power yourself to set up and run your own tasks, ensuring that all the computer maintenance gets done. This section tells you how.

The Task Scheduler isn't the same thing as the Task Manager. See Chapter 2 in Book II for information on the Task Manager.

Opening the Task Scheduler

Windows keeps all its scheduled tasks, as well as the tasks you may create and schedule, in the Task Scheduler window. Here's how to get there:

1. **Open the Control Panel's Administrative Tools icon.**

2. **Open the Task Scheduler icon.**

3. **Type the administrator's password or click the Continue button.**

> The Task Scheduler window appears. Allow me to take you on the grand tour.

4. **On the left side of the window, select the top item, Task Scheduler (Local).**

> You see the Task Scheduler Summary, as illustrated in Figure 3-1. It provides a quick review of your tasks, including a review of which tasks have run and which are active.

Task folders   Review of recent and current tasks   Actions panel

Figure 3-1:
The Task Scheduler overview.

Update information

5. On the left side of the window, choose the item Task Scheduler Library.

Tasks are organized into folders. The Task Scheduler Library folder is kind of like the "root folder" for all tasks. You may see a few tasks listed there, as shown in Figure 3-2.

Selected folder   Tasks found in selected folder   Create new task

Figure 3-2:
Viewing tasks in the Task Scheduler overview.

Customize selected task/review task details   Delete task | Test-run ta:
Disable task

Additional tasks in the Task Scheduler window are organized by owner. You see a folder for Microsoft, which contains subfolders for Windows and Windows Defender, as shown in Figure 3-2. The Windows folder is open in the figure, showing additional subfolders for tasks related to specific programs or tools in Windows.

Finally, at the bottom of the window, you may see other folders. I created a personal folder for my own tasks: Dan's Tasks (refer to Figure 3-2).

The remaining steps illustrate how a task works and how information about the task is presented in the Task Scheduler window.

6. Select the System Restore folder.

You may need to open the Microsoft folder, and then the Windows folder, to find the System Restore folder.

The System Restore folder contains tasks related to the System Restore utility — specifically, tasks that periodically create restore points for system recovery. The top part of the window describes the tasks for the System Restore folder. One task that's listed, SR, is shown as Ready (unless you disabled System Restore). You can also see the next and last run times, which verifies that the task is performing properly.

On the General tab at the bottom of the screen, you see the task's description: "This task creates regular system protection points." You can also see that the task is scheduled to run whether you're logged in or not.

7. Click the Triggers tab.

A *trigger* is an event or action that prompts a task to run. It can be a time during the day, such as midnight (which is when my computer says that a restore point is set), or it can be an action, such as system startup.

8. Click the Actions tab.

An *action* is what a task does — a program that's run, a message that's displayed, or another thing that happens. It's the task itself, basically, such as setting a restore point, defragmenting the hard drive, or sending an e-mail message.

 Yes, the action shown for setting a restore point is technical. It's gross-looking. But keep in mind that you're viewing a Windows task. The tasks you set up will not be as complex. (They can be, but they probably won't.)

9. Click the Conditions tab.

The settings on the Condition tab refine when the task is run. The action, or task, doesn't run unless all the conditions are met.

10. Click the Settings tab.

The Settings tab lists further control over the task — minor things that control how and when the task is run and when to stop a task that might run amok.

11. Click the History tab.

You find on the History tab some information about when the task was last run and whether it ran successfully. That's your way to test whether your tasks are doing what you set them to do.

12. Close the Task Scheduler window when you're done poking around.

You can choose any task in any folder to study how it's set up, how it works, and whether it's run. In fact, reviewing the already created tasks is a helpful way to learn different ways to configure your own tasks, which is covered in the next section.

✦ Although the Task Scheduler window isn't the same as the Task Manager, you can use the Task Scheduler window to view any of its tasks that are running: Choose the item Display All Running Tasks from the right, Actions part of the Task Scheduler window. You see a list that shows only the scheduled tasks that are running.

✦ To see all programs and processes running in the computer, open the Task Manager window: Press Ctrl+Shift+Esc.

✦ The Task Scheduler supplies information to the Event Viewer, which can also be used to determine whether a task has run, as well as to provide information on just about everything going on in Windows. See Book II, Chapter 7 for information.

✦ Chapter 8 in Book II is on the topic of system recovery, which is where I praise the System Restore utility.

Making your own task folder

It's best to place your own tasks into a special folder in the Task Scheduler window. That keeps them organized, and if you're the kind of person who appreciates a schedule, you're most likely the same type of person who likes to be organized. Maybe not. Anyway. Here are the steps to create your own task folder:

1. **Open the Task Scheduler window.**

Specific directions are found in the preceding section.

2. **From the left side of the window, select the Task Scheduler Library folder.**

3. **From the right side of the window, Actions, choose the command New Folder.**

The Enter Name of the New Folder dialog box appears.

4. **Type a name for the folder.**

For example, you can type My Tasks. Well, because this is Windows Vista, you probably want to type just Tasks because that *My* archetype is so Windows XP.

5. **Click the OK button.**

The folder is created and ready for you to stuff with tasks.

If you plan to go nuts with tasks, you can create subfolders in your folder. Simply repeat these steps, but in Step 2 choose your own folder.

You can't rename a folder, which seems odd to me. You can, however, remove a folder by selecting it and then choosing Delete from the Actions side of the Task Scheduler window.

Creating a new task

A *task* is simply something that the computer does. Sadly, you can't create a task that makes the computer do something it doesn't do already. For example, my task that tried to get my laptop to ride a unicycle while juggling USB wireless mice failed miserably.

You create a task by using one of two options in the Actions part of the Task Scheduler window: Create Basic Task or Create Task.

The Create Basic Task option lets you set up a new task quickly, especially when you're just starting out. You don't miss anything by choosing this option, because the final step allows you to customize your task by using the task's Properties dialog box, shown in Figure 3-3.

Figure 3-3: The type of message displayed by the Task Scheduler.

The Create Task option, also found in the Actions part of the window, basically just starts the process with a dialog box that contains all the options and settings (refer to Figure 3-3). There's no walkthrough, as there is with the Create Basic Task option, unless you just work through the tabs from right to left.

The key to setting up a task is scheduling when the task takes place, which is the *trigger*. Tasks can happen at given intervals or after certain events.

The intervals can be daily, weekly, or monthly and then refined to take place at a specific time, day, or week, or to even repeat. You can also schedule a task to take place when the computer starts, when you log in to Windows, or after another task has run or an event has taken place.

The final element is what the task does: the *action*. You can create only three types of tasks:

Run a program. You choose a program to run or to open a file. Windows lets you find the program, but to run some utilities, you must specify command line options, which are both confusing and difficult to discover.

Send an e-mail message. You can send a message you compose to any e-mail recipient. The message can contain an attachment, or it can be just text. The message content is static, however; you merely schedule when the message is being sent.

Display a message. A dialog box, similar to the one shown in Figure 3-4, appears at whatever time or after whatever event you specify.

Figure 3-4: The type of message displayed by the Task Scheduler.

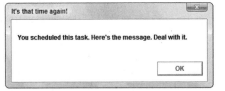

It's that time again!

You scheduled this task. Here's the message. Deal with it.

OK

You're not limited to doing only one of these tasks at a time. It's possible to stack tasks so that one executes after the other. For example, you can run a program and then send an e-mail to confirm that the program has run.

The following sections describe how to create specific tasks and use the various features found in the Task Scheduler window.

✦ The section "Creating a task to run a program," next in this chapter, uses the Create Basic Task method of creating a task.

✦ The section "Creating a task to display a pop-up message," found later in this chapter, uses the Create Task method, which is more advanced.

✦ The *trigger* is the event that causes a task to run. It can be a certain time, an interval of time, or an event, such as starting Windows or logging in to the PC.

✦ The action is limited to only the three items mentioned in this section.

✦ One of the best ways to customize an action is to run a script, such as batch file or some type of automation routine that carries out activities in Windows. Such scripting languages can be an entire universe unto themselves, and people get wrapped up in writing scripts that do amazing things. Sadly, the topic of scripting is beyond the scope of this book.

Creating a task to run a program

Unlike previous versions of Windows, most of the utilities you can schedule are already listed as tasks in the Task Scheduler window. These utilities include Defrag, Backup, System Restore, and Check Disk. Other utilities you have might also use the Task Scheduler to set themselves up. That leaves few options available for running a task as part of general Windows maintenance.

I don't intend to make this a two-paragraph section, however. The following two sets of steps describe how to schedule a task that prints a document. It's probably nothing that you're eager to do, but the example illustrates some important points about running programs as tasks.

The first step is to create the document:

a. **Open Notepad.**

From the Start button menu, choose All Programs⇨Accessories⇨ Notepad.

b. **Type some text.**

I typed `You left the printer on.`

c. **Save the document to your Documents folder.**

Press Ctrl+S and then type a name, such as `print-sample.txt` or something else you can recognize.

d. **Close Notepad.**

Now that the text document is created, you can build a program task that automatically prints the document at a specific time or on a schedule. Follow these steps to create that task:

1. **Open the Task Scheduler window.**

Specific directions are found in the section "Opening the Task Scheduler," earlier in this chapter.

2. Choose the folder in which to create your new task.

I create my tasks in the Dan's Tasks folder. If you haven't yet created a folder, see the earlier section "Making your own task folder."

3. Choose Create Basic Task from the list of actions on the right side of the window.

The Create Basic Task Wizard appears.

4. Type a name for the task in the Name text box.

For the Notepad example, type **Print Document Test.** The task name should reflect the task.

5. Type a description in the Description box.

Yeah, I was once one of those people who never typed descriptions. That's because I figured that I could just remember everything. Now that I'm older and wiser, I type descriptions for everything. My suggestion for the Notepad example is to type **Print a document on the printer every day at noon**, as shown in Figure 3-5.

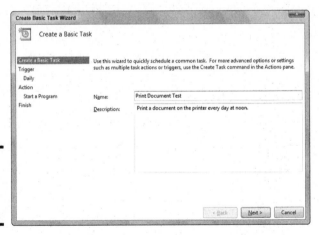

Figure 3-5:
The task is named and described.

6. Click the Next button.

Your next step is to decide what event must take place to trigger the task.

7. Choose Daily.

Basically, you're just narrowing things down for Windows. You customize the trigger in the next window.

8. **Click the Next button.**

   For time-driven triggers, you must specify the start time and interval. For event triggers, such as logging in to Windows, there's no additional step here, so you should skip to Step 11.

9. **Enter the starting date and time, plus any additional time settings.**

   For the Notepad example, set the time to noon, which is 12:00:00 PM. Set the repeat time to 1 day, to have the event trigger every day at noon.

10. **Click the Next button.**

    You need to choose an action, or the actual thing that the task does.

11. **Choose Start a Program.**

    Use the Browse button to set the program name, any options, plus the Start In folder, if necessary. Yep, that's all complex stuff. For the Notepad example, the next few steps describe what to type.

12. **In the Program/script box, type** %windir%\notepad.exe.

    Do not put a period at the end of the command. Computer commands do not end in periods, though a period is specified at the end of the sentence in this step (because, otherwise, copy editors would have a conniption fit).

13. **In the Add Arguments (Optional) box, type** /p print-sample.txt.

    Do not put a period at the end of the command.

14. **In the Start In (Optional) text box, type** %userprofile%\documents.

    Do not put a period at the end of the command.

    See Figure 3-6 to confirm that you entered everything correctly.

Figure 3-6:
Setting up
the program
to run.

15. **Click the Next button.**

The final window presents a summary of everything you've done.

16. **Click the Finish button.**

The task has been created. Does it work? I don't know. Windows executes the task at the date and time (or event) specified. You have to review the task's History panel to confirm that it works. But there's an easier way:

With the task selected in the top part of the window, click the Run command in the Actions panel.

By clicking the Run command, you direct Windows to instantly run the task. So even though it's not on schedule, the task runs just as though the trigger event had occurred. In this case (as long as the printer is turned on), the document you created is printed.

✦ The task you created is a real task, and it runs on a schedule. If you don't want something to print every day at noon, disable or delete the task. See the section "Disabling a task" or "Deleting a task," later in this chapter.

✦ If the task was unsuccessful, you need to edit it. See the section "Editing a task," later in this chapter.

✦ There are command line options for just about every program that runs in Windows. Although that may seem like a throwback to the days of DOS, the truth is that the power in Windows relies heavily on that command line backbone. Just about every task that's run in Windows uses those command line options.

✦ Command line options are rarely documented in Windows itself. The Microsoft support page on the Web can be of some help: http:// support.microsoft.com. I happen to know Notepad's print command structure because, well, I'm a nerd. But it's also easy to remember the command /P to print.

✦ The word %windir% is the *environment variable* used by Windows to refer to the folder from which Windows was started. By using the %windir% variable, you ensure that the task runs on any computer with Windows Vista installed, no matter which drive may be the system drive.

✦ The word %userprofile% refers to the User Profile folder, where your documents and files are stored. It works no matter which user is running the task. See Chapter 5 in Book II for more information on the User Profile folder in Windows Vista.

Creating a task to send e-mail

The e-mail task is a bit silly, mostly because the e-mail message you send is *static:* You cannot customize the message to relate any information that changes. You can add an attachment, which might be a file that's updated, such as a log file. But beyond that, the e-mail action seems to be limited.

Use the steps from the preceding section as your guide to create an e-mail task. Here are the specifics:

1. **Name the task** E-mail Test **and add your own description.**

2. **Set the trigger to Weekly and set the time as every Monday at 9 A.M.**

3. **For the action, choose Send an E-Mail.**

4. **Fill in the e-mail message as follows:**

> *From:* Your e-mail address.
>
> *To:* The recipient's e-mail address, which can be your own e-mail address or whoever you want to receive the message.
>
> *Subject:* The message subject.
>
> *Text:* The message text.
>
> *Attachment:* Any files you want to attach. Use the Browse button to help you locate the file.
>
> *SMTP Server:* The most important field. That's because the Task Scheduler doesn't use your PC's e-mail program. Instead, it's the Task Scheduler itself that sends the message. As such, it requires the name of an e-mail server to handle the request. (See Book IV, Chapter 3 for more information on what an SMTP server is and how to find out which one to use.)

The completed screen for my computer is shown in Figure 3-7. Note that the SMTP server I specified in the figure isn't a real SMTP server; you should use your own ISP's server.

After finishing the Create Basic Task Wizard, test-run the task: Select the task at the top of the window and click the Run link, found in the Actions area on the right side of the window. If all goes well, you should receive the e-mail message instantly.

This task continues to run until you delete or disable it. See the sections "Deleting a task" and "Disabling a task," later in this chapter.

Figure 3-7:
Configuring
the mail
message
to send.

Creating a task to display a pop-up message

The simplest type of task you can create displays a pop-up message. Here are the steps to create such a task by using the Create Task method:

1. **Open the Task Scheduler window.**

Specific directions are found in the section "Opening the Task Scheduler," earlier in this chapter.

2. **Choose a folder for the new task.**

3. **Choose Create Task.**

The Create Task dialog box appears. It looks similar to the task's Properties dialog box (refer to Figure 3-3).

You start on the General tab.

4. **Type a name for the task in the Name text box.**

For this example, type **Reminder** in the Name box.

5. **Type a description in the Description box.**

For this example, type **A message that pops up and reminds you of things way too often**.

6. **Click the Triggers tab.**

7. **Click the New button.**

How about having the message pop up every hour on the hour?

8. **Choose Daily.**

9. **Edit the start time so that the hour value ends in 00:00.**

   For example, if the current time is 10:39:19, edit it to read 10:00:00.

10. **Place a check mark by the option Repeat Task Every, and then choose 1 Hour and then a 1 Day for the duration.**

11. **Click OK.**

12. **Click the Actions tab.**

13. **Click the New button.**

14. **From the Action button menu, choose Display a Message.**

    The window changes to reflect the new choice.

15. **Fill in the message title.**

    The message title appears atop the window, such as "It's that time again!" (refer to Figure 3-4). For this example, type **Gentle reminder**.

16. **Write the message.**

    The message itself appears in the dialog box. For this example, type the text **You've been gently reminded**.

    The dialog box sports only an OK button.

17. **Click OK.**

    You're pretty much done at this point. The Conditions tab provides supplemental options for refining when the task does or doesn't run. Likewise, the Settings tab provides you with more options.

18. **Click OK to create the task.**

The completed task appears in the list of tasks at the top of the window. To test-run it, select the task (if necessary) and then choose Run from the Actions side of the Task Scheduler window. The pop-up window appears, but it may show up behind the Task Scheduler window; click the Gentle Reminder button on the taskbar to see your results.

See Video 631 to see a walk-through of how to create a pop-up message task.

Test-running a task

To ensure that a task works, follow these steps with the Task Manager window open:

1. **From the left side of the Task Scheduler window, choose the folder containing the task you want to test-run.**

2. **Select the task from the top-center portion of the window.**

3. **Click the Run item in the Actions part of the window (on the right).**

The task goes about doing its thing.

REMEMBER

✦ Some tasks don't provide any visual feedback. To confirm that the task has run, see the later section appropriately named "Confirming that a task has run."

✦ Also refer to earlier sections in this chapter that discuss creating a new task and test-running the task after it's created.

✦ The Run item isn't available when a task has been disabled. Enable the task and then test-run it.

✦ To enable a task, see the section "Disabling a task," later in this chapter.

Halting a task

Tasks are shown in the top-center portion of the Task Scheduler window. They're shown in the "Details" view in separate columns: Name, Status, and Triggers. The Status column displays three task states:

Ready: The task is ready to go, waiting for its given triggers.

Disabled: The task has been disabled and will not run.

Running: The task is currently doing its scheduled thing.

You can disable a task that's ready. You can enable a task that's been disabled. To stop a running task, follow these steps:

1. **Select the task.**

2. **Choose the End option from the Actions list on the right side of the window.**

   A warning dialog box appears, asking whether you want to end all instances of the task.

3. **Click Yes.**

   The task is stopped.

Ending a task doesn't disable it. The task merely stops running — just as though you quit a program. To disable a task, preventing it from running in the future, see "Disabling a task," later in this section.

Confirming that a task has run

Never assume that automation takes place. Perfecting a task, test-running it, even selecting the proper goat as a sacrifice — none of these events is an assurance that the computer is behaving itself. To confirm that a task has run and run properly, follow these steps:

1. **Open the Task Scheduler window.**

Specific directions are found earlier in this chapter.

2. **From the left side of the window, open the folder containing the task.**

As an example, open the Defrag folder, found in the `Microsoft\` `Windows` folder. You can check the status of automatic defragmentation on your PC by confirming that the Defrag utility has run.

3. **Choose a task from the top-center portion of the Task Scheduler window.**

To check on the Defrag utility, choose the ScheduledDefrag task.

4. **In the bottom-center part of the window, click the History tab.**

You see a list of all recent times that the task has executed, as shown in Figure 3-8. You can click to highlight a specific event and see details toward the bottom of the window, or you can double-click an entry to see more information in a dialog box.

Figure 3-8:
Information
on an
executed
task.

5. **Close the Task Scheduler window when you're done.**

When the task fails to run, an error message is displayed, hopefully with an explanation, though often the reason that a task fails to run is that the computer was turned off. In fact, the Windows Backup routine displays a notification area pop-up balloon informing you of missed backups.

✦ Backup tasks are found in the Microsoft\WindowsBackup folder, though the tasks themselves are created using the Backup program, not the Task Scheduler.

✦ Backup is covered in Chapter 1 of this minibook.

✦ If there's a problem reading the history log, the Task Scheduler displays a pop-up warning window. That warning doesn't mean that something is wrong with your task, but rather that there's a problem reading the log.

Editing a task

To review or modify an existing task, follow these steps:

1. **Open the Task Scheduler window.**

2. **Open the folder containing the task.**

Folders are listed on the left side of the window.

3. **Select the task from the top-center portion of the window.**

4. **From the list of actions, choose Properties.**

The task's Properties dialog box appears, similar to the one shown earlier, in Figure 3-3.

5. **Modify the task.**

Use the various settings on the tabs to customize the task. You can reset the triggers, hone the action, or mess with any of the optional settings and controls.

6. **Click OK to save the changes.**

I also recommend that you test-run the task, just to be sure. See the section "Test-running a task," earlier in this chapter.

Do not edit any tasks in Windows, such as any of those in the Microsoft folder or its subfolders. Those tasks can be modified using the utilities themselves. For example, if you want to modify the backup scheduler, do so using the Backup program, not the Task Scheduler window.

Disabling a task

All tasks run all the time — unless you disable them. Disabling a task doesn't delete the task (which is covered in the next section). It merely prevents the task from running again.

To disable a task, select the task in the Task Scheduler window, and then choose the option Disable from the list of actions on the right.

Tasks remain disabled until you reenable them. To reenable a disabled task, select the task and choose the Enable action.

✦ Disabled tasks are flagged as such in the top part of the window, in the Status column.

✦ You cannot stop a disabled task, which makes sense because the disabled task isn't running anyway.

✦ You must reenable a task to test-run it.

✦ Do not disable any tasks in the Microsoft folder. If you want to disable an automated activity in Windows, use the methods described in this book. Most Windows tools and utilities can be disabled using the tool or utility program itself.

✦ Tasks can also be disabled in their Properties dialog box: Click the Triggers tab and then edit one of the triggers. In the Edit Trigger dialog box, remove the check mark by the Enabled option (at the bottom part of the window) to disable that trigger. By disabling all triggers, you disable the task.

Deleting a task

I don't recommend that you delete a task. Instead, consider disabling it first, as described in the preceding section. If you really want to get rid of a task, you can delete it: Select the task from the top part of the window, and then choose the Delete action from the Actions list along the right side of the window.

Don't delete any task you did not create. Never delete any task in the Microsoft folder.

Windows XP Scheduled Tasks

Windows XP provides you with the Scheduled Tasks window. It's a place where you can create your own tasks — programs that run to do various things — automatically on a schedule. It's part of that automation thing that makes computer maintenance easy. This section explains how that works.

Opening the Scheduled Tasks window

To review any tasks you created, or to create a new task, you must visit the Windows XP Scheduled Tasks window: From the Start button menu, choose All Programs⇨Accessories⇨System Tools⇨Scheduled Tasks. The Scheduled Tasks window appears, as shown in Figure 3-9.

Figure 3-9:
The
Scheduled
Tasks
window.

To ensure that you're getting the full effect of the Scheduled Tasks window, choose View⇨Details from the menu. That way, you can see the schedule for each task and the next run time and last run time, as shown in the figure.

In Figure 3-9, three icons are shown.

The first icon, the one that's always in the window, is the Add Scheduled Task icon. Opening that icon runs the Scheduled Task Wizard, which helps you create your own tasks.

The second type of icon represents tasks you create. In Figure 3-9, two tasks I created are listed. The first, titled `defrag`, automatically runs the hard drive defragmentation utility, which keeps the PC's hard drives running smoothly. (You learn how to create this task in the next section.)

The second task icon is titled `reboot`. It automatically restarts the computer, but it's disabled. You can confirm by checking the Next Run Time column, which shows that the task will "never" run again. Well, unless it's reenabled.

The remaining sections in this chapter discuss how to use the Scheduled Tasks window to create, use, and modify your own tasks.

Creating a task

Not all computer maintenance is automated in Windows XP. As a prime example, consider the Defrag utility (mentioned in Chapter 2 of this mini-book). It's a tool you should run often to keep the hard drive performing at top efficiency. Yet Windows doesn't automatically run Defrag by itself. Instead, you must automate the process by creating a new task. Follow these steps:

1. **Open the Scheduled Tasks window.**

From the Start button menu, choose All Programs⇨Accessories⇨System Tools⇨Scheduled Tasks.

2. **Open the Add Scheduled Task icon.**

The Scheduled Task wizard appears.

3. **Click the Next button.**

Windows presents a list of scrolling programs, along with a Browse button. You can choose a program from the list, but, sadly, the Defrag program didn't make the cut. You have to use the Browse button to locate Defrag manually.

4. **Choose the program to run, and click the Next button, or click the Browse button to locate the program.**

For the example of creating a Defrag task, click the Browse button and then follow these substeps:

a. From the Address bar in the Select Program to Schedule Window, choose drive C, the PC's main hard drive.

b. Open the `Windows` *folder.*

c. Open the `System32` *folder.*

d. Click to select the `defrag.exe` *program.*

The program might be called `defrag` or `defrag.exe`, depending on whether you configured Windows to display filename extensions.

e. Click the Open button.

5. **Type a name for the task.**

The program name is probably set up already in the wizard. If it's okay, such as `defrag`, keep it. Otherwise, you can be more descriptive and type something else.

6. **Choose the task trigger.**

The trigger is either a time interval — Daily, Weekly, Monthly — or a one-time event, such as Once, When My Computer Starts, or When I Log In.

For the Defrag task, choose Weekly.

7. **Click the Next button.**

8. **Refine the run time, if prompted.**

For a weekly task, the next screen lets you choose the days of the week, start time, and repeat interval. I set up Defrag on my computer to run every Monday at 9:44 AM. (That's because it's a Monday, and I'm probably not doing anything at my computer at 9:44 AM.)

For a daily task, you can choose when to run the task, as well as how often a day to run it. Monthly tasks have similar options.

The One Time Only option lets you set only the day and time for the task to run.

The other two triggers, When My Computer Starts and When I Log In, are preset to run the task only at those times.

9. Click the Next button.

Your user account name is specified in the Enter User Name box. That's because all tasks in Windows must be assigned to a user. It's a security measure, though it's not that sincere (not as strong as Windows Vista, which itself isn't that strong).

Because your account will be running the task, you need to specify your account password.

10. Type your Windows account password in the Enter the Password text box.

11. Type your password a second time, in the Confirm Password text box.

12. Click the Next button.

A summary screen lists information about the task.

13. Click the Finish button.

And the task is created.

The task exists as an icon in the Scheduled Tasks window. But more importantly, the task exists in the computer's brain. Every Monday, the Defrag program will run, defragmenting your PC's hard drives automatically. That's the reason behind setting up the task and how tasks help automate maintenance on your PC.

The task doesn't run right away. In fact, your next task [sic] is to test-run the task you just created, to ensure that it works. Continue in the next section.

✦ If you created the Defrag task, it doesn't work as written. You need to modify the Defrag command to make it work properly. See the section "Editing a task," later in this chapter.

✦ Tasks don't run when the computer is turned off. Ensure that you schedule your PC's tasks to run when the computer is on.

✦ Some activities in your PC can be set up to run automatically from within the program itself. For example, your PC's antivirus program probably makes automatic updates based on its own schedule. You can change that schedule, or disable the updates, using the antivirus program.

Running a task

I recommend that you test-run any new task you create. Here's how it's done:

1. **Open the Scheduled Tasks window.**

2. **Right-click the icon representing the task you want to run.**

3. **Choose the Run command from the shortcut menu.**

   The task busies itself. Any feedback you see reflects what the task is doing. Some tasks have no visual feedback.

4. **Close the Scheduled Tasks window when you're done.**

You can also use these steps to run a task off-schedule. For example, when you have a task that performs a complex operation and you know that the computer will be turned off in the future, you can manually run the task at once by following the steps in this section.

Confirming that a task has run

Some tasks are like a submarine: They're running, but you can't see them from shore. That's because the task whizzes away in the background, doing its thing and not bothering you or otherwise being obvious. That's okay for regular operations, but when you want to confirm that the task ran, it makes things difficult.

To confirm that the task has run, you need to check the task logs. Follow these steps:

1. **Open the Scheduled Tasks window.**

2. **Choose Advanced⇨View Log.**

   The log file is loaded into the Notepad program. The text you see in the Notepad window reflects recent log activity, though the list isn't sorted chronologically. You need to do some searching to find the most recent entries.

3. **Press Ctrl+F to summon the Find dialog box.**

4. **In the Find What box, type** most recent **and click the Find Next button.**

   You zoom to a line in the file that contains the following text:

   ```
   [ ***** Most recent entry above this line ***** ]
   ```

5. **Click the Cancel button to close the Find dialog box.**

   The log file starts at the Most recent entry line and works its way up from there.

6. Close the Notepad window when you're done looking at the logs.

7. (Optional) Close the Scheduled tasks window.

A typical task has two entries. For example, the Defrag task should show entries like this:

```
"defrag.job" (defrag.exe)
       Started 10/19/2009 9:44:01 AM
"defrag.job" (defrag.exe)
       Finished 10/19/2009 9:55:06 AM
       Result: the task completed with an exit code of (0).
```

The first entry (at the top) shows when the task was started. The next entry describes when the task has completed, as well as the results.

When a task screws up, you see something like this displayed:

```
"defrag.job" (defrag.exe)
       Started 10/12/2009 9:44:01 AM
"defrag.job" (defrag.exe)
       Finished 10/12/2009 9:44:01 AM
       Result: the task completed with an exit code of (2).
```

Your key to determining that the task screwed up is first knowing the task and checking the start and finish times. In this example, it's impossible for Defrag to run instantly: The start and finish times are the same. Sometimes, they're just really close.

Also, the `exit code 2` message usually isn't a good sign. You'd have to look it up in your online documentation to see what it means, but it's not good.

✦ The Scheduled Tasks log file is named `SchedLgU.txt`, and it's located in the Windows folder. It's a plain text file.

✦ An *exit code* is a value that all programs produce for the operating system when the program quits. It's a way for programs that run automatically (such as those run by the Scheduled Tasks window) to communicate with the operating system.

✦ Generally speaking, any exit code other than zero means that an error occurred.

✦ Every time the Task Scheduler starts, you see an entry giving the starting time.

✦ All tasks run. Whether the task was successful must be determined by examining the log.

Editing a task

After you create a task, you might want to take a stab at modifying or editing it. For example, the Defrag task, created earlier in this chapter, doesn't run properly. That's because the Defrag command needs to know which drive to defragment. To specify the drive letter, you need to edit the task. Here's how:

1. **Open the Scheduled Tasks window, if it's not open already.**

2. **Right-click the icon for the task you want to edit.**

For example, right-click the Defrag icon to fix that task if you find that it's not working, based on the directions earlier in this chapter.

3. **Choose Properties from the shortcut menu.**

The task's dialog box appears, as shown in Figure 3-10.

Figure 3-10:
A task's
dialog box.

The task's dialog box has three tabs, each of which lets you review or modify what the task does or when it runs, as well as other settings.

4. **Fix the Defrag task by editing the Run text box to include the disk drive to defragment.**

In Figure 3-10, you can see that I added `C:` to the line, which means that the Defrag program will defragment drive C when the task runs.

5. **Click the Schedule tab to modify the schedule.**

6. **Click the Settings tab to review various options and stuff.**

7. **Click OK to close the task's dialog box.**

8. **If prompted, type your password twice.**

All tasks must be assigned to a user, so you need to provide the password so that the task is run by your account.

You might consider test-running the task to ensure that it's still working properly or that it's been fixed. See the section "Running a task," earlier in this chapter.

Disabling a task

All tasks shown in the Scheduled Tasks window run at their appointed times. That is, unless a task has been disabled. To disable a task, follow these steps:

1. **Right-click the icon for the task you want to disable.**

2. **Choose Properties from the shortcut menu.**

3. **In the task's dialog box, on the Task tab, remove the check mark by the item Enabled (Scheduled Task Runs at Specified Time).**

Use Figure 3-10 as a guide.

4. **Click OK.**

Disabled tasks appear with a red X in their icons, as shown in the margin (though the red X isn't red). In Details view, the Next Run Time column shows the task as Disabled.

Unlike deleting a task (covered in the next section), a disabled task simply sits and waits. It doesn't run. It does run, however, if you reenable the task. To do so, repeat these steps, but in Step 3 place the check mark by the item Enabled (Scheduled Task Runs at Specified Time).

Deleting a task

To discard a task you never use, or perhaps a test task you created, follow these steps:

1. **Select the task icon in the Scheduled Tasks window.**

2. **Press the Delete key on the keyboard.**

3. **If prompted, click the Yes button to confirm the file deletion.**

I recommend that you consider disabling a task as opposed to deleting it outright. Unlike deleting a task, when you disable a task, it's easier to revive it, to *reenable* the task. A deleted task has to be either recovered from the Recycle Bin or re-created from scratch.

Yes, deleted tasks are placed into the Windows Recycle Bin. The task appears by name in the Recycle Bin window. Tasks use the filename extension job.

Chapter 4: A Time to Clean

In This Chapter

✓ Obtaining cleaning stuff

✓ Cleaning outside the PC

✓ Dealing with a dirty keyboard

✓ Washing a keyboard

✓ Fixing a dirty mouse

✓ Making the screen sparkle

✓ Shining an optical disc

✓ Blowing the dust out of the case

I'll bet that you've never cleaned your PC. Even my mother, who could hear a raisin hit the kitchen floor while she was standing in another time zone, has probably never cleaned her computer. No one gives a clean PC a second thought. Oh, there may be dusting. There may be concern over "things" on the screen. But cleaning is something you as a PC user have probably seldom considered. So read this chapter.

Your Cleanliness Arsenal

You're lucky: Some cleaning chores involve big equipment, high-pressure steam cleaning, toxic chemicals, and maybe even high explosives. Although it's possible to use those things to clean your PC, it's not necessary. That's because the things you need in order to clean your computer are probably items you already have around the home or office. Here's my list:

Air can: A can of air is like a can of cheese — I wouldn't recommend consuming either one. You can find cans of compressed air used for cleaning at any office-supply or computer store. The air can, shown in Figure 4-1, contains pressurized gas that you can use to blow dust and crud out of the keyboard, mouse, console, and other places tiny and filthy.

Cleaning fluids: You don't need anything fancy to clean your computer. I use Formula 409 or Fantastic to clean the case. Soapy water works. Avoid alcohol and ammonia.

Figure 4-1:
An air can.

Sponge or paper towels: For wiping down surfaces, nothing beats the standard kitchen sponge, a paper towel, or even a nice software dishcloth. Don't use those moist towelette types of cleaners because they contain alcohol, which is not optimal for certain parts of the computer.

Tweezers: Nothing beats a good pair of tweezers for retrieving specific pieces of junk from a keyboard or for pinching hair out of an optical mouse sensor.

Vacuum: I bought a tiny, portable vacuum to help clean my computer. You don't have to go that far, as long as your household vacuum sports accessories, such as a drapery cleaner, shown in Figure 4-2.

Figure 4-2:
Portable
vacuum
cleaner.

Wipes for the LCD monitor: Cleaning the computer monitor requires special care, which is covered later in this chapter. If you can, take the time to find some wipes designed specifically to clean the delicate surface of an LCD monitor. Generic wipes are available, and some pricey brand names. Just don't use alcohol- or ammonia-based wipes.

I'm not recommending that you run out and buy anything right now. Instead, follow my advice in this chapter, and if you discover anything extra that you can use to make the cleaning job easier, go out and get it.

Cleaning a PC isn't something you're going to do all the time. I clean my stuff every so often, mostly when I attach something new to the console and notice how disgusting the situation is behind my computer desk. Or, I'll do an inside-the-case cleaning job when I add new hardware. But — and this is for all you moms out there — don't obsess over cleaning your PC.

+ Air cans don't contain "air." They contain pressurized gas. I mention this fact because you shouldn't inhale the gas. Nor should you turn the can upside down to shoot out a lovely plume of white fog, which is something I've never done nor would I recommend that anyone do.

+ Although I use a can of air to clean things, I prefer to use the vacuum cleaner. Air cans tend to blow stuff around as opposed to getting rid of it outright.

+ Avoid using strong chemicals when cleaning your PC. These chemicals include ammonia, alcohol, bleach, and any acids, such as vinegar.

+ It's still okay to *drink* alcohol while you use your computer. But I caution you not to compose and send e-mail while intoxicated.

+ USB-powered vacuum cleaners are very popular with the laptop set.

+ If you plan to use high explosives to clean your PC, be sure that someone uses a video camera to record the event. Not only will it be entertaining to watch later, but you also might win $10,000 on *America's Funniest Computer Cleaning Videos*.

Outside the Box

You may have trouble thinking "outside the box," but you shouldn't have any problems cleaning outside the computer's box. That's because the muck and grime — okay, mostly dust — that clings to the exterior of your PC is easy to locate and clean up. This section covers various things to clean on the outside of the computer system.

Cleaning surfaces and stuff

Generally speaking, I wipe down the outside of the monitor and console using nothing more than a dry cloth. For some things, I wet a paper towel with some household cleaner, such as Formula 409, and then do some rubbing to remove any build-up. But the console and monitor surfaces (not the screen) mostly collect dry dust. It's not a pain to clean.

Behind the console, and in the nest of cables beneath the computer desk, you'll probably find a lot of dust bunnies, and maybe some peanuts, paper, that old CD you thought you had lost, and other junk. Tidy that stuff up using a portable vacuum cleaner or the hose-and-wand attachment from an upright vacuum.

You can also clean the printer using a damp cloth or paper towel. However, because the printer seldom sees as much handling as a console or monitor, it doesn't get dirty as fast.

✦ When using liquids to clean the outside of a computer, avoid spilling any liquid inside the computer.

✦ Do not spray cleaner on the computer case; instead, first spray it on a paper towel and then clean the case.

✦ There's no need to turn the computer off to clean it.

✦ Video 641 demonstrates how to clean a PC.

Cleaning the console vents

The most important things to clean on any computer are the air vents on the console. Air must circulate inside the box, or else the computer's components get too hot and make Mr. PC uncomfortable. That's when problems start. In fact, cleaning the air vents on your PC is probably the best way to ease the computer's woes.

The computer has two sets of air vents, as shown in Figure 4-3, found on the front and back. Clean both. If the vents are clogged with pet hair, you might be able to clean them out by hand. I prefer to use a vacuum cleaner to get the gunk out. An air can works, but don't try to blow the gunk into the console.

✦ The *console* is the main PC box. The old IBM term was the *system unit*. Some folks call it the *CPU*, though that term isn't correct. Nope, it's really the console, the main box into which all the computer goodies plug.

✦ See the section "Inside the Box," later in this chapter, for information on removing the crud from inside the PC, which is where it goes when you use an air can to clean the vents.

Fan vent

Air vents

Figure 4-3:
Where the
vents are
found on a
PC console.

Console front

Console rear

Cleaning the keyboard

I prefer to use a vacuum cleaner to de-crud the keyboard. I feel that the vacuum more adequately removes the debris from between the keys than a can of air does, which I think merely blows the stuff around. For intermediate crud, I use tweezers.

Sometimes, it helps to turn over the keyboard and give it a good shake. Be prepared for gross stuff to come out.

The best way to avoid a dirty keyboard is to *not eat* while you use the computer.

You can clean keycaps by using a pencil eraser. Keep in mind that the more you use a computer keyboard, the more likely it is that certain key cap labels wear off. On my keyboards, it's always the A key's label that goes first.

If you use a pencil eraser to clean key caps, take a vacuum to the keyboard immediately afterward to rid the keyboard's guts of eraser stubble.

Dealing with liquid spilled in a keyboard

The worst thing that can happen to the keyboard is water damage, such as spilled coffee or juice. Such a mishap may not ruin the keyboard, but it depends on the type of keyboard, whether it's mechanical or magnetic.

The first thing you should do after spilling liquid into the keyboard is to detach it. If you're using a USB keyboard, simply unplug it. The older PS/2 connector keyboards shouldn't be disconnected without turning off the PC first. Otherwise, by disconnecting the PS/2 connector, you may accidentally damage the keyboard connection circuitry or the PC's motherboard. That's a bad thing.

After removing the keyboard, try to give it a bath. Fill a washtub with cold, soapy water. Immerse the keyboard in the water and give it a few good shakes. Then let the keyboard drain on a towel. Let it sit overnight or until it's completely dry — typically, overnight.

The next day, after the keyboard is dry, attempt to plug it back into the PC and see whether it can be used. Often, the keyboard recovers just fine. If not, replacement keyboards are cheap.

✦ Mechanical keyboards are more expensive than their magnetic and membrane cousins. They do, however, stand a greater chance of being cleaned using the water-immersion method.

✦ Cheaper keyboards use magnets and membranes to make the keys connect. In that case, immersing the keyboard to clean it may render the thing useless. Of course, it was probably rendered useless immediately after you spilled coffee into it, so the point is moot.

Cleaning a mouse

The mouse needs cleaning more than any other part of the computer. Optical mice especially seem to collect junk and hair on the desktop, which causes the mouse pointer to behave erratically on the screen. A good cleaning fixes the problem.

To clean an optical mouse, first position the mouse pointer on the screen in a way that, if you accidentally click the mouse, nothing "bad" happens. Then place the mouse upside down in one hand and use a pair of tweezers in the other hand to remove gunk from the mouse's optical "eye." You might also use a blast of air to finish the job.

Mechanical mice rely on a rolling ball to detect movement. To clean a mechanical mouse, follow these steps:

1. **Roll the mechanical mouse over on its back.**

2. **Remove the base plate that holds in the mouse's ball.**

3. **Remove the mouse ball.**

4. **Clean the mouse ball by wiping it with a damp cloth.**

5. **Clean the sensors inside the mouse by using a pair of tweezers and an air can.**

   Rolling sensors inside the mouse detect movement of the mouse ball. Often, crud wraps itself around the rollers, which you can remove by using tweezers. (Sometimes, an X-Acto knife may be needed to scrape off the gross filth encrusting the rollers.)

   You might also consider cleaning out the cavity that the mouse ball occupies, to remove bits of fingernail, potato chip, and hair.

6. **Replace the mouse ball.**

You can now continue to use the mechanical mouse, which should be more responsive to your input.

✦ Yes, a tiny hair — even a blond one — can obscure the optical mouse's ability to properly interpret movement.

✦ There's no way to avoid a dirty mouse. Because mice roll on the desktop, they collect crud as you work. Fortunately, a dirty mouse manifests itself by exhibiting unreliable mouse pointer behavior. So the mouse doesn't stay dirty undetected.

Cleaning the screen

The traditional glass or CRT monitor was easy to clean. What I did was spray some standard glass cleaner on a paper towel and then rub the monitor's screen to remove the various sneeze globs and pixel dust. The key was to not get any of the glass cleaner inside the monitor. As long as you spray a conservative amount of cleaner on the paper towel, you'll meet that goal.

Cleaning an LCD monitor is trickier because not only should you not spray anything on the monitor, you also need to avoid using alcohol or ammonia to clean the thing. The best way to clean an LCD monitor is to use an LCD monitor-cleaning kit. For general cleaning, a lint-free cloth works fine. In fact, your monitor may have come with such a cloth.

✦ For detailed information on cleaning an LCD monitor, see Book III, Chapter 4.

✦ Clean a monitor when it's turned off. That way, you can best see the screen.

Book VI
Chapter 4

A Time to Clean

+ Watch Video 342 to see me cleaning a laptop's monitor. Video 642 shows me cleaning a CRT monitor.

Buffing an optical disc

There's no need to periodically thumb through your collection of data discs and clean them. Only when there's a problem reading the disc should you investigate cleaning it as a solution.

To clean a disc, gently wipe it with a dry, lint-free cloth. Wipe from the center hole outward; do not wipe in a circle. That's pretty much all you can do.

+ Cracks and scratches in an optical disc render it useless. Although you can try to clean the disc as described in this section, when you continue to have problems, I recommend throwing out the disc.
+ Never attempt to clean the inside of an optical drive.

Inside the Box

Some people use a computer for years and never clean inside the thing. Perhaps if you live in a completely dust-free, sterile environment might there be nothing inside the console to clean. But most of us don't live inside a sterile environment. Some of us have pets. Worse, many of us have children. Dust, debris, and other things float inside the console. It's gross.

To clean out that stuff inside your PC's console, start by opening the case.

Never open a computer console unless you properly shut down the computer and turn it off. The computer must be unplugged before you open the case.

After you open the case, you can use a can of air to blast away the years of accumulated crust. Of course, I'm not an air can fan. When I open my PCs and shoot in a can of air, I find that all the dusty remains blow up into my face. I prefer a vacuum cleaner with the tube or drapery attachment.

Don't forget to clean the inside of the vents.

When you're done cleaning, close the case. The computer runs better because the air circulation inside the console is better without all the dust.

✦ There's no need to schedule regular maintenance inside the console. I do it only when I upgrade hardware. There are some PC's I've owned that I've never opened or cleaned. But:

✦ I would clean the inside of a PC that's experiencing the types of erratic errors that are brought on by the case being too hot. See Book I, Chapter 3 for more information on the type of random restarts created by a hot PC.

✦ Enjoy Video 643 to see how I clean the inside of a computer console.

Appendix A: About the DVD

In This Appendix

✔ System requirements

✔ DVD setup

✔ What you'll find on the DVD

✔ Customer care

System Requirements

Ensure that your computer meets the minimum system requirements shown in the following list. If your computer doesn't match up with most of these requirements, you may have problems using the software and files on the DVD. For the latest and greatest information, please refer to the ReadMe file located at the root of the DVD-ROM. Here are the items you need:

✦ A PC running Microsoft Windows XP or Windows Vista

✦ An Internet connection

✦ A DVD-ROM drive

If you need more information on the basics, check out my book *PCs For Dummies*, published by Wiley Publishing, Inc.

DVD Setup

To install the items from the DVD to your hard drive, follow these steps.

1. **Insert the DVD into your computer's optical drive.**

The license agreement appears.

Ensure that you have AutoPlay enabled; otherwise the automatic configuration program doesn't run. Refer to Book I, Chapter 4 for more information on AutoPlay.

2. **Read through the license agreement.**

3. **Click the Accept button if you want to use the DVD.**

After you click Accept, the License Agreement window will no longer appear when you insert the disc.

4. **Install the programs per the directions on the DVD interface.**

What You'll Find on the DVD

The following sections provide a summary of the videos and software you'll find on the DVD. If you need help installing the items provided on the DVD, refer to the installation instructions in the preceding section.

Shareware programs are fully functional, free, trial versions of copyrighted programs. If you like particular programs, register with their authors for a nominal fee and receive licenses, enhanced versions, and technical support.

Freeware programs are free, copyrighted games, applications, and utilities. You can copy them to as many PCs as you like — for free — but they offer no technical support.

GNU software is governed by its own license, which is included inside the folder of the GNU software. There are no restrictions on distribution of GNU software. See the GNU license at the root of the DVD for more details.

Trial, demo, or *evaluation* versions of software are usually limited by either time or functionality (such as not letting you save a project after you create it).

Author-created material

The DVD is adorned with a plethora of instructional videos. The videos were created to supplement information presented in the book; occasionally it's easier to see something being done than it is to read about it.

There are two types of videos:

Screen Captures. These videos are recordings taken directly from a Windows Vista computer. I narrate the activities shown on the screen.

Live Demonstrations. In these videos, I show you some of the maintenance and repair options for computer hardware. Yep, that's me.

Each video is numbered. The number refers to the Book and Chapter in which the video reference can be found. So, for example, Video 431 refers to Book IV, Chapter 3, and it's the first video found in that chapter.

Within the book's text itself, you'll find an "On the DVD" icon (shown in the margin). The icon flags where a video supplements information presented in that particular part of the book.

Note that you can also view the videos on any handheld device with video display. Just copy the .mov files from the DVD to your handheld device.

AVG Anti-Virus Free

Freeware.

For Windows. AVG includes anti-virus, anti-spyware, and other PC security tools. You'll find a copy of the free version on the DVD, or it can be obtained on the Internet at `http://free.avg.com/`.

PerfectDisk 2008

Trial version.

For Windows. PerfectDisk 2008 is a disk defragmentation utility that includes scheduling options. It's available on the DVD as a 30-day trial in case you don't have an Internet connection. If you do have an Internet connection, you can download your copy of PerfectDisk 2008 at `http://ftp.raxco.com/pub/download/pd90/PD2008_WS.exe`.

Vopt9

Trial version.

For Windows. In case you don't have an Internet connection, the DVD includes a copy of the Vopt9 disk defragmentation utility. Otherwise, you can obtain a copy by visiting the GoldenBow Web site at `www.goldenbow.com/nudownload.htm`.

Appendix A

About the DVD

Customer Care

If you have trouble with the DVD-ROM, please call the Wiley Product Technical Support phone number at (800) 762-2974. Outside the United States, call (317) 572-3994. You can also contact Wiley Product Technical Support at **http://support.wiley.com**. John Wiley & Sons provides technical support only for installation and other general quality-control items. For technical support on the applications themselves, consult the program's vendor or developer.

To place additional orders or to request information about other Wiley products, please call (877) 762-2974.

Index

Notes

Wiley Publishing, Inc.
End-User License Agreement

READ THIS. You should carefully read these terms and conditions before opening the software packet(s) included with this book "Book". This is a license agreement "Agreement" between you and Wiley Publishing, Inc. "WPI". By opening the accompanying software packet(s), you acknowledge that you have read and accept the following terms and conditions. If you do not agree and do not want to be bound by such terms and conditions, promptly return the Book and the unopened software packet(s) to the place you obtained them for a full refund.

1. **License Grant.** WPI grants to you (either an individual or entity) a nonexclusive license to use one copy of the enclosed software program(s) (collectively, the "Software," solely for your own personal or business purposes on a single computer (whether a standard computer or a workstation component of a multi-user network). The Software is in use on a computer when it is loaded into temporary memory (RAM) or installed into permanent memory (hard disk, CD-ROM, or other storage device). WPI reserves all rights not expressly granted herein.

2. **Ownership.** WPI is the owner of all right, title, and interest, including copyright, in and to the compilation of the Software recorded on the disk(s) or CD-ROM "Software Media". Copyright to the individual programs recorded on the Software Media is owned by the author or other authorized copyright owner of each program. Ownership of the Software and all proprietary rights relating thereto remain with WPI and its licensers.

3. **Restrictions On Use and Transfer.**

   (a) You may only (i) make one copy of the Software for backup or archival purposes, or (ii) transfer the Software to a single hard disk, provided that you keep the original for backup or archival purposes. You may not (i) rent or lease the Software, (ii) copy or reproduce the Software through a LAN or other network system or through any computer subscriber system or bulletin-board system, or (iii) modify, adapt, or create derivative works based on the Software.

   (b) You may not reverse engineer, decompile, or disassemble the Software. You may transfer the Software and user documentation on a permanent basis, provided that the transferee agrees to accept the terms and conditions of this Agreement and you retain no copies. If the Software is an update or has been updated, any transfer must include the most recent update and all prior versions.

4. **Restrictions on Use of Individual Programs.** You must follow the individual requirements and restrictions detailed for each individual program in the About the CD-ROM appendix of this Book. These limitations are also contained in the individual license agreements recorded on the Software Media. These limitations may include a requirement that after using the program for a specified period of time, the user must pay a registration fee or discontinue use. By opening the Software packet(s), you will be agreeing to abide by the licenses and restrictions for these individual programs that are detailed in the About the CD-ROM appendix and on the Software Media. None of the material on this Software Media or listed in this Book may ever be redistributed, in original or modified form, for commercial purposes.

5. **Limited Warranty.**

   (a) WPI warrants that the Software and Software Media are free from defects in materials and workmanship under normal use for a period of sixty (60) days from the dpate of purchase of this Book. If WPI receives notification within the warranty period of defects in materials or workmanship, WPI will replace the defective Software Media.

   (b) WPI AND THE AUTHOR(S) OF THE BOOK DISCLAIM ALL OTHER WARRANTIES, EXPRESS OR IMPLIED, INCLUDING WITHOUT LIMITATION IMPLIED WARRANTIES OF MERCHANTABILITY AND FITNESS FOR A PARTICULAR PURPOSE, WITH RESPECT TO THE SOFTWARE, THE PROGRAMS, THE SOURCE CODE CONTAINED THEREIN, AND/OR THE TECHNIQUES DESCRIBED IN THIS BOOK. WPI DOES NOT WARRANT THAT THE FUNCTIONS CONTAINED IN THE SOFTWARE WILL MEET YOUR REQUIREMENTS OR THAT THE OPERATION OF THE SOFTWARE WILL BE ERROR FREE.

   (c) This limited warranty gives you specific legal rights, and you may have other rights that vary from jurisdiction to jurisdiction.

6. **Remedies.**

   (a) WPI's entire liability and your exclusive remedy for defects in materials and workmanship shall be limited to replacement of the Software Media, which may be returned to WPI with a copy of your receipt at the following address: Software Media Fulfillment Department, Attn.: *Troubleshooting and Maintaining Your PC All-in-One For Dummies*, Wiley Publishing, Inc., 10475 Crosspoint Blvd., Indianapolis, IN 46256, or call 1-800-762-2974. Please allow four to six weeks for delivery. This Limited Warranty is void if failure of the Software Media has resulted from accident, abuse, or misapplication. Any replacement Software Media will be warranted for the remainder of the original warranty period or thirty (30) days, whichever is longer.

   (b) In no event shall WPI or the author be liable for any damages whatsoever (including without limitation damages for loss of business profits, business interruption, loss of business information, or any other pecuniary loss) arising from the use of or inability to use the Book or the Software, even if WPI has been advised of the possibility of such damages.

   (c) Because some jurisdictions do not allow the exclusion or limitation of liability for consequential or incidental damages, the above limitation or exclusion may not apply to you.

7. **U.S. Government Restricted Rights.** Use, duplication, or disclosure of the Software for or on behalf of the United States of America, its agencies and/or instrumentalities "U.S. Government" is subject to restrictions as stated in paragraph (c)(1)(ii) of the Rights in Technical Data and Computer Software clause of DFARS 252.227-7013, or subparagraphs (c) (1) and (2) of the Commercial Computer Software - Restricted Rights clause at FAR 52.227-19, and in similar clauses in the NASA FAR supplement, as applicable.

8. **General.** This Agreement constitutes the entire understanding of the parties and revokes and supersedes all prior agreements, oral or written, between them and may not be modified or amended except in a writing signed by both parties hereto that specifically refers to this Agreement. This Agreement shall take precedence over any other documents that may be in conflict herewith. If any one or more provisions contained in this Agreement are held by any court or tribunal to be invalid, illegal, or otherwise unenforceable, each and every other provision shall remain in full force and effect.